REYNOLDS SEC. SCHOOL

YEAR ISSUED	STUDENT'S NAME	DIV.	HOME ROOM	COND.

Management and Foods

Management
and Foods

GOVERNMENT OF THE PROVINCE OF BRITISH COLUMBIA
DEPARTMENT OF EDUCATION • VICTORIA

MANAGEMENT AND FOODS

Published by the Publication Services Branch
in co-operation with the Curriculum Development Branch
of the Department of Education.

Copyright © 1975 Department of Education,
Province of British Columbia.

ISBN   0-9690498-5-4

Author: MYRTLE SIEBERT

Editor: JOYCE KENNEDY

LITHO'D IN CANADA • AGENCY PRESS LIMITED 210-33L

History

Under the supervision of Miss Jessie L. McLenaghen (Provincial Director of Home Economics 1926-1946), the Department of Education, Government of the Province of British Columbia, published the book, "Recipes for Home Economics Classes" in 1927, for elementary and junior high school pupils of home economics.

Although the primary purpose of the book was to eliminate the copying of notes and recipes in classtime, it also stimulated home practice and assisted in securing the interest and co-operation of parents. Because this book proved to be a great advantage in the classroom, it was enlarged in 1928 to include the needs of senior students. The title was changed to "Foods, Nutrition, and Home Management Manual." In 1932, additional home management was included to suit the revised content of the home economics option for matriculation.

In keeping with the change of times and of products on the market, Miss Bertha Rogers (Inspector of Home Economics 1941-1946 and Provincial Director of Home Economics 1946-1959), with the assistance of Miss Mildred C. Orr (Inspector of Home Economics 1945-1959 and Provincial Director of Home Economics 1959-1968), revised the book in 1957. Again, "Foods and Home Management" was published by the Department of Education.

Beginning in 1961 there was a major review of all home economics courses and the revisions were introduced into British Columbia schools between 1962 and 1966. In 1970, the Home Economics and Community Services Textbook Selection Committee recommended that, along with the textbooks selected for each of the courses, there continued to be a need for a basic book related to foods and to management. This 1975 edition, "Management and Foods", is the outcome of the recommendation. The book reflects recent changes in life styles, methods and the availability of products and equipment. The change to the metric system in Canada has been taken into consideration.

Jean Irvine,
Co-ordinator of Home Economics,
Department of Education.

Contents

VIII

Acknowledgements

For suggestions of material to be included in the book, manuscript review, recipe testing, and for their continued support, we are indebted to the following consultants:

MARGARET HARVIE, *B.Sc. (H.Ec.) (Alta.)*

JEAN IRVINE, *B.Sc. (H.Ec.) (Man.)*

MURIEL JOHNSON, *B.H.Sc. (Sask.)*

EVELYN KERR, *B.Ed. (Brit. Col.)*

CAROLE LYONS, *B.Ed. (Brit Col.)*

ELAINE MURPHY, *B.Sc. (Agr.) (Brit. Col.)*
        B.H.E. (Brit. Col.) M.A.L.S. (Reed)

MARIA ROBERTS, *Dip. H.Sc. (Australia)*

Parts of the book as follows were excerpted directly (except for necessary omissions or changes due to metric conversion) from "Handy Nutrition," a publication of The Associated Milk Foundations of Canada.

Proteins (excepting Vegetable Proteins)

Fats

Carbohydrates

Calcium and Phosphorus

Iron

Vitamin A

Vitamin D

Other Fat-Soluble Vitamins

Thiamine

Riboflavin

Niacin

Other B Vitamins

Vitamin C

Other Dietary Essentials

For permission to use certain recipes and charts, credit is due:

LAURA SECORD CANDY SHOPS, *Vancouver*

"HANDBOOK OF FOOD PREPARATION," SIXTH EDITION, OF AMERICAN HOME ECONOMICS ASSOCIATION, *Washington, D.C.*

This book represents a synthesis of information rather than individual viewpoints. Important contributions on many aspects of the subject were made by the following advisors:

DONNA ALDOUS, *Department of the Environment, Canada*
SALLY HENRY, *Maple Leaf Mills Ltd.*
MELVIN LEE, *University of British Columbia*
KAREN LOOSE, *B.C. Dairy Foundation*
JOYCE MACKAY, *B.C. Dairy Foundation*
BEATRICE M. MILLAR, *B.C. Hydro & Power Authority*
FRED MINTY, *Metric Consultant*
DORIS NOBLE, *Health and Welfare, Canada*
EDNA RAYNOR, *Department of the Environment, Canada*
SANDRA REID, *B.C. Dept. of Agriculture*
WENDY SANFORD, *Chairman, Metric Committee*
        Canadian Home Economics Association
CORINNE TRERICE, *Associated Milk Foundations of Canada*
MARY E. WILSON, *Sunkist Growers, Inc., Calif.*
PATRICIA WOLCZUK, *B.C. Department of Health*

Photographs in Part 3, Basic Cookery, are used by kind permission of the following firms, associations and **gov**ernment departments:

AGRICULTURE CANADA
ALBERTA HOG PRODUCERS MARKETING BOARD
BALL BROTHERS COMPANY, *Muncie, Indiana*
BEEF INFORMATION CENTRE, *Toronto*
BLUE GOOSE, INC., *Fullerton, California*
B.C. DEPARTMENT OF AGRICULTURE
B.C. FISHERIES ASSOCIATION
B.C. HYDRO AND POWER AUTHORITY
THE CANADIAN LIFE INSURANCE ASSOCIATION, *Toronto*
DAIRY FOODS SERVICE BUREAU, *Toronto*
ENVIRONMENT CANADA
GENERAL FOODS KITCHENS, *Toronto*
HOLLAND CHEESE CONSUMER BUREAU, *Toronto*
MAPLE LEAF MILLS LIMITED, *Toronto*
NABOB FOODS LIMITED, *Vancouver*
NATIONAL DAIRY COUNCIL, *U.S.A.*
NEW ZEALAND MEAT PRODUCERS BOARD
STANDARD BRANDS FOOD COMPANY, *Montreal*
SUNKIST GROWERS, INC., *California*
SWIFT CANADIAN CO., LIMITED, *Toronto*
WHEAT FLOUR INSTITUTE, *Chicago, Ill.*

Part 1

Management

The Management Principle in Action

Each day we must make decisions – to eat breakfast or not, to take a lunch to school, (whether to go at all!), how to spend our free time and with whom, how to spend our money and where to spend it. Later in life we must decide on vacations, whether to marry, whom to marry, where to live and what our life style will be. We must decide whether we will have children, how many and when. Some decisions are obviously more important than others. Despite this, each decision we make affects the sense of fulfilment or frustration we experience in life, and to a large extent we control our own destinies through our decisions.

A decision is a choice of one action instead of another. To gain satisfaction from life we must make our choices on the basis of our *values*. Values are simply those things which matter to us. Friends, family, tolerance, honesty, material possessions, privacy – all these are values. There are many more and no two people share exactly the same values in the same priority.

Knowing the order of importance of your values is necessary if you are to make decisions with which you can be content. For example, if you truly value family above friends, you decide to attend a family birthday dinner instead of a friend's party. If you value privacy above comfort, you choose to live alone in a small room rather than to share a large comfortable house with others. It is important to remember, though, that value order changes from time to time and must be continually reviewed.

Value and *goals* are closely related. Values help us to set our goals. Perhaps you value independence. Your goal could then be to save money so you could be financially independent. You could also decide to accept full responsibility for your actions to gain further independence.

To reach your goals you must manage well. *Management* is defined as achieving the greatest satisfaction possible with available time, energy and resources. Whether you choose a hot breakfast rather than a cold one is determined by the degree of satisfaction you receive from each, the time available, your energy level and the foods present in the cupboard. The use of time, energy and resources are interrelated and interdependent. The emphasis on each of these will vary from job to job. Governing all three areas will be your own interpretation of the phrase "achieving the greatest satisfaction possible."

In order to manage well, you can make use of the management principle. This entails planning, doing, and evaluating what was done and whether goals were reached. If you value good looks, your goal could be to lose five kilograms. To employ the management principle you would plan to eat those foods low in kilojoules which could be prepared in the time available, with energy available and from ingredients you could afford. The doing would involve preparing and eating nutritious low-kilojoule meals. This doing always requires self-discipline and here is where most people fall down. But if your value is genuine, the doing is easier.

Evaluation would take place each time you got on the scales. If your goal is not being achieved then you must reconsider it. Perhaps a five kilogram goal was too high. Planning may have been unrealistic. Actually doing as you planned may have been difficult. If so, you must decide the reason for failure and formulate another plan. All this results from evaluation. Your values may also need reassessment. Perhaps you do not value good looks as highly as you value good food.

The management process can be applied to all areas of life — how you organize your day to accomplish what matters most, how you spend your money to attain material goals and how you develop personal relationships to give you satisfaction. The management process can lead to personally successful living within any family or group living organization, and within society as a whole.

Values, then, are those things, material and not material, which matter to you. A conscious knowledge or awareness of their order of importance at any one time in your life is essential if you are to be content with your decisions. Establishment of a value order leads to self knowledge. Goals are developed from your order of values and give you purpose in life. Goals are specific objectives, set by your values. They may be immediate or long-term. Utilization of the management process can help you reach your goals and achieve a feeling of satisfaction with your own life and your relationships with others.

Kitchens

Management in the Kitchen

The management process can be used to advantage in all areas of home life, and it is particularly useful in the kitchen where a great deal of time is spent, much energy expended, and a number of expensive resources are centred. Whether the job is preparing lunches, peeling potatoes or storing vegetables, values, goals, planning, doing and evaluating are involved.

The value placed on good meals, on time used, and on the equipment necessary must first be decided. From these, specific goals are set and planning proceeds. Most of us want to gain the greatest satisfaction from time, energy and resources spent in the kitchen.

Kitchen Organization

Few people have an opportunity to design their own kitchen and even those who do are seldom able to develop a perfect kitchen.

Any kitchen can be organized to improve its efficiency by cutting necessary movements to a minimum. The first step toward this objective is a careful analysis of your present kitchen.

THE WORK TRIANGLE

The *work triangle* is an imaginary shape formed by lines which connect the sink, the refrigerator and the range. The perimeter of this triangle should not exceed 6.5 metres and ideally is between 5 and 6 metres. This is the distance travelled between these three areas by the person working in the kitchen.

Because it is most frequently used, the sink is best located between the range and the refrigerator. Where possible, the refrigerator should be situated close to the back entrance in order to save steps when putting away groceries. The range should be placed close to the food service area.

TYPES OF KITCHEN LAYOUTS

The kitchen which you work in will probably be one of the types described here. The three main pieces of equipment, except in rare circumstances, will be permanently installed and major remodelling of the kitchen would be required to place them differently. Acceptance of any disadvantages in the type you have, coupled with an objective analysis of the possibilities for improvement, is the first step to reorganizing your present kitchen to greater efficiency. If a new kitchen is being planned, however, these layout alternatives should be carefully considered in relation to the total house plan before the building is started.

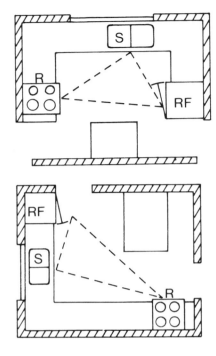

1. "U" Shaped Kitchen

This arrangement has counters and appliances on three sides allowing work to progress in step-saving sequence from one work centre to another. The main advantage of this type is that it has no traffic through the work triangle. The space provided by the fourth wall is ideal for a dining area or activity space.

2. "L" Shaped Kitchen

Here the cupboards and appliances line two adjoining walls to form an L-shaped plan. This leaves the remaining two walls free for use as dining area, storage wall, or space for large equipment as freezer, washer, dryer, desk. Usually this arrangement has no traffic through the work triangle.

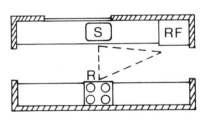

3. Corridor or Two-Wall Kitchen

This arrangement has counter and appliances on opposite sides of the work area. It is usually used in a narrow room, preferably only 2.5 to 3 metres wide with the distance between the edges of the two counters only 1.25 metres. There is little space available for other activities as in the "L" or "U" type. Dead corners are eliminated but there is usually traffic through the work triangle.

4. One-Wall Kitchen

The simplest way to combine work centres into an assembly is to place them in a straight line. However, this makes for a very long work triangle and uses up a large wall area. This plan is used in small apartments and summer cottages. It

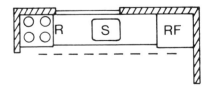

would very seldom be practical in a home; e.g., where it occupied one wall of a family room.

5. Individual Activity Centres

This arrangement should be used only if the location of windows and doors makes other plans impossible. No two appliances are joined by continuous counter and cupboards; therefore, a maximum number of steps will be used to do any task. Kitchens arranged this way can often be improved by adding or improvising counter and storage space adjacent to the individual appliances.

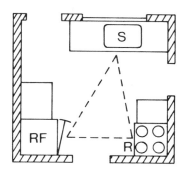

WORK CENTRES IN THE KITCHEN

Whether you are planning a new kitchen or reorganizing your present one, the information outlined in this section will be important. Activities in the kitchen can be grouped around the three or four main pieces of equipment used. A *work centre* is a well defined area of the kitchen where specific kinds of work are done and the required equipment is located. Organizing a kitchen into work centres drastically reduces the time, energy and frustration frequently associated with working in the kitchen.

Where each work centre is located will depend on the location of the major appliances and the counter areas. It will also be influenced by the kinds of foods most frequently prepared for meals, and the other activities which take place in the kitchen. More important, specific areas of the kitchen should be chosen to do similar types of preparation.

The main centres of activity in the kitchen should include storage cabinets, counters and appliances required for that type of activity. The clean-up centre can include a dishwasher and a sink. The cooking and serving centre might be divided by providing a separate bake centre if a wall oven is being used.

The recommended sequence of work centres for a right-handed person is from right to left; that is, the refrigerator centre followed in turn by the mix, sink and range-serve centres. However, having each centre complete in itself, with adequate counter and storage space, is more important than the sequence. An isolated centre is satisfactory if it is a complete centre with its own work counter and storage space and is not just an appliance. Adequate counter space is required in each of the centres but the counter space of one work centre can overlap another provided both centres are not normally used at the same time.

1. **Food Storage or Refrigerator Centre**

The refrigerator, and freezer if your kitchen can accommodate one, are the main appliances located in this area. Here food is received, sorted, prepared for storage and, as far as possible, stored. Some supplies go to the sink for handling before they are placed in the refrigerator while other items may go into cabinets or the freezer.

Refrigerators are normally hinged at the right and should be at the right end of the counter for convenience in transferring foods to and from the refrigerator. When placing a refrigerator at the left end of the counter or using a left hinged one, be sure to provide counter space on the side the refrigerator door opens.

2. **Mix Centre**

The mix centre is where ingredients are combined during food preparation. The most convenient location for this centre is between refrigerator and sink centres or between sink and range-serve centres. The latter arrangement involves more travel because the distance to the refrigerator is greater.

3. **Clean-up or Sink Centre**

The clean-up centre is by far the most frequently used centre. It should be centrally located and close to the mix and range-serve centres. A sink is usually placed under a window. This is a personal preference. When planning the location of the sink in an "L" or "U" shaped assembly, it is important to allow standing space on both sides of the sink. For minimum and medium sized kitchens, 25 cm of counter frontage is needed, measured from the edge of the sink bowl to the corner of the counter cupboards. In larger kitchens, 40 cm is recommended.

Where a dishwasher is to be permanently installed in the kitchen, its placement will be affected by the arrangement of the work centres and the shape of the kitchen. It is not important from the standpoint of efficiency whether the dishwasher is placed to the left or the right of the sink. It is recommended that a corner sink not be used with a dishwasher for it does not allow adequate work space at the sink when the dishwasher door is opened.

4. **Cooking and Serving or Range-Serve Centre**

The range-serve centre is designed for cooking the meal and serving it to the dining area. The range or built-in surface unit should not be installed under a window because of the fire hazard with curtains and the difficulty of reaching and opening the window. It is important to locate the burners to provide adequate space for pot handles so that they need not project into traffic lanes. The 25 cm space between cooking units eliminates this problem but units without this space require a counter on both sides to provide an area for handles. Ideally, the range-serve area should contain a ventilating hood to remove the heat, odour, moisture and smoke.

5. Baking or Oven Centre

During meal preparation, the oven is used much less than the sink, refrigerator or cook top. Therefore saving steps is not an important factor in establishing the oven location. When a wall oven is used it should be located to avoid blocking the flow of work from one counter to another. A built-in oven and the refrigerator, while both take up wall space, should each be located at the end of an assembly.

Kitchens need adequate ventilation to remove stale odours and moisture from the air. To prevent their accumulation, an exhaust fan can be located directly above the range. It must be the same size as the entire area of the stove surface, be properly installed, and vented to the outdoors. Investigate various types carefully before purchasing. They vary in efficiency.

Each work centre should have adequate lighting. A central ceiling light is advisable. There should be electric outlets in each work centre, wired to carry adequate current.

A planning centre including counter top and drawer space for paper, pens, receipts, and equipment instructions is a convenience. A phone can be situated here.

The eating area may be situated in the kitchen close to the range or it may be in another room. Counter space beside the range or cook-top is important for efficient food service. The eating area should be made as attractive as possible and in some arrangements the installation of dividers can separate this area from the main part of the kitchen.

ARRANGEMENT OF EQUIPMENT IN WORK CENTRES

Once work centres are established, the important task of arranging specific pieces of equipment can be done. Many people make the error of throwing equipment and utensils into any drawer or cupboard handy when they first move into their home. This is a mistake. As you unpack, leave the kitchen equipment out. Think carefully about where each piece will be used and place it there. It is extremely difficult to reeducate people to logical storage habits once they become accustomed to where an article was originally stored.

After you have used the kitchen for a few months, ruthlessly pull out seldom used pieces and store them elsewhere. Within limits, the less equipment kept in often used storage areas, the better.

If you are less than satisfied with the way your kitchen works for you perhaps the equipment and/or food items are badly placed. Try to arrange for a day when the kitchen will not be needed. Then remove all the contents of cupboards and drawers. Put items back slowly with careful consideration of the reason for that particular placement. Be aware of the work centres which exist or which you have identified and think of the activities to take place in each of these centres. As much as possible, be careful to place the needed equipment and supplies for each centre in, or close to that centre. Listed here are the principles which apply to good placement of kitchen equipment:

1. Locate articles at the point of first use. This is perhaps the most important principle. The logical placement of articles where they will be needed, instead of where they have always been or where there is space, will cut steps and time. For example, place potholders, cooling racks and other tools used for handling hot items near the range, in the cooking centre. Place paring knives, vegetable peeler, colander, near the sink where they will be used. Have plastic containers used to store food in the refrigerator near that centre.

2. Locate articles within sight and reach. Place regularly used articles within your range of vision up, down and sideways and requiring only a slight turn of the head. Less frequently used articles can be stored where bending, or reaching from a stool or ladder, will be required.

3. Place most frequently used items within elbow pivot range. The elbow pivot is the imaginary circle traced by your hand as you move your lower arm, elbow bent at your side. Less frequently but regularly used items are kept within the full arm pivot range. This is the curve made by the sweep of your hands when your arms are out straight.

4. Consider the mass of articles being stored. Place the heavier pieces within the curve made by the elbow pivot. Lighter items can be stored within a full arm's reach. Reaching for heavy items can be dangerous. Therefore, place only very light articles used infrequently beyond your full arm reach. An important safety precaution is to use a kitchen ladder or sturdy stool when any article must be stored beyond your reach.

PLANNED KITCHEN STORAGE

SPICE RACKS

STEP SHELVES FOR SPICES

STEP SHELVES FOR DISHES

PULL OUT SHELVES

SWING OUT SHELVES

LAZY SUSAN CUPBOARD

PLANNED KITCHEN STORAGE

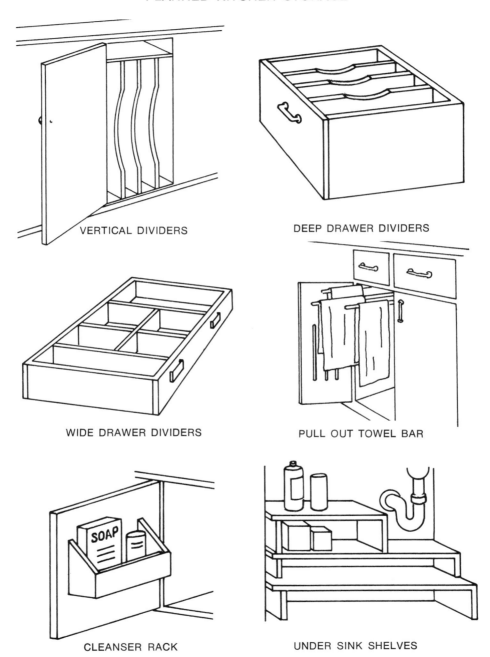

VERTICAL DIVIDERS

DEEP DRAWER DIVIDERS

WIDE DRAWER DIVIDERS

PULL OUT TOWEL BAR

CLEANSER RACK

UNDER SINK SHELVES

FOOD STORAGE

Good storage techniques save money. Poorly stored food perishes rapidly, and loses flavour and nutritional value. Most unrefrigerated foods keep best in a cool, dry place. If you do not possess storage space where temperatures remain between 10°C to 20°C (a little below suggested room temperature), buy these foods in small quantities to avoid deterioration. Part III, Basic Cookery, of this text contains specific instructions for storing foods.

Packaged foods such as flours, cereals, crackers, cake and pudding mixes are stored in tightly sealed containers to avoid infestation by insects, and moisture loss or absorption. Packaged foods containing fat, like whole wheat flour, should be bought in small quantities to prevent rancidity during prolonged storage. Nuts and coconut both contain fat and are best refrigerated, as they are used in small amounts and do not keep well at room temperature.

Refrigeration is a drying process. All foods so stored must be well wrapped to prevent staleness. The refrigerator is not an ideal storage spot for baked products unless room temperatures are high and mould is a problem. Store bread in original wrapping in a bread box or freezer if for a short time. Although a freezer is an expensive bread box, bread and baked goods can be frozen for 12 months if properly wrapped. It is also safe to thaw and refreeze if necessary. Baked goods, if not frozen, should be separated into crisp and moist types and stored in separate tins in a cool place.

The chart following is a guide to storing perishables requiring refrigeration at 2°C to 7°C.

Refrigerator Storage

FOOD	HOW TO COVER	APPROXIMATE TIME LIMIT	COMMENTS
Milk, cream	Tightly	3 days	Reseal tightly after each use.
Butter, margarine	Tightly	2 weeks	Absorption of unwanted odours and rancidity cause disagreeable flavours.
Eggs, in shell	Loosely	Several weeks	Moisture evaporates through the shell if air is dry or warm and deterioration starts quickly.
– yolks	Tightly	2-3 days	Cover with water to store.
– whites	Tightly	1 week	
Cheese Unripened: Soft & semi-soft varieties	Loosely	3 days	These cheeses lose quality and spoilage starts quickly. They should be used promptly.

FOOD	HOW TO COVER	APPROXIMATE TIME LIMIT	COMMENTS
Cheese Ripened: Very hard, hard	Tightly	Several months	These cheeses keep well when not exposed to the air. Keep in original wrapper; after opening, wrap in foil, wax paper, or plastic wrapping.
Process spreads	Tightly	Several weeks	Keep in jars.
Meats Small Cuts, organ meats	Loosely	2 days	Original wrapping should be removed. Covering should be loose to permit some evaporation and drying of surface to discourage bacterial growth. Storage time for pork cuts is somewhat shorter than for other meat cuts.
Large cuts beef, lamb, veal	Loosely	1 week	
Cold cuts	Loosely	6 days	Leave in original wrapper.
Ground meat	Loosely	1-2 days	
Cured meat	Loosely	7-10 days	
Fish	Tightly	1-2 days	Better if used promptly because fish spoils quickly.
Poultry	Loosely	2-3 days	Same as meat. Remove giblets. Remove stuffing and store separately.
Poultry, cooked	Tightly	2-4 days	
Fresh fruits Citrus juice	Tightly	2-3 days	After 24 hours, deterioration in flavour starts and there is a gradual loss of vitamin C.
Berries	Uncovered and spread out	2 days	Subject to rapid deterioration. Don't wash or stem.
Apples	Uncovered	3 weeks (keep dry)	Some varieties of apples may be kept for months. Keep in perforated plastic bags or vegetable crispers.
Pears and Peaches	Uncovered	3 weeks	
Citrus fruits	Uncovered	5 weeks (keep in damp air)	
Melons	Uncovered	1 week (keep dry)	
Vegetables such as lettuce, spinach, cabbage, cauliflower, broccoli, snap beans, celery	Loosely	5 days	Should be protected against loss of moisture to delay wilting and spoilage; e.g., use plastic bags or a food crisper.

FOOD	HOW TO COVER	APPROXIMATE TIME LIMIT	COMMENTS
Nut meats	Very tightly	6 months	Rancidity of oil in nuts caused by air and warm atmosphere makes flavour disagreeable.
Salad oils and dressings after opening	Tightly, using original cover	Several months	Rancidity caused by air and too high temperature causes disagreeable flavours. Wiping off of bottle or jar opening is a good practice.
Desserts such as milk puddings, custard pies, éclairs, cream puffs	Loosely	1 day	Desserts made of milk and cream should be eaten very soon, for spoilage is rapid.
Fresh herbs	Tightly	3 weeks	Wash and drain and put in plastic bags.

Equipment

Choosing Equipment

Whether you are planning to buy a stove or a can opener, one basic principle applies. *Buy for purpose.* There is no point in purchasing a top-of-the-line range if you do very little baking or entertaining. There is no point in buying an electric can opener if you seldom open a can. The idea of buying for purpose seems very simple, yet few people really consider their purchases before making them. Consequently they are frequently disappointed afterwards.

Before making a purchase, investigate the kinds of equipment available, what each will do for you, and the reasons for the price differences. There are many consumer publications available to assist you here. Ask questions. That is your right and your responsibility as a consumer.

Make your final decision at home or, in any case, out of the store and away from sales pressures. Base your decision on these factors:

1. The purpose for which you want the equipment.
2. The amount of money you are prepared to pay.
3. The reliability of the dealer and manufacturer.
4. Construction.
5. Operating directions, guarantees, warranties.
6. Cost.

CHOOSING MAJOR APPLIANCES

Major kitchen appliances include the range, refrigerator, washer, dryer and dishwasher. They are expensive pieces of equipment and upon their choice, efficiency, maintenance and use will depend the ease with which housekeeping chores are done.

Apart from the general considerations for choosing and purchasing equipment already mentioned, consider these points:

Range

1. Oven size, rack arrangement possible.
2. Top surface area, excluding elements.
3. Ease of cleaning • top elements.
   • oven.
   • back splash.
4. Arrangement of large and small surface elements for convenience.
5. Safety and convenience of control switches.
6. Need for specific features such as automatic oven control, self-cleaning oven.
7. Simplicity of directions for operation and maintenance.

Refrigerator
1. Direction of door opening for convenient access to counter space in work triangle.
2. Size suitable to available space and projected family needs.
3. Proportion of frozen food storage space to refrigerator space.
4. Possible rack arrangement.
5. Non-corrosive racks.
6. Need of special features such as "frost-free" in refrigerator and in frozen food compartment, temperature controlled butter compartment, ice dispenser.

Washer
1. Space available for model chosen.
2. Separate or combined with dryer.
3. Tub size in relation to family size.
4. Time-fill or pressure-fill. (Time-fill is not satisfactory if water pressure is low.)
5. The perfection of finish. A non-porous finish on tub and lid may be subject to rust corrosion.
6. The number and combination of cycles needed by the family, dependent on types of clothes being washed.
7. Length of time required by cycles.
8. Convenience of control location.
9. Simplicity of instructions.

Dryer
1. Model needed – separate or in some combination with washer.
2. Electric or gas model.
3. Number and combination of cycles needed – either timed or automatic which may include permanent press, delicate, damp dry and air fluff.
4. Temperature selection.
5. Corrosive resistant finish.
6. Simplicity of instructions for use and care.
7. Added features – purpose and usefulness.
8. Cost of installation and maintenance.

Dishwasher
A detailed investigation of efficiency of various brands is most important.
1. Suitability of model for space available – built-in, portable, convertible.
2. Necessary capacity for family use and size.
3. Amount and temperature of water required.
4. Noise level during operation.
5. Number and combination of cycles.

6.   Simplicity of operation, loading and maintenance.

7.   Cost of installation and maintenance.

Garbage machines

Kitchen waste disposers and trash compactors are efficient and convenient for the disposal of kitchen waste if they are used according to manufacturer's directions. When purchasing, consider the following points:

A.   Waste Disposers. A kitchen waste disposer is an electrical appliance which can be installed on any standard sink drain opening. It will grind most types of food waste to a consistency to be rinsed away with other household waste water. Check manufacturer's instructions carefully.

    1.   Type desired:
- continuous feed
- batch feed

    2.   Special features:
- deep grind chamber
- splash deflector
- cutting blades, grinding and anti-jamming features
- anti-vibration sink mounting, noise level

    3.   Installation:
- costs and complications

    4.   Instructions for operation and maintenance.

    5.   Water temperature requirements.

B.   Trash Compactors: A trash compactor is an electrical appliance that reduces household trash to approximately one-quarter of its original bulk. It does not replace a kitchen waste disposer but compacts items which the waste disposer cannot handle.

    1.   Type:
- free standing
- built-in

    2.   Loading method.

    3.   Available features – use and desirability.

    4.   Availability and cost of bags.

    5.   Installation requirements.

CARE OF LARGE APPLIANCES

Looking after large appliances is mainly a matter of keeping them clean and not overloading them. For example, careful loading of a dishwasher is important. Cleaning of appliance surfaces and the kitchen generally is a day to day job. The cleaning methods will depend upon the type of surface. A wash with warm soapy water, rinsing, followed by drying, is recommended for most. Some appliance manufacturers recommend application of a polish or wax. If so, be sure to use the suggested kind.

With all appliances, following the manufacturer's directions for use and care is the best policy. To do this effectively the instruction booklet which accompanies each appliance must be kept safe and readily accessible. In addition, the information which follows may be helpful.

The refrigerator must be cleaned inside regularly, even if it is frost-free. First turn the control off. Then empty the refrigerator completely and wash all surfaces with mild soap and water. Baking soda added to the water sweetens the smell. Acids in such foods as milk, salad dressings and pickles can destroy the non-porous finish in a porcelain enamel refrigerator. Wipe up these spills immediately. The refrigerator should then be rinsed with clean water and dried thoroughly. Racks are washed and dried and crispers cleaned out. Unwanted food leftovers should be discarded. Food containers can then be wiped off and replaced in an orderly fashion.

The range surface must be cleaned daily to prevent a large cleaning job later. Wipe up spilled food immediately to prevent burning on and, for the same reason, check surface element rings and drip pans after every meal.

As is the case with a refrigerator lined with porcelain enamel, the surface finish of a range should have acid food spills wiped up immediately. Rough treatment will scratch or chip these surfaces. Do not drop objects on them, and never use abrasive cleaners as they will scratch the surface. Avoid sliding pots across the surface of the range. Metal pots which are larger than the element may cause cracking in the porcelain enamel around the element. Therefore, choose pots to fit the element.

Ovens need regular cleaning to maintain accurate temperature control and prevent kitchen odour. Commercial cleaner directions should be carefully followed. Most cleaners are caustic and are harmful to the lungs and skin and can damage kitchen surfaces. Avoid covering the thermostat control and the heating elements with cleaning agent. In the case of self-cleaning type ovens, follow the manufacturer's directions exactly.

Automatic washers and dryers will not function properly if overloaded. They need wiping out after use, to remove lint and foreign material. Lint screens must be cleaned regularly. When not in use, the washer lid should be left open to help prevent rust accumulation in any breaks in the finish around the lid.

CHOICE AND CARE OF SMALL ELECTRIC APPLIANCES

There is a variety of these, many of which are convenient but not essential. Discussed in this section will be the choice and care of commonly used small appliances. In all cases keep manufacturer's instruction sheets and follow directions for use and care.

Electric Kettle

Consider the capacity of the kettle, the placement of the handle and pouring spout. There should be a cut-off or reset button on the bottom of the kettle to break the current flow when the kettle boils dry. This can be reset when the kettle cools.

Kettles need periodic cleaning to remove mineral residue from the bottom of the inside. Harmless chemical removal agents are available for this purpose. Regular washing with hot soapy water and then clear water, followed by polishing with a clean soft cloth is recommended. Care must be taken not to immerse the kettle in water, unless it is constructed for this.

Toaster

Buy a two- or four-slice toaster, depending on family size. Look for fine wire elements evenly distributed on the interior heating surface. A regulator to control the degree of browning is useful.

Keep the crumb tray on the bottom clean at all times to avoid a fire hazard. Do not return buttered toast to the toaster. Never poke at wedged bread with a fork or sharp instrument, not even when the toaster is disconnected. This could damage the wire heating elements. To release stuck toast, disconnect the toaster, open the bottom, and carefully remove the bread.

The exterior is kept clean in the same manner as the kettle. Regular cleaning is recommended.

Coffee Maker

Purchase a size suitable for family use. Choose a broad low model in preference to a tall slim one because this shape is less easily knocked over. A wide spout is easier to clean than a narrow one. The strength of coffee should be controllable and a re-heat setting is useful. An indicator light will tell when coffee is brewed.

Keep the inside scrupulously clean. Otherwise, coffee oils can accumulate inside. These become rancid and give the coffee an unpleasant, bitter flavour. Therefore, clean with hot soapy water and rinse well each time the pot is used.

Electric Fry Pan

An electric fry pan can be used in many ways, even to bake a cake. Buy a size convenient for your use, shallow or deep as you prefer. There is controlled heat for exact cooking and an indicator light to tell when the dialed temperature has been reached. The lid should fit snugly to maintain heat when steam is needed.

Most fry pans are water immersible, but check instruction sheets carefully. Wash regularly with hot soapy water, but avoid harsh abrasive cleansers, especially if there is a non-stick interior finish. When liquid is left in an aluminum pan for a long period, the metal will pit. Once each year or more often, depending on usage, electric fry pans should be cleaned on the outside with a commercial cleaning agent. As aluminum is slightly porous, grease gradually works through the metal of the pan and is deposited on the outside. Accumulation of grease can interfere with even heat distribution. A very heavy build-up can be removed at an appliance service shop. As with all appliances, follow manufacturer's directions for use and cleaning.

Hand Mixer

Choose a reliable brand with a strong motor and sturdy construction. The removable beaters should be strong and unbendable.

Use a handmixer only for those jobs for which it was designed. For instance, they are not meant for heavy doughs or bread making. Never wrap the cord around the mixer as, gradually, wires are bruised and broken in the cord. This is true of all appliances where electric cords are used.

The mixer should not be immersed in water, but wiped off carefully after each use. The cord, too, should be kept clean. The mixer should be professionally cleaned and serviced periodically to remove accumulated foods and to oil the motor.

Iron

A reliable brand should be chosen. In most homes, (especially those where sewing is done), the iron gets steady use. A medium weight is easy to handle but has enough weight to eliminate the necessity of heavy pressure being exerted on hard-to-iron fabrics.

Follow directions for care and use of iron. Water-filled irons should be filled according to instructions, emptied after use and stored upright. If distilled water is not used, periodic cleaning is necessary to remove accumulated minerals from the tank. There are special agents for this job. The ironing surface should be kept clean and smooth. Only the gentlest of abrasive cleansers should be used to remove anything stuck on this surface, and then only if absolutely necessary. Care should be taken when ironing to avoid metal scratches on ironing surface.

Cords and Plugs

As stated previously, cords should not be wrapped around appliances as this shortens their life. Always pull cords out by the plug to ensure wires do not become disconnected. When appliance has a separate cord and plug, insert the plug into the appliance first, then into the socket.

NON-ELECTRIC EQUIPMENT AND TOOLS

Equipment in this group includes sauce pans, pots, kettles, frying pans, baking equipment and kitchen cutlery. Information is given here for general choice and care of these items.

Sauce Pans

Technically, a sauce pan has one handle, a pot two and a kettle has a bail handle like a pail. More important than correct terminology, are the materials used and the design and construction.

Wherever heat is to be employed, the materials used in manufacturing are important. Metals and ceramic material should carry heat evenly and quickly. Aluminum and iron are the best conductors. Stainless steel can be used if construction includes a bottom surface or core of a more even-heating metal. Otherwise, stainless steel has a tendency to "spot burn". Metals are used in combination to take advantage of the specific qualities of each. For instance, aluminum is highly satisfactory as a heat conductor but it pits and stains. Stainless steel is an uneven conductor but it does not pit or stain. These two metals are now used in combination, aluminum exterior and stainless steel interior. Porcelain, heat-proof glass and enamel-ware are becoming more popular as improved technology helps prevent chipping, breaking and spot burning.

Within practical weight limits, the thicker the metal used the better the container. Cast metal is superior to pressed metal because there are no seams and utensils can be heavily constructed. The heavier utensils are sturdier, and bottoms do not warp, so heat is evenly distributed and not wasted.

A good sauce pan or pot has smooth flat sides and a flat bottom which will fit one of the two sizes of elements on the stove. It is well balanced and will not tip when the lid is removed. The lid should fit snugly. Handles should be strong and fit the hand comfortably. Handles and knobs should be securely attached with heavy screws and washers where necessary.

Non-stick interior surfaces are being steadily improved. Because they are fused into the metal, metal utensils can be used in them without destroying the finish. Abrasive cleansers are not recommended. These surfaces require no fat in cooking and are suitable for low fat diets. Non-stick surfaces are especially useful in fry pans, muffin pans and cookie sheets.

Glass and ceramic materials are subject to chipping if carelessly handled. They hold heat well and for this reason a reduction in cooking temperatures ($10°C$ to $15°C$) is recommended when these materials are used.

Double Boilers

A double boiler is one sauce pan or pot which fits into another, slightly larger, pan or pot containing water. These are used when careful heat control is needed. Buy a sauce pan-type double boiler instead of a pot-type double boiler. Long single handles on each sauce pan will prevent burns often incurred with pots and two handled double boilers.

Fry Pans and Skillets

All qualities required in sauce pans and pots are wanted in these, too, especially good handles and extra metal thickness. Tightly fitted lids are necessary for steam cooking. Follow any directions for "seasoning". This term means slowly heating the fry pan to high heat, after first applying a thin coating of cooking oil. This usually prevents warped bottoms which occur when new fry pans are subjected quickly to high temperatures. There is also less chance of spot-burning when the pan is properly seasoned. Some better fry pans are seasoned during manufacture.

Dutch Ovens

These are large heavy pots or kettles with tightly fitted lids, and are used for long, slow moist-heat cooking. Various materials are used. These pots are very suitable for the tougher and lower cost meat cuts.

Pressure Cookers or Pressure Pans

These are made from strong metal, with an air-tight rubber-flanged lid. They shorten cooking periods by increasing the internal pressure and thus raising the temperature. Pressure cookers are used for cooking tougher meat and poultry and certain vegetables, although they are not recommended for all foods. They are great time and fuel savers. A pressure canner is an essential piece of equipment for the home canning of all foods other than fruit. See Food Preservation, page 403.

It is imperative that directions be carefully followed when using pressure cookers, as incautious use can be very dangerous.

Baking Utensils

Most equipment will depend on the kinds of baking done and related personal preference of the cook. Remember that required baking time will be cut in proportion to the darkness of the metal of the utensil. Older, darker cookie sheets and bread pans will require less baking time than light coloured, newer ones, for example. Remember, too, that glass and ceramic containers are highly heat absorbent and reducing the oven temperature. at least 10°C is suggested when using these materials.

Clay Pots

At least three different types of clay cookers are available, each having a number of variations. Some types have an enameled or glazed external surface; the more porous ones are made entirely of crockery; others have a minimum of decorative glazing. Some of these are used in the oven, others are heated by their own thermostatically controlled electrical element. Look at them all and be aware of the limitations of each before making a choice. Follow manufacturer's instructions for care. Not to be overlooked is the possibility of fashioning a clay baker yourself provided the materials and necessary instruction are available. See page 220 for notes on this moist heat cooking method.

All types of clay cookers require careful cleaning to prevent the absorption of unwanted flavours and odours; the use of detergents is not advised. A long soaking period in hot water, followed by a vigorous scrubbing with a firm brush or non-metallic cleaning pad will usually remove any remaining food particles. Sometimes a little vinegar in the final rinse water will leave the baker fresher.

Kitchen Tools

Small hand tools such as cutlery, graters, sifters and strainers are included in this group. Generally, one applies the basic principle of purchasing here – buy for purpose. See page 16. Examine individual pieces for construction weaknesses and flaws before purchase. Well secured handles are important.

Knives

Good, sharp knives are essential for efficient, safe work. More people cut themselves on dull, unreliable knives than on sharp knives. There are many different types of knives available. The best are made from vanadium, and are hollow ground, having a blade which is concave on both sides. The end of the blade set into the handle is called the tang and should extend into the handle by half the handle length. The blade should be securely fastened into the handle by two or more compression rivets.

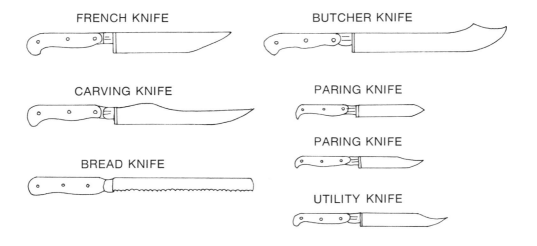

FRENCH KNIFE

BUTCHER KNIFE

CARVING KNIFE

PARING KNIFE

PARING KNIFE

BREAD KNIFE

UTILITY KNIFE

GUARANTEES AND WARRANTIES

Guarantees do not necessarily protect the consumer. They do, in fact, limit the responsibility of the manufacturer or seller. What is often called a guarantee is, in law, a warranty or a condition. It is a promise concerning quality, performance, condition or fitness of the article.

Warranties fall into two categories, either "implied" or "expressed". Implied warranties are developed from government legislation, such as the Sales of Goods Act. They are implied, because they are fixed on the seller by law. Express warranties are specific promises made by manufacturer or retailer concerning such things as quality, performance or condition.

All guarantees and warranties should be read carefully. Always have them in writing. If cards are required to be mailed to firms to ensure guarantees are valid, do this within the time limit given.

When reading a guarantee or warranty, it is for your protection to know:

1.   Conditions which make guarantee applicable.
2.   Time span applicable – whose "life time"?
3.   Who is responsible and under what circumstances?
4.   Length of period honoured.
5.   Where repairs are done. Who pays shipping charges?

Your best protection is to use care when purchasing and buy for purpose. Check other people's experiences and read consumer bulletins. Know the dealer's and manufacturer's reputations and the length of their business careers.

Making Wise Selection of Goods

Consumers are increasingly aware of the tremendous sales pressures to which they are subjected. Persuasive voices are urging continually from radio, television, newspapers, billboards and magazines, tempting them into buying much they do not need. The following suggestions may help the consumer to make a wise selection of goods.

LEARN TO JUDGE QUALITY

There are many articles offered for sale in different grades of quality. Generally the highest quality merchandise sells at the highest price. However, in judging quality, price is not always a safe guide. Sometimes:

1.   Identical merchandise is packaged under different trade names and offered for sale at different prices.
2.   Certain products made by different companies may be almost identical, since they are manufactured to meet government standards, yet may have different prices.

3. Goods of identical quality may sell at considerably higher prices in some stores than in others because of extra services offered, such as free delivery, special surroundings and more salespeople. Since price is not always a reliable guide, how can consumers judge quality?

Buy by grade

The majority of Canadian food products that are sold in retail stores are graded according to quality with the grade mark appearing on the container or product. These grades are established by the Canadian Department of Agriculture. The word "Canada" in a grade name simply means that the product has been graded according to federal standards. A standard is a measuring device that helps to define quality and a grade is simply a means of identifying a standard. The intelligent consumer becomes familiar with the meaning of the various grades.

Buy by label

The basic function of the label is to give an accurate description of the contents so that the purchaser may not be deceived. Canada's Food and Drug Act insists on truthful labelling. By reading a food label, for example, the customer can find out such things as:

1. Form – solid, sliced, powdered.
2. Method of processing – baked, powdered.
3. Net contents – mass or numbers.
4. Origin – beef, pork, chicken.
5. Kind – chocolate, whole wheat.
6. Declarations – of added preservatives, food colour, artificial flavouring; conditions for use; list of ingredients.
7. Dietary claims – sodium content, type of sweetener.

The jar of vitamin tablets lists its nutritional values. In fact, a "label reader" can obtain a wealth of information about the quality of the product. Certification labels are helpful in indicating that a product meets the requirements of independent testing agencies; for example, the C.S.A. label of the Canadian Standards Association provides assurance of the safety of an electrical appliance.

Buy through advertisements

Advertisements can provide some information for judging product quality. However, since advertisers are basically concerned with selling their products and therefore have a tendency to describe them in glowing terms, the customer has to look for actual descriptions, just as in reading a label.

Buy by consulting consumer magazines

Consumer Reports and Canadian Consumer, for example, provide good information in the form of articles and ratings. These impartial ratings are made on several competing brands of goods on the basis of use-testing and examination. The Federal Government sends out regular newsletters which help consumers make choices.

It is not only important to be able to judge quality but even more important to be able to fit the quality to the need. Often goods of high quality and high price do not serve people's purposes any better than do goods of lower grades.

LEARN TO RECOGNIZE A BARGAIN

Sometimes articles are advertised at reduced prices because a merchant wishes to get rid of odd sizes or slightly obsolete goods. The article marked with "made to sell for $20.00, now $14.95" may have been produced to sell for under $15.00. The consumer must not expect all "sales" to be genuine.

When is a bargain really a bargain? In the first place, it is a bargain only if it satisfies a real need. There is no point in bringing home a "bargain" only to have it stay around the house unused. Again, it is a bargain if, upon comparison with the price of the article in other stores, it is found that there is a substantial reduction in price. The following are considered price reductions that attract wise shoppers:

1. Shopworn goods, "seconds" with slight imperfections, and demonstration models can often be just as useful as higher priced items.
2. End-of-season or clearance sales often provide real bargains.
3. Sometimes merchants cut prices for a day or a week in order to move a large volume of goods, for example, "Dollar Days" or "Anniversary Sales".
4. It is wise to notice price reductions that are seasonal. During the growing season, fresh fruits and vegetables are sold at their lowest prices; near the end of the year, car dealers make room for the new models, and so they sell their old cars at considerable reductions.
5. Purchasing goods in quantity can sometimes contribute to savings. Purchasing more than can be used or stored conveniently is not a saving.

EXAMINE THE PACKAGE CAREFULLY

It is the contents that count, not the package. Attractive packaging may be deceptive in a variety of ways; these precepts should be followed:

1. Do not be misled by the shape of the package. The shape of a bottle, for example, may give an incorrect impression as to the quantity. Some containers are much larger than necessary to hold the contents. Calculate the unit price in the "giant economy size" to discover what actual economy is achieved by the quantity purchase. On "specials" calculate the unit price and compare with the price of the same article when it is not on special.
2. Examine packages carefully. Attractive packaging may deliberately be hiding mediocre or inferior quality.

Meal Management

Meal Planning

Managing menus, food purchasing and food preparation are among the most important and demanding jobs done in the home. The general health and energy level of group members is determined very considerably by nutritional quality of foods presented. (Human nutritional needs are discussed in Part II.) The enjoyment of meals served, to a great extent is dependent on the organizational ability of those responsible for food preparation and service.

Careful planning, in advance, for meals has many advantages. Meals can be made more consistently nutritious and interesting. Costs can be controlled more readily and preparation can be simplified as jobs can be dovetailed. Actual meal preparation becomes less complicated when all necessary materials are available through planning. Time required for food preparation can be better utilized and meals can be served more efficiently.

When lack of organization causes meals to be served later, quarrels often occur. Blood sugar levels are low and this is irritating to brain cells. This, in turn, causes a person to be irritable.

If value is placed on good food, pleasantly served, the management principle should be used. One must plan, do, and then carefully evaluate what has been done.

Considerations before planning meals

1. The money available.
2. Meal patterns of group.
3. Ages of those fed.
4. Energy requirements for activity levels of group members.
5. Any special diets.
6. Food preferences.

Considerations when planning menus

1. Canada's Food Guide requirements.
2. Foods available and in season.
3. Interesting flavour combinations.
4. Variation in colour, texture, moisture content and food shapes.
5. Introduction of new foods.

6. Service of only one fatty or hard-to-digest food at one meal.

7. Service of only one strongly flavoured food at one meal.

8. Ease of preparation of various foods served at one meal.

9. Variation in foods served day to day.

10. Utilization of left-over food. (Proper quantity control minimizes this consideration.)

A good practice is to plan menus five or six days in advance. Menus can easily be altered or other foods substituted to meet changing group needs; for example, if guests arrive unexpectedly or if people are not particularly hungry. Generally, however, planned menus should be used. As mentioned previously, needed supplies are then available and advantage can be taken of advertised food specials.

Complete food requirement lists should be made from menus. If a continuing list is kept of other items as supplies are depleted, a final shopping list can be made. Before shopping, organize the list in groups as they will be found in the store. This keeps time and energy spent in the store to a minimum. When you go shopping, keep these points in mind:

1. Take the list with you.

2. Shop alone if possible. (Avoid shopping when you are hungry!)

3. Know current prices of foods. Keep a record if necessary. This is the only way to know if an item is actually on sale.

4. Calculate unit cost of foods. Compare on this basis. Use a pocket calculator or pencil and paper to help select the better buy.

5. Read labels for such information as: mass, volume, grade, cost, nutritional content and additives. Do not be misled by packaging. Large containers do not necessarily mean greater content.

6. Become familiar with government grading standards. Government publications are available for this and many are given in other sections of this book.

7. Buy grade or quality needed for purpose. All food sold at retail outlets is quality controlled by government agencies. Grade choice should be made for purpose alone.

8. Become knowledgeable as you shop. Discover the meaning of such terms as: homogenized, hydrogenated, reconstituted, converted.

9. Use a variety of brands. Try a new one if the price is cheaper and the grade acceptable for purpose. Use store brands where possible, rather than nationally advertised brands, when there is a saving and grades are the same.

10. Buy in bulk when cheaper if storage space is available and quality will not deteriorate during storage. Bulk buying is not always less costly. Calculate unit cost saving each time you buy.

11. Be realistic about what partially prepared foods actually cost. Are you paying dearly for someone else's labour when you could do the job yourself? Is time saved being usefully spent?

12. Purchase frozen foods last.

13. Check prices as costs are rung up at the till. Mistakes can be made here, especially on sale items.

14. Be respectful of merchandise. Do not damage fresh fruits and vegetables, or open containers. Resist sampling food, unless invited to. Cost of losses to the store are passed on to the consumer.

15. When you reach home, store foods properly to ensure nutritional content is maintained and spoilage retarded for as long as possible. Get frozen foods in the freezer immediately.

Meal Preparation

After menus have been planned and food purchased comes the actual preparation of meals. It is important to have all foods for the meal ready at one time and to dovetail operations as work proceeds. In order to be as economical as possible with time and energy organized movements are essential. The following management techniques will help you:

PLAN AHEAD

1. Make a work plan. Experienced cooks plan in their heads but until you have prepared meals for some time it is good practice to write down what you must do and when you must do it. List foods and cooking times. Then work backwards from the time of meal service, arranging to prepare foods so they will all be ready on time.

2. Dovetail operations: Heat the fry pan as you shape meat balls. Bake cookies as you iron. Utilize the heat in the oven to bake brownies as the casserole heats, or dry bread crumbs while the roast cooks.

3. Prepare more than you need. Butter crumbs and store the extra, mince onion or parsley and freeze excess. Make two casseroles or cakes and freeze one.

4. Use paper products: Prepare meat or grate cheese on waxed paper. Use a paper bag to flour foods. Keep a small paper bag on the counter for garbage.

5. Clean up as you work. Put away containers as you finish using them. Rinse and soak dishes to make washing them easier. Keep soapy water in a sink and wash and dry equipment as soon as possible. Keep counters tidy.

6. Use the proper tool for the job. Choose a French knife rather than a paring knife to mince onion. Select the proper sized bowl in the first place and save having to transfer the mixture to a large one later. Use oven-to-table ware when possible.

7. Learn the approximate cooking times of frequently prepared foods. Use a timer rather than rely on your memory.

ELIMINATE UNNECESSARY MOTIONS

1. Avoid unnecessary handling. Use trays when collecting dishes or a number of supplies.

2. Use both hands. Hold the lid of a sauce pan with one hand and stir the sauce with the other hand.

3. Avoid retracing steps. Get all supplies from the refrigerator at one time. Get out at one time all the pots needed for the different vegetables. Properly equipped and arranged work centres are important for this to be possible.

APPLY PHYSICS PRINCIPLES

1. Use big muscles and large knives and cut downwards rather than use small finger muscles and small knives and cut up. This is efficient use of the lever principle. (It is also safer.)

2. Let gravity of falling water separate lettuce leaves and force dirt particles from salad greens and leafy vegetables.

3. Let the wheel save energy. Use trolleys when moving foods to the table and to clear dishes from the table.

TABLE SETTING AND MEAL SERVICE

Table setting and meal service have a distinct effect on the enjoyment received from eating. Confusion caused by forgotten serving spoons, and improperly placed cutlery, distracts from good food and conversation. To avoid such distractions, table setting should be complete and follow the conventional pattern of placement suitable under the particular circumstances. If conventional patterns for table setting and meal service are used in the home, young people learn what to expect when they go out to eat. They then can be relaxed and enjoy the occasion, knowing that they are behaving acceptably.

TABLE SETTING

Table setting for family meals is usually dovetailed with meal preparation unless it is another person's responsibility. Table setting for entertaining requires more time and extra care. Adequate time must be allowed for this in order that service should run smoothly. Whatever the circumstances, certain factors should be considered. A well set table has the following characteristics:

1. It is complete. All necessary equipment is present for efficient service.

2. It is attractive. Surroundings are calm, comfortable and as pleasant as possible.

3. It is set in a conventionally acceptable way.

General Suggestions

1. Arrange eating area attractively. Table cloths or mats should be clean and neatly arranged on the table. Plastic has become more acceptable but must be wiped off regularly and should be changed occasionally for the sake of variety. A centre piece is a pleasant addition to any table. It should be simple and not more than 35 cm high.

2. All dishes, glass and cutlery must be clean and free from smudges.

3. Allow 45 to 60 cm space for each cover. A *cover* is the term used for all the equipment one person requires for a meal.

4. Use only that cutlery and those dishes needed. Knives, for instance, are not always required. Hotel service varies in that all cutlery which could be needed is set at each cover. Unnecessary pieces are removed when food is ordered.

5. Arrange utensils neatly. Handles of cutlery should be either perpendicular or horizontal to the edge of the table.

6. Have all necessary equipment on the table before serving the food. Check for such things as serving spoons, hot pads and napkins.

7. Plan to heat main dish plates and serving dishes if the main course foods are hot.

8. Follow this pattern when setting an individual cover. Add or remove pieces as required by the menu.

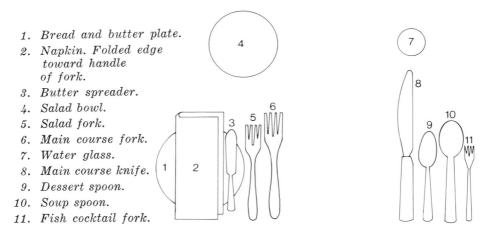

1. *Bread and butter plate.*
2. *Napkin. Folded edge toward handle of fork.*
3. *Butter spreader.*
4. *Salad bowl.*
5. *Salad fork.*
6. *Main course fork.*
7. *Water glass.*
8. *Main course knife.*
9. *Dessert spoon.*
10. *Soup spoon.*
11. *Fish cocktail fork.*

NOTE: Pieces are added to right and left as needed. They are placed in order of use, beginning from the outside. The ones furthest from the plate are used first.

Other Details

Dessert spoons can be placed as shown. Dessert forks, used last, could be placed closest to the plate on the left side. Cutlery for dessert may also be served with the dessert or placed at the top of the main course plate.

Beverage spoons are served as required, with the beverage.

If a fork only is used for the main course, it can be placed to the right of the plate, in the position usually taken by the knife.

At very formal meals a service plate is used. All food plates are placed on this larger plate. It is removed only for the dessert course. Cocktail glasses and sherbet glasses are served on small plates. Soup and salad bowls are also served on plates. A finger bowl may be used. This is placed above the main course plate and used to carefully clean one's fingers after eating finger food. Lemon slices are often placed in finger bowls to add a pleasant fragrance to the water.

Table setting in the home is becoming more simple as life styles change. But the general suggestions given for table setting should be followed. The importance to most people of pleasant food, conveniently and quietly served, should be remembered.

MEAL SERVICE

There is a variety of service styles conventionally accepted. Family service must be adapted to the ages and number being served, and to the space and time available. Food can be served on plates from the kitchen, served from bowls placed conveniently about the table, or by the host and hostess at the table.

Buffet service is popular for entertaining, especially when space is limited. There are set patterns for setting buffet tables and information is readily available on this topic.

At sit-down meals it is important that a pattern be established for placing and removing individual plates, cups and glasses. This makes service more convenient and prevents confusion among those being served. An established procedure is to serve individual portions from the left and remove empty plates from the left also. If this is done using the left hand there will be less chance of bumping the arm, shoulder or head of the guest. All beverages are served or removed from the right, and in this case using the right hand would be preferable.

Clearing all main course foods from the table before serving the dessert and beverage leads to less clutter and confusion. Only those foods or utensils used for, or after, dessert are left on the table. In some cases, dessert and coffee are served away from the table, in the living room. This is a pleasant technique to use when guests are present.

If coffee or tea are served at the table, it is more convenient if these are served to guests than it is to place cups at settings as is done in restaurants. Cups should be filled as desired and spoons placed on saucers if needed. The spoons should be put parallel to the handle of the cup and the cup and saucer passed in such a way that the cup handle is conveniently placed to be picked up.

If more detailed information is required on specific types of service, there is a variety of books written on this topic.

ENTERTAINING

Entertaining should be fun for the host and hostess as well as for invited guests. Good parties do not "just happen". They are planned in advance much like a military operation. If they are properly planned, everyone can relax and enjoy themselves.

Here are a few suggestions to help you plan a great party:

1. Decide first how much money you can spend.

2. The money available will determine the number of people you can ask. Of course, the extent of your china and cutlery supply as well as the space you have in your home will also have a bearing on the number of people you invite.

3. Plan to ask people 2-3 weeks in advance. This way you are sure that everyone you would like to invite will be available. Ask people at the time you invite them if there are any foods they cannot eat.

4. Choose guests carefully. We all enjoy meeting new people. Mix and match your guests. Some people are excellent guests. They mix well, avoid unpleasant topics and move about the room freely attempting to draw others into the conversation. Every party needs a few of these.

5. Plan your menu carefully.

   Consider   a.   the number of people to serve

   b.   the age of guests

   c.   the time of year and availability of various foods

   d.   the types of service dishes needed

   e.   the kind of table service you must use; e.g., fork food at buffet parties

   f.   the foods that will require oven space – oven temperatures can be a problem

   g.   choose no foods needing extensive last minute attention

      h. the aesthetic elements of food preparation; e.g.
           colour
           textures
           moisture content
           flavour combinations
           richness of food
           repetition of flavours and textures from one course
           to another
      i. plan to prepare as much of the food ahead as possible.

6. Make a written work plan. List jobs to do, including table setting, floral arrangements, room and seating arrangements, collection of needed dishes, cleaning of silver, polishing of glass. Reorganize the list, starting with the jobs that can be done farthest ahead of time. Organize your work so you have at least two hours to yourself in the afternoon. Recheck the list to see nothing is forgotten.

7. Make a grocery list from your menu. Remember napkins, lump sugar, candles, etc. Check supplies on hand. This way you avoid the frustration of wasted time.

8. Plan the table arrangement. Think about the positioning and arrangement of food. This will vary depending on the type of service you choose.

9. Arrange the room. Perhaps you should rearrange the position of the food table to allow you and guests to move smoothly to and from the table. Give thought to the movement of guests while they are chatting. Group chairs in conversational arrangements. Attempt to have small tables handy. Place precious items where they will not be broken.

10. Clear all counters in the kitchen. Do all the dishes. Get out towels and plan to heat plates and serving dishes if necessary. Check the table again.

11. Consider music and lighting to create the desired mood. Soft light is most relaxing.

12. Be prepared to mix with your guests. Move them about and always be on the look out for trapped guests and lonely guests. Either the host or hostess should always be with the guests.

13. Serve food when it is convenient to you, and when you "feel" your guests are relaxed and ready. Suggest at a buffet that one or two women start eating first.

14. Before suggesting second helpings at a buffet, check the table for neatness and replenish plates of food.

15. Before serving dessert and coffee, clear the table of all main course foods, salt and pepper, etc.

16. When guests are finished eating, quietly remove soiled plates, etc. Do not stack in the party area.

17. When the last guest is gone, sit back and take off your shoes. Discuss the party and recall what points will need more thought next time.

CLEAN UP

Many people like to cook. Few enjoy cleaning up afterwards. To make this task as pleasant as possible, follow these suggestions:

During Clean Up

1. Keep counters neat.
2. Rinse and soak utensils in water of an appropriate temperature.
3. Wash as many preparation utensils as possible before serving the meal.

After The Meal

1. Use trays, if practical, to clear the table.
2. **Put left-overs into refrigerator containers before serving the dessert.**
3. Use paper towels to wipe out greasy containers before washing. Use a rubber scraper to clean out sauce or gravy pans.
4. Place cutlery to soak in a tall container; do not immerse wooden or hollow handles in water.
5. Rinse plates before washing.
6. Wash glass, cutlery, plates and pots in that order.
7. Rinse dishes with boiling water and leave to dry. Wipe cutlery to avoid streaks.
8. If a dishwasher is used, prepare dishes and load machine as directed.

After Dishes Are Done

1. Wipe off all counters.
2. Wipe off range and clean drip pans if necessary. Clean and polish metal parts of range.
3. Wipe finger marks off cupboard doors.
4. Clean out the sink.
5. Sweep or wipe the floor.

After you have completed one week's meal service, evaluate carefully your planning and preparation of meals. If you are not satisfied, reassess what you have done and make changes where necessary. That is management.

Housekeeping and Safety

Types of Dirt and Cleaning Agents

In a home we wage a never ending war against dirt of various kinds. We value cleanliness as a means of preventing illness caused by air-borne and soil-borne bacteria and viruses. Aesthetically, most people enjoy an orderly, clean environment.

Types of Dirt

Dirt or soil in a home is defined as any matter out of place. Sand at the beach is expected, sand on the kitchen floor is dirt.

1. Loose dirt: This is easily removed by brushing, shaking or vacuuming unless it is combined with moisture or oil.

2. Water soluble dirt: These dirts dissolve in water, either hot or cold depending on the particular soiling agent. Included in this group are sugar solutions and starchy foods.

3. Dirt insoluble in water: These soiling agents do not dissolve in any temperature of water. They are usually oil based. Allowed to remain on surfaces, they have a tendency to "set" and become very hard to remove.

4. Corrosion or tarnish: These are developed through chemical action on metals caused by exposure to air or specific liquids. Iron rust in cast iron fry pans is an example. Silver tarnish is another.

Types of Cleaning Agents

1. Water is widely used. It is seldom harmful unless too much is used, the temperature is too high, or the exposure period is too long. Depending on the type of soil and on the surface to be cleaned, water used can be cold, warm or hot.

2. Alkaline water solutions: Alkalis cut grease and are superior cleaning agents to water, unless they cause chemical reactions on the surface cleaned, as in the case of aluminum or wool. Soaps, soda, lye, ammonia, water softeners and general purpose detergents make alkaline solutions with water. Strong alkaline solutions such as drain cleaners, must be handled carefully and according to directions as they are caustic to the skin and poisonous if taken internally.

   Use alkaline cleaners in as weak a solution as possible to do the job. Rinse any surface on which they are used. Properly used, alkaline solutions are valuable cleaning agents.

3.   Soap is made from fat and alkali in the form of lye. Good soap, properly balanced in the proportion of fat to lye, is neither acidic nor alkaline. It is neutral. When this is the case, it is safe to use on most surfaces.

Soap acts as wetting agent. It breaks down surface tension in water and causes water to spread or penetrate the surface being cleaned. Soap assists cleaning, also, by helping oil combine with water to form an emulsion which is then carried away by the water.

The disadvantage of soap is its tendency to form a soap curd by combining with minerals in hard water. The curd floats like a scum on the water surface and is hard to rinse out.

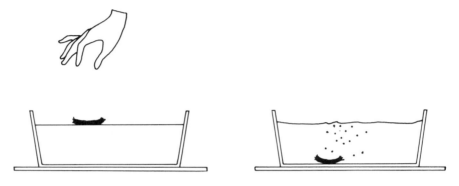

Wetting Action

4.   Synthetic detergents: These are chemically prepared from petroleum products. They are similar in action to soap but do not combine with minerals in water to form a curd. This is a great advantage in most areas where there are minerals dissolved in the water. Synthetic detergents are better wetting agents than soaps and cut grease better.

5.   Acid water solutions: The acid helps cut grease. Commonly used acid solutions are made from vinegar and lemon juice. Acid solutions also act as mild bleaching agents and can be used on some metals to brighten the surface. An example of this is the action of a vinegar solution on aluminum. Weak acid solutions are seldom damaging to the surfaces being cleaned.

6.   Fat solvents: These are agents in which fat or oil is soluble. Dry cleaning fluids are fat solvents, as are gasoline and spot removers. Gasoline is extremely dangerous to handle and should never be used in the home for cleaning purposes or starting fires. Handle all fat solvents carefully as they are highly flammable.

7.   Fat Absorbents: These usually come in powder form and as the name

states, absorb grease or fat. They are then brushed or vacuumed off. Some rug cleaners are made of fat absorbent powders and liquid solvents and are handled the same way. Corn meal, talcum and Fuller's Earth are fat absorbent cleaners.

8. Abrasives: These wear away dirt. There are fine abrasives such as silver polish; medium abrasives such as powdered bathroom cleaners and harsh abrasives such as steel wool, cleaning pads and sand paper. Abrasive cleaners are effective but can scratch surfaces. They must be used according to directions and with discretion.

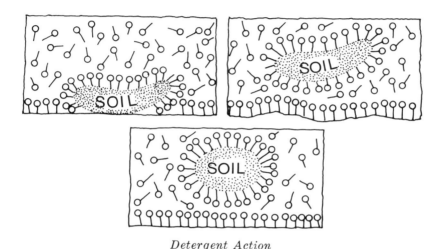

Detergent Action

Additional Cleaning Techniques

Laminated Plastic

Laminated plastic materials are used to cover work counters, back splash areas, table surfaces and sometimes as wall panelling. These surfaces are stain- and heat-resistant but in spite of this require careful treatment. Avoid placing electric fry pans or hot pots directly on these surfaces because they can scorch and buckle. Always use a heat pad of some kind. Heavy use can scratch the surface and this increases the risk of staining. Protect laminated surfaces with a cream wax cleaner. Immediately wipe up spills from stain-inducing materials such as mustard and fruit juice. Do not use abrasive cleaners. These can damage the surface as do bleaches with a chlorine base.

Ceramic and Plastic Wall Tiles

Soap and water cleaning and a protective coat of cream wax are sufficient for these surfaces.

Painted Walls

A solution of ammonia and water, or commercial paint cleaning agents can be used. To avoid streaking, start at the bottom of the wall and work up to the top. Wall washing can be cut to a minimum by careful cooking techniques such as controlling cooking temperatures and using lids on pots when possible.

Unfinished Wooden Surfaces

These are found on cutting boards, rolling boards and chopping blocks. They must be kept scrupulously clean to avoid bacteria contamination, especially when meat, poultry or fish are handled. Do not cut or chop foods on the same surface used for rolling pastry or kneading bread. Food particles can be trapped in cuts and crevices and are hard to remove. When cleaning up flour mixtures, dry scrape the surface first. Do not immerse the board in water. Clean carefully, rinsing with a minimum of water to prevent warping of the wood.

Floors

All floors should be kept clean. This is especially true of kitchen floors. Spills must be completely wiped up when they occur, to prevent slips and falls. For the same reason, objects should not be left on the kitchen floor, anywhere near a traffic path.

Floors should be cleaned in accordance with instructions for the specific covering used. Many coverings require only soap and water cleaning. When water is used a disinfectant can be added. Where wax protection is suggested, an appropriate wax should be chosen. Surfaces should be stripped of wax regularly to avoid build-up and discolouration. Many commercial wax strippers are available for this purpose.

Wax finishes protect floors and improve the appearance of the floor covering. Care should be taken to choose the correct wax for the floor and to ensure the surface is not so slippery as to be a safety hazard.

Waxes are either paste or liquid, polishing or self-polishing, with spirit base or water base.

Spirit-base waxes should not be used on asphalt or rubber tile floors because the spirit solvent used for the wax can damage this. This wax is good for wooden floors.

Water-base waxes are suitable for rubber or asphalt tiles. Either wax can be used on linoleum, vinyl, terrazo or ceramic floorings.

Many floor coverings do not require wax protection. Follow directions carefully for maintaining specific types of floor coverings.

Garbage Cans

To prevent foul odours, keep these scrupulously clean. Wash and disinfect them each time they are emptied. Use bags for disposal and rinse out cans and cartons before throwing them out. Whenever possible, retain containers, rinse and use them for storage in the home.

Kitchen Drains

Coffee grounds, tea leaves and fat clog drains. Never put these down the sink. To keep drains running freely, regularly use one of the commercial agents available to clear drains. These are highly caustic and can be dangerous if directions are not followed carefully.

Bread Boxes

Regularly clean these out. Before odd pieces of bread can mould, place them on cookie sheets and dry for melba toast, croutons or crumbs. Store air tight in a dry place.

Wash out bread boxes with hot soapy water. (Add baking soda to sweeten the smell.) Rinse, dry and air thoroughly.

Safety Precautions

Most accidents are avoidable if precautions are taken:

1. Keep traffic paths clear at all times. Avoid unrelated movement through the work triangle if possible.
2. Wipe spills immediately to avoid falls.
3. Keep pot handles turned to back or protected side of range top.
4. Use adequate heat protection when handling hot containers.
5. Release steam from pots away from your body.
6. Make sure all handles are secure.
7. Never leave fat cooking unattended. Control temperatures carefully.
8. **Have a small kitchen fire extinguisher handy at all times.**
9. Keep a small first aid box in the kitchen. Put burns under cold running water and do not add cream or fat. Call the doctor if doubtful about the seriousness of the burn. Keep hospital and fire department numbers by the phone.
10. Use a kitchen ladder or well-balanced stool for reaching difficult storage areas.
11. Never place knives in dishwater until they are to be washed. Then wash individually, remove from water immediately and dry carefully.
12. Store all sharp or pointed tools in specially designed holders or containers, close to where they are used.

Storage and Use of Cleaning Agents

Many of these are poisonous. Keep them well out of children's reach at all times. Follow directions for use and do not use them in combination unless directed. Toxic gases can be released when two or more are indiscriminately mixed for use.

Part 2

Nutrition

Choosing Food

Daily Food Guide

1. MILK AND MILK PRODUCTS

• Children	2-3 servings
• Adolescents	4 servings
• Adults	1-2 servings
• Expectant and Nursing mothers	4 servings

Examples of One Serving

250 ml milk – whole, 2% or skim
30 g firm cheese
250 ml cottage cheese
250 ml yogurt
250 ml ice cream

Milk can be used as a beverage, as cheese, as ice cream or in other foods like sauces, puddings and soups.

• All growing persons and expectant or nursing mothers need 10 micrograms cholecalciferol vitamin D daily, obtainable in fortified milk and margarine. If the milk used is not fortified, vitamin D supplements are available.

2. MEAT AND ALTERNATES

Daily need: 2 servings

Fish, poultry and eggs are included in this group. Vegetable proteins such as dried beans and peas, peanut butter, and nuts can be used in place of meat.

Examples of One Serving

60-90 g lean meat, fish or poultry
90 g of meat such as weiners, luncheon meat or salami
2 eggs
60 ml peanut butter
250 ml baked beans

3. FRUITS AND VEGETABLES

Daily need: 4 servings or more.

Sources of vitamins C and A are important. Eat a vitamin C rich source every day. Choose a variety of colourful fruits and vegetables.

Vitamin C rich sources are:

• orange, grapefruit or their juices
• vitaminized apple juice

- fresh strawberries
- broccoli, brussels sprouts
- tomato, tomato juice
- raw cabbage, baked potatoes

Vitamin A rich sources are :

- carrots, sweet potato, winter squash
- apricots, cantaloup, fresh peaches
- spinach, beet greens, swiss chard and other dark green vegetables.

Examples of One Serving
125 ml fruit, vegetables or their juices

4.   BREADS AND CEREALS
Daily need: 3 servings
Whole grain or enriched cereals, breads and pastas should be chosen.

Examples of One Serving
175 ml cooked cereal such as oatmeal
250 ml flaked cereal or other ready-to-eat variety
  1 slice whole grain or enriched bread
175 ml enriched pasta such as spaghetti, macaroni or noodles
125 ml cooked brown or converted rice

STANDARDS AND GUIDES
As early as the 1800's, standards were set down by countries to show the minimum requirement of foods necessary to maintain health. Many people have no clear picture of what foods are important to their health and why they are important. Nutrition is a complex study, one which is becoming even more complicated, and governments, recognizing the importance of proper nutrition to the health of the nation, have developed standards for use by health professionals and food guides for general use.

The Canadian Dietary Standard recommends specific nutrient and energy requirements for Canadians of all ages and activity categories. These recommendations, compiled by a group of nutrition, medical and public health authorities serving as advisors to the Minister of National Health and Welfare, are intended to provide a guide in planning normal diets and food supplies for both individuals and groups. The revised standards 1974 are found on page 48. A *daily food guide* is an interpretation of these standards which the average citizen, having little or no knowledge of nutrition, can follow. It states that if the foods listed are eaten each day one can be reasonably sure of getting all the needed food nutrients in the proper amounts.

Food habits are a very personal thing and are closely tied to ethnic and religious customs. For this reason any food guide must be very general and allow plenty of scope for substituting one food for another. Also, it must be in a form which is easily understood by everyone and therefore it is highly simplified. Students interested in nutrition and persons wanting to learn more about what to eat to be healthy will require much more information than a food guide can give.

NUTRIENT CONTRIBUTIONS OF THE FOUR MAIN FOOD GROUPS

1. Milk Group

Protein – high quality (complete protein)
Calcium
Phosphorus
Riboflavin
Vitamin A (if fortified)
Vitamin D (if fortified)

2. Fruit and Vegetable Group

Vitamin C (ascorbic acid)
Vitamin A
Iron
Calcium (in leafy dark green vegetables
    except beet greens, chard and spinach)
Incomplete proteins

3. Meat Group

Complete protein
Iron
Niacin
Riboflavin
Thiamine (as in pork)
Other B vitamins
Vitamin A (in liver)
Phosphorus

4. Bread and Cereal Group

Thiamine
Niacin
Riboflavin
Iron
Carbohydrates
Incomplete protein

OTHER FOODS

Butter and fortified margarine contain vitamin A. Many foods contain saturated and unsaturated fatty acids and provide mainly kilojoules.

SYSTEM FOR SCORING YOUR DAILY FOOD CHOICES

FOOD GROUP	MINIMUM REQUIREMENTS	MAXIMUM POINTS
Milk and Milk Products		
Score 2 points for each serving	Children 2-3 servings	6
	adolescents, pregnant and	
	nursing mothers 3-4 servings	8
	adults 2-3 servings	6

Examples of servings: 250 ml milk; 250 ml cottage cheese; 250 ml yogurt; 30 g firm cheese; 125 ml ice cream equals half a serving

Meat and Alternates		
Score 3 points for each serving	All persons 2 servings	6

Examples of servings: 60-90 g lean meat, fish, poultry; 90 g luncheon meat, weiners, salami; 2 eggs; 250 ml baked beans; 60 ml peanut butter

Fruit and Vegetables		
Score 2 points for all servings		
Score 1 additional point for a Vitamin C rich serving	All persons 4 servings	9

Examples of vitamin C rich servings: 1 orange, ½ grapefruit, 125 ml of their juices; 125 ml vitaminized fruit juices; 125 ml raw or frozen strawberries; ½ small canteloup or ¼ large; 125 ml broccoli

Examples of other vegetables and fruits: fresh, canned, frozen or dried; 125 ml carrots, green beans, peas; 125 ml all vegetable greens; 125 ml winter squash, sweet potatoes; 1 medium potato; 125 ml apricots; 1 apple; 1 banana

Bread and Cereal Products		
Score 2 points for each serving	All persons 3 servings	6

Examples of a serving: 1 slice enriched bread; 250 ml ready to eat cereal; 175 ml whole grain or enriched cooked cereal; 175 ml cooked enriched pasta; 125 ml cooked or converted rice

Vitamin D		
Score two points for a source	Needed by:	
	children, adolescents, pregnant	
	and nursing mothers	2
10 micrograms cholecalciferol Vitamin D supplement		

		TOTAL POINTS
Score of 25-31 Good	Children	27-29
Score of 18-24 Fair	Adolescents, pregnant and	
Score of less than 18, try to improve	nursing mothers	29-31
	Adults	27-29

RECOMMENDED DAILY NUTRIENT INTAKES (Revised 1974)

Based on the recommendations of the
Committee for Revision of the Canadian Dietary Standard
Bureau of Nutritional Sciences, Health and Welfare Canada

Age (years)	Sex	Mass (kg)	Height (cm)	Energy (kJ)	Protein (g)	Calcium (mg)	Iron (mg)	Vitamin A (µg RE)[6]	Thiamin (mg)	Riboflavin (mg)	Niacin (mg)	Ascorbic Acid (mg)	Vitamin D[7] (µg chol.)
0 - ½	Both	6	—	Mass×490	Mass×2.2[1] or ×2	500[5]	7	400	.3	.4	5	20[7]	10
½ - 1	Both	9	—	Mass×452	Mass×1.4[4]	500	7	400	.5	.6	6	20	10
1 - 3	Both	13	90	5 858	22	500	8	400	.7	.8	9	20	10
4 - 6	Both	19	110	7 531	27	500	9	500	.9	1.1	12	20	5
7 - 9	M	27	129	9 205	33	700	10	700	1.1	1.3	14	30	2.5[8]
	F	27	128	8 368	33	700	10	700	1.0	1.2	13	30	2.5[8]
10 - 12	M	36	144	10 460	41	900	11	800	1.2	1.5	17	30	2.5[8]
	F	38	145	9 623	40	1 000	11	800	1.1	1.4	15	30	2.5[8]
13 - 15	M	51	162	11 715	52	1 200	13	1 000	1.4	1.7	19	30	2.5[8]
	F	49	159	9 205	43	800	14	800	1.1	1.4	15	30	2.5[8]
16 - 18	M	64	172	13 389	54	1 000	14	1 000	1.6	2.0	21	30	2.5[8]
	F	54	161	8 786	43	700	14	800	1.1	1.3	14	30	2.5[8]
19 - 35	M	70	176	12 552	56	800	10	1 000	1.5	1.8	20	30	2.5[8]
	F	56	161	8 786	41	700	14	800	1.1	1.3	14	30	2.5[8]
36 - 50	M	70	176	11 297	56	800	10	1 000	1.4	1.7	18	30	2.5[8]
	F	56	161	7 950	41	700	14	800	1.0	1.2	13	30	2.5[8]
51+	M	70	176	9 623[2]	56	800	10	1 000	1.4	1.7	18	30	2.5[8]
	F	56	161	7 531[2]	41	700	9	800	1.0	1.2	13	30	2.5[8]
Pregnant				+1 255[3]	+20	+500	+1[5]	+400	+.2	+.3	+2	+20	+2.5
Lactating				+2 092	+24	+500	+1[5]	+400	+.4	+.4	+7	+30	+2.5

[1] Energy recommendations assume a characteristic activity pattern for each age group. One kilojoule (kJ) is the unit of energy approximately equal to .239 kilocalories of heat energy.

[2] The recommended energy allowance for 66+ is reduced to 8 368 for men and 6 276 for women.

[3] This is the increased energy allowance recommended during the second and third trimester. An increase of only 418 kJ is recommended during the first trimester.

[4] The protein allowance decreases from 2.2 g for each kg of body weight to 2 g per kg of body weight after the first two months of age. If the protein is not from breast milk or its protein equivalent then the protein requirement is greater.

[5] The recommended total intake of 15 mg iron daily during pregnancy and lactation assumes the presence of adequate stores of iron. If these stores are suspected of being inadequate, then additional iron as a supplement is recommended.

[6] To convert retinol equivalents (µg RE) to International Units use this formula:
    One retinol equivalent (µg RE) = 3.3 IU retinol (1 microgram) i.e. from animal sources.
    One retinol equivalent (µg RE) also = 10 IU β-carotene (6 micrograms) i.e. from vegetable sources.

[7] One microgram cholecalciferol (µg chol.) is equivalent to 40 IU of vitamin D activity.

[8] This recommended vitamin D allowance should be increased to 5 µg chol. daily for those who are confined indoors or are otherwise deprived of sunlight for extended periods.

NUTRIENT VALUES OF SOME COMMON FOODS

ABREVIATIONS USED:

A.P. - as purchased	— - indicates no available data	µg RE - microgram retinal equivalent
E.P. - edible portion		
cm - centimetre	g - gram	kJ - kilojoule
mm - millimetre	mg - milligram	dr. - dried
ml - millilitre		pcs. - pieces

	can. - canned
	med. - medium
	fr. - fresh
	tr. - trace
	diam. - diameter

FOOD	PORTION Amount	Mass	Energy kJ	Fat g	Carbohydrate g	Protein g	Calcium mg	Iron mg	Vitamin A µg RE	Thiamine mg	Riboflavin mg	Niacin mg	Ascorbic Acid mg
MILK PRODUCTS													
Buttermilk	250 ml	269 g	391	tr.	13	9	311	.2	tr.	.11	.47	.2	2
Evaporated, can.	125 ml	139 g	794	tr.	13	10	349	.2	135	.06	.46	.3	17
Dried, skim	50 ml	15 g	376	tr.	13	9	322	.2	tr.	.09	.49	.3	2
Fluid, skim	250 ml	269 g	387	tr.	13	9	319	.2	tr.	.10	.46	.2	2
Fluid, whole (3.5%)	250 ml	268 g	704	9	13	9	306	.2	116	.10	.44	.2	2
Cream (18%)	25 ml	26 g	195	5	1	1	26	tr.	61	.01	.04	tr.	tr.
Cream (32%)	25 ml	26 g	328	8	1	1	20	tr.	100	.01	.03	tr.	tr.
Ice Cream, plain	125 ml	71 g	750	11	12	3	146	.1	135	.03	.22	.1	tr.
CITRUS FRUITS & TOMATOES													
Grapefruit, 10 cm diam., A.P.	half	241 g	45	tr.	12	1	19	.5	1	.05	.02	.2	44
Grapefruit juice, can.	125 ml	136 g	55	tr.	13	1	11	.6	1	.04	.02	.2	46
Lemon, med., A.P.	one	110 g	6	tr.	6	1	19	.4	1	.03	.01	.1	39
Orange, 7 cm diam., A.P.	one	180 g	272	tr.	16	1	54	.5	26	.13	.05	.5	66
Orange juice, fr.	125 ml	136 g	255	1	14	1	15	.3	28	.12	.04	.6	68
Orange juice, frozen − diluted	125 ml	137 g	300	tr.	16	1	14	.1	30	.12	.01	.6	66
Orange juice, can.	125 ml	137 g	300	tr.	15	1	14	.6	28	.09	.03	.4	55
Orange & grapefruit juice, can.	125 ml	138 g	299	tr.	20	1	12	.4	8	.07	.03	.3	52
Tomato, 6 cm diam., A.P.	one	150 g	146	tr.	7	2	20	.8	135	.10	.06	1.0	34
Tomato, can.	125 ml	133 g	115	tr.	6	1	8	.7	119	.07	.04	.9	23
Tomato juice, can.	125 ml	134 g	104	tr.	6	1	9	1.2	107	.07	.03	1.0	21
Tomato sauce, can.	50 ml	60 g	291	5	5	1	6	.4	76	.03	.03	.4	4
OTHER FRUIT													
Apple, 6 cm diam., A.P.	one	150 g	293	tr.	18	tr.	8	.4	5	.04	.02	.1	3
Apple juice, vitaminized, can.	125 ml	136 g	276	tr.	17	tr.	8	.8	—	.01	.02	.1	48
Apple sauce, sweetened, can.	125 ml	140 g	529	tr.	33	tr.	6	.7	6	.03	.02	.1	2
Apricots, dr., about 10 halves	50 ml	33 g	359	tr.	22	2	22	1.8	357	tr.	.05	1.0	4
Bananas, 20 cm long, A.P.	one	175 g	418	tr.	26	1	10	.8	23	.06	.07	.8	12
Blueberries, fr.	125 ml	77 g	196	tr.	12	tr.	12	.8	8	.02	.04	.3	11
Canteloup, 13 cm diam., A.P.	half	385 g	251	tr.	14	1	27	.8	654	.08	.06	1.2	63
Cherries, large, fr., A.P.	ten	78 g	180	tr.	10	1	13	.3	44	.04	.03	.3	6
Cherries, pitted, can.	125 ml	134 g	242	tr.	14	1	20	.4	91	.04	.03	.3	7
Dates, pitted, A.P.	50 ml	39 g	451	tr.	29	1	23	1.2	2	.04	.04	.9	0
Grape juice, can. or bottled	125 ml	84 g	380	tr.	23	1	15	.1	—	.06	.03	.3	22
Grapes, Canadian type, A.P.	1 ml	100 g	42	tr.	10	1	10	.3	6	.03	.02	.1	2
Peaches, 5 cm diam., A.P.	one	114 g	146	tr.	10	1	9	.5	132	.02	.05	1.0	7
Peaches, can.	125 ml	140 g	460	tr.	29	1	6	.4	61	.01	.03	.8	4
Pears, 7 cm diam., A.P.	one	182 g	418	1	25	1	13	.5	3	.04	.07	.2	7
Pears, can.	125 ml	140 g	449	tr.	28	1	7	.3	tr.	.02	.03	.2	2
Pineapple, can.	125 ml	143 g	449	tr.	28	1	16	.4	7	.11	.03	.3	9
Pineapple juice, can.	125 ml	137 g	311	tr.	19	1	20	.4	7	.07	.02	.3	12

NUTRIENT VALUES OF SOME COMMON FOODS *(continued)*

FOOD	PORTION Amount	PORTION Mass	Energy kJ	Fat g	Carbohydrate g	Protein g	Calcium mg	Iron mg	Vitamin A µg RE	Thiamine mg	Riboflavin mg	Niacin mg	Ascorbic Acid mg
Plums, 5 cm diam., A.P.	one	60 g	105	tr.	7	tr.	7	.3	14	.02	.02	.3	3
Prunes, dr., med., A.P.	six	48 g	439	tr.	27	1	21	1.6	66	.03	.06	.6	2
Raisins, seedless	50 ml	36 g	442	tr.	28	1	22	1.3	1	.04	.03	.2	tr.
Raspberries, fr., A.P.	125 ml	68 g	161	tr.	9	1	15	.6	9	.02	.06	.6	17
Rhubarb, cooked, sugar added	125 ml	150 g	886	tr.	54	tr.	117	.9	12	.03	.08	.4	9
Strawberries, fr., A.P.	125 ml	82 g	127	tr.	7	1	17	.8	5	.02	.06	.6	48
Watermelon, slices: 25 cm diam. & 2 cm thick	one	925 g	481	1	27	2	30	2.1	251	.13	.13	.7	30
VEGETABLES													
Asparagus spears, 1 cm diam. E.P.	four	60 g	42	tr.	13	1	13	.4	54	.10	.11	.8	16
Asparagus, green, can.	125 ml	80 g	17	tr.	3	2	17	1.3	68	.05	.08	.7	12
Beans, lima, fr.	125 ml	94 g	437	1	19	7	44	2.4	26	.17	.09	1.2	16
Beans, snap or green, fr.	125 ml	69 g	212	tr.	4	1	35	.4	37	.05	.06	.3	8
Beans, snap or green, can.	125 ml	69 g	212	tr.	4	1	31	1.0	32	.02	.03	.2	3
Beets, fr.	125 ml	94 g	146	tr.	7	1	13	.5	2	.03	.04	.3	6
Beets, can.	125 ml	91 g	143	tr.	8	1	18	.7	2	.01	.02	.1	3
Beet greens, fr.	125 ml	80 g	58	tr.	3	1	79	1.5	407	.06	.12	.2	12
Broccoli, 1 cm pcs., E.P.	125 ml	85 g	209	tr.	4	3	75	.7	213	.08	.17	.7	77
Brussels sprouts	125 ml	85 g	92	tr.	6	4	28	.9	45	.07	.12	.2	74
Cabbage, red, raw, shredded	125 ml	39 g	11	tr.	3	1	16	.3	6	.03	.02	.2	24
Carrots, 3 cm base diam., 15 cm long, E.P.	one	50 g	84	tr.	5	1	18	.4	550	.03	.03	.3	4
Carrots, cooked, diced	125 ml	80 g	29	tr.	6	1	26	.5	837	.04	.04	.4	5
Cauliflower, fr., E.P.	125 ml	51 g	68	tr.	3	1	11	.5	5	.05	.05	.3	35
Celery, raw, pcs.	125 ml	50 g	39	tr.	2	1	21	.2	13	.02	.02	.2	5
Corn, sweet, ear, 4 cm diam., 13 cm long	one	140 g	293	1	16	3	2	.5	42	.09	.08	1.0	7
Corn, sweet, can., cream style	125 ml	127 g	396	tr.	20	2	6	.7	25	.03	.07	1.1	7
Cucumber, sliced, 5 cm diam. 3 mm thick	six	50 g	21	tr.	2	tr.	8	.2	tr.	.02	.02	.1	6
Lettuce, crisp, head, large leaves	two	50 g	42	tr.	2	1	34	.7	95	.03	.04	.2	9
Mushrooms, fr., average	four	70 g	326	7	3	2	8	.7	17	.05	.28	2.9	tr.
Onions, 6 cm diam.	one	110 g	167	tr.	10	2	30	.6	4	.04	.04	.2	11
Parsnips, fr., E.P.	125 ml	85 g	230	tr.	13	1	39	.5	4	.06	.07	.1	9
Peas, green, fr., E.P.	125 ml	88 g	265	tr.	11	5	10	1.6	37	.24	.09	2.0	18
Peas, green, can.	125 ml	77 g	258	1	11	5	18	1.6	39	.09	.05	.8	7
Peppers, green, E.P.	one	74 g	63	tr.	4	1	7	.5	31	.06	.06	.4	94
Potatoes, med., fr., baked	one	136 g	377	tr.	21	3	9	.7	tr.	.10	.04	1.7	22
Radish, small, E.P.	four	40 g	21	tr.	1	tr.	12	.4	tr.	.01	.01	.1	10
Spinach, fr., E.P.	125 ml	99 g	167	tr.	3	3	92	2.0	802	.07	.14	.6	28
Squash, summer, diced	125 ml	116 g	69	tr.	4	1	29	.5	45	.06	.09	.9	12
Squash, winter, mashed	125 ml	113 g	272	tr.	18	2	31	.9	431	.06	.15	.8	15
Sweet potato, 13 cm × 5 cm, baked	one	110 g	230	1	36	2	44	1.0	891	.10	.07	.7	24
Turnip, cubed	125 ml	110 g	198	tr.	8	1	59	tr.	61	.07	.07	.6	29

NUTRIENT VALUES OF SOME COMMON FOODS *(continued)*

FOOD	PORTION Amount	Mass	Energy kJ	Fat g	Carbohydrate g	Protein g	Calcium mg	Iron mg	Vitamin A μg RE	Thiamine mg	Riboflavin mg	Niacin mg	Ascorbic Acid mg
WHOLE GRAIN CEREALS													
Flour, whole wheat	250 ml	132 g	1 841	2	94	19	39	4.0	0	.77	.22	7.9	0
Oatmeal or rolled oats, dry	50 ml	18 g	287	1	12	2	9	.8	0	.11	.02	.2	0
Oatmeal or rolled oats, cooked	125 ml	132 g	299	1	13	3	12	.8	0	.10	.03	.1	0
Rice, brown, cooked	125 ml	88 g	456	tr.	24	2	10	.5	0	.11	.01	1.1	0
Wheat flakes	250 ml	31 g	484	tr.	25	3	11	.9	0	.02	.07	1.4	0
Wheat germ	15 ml	—	84	1	3	1	4	.4	0	.11	.04	.2	0
Wheat, shredded, large (12 of the spoon size)	one	25 g	335	tr.	18	1	10	.8	0	.06	.02	1.3	0
REFINED CEREALS													
Barley, pearl, raw	25 ml	22 g	322	tr.	17	2	4	.4	0	.03	.01	.7	0
Cornflakes, enriched	250 ml	23 g	363	tr.	20	2	1	3.3	0	.50	.83	.5	0
Cornmeal, dry	50 ml	30 g	460	tr.	24	2	2	.3	13	.04	.01	.3	0
Farina, enriched, cooked	125 ml	134 g	242	tr.	11	2	99	8.5	0	.03	.01	.2	0
Flour, all-purpose, enriched	250 ml	121 g	1 777	1	86	14	20	3.5	0	.55	.33	4.4	0
Macaroni or spaghetti, cooked	250 ml	154 g	202	1	35	6	12	.7	0	.02	.02	.4	0
Noodles, egg, cooked	250 ml	176 g	920	1	41	8	18	1.1	36	.06	.03	.7	0
Rice, white, short grain, cooked	125 ml	94 g	495	tr.	28	2	8	.2	0	.02	.01	.5	0
Rice, puffed, enriched	250 ml	31 g	488	tr.	26	2	6	4.4	0	.66	1.10	6.6	0
Wheat, puffed, enriched	250 ml	17 g	251	tr.	13	2	5	.7	0	.44	.82	4.9	0
BREADS & CRACKERS													
Bread, dark rye or pumpernickel slices	one	32 g	330	tr.	17	3	27	.8	0	.07	.04	.4	0
Bread, raisin, slices	one	25 g	272	tr.	13	2	18	.3	0	.01	.02	.2	—
Bread, white, enriched, slices	one	30 g	343	1	15	2	20	.5	0	.07	.05	.7	0
Bread, whole wheat (60%), slices	one	30 g	301	1	15	3	15	.7	0	.05	.03	1.0	0
Crackers, graham, 6 cm square	four	28 g	460	3	21	2	11	.4	0	.01	.06	.4	0
Crackers, saltine, 5 cm square	four	11 g	209	1	8	1	2	.1	0	tr.	tr.	.1	0
BEEF													
Ground beef, lean (less than 15% fat), broiled		85 g	774	10	0	23	10	3.0	6	.08	.20	5.1	—
Ground beef, regular (less than 30% fat), broiled		85 g	1 025	17	0	21	9	2.7	9	.07	.18	4.6	—
Oven roast, lean (e.g. round)		85 g	688	3	0	25	11	3.2	3	.06	.19	4.5	—
Oven roast, fat (e.g. rib)		85 g	1 569	34	0	17	8	2.2	21	.05	.13	3.1	—
Pot roast or stewing beef		85 g	1 025	16	0	23	10	2.9	9	.04	.18	3.5	—
Steaks, fat (e.g. sirloin), broiled		85 g	1 381	27	0	20	9	2.5	15	.05	.16	4.0	—
Corned beef, can.		85 g	774	10	0	22	17	3.7	6	.01	.20	2.9	—
LAMB													
Lamb chop, lean and fat, broiled	one	112 g	586	6	0	21	9	1.5	—	.11	.20	4.5	—
Lamb leg, lean and fat, broiled		85 g	983	16	0	22	9	1.4	—	.13	.23	4.7	—
PORK													
Bacon, back, slices	one	21 g	272	4	3	6	4	—	0	.18	.03	1.1	0
Bacon, side, slices	two	15 g	377	8	1	5	2	.5	0	.08	.05	.8	0

NUTRIENT VALUES OF SOME COMMON FOODS *(continued)*

FOOD	PORTION Amount	PORTION Mass	Energy kJ	Fat g	Carbohydrate g	Protein g	Calcium mg	Iron mg	Vitamin A μg RE	Thiamine mg	Riboflavin mg	Niacin mg	Ascorbic Acid mg
Ham, cured, boiled, sliced		85 g	842	15	0	16	9	2.4	0	.37	.13	2.2	0
Pork chop, thick, with bone	one	98 g	1088	21	0	16	8	2.2	0	.63	.18	3.8	0
Roast pork		85 g	1297	24	0	21	9	2.7	0	.78	.22	4.7	—
VEAL													
Cutlet or chop, boneless cooked		85 g	774	9	—	23	9	2.7	—	.06	.21	4.6	—
Leg, roasted		85 g	961	14	0	23	10	2.9	—	.11	.26	6.6	—
Stew meat		85 g	409	7	0	8	4	1.2	0	.05	.10	2.6	0
POULTRY													
Chicken, roast		85 g	722	11	0	12	17	1.3	0	.07	.14	6.8	0
Chicken, fried, breast	half	94 g	649	5	1	25	9	1.3	21	.04	.17	11.2	—
Turkey, roast		85 g	669	6	0	25	24	5.0	3	.06	.14	5.8	0
VARIETY MEATS													
Beef heart, braised		85 g	669	5	1	27	5	5.0	6	.21	1.04	6.5	1
Beef kidney, cooked		85 g	640	9	1	16	10	8.6	347	.16	1.80	3.5	0
Beef liver, fried		85 g	810	9	4	22	9	7.0	13535	.22	3.53	14.0	22
Bologna, 8 cm diam., sliced	one	13 g	167	3	tr.	2	1	.3	—	.04	.03	.4	—
Salami, dry		13 g	251	5	tr.	3	2	.5	—	.05	.03	.7	—
Sausage, pork links	one	13 g	260	6	tr.	3	1	.3	0	.11	.05	.5	—
Weiners	one	56 g	669	15	1	7	3	.8	—	.08	.11	1.4	—
FISH													
Cod, fried in butter		85 g	611	4	—	23	26	.8	46	.07	.09	2.5	—
Haddock, fried, breaded		85 g	586	5	5	17	34	1.0	—	.03	.06	2.7	2
Halibut, grilled with butter		85 g	611	6	0	21	14	.7	174	.04	.06	7.1	—
Salmon, can., with bones		85 g	502	5	0	17	167	.7	18	.03	.16	6.8	—
Salmon, fr., fried in butter		85 g	649	6	0	23	—	1.0	42	.14	.05	6.2	—
Sardines, can. in oil		85 g	732	9	0	20	372	2.5	57	.02	.17	3.0	—
Trout, raw		85 g	594	9	0	16	17	.9	—	.08	.17	3.0	—
Tuna, can.		85 g	711	7	0	24	7	1.6	21	.04	.10	10.1	—
SHELLFISH													
Crab, can.		85 g	356	2	1	15	38	.7	—	.07	.07	1.6	—
Lobster, boiled with butter	one	334 g	1289	25	1	20	80	.7	276	.11	.06	2.3	0
Scallops, cooked	five	85 g	398	1	—	20	98	2.6	—	—	—	—	—
Shrimp, large, fried	five	85 g	800	9	9	17	61	1.7	0	.03	.07	2.3	—
Shrimp, small, A.P.	150 ml	85 g	324	1	2	20	54	1.4	0	.02	.03	2.7	—
OTHER PROTEIN FOODS													
Cheese, cheddar, 3 cm cube	27 ml	30 g	519	9	tr.	7	226	.3	116	tr.	.14	tr.	0
Cheese, cheddar, processed	27 ml	30 g	470	10	tr.	7	234	.3	112	tr.	.13	tr.	0
Cheese, cottage, creamed (4% fat)	30 ml	30 g	131	1	1	4	28	.1	15	.01	.07	tr.	0
Cheese, cottage, not creamed	34 ml	30 g	106	tr.	1	5	27	.1	1	.01	.08	tr.	0
Eggs, large, fried	one	55 g	547	10	—	6	28	1.1	222	.05	.15	0	0
Eggs, large, whole, without shell	one	50 g	335	6	tr.	6	27	1.1	177	.05	.15	tr.	0
Peanut butter	15 ml	16 g	426	9	3	4	10	.3	—	.02	.02	2.6	0
Peanuts, roasted, salted	50 ml	32 g	773	16	6	8	24	.7	—	.10	.04	5.4	0
Walnuts, English, chopped	50 ml	28 g	736	18	4	4	28	.7	tr.	.10	.04	.4	—
FATS													
Butter	15 ml	15 g	448	13	tr.	tr.	3	0	151	—	—	—	0

NUTRIENT VALUES OF SOME COMMON FOODS *(continued)*

FOOD	PORTION Amount	Mass	Energy kJ	Fat g	Carbohydrate g	Protein g	Calcium mg	Iron mg	Vitamin A µg RE	Thiamine mg	Riboflavin mg	Niacin mg	Ascorbic Acid mg
Lard	15 ml	14 g	505	14	0	0	0	0	0	0	0	0	0
Margarine, hard or soft	15 ml	15 g	439	13	tr.	tr.	3	0	154	—	—	—	0
Mayonnaise	15 ml	15 g	439	12	tr.	tr.	3	.1	13	tr.	.01	tr.	0
Oil, salad or cooking	15 ml	15 g	549	15	0	0	0	0	—	0	0	0	0
Salad dressing, French	15 ml	16 g	259	6	2	tr.	2	tr.	—	tr.	tr.	tr.	0
Salad dressing, French, diet	15 ml	17 g	59	tr.	2	tr.	2	.1	—	—	—	—	0
Shortening, vegetable	15 ml	14 g	486	14	0	0	0	0	0	0	0	0	0
SWEETS													
Candy bar, average	one	35 g	703	8	22	3	31	.9	—	.02	.06	2.0	0
Caramels, plain or chocolate	one	10 g	173	1	8	tr.	15	.1	tr.	tr.	.02	tr.	tr.
Chocolate, baking, sweet	25 ml	25 g	565	9	14	1	24	.4	tr.	.01	.04	.1	0
Cookies, chocolate chip	one	10 g	209	3	6	1	4	.2	3	.01	.01	.1	0
Devil's food layer cake, chocolate icing, 22 cm diam., 1/16 pcs.	one	69 g	983	9	40	3	41	.6	30	.02	.06	.1	0
Fruitcake, dark, 20 cm loaf, 1/30 pcs.	one	15 g	228	2	9	1	11	.4	6	.02	.02	.1	0
Honey, strained	15 ml	20 g	245	0	18	tr.	1	.1	0	tr.	.01	.1	tr.
Jams and preserves	15 ml	20 g	207	tr.	13	tr.	4	.3	tr.	tr.	.01	tr.	—
Sponge cake, plain, 25 cm diam., 1/12 pcs.	one	66 g	816	4	36	5	20	.8	90	.03	.09	.1	0
Sugar, brown	15 ml	15 g	226	0	14	0	12	.5	0	tr.	tr.	tr.	0
Sugar, white, granulated	15 ml	12 g	177	0	12	0	0	tr.	0	0	0	0	0
Syrup, chocolate, thin	15 ml	34 g	339	1	22	1	5	.5	tr.	.01	.03	.2	0
Syrup, corn	15 ml	19 g	215	tr.	10	tr.	3	.3	0	0	0	0	0
White layer cake, chocolate icing, 22 cm diam., 1/16 pcs.	one	71 g	1046	8	45	3	70	.4	40	.01	.06	.1	0
MISCELLANEOUS													
Cola, carbonated	250 ml	269 g	443	0	27	0	—	—	0	0	0	0	0
Gelatin dessert, prepared with water	125 ml	132 g	368	0	21	2	—	—	—	—	—	—	—
Ginger ale	250 ml	267 g	351	0	21	0	—	—	0	0	0	0	0
Muffins, plain, 7 cm diam.	one	40 g	502	4	17	3	42	.6	12	.07	.09	.6	tr.
Muffins, bran	one	35 g	360	3	14	3	35	1.3	18	.07	.09	1.5	2
Pancakes, plain, mixed with egg and milk, 10 cm diam.	one	27 g	25	2	6	2	58	.3	21	.04	.06	.2	—
Pie, apple, 2-crust, 23 cm diam., 1/6 pcs.	one	160 g	1715	18	61	3	1	.5	10	.03	.03	.6	2
Pie, lemon meringue, 23 cm diam., 1/6 pcs.	one	140 g	1494	14	53	5	20	.7	72	.05	.11	.3	4
Pizza (cheese), 36 cm diam., ⅛ pcs.	one	75 g	774	6	27	7	107	.7	87	.04	.12	.7	4
Popcorn, popped, oil and salt	250 ml	10 g	184	2	5	1	1	.2	—	—	.01	.1	0
Pickles, dill, med.	one	50 g	23	tr.	1	tr.	13	.5	5	tr.	.01	tr.	3
Soup, cream of mushroom, with milk	250 ml	270 g	990	15	18	8	210	.6	83	.06	.37	.8	1
Soup, tomato, with milk	250 ml	275 g	805	8	25	8	185	.9	316	.11	.28	1.4	17
Soup, vegetable beef, with water	250 ml	270 g	368	2	11	6	13	.8	300	.06	.06	1.1	—
White sauce, med.	50 ml	55 g	373	6	5	2	63	.1	76	.02	.09	.1	tr.

The Nutrients

Proteins

Food proteins are complex compounds, necessary for growth, maintenance and repair of body tissues and optimum good health. They are made up of simpler substances known as amino acids. Some 22 different amino acids have been identified, and about 12 to 18 of these are usually present in any food protein. Ten amino acids, referred to as essential or indispensable, must be supplied in sufficient amounts by food. If any one of the 10 is missing, or if they are not present in the correct ratio, normal growth is not possible. The others, referred to as non-essential, can be built up in the body from fragments of amino acids plus other available substances; individually they are not required since one can replace another.

Proteins in foods vary according to the kinds and amounts of amino acids they contain. They are often classified as complete or incomplete. Complete proteins contain all essential amino acids in reasonable amounts. They are usually found in foods from animal sources, such as milk (all types), cheese, eggs, meat, fish and poultry. The exception is gelatin, which lacks some of the essential amino acids. Incomplete proteins, as their name implies, are lacking or low in one or more essential amino acids. Proteins in most foods of vegetable origin, such as cereals, breads, dried legumes and nuts, are the incomplete kind, although the quality of peas, beans and other legumes is generally higher than many other plant proteins. Fortunately the amino acid selections in different food proteins can supplement one another. If incomplete protein foods (cereals, pastas, legumes or nuts) are mixed with, or eaten with complete protein foods (milk, cheese, meat, fish, etc.) they are as effective in performing their functions as the complete proteins are alone. In fact, the two types of foods together offer more amino acids in ideal proportions than either food by itself. Thus, casseroles, soups, puddings, sandwiches, cereal with milk, and other protein food mixtures or combinations, are wise food choices. It is important to note, however, that the incomplete and complete protein food "partners" must be eaten at the same meal if the amino acid supplementation is to take place.

When foods are eaten, their proteins are broken down during digestion into their component amino acids. These are carried by the blood stream to all body cells. Two remarkable substances called deoxyribonucleic acid (the DNA molecule) and ribonucleic acid (the RNA molecule) are responsible for using these amino acids to synthesize tissue protein. Together they select and arrange the proper amino acids to build each type of body protein, (muscle, blood, nerve, enzymes, etc.). This is the basic mechanism of genetic control or inheritance.

There are no specific protein reserves in the body as there are for some other nutrients. When more protein is eaten than is needed, it serves as a source of energy or is converted to fat. The protein needs of the body should be met regularly with a variety of foods that supply all essential amino acids. When sufficient amino acids are not supplied in food, body proteins may be used. However, the cells soon reach a point where they can spare no more protein and symptoms of nutritional deficiency appear. The protein deficiency disease kwashiorkor is common in young children in countries where cereal foods are the main staple diet and where animal protein foods are in short supply.

Vegetable Proteins

The importance of complete proteins from animal sources has been explained. All of the essential amino acids are found in meat, poultry, fish, eggs, milk and cheese, so that one of these can be the only protein served at a meal. Any of these animal sources can be used to supplement the incomplete type of protein found in most plant sources. When served together, a greater number of amino acids can be supplied to the body than either will provide when served alone.

However, persons restricting their protein intake to incomplete proteins alone must be very careful in their selection of food combinations. Unless a supplement of milk, milk products or eggs is used, vegetarian diets must provide all of the essential amino acids **at each meal** by combining incomplete protein foods which complement each other. By using them in combination, those amino acids which are deficient in one may be supplied by another vegetable protein. Here are examples of combinations which can **be used – any food from a grouping on the left can be served with any food chosen from the corresponding group on the right to provide a complete protein:**

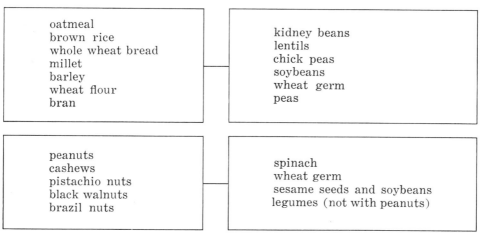

oatmeal brown rice whole wheat bread millet barley wheat flour bran	kidney beans lentils chick peas soybeans wheat germ peas
peanuts cashews pistachio nuts black walnuts brazil nuts	spinach wheat germ sesame seeds and soybeans legumes (not with peanuts)

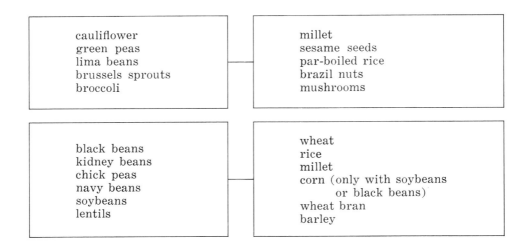

cauliflower green peas lima beans brussels sprouts broccoli	millet sesame seeds par-boiled rice brazil nuts mushrooms
black beans kidney beans chick peas navy beans soybeans lentils	wheat rice millet corn (only with soybeans or black beans) wheat bran barley

Fats

Fat is an essential nutrient, serving as the carrier of important fat soluble vitamins (A, D, E, K) and providing a concentrated source of energy. A limited amount of stored body fat is desirable to provide a reserve supply of energy, to insulate and protect body parts, and to improve appearance.

Foods containing visible fats come from both animal and vegetable sources, and are easily recognized. Other common foods, including pork, beef, fish, cheese, whole milk, egg yolk, nuts, chocolate and olives, contain fairly high percentages of fats that are not so obvious. Since fats produce more than twice the kilojoules produced by equal masses of protein or carbohydrates, these "invisible" fats should not be overlooked.

Food fats, more properly called lipids, are complicated chemical compounds. Some are liquid at room temperature and are called oils. Others are solid or semi-solid, and are called fats. Most contain a molecule of glycerol (glycerin) combined with three molecules of fatty acids. Variations in the kinds and combinations of these fatty acids produce different kinds of fats.

About ten different fatty acids are found in the fats or lipids in common foods. Three of these cannot be made in the body, but are known to be necessary for good health. They are classified as the essential fatty acids. If other fatty acids are not in the food we eat, they can be manufactured in the body from by-products of protein and carbohydrate digestion that are not used for building, repair or energy.

There are three types of fatty acids, saturated, monounsaturated and polyunsaturated, depending upon the degree to which hydrogen atoms are bound (or attached) to the remainder of the fatty acid molecule. The essential fatty acids are all polyunsaturated. Firm or solid fats, such as those in meats and butter, usually contain a high proportion of saturated fatty acids. Olive oil is the most common example of a food containing a high percentage of monounsaturated (almost saturated) fatty acids. Other common vegetable oils (corn, cottonseed, peanut and soya) contain high proportions of polyunsaturated fatty acids. The exception is coconut oil, which is high in saturated fatty acids, and which remain firm at 20°C. The fats in poultry and fish are largely made up of mono- and polyunsaturated fatty acids, and their fat is correspondingly soft and pliable.

Most of the digestion of fats takes place in the intestine. Bile from the liver disperses the fat into tiny particles to form an emulsion, and enzymes (some from the pancreas) split off some of the fatty acids. Monoglycerides (a molecule of glycerol with one fatty acid), fatty acids, some glycerol and some fat are absorbed into the intestine wall where the lipid structure reforms. The lipids then pass, mainly by way of the lymph system, to blood vessels and are transported to body cells. If not used for energy, fat is deposited under the skin, between muscles and around internal organs. This deposited fat represents reserve fuel in a dynamic state. It may come from dietary fat, carbohydrate or proteins. Newly absorbed or synthesized fat is continually deposited to replace that which has been removed and oxidized.

Elderly persons, or those who are fatigued or suffering from infection, may find fats difficult to digest, probably because their digestive processes are less efficient. Most older persons are less active and, therefore can do with less of these high energy foods.

The body needs both saturated and unsaturated fats for good health. Some authorities believe excessive intakes of fat, particularly from animal sources, may be related to the development of atherosclerosis and heart disease. While a direct relationship between diet and atherosclerosis has not been proven, most physicians recommend a choice of foods to supply moderate amounts of fat from both animal and vegetable sources. This practice, and a reduction in total intake of kilojoules, including those from food fats, will help to prevent obesity, an acknowledged contributing factor in heart disease. Increasing energy expenditure by regular exercise also helps. Choosing skim or 2% milk and lean meats will help reduce fat intake without sacrificing important protein, minerals and water soluble vitamins. Since excess carbohydrates, and excess amounts of amino acids from protein digestion may also be converted to body fat, it is important to match total daily food intake to total daily energy needs.

Carbohydrates

There are two main types of carbohydrates in foods – starches and sugars. These provide the body with its most economical sources of energy.

Starch is the complex carbohydrate found in cereal grains (including flours, breads and pastas) and in some vegetables (e.g., potatoes, corn, dried beans). It is a polysaccharide made up of thousands of molecules of a simple sugar called glucose, and must be broken down during digestion into glucose before the body can use it. This breakdown is started in the mouth by an enzyme in the saliva and is completed in the small intestine. Glucose molecules, the smallest units of starch digestion, are carried by the blood to the liver. Most available glucose travels on to body cells to be burned (metabolized) with oxygen to provide energy. The body stores small amounts of glucose in liver and muscle tissue as glycogen, which is made up of thousands of glucose molecules joined together. This is readily converted to glucose when the body needs extra energy.

Sugars, the second common type of carbohydrate, are found in fruits and vegetables, usually in the form of fructose, glucose or sucrose. Some fruits and vegetables contain much more sugar than others, and thus provide more kilojoules. Sucrose (table sugar) is a disaccharide, meaning it is made up of two simple sugars, glucose and fructose, joined together. During digestion in the intestine, enzymes break these down into simple sugars known as monosaccharides. Fructose (which has the sweetest taste of all sugars) and glucose are monosaccharides. Glucose is the most common monosaccharide and the form most readily used by the body for energy.

Milk is the only common food from an animal source that contains any appreciable amount of carbohydrate. Milk's sugar is called lactose, a dissaccharide (galactose and glucose) that gives milk its characteristic sweet flavour.

The foods known as white or brown sugar are almost entirely carbohydrate in the form of sucrose, differing only in their degree of purification. These sugars and similar sweets (syrups, honey, molasses, jams, jellies and marmalades) should not be eaten as the main source of food energy. They offer few, if any, nutrient values and often contribute to tooth decay. In fact, excessive amounts of any foods containing a high percentage of starch or sugar are not desirable. They may satisfy the appetite and meet energy needs without providing all necessary nutrients. Particularly if eaten between meals, they are potential causes of dental caries. And always, the tendency toward a high consumption of this type of food is the warning signal of obesity. Some researchers suggest that excessive consumption of sucrose (or its derivatives) not only contributes indirectly to increased incidence of atherosclerosis and heart disease through obesity, but is directly involved as a significant factor. However, reasonable amounts of carbohydrates are necessary each day; first, so proteins will not have to be used for energy; second, so fats are utilized more efficiently. If more carbohydrate is available than is used for energy production and glycogen storage, the excess is converted into body fat.

Minerals

Although mineral elements account for only 4% of the body weight, they are a critically essential part of human nutrition. In general, they have two main functions. The first one is as an actual constituent of the body in both hard and soft tissues. For example: calcium, phosphorus and magnesium are very important in the structure of bones and teeth. Iodine is found in the thyroid gland and in its secretion, thyroxine. Many of the hormones, enzymes and other body components include minerals in their makeup.

In their second important role, minerals act as regulators and are necessary to certain body functions. For example, minerals are important to the functioning of nerves. Certain minerals are involved in maintaining an acid-base balance in the body. Minerals also contribute to the movement of body liquids by osmotic pressure. They are a valuable catalyst for a number of reactions in the normally functioning body.

The exact role and daily requirement of many mineral elements is not yet known. Those of major nutritional concern are calcium, phosphorus and iron. When recommended amounts of these are provided, needs for others are usually met. A discussion of the importance of these three minerals makes up the major portion of this section. Other minerals are mentioned briefly in an attempt to show the wide range of their important functions.

CALCIUM AND PHOSPHORUS

Calcium (Ca) and phosphorus (P) together make up the major part of the mineral content of skeletal tissues. About 99% of the body's calcium and 70 to 80% of its phosphorus are in the bones, in an almost constant 1:1 ratio. These minerals are largely responsible for the rigidity and strength of bones and teeth. The bones provide a mineral reserve which may be drawn upon when other sources are not adequate. The calcium level of the blood, important in normal functions of nervous tissue, may be maintained from these reserves.

Calcium functions in bone formation with several other essential nutrients, including phosphorus, fluoride, potassium, sodium, magnesium, and vitamins A, C and D. Although the dietary supply of calcium may be adequate, its absorption and utilization by the body depend upon the presence of vitamin D. For healthy bone and tooth formation, vitamins A and C must also be available.

Calcium is needed by persons of all ages. Infants, children and adolescents need extra supplies for normal development of bones and teeth. Adults need some for maintenance and repair of bones, and they also require it to maintain normal muscle tone and nerve function, to regulate the heart beat and to aid normal blood clotting. These requirements continue into old age, so nutrients such as calcium remain important in the maintenance of health throughout life. Expectant and nursing mothers have greatly increased needs for this mineral. During the latter part of pregnancy the fetus demands calcium for skeletal and tooth formation. Then the mother must supply her own normal requirements plus those of her developing baby. While nursing her baby, she must again meet her own needs plus that needed for milk production. All persons lose calcium daily in faeces and urine, so an adequate supply must be provided in foods to prevent depletion of reserves in the bones. If this depletion continues, bone fragility will result.

Phosphorus is as important as calcium, and is involved in many of the same body functions. It is also very important in energy metabolism. Because the two minerals almost always occur together, the significance of phosphorus as an essential nutrient is often overlooked. Fortunately, foods rich in calcium are also good sources of phosphorus.

It is difficult to meet calcium (and phosphorus) requirements with foods unless milk and cheese are included daily in amounts recommended in Canadian food guides. Other dairy foods made from milk, and some green leafy vegetables are also good sources. Greens of the goosefoot family, such as spinach, beet tops and chard, contain oxalic acid which combines with their calcium to form an insoluble substance which limits the amount of calcium the body can absorb or use.

Calcium and phosphorus are stable and relatively insoluble in water so that cooking, freezing, canning or processing do not cause losses.

IRON

The minute amount of iron (Fe) in the body, about 5 grams in a healthy adult, is in no way indicative of its nutritional importance. This mineral is one of the most vital elements in body metabolism. It is stored in almost all body tissues, with major iron reserves found in the liver, spleen and bone marrow.

Iron is a necessary part of the hemoglobin in red blood cells, making possible the transport of oxygen and carbon dioxide. The blood cells continually wear out and break down, releasing their iron. Most of this iron can be recovered and re-used but there is always a small loss. Thus there is a continuous need for new supplies of iron from food. If iron intake is habitually low and reserve supplies are gradually depleted, an iron deficiency anaemia will develop. Additional iron is lost any time blood is lost. Any excessive bleeding may lead to anaemia unless iron intake is increased. Iron from foods must also provide for the expanding volume of blood in growing persons. During pregnancy and lactation, the need for iron is greatly increased. The mother must provide iron for the developing fetus; to increase her own blood volume; and to supply her baby with a store of iron to last for several months after birth until the baby's own diet contains iron-rich foods.

Many factors influence the body's degree of utilization of iron in foods. These include: the chemical form of the mineral, the nature of the particular food source and the extent of the body's current iron reserves. The iron level in the body is regulated by the absorption of iron from foods. Normally, only 5% to 20% of available food iron may be absorbed and utilized. The presence of certain other nutrients, especially vitamin C, also affects the efficiency with which iron in foods is utilized. Thus the prevention of nutritional anaemia depends on adequate total nutrition, provided by a variety of foods containing all essential nutrients.

Foods which contain good supplies of iron include liver, red meats, egg yolks, dried legumes, leafy green vegetables and whole grain or enriched cereals. Of these, meats have the highest availability of iron. There is no loss of this mineral during storage, processing or cooking of foods, except very small losses if cooking water is discarded.

OTHER MINERALS

Because of the limited information available the other minerals which are needed in macro amounts — sodium, potassium, chloride, magnesium and sulphur — will be considered only briefly. Sodium, potassium and chloride are electrolytes involved in cellular metabolism, and are related to cardiovascular function. The most common source of sodium is ordinary table salt which is in the form of sodium chloride. Therefore, foods which use a salt brine, such as pickles, have a high sodium content. Potassium is widely distributed naturally in plant foods and a deficiency is, therefore, unlikely. Chloride in the blood is used for the formation of hydrochloric acid which is secreted into the stomach from the gastric glands. It functions with the gastric enzymes in the stomach assisting in the digestion process. The only time the body may suffer from insufficient chlorine is after a severe attack of vomiting.

Magnesium is important in bone formation and the metabolism of calcium and phosphorus. It is relatively abundant in food. Owing to its presence in chlorophyll, magnesium is found in large amounts in all green vegetables. Sulphur is found in every cell and is present in a number of the body's secretions such as bile and saliva.

A number of other minerals are known to be important, but their function in human nutrition is not fully understood. These elements are needed by the body in very small amounts and are known as trace elements or micronutrients. The first essential trace minerals to be identified were iron, iodine, copper, manganese, zinc and cobalt. Some of these mineral elements have now been studied extensively to determine their nutritional functions and the amounts needed for normal nutrition. The dietary importance of iron, for example, is well known and has already been discussed.

One of the first micronutrients to be isolated was iodine. This mineral is essential for proper functioning of the thyroid gland, which regulates many metabolic processes. In Canada, through federally legislated compulsory iodization of table salt, most individuals' requirements for iodine are met. However, care should be taken to provide the person on a low sodium (salt free) diet with an alternate source of this essential mineral.

Copper is widely distributed in food and water. The quantity to be found is dependent on the soil's copper content, but it occurs in most natural food along with the other mineral elements. A part of many enzymes involved in metabolism, copper is necessary for the utilization of iron in the production of blood hemoglobin.

Because manganese is found in many foods, it is unlikely that human deficiency of this mineral occurs. As yet the human requirement of manganese has not been established and the role which it plays in digestion, metabolism and blood formation is uncertain.

Cobalt is involved in the formation of red blood cells. Since there is plenty of it in the average diet, there is little danger of a deficiency occurring.

Zinc has long been known to be present in living organisms, where it plays an essential role. Recently zinc has been found to be even more important than was originally thought, especially in the areas of growth and sexual development.

As scientific research in trace mineral nutrition continued during the 1950's, three other elements were identified. These are molybdenum, selenium and chromium. By feeding diets deficient in these minerals to laboratory animals it was demonstrated that the latter two at least are essential. Chromium appears to alter the glucose utilization pattern. Rats fed chromium deficient diets showed symptoms similar to those of diabetes. This would indicate it may function in the insulin glucose cycle but is not claimed to be a cure for diabetes.

As new control methods have been developed, identification of other micronutrients has become possible. More recent additions have been fluorine, tin, vanadium, silicon and nickel. Fluorine has been known for some time to be necessary in the prevention and control of dental caries. However, it also has an essential role in nutrition as a requirement for growth of animals. The major source of fluorine in human nutrition is that naturally present in, or added to, water supplies.

Silicon has not yet been related to human nutrition but has been shown in laboratory animals to be related to skin and bone tissue. It is known to play some role in calcification of bone and is an important component of cartilage and connective tissue. Nickel is probably essential but laboratory results are as yet not clear. Experiments have shown that vanadium affects the feathers and bones in young chickens and growth in rats. Tin is definitely essential to rats.

Vitamins

The word vitamins refers to a group of essential chemical substances which occur naturally in various foods. As a group they are important in two broad categories: prevention of disease and regulation of body processes. Individually, each vitamin performs specific functions in the body.

Because the body is unable to manufacture most vitamins, they must be obtained from food sources. Plant foods, or animals which have fed on plant food, contain a variety of vitamins but no single food contains all of the vitamins in sufficient amounts for health. The amount of each vitamin required daily for optimum body performance has been carefully studied. Of those for which requirements have been established, some are open to further discussion since it appears that amounts needed depend upon the individual person.

It should be noted that the discovery of specific vitamins grew out of a need to determine the cause of certain diseases which were at the time not recognized as deficiency diseases. A deficiency disease is one that is caused by a lack of a specific nutrient in the diet. Examples of deficiency diseases are beri-beri, scurvy, pellagra. While studying the symptoms and attempting to treat the disease, investigators first established the existence of the needed vitamin. In the case of a vitamin deficiency, the disease or symptoms of the deficiency can be cured or prevented by giving only the missing vitamin.

In fact, many deficiencies are multiple and it is difficult to distinguish one from another. A diet that is inadequate in one respect, is usually poor in another. Therefore, it is seldom that an individual suffers a deficiency of only a single nutrient. If the diet consists of only one food, the deficiency is sure to be a multiple syndrome as is the case in many parts of the world.

As individual vitamins were isolated during the early part of this century, they were labelled with letters of the alphabet. Today some vitamins are still commonly referred to by letter. However, as their chemical composition was determined, they were assigned specific chemical names. These are now becoming better known.

Vitamins are usually classified on the basis of their solubility. Vitamins

A, D, E, and K are soluble in fat and vitamin C and the B vitamin group are water soluble. Fat soluble vitamins are stable and are not easily lost during the cooking of food. They are absorbed with the fats in food. If the body obtains more than it can use, fat soluble vitamins cannot be excreted in the urine since they are not water soluble. Therefore, they are stored in the body and if excessive amounts are present, can produce toxicity.

Water soluble vitamins are not stored in appreciable amounts so the possibility of overdosage is eliminated. Excess quantities are excreted in the urine. Thus, it is especially important that sufficient quantities of these are provided daily.

VITAMIN A

This vitamin is important in normal growth, good vision, healthy skin and resistance to infection. It is needed by persons in all age groups and is particularly important during growth, pregnancy and lactation. An early sign of vitamin A deficiency is a condition known as functional night blindness; i.e., the inability of the eyes to adjust quickly to dark after exposure to bright light.

Many common foods contain vitamin A; e.g., whole milk and cheeses made from it, butter, fortified margarine, liver and egg yolk. Other foods, particularly green leafy and yellow vegetables and yellow fruits, contain carotene, the precursor of vitamin A. Since the body can convert carotene into vitamin A, its presence in a food (usually marked by a deep green or yellow colour), is an indication of that food's value as a source of the vitamin. Both vitamin A and its precursors are destroyed by oxidation, particularly at high temperatures. Acids or alkalis have little effect on their stability.

A daily serving of a green or yellow vegetable or a yellow fruit will supply a child or an adult with sufficient vitamin A for normal nutrition. Although whole milk is an excellent source, the vitamin A values of partly skimmed and skim milk decrease in direct proportion to their fat content . . . unless they are fortified with it. Since vitamin A is more readily absorbed in the presence of fats, factors which limit fat absorption affect the absorption of vitamin A. Mineral oil, when taken internally, is such a factor and should be used routinely only on the advice of a physician.

The liver is the main storage site of vitamin A in the body, and lesser amounts may be stored in the kidneys, lungs and fatty tissues. While moderately large amounts are not considered harmful, very high intakes of vitamin A are toxic.

VITAMIN D

Vitamin D is referred to as a single nutrient although there are several vitamins D that perform identically. A fat soluble vitamin, it is moderately stable to heat, oxidation, acids and alkalis.

This is the vitamin necessary for the proper use of calcium and phosphorus by the body and for sound teeth and strong bones. It is needed to prevent rickets, a deficiency disease which results in stunted growth and deformed bones. Rickets most commonly develop in infants and young children during their period of rapid growth. Since vitamin D is essential for calcium and phosphorus utilization, it is clearly needed by all actively growing persons including adolescents and pregnant and nursing women. It is probably also needed in smaller amounts by all adults. The relationship of vitamin D and calcium in the prevention of osteomalacia (brittle bones) in older persons is now recognized, although their exact requirements are not known. These nutrients may be a factor in osteoporosis, also seen in older persons.

Natural foods, except fish liver oils, are poor sources of vitamin D. For those who need a daily supply, a normal diet of unenriched foods will not meet requirements. The ultraviolet rays in sunlight can produce vitamin D if they come into direct contact with the skin. In fact, it is often referred to as the "sunshine vitamin". However, smog, fog, clothing, windows or any other material which shuts out the sun's ultraviolet rays will interfere with this process. The most reliable sources of vitamin D, therefore, are pharmaceuticals or foods which are vitamin D enriched. All types of milk (fluid, evaporated and powdered), margarine and infant formulae preparations are now the *only* foods processed in Canada which may be enriched with vitamin D. The levels of such enrichment are specified in the Food and Drug Act and Regulations, so that a "reasonable daily intake" of the foods will provide the recommended 10 micrograms cholecalciferol of vitamin D. Use of vitamin D enriched milks, identifiable by their labels, should be encouraged to meet both calcium and vitamin D requirements. When sufficient amounts of the enriched milks are provided daily, no additional supplement should be necessary. If vitamin D milk is not available or is not used, a vitamin D supplement (10 micrograms cholecalciferol per day) is recommended for all growing persons and for women during pregnancy and lactation.

Excessive intakes of vitamin D (e.g. 50 to 100 times the recommended daily amount for children) are known to be toxic. In young infants, the "margin of safety" may be less, and intakes generally exceeding the recommended daily levels (10 micrograms cholecalciferol) should be avoided.

OTHER FAT SOLUBLE VITAMINS

Vitamin E

Vitamin E plays an important part in protecting the body's supplies of vitamin A. It functions as an anti-oxidant, and seems to be important in maintaining the functions of all membranes, and perhaps in some metabolic reactions.

There are indications that increasing the intake of polyunsaturated fatty acids increases the individual's requirement for vitamin E. Excess amounts of polyunsaturates may cause, at least in part, poor growth, dermatitis and decrease in longevity – symptoms of vitamin E deficiency. Fortunately, most food sources of polyunsaturated fatty acids carry vitamin E with them.

Vitamin E occurs so widely in foods that deficiency is rarely seen. The best food sources are vegetable oils, including those of wheat germ, corn and soybean, and products containing them such as margarine and whole wheat bread.

Vitamin K

Vitamin K is necessary for the synthesis of prothrombin, which is required in normal blood clotting. It occurs widely in foods, and deficiency is seldom seen except where malabsorption conditions occur in digestive diseases.

THIAMINE

Thiamine was the first of the B-vitamin group to be isolated as a single vitamin (1926). Almost automatically it became known as vitamin B_1.

Its primary function is in the release of food energy from sugars and starches. For this reason, daily thiamine requirements are based on the energy needs of the individual. Thiamine is also important in growth, maintenance of good appetite and normal functioning of the nervous system.

Most foods, except fats and sugars, contain some thiamine. Few foods are considered excellent sources but good variety in meal planning will help to ensure an adequate daily supply. The best food choices for thiamine are pork products, legumes, potatoes and whole grain or enriched flours and cereals. Much of this vitamin is lost from highly refined cereals.

Thiamine is readily absorbed in the body but only minimal amounts are stored, usually in the liver, heart, kidneys or muscles. Thus an adequate daily intake is important. Intakes in excess of needs are not potentially harmful and normally are excreted in the urine. Because it is soluble in water, losses of thiamine which occur during cooking may be reclaimed by using cooking water or meat juices. Prolonged heat exposure, especially in an alkaline medium (e.g., adding baking soda when soaking or cooking legumes) can destroy much of a food's thiamine content. Toasting bread or high-heat roasting and "puffing" cereals will reduce their thiamine content. Commercial canning or freezing of foods result in very slight thiamine losses.

RIBOFLAVIN

Riboflavin was recognized as a separate factor in the B-group long before it was finally isolated in the mid-1930's. It was formerly known as vitamin B_2.

This vitamin is important in growth and reproduction, normal appetite and digestion, normal functioning of the nervous system and helping to maintain a healthy condition of the skin and eyes. It is important for all age groups, since it plays an essential role in the body's enzyme system, releasing energy to the cells when carbohydrate, protein and fat are metabolized. Riboflavin requirements are also based on the body's energy needs with increased needs during periods of rapid growth and during pregnancy and lactation.

Milk is probably the chief source of riboflavin in the average Canadian diet. Although several foods are good sources, it is difficult to meet normal needs at any age unless milk and milk products are eaten. 250 ml of milk provides over 50% of the daily riboflavin requirement for an average kilojoule intake. Other important sources of riboflavin are cheese, eggs, meats (particularly organ meats), leafy green vegetables, salmon and enriched cereals and breads.

Storage of riboflavin in the body is limited, and normally any daily excess is excreted. Thus a reliable daily supply is important. This vitamin is fairly stable to heat, but is broken down by direct sunlight. For this reason, milk in glass bottles should be carefully protected during transit, and stored in a darkened refrigerator until used. Riboflavin losses are minimal when foods are canned or frozen.

NIACIN

Niacin or nicotinic acid is a third key member of the B-vitamin group. It occurs in two forms – nicotinic acid (niacin) and nicotinomide (niacinamide), either of which is satisfactory in human nutrition. Unlike others in the B-group, this vitamin can be synthesized in the body. Sixty milligrams of the amino acid tryptophan provide a niacin equivalent of one milligram. Thus, foods which may be low in niacin but high in the amino acid (such as milk) are considered to have a high "niacin equivalent" value. However, the diet must always provide some preformed niacin.

This vitamin is important in growth and reproduction, for the normal function of the gastro-intestinal tract and the prevention of pellagra. With symptoms involving the skin and gastro-intestinal tract, pellagra is essentially a disease of the nervous system which can lead to insanity. Like the two previous members of the B-group, niacin is required in the release of energy to the cells. Needs increase during pregnancy and lactation.

Niacin is plentiful in both plant (as nicotinic acid) and animal foods (as nicotinamide). Meat, fish, poultry and enriched cereals, flours and breads are excellent sources. Milk's supply of tryptophan makes it a valuable source of the niacin equivalent.

A small amount of niacin may be stored in the body, but a daily supply from foods is necessary to meet normal needs. Some of this must be one of the natural forms of niacin, which may be supplemented with the niacin synthesized from tryptophan.

This vitamin is fairly soluble in hot water but only slightly soluble in cold water. It is exceptionally stable to heat. Any cooking losses which might occur may be reclaimed by using cooking waters and meat juices. Freezing and canning of foods have no appreciable effect on their niacin content.

OTHER B VITAMINS

Other members of the B-vitamin group which have been isolated include pyridoxine (B_6), cyanocobalamine (B_{12}), folic acid (folacin), pantothenic acid, biotin, inositol and choline. All are known to be necessary for health although the latter two may be formed in the body under normal conditions. They appear to play essential roles in a variety of body processes but all their specific functions and daily requirements have not been determined. Folic acid and vitamin B_{12} have been associated with the body's maintenance of healthy blood. Vitamin B_6 is involved in protein and energy metabolism; pantothenic acid and biotin are involved in energy metabolism; choline and possibly inositol are required in fat transport in the body. Precise recommendations for some of these nutrients have not been established in Canada as yet.

When foods are chosen each day to meet the needs for thiamine, riboflavin, niacin and folic acid, other B vitamins appear to be provided in adequate amounts for the normal, healthy individual.

VITAMIN C

Vitamin C is stored in the body in only limited amounts. In foods, it is the least stable of all the vitamins. Thus great care must be taken to provide sufficient amounts in daily foods to meet the body's needs, and to allow for losses during storage, preparation, cooking and serving.

Otherwise known as ascorbic acid, vitamin C is necessary for healthy teeth, gums and blood vessels. It helps form and strengthen the cementing substance which holds the body cells together, and thus prevents scurvy. This was the deficiency disease so prevalent among early sailors who were deprived of fresh fruits and vegetables, until they found that a daily ration of fresh limes would prevent the weakness and other dreaded symptoms. In the enlightened 1970's cases of scurvy can still be found among infants whose formulae contain no source of vitamin C and among others whose diets are entirely lacking in fruits and vegetables.

The most common, reliable sources of vitamin C are the citrus fruits, vitaminized apple juice and tomatoes (and their pure juices). Cantaloup and strawberries are excellent sources, with several vegetables and potatoes offering significant amounts. If a fruit drink is used instead of a pure juice, the label should be checked to make sure its vitamin C content is adequate.

Probably the most critical factors in providing the daily requirement of vitamin C are the handling and preparation of foods before eating. Warmth and exposure to air, which result in wilting, markedly decrease the vitamin C content of raw fruits and vegetables in the garden, in the store or in the home. This unstable vitamin is readily dissolved in water. Proper cooking methods, using fairly large pieces, minimum amounts of boiling water and short cooking times will keep vitamin C losses to a minimum. Adding soda during soaking or cooking hastens destruction of this vitamin, and "holding" hot vegetables also increases losses of vitamin C. Commercial canning and freezing methods are controlled from harvest to final product to minimize losses of vitamin C. When cans or packages of these foods are opened for cooking or serving, they are as susceptible as any fresh food to losses of vitamin C through oxidation.

Intakes of vitamin C in excess of daily needs are excreted in the urine, with no indication of any adverse effects. In fact, it is probably wise to allow for a margin of safety to counteract the high degree of perishability of this nutrient.

Other Dietary Essentials

Water is the most important single item in man's dietary intake, and the need for it is second only to oxygen. A person can live for weeks without food, but death results within a few days when water is not available. About 70% of body mass is water. It is necessary in all body cells to provide the medium for essential chemical processes, for the transport of oxygen and nutrients to the cells, and for the transport of waste products for elimination. It helps to regulate body temperature, serves as a lubricant and aids digestion and elimination. A healthy adult needs about a litre of water a day in addition to the water provided by foods. Depending upon activity and environmental temperature, water requirements may be greatly increased.

Cellulose (or roughage) is necessary in many body functions. Although not considered to be a nutrient because it is not digested, cellulose absorbs water and provides the necessary bulk for normal elimination of body wastes through the intestinal tract. It is normally obtained from fruits, vegetables and whole grain cereals.

SOURCES AND FUNCTIONS OF FOOD NUTRIENTS

NUTRIENT	FUNCTIONS IN	SOURCES
Proteins	• building and repairing all types of body tissues • regulating body processes • forming antibodies to fight infection • supplies energy	Complete: milk, cheese, eggs, meat, fish, poultry Incomplete: dried legumes (peas, beans, lentils), nuts, cereals, breads, vegetables.
Fats	• supplying energy • transporting vitamins A, D, E, K, • protecting and insulating body parts • supplying the essential fatty acids	Fish, meat, salad oils and dressings, margarine, butter, whole milk, cream, cheddar cheese, ice-cream.
Carbohydrates	• supplying energy • sparing protein • assisting in utilization of fats	Starches: breads, cereals, pastas, potatoes, corn. Sugars: dried fruits, canned fruits, fresh fruits, frozen fruits, milk, sugars, syrups, jams, jellies, marmalades, honey, molasses.
Calcium	• forming strong bones and teeth and maintaining and repairing the skeleton • maintaining muscle tone, normal heart beat and healthy nerve function • aiding normal blood clotting	Milk (any type), ice cream, cheese (any type), yogurt, canned salmon and sardines (with bones), broccoli, navy beans (dried), string beans, turnips, carrots, dried apricots, cantaloup.
Phosphorus	• forming strong bones and teeth and maintaining and repairing the skeleton • facilitates absorption and transportation of nutrients • regulates the release of energy	Meat, fish, poultry, eggs, nuts, milk, cheese.
Iron	• building hemoglobin in red blood cells to transport oxygen and carbon dioxide • preventing nutritional anemia	Liver, red meats, egg yolks, dried beans, peas and lentils, green leafy vegetables, whole grain and enriched cereals, pre-cooked infant cereals, flours, bread and pastas.
Fluorine	• prevention and control of dental caries • prevention of osteoporosis	Drinking water (natural or fluoridated water supplies), salt water fish, tea.
Iodine	• proper functioning of the thyroid gland	Iodized salt.
Magnesium	• formation of bone • metabolism of calcium and phosphorus	Cocoa, nuts, whole grains, spinach, liver, clams, oysters, crabs.
Zinc, copper, cobalt, manganese, chromium, molybdenum and selenium	• known to be important but functions in human nutrition are not fully understood	The average Canadian diet would provide the required amount.

SOURCES AND FUNCTIONS OF FOOD NUTRIENTS *(continued)*

NUTRIENT	FUNCTIONS IN	SOURCES
Vitamin A	• normal growth and formation of skeleton and teeth • maintaining normal vision • resisting infection by keeping skin and lining layer of body healthy • normal reproduction and lactation	Dark green and yellow vegetables, yellow fruits, egg yolks, liver, butter, cream, whole milk, cheeses, fortified skim or 2% milk, fortified margarine.
B Vitamin Group Thiamine	• releasing food energy from carbohydrates • normal growth • maintaining good appetite • normal functions of the nervous system	Pork and pork products (including organ meats), dried legumes (peas, beans, lentils), whole grain or enriched cereals, flours, bread, potatoes and pastas.
Riboflavin	• normal growth and development • maintaining good appetite and normal digestion • helping to maintain healthy skin and eyes • helping to maintain a normal nervous system • releasing energy to body cells during metabolism	Milk and milk products (except butter), cheese, eggs, meats, (particularly organ meats), salmon, leafy green vegetables, enriched cereals, flours, bread and pastas.
Niacin	• normal growth and development • maintaining normal function of the gastro-intestinal tract • normal function of the nervous system	Meat (particularly organ meats), fish, poultry, enriched cereals, flours, breads and pastas, tomatoes, peas, potatoes, peanuts and peanut butter, milk, cheese and eggs.
Vitamin B$_6$ (Pyridoxine)	• protein and energy metabolism	Meat, liver, vegetables, whole grain cereals, eggs.
B$_{12}$	• maintenance of healthy blood	Liver, kidney, milk, meat.
Folic Acid	• maintenance of healthy blood	Liver, kidney, mushrooms, asparagus, broccoli, lima beans, spinach, lemons, bananas, strawberries, cantaloup.
Pantothenic Acid	• energy metabolism	Liver, kidney, egg yolk, nuts, legumes.
Vitamin C (Ascorbic acid)	• maintaining healthy teeth and gums • maintaining strong blood vessel walls • helping to form and strengthen the cementing substance which holds body cells together	Orange, lemon, grapefruit, lime, tangarine and their juices, vitaminized apple juice, vitaminized fruit drinks, tomatoes and their juice, cantaloup, strawberries, broccoli, cauliflower, brussels sprouts, cabbage (green), baked white potatoes, turnips.
Vitamin D	• utilizing calcium and phosphorus in the development and maintenance of sound bones and teeth	Vitamin D enriched milks (fluid, evaporated and powdered), vitamin D enriched infant formulae preparations, vitamin D enriched margarines, vitamin supplements or fish liver oils.
Vitamin E	• protecting body's supplies of vitamins A and C • maintaining health of membranes by being an antioxidant • blood cell formation	Vegetable oils; e.g., corn and soybean, wheat germ, margarine and whole wheat bread.
Vitamin K	• normal clotting of blood	Green and yellow vegetables. Synthesized by intestinal bacteria.

The Digestive Process

While studying the nutrients that supply the body with heat and energy, with material for growth and repair and substances which regulate the mechanism of the body, it becomes evident that these nutrients are consumed in a complex assortment of foods. All nutrients must be separated and simplified before the body can utilize them. *Digestion* refers to the processes by which the nutrients in foods are changed into their simplest forms. They become liquid in content, by the progressive inflow of digestive juices which prepare them for absorption in the latter part of the digestive tract.

Absorption is the passage of the products of digestion through the walls of the digestive tract into the circulatory system. The body's circulatory system carries these simplified nutrients to cells throughout the body. The chemical process that takes place within the cells is called *metabolism*. A little knowledge of these processes helps one to understand the relationship of the foods eaten to the ultimate nourishment of the body.

Digestion

The digestive tract, also known as the gastro-intestinal tract and alimentary canal, is composed of the mouth, gullet (or oesophagus), stomach, small intestine and large intestine. In adults the *small intestine* which is divided into three parts: the duodenum, the jejunum and the ileum, is about six metres in length. The *large intestine* is a broader organ measuring about two metres in length. Various glands such as the salivary glands of the mouth, the gastric glands of the stomach, the liver and the pancreas, secrete digestive juices into the intestine which break down the food by chemical action into simpler, soluble substances which can be absorbed into the blood.

Throughout the entire process of digestion the food is pushed along the digestive tract by the muscular relaxation and contraction of the muscles within the intestinal walls. This wave-like action is known as *peristalsis*. Sometimes it is possible to feel these peristaltic movements in your own abdomen.

During digestion, changes in the chemical and physical nature of nutrients are aided by the presence of *enzymes* in the digestive juices. These enzymes are protein in substance and behave as catalysts in speeding up chemical reactions but remaining unchanged themselves at the end of the reaction. Different enzymes are needed for reducing the various nutrients. The protein-splitting enzyme is a *protease;* the fat-splitting enzyme is a

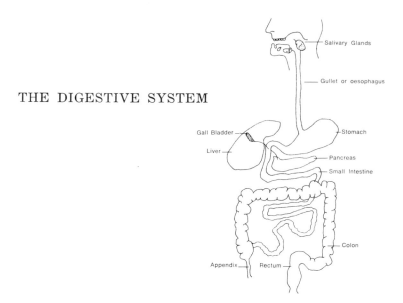

THE DIGESTIVE SYSTEM

lipase, the starch-splitting enzyme is an *amylase.* Some enzymes can function only in an acidic environment, as for example the protease enzyme in the stomach; others can operate only in an alkaline environment, for example the amylase enzyme in the mouth and small intestine. Some enzymes are more, or less, heat sensitive than others.

Digestion begins in the mouth. The teeth masticate the food, cutting and grinding to reduce its size while the tongue and mouth muscles by their movements mix the food with the saliva secreted by the salivary glands. These juices also moisten and lubricate the food to allow the soft ball or *bolus* of food to pass easily down the oesophagus. The amylase or starch-splitting enzyme in the saliva, called *ptyalin,* converts any starch in the food to maltose or dextrin. But this is possible only if the solution is neutral or slightly alkaline and when the cellulose covering of the starch grains has been ruptured by cooking. In this form the starch grains are more accessible to the digestive enzyme. When starch grains are cooked with fat, as in pastry or batter-dipped fried foods, the digestive action of the amylase is considered hindered and indigestion, to some degree, may occur.

The secretion of *saliva* is a reflex action in response to the stimulus of taste, sight and smell and even pleasant surroundings. But salivation is also closely linked with the emotions. The mere thought of food, particularly when hungry, is often sufficient to "make the mouth water." But fear, excitement or worry may inhibit secretion.

The bolus enters the stomach via the gullet. The *stomach* is a pear-shaped, extremely muscular organ which will expand to contain the amount of food consumed. Its chief function is that of a reservoir which deals out its contents in conveniently manageable quantities to the first part of the small intestine called the *duodenum*. Another useful function is to bring foods of different temperatures all to body temperature, 37°C, and to melt fats. The stomach's great supply of blood vessels makes it well adapted to these purposes.

The powerful muscles in the walls of the stomach exert further mechanical action on the food. This churning brings the food in close contact with the gastric juices and reduces the bolus to a more liquid consistency now known as *chyme*.

The flow of *gastric juices* into the stomach is stimulated partly by the chemical nature of the food passing into it and partly by psychological factors. The dextrin produced by the initial digestion of the starch in the mouth, and water in the saliva, have a stimulating effect on the gastric glands. Herein lies the justification for nibbling on a roll or cracker before taking soup. The meat extractives in soups are powerful stimulants on the gastric glands. Hence, the service of soups at the beginning of a meal. The psychological factors of smell and sight, which promote the flow of saliva, also stimulate the flow of the gastric juices. Likewise, this flow is stopped by worry, excitement, anger, unpleasant sights and odours and digestion is thus hindered.

The acid environment in the stomach, which brings to an end the amalyese action on starches from the mouth, is due to the presence of a diluted form of hydrochloric acid. This acid acts as an antiseptic on some foods that are not completely wholesome for consumption.

The enzymes present in the gastric juices are protein-splitting proteases. One of the enzymes, *pepsin*, helps in the digestive conversion of some proteins into peptones. The gastric juices of infants and young children also contain a protease enzyme, *rennin*, which coagulates milk in readiness for digestion in the small intestine.

The length of time that food remains in the stomach is generally from three to five hours, but it could remain there for more or less time. A lot depends upon the kind of foods eaten. Carbohydrate foods tend to leave the stomach more rapidly than protein foods, and protein foods more quickly than meals that are high in fat content. This explains the satisfied contented feeling of fullness that one experiences for some hours after a meal of roasted meat, baked vegetables and pudding. Such a meal of protein and fat foods is said to have *satiety value*.

The thorough impregnation of the chyme with the acid gastric juices has a relaxing effect on the circular, muscular, sphincter valve, the *pylorus* or pyloric sphincter, at the base of the stomach, and on the first portion of the small intestine. This relaxation of the muscles allows small quantities of chyme to enter the duodenum, a little at a time. The environment of the small intestine is alkaline. Consequently, the admission of the acid contents from the stomach stimulates the flow of the alkaline pancreatic juices from the pancreas and the flow of bile from the liver.

The *bile* is a bright yellow liquid which is being constantly manufactured in the liver. As it is not always needed at the time of production, it is stored in a bag about the size and shape of a small pear that resides under the liver. This organ is called the *gall bladder*. During its storage the bile is concentrated by the removal of water and it becomes thicker and golden green in colour. The bile juices contain bile salts which emulsify the fats, which in turn increases the activity of the pancreatic lipase or fat-splitting enzyme. The final product of these actions are two simple forms of fat: fatty acids and glycerol.

The pancreatic juice also contains a protease enzyme called *trypsin* which changes proteins and peptones to amino acids, and an amalyese which continues the work of the salivary amylase, breaking down the starch into the disaccharides, maltose, sucrose and lactose.

Besides the manufacture of the digestive pancreatic juices, the *pancreas* is also responsible for the production of a hormone called *insulin*. There are specialized cells or *endocrine glands* within the pancreas and these produce this insulin and empty it directly into the blood stream. They are not directly connected with the digestive system. In the blood, the insulin regulates the amount of sugar released into the blood from the liver and causes sugar that is already there to be used faster by the muscles. *Diabetes* is the disease that results when these endocrine glands lose their power to manufacture insulin. The person who has this disease may have to take insulin through a hypodermic needle into the arm or leg, from where it is absorbed into the blood.

As the chyme passes on from the duodenum further down the small intestine it has poured onto it, from the glands within the lining walls of the intestine itself, an intestinal juice. These juices contain proteases which complete the final breakdown of all proteins to amino acids. Also present are the sugar-splitting enzymes maltose, sucrose, and lactose, which convert the disaccharides to monosaccharides or single sugars. Respectively, *maltose* becomes two molecules of glucose, *sucrose* yields one molecule of glucose and one molecule of fructose, and *lactose* liberates one molecule of glucose and one molecule of galactose.

The food or *chyle* as it is now termed, being as it is such a highly liquid state, moves along the length of the small intestine by the peristaltic action of its muscles. All of it that is digestible has been rendered to substances that are simple and soluble enough to pass through the intestine and into the surrounding blood capillaries and lacteals of the lymph system to be utilized by the body.

Absorption

Absorption, or the passage of the products of digestion through the walls of the digestive tract, takes place for the greater part in the small intestine. Within the mucous lining of the intestinal walls are large folds with tiny hair-like projections called *villi*. These villi expose the maximum possible surface area to the digested nutrients for their absorption into the body's circulatory system. This is an intensive system of food transportation to the body's tissues.

CROSS SECTION OF
SMALL INTESTINE
(Magnified)

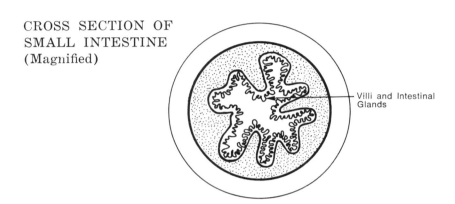

Villi and Intestinal
Glands

Each villus is provided with a small lymph vessel called a *lacteal* and a network of capillary blood vessels. During digestion these villi are surrounded by chyle and the soluble substances produced as a result of digestion.

CROSS SECTION
OF A VILLUS

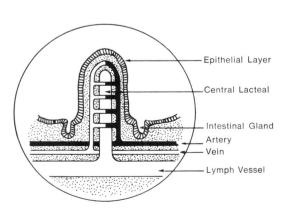

Epithelial Layer

Central Lacteal

Intestinal Gland
Artery
Vein
Lymph Vessel

The glucose and amino acids diffuse into the capillaries of the villi and pass by way of the portal vein into the liver. The glucose in demand by the body and the amino acids then pass from the liver into the general circulation and from here to the tissues and the organs of the body.

The fatty acids and glycerol are also absorbed into the walls of the small intestine. Some of the fatty acids and glycerol molecules reunite and enter the blood stream as microscopic droplets of fat. These droplets are not in solution in the blood but are held in suspension much as the fat of homogenized milk. But most of the digested fat (60 to 70 percent of it) is first conveyed in the lymph vessels or lymphatic system and later enters the blood system. Single glycerol molecules which can be metabolized by the cells for energy production enter the capillaries and are conveyed to the liver via the portal vein. On its passage through the liver, the glycerol is rendered readily available for energy production in the body cells.

Some available minerals and vitamins which do not require digestion as do proteins, fats and carbohydrates can be absorbed through the walls of the stomach. Such minerals include sodium and potassium. Small quantities of alcohol, readily available glucose and water soluble vitamins B and C are also absorbed from the stomach. Remaining water soluble vitamins and all fat soluble vitamins are absorbed from the small intestine. The minerals iron and calcium are also absorbed from the small intestine. Unavailable calcium and excess iron are eliminated from the body in the faeces. Water soluble vitamins absorbed in excess and which cannot be stored in the body are eliminated by the kidneys and excreted from the body in the urine.

The large intestine contains no digestive juices, but is rich in bacteria called intestinal flora. By the time the food mass reaches it all the digestible food has been removed. The material left is largely cellulose and water. Cellulose, a starch-like carbohydrate present in bulky vegetable and fruit tissues and in cereal grains is not digested by humans. It is, however, important in the mechanics of the digestive process because it provides bulk which aids in discarding the residues of digestion. The water is absorbed from the residue all along the large intestine so that it reaches the rectum in a semi-solid or solid form. This residue, the leftovers from digestion, are termed faeces. These exert a pressure on the muscles of the rectum which leads to their expulsion or elimination from the body in a "bowel movement".

It is important to note that some of the bacteria in the large intestine produce certain of the B-group of vitamins, which to a small extent supplement the body's supply. Being water soluble, these vitamins would enter the body's system along with the absorbed water.

Before completing a discussion of the digestive tract it is of interest to mention the *appendix,* a very small unprepossessing organ about the size of one's little finger which, for all its smallness, can be a bigger trouble-maker than all 8 metres of the intestines. It is called the vermeform appen-dix which means, and appropriately so, "worm-shaped attachment". It is situated right at the muscular doorway between the small and large intest-ine. Food particles can become trapped within it and it does on occasions become infected, resulting in the rather painful ailment known as appen-dicitis. This infected organ is easily removed if diagnosed early, by an operation called an appendectomy. Complications can result if it is not recognized and treated in time. Animals have a similar organ, though one that is of necessity fully developed and functioning as part of their diges-tive system. It is called the caecum and is of ultimate importance in their digestion of cellulose, their major source of food energy.

Metabolism

With the blood stream serving as the conveyor, nutrients are carried to every cell in every tissue of the body. The chemical processes that take place within all cells to build tissue or to release energy is called *metabolism.* It is at this point that the adequacy of the diet meets its real test. Continued nutrient shortages will result in poorly nourished cells and this will eventually become manifest in a poorly nourished body.

Glucose is normally found in the blood in fairly steady concentration. It supplies immediate energy for cells and tissues that carry on the work of the muscles as in physical exercise and in the internal work of the body organs. Only a small amount of sugar is stored in the body and this is in the form of animal starch or *glycogen*. About two-thirds of the glycogen is stored in the muscles and one-third in the liver. A small but essential amount is retained in the blood as glucose, called *blood sugar*. The glucose level of the blood normally remains stable, this level being controlled by the hormone insulin. When in use, muscles have this energy need replenished by glucose from the blood. The blood sugar is, in turn, replenished by the glycogen from the liver which can change, when needed, back to glucose.

The liberation of the available energy of the blood sugar is a complicated process involving the absorption of oxygen from the blood stream and the liberation of carbon dioxide and water as breakdown waste products. The energy appears in various forms as heat, as muscular work and as chemical energy in a variety of forms associated with the life giving function of all cells and tissues. Besides being stored as glycogen, excess glucose can be reduced to fat in the form of adipose tissue and retained as a more concen-trated fuel reserve. The body fat is retained chiefly in the abdominal region.

Fat, in addition to glucose, is used to carry on the work of the muscles and internal activities of the body. Fat that is not needed immediately is stored as body fat. When needed it can be moved into the blood stream again and drawn up, as required, by tissues. Since both carbohydrates and proteins can be converted into fat in the body, all foods are a potential source of body fat. It follows then that the amount of fat stored will reflect the total amount of food that has been eaten in excess of immediate energy needs. About half of the body fat is stored directly under the skin and half serves as a protective cover for internal organs as the heart and kidneys.

The complete *oxidation* of fat in the body is a more difficult and complicated process than that of glucose. When completely oxidized to liberate energy, fat yields, as does glucose, carbon dioxide and water as waste byproducts. The oxidation of fatty acids refers to the breakdown of long carbon chains to shorter carbon chains, for example reducing an 18 carbon chain to a 4 carbon chain. Incomplete or partial oxidation of fats will occur in a diet where consumption of fat and carbohydrates are poorly balanced. This is because complete fat oxidation is interrelated with glucose oxidation. Incomplete fat oxidation will lead to a state known as *ketosis*. Ketosis results from the presence of ketones which are fatty acids of a 4 carbon chain type.

The essential compounds for the building up of many different cell proteins are the *amino acids*. In addition to the atoms of carbon, hydrogen and oxygen found in the glucose or fat molecules, proteins provide nitrogen. The nitrogen is very necessary to the development, maintenance and life of every cell in the body.

The tissues and organs of the body have the capacity to select from the variety of amino acids present in the blood the ones they need for building, sustaining and repairing their own structures. In so doing, the amino acids are regrouped into combinations needed for new and rebuilt tissues, as for making certain active compounds such as hormones and enzymes. Excess amino acids, or those left over from this regrouping, are returned to the liver where the nitrogen is removed from its molecular structure and excreted from the body as urea in the urine. The carbon, hydrogen and oxygen that remains can then be reorganized to be used for energy as carbohydrate and fat molecules. If the energy is not needed at once body fat is formed and stored for future use. The use of excess protein as fuel instead of as a building and repair substance is, however, uneconomic. Wastage of protein in this manner can be avoided by the practice of eating balanced carbohydrate and protein meals.

It is evident that the digestion, absorption and metabolism of food is a step-by-step, interrelated and complex process. Many gaps still remain in the scientific understanding of these reactions and much is yet to be learned about the interrelationships of vitamins and minerals and their roles in digestion and metabolism.

Part 3
Basic Cookery

Appetizers

Early cooks soon learned that the appetite is stimulated by the sight and smell of food. They observed that bitter substances frequently awaken lost appetite by releasing digestive secretions. Thus the appetizer, a small portion of food served before a meal or as the first course, was originated. Every country has its version of these tempting morsels — the Slav *zakuska*, the Italian *antipasto*, the Scandinavian *smorgasbord*, and the French *hors d'oeuvre*.

The quantity and variety of appetizer will depend upon the occasion. It may be a reception, a cocktail party, an informal get-together of a few friends, a holiday open house or a sports fans' Grey Cup celebration. Whatever the occasion some form of appetizer is always in order. If dinner is to follow, one or two really tempting appetizers, offered in small quantity, will be enough. In fact, to avoid satisfying the guests' appetite before the meal, more should not be served. If, on the other hand, your party is likely to last for several hours, your guests will crave more substantial fare; fondues, chafing dish specialties, skewered appetizers broiled over a hibachi or an outdoor barbecue, spicy meatballs simmering in a casserole over a candle warmer.

The characteristics of properly prepared appetizers are much the same as those of salads:

1. They should have eye appeal.
2. They should contain stimulating ingredients with taste appeal.
3. They should be bite-sized pieces, easy to eat.
4. Hot appetizers must be served piping hot.
5. Serve cold appetizers well chilled.
6. The appetizer should not repeat the ingredients of the main meal.

Simplicity, harmony of colour, pleasing contrasts, attractive arrangements and presentation are the key points. Over-garnishing can be unappealing and costly.

Appetizers are generally classified into seven or eight categories:

1. Cocktails.
2. Hors d'oeuvre.
3. Canapés.

4.   Relishes.

5.   Dips.

6.   Nibbles.

7.   Soups and consommés.

8.   Petite salads.

1.   COCKTAILS

A cocktail is an appetizer made from seafood, vegetables or fruit, usually served with a sauce or dressing, and eaten at the table. Ingredients frequently used are shrimp, crab, lobster or other shellfish, with a vegetable base, or mixed fresh fruits. These are arranged in well chilled glass dishes to be eaten with a cocktail fork or spoon (which is placed to the right of the knife when the table is set).

Chilled vegetable or fruit juices with added seasonings are also used as appetizer cocktails. Shrimp cocktail with a tangy seafood sauce is a favourite. Melon balls on lettuce is another. Sectioned grapefruit topped with a maraschino cherry and mint or candied ginger will whet any appetite.

2.   HORS D'OEUVRE

Hors d'oeuvre are tasty, colourful snack foods served before the main meal. Because they are usually served to standing guests, hors d'oeuvre should be small enough to be eaten with the fingers with a toothpick. A small fork should be provided when they are served at the table. Whether served piping hot or thoroughly chilled they are almost always "finger food".

So that the appetite for the next course is not dulled they should be light, very delicate, and have a distinct, sharp taste.

Hors d'oeuvre can be made with any combination of food, provided the selections are served in small quantities.

The hors d'oeuvre should not repeat the ingredients of the main dish or be too similar to it. For example, if pork is the main course avoid ham hors d'oeuvre.

There are two types of hors d'oeuvre: those served piping hot and those served cold. Rolled stuffed meats, baked oysters on the half shell, shrimp, miniature meatballs, pizzas and sausage rolls, angels on horseback (oysters wrapped in bacon), devils on horseback (chicken livers with a dash of tabasco sauce, wrapped in bacon), bite-size cheese or meats, spiced fruits and vegetables, devilled eggs, stuffed mushroom caps and caviar are all delicious served as hors d'oeuvre.

NOTE: An attractive way of serving appetizers on toothpicks is to stud pineapples, melons, grapefruit or cheese with toothpicks holding these tidbits.

3.   CANAPÉS

Canapés are tiny open-faced sandwiches having as their base bite-sized pieces of crisp bread, pastry or biscuits in assorted shapes. The word "canapé" is derived from the French meaning "sofa". It was considered that the small bread bases acted as a "seat" for the delicacies which topped them.

The bread bases are spread with a rich savoury paste or butter, cut into various small shapes and highly decorated to give them eye appeal. Toasted bread may be more desirable than some of the other bases because it will not absorb the moisture of the spread too quickly and it can be cut into more interesting shapes.

It is best to use firm textured bread or bread at least one day old. If this is not available, the bread can be partially frozen before cutting. Pumpernickel, white, rye, whole wheat and rye breads trimmed free of all crusts are suitable for canapés provided that the filling and bread complement each other. White cream cheese provides an attractive contrast with black pumpernickel, crab meat and white bread are a good combination. The bread may be cut into diamonds, triangles and squares or shaped with cookie cutters.

Canapés are a beautiful beginning for a party. Few guests can resist the temptation to return to the canapé tray again and again. Allow four to six canapés per person.

Canapé Butters

Use one or more of these as a spread for canapés. They make a delicious complementary base for sliced ham, turkey, roast beef, tongue, radishes, tomatoes and cucumbers. Spread on toast rounds.

CHIVE BUTTER
Combine 75 ml soft butter or margarine, 30 ml finely chopped chives, and 7 ml of lemon juice, mixing well. Yield: approximately 100 ml.

CURRY BUTTER
Combine 75 ml soft butter or margarine and 2-3 ml curry powder, mixing well. Yield: approximately 75 ml.

WATERCRESS BUTTER
Combine 75 ml soft butter or margarine, 50 ml finely chopped watercress, 7 ml lemon juice and a dash of Worcestershire sauce. Mix well. Yield: approximately 100 ml.

CHILI MAYONNAISE
Combine 30 ml chili sauce and 75 ml mayonnaise or cooked salad dressing. Mix well. Yield: 100 ml.

MUSTARD MAYONNAISE
Combine 5 ml prepared mustard, 75 ml mayonnaise or cooked salad dressing and a dash of garlic powder. Mix well. Yield: 75 ml.

HORSERADISH CREAM CHEESE
Combine 200 g soft cream cheese and 30 ml prepared horseradish (drained). Mix well. Yield: approximately 200 ml.

HINT: The addition of cream cheese to butter prevents soaking of the bread base.

To make less work for spur-of-the-moment entertaining, fill your freezer gradually with an assortment of butters, spreads and bread bases that can be assembled quickly in many different combinations to make a wide variety of canapés.

4.   RELISHES

Relishes include radish roses, carrot curls, vegetable sticks, celery hearts, stuffed olives, ripe olives, pickles and cherry tomatoes. At a sit-down meal they are placed on the table in a bowl with crushed ice to maintain the crisp character of the vegetables and may be left on the table throughout dinner.

5. DIPS

A dip is a very thick sauce served in a small dish and scooped up with bite-sized pieces of food. Foods suitable for dipping include: potato chips, crackers of all kinds, raw vegetables and cold cooked shellfish. Today there are limitless varieties of chips and crackers on the market that can be served with dips to create different and unusual taste sensations. Fresh vegetables such as cauliflowerets, broccoli pieces and carrot or celery sticks are an interesting change.

Dips are usually prepared from a cheese base with various ingredients added to create unusual flavours. Inexpensive dips may be prepared by creaming cottage cheese in a blender and seasoning it with powdered soups such as French Onion. All dips should be well chilled but brought from the refrigerator half an hour before serving.

The consistency of a dip is all-important. If it is too thick the cracker or chip will crumble; if too thin, the dip will run and drip on clothes and furniture.

6. NIBBLES

Salted nuts, bits of cheese, pickles and some of the relishes mentioned are often referred to in this way. An assortment of suitable ready-to-eat cereals mixed with pretzels, nuts and seasonings is a nibble-style appetizer sometimes called "nuts and bolts". These ingredients are coated with melted butter and heated slowly in the oven, with frequent mixing, until the flavours are well blended.

7. SOUPS

A small bowl or cup of soup is a good start to a meal, provided the serving is not too large or the soup not too filling. Cold soups are light with a subtle flavouring which makes them the perfect appetizer for a summer meal.

Sauces and Gravies, Soups and Stocks

The methods of preparation of sauces, gravies and soups are interrelated. A good stock is everything in making a good soup and the base for most sauces.

Stock is made by simmering meat and bones with vegetables and seasonings.

Sauce is a flavoured liquid which is served with food to improve its flavour, appearance and nutritive value.

Gravy is really a sauce having the flavour of the extractives from the meat used.

Soup is a liquid food served as an appetite stimulant at the beginning of the meal or as the principal part of a meal.

These four topics will be discussed in the same chapter. Many of the terms used will be more familiar in the commercial kitchen and certain techniques are more common there also. It is generally accepted that a better understanding of work "behind the scenes" contributes to the enjoyment of a restaurant meal. This is one area where practices in the home and commercial kitchens overlap.

Sauces

A sauce is a rich, flavoured liquid which is served with food to improve its flavour, appearance and nutritive value. It should never be used to change or mask the flavour of the food it is being served with but should instead enhance its natural flavour.

Sauces vary widely in their flavour, consistency and temperature. Some are served with the main course, others are strictly dessert sauces. Most main course sauces are savoury and served hot but there are exceptions. For example, raisin, pineapple and sweet and sour sauces are sweetened; tartar sauce is served cold. Thickeners for sauces vary also. Most are starch thickened, a few are egg thickened and others, including the various butter and basting sauces, have no thickening at all.

Sauces are very difficult to classify. Home use of sauces is largely dependent upon the recipe selections and competence of the home cook, together with the preferences of family members. This chapter describes the preparation of white sauce and gravy. Reference has also been made to sauces used in the commercial kitchen, but these are usually prepared in large quantities and no attempt has been made to provide recipes for them. Here are notes about some sauces that you may not have thought to include in this category:

Tartar sauce is made from mayonnaise and chopped pickle of some kind with other ingredients added to contribute to its thick consistency and coarse texture. Tartar sauce especially complements the flavour of seafood and it is usually served at the side of the fish.

Some salad dressings have a sauce base; for example, cooked salad dressing, mayonnaise.

Seafood cocktail sauce is one of the spicy sauces that are served cold.

Hard sauce is very thick due to the high proportion of icing sugar that is used in making it. It is served cold on steamed puddings.

Preparing a White Sauce

The preparation of white sauce is based on the principles of milk cookery (see page 199) and the principles of starch cookery (see page 353). The basic ingredients used are flour, for thickening; fat, usually butter or margarine; and a liquid, usually milk or cream. A broth or vegetable juice is sometimes substituted for part of the liquid. Seasoning is important. A small amount of salt and pepper is usual. Other additions may be onion or chives, curry powder, paprika or cheese.

Being able to make a good white sauce is an important cooking skill, not only for its use over foods but also for its place as part of many other dishes. For example, it is the basis of creamed and scalloped dishes, soufflés, croquettes and many casseroles, as well as cream soups. The white sauce for each of these types of dishes differs only in consistency. Proportions of

Measuring the ingredients.

Adding flour to the melted fat.

Stirring in cold milk.

Checking the consistency.

flour to liquid are changed to alter the thickness of the sauce. A chart of proportions for white sauce is found on page 460.

A good white sauce will be glossy in appearance, smooth in texture — like cream, of desired consistency and with a well cooked and well seasoned flavour. There should be no raw starch taste. It is well to remember that flour tends to lump when it is combined with a hot liquid or when the combined flour and liquid are cooked rapidly. To prevent this happening, the flour is mixed well with the melted fat and cooked slightly without browning. At this point the mixture is known as a white *roux*. The liquid is added a little at a time with constant stirring to keep the mixture smooth. To the beginning cook it may seem as though three hands would be an advantage when adding and stirring in the liquid. Some recipes suggest the milk be heated first. This practice will speed the cooking process but adds to the dishwashing chore. Using a cold liquid instead helps to further prevent formation of lumps. When preparing large quantities of sauce the first portion of the liquid added could be cold and the rest heated.

When all of the liquid has been added, the mixture is cooked over low heat or over boiling water and stirred continuously until completely thickened. Never leave the sauce standing over direct heat without stirring as it sticks and scorches easily. Some recipes suggest a further cooking period. Provided there is no taste of raw starch, this seems unnecessary and may even cause overcooking of the starch and a consequent thinning of the product. A lid placed on the pan as it waits over boiling water until serving time will prevent a skin forming on top.

Preparation of a Gravy

Gravy is a type of sauce. It has the same method of preparation and the same consistency. The main difference between a sauce and a gravy is in the flavour. Sauces often contrast the flavour of the food with which they are served. All gravies contain the flavour of the meat from which they are made and with which they are served. Gravies are sauces that are prepared from the juices extracted from meat or poultry. At least part of the fat used to make the roux should be fat drippings from the meat used. "Au jus" refers to an unthickened gravy.

There are two recognized methods of preparing a gravy. These are presented in recipe form on page 489.

1. From pan drippings of meat cooked by a dry heat method. If too much fat remains in the pan some is poured off. Then the flour is mixed and heated with the fat in the cooking pan to form a roux. Lumps are less likely to form if the flour is added by sprinkling over the fat while stirring. Liquid is added slowly with constant stirring until the mixture is thickened and the desired consistency is obtained. Full flavour is achieved by stirring down the browned particles at the sides of the pan as these are really concentrated meat juices. Vegetable stock may improve the food value as well as the flavour of the gravy. This method is very similar to the method used for making a white sauce.

2. From meat cooked by a moist heat method. This method uses the liquids in which the meat has been cooked and which contain the flavourful meat juices. Vegetable or meat stock or water can be used to extend the remaining liquid, as required.

The thickener, which could be flour or cornstarch or some of both, is first mixed with a cold liquid. A simple way is to shake liquid and thickener together in a tightly covered container to form a smooth thin paste. In the commercial kitchen this is known as "slurry". Best results are obtained if the liquid is cold (to prevent lumping) and placed in the container first (for easier mixing) before the thickener is added.

The thickening mixture is poured slowly into the boiling meat juices with constant stirring. A beginning cook will probably have to measure amounts. The experienced cook will add only enough "slurry" to obtain the desired thickness in the gravy.

Basic Sauces in the Commercial Kitchen

Chefs and commercial cooks seem to agree that of the sauces that are served warm there are five upon which all the others are based. They call these sauces the primary, leading or "mother" sauces and the ones that are made from these the secondary, or little sauces. Several of these basic sauces have a history in French cookery and the French name is often applied, especially in quantity food production. Here is a chart showing the five primary sauces used in commercial kitchens and some of the secondary sauces that can be derived from them. Also included is the French name and the characteristic colour of the sauce.

Primary Sauce	Colour	French Name	Secondary Sauces	
Cream	white	Béchamel	egg mustard Mornay cheese	mock Hollandaise a la king newburg
Velouté	blond	Velouté	horseradish chicken curry	bonne femme supreme allemande
Brown	brown	Espagnole	onion mushroom Bordelaise	
Tomato	red	Tomat	barbecue pizza creole Italian	
Hollandaise	yellow	Hollandaise	Béarnaise	

Following are the descriptions of the five primary sauces. The reader will need to be familiar with the terms "stock" and "roux".

1. Cream Sauce is a delicately flavoured sauce derived from milk or cream and thickened with a white roux. It is used for creamed dishes and many cream sauce variations. By this definition, a cream sauce is better known in the home kitchen as a white sauce. However, discriminating cooks know that a true Béchamel of the French tradition is actually a veloute made from rich veal or chicken stock and then thinned with rich milk or cream. This is why some writers and cooks reserve the term white sauce for a sauce made from milk.

2. Velouté Sauce is made from a plain roux and a white stock, either chicken or fish, depending upon how it is to be used.

3. Brown Sauce is made from brown stock thickened with a brown roux. It is used extensively in the preparation of all types of red meat and game dishes.

4. Tomato Sauce is prepared from a meat stock and a tomato product with a roux for thickening. The seasonings are usually stronger than in other meat sauces. It is used in the production of tomato flavoured foods as well as by itself with meat, poultry, fish, vegetables and macaroni dishes.

5. Hollandaise Sauce is thickened by egg yolk. It has a high proportion of butter and is one of the more difficult sauces to make. It is included here as a basic sauce because there are a number of secondary sauces derived from it.

Thickeners for Sauces and Gravies

The usual thickeners for sauces are starch, a roux, or eggs, especially the yolks. Cornstarch gives a clear sauce which tends to thicken more as it cools. It is frequently used in dessert sauces and those served cold. In addition, it is especially suitable for Chinese style sauces; for example sweet and sour sauce. Cornstarch has nearly twice the thickening power of flour.

Egg yolks are the thickener in Hollandaise sauce and its derivatives, and also in custard sauce. Egg is sometimes stirred into a sauce which has already been thickened in some other way. It adds a rich colour and flavour to the sauce as well as providing additional thickening.

A roux is a thickening agent made by cooking together flour and fat. If properly prepared the mixture keeps well and can be stored in the refrigerator to use when needed. The fat used for roux is usually butter (because of its flavour) or margarine or a mixture of the two. Chicken fat also gives good flavour and is suitable if the sauce is to be served with poultry. The fat is first melted, then the flour added and the mixture cooked for about ten minutes over moderate heat until the roux is frothy and leaves the bottom of the pan easily. It will have a slightly gritty texture, a golden colour and will have lost the taste of raw flour.

Roux is classified by colour — white, blond or brown. The colour is determined by the amount of browning of the flour. Browning is usually done in advance in a heavy frying pan or by roasting in the oven. It is also possible to brown the flour while it is being cooked with the fat. Done this way it is difficult to know how much colour is due to browning of the flour and how much to browning of the fat. Because flour loses some of its thickening power when browned, two to three times as much brown flour as white is needed for the same thickening quality. A white roux uses equal proportions of flour and fat. To prevent lumps when using the roux, blend the cold roux with a hot liquid. If the roux is hot, use a cold liquid.

Dry roux has no fat and is used when a less rich product is desired. It is simply flour that has been heated in the oven until slightly gritty.

Sometimes flour or other starches are blended with liquid and used for thickening. This starch-liquid mixture is known as a "slurry" or "whitewash". It is used in a similar way to the second method for gravy outlined on page 489.

A "beurre maine" is made of equal parts of flour and butter kneaded together. Small pea-sized balls of this are pinched off and dropped into a near boiling sauce, then mixed until smooth. It is used mostly in commercial kitchens, to correct the consistency of a sauce or soup that is too thin.

SOUPS

A soup is a liquid food. Thin, less satisfying soups can be served at the beginning of a meal as a stimulant to the appetite. Thick, or more substantial soups could be served as the principal part of a light supper or informal lunch.

Unlike sauce, a soup is not intended to complement another food. Its thickness will vary according to its type and the ingredients used. Regardless of type, a good soup will satisfy these requirements:

1. An appetizing colour and aroma.

2. A delicate, satisfying flavour distinctively that of the main ingredients.

3. Seasonings should be carefully added and are intended to bring out the characteristic flavour of the soup, not hide it. Taste the product before serving and adjust seasonings accordingly.

4. The soup should not be greasy. Tiny dots of fat on the surface of broth soups are acceptable.

5. Serve hot soups piping hot in heated dishes and jellied soups in chilled containers.

6. Serve the soup with an attractive garnish.

   Examples:

   a. Thin soup – finely chopped parsley, thin lemon slices, finely chopped green onion tops or chives.

   b. Cream Soups – toasted croutons, shredded toasted almonds, chopped chives or green onions, crumbled bacon, julienned meat.

   c. Other Thick Soups – chopped parsley or celery tops, thin sliced frankfurters, sliced lemon (seafood chowder).

7. Choose a suitable accompaniment. Examples: crackers, bread sticks, croutons, melba toast, pretzels, cheese or garlic toast.

Classification of Soups

There are so many kinds of soups that it is difficult to classify them. Some cooks divide them according to the type of stock from which they are made:

meat stock, meatless or vegetable stock and cream sauce. A simpler system to understand would be to divide all soups into thin and thick soups and then allow subdivisions within these two.

1. Thin Soups – Most thin soups are prepared without the use of starch, from a clear, rich liquid or stock.

   a. Clear soups will be thin and of a watery consistency but will have a good flavour.

      Bouillon is made from a brown stock that has been clarified. It has a distinct beef flavour and a darker colour than consommé.

      Consommé is made of beef stock which is usually combined with veal or chicken stock. Its flavour, from a blend of seasonings, is veal or chicken stock. Its flavour, from a blend of seasonings is delicate and its body and clarity is usually superior to that of bouillon. Broth is less clear than bouillon and consommé and does not usually have the same depth of flavour.

   b. Stock soups are made by adding vegetables, and rice and/or cereal products to the clear stock. The consistency will vary with the amount of foods added.

2. Thick Soups derive their thickness from the ingredients added to the stock, and these may be a roux (a fat and flour mixture) or other starch thickener, starch vegetables, macaroni products, or meat, fish or vegetables.

   a. Cream Soups are soups that have been prepared from a thin to medium white sauce, a roux-thickened cream sauce, or velouté sauce, with other ingredients added. Examples are: Cream of Mushroom, Tomato, Cream of Chicken. Bisques are heavy cream soups containing shellfish.

   b. Purée Soups are self-thickened by cooking the predominating ingredient into a pulp. Examples are: split pea soup, navy bean soup, potato soup.

   c. Potage is a broth heavy with vegetables, meats and pasta and is usually served as the main part of a meal.

   d. Chowders are a special type of thick soup named according to the predominating flavour which might be a seafood, as in clam, oyster or fish chowder or a vegetable, such as corn. Most chowders contain bits of bacon or salt pork, diced potatoes, onions and often other vegetables. There are two types of clam chowder:

      New England (or Boston) Clam Chowder has a milk base.

      Manhattan (or New York) Clam Chowder contains a fish stock with tomatoes.

Although it is usual to think of soups as being served hot, there are many cold ones as well.

They can be either thin or thick. Jellied consommé is a refreshing appetizer on a hot day. Vichyssoise is a cream of potato soup that is served cold. A cold soup made of fruit is particularly popular in the Scandinavian countries. Borsch, a beet soup, is often served chilled. Gazpacho is a Spanish specialty made of whole tomatoes.

Food Value of Soups

The nutrients in soup vary with the kind of soup. Thin, clear soups have little food value other than the minerals and water soluble vitamins which have been cooked out into the stock. Thick soups and cream soups can add food value to the meal according to the ingredients used. As well as vitamins and minerals they may contain proteins, fat and carbohydrates.

Stock

A stock is the liquid which results from boiling vegetables and the bones and flesh of meat, poultry or fish until the flavour and soluble nutrients have been extracted. Stocks are the basis of many soup and sauce preparations and as such are important in the home kitchen.

There are a number of different kinds of stocks used in the commercial kitchen. From these are made soups, sauces and gravies. With improvements in food technology, many good soup bases are available on the market. These can be used to make excellent soups and will reduce costs and cleanup time in the kitchen. However, when the bones and other materials for making stock are on hand they are generally used, with some of the ready-made base added to extend the flavour and quantity.

Types of Stock

1. Meat Stock is the liquid strained from bones and meat that have been simmered in water.

    This type may be classified according to its colour.

    a. Brown Stock results when beef or veal bones and meat are browned before they are added to the water. Some fat is added to assist the browning and the usual vegetables are used.

    b. White Stock is made from unbrowned veal or poultry bones and meat simmered with vegetables for 6-8 hours.

    A mild delicately flavoured stock can be made from the bones of beef, veal and poultry used separately or in combination. Pork and ham, lamb and mutton, each make stock which has a distinct flavour and should be used separately.

2. Vegetable Stock is the water from boiled vegetables such as: potatoes, carrots, celery, onions, green vegetables and the liquid from mild flavoured canned vegetables. Vegetable stock may be used as part or

all of the liquid in certain soups, sauces and gravies. Where used, flavour is improved and food value increased.

3. Fish Stock is prepared by simmering the skeleton, head and skin of fresh or frozen fish. It is limited to use in soups and chowders made with seafood.

Preparing a Good Stock

For a good quality stock the finest bones and meat and vegetables are carefully prepared and slowly simmered for at least eight hours. As the stock simmers the volume is reduced and the flavour becomes more concentrated. Attention to these details is important:

1. Use correct proportions of bones and water. Basic proportions are:
    2 kg meat and bone
    4 litre water
    500 g chopped vegetables

2. Trim off all fat from the bones and meat used. For more flavour add meat scraps.

3. Cut and split bones to allow full extraction of marrow and juices.

4. Start a stock from cold salted water to give the greatest flavour. The salt helps with extraction of flavour from bones and meat.

5. Add vegetables. The best flavour is obtained from onions, carrots and celery. Root vegetables may be unpared but should be well scrubbed. The mixture of chopped vegetables is called a "mirepoix". Leftovers, if clean and wholesome, are used; for example, roast bones, meat and vegetable trimmings, celery tops.

6. Long, slow simmering time is needed. Boiling makes the stock cloudy.

7. When cooking is finished pour the stock through a sieve or colander.

8. Chill and remove the fat layer which forms on top.

9. If stock is to be used for a clear soup it will need to be clarified. To clarify stock follow these steps:
    a. To each litre of stock add 1 egg white and 1 crushed egg shell.
    b. Heat stock to the boiling point and simmer until egg coagulates.
    c. Strain stock through several thicknesses of cheesecloth.

Sandwiches

The ever popular sandwich defies definition. The base is always some form of bread. On the bread is spread butter or margarine. In some special kinds of sandwiches the butter may be omitted or in the case of a grilled sandwich, it may be spread on the outside. There is always a filling which may be between the bread layers or on top of a single layer of buttered bread.

Sandwiches have many forms and many uses. The infinite variety of breads and fillings leaves little reason for the same kind of sandwich to be prepared and served so often that the eater tires of it. Sandwiches may be closed or open-faced, flat or rolled, cold or hot. They may be plain or fancy, large or small, served attractively garnished on a plate or wrapped in plastic wrap or waxed paper to go into the lunch box. No matter the kind, most sandwiches have these parts:

BREAD

Yeast bread is most often used since it is easily sliced and firm enough to hold the filling. Bakery bread is available sliced thin for sandwiches or in the regular thickness which is suitable for many uses. Unsliced bread has an advantage since it can be sliced any way desired. This is especially important for making fancy sandwiches. The trick of turning out straight uniform slices requires some practice with a serrated knife.

The kind of bread chosen will add much to the quality of the sandwich made. Many flavourful varieties other than white or brown are available. Try pumpernickel, cracked-wheat, cheese, raisin, rye, French, oatmeal or whole wheat. Hard or soft rolls make interesting sandwiches as do hamburger or hot dog buns.

Quickbreads such as muffins, biscuits or pancakes can be used to make a special kind of sandwich. Slices of fruit and nut loaf are good bases for sweet or party sandwiches.

FILLING

The possibilities for sandwich fillings are as extensive as the foods in the kitchen, ranging from slices of meat to elaborate and inventive combinations of ingredients. Many people, however, rely on a few standard fillings which they prepare regularly. No wonder they quickly tire of sandwiches!

Most sandwich fillings fall into one of three groups: either protein, vegetable or sweet. The protein fillings are the most satisfying and because of the nutrients they provide should be used at mealtime. Fillings in this classification include meat, poultry, fish, cheese, eggs, peanut butter or nuts. Usually a protein filling is combined with one or more of these: lettuce or other crisp vegetables, pickles, relish, spiced sauce, mustard, ketchup, mayonnaise, salad dressing.

Vegetable or relish fillings are not suitable at mealtime unless accompanied by a protein food. Served alone they satisfy hunger only temporarily. More often this kind of sandwich is used for a between meal snack or daintily sized and attractively garnished to accompany a beverage.

Sweet fillings include those made with jam, jelly, honey or fruit. When more staying power than that provided by an essentially carbohydrate sandwich is wanted, a sweet filling is sometimes combined with cheese, nuts or peanut butter. Most sandwich fillings can be used in all types of sandwiches but the texture of the filling and the amount used will depend on whether the sandwiches are hearty or dainty. Whenever a recipe is not being used, and sometimes when one is, a large dash of imagination will serve to improve sandwich fillings.

BUTTER

Butter or margarine is another basic ingredient of the sandwich. Its function is threefold. It adds rich flavour and food value, serves to hold the bread and the filling together and it prevents moist fillings from soaking into the bread.

For easier spreading butter should be soft. It can be creamed until light and fluffy but should not be melted for in this state it would soak into the bread. A pliable knife or small spatula is the best implement for even, smooth spreading.

Sometimes seasoning ingredients are added to creamed butter. These mixtures are used as spreads or fillings for dainty, fancy sandwiches and canapés or as a base for other fillings in more substantial sandwiches. Savoury butter spreads may be referred to as seasoned butter, sandwich butter or canapé butter. Some examples of canapé butters are to be found on page **86**, Appetizers. Any good recipe book will give other suggestions.

KINDS OF SANDWICHES

1. **Hot Meat Sandwiches**

    These consist of slices of meat or poultry on bread or toast and served with gravy or a sauce.

2. **Grilled Sandwiches**

    Two slices of bread with a filling between are buttered on the outside and browned on a hot skillet or griddle.

3. **Broiled Sandwiches**

    A single layer of bread or a bun half is spread with filling and browned under the direct heat.

4. **Toasted Sandwiches**

    This type includes any sandwich made with toasted bread. A popular example is the clubhouse sandwich made with three slices of bread and several different fillings.

5. **Beef Dip**

    Many layers of thinly sliced roast beef are placed between pieces of French bread or a large crusty roll and served with a side dish of juices from the beef, for dipping.

Cold sandwiches are most often served and play an important role in the packed lunch. When served as a main part of the meal a hot food such as soup or beverage is a welcome contrast. Here are some examples:

1. **Plain Sandwiches**

    Two slices of bread are used to hold an endless choice of fillings. Sliced meats, poultry or cheese are popular. Other fillings are more moist and soft textured and often consist of minced meat, chopped egg, cooked fish combined with mayonnaise or salad dressing.

2. Party Sandwiches

These are of miniature size, usually large enough for only one or two bites. They are made using assorted flavours and cut into interesting shapes. Usually bread crusts are removed and the sandwich tray is artistically garnished.

3. Sandwich Loaf

This is popular for a party. Lengthwise slices of alternatively white and brown bread are spread with several different fillings. When put together into the loaf shape again the exterior is spread with softened cream cheese and chilled. Serving time reveals an interesting surprise of flavours within each slice.

PREPARING SANDWICHES

1. It is good management, where possible, to set aside one area of the kitchen as a centre for preparing sandwiches. Near the refrigerator and the breadbox a cupboard shelf and a drawer can be equipped with sandwich making necessities. These include cutting board, bread board, sharp knives, small bowls, spoons and forks, pliable knife or spatula, waxed paper and plastic wrap. If fancy sandwiches are made frequently the utensils needed to make them could be stored here, too.

2. To make sandwiches more interesting choose a variety of bread and rolls. Coarse textured bread slices best with a serrated knife. Use a sawing motion. For easier slicing of fresh bread the loaf can be chilled in the refrigerator first.

3. Day-old bread is best for most types of sandwiches, though very fresh bread is needed to make rolled sandwiches or pinwheels so that slices will not crack when rolled.

4. **Remove crusts before making most fancy-type sandwiches; e.g., rolled, pinwheels, fancy shaped, open faced. This prevents waste of butter and fillings. Ribbon and plain sandwiches are easier to make if crusts are trimmed after they are made. Save the crusts for crumbs, casseroles, puddings, croutons.**

5. Frozen sliced bread is convenient for making picnic or lunch box sandwiches. It is easy to spread and the frozen slices help to keep the filling and other ingredients in the lunch box cool. Also, lettuce and other vegetables used for filling will stay crisp.

6. A thin layer of soft butter or margarine protects the bread from moist filling ingredients. Softened cream cheese has a similar effect and may be substituted for the butter or mixed with it in some fancy sandwiches.

7. Fillings should be well seasoned to complement the blandness of the breads. Taste as you add a little seasoning at a time until the right flavour is achieved. A crisp crunchy ingredient adds interesting texture. When combined in a moist filling mixture it should be finely chopped to make flavour and texture more appealing. Meat for sandwiches should be sliced very thin using several slices instead of one thick slice.

8. When making sandwiches use good management principles. Especially when making them in quantity, organize the work area so that there will be no wasted motion. Use assembly-line methods making all of one kind of sandwich before going on to the next. Allow sufficient space for cutting the bread, placing slices in pairs to spread with butter and filling, combining layers, cutting and wrapping.

Storing Sandwiches

Most sandwiches (with the exception of lettuce and tomato) can be made up ahead of time. They should be carefully wrapped in waxed paper and stored in a cool place, preferably in a refrigerator. Open face and other unwrapped sandwiches can be stored in baking pans lined with waxed paper and then covered with another sheet of waxed paper and a damp cloth. The damp cloth should not touch the sandwiches as it may make them soggy. The waxed paper and cloth may be held in place with clothes pegs clipped to the edges of the pan or with large elastic bands placed around the pan. Sandwiches will keep fresh for 12 to 24 hours when stored in this manner.

Freezing

For longer storage, sandwiches can be frozen. Fillings made of meat, poultry, fish, cheese or nuts freeze well. Only a few ingredients are unsuitable to use in sandwiches that are to be frozen. These include eggs, which become tough and dry; lettuce, celery, tomatoes, cucumbers and watercress, which lose crispness; fruit jelly, which tends to soak into the bread during thawing; and oil dressing, which may separate during freezing.

Only freshly prepared sandwiches should be frozen and they should be wrapped and put into the freezer immediately. Fancy sandwiches such as checkerboard, rolled, etc., and plain sandwiches too, are best left whole. They will look better and taste fresher if cut just at serving time.

Sandwiches can be frozen individually or a number with the same kind of filling packed together. Large quantities wrapped together will result in uneven thawing so it is best to wrap sandwiches in small packages.

Sandwiches wrapped in heavy waxed paper will keep well in the freezer for a week or two but for longer storage they should be wrapped in moisture-vapour-proof freezer materials. For individual lunch box sandwiches small plastic bags are handy. Each bag should be clearly marked with name of the filling and date of freezing, and the bag should be tightly closed to keep the sandwich from drying out.

Thawing

The thawing time should be planned so that sandwiches will be ready just in time for serving. (If they are thawed too soon, store in the refrigerator.) Small open face sandwiches will thaw at room temperature in about $\frac{1}{2}$ hour; small packages (up to $\frac{1}{2}$ loaf) or other sandwiches in 2 to 3 hours. Take lunch box sandwiches from the freezer just before leaving for work or school in the morning and they will be thawed but still fresh and cool at lunch time. Outer wrappings of frozen sandwiches should not be removed until the sandwiches are partially thawed.

SUGGESTIONS FOR ROLLED SANDWICHES

1. Cream cheese with maraschino cherries.
2. Peanut butter and banana.
3. Cream cheese and asparagus.

SUGGESTIONS FOR OPEN FACED SANDWICHES

1. Cream cheese with orange marmalade, cranberry jelly or crushed pineapple.
2. Cream cheese and pimento with a few drops of food colouring.
3. Cream cheese with $\frac{1}{4}$ part blue cheese and a dash of Worcestershire sauce.

SUGGESTIONS FOR FANCY SANDWICH FILLINGS

1. Ground cooked meat with pickle relish or chopped pickled onion and mayonnaise and horseradish.
2. Crumbled crisp bacon with peanut butter and mayonnaise.

3. Liverwurst, olives and salad dressing.
4. Diced cooked chicken, finely diced celery, chopped sweet pickle and mayonnaise.
5. Two parts each of chopped cooked chicken and walnuts with one part drained crushed pineapple moistened with salad dressing.
6. Sardines and chopped hard cooked egg, moistened with lemon juice.
7. Tuna, crab or lobster with finely cut celery moistened with mayonnaise.
8. Diced hard cooked egg with minced onion and green pepper and finely chopped ham moistened with mayonnaise.
9. Chopped hard cooked egg, chopped stuffed olives and salad dressing.
10. Cottage cheese, minced green pepper, onion salt and paprika.

SUGGESTIONS FOR GARNISHES

Garnishes are used to add colour, tang or texture contrast to the sandwich. Choose one which will harmonize with both the filling and type of sandwich. Delicate garnishes add to a plate of dainty sandwiches but larger garnishes look better with more substantial sandwiches. A garnish must always be edible!

1. Carrot curls, sticks or slices.
2. Celery curls, fans, sticks or stuffed.
3. Pickles, as dill, sweet, cucumber, gherkins, onions, beets, olives.
4. Fruit such as apple slices, cubes, rings or balls; spiced peaches, crab-apples.
5. Vegetables as green onion, radishes (plain or in roses), green pepper in slices or rings, tomato wedges or slices, cucumber in slices, sticks or fans, cauliflower.

Cereals and Cereal Products

Cereals are the edible seeds produced by certain plants of the grass family. They are the start of new plant life and, as such, are rich storehouses of food elements needed by living things. Since the beginning of time, when people discovered that the kernels of grain growing on the top of certain grasses were good to eat, cereals have been our chief means of subsistence. Ancient peoples believed that the protection of grain was the concern of the goddess Ceres. From the name Ceres came the word cereal. The first crude bread was formed when people learned to pound the grain between stones and mix it with water into a mash which was dried in the sun or baked on hot stones.

Because of their good keeping quality and low cost, cereals and cereal products are staple foods everywhere. In many countries bread made from wheat is called the "staff of life". Wheat is the most important of the cereal grains as it provides nourishment for more nations of the world than any other food. Rice, a close second, is still the most extensively used cereal in countries with the greatest population, India, China and Japan.

Cereals are an important part of the food intake in developing countries and in the diets of low income families. Because of the minerals and vitamins they contain it is important that whole grain, enriched or restored products be chosen rather than refined or unenriched products.

STRUCTURE AND NUTRITIVE VALUE OF CEREAL GRAINS

The nutrients provided by cereals include carbohydrate, vitamins, minerals, fat and protein. These are not distributed evenly throughout the cereal grain nor are they in the same proportions in each type of grain. Each kernel has three separate sections and each section performs a special function.

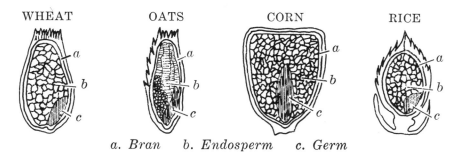

WHEAT   OATS   CORN   RICE

a. Bran   b. Endosperm   c. Germ

Bran   The outer layer of the grain which remains after the protective skin or husk is removed in preparation for milling human food. Bran is of cellulose composition with mineral deposits of iron and phosphorus giving a rigid structure. Thiamine is the most significant vitamin present although bran also contains riboflavin and niacin.

Germ   The portion that sprouts when the seed is allowed to grow, which explains why this part has the best nutritive value. A rich source of "B" vitamins, especially thiamine, the germ also contains some vitamin E and the mineral iron. Because of the presence of fat it has poor keeping qualities.

Endosperm   Makes up the largest portion of any cereal grain. Nutritionally it is inferior since it contains mainly starch and some vegetable protein but lacks vitamins, minerals and cellulose. It furnishes nourishment to the growing seed. Endosperm is the only part of the kernel that remains in highly refined cereals, polished rice and white flour.

It has already been stated that all cereals and cereal products are a rich and inexpensive source of energy. Their vitamin and mineral content will depend upon the parts of the cereal grain used and whole grain cereals are by far the most valuable nutritionally. Cereals are deficient in vitamins A, D and C, although yellow corn products contain good amounts of vitamin A. At breakfast, vitamin A can be furnished by whole milk on the whole grain cereal or by butter on the toast or by serving eggs as well. Vitamin C is added to breakfast by including a citrus fruit or vitaminized apple juice. Vitamin D is obtained by using irradiated milk.

Kinds of Cereal Grains

1. Wheat   The climate of much of the western world is well suited to the growing of wheat. Because wheat has the highest percentage of protein of all the cereals wheat flour is valued for making bread and other baked products that need a strong gluten framework. Smaller amounts of wheat are used to make breakfast cereals. Durum wheat is especially suited to the manufacture of macaroni products which are known as alimentary pastes.

2. Oats

In Canada, oats rank second to wheat as cereal grain produced for food. Oats are used chiefly in making breakfast cereals. Because usually the whole grain is used with only the outer husk removed, these cereals are rich in nutrients. Breakfast cereals made from oats are also used as an ingredient in breads, cookies and desserts.

3. Corn

Next to wheat, corn is the grain most used in the United States. It is made into breakfast cereals, cornmeal, hominy and grits. By-products are cornstarch, corn oil and corn syrup. Corn is used extensively as a cereal in Canada but because production in this country is limited, it is mostly imported.

4. Rye

Rye is used principally for breadmaking flour. Pure rye flour as made in Russia, Germany, Poland and the Scandinavian countries is almost black and very heavy. Because the protein in rye flour is not as strong as in wheat flour the loaf is not light and porous. Therefore, we combine rye flour with wheat flour to make a lighter coloured, more porous rye bread.

5. Barley

Barley cereal is used for thickening and flavouring soups. It may be in the form of pot barley, which is the whole grain, or pearl barley, which is the refined cereal. Malt is made from barley. It is the flavouring material in malt syrups, malted milk, and malted breakfast foods. Barley has a high mineral content.

6. Buckwheat

Buckwheat is used mainly for the manufacture of pancake flour. Some buckwheat groats are used as a breakfast cereal.

Types of Breakfast Cereals

NUTRITIVE VALUE CLASSIFICATION

1. Whole Grain Cereals

Are made from the entire kernel of the cereal grain. They contain significant amounts of the vitamins, thiamine, riboflavin and niacin and of the minerals iron and phosphorus while providing an excellent and economical source of starch and vegetable protein.

2. Refined Cereals   Are processed by intensive milling and contain mostly the endosperm of the grain. They are sometimes enriched with vitamins and minerals or by the addition of wheat germ to bring their food value nearer that of the whole grain cereal. Enrichment is controlled by Federal regulations. Unless enriched they contribute only kilojoules and some incomplete protein.

MARKET FORMS AVAILABLE

1. Regular Cereals   Are the least processed of all cereals and therefore require long cooking. There are very few found in this form. Examples are oatmeal, rolled oats, cracked wheat.

2. Quick Cooking Cereals   Are made by dividing the cereal kernel more finely than the regular cereal is divided. Therefore, only a few minutes cooking is required. Most uncooked cereals are sold in this form. For example, quick cooking rolled oats are cut into thinner flakes than the regular rolled oats.

3. Instant Cereals   Need only to be mixed with hot liquid such as milk or water before serving. Although they save time in preparation they cost more and may have a less acceptable flavour and consistency.

4. Baby Cereals   Are precooked with vitamins and minerals added. Their fine texture is specially suited to infants and convalescents.

5. Ready-to-Eat Cereals   Are produced from corn, oats, wheat and rice in a variety of flavours, shapes, sizes, colours, and textures. During processing the cereal grain is precooked and then flaked, shredded, puffed, or popped in an almost endless variety. About one quarter of those on the market today are pre-sweetened. Most cost more per serving than uncooked cereals. The processing of refined cereals destroys most naturally occuring nutrients leaving essentially a carbohydrate food. There is an attempt to replace this loss by addition of B vitamins and iron.

HOW TO BUY BREAKFAST CEREALS

1. Choose a package that is clean and dry and the right size for the needs of your family.
2. Read the label carefully to determine the kind of grain, food value, cooking instructions and other pertinent facts.
3. Compare the cost per serving of the different kinds of cereals and consider the food value for the price.
4. Because the nutritive value of cereal products is determined by the parts of the grain used, whole grain cereals which are made from the bran and germ as well as the endosperm, will provide the most vitamins and minerals for the money spent. "Enriched" cereal products are the next best buy. The least nutrients for your money will be obtained from refined cereal products.

HOW TO STORE BREAKFAST CEREALS

1. Store packaged cereals in the original container with the waxed paper lining rolled down and the lid of the box closed to prevent cereal from

becoming stale. Store bulk cereals in a covered container such as a glass jar.

2. Examine all cereals frequently in hot weather to check their condition. To prevent rancidity, whole grain cereals should be kept in a cool, dry place.

Principles of Cereal Cookery

Because starch makes up at least three-quarters of the cereal grain, it is the principles of starch cookery which determine the procedure used for cooking breakfast cereals. The objectives of all cereal cookery are to improve the flavour, soften the cellulose, gelatinize the starch and produce a product that is free of lumps. For Principles of Starch Cookery see page 353.

So that lumps cannot form, the cereal granules are first separated from each other. This is usually done by stirring the cereal slowly into rapidly boiling water. When the cereal particles come in contact with the boiling water their outer surface becomes sticky. Hence constant stirring to prevent lumping is recommended until the water boils again. The finer the cereal, the greater the tendency to form lumps.

As the starch cooks the starch grains absorb water, causing the cereal to increase in bulk. Some cereals, such as cream of wheat, absorb more water than others. Various cereal grains will use different amounts of water to achieve the right consistency. (See chart page 111.)

The heat of the cooking converts the water absorbed by the starch granules into steam, which bursts the granules and releases the soluble starch inside. The starch which had filled the cells flows out and causes the cereal to thicken as it cooks.

The term gelatinization refers to the thickening which occurs when starches are cooked. Since cereal is quite bland in flavour, its texture must be made appetizing by using the right proportion of water to cereal and allowing the correct cooking time to produce gelatinization. Adding salt is an important aid to flavour but cooking also develops the flavour of cereals.

When the boiling water permeates and softens the starch granules they become more accessible to the enzymes of the human digestive tract. Raw starch is only about fifty percent digestible. Cooked starch is about ninety percent digestible.

Since many of the cereals available today have been precooked, following the directions on the cereal package is recommended procedure. However, sometimes directions are not clear or are unavailable. The chart which follows, of proportions and cooking time for regular cereals provides a workable guide.

PROPORTIONS AND TIMES FOR COOKING "REGULAR" CEREALS

TYPE	EXAMPLES	CEREAL	WATER	SALT	DIRECT HEAT	DOUBLE BOILER
Fine Cereal	Cream of Wheat Cornmeal Farina Wheatlets	40-50 ml	250 ml	1 ml	10-15 minutes	20-30 minutes
Rolled or Flaked Cereal	Rolled Oats Flaked Wheat	75-85 ml	250 ml	1 ml	30 minutes	45 minutes
Coarse Cereal	Cracked Wheat Oatmeal	60 ml	250 ml	1 ml	45 min 30 min	2 hours 1 hour

NOTE: *The yield will be about the same as the amount of liquid used.*

METHOD OF COOKING CEREAL
1. Bring measured salted water to a boil over direct heat.
2. Sprinkle measured cereal slowly into boiling water, stirring constantly.
3. Continue stirring to prevent sticking as cereal thickens (2-5 minutes).
4. Reduce heat and cook by method (a) or (b):

    a – Cover pot and cook over low, direct heat for shorter time indicated.

    b – Cover pot and finish cooking over boiling water for longer time.
5. Stir several times during cooking to prevent lumps forming and to ensure a better consistency. If the cereal becomes too thick add more boiling water to prevent it from sticking to the pan. Taste for salt before serving. Cook until there is no starchy flavour remaining and a desired consistency is reached.

NOTE: *An alternate method for fine cereals, such as cream of wheat and corn meal, is to mix the cereal with a small amount of cold water before stirring it into the boiling water.*

QUICK COOKING CEREALS
The times in the chart above serve as a guide for cooking "regular" breakfast cereals. Shorter or longer times may be desirable to suit individual preferences. Quick-cooking cereals, however, vary in the cooking time required; therefore, prepare according to package directions when first trying a cereal. Then vary proportions and cooking time as family preferences indicate.

Qualities of a Well Cooked Cereal
1. A smooth uniform texture without lumps and of a flowing consistency.
2. A nutlike flavour, properly salted and thoroughly cooked so that there is no taste of raw starch.
3. A good hot serving temperature.

Tips for Cooking and Using Cereal

1. When combining two or more cereals allow time for the cereal which requires the longest cooking time.

2. For packaged cereals use the chart as a guide and compare it to directions given on package. In some cases, increasing the cooking time recommended by the manufacturer may be desirable to avoid the taste of raw starch.

3. For extra food value, 30 ml of wheat germ per 250 ml of uncooked cereal may be added to the cereal just before the end of cooking.

4. For added laxative quality use 15 ml to 50 ml flax seed or 50 ml to 75 ml bran per 250 ml of uncooked cereal.

5. Fruit juice, such as apple juice, may be substituted for water when cooking cereal.

6. Add extra flavour, interest and food value with a pat of butter or chopped dried fruits (apricots, apples, prunes, peaches, raisins).

7. Serve with white or brown sugar, maple syrup or honey, and milk or cream.

8. When planning to reheat cooked cereals be sure to pour a thin layer of cold water over the cereal to prevent a hard skin forming overnight. Then reheat over hot water keeping the pot tightly covered. To prevent lumping, do not stir until heated.

9. To heat or crisp ready-to-eat cereals, pour the cereal into a shallow baking pan. Place in a moderate oven (180°C) with the door slightly ajar. Leave until heated through. Never put the whole package in the oven.

10. Cereals may be used in many ways other than as a breakfast food. Recipes for cookies, quick breads, crumb crusts and dessert toppings include various cereals. Uncooked granular cereal or fine crumbs made by crushing ready-to-eat cereals can be used for coating pan fried or deep fried foods such as croquettes, chops, fish or poultry. The food should be dipped in egg-milk mixture before rolling in the cereal or cereal crumbs.

    Cereals may also be used as a meat extender and when a whole grain or enriched one is chosen the nutritive value of the meal is inexpensively improved. In a meat loaf recipe substitute any one of these for 250 ml soft bread crumbs or 125 ml dry bread crumbs:

    375 ml whole wheat flakes, uncrushed
    165 ml fine cereal crumbs
    250 ml rolled oats, uncooked
      80 ml farina, uncooked
      80 ml whole wheat cereal, uncooked

Wheat Flour

Canada is one of the world's leading exporters of wheat. Millions of hectares of this grain are grown yearly, the principal variety being hard spring wheat. Hard spring wheats are sown in May for harvesting in late August or September. They may contain from 12 to 14 percent protein and are used mainly for bread flour. Soft fall wheats may contain 8 to 10 percent protein and are used for pastry and cake flours.

The familiar white flour is a finely milled and sifted wheat product. It contains mostly the endosperm of the grain. Since they give flour a dark colour the bran and the germ containing vitamins and minerals necessary for good health are removed. In order to replace these lost minerals all of the white flour sold in Canada is enriched.

KINDS OF FLOUR

All purpose Flour	is a white flour milled from hard spring wheat. It contains a protein which, when moistened, forms the substance called gluten. Gluten gives the elasticity needed in the making of bread. Although all purpose flour is an excellent bread flour it is also satisfactory for general baking and for making puddings, sauces, gravies, etc. When substituting all purpose flour for cake flour in a recipe it is recommended you use 10 per cent less than specified.
Bread Flour	is milled from hard spring wheat. It is usually sold to bakers because it makes excellent bread with bakery equipment but has too much gluten-forming protein for home use.
Pastry Flour	is a white flour milled from soft winter wheat and is often labelled "cake and pastry" flour. It has less protein than all purpose flour and is therefore best suited for making pastries, cakes, cookies and quickbreads. A finely milled flour, it is smooth to touch. Because of its high starch content and little protein it packs in the hand when pressed. All purpose flour contains more granular protein and does not pack when pressed.
Cake Flour	is a highly refined white flour made from soft wheat. Since it is very low in protein it is best suited for cake making, especially angel and sponge cakes that are leavened by air. It is more

	finely grained than pastry flour and is velvety to the touch.
Graham Flour	is white flour milled from hard spring wheat, to which bran and other parts of the wheat kernel have been added. These additions give a brownish colour to the flour which is used with various proportions of white flour in making yeast breads and quick breads.
Whole Wheat Flour	is a brownish coloured flour that contains all the natural parts of the wheat kernel up to at least 95 percent of the total weight of the wheat from which it was made. Although whole wheat flour contains more protein than all purpose flour, the tiny particles of bran cut and break the gluten strands, giving a slightly heavier product. Whole wheat flour is used with various proportions of white flour, which forms the needed gluten, in making yeast breads and quick breads.
Self-Raising Flour	is a blend of white flour, salt and baking powder. It can be used with most recipes by omitting the salt and baking powder called for in the recipe. It is not available in all parts of Canada but is more common in Australia, Great Britain and many European countries.

If bleaching or maturing agents have been added to any of these flours, the ingredients and amounts used are regulated by law and the label of the bag or package will be marked to indicate what has been added. These additives are used to improve the baking performance of the flour, which formerly was achieved by storing or aging the flour before marketing.

HOW TO BUY FLOUR

1. Buy white flour in the largest amounts that use and home storage permit, in order to save time and money.
2. Buy whole wheat and Graham flours in amounts that can be used up in a reasonable length of time as these do not keep well in hot weather.
3. Buy flour according to the type needed for the use for which it is intended. This will ensure a more satisfactory baked product.
4. Read labels to determine the type of flour and contents of the package. Then compare brands to obtain the best value.

HOW TO STORE FLOUR

1. Keep containers tightly covered in a cool dry place to exclude atmosphere moisture and insects.
2. Store whole grain flours in a cool, dark place to prevent rancidity.

Rice

Rice is one of the principal cereals, second only to wheat in world importance. It thrives in a hot moist climate and in some areas of the world it is possible to grow three crops a year. A dietary mainstay in Asia and the Far East, in other parts of the world it is used as an accompaniment to protein foods, as an ingredient in main dishes and in special desserts. Although not grown in Canada, it is grown in some of the United States.

Like all cereal seeds, rice has a husk on the outside, the main part of the seed is the endosperm, and the germ forms the small part of the seed that will ultimately grow into the plant. The endosperm is mostly starch. The husk and the germ contain most of the vitamins, protein and fat.

During milling the husk and the germ are normally removed leaving only the endosperm, as in white rice. In countries which use rice as their staple food the thiamine deficiency disease beri-beri is fairly common. To increase the amount of thiamine in rice it is possible to soak and then steam it before milling. This process loosens the husk, distributes the thiamine through the grain and improves its keeping qualities. Converted rice is prepared by this special process.

KINDS OF RICE

There are numerous varieties of rice. After harvesting, all the seeds are cleaned and then screened to separate them into the three basic types — long, medium and short grain rice. Long grain rice is produced as a result of a longer growing period and more irrigation. Milling removes the bran, resulting in polished rice of varying lengths. There are many kinds of rice displayed on the grocer's shelf.

White Rice   is the white starchy endosperm of the rice grain. It is less flavourful than brown rice. Long grain white rice is light and fluffy when cooked, for the grains tend to separate and keep their individual shape well. It is useful served alone or in almost any rice dish. Medium and short grain varieties are tender and moist, for the grains tend to cling together. They are especially useful in a dish requiring a tender easily moulded rice, such as in pudding.

Converted, Special Process or Parboiled Rice

These three terms refer basically to the same thing. The unmilled rice is processed with heat or steam under pressure and then dried. This partial cooking process allows the nutrients in the outer layers to diffuse into the endosperm so the milling which follows does not remove the nutrients. This type of rice can be described as creamy in colour, somewhat chewy, with each grain distinct when cooked and a flavour falling somewhere between that of brown rice and white rice.

Precooked, Instant or Five Minute Rice

These terms refer to a rice that has been milled, completely cooked, and then dried. It requires only the absorption of boiling water to make it ready for serving. It is white in colour, bland in flavour, and somewhat soggy when reconstituted.

Brown Rice

is whole, unpolished rice from which only the hull and some of the bran has been removed. It is, therefore, richest in vitamins and minerals. Cooked brown rice is a light brown colour with fluffy particles. It has a nut-like flavour and is well suited for use in casseroles, main dishes and special stuffings.

Wild Rice

is not a true rice although it belongs to a related plant family. It is the seed of a grass that grows naturally in the Great Lakes region. It is best known as an accompaniment to game or game birds. See page 118 for more information on wild rice.

COOKING RICE

A first consideration in cooking rice is to choose the right rice for the use intended. Popular uses are outlined above. Secondly, the nutritive value should be considered. Unpolished brown rice has the highest vitamin content. Converted rice retains a large portion of nutrients after milling. Unenriched white rice is chiefly starch. The third consideration is time available. Each of the kinds of rice requires a different cooking time. Brown rice cooks most slowly; precooked rice takes only five minutes to prepare.

Even experienced cooks sometimes have difficulty cooking rice. The problem is one of retaining the form of the kernel while at the same time cooking the kernel until tender. One reason may be the variation in moisture content of rice. Be sure to read the directions for cooking on the rice package. A simple easy-to-remember formula for cooking all except pre-cooked and wild rice combines:

    250 ml rice
    500 ml water
      3 ml salt

Accurate measurement is very important. Remember that rice swells when cooked:

    250 ml of white, brown or converted rice becomes 750-1 000 ml.
    250 ml of precooked rice becomes 500 ml.
    250 ml of wild rice becomes 1 000 ml.

Here are some guidelines that will contribute to success:

1. Use a rice cooker or other heavy pan with a tight-fitting lid.

2. Do not wash the rice before cooking or rinse it afterward as this washes away water-soluble nutrients.

3. Place measured rice, cold water, and salt into the pan.

4. Bring to the boil, cover, and reduce heat to low or simmer.

5. Do not stir rice after it boils as this breaks up the grains and makes the rice gummy.

6. Do not lift the lid of the saucepan after the rice has started boiling or some of the measured water will be lost and the cooking time altered.

7. Time rice carefully, allowing:

    15-20 minutes for white rice,
    25-30 minutes for converted rice,
    45-50 minutes for brown rice.

8. To test if rice is cooked, press a single kernel between the thumb and forefinger. It should feel tender throughout with no "bone" in the centre.

9. To keep rice warm before serving leave it in the pot, covered, for 5-10 minutes, or place it in a warm, not hot, oven. If left longer it will pack down.

When you have tried this formula for cooking rice you may decide to attempt variations. For a firmer rice with well separated kernels try 400 ml water instead of 500 ml. If you prefer softer rice use more water. For drier rice, remove the cover after cooking and leave on very low heat for five minutes.

Another way of maintaining a low heat after the liquid and rice have been brought to the boil over direct heat is to place the covered pan over boiling water. Rice may also be oven baked. Use the same proportions and bake, covered, at 180°C. White rice takes 30-35 minutes to cook in the oven, the other kinds take longer.

Rice can be cooked ahead and reheated. To reheat, place in a pan, sprinkle with water, and allow to steam for 8-10 minutes. Leftover rice can be refrigerated for up to a week or frozen for up to six months. Look in the index of this book for recipes for cooking and using rice.

Wild Rice

Wild rice is the grain of a water grass which grows naturally in the shallow water along the edges of lakes and ponds in parts of Manitoba and Ontario. In past years it provided an important food for the people of the Great Lakes region. Today the grass provides food and shelter for fish and water fowl and is valued for that reason as well as for its appeal as an epicurean dish.

When ripe, the kernel is long and greenish black in colour. Wild rice must be harvested as soon as it is ripe, otherwise the grains drop off and are lost. Harvesting is done by hand from a canoe. One person paddles while the other flails the ripe kernels into the canoe with big sticks. Because of the difficulties of harvesting the crop, wild rice has always been expensive, but labour costs and the increasing demand for it in today's food markets have raised the price still further.

Wild rice is a favourite accompaniment to game and game birds and to tame birds such as goose, duck and game hen. It can be served in small quantities as an accompaniment dish or mixed with brown or white rice in a casserole or stuffing.

Before wild rice is used in most recipes it should be soaked to soften it. This may be done by allowing the rice to stand overnight in cold water. A more convenient method has been developed which retains the desired flavour and texture of the rice. Here are the steps:

1. Wash the required amount of wild rice under cold running water (250 ml raw rice will swell to 1 000 ml when cooked).

2. Stir measured rice into 3 times the amount of boiling water.

3. Parboil for 5 minutes.

4. Remove from the heat. Let soak covered in the same water for 1 hour.

5. Drain, wash and cook as directed in the recipe being used.

1. Manicotti 2. Lumaconi (jumbo shells) 3. Noodles Fini (fine) 4. Tubettini (med. cut macaroni) 5. Noodles Extra Larghe (extra broad) 6. Stivaletti (ready cut macaroni) 7. Rotini (turrets) 8. Egg Tagliatelle 9. Anellini (rings) 10. Galle (bow ties) 11. Egg noodles (birds nest) 12. Acini Pepe (lead shots) 13. Spaghetti 14. Penne Lisce (pens) 15. Conchiglie (medium shells) 16. Spinach noodles 17. Spirals 18. Lasagne 19. Mafalda

Pasta

MAKING PASTA

Pasta is the Italian name describing the group of foods which includes spaghetti, macaroni and noodles. They are frequently called macaroni products. All pasta is made from the same basic ingredients: flour and water. The best macaroni products are made from a special variety of wheat called durum, which is extremely hard spring wheat with a very high gluten content that provides tenacity and strength.

The same procedure is followed for making macaroni products, whatever the shape. First the coarsely ground durum flour, semolina, is mixed with water to make a very stiff dough, and kneaded until smooth. The dough is enriched by the addition of thiamine, niacin, riboflavin and iron and if the end product is to be noodles, egg solids are added. The dough is then forced through special machines that produce the desired size and shape of pieces which are then dried slowly in special driers before packaging.

KINDS OF PASTA

Within the three categories of spaghetti, noodles and macaroni, there are numerous different shapes and sizes, many with interesting and imaginative names. Spaghetti is the general term for the solid rod form of pasta. Round rods may be made in many different diameters ranging from fidellini, the smallest, up through vermicelli, spaghetti to spaghettoni, the largest size. Solid rods may be made in an oval shape, too.

Noodles, or egg noodles, are flat products. These may be fine or narrow, medium wide or broad. Some may be extra long and called "folded". Fettucini means "ribbons" in Italian, a descriptive word for many of these flat shapes. All of these flat shapes can be made curly on one or both sides. The large ones of this group are known as lasagne.

Macaroni is the third group of pasta products. They are round with a hole in the middle and the variety is almost endless. All can be cut into any length, from thin slices to long tubes. Probably the best known are the elbow macaroni products. As well there are so-called specialty products which include sea shells, smooth and ridged, varying in size from very small to very large. There are snails and nut shells both smooth and ridged and at least two sizes of alphabet noodles. Also available are wheels, stars, bows, curls and twists — the possibilities are unlimited.

USES OF PASTA

The uses of pasta are as limitless as the forms. Although some recipes call for certain types of macaroni product, interchanging of shapes is possible as long as the exchange is made among products of similar shape and size, and as long as the cooked volume is approximately the same. Uses of macaroni products may be arranged into three groups:

1. As a main dish – macaroni and cheese, lasagne, chicken tetrazzini.

2. As an accompaniment to a protein food (in place of potato or rice)
    - buttered and seasoned macaroni with pork chops
    - spaghetti with meatballs or chicken cacciatore
    - noodles with chicken fricassee or beef stroganoff.

3. As an ingredient
    - in a main dish – tuna noodle casserole
    - in soup – chicken noodle soup
        – minestrone
    - in salad – macaroni salad.

COOKING PASTA

Properly cooked pasta will be still firm and chewy but not yet soft or mushy. This is not difficult to do if a few basic principles are considered. To avoid waste, cook only the amount you need. Individual appetites vary so that allowing 125-250 ml of cooked pasta is only useful as a guide. The amount required will also depend upon the way it is to be used and on the other foods being served with it. Macaroni products all expand to about twice their original size when cooked. Cook the pasta in a large amount of rapidly boiling water to allow the starch granules enough room to swell. Put the dry pasta slowly into the boiling water so that the water continues to boil. Spaghetti ends should be dipped into the water and pushed down as the rods soften. Wide noodles require careful handling to prevent tearing.

The addition of salt is important to achieving a pleasant-tasting macaroni product. Vegetable oil added to the cooking water reduces the tendency for the pasta to stick together and helps to prevent the water boiling over. Boiling over can also be prevented by lightly greasing the upper 5 cm of the saucepan.

Probably the most difficult principle to be learned by the beginning cook is knowing when pasta is cooked enough. Cooking times will depend upon the thickness of the macaroni product and on the brand. If the pasta is to be combined with other ingredients, and then cooked further, as in a casserole, the recommended cooking time should be reduced by one third. If it is not to be cooked further the most satisfactory method is taste-testing. Learning from the Italians, we say it is cooked "al dente", meaning it is tender yet chewy when tasted "under the tooth".

As soon as the pasta is cooked enough it should be poured quickly into a colander or sieve and drained. Only if it is to be chilled for use in a salad should it be rinsed. Then use cold water, drain and refrigerate immediately. The practice of rinsing pasta with boiling water tends to prevent sticking of the cooked product but it also rinses away some of the water soluble nutrients.

CHART FOR COOKING PASTA

Type of Pasta	Amount Uncooked	Water	Salt	Cooking Time	Yield Cooked
Spaghetti	250 g	2 litres	10 ml	15-20 minutes	1 litre
Noodles	250 g	2 litres	10 ml	15-20 minutes	1 litre
Macaroni – small	250 g	2 litres	10 ml	15-20 minutes	1 litre
Macaroni – large	250 g	2 litres	10 ml	10-15 minutes	1 litre

METHOD OF COOKING PASTA

1. Bring water to a full rolling boil in a large saucepan. Lightly greasing the upper 5 cm of the saucepan will prevent boiling over.

2. Add salt. The addition of 15 ml of vegetable oil to the cooking water helps to keep the pasta from sticking together and also prevents boiling over.

3. Add pasta slowly to the rapidly boiling water so that the water does not stop boiling.

4. Cook uncovered allowing the cooking time indicated on the package. When directions are not available, this chart will serve as a guide. If pasta is to be used in combination with other foods and cooked further, reduce cooking time by one third.

5. Cook until just tender. Test by cutting with a fork against the side of the pan. When taste-tested, pasta should be tender but still chewy.

6. When cooked, drain the pasta in a colander or sieve, then transfer it to a heated deep serving dish or heated plates. Serve immediately. (Rinse, using cold water, only if the cooked pasta is to be chilled for use in a salad or other dish to be served later.)

NOTE: Refer to section on cereals for more information on "Cooking Pasta" page 121.

Casseroles

A casserole is a combination of foods baked together in an oven-proof serving dish. Because it constitutes the main part of the meal a minimum of additional foods will complete the meal.

Casseroles usually consist of four parts: a protein food, a sauce, a starchy ingredient and a topping. Casserole recipes are seldom precise. Most of them allow plenty of opportunity for the cook to add or subtract ingredients, such as seasonings, or to use foods that are available, perhaps leftovers, in order to obtain a meal which suits those being served.

The principal advantage of a casserole is that it can be assembled well in advance of serving time and requires little or no attention while it is baking. These factors acquire special significance when applied to entertaining. Plan to prepare ahead and refrigerate, or freeze, the casserole. Then if guests are late or they linger over appetizers there need be no concern, as the casserole will remain in good condition if when it is cooked the temperature is reduced.

Casseroles lend themselves nicely to buffet service because most oven proof dishes retain heat well, and if a candle warmer is used they can be kept hot for extended periods. As the food is served in the dish in which it was cooked and only a few other foods are generally needed, dishwashing is reduced to a minimum.

Casseroles can be economical, especially when they utilize ingredients which are in season, on sale, or left from another meal. Possibly the main economy is that a relatively small amount of a more expensive protein food can be extended by combining it with other casserole ingredients. Sometimes a vegetable protein is used to extend the complete animal protein thus providing more usable protein to the body. Other times the flavour of complete protein is extended so that a small portion of the protein food will satisfy each family member.

Contrary to a widely accepted idea, a casserole meal is not necessarily inexpensive. Its total cost will depend upon the individual ingredients used in the casserole and the other foods served. Many casserole recipes combine packaged or partially prepared foods. Some of these are more expensive than those prepared at home from the basic ingredients. When a concentrated canned cream soup is the sauce this can often be replaced by a white sauce, made in part or completely using reconstituted skim milk powder. Recipes which require an assortment of seafoods can frequently be adapted to incorporate the least expensive ones which are readily available. Similarily a simple family recipe can be varied for an elegant company meal by the inclusion of one or two special, and possibly expensive, ingredients.

Most casserole mixtures freeze well. Busy cooks reduce preparation time by doubling or tripling a suitable recipe. Then one amount can be served that day and the rest frozen for use at a future time. Casseroles retain maximum quality for only two months although they can be kept longer. It is important then that they be labelled with the date the food should be used as well as the time and temperature required for reheating after thawing. See page 430 for how to freeze casseroles.

When preparing casseroles for freezing it is advisable to under-cook the mixture slightly. This way the freezing, thawing and reheating steps are less likely to result in an overcooked or dry product. Certain foods do not freeze well if included in a casserole; for example, potatoes and hard cooked egg. Others, such as onions, lose some flavour. Herbs and sour cream are best left out until just before reheating.

A *scalloped* dish is of the same family as a casserole. A scallop is cooked food arranged in layers with a sauce and usually covered with a topping. Most scallops are made with cooked vegetables or meat, fish or poultry but sometimes other foods such as noodles or hard cooked eggs are used. The dish is baked in the oven long enough for the mixture to bubble and the topping to brown. Therefore, if a vegetable is the principal ingredient the scallop will arrive at the table in better condition if the vegetable is not fully cooked when combined with the sauce.

Most casseroles consist of four parts. The chart on page **470** illustrates how these may be combined in a variety of ways to produce an interesting recipe.

1. PROTEIN – When an incomplete protein is supplemented with a small amount of complete protein, as in a bean casserole, the protein food may be the basis of the casserole. More often a complete protein, such as meat, fish, poultry, cheese or eggs is extended by a carbohydrate food. Ground meat is often used, sometimes cheese cubes or cottage cheese and frequently the protein food is a leftover from a previous meal.

2. STARCH – Probably the most popular starchy ingredients are the numerous forms of pasta which include spaghetti, noodles and macaroni in all shapes and sizes. Many casserole recipes use rice in either the long grain white, brown, converted or pre-cooked forms. A time-honoured favourite recipe for using leftover roasted meat, shepherd's pie, uses mashed potatoes on top. There are different ways of using biscuit or pastry dough in a casserole. Some recipes incorporate chow mein noodles, many use potato chips and others rely on beans for both starch and protein content.

3. SAUCE – The sauce provides moisture and much of the flavour so that it should be chosen with care and seasoned to give the desired flavour. White sauce is frequently used, canned cream soup is popular and gravy can make up at least part of the moisture when leftover meat is the protein food. Other possibilities include tomato products either canned or puréed or juice and milk products such as milk, cream or sour cream.

4. TOPPING – The purpose of a topping is to insulate the casserole and in this way help retain moisture. It also improves both colour and flavour. A frequently used topping is buttered crumbs. Others are broken potato chips, grated or sliced cheese, pastry or biscuit dough.

Salads

Salads occupy an important place in our daily needs because of the nutrients which they contain and the texture, flavour and colour which they contribute toward making the meal appealing. In addition, salads can be used effectively for different purposes in a meal. They are equally delicious as an appetizer, as an accompaniment to the main dish, as a hearty meal in itself or as a delightful dessert.

TYPES OF SALADS

1. Appetizer

Appetizer salads are designed mainly to whet the appetite and set the stage for the rest of the meal. They must be light and relatively small. Possibilities include raw vegetables with a dip, a relish tray, assorted salad greens, tart fruit, seafood with a tangy sauce.

2. Accompaniment

As its name implies, this type of salad is eaten with the main course and, therefore, should complement the other foods. There have been many varieties developed, ranging from the popular tossed green salad to simple garnish salads which add eye appeal to the protein dish. Jellied salads have an infinite variety of flavours and textures from the ingredients used.

3. Main Dish

This kind should have some protein food such as meat, poultry, fish, eggs or cheese as the main ingredient. The protein food used in combination with salad greens and a zesty dressing is a satisfying meal. If desired, add a hot soup, bread accompaniment, dessert and beverage.

4.   Dessert

A dessert salad is a perfect finish to a hearty meal or it may be served alone as a party refreshment. The three best known kinds are colourful fruit arrangements, gelatin moulds and frozen fruit salads. The gelatin and frozen types are especially suitable when much of the food preparation must be done well in advance. Frozen fruit salads are usually made in refrigerator freezing trays or loaf pans and are cut into slices to serve.

NUTRITIONAL VALUE OF SALADS

Because of the minerals and vitamins which they supply, salads have an important role to play in good nutrition. The foods used to make the salad will determine its nutrient contribution. Raw vegetables and fruits usually have better food value than cooked ones. Tossed green salad eaten with a meal can count as one serving of a leafy vegetable when examining your daily food intake. Smaller amounts such as those used in a garnish salad or appetizer salad would make only part of the day's vegetable requirement.

Main dish salads, by definition, supply protein. Generally these salads have some carbohydrate value as well. Potato and macaroni combinations have a high kilojoule count because of the starch they contain.

The kilojoule count in most salads is low. For this reason they are included often in reducing diets. Not all salads have a low kilojoule count. Persons trying to reduce should examine salads carefully for "hidden" carbohydrates and fats. The type and amount of salad dressing affects the kilojoule count of your salads. The richest dressings contain fat or cream. Cooked salad dressing contains less fat than mayonnaise. People who are very serious about losing mass will try seasoned vinegar or lemon juice for their tossed salads.

SELECTION AND STORAGE OF SALAD GREENS

A good salad begins with careful selection of the ingredients which go into it. Choose the freshest greens available. Avoid any which appear bruised or wilted, because they will have less food value and poorer flavour. When a store offers only limp, tired heads of iceberg lettuce, check the produce counter for good quality cabbage, spinach, romaine or some other green vegetable to use instead. With so many different kinds of salad possibilities there is no excuse for always serving the same kind.

How you care for the salad greens you have selected will depend upon when you plan to use them. Remember that excess moisture during storage increases the rate of spoilage. Therefore, if they are to be kept for several days store them without washing. Simply remove any bruised or very wilted leaves and place the greens in a plastic bag in the refrigerator, preferably in the crisper section.

If you plan to use them in a salad within 24 hours, wash the vegetables thoroughly to remove any soil or possible residues from sprays. Check for garden pests. Drain well on a rack, tea towel or paper towels. Gently tossing the separated leaves on a towel helps to remove all the water from leaf lettuce and other loosely bunched greens. Wrap in a towel and store in a plastic bag in the refrigerator until ready to use.

If the greens have been refrigerated unwashed, then follow the same procedure early in the day on which the salad is to be served. It is the secret to crisp salads. Lettuce and other salad greens require several hours at least, to become crisp. Washing just before use without allowing time to crisp is not as effective. Also there is often not enough time for the vegetables to drain completely and any remaining water thins the dressing and results in a watery limp salad.

INGREDIENTS USED TO MAKE SALADS

Choose and care for these as described in the preceding section.

TYPES OF LETTUCE

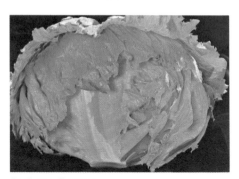

Iceberg Lettuce

1. Iceberg – Also known as head lettuce, this is the most popular kind. It has a compact firm head, crisp texture medium green leaves on the outside and a very pale inside. The tightly packed curly edged leaves overlap slightly.

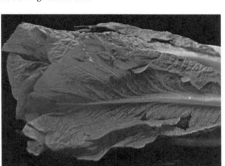

Romaine

2. Romaine – It is an elongated head made up of firm, crisp, bright green leaves having firm white ribs. The characteristic flavour of romaine is sharper than iceberg or leaf lettuce.

Curly Endive (Chicory)

3. Curly Endive (Chicory) — Endive is a bunchy head of leaves with lacy crimped dark green edges and firm white ribs and core. The flavour is sharp, tangy and sometimes slightly bitter.

Escarole (Broad Leaf Endive)

4. Escarole (Broad Leaf Endive) — Escarole has flat tightly curled dark green leaves sometimes edged in yellow. It usually has a much milder flavour than that of curly endive and also a softer texture.

Boston Lettuce (Butterhead)

5. Boston Lettuce (Butterhead) — This is a small head of mild flavoured, tender, delicate leaves which separate easily. It is usually a pale green colour.

Leaf Lettuce

6. Leaf Lettuce — This is made up of a loose, non-heading bunch of fan-shaped leaves branching from a small stalk. Its crimp-edged leaves are bright green and sometimes tinged with red and have a delicate flavour.

OTHER INGREDIENTS USED IN SALADS

Watercress – has tiny dark green crisp leaves branching from slender stalks. It contributes vitamins, a spicy biting flavour and brilliant colour which makes it an interesting salad ingredient or garnish.

Watercress

Spinach – is a valuable addition to other greens for its deep green colour, lively flavour and important vitamins and minerals.

Spinach

Parsley – has small, finely divided, tightly curled leaves grouped at the top of a slender stem.

Parsley

Swiss Chard

Swiss Chard – has a rich dark leaf attached to a firm white stem. It is most suitable for salad making when young and tender before the flavour has fully developed.

Mint

Mint – has deep green, pointed, slightly crinkly leaves branching from an upright stalk.

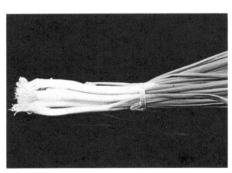

Green Onions

Green Onion – is a mild flavoured onion with bright green, tubular top attached to a white, slightly enlarged bulb. Both parts are used.

Chives

Chives – have a narrow tubular shape and a flavour much like green onions although milder.

Storage

Parsley is best stored standing in a glass jar or plastic container having a small amount of water in the bottom. If they are still attached do not remove the roots, otherwise trim the stem ends. Remove the cord or elastic and any wilted or yellow leaves before refrigerating. Chives keep well this way, too. Wrap green onions in waxed paper. Remove the roots and trim outside layers and ends just before using. A tightly covered jar is a convenient container in which to store mint.

CHOOSING, STORING AND USING CABBAGE

Look for cabbage that is fairly heavy for the size of the head and has a minimum of damaged outside leaves. A well refrigerated produce counter is important to obtaining fresh, crisp cabbage.

Before refrigerating at home, remove bruised, limp and very coarse leaves. Cut a thin slice off the butt end, or core, but avoid overtrimming because the butt contains moisture that keeps the head fresh longer. Store unwashed in a plastic bag.

When ready to use cabbage, wash the head under cold running water, drain well and roll in towelling. Shred Chinese cabbage by slicing the head crosswise. To shred or chop other varieties cut the head in half first. Then quarter if desired and cut. The heart will help to hold the leaves together as you work. To prevent nutrient losses cabbage should not be shredded until just before serving time.

OTHER SALAD VEGETABLES

These vegetables have a place in many foods other than salads. Since they have been discussed in the Vegetable section, only specific instructions for storage are included here.

Celery

Store celery in the refrigerator after first removing discoloured tips, extra leaves and any damaged stalks. Trim a thin slice off the root end. If properly cared for when fresh the whole head may be used including the leaves, which add a special flavour to green salad or cole slaw. Even the hard core is a crisp contrast when thinly sliced.

Tomatoes

They keep well if they are not bruised, cracked or over-ripe. Pale, under-ripe tomatoes will not ripen in the refrigerator but will ripen if left for a few days at room temperature in indirect light.

Cucumbers

These require air circulation and will develop soft spots if stored in a plastic bag.

Green or Red Peppers
They are best stored unwrapped in the refrigerator. Plastic bag storage for these makes them soft and slimy.

Radishes
Before refrigeration remove leaves leaving root ends intact.

Cauliflower
During storage the leaves should remain in place. Cut a thin slice off the root end but do not overtrim because the butt contains moisture which keeps the head fresh longer.

Carrots
Cut off green tops before refrigerating. Store in plastic bag.

MAKING A SALAD
For success in salad making follow these steps:
1. Choose the freshest vegetables and fruits available. Buy only what you can use within a few days to maintain this quality.
2. Store salad ingredients carefully (see page 128). Examine fresh fruits and vegetables daily to check their condition. Plan to use them before they start to wilt or to develop soft spots.

3. Wash and dry fresh vegetables. All salad ingredients, including greens and others that may be fresh, cooked or canned, must be thoroughly chilled. Allow enough time.

4. Instead of cutting, tear lettuce into pieces. This does not damage the cell structure as much and the salad will not wilt as quickly as when lettuce is cut with a knife.

5. Salad foods should be in bite-sized pieces at least large enough to keep their identity. Also aim for ease in eating the food with the fork. Cole slaw is an exception to the "bite-size pieces" guide but the dressing used binds it together making it easier to eat.

6. When mixing salads toss gently to avoid bruising the delicate cell structure of the ingredients. Do not stir.

7. Salt added to vegetables draws out moisture and makes them limp. To prevent wilted greens add dressing and seasonings just at serving time or better yet serve dressing at the table.

8. Choose an attractive garnish but use it sparingly. Depend upon the natural colour and arrangement of the foods to give an attractive, appetizing salad.

SERVING A SALAD

1. Use a chilled salad bowl or serving plate for arranging a large salad. Place the container in the refrigerator to cool while you prepare the salad ingredients.

2. In keeping with the "hot foods hot and cold foods cold" guide, use separate plates for salad if it is to accompany a hot main course. Use small side plates or little wooden or pottery bowls and place them to the left of the dinner plate.

3. When you set out a small salad for each person, it helps to make an attractive place setting. In this way also there are no leftovers nor is there a chance of there not being enough salad for everyone.

4. Don't let greens extend beyond the edge of the plate. Avoid a cluttered effect and allow the plate to "frame" the salad.

5. When a gelatin salad is done in a ring mould, a small bowl of dressing can be placed in the centre.

MOULDED GELATIN SALADS

Gelatin based salads have a special place in meal planning. Either as an individual serving or on a "serve yourself" platter they frequently appear on the menu during hot weather or as part of a buffet for guests. Whether you make one for the family or for guests these few suggestions will increase your chances of success:

1. Prepare gelatin salads a day ahead so they will be thoroughly set before unmoulding.

2. You may reduce the amount of liquid suggested on the package of fruit flavoured gelatin or the unflavoured gelatin envelope.

3. Chill gelatin until slightly thickened, which means the consistency of unbeaten egg whites, before adding the solid ingredients. This holds them evenly distributed as you stir them in.

4. Have fruits and vegetables well drained so as not to dilute the gelatin and reduce its setting power.

5. To make moulded layered salads be sure each layer is firmly set before adding the next layer.

6. For a mould use a large ring, fancy mould, shallow baking pan, individual moulds or any suitable sized container you have on hand.

7. To make unmoulding easier, fill the mould as full as possible.

8. To unmould the salad, first loosen the edge of the mould with a pointed knife that has been dipped in warm water. Then quickly immerse the mould just to the top in lukewarm water – hot water will melt the salad. Place serving dish over top of mould, invert and carefully lift the mould off. If salad does not come free, repeat the procedure.

9. If the mould is a large one moisten the surface of the gelatin and the surface of the serving plate. The two wet surfaces makes it easier to centre the salad on the plate. Wipe away excess moisture with a towel.

10. Garnish a large salad with greens after unmoulding. (It may break if unmoulded on crisp greens.) Individual salads may be turned out directly onto greens.

SALAD DRESSINGS

The type of salad dressing used should vary with the salad but will also be influenced by the personal preferences of those eating it. The three main classes of dressings are:

1. French Dressing, a mixture of oil, vinegar and seasonings. When allowed to stand the ingredients separate, with the oil on the top and vinegar below. Separation occurs because there is no emulsifier used.

2. Mayonnaise, made by slowly blending oil into a seasoned vinegar and egg mixture. The egg acts as an emulsifier so that the vinegar and oil do not separate. Many variations are possible including Thousand Island Dressing which contains chili sauce or a tomato sauce and chopped olives and vegetables.

3. Cooked Dressing has a white sauce with egg base to which the acid, vinegar or lemon juice is slowly added. The starch used for thickening and the added egg prevent separation.

Main dish salads made with meat, poultry, fish, eggs, cheese or potatoes usually go well with a mayonnaise type of dressing or a cooked salad dressing. Some of the more substantial salads, however, are also good with a tart French dressing. French dressing is a likely choice for vegetable salads and fruit and vegetable combinations. Fruit salads take a sweet clear French dressing, perhaps made with fruit juices or with mayonnaise that has been mixed with whipped cream or sweetened fruit juice. A salad dressing is appropriate when it complements the flavour of the salad, contributes an accent in flavour and colour, and blends well with the texture of the salad ingredients.

Vinegars used to make salad dressings are of three basic types: cider, wine and white. White vinegar is the most familiar kind. Cider vinegar is amber coloured and more mellow in flavour than white vinegar. Wine vinegar has a flavour and colour characteristic of the wine from which it was made – red or white and sweet or dry.

To make a herb vinegar from any of these, simply add the herbs you desire and let the mixture stand until it reaches the flavour you want. The herbs can be strained out to prevent further flavouring or left in if you prefer.

Most salad dressings are made in advance and stored in the refrigerator. This allows the flavours to mingle and the dressing to chill before its addition to the crisp cold greens. Occasionally a salad recipe has its own special dressing which is mixed with the other ingredients as the salad is made. Examples are bean salad and Caesar salad.

Vegetables

When discussing vegetables it is sometimes convenient to think of them in groups or classes. They can be grouped according to the part of the plant used, according to the flavour of the vegetable, and according to the predominating colour. Sometimes vegetables are grouped according to the principal nutrient they contain.

CLASSIFICATION ACCORDING TO THE PART USED

1. Seed

Vegetables that ultimately form the seed from which a new plant will grow have a higher protein content than any other of the fresh vegetables. Examples of seed vegetables are: peas, beans, corn.

Green Beans

Broad Beans

Wax Beans

Bean Sprouts

2. Flower

As the name indicates, these vegetables more closely resemble a flower than does any other group. They have a high vitamin and mineral content but contain few kilojoules. Examples are: cauliflower, broccoli and artichoke.

Cauliflower

Broccoli

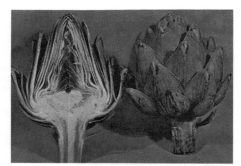

Artichoke

3. Leaf

Because leaves are the manufacturing part of the plant, they are low in fats and carbohydrates but high in vitamins and minerals. Bright leaves have more vitamin A than pale ones. Examples are: spinach, lettuce, endive, cabbage, brussels sprouts, chard, kale.

Brussels Sprouts

Kale

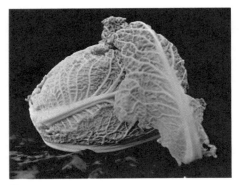

Savoy

Chinese Cabbage

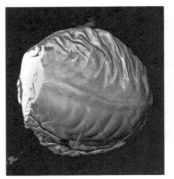

Red Cabbage

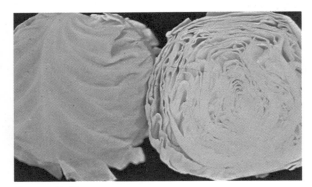

Green Cabbage

4.   Fruit

Fruit vegetables are important for their high vitamin and mineral content and good flavour. Most are low in carbohydrate. Examples are tomato, cucumber, peppers, eggplant, squash and pumpkin.

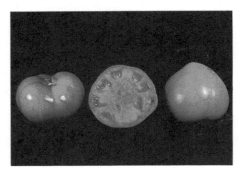

Tomatoes

Cherry Tomatoes

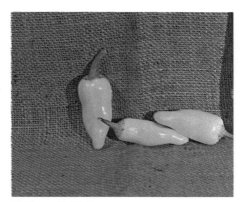

Yellow Chili Pepper

Hot Chili Pepper

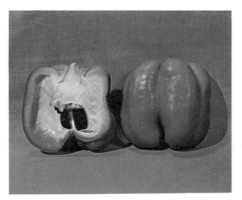

Green Bell Pepper

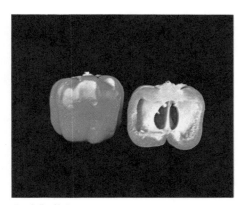

Red Bell Pepper

Standard Eggplant

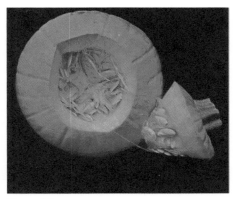

Pumpkin

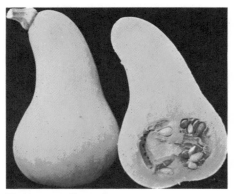

Butternut Squash

Acorn Squash

Hubbard Squash

Banana Squash

Yellow Crookneck Squash

Zucchini

5. Stalk or Stem

Since the main function of this part of the plant is to carry the soluble nutrients from one part of the plant to the other, it is rarely used as a place of storage. Therefore, stalk vegetables have value not for energy but as a source of minerals, vitamins, cellulose and flavour. Examples are: celery, asparagus, chives.

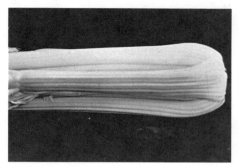

Celery

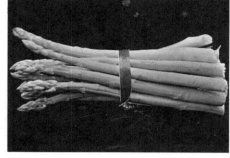

Asparagus

Onions

6. Bulb

Bulb vegetables are especially valuable for the flavours which they contribute. Examples are: onion, green onion, garlic, leeks, shallots.

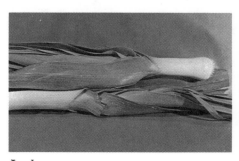

Leeks

Clove Garlic

7. **Root**

Root vegetables contain valuable vitamin and mineral deposits. Their carbohydrate content is lower than that of tubers and is mainly in the form of sugar rather than starch. Examples are: carrots, parsnips, radishes, beets, turnips, rutabagas.

Carrots

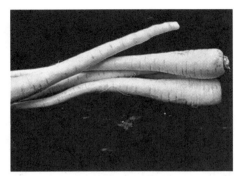

Parsnips

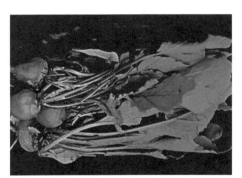

Beets

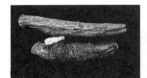

Horseradish Root

Radishes

Turnips

8. Tuber

Since this is the storage place for energy for the plant, tubers provide carbohydrate and vitamins. Potatoes provide a good source of vitamin C and sweet potatoes and yams provide vitamin A.

Potatoes

Yams

Sweet Potatoes

CLASSIFICATION ACCORDING TO FLAVOUR

Strong flavoured vegetables include those with a cabbage-like flavour such as cauliflower, brussels sprouts, broccoli, kale and turnip and those with an onion-like flavour such as leeks and onions.

This classification is based upon the presence or absence of certain sulphur compounds which are partly responsible for the characteristic taste of the strong-flavoured vegetables. During cooking, these sulphur compounds tend to break up, forming hydrogen sulphide, which has a well known and easily recognized odour and flavour. High heat and long cooking cause these unpleasant odours to develop fully.

Method 1:   If a strong flavoured vegetable is cut in small pieces and cooked, covered, in a small amount of boiling water the heat will penetrate quickly and cook the vegetable before much of the objectionable flavour has developed. Nutrients will escape from the many surfaces of the small pieces and use of the vegetable water would be important.

Method 2:   If the vegetable is left whole or cut in large pieces and cooked uncovered in a large quantity of boiling water, the vegetable acids responsible for the undesirable side effects are diluted by the water and the volatile acids escape with the steam. Using this method, an even greater loss of water soluble nutrients occurs.

Compromise This is the recommended method for cooking strong flavoured
Method:　　vegetables. Bring the cut or whole vegetable quickly to the
　　　　　　boil in a minimum of water. Leave the lid off until the boil
　　　　　　is reached and the brightest colour appears. Then cover, re-
　　　　　　duce heat and cook only until tender. This method assures not
　　　　　　only a good flavoured product but one that has maximum food
　　　　　　value. The colour will be attractive, not browned as results
　　　　　　with overcooking.

CLASSIFICATION ACCORDING TO COLOUR

Much of the appeal of an appetizing meal is in the attractive and varied
colours of the vegetables served. Changes that occur during cooking make
a vegetable quite unattractive unless special precautions are taken. Four
variables – water, heat, acidity and alkalinity – must be controlled during
the cooking process. Proper cooking methods to retain the pigments will
ensure vegetables which have the best possible colour.

The pigments found most frequently in vegetables are chlorophyll,
anthocyanins, flavones and carotenoids. Each of these reacts in a characteristic way when subjected to the four cooking variables. The chart "Effects
of Cooking Variables on Food Pigments" summarizes these reactions.

Most water is alkali, hard water more so. Baking soda is also alkali. Its
addition, however, destroys vitamin C and makes the vegetables mushy.
Most vegetables contain varying amounts of organic acids which are released as cooking proceeds. Where an acid medium gives a desirable effect,
adding five millilitres of vinegar or lemon juice near the end of the cooking
period is suggested. A sour sauce can also be used. Adding a few slices of
tart apple to red cabbage will provide the desired acid.

EFFECTS OF COOKING VARIABLES ON FOOD PIGMENTS

PIGMENT	COLOUR	WATER	HEAT	ACID	ALKALI	METAL
Chloro-phyll	green	very slightly soluble	turns a bronze green	turns a bronze green	brightens and intensifies the green	copper and zinc brighten and intensify the green
Antho-cyanins	red to blue	soluble	stable	brightens or turns red	dulls or turns to blue	tin or iron turns pigments purple, blue or green
Flavones	white	soluble	stable	turns to yellow	turns to yellow	iron turns pigments green
Caroten-oids	yellow or orange	insoluble	stable	stable	stable	or brown stable

Summarizing information on the chart, these methods are the most suitable for vegetables containing the four pigments.

1. **Chlorophyll**

   Cook green vegetables for a short time with the lid off to allow the volatile acids to escape, then cover and reduce the temperature. Do not overcook or add baking soda.

2. **Anthocyanins**

   Reactions to the cooking variables are exactly opposite to those that occur when green vegetables are cooked. Therefore, cook all red vegetables covered so they benefit from their own acid content, and add an acid if possible.

3. **Flavones**

   Cook white vegetables in an acidic medium created by covering the pan; cook in as short a time as possible and only until tender. If yellowing does occur, a small amount of vinegar may be added to the cooking water.

4. **Carotenoids**

   Ordinary cooking conditions have very little effect on the colour or nutrient content of yellow vegetables. Their colour is little affected by acid, alkali, the amount of water or the cooking time and their nutritive value is protected during cooking by the insolubility of carotenoids in water. Prolonged cooking may darken the colour due to the caramelization of sugar.

Food Value of Vegetables

The best way to insure that all of the valuable nutritive elements found in vegetables are present when you eat them is to be sure they are freshly picked, properly stored, and eaten raw as often as possible. Here is an outline of these nutrients and some of the vegetables in which they are to be found:

1. **Vitamins**

   A – found in abundance in leafy green and bright orange and yellow vegetables.

   C – found in tomatoes, vegetables of the cabbage family including green cabbage, broccoli, brussels sprouts, cauliflower, kale, etc.

   B – riboflavin is found in leafy green vegetables.

   B – thiamine is found in dried peas, beans, lentils, potatoes.

   B – folic acid is found in mushrooms, asparagus, broccoli, lima beans, spinach.

2. **Minerals**
   Iron – in green vegetables and legumes, also potatoes.
   Calcium – in green leafy vegetables, carrots, turnip tops.
   Iodine – present only if it was present in soil.

3. **Carbohydrate**
   Starch – in potatoes, parsnips, corn and beans.
   Sugar – in peas, sweet potatoes.

4. **Protein**
   Incomplete protein (vegetable sources) found in beans, peas, lentils, soya beans.

5. **Cellulose**
   Found in all vegetables, especially celery, cabbage, beets, green leafy vegetables.

6. **Water**
   Large amounts in all vegetables especially leafy ones.

Choosing and Storing Vegetables

Vegetables are available in many forms: fresh, frozen, canned, dried, dehydrated, freeze-dried. The form you use will depend on quality, cost, use, storage space and preparation time. Learning to make wise selections can only come through experience. To add to the problem, a choice that might be valid one week may be inappropriate the next.

FRESH VEGETABLES
The chart on page 151 "How to Buy, Store and Prepare Fresh Vegetables", is a good guide for selection, storage, and use of the most common fresh vegetables. In addition, "Chinese Vegetables . . . How to Buy, Store and Prepare" on page 154 is a handy reference for the many homemakers who have access to stores selling these interesting and nutritious vegetables.

Selecting good quality fresh vegetables is especially difficult. Perhaps these general suggestions will help:

1. **Personally select all vegetables.**

2. Buy vegetables that are in season. Their colour, flavour, texture and food value will be at their best and in most cases the price will be less than at any other time. Some root and tuber vegetables that store well are available for most of the year.

3. Consider many other factors besides cost. Sometimes inferior quality produce is sold at reduced prices but the amount of waste and the nutrients that have been lost during storage make it poor value.

4. Select on the basis of use. The largest size is not always the best. Sometimes smaller vegetables are more suitable to the form in which you plan to use them. Frequently they have better texture and food value also and may be better suited to the size of your family (See 5. below.)

5. Buy only quantities that you can use while they are still fresh.

6. Colour and crispness are a key to quality. Colour should be bright and characteristic of the vegetable. Vegetables, especially green and leafy ones, should be crisp with no signs of wilting. An unwilted top and outside leaves with minimum of trimming indicates maximum vitamin content and best flavour.

7. Buy by grade. Most vegetables are sold as Canada No. 1 or Canada No. 2 grade. In the latter grade, greater tolerances are allowed for injury and other surface defects but these do not affect eating quality and are usually removed on peeling. The grade name is usually marked on the package or is indicated on the produce counter.

8. Learn to recognize the blemishes which will affect quality and which ones affect only appearance. Irregular shapes do not affect the cooked product or its food value and are usually sold at a lower price. Bruises or decayed spots indicate a reduction in quality that is seldom good value, regardless of cost.

9. Unnecessary or rough handling of fresh vegetables causes spoilage and the losses incurred by the retailer will ultimately be paid for by the consumer. Therefore, examine fresh produce with care to prevent its injury.

FROZEN VEGETABLES

Frozen vegetables are waste free and ready to cook and their food value, colour, flavour and texture compares favourably to fresh ones. Because freezing, unlike canning, does not destroy but merely inactivates the organisms which cause food spoilage, it is important that frozen vegetables remain solidly frozen until they are ready to be cooked. These are some suggestions for selecting frozen vegetables:

1. Purchase only solidly frozen vegetables. Avoid cartons that are stained indicating that they have been thawed and refrozen.

2. Avoid packages that contain relatively large chunks frozen together. Except in the case of leafy vegetables or others that form a block when blanched, this would indicate improper freezing to begin with, or thawing and then refreezing.

3. Providing you have adequate freezer storage space, polybagged vegetables are usually a better buy than the smaller size waxed or polycoated cartons. Most vegetables bagged in the larger quantity are quick frozen individually and loosely packed so that the amount required for a meal can be taken out and the remainder stored.

4. Unsized vegetables are cheaper than those that are sized. Vegetables and vegetable combinations frozen in sauce will be more expensive than plain ones to which you add a home made sauce.

Additional information on frozen vegetables is to be found on page 430 "Freezer Storage Chart"; page 431 "Refreezing Food; and page 442 "Cooking and Serving Frozen Vegetables".

CANNED VEGETABLES

Although vegetables suffer some nutrient loss during the canning process, they remain rich in important food values and are a good substitute when fresh or frozen vegetables are not available or are too expensive. The leafy green vegetables lose some flavour, colour, texture and vitamins when canned. Almost every kind of vegetable is represented in some form among the canned goods. Can sizes and quality vary. The main principle to follow when buying canned vegetables is to choose on the basis of the use for which the canned vegetable is intended. While the highest quality may be desirable for heating and serving as a separate dish, second quality is usually quite suitable for use in combination dishes such as stews, casseroles, and soups. Grades of vegetables are the same as for fruit and are based upon government inspection. Remember that grade indicates differences in tenderness, uniformity and colour but not differences in wholesomeness or nutritive value.

In addition it is good practice to choose a size of can that will suit the number of people being served or the recipe being used. If a larger size than needed for one meal is on "special" be sure the remainder will be used and not discarded. Descriptive labels give good information to the consumer and often include recipes and serving suggestions.

Canned vegetables keep well for a long time when stored in a cool, dry, dark place. Room temperature or cooler is preferred. For prolonged storage of canned vegetables a temperature of 10°C or less is recommended. They should not be allowed to freeze. Dampness will rust cans and loosen labels. Although a high temperature will, in time, affect the colour and flavour of canned foods, it will not appreciably affect their wholesomeness.

DRIED VEGETABLES

Of the dried vegetables, the most familiar are the legumes which include beans of various kinds, peas, either whole or split, and lentils. Additional vegetables are constantly being introduced in the dried form. They include: potatoes, in granules and flakes, onions, parsley and chive flakes and green onions.

Although dried vegetables have lost all of their vitamin C content and some of their vitamin A during processing, they are rich in minerals. Legumes, especially the soybean since it contains a superior quality protein, are a good source of protein.

Dried vegetables have always been relatively inexpensive but their greatest advantage is probably that they are easily stored and take up little space. They may simply be kept on a shelf at room temperature. Opened packages should be closed carefully or the contents transferred to a tightly covered container to prevent infestation by bugs or insects. Since they require no refrigeration and are light to carry they are a popular choice of travellers and outdoors enthusiasts.

HOW TO BUY, STORE AND PREPARE FRESH VEGETABLES

VEGETABLE	SEASON FOR B.C. GROWN	LOOK FOR . . .	STORE	USE	TO PREPARE WASH VEGETABLES WELL UNDER RUNNING WATER
Asparagus	April to June	Straight, tender, crisp bright-green stalks with tightly closed tips. Bunches having stalks of uniform size and thickness.	In plastic bag in refrigerator.	Within 1-2 days.	Break off base where it snaps easily. Remove sand from under scales.
Beans, Green and Wax (Yellow)	June to September	Young, crisp, tender, fairly straight beans free from blemishes. Beans of uniform size with well-formed seeds.	In plastic bag in refrigerator.	Within 5 days.	Remove ends. Leave whole, cut in 3 cm pieces or French by cutting lengthwise in strips.
Beets	June to August	Clean, firm, smooth beets free from cracks or other blemishes. Beets of uniform size to cook together.	In cool moist place or in refrigerator, 3 cm stem and all roots attached.	Within several weeks.	Wash without bruising skin.

HOW TO BUY, STORE AND PREPARE FRESH VEGETABLES

VEGETABLE	SEASON FOR B.C. GROWN	LOOK FOR . . .	STORE	USE	TO PREPARE WASH VEGETABLES WELL UNDER RUNNING WATER
Beet tops	June to August	Fresh crisp leaves.	Refrigerate in plastic bag.	Within 1-2 days.	Wash in lukewarm then cold water. Leave a little water on leaves for cooking.
Broccoli	August to November	Tender firm stalks with compact green heads.	In plastic bag in refrigerator.	Within a few days.	Trim coarse leaves and woody stems. Cut lengthwise in several serving-size pieces. Make 2 or 3 cuts part way up thick stalks.
Brussels Sprouts	October to December	Firm compact heads with fresh green leaves. Sprouts of uniform size to cook together.	In plastic bag in refrigerator.	Within 1-2 days.	Trim stems and outer leaves. Make 2 crosswise cuts in base.
Cabbage Red & Green Savoy Chinese	July to September August to November May to October	Firm heads with crisp green or red leaves. Later varieties heavy for their size. Savoy cabbage has distinct crinkly green leaves.	In closed container in refrigerator. Cut thin slice from stalk.	Within 2 weeks.	Trim outer leaves and stem. Cut in wedges (leaving portion of heart attached) or chunks or shred.
Carrots	May through December	Bunched young carrots with fresh green tops. Packaged mature carrots firm, well shaped, smooth, free from blemishes and green colour.	In cool moist place or refrigerator. Remove tops.	Young carrots within 2 weeks. Others within several weeks.	Brush or scrape young carrots, peel others. Leave small fingers, 2-3 cm chunks or thin slices.
Cauliflower	June to July and October to December	Firm, creamy-white, smooth head that is compact and heavy.	In refrigerator. Leave outer leaves attached. Cut thin slice from stalk.	Within 1 week.	Trim outer leaves and stem. Leave whole, cutting out 3 cm of core, or separate into flowerets.
Celery	July to October	Crisp, fresh, green bunches with straight stalks free from blemishes.	In plastic bag in refrigerator. Cut thin slice from base.	Within 1 week.	Trim root and leaves. Separate stalks. Slice diagonally 0.5 - 1 cm thick.
Corn	July to October	Freshly picked corn with bright-green husks tightly wrapped around well-filled ears. Creamy-yellow, plump kernels.	In refrigerator. Leave husks on.	Preferably same day.	Remove husks and silk. Cut off most of stalks.
Eggplant	August to October	Well-shaped, firm, heavy eggplant. Smooth, satiny purple skin free from blemishes.	Uncovered in refrigerator.	Within 1 week.	Remove stem. Peel if desired. Slice 1 - 1.5 cm thick.
Green Peppers	July to October	Crisp, bright-green peppers with smooth skin. Symmetrical shape for stuffing	Uncovered in refrigerator.	Within 3-4 days.	Halve lengthwise. Remove stem, seeds and membrane. Stuff halves or cut into chunks or strips
Mushrooms	All Year	Fairly clean, white, firm mushrooms. Caps not fully opened.	Uncovered in refrigerator.	Within 1 week.	Trim stalk. Slice lengthwise.

HOW TO BUY, STORE AND PREPARE FRESH VEGETABLES

VEGETABLE	SEASON FOR B.C. GROWN	LOOK FOR . . .	STORE	USE	TO PREPARE WASH VEGETABLES WELL UNDER RUNNING WATER
Onions	July to December	Firm onions with dry, brownish-yellow skins. Not sprouting.	Uncovered in dry, airy place.	Within several weeks.	Remove dry skin, root and stem. Leave whole or halve, quarter or slice.
Parsnips	September to December	Firm, straight, smooth parsnips free from blemishes.	In cool place or refrigerator.	Within several weeks.	Trim stem and root ends, peel. Leave small parsnips whole, cut others in fingers or thin slices.
Peas	May to July	Freshly picked, crisp, bright green pods, well filled but not bulging.	In plastic bag in refrigerator.	Preferably same day.	Shell.
Potatoes	Summer Varieties June to September Netted Gems All Year	Fairly clean, well-shaped potatoes, relatively free from blemishes, no green colour caused by exposure to sunlight.	New potatoes — in refrigerator. Others — in cool 10°C dark, airy place.	New potatoes within 1 week. Others within 4-9 months.	Scrub, leave skins on or peel. Leave whole or halve, quarter, slice or cut in fingers.
Spinach	April to October	Fresh, clean, crisp green leaves.	In plastic bag in refrigerator.	Within 1-2 days.	Trim roots and heavy stems. Wash bulk in lukewarm then cold water. Wash packaged in cold water. Leave a little water on leaves for cooking.
Squash, Vegetable Marrow	Summer: July to October	Summer varieties — tender skin, free from soft spots, heavy for size.	Summer varieties — in refrigerator.	Within 1 week.	Summer varieties — leave skin on; remove seeds if desired.
	Winter: August to December	Winter varieties — hard shell, free from soft spots or damage.	Winter varieties — in cool dry place or at room temperature.	Within several months if in cool dry place, or 1 week at room temperature.	Winter varieties — leave skin on or peel. If to be mashed, remove seeds. Halve, quarter, slice, dice or cut in chunks.
Swiss Chard	April to October	Fresh, crisp, green leaves. Crisp, fairly clean, light-green stalks. Young chard for best flavour.	In plastic bag in refrigerator.	Within 1-2 days.	Trim stalks and outer leaves. Wash in lukewarm then cold water. Cut leaves from midribs, chop coarsely. Cut midribs and stems in 3 cm pieces.
Tomatoes	Field: July to October Hothouse: April to December	Plump firm tomatoes. Uniform red colour, firm skin.	Ripe ones — uncovered lowest part of refrigerator. Others — ripen away from direct sunlight.	Within 1 week.	Remove stem. Leave whole; or halve, quarter or slice. To peel dip in boiling water 30-60 seconds, cool briefly in cold water.
Turnips (White) Rutabagas (Yellow)	July to September September to March	Firm heavy turnips with few scars and roots. Fresh, crisp, green tops.	In cool moist place or at room temperature.	Within 1 week if at room temperature. Within several weeks if cool.	Peel whole small white turnips; cut in 1 cm slices before peeling. Dice, shred or cut in fingers or chunks. Leave small turnips whole, if preferred.

CHINESE VEGETABLES ... HOW TO BUY, STORE AND PREPARE

NAME	SEASON	LOOK FOR ...	STORE	PREPARE
Bok Choy (white vegetable)	April through October	Tender, delicate vegetable with long smooth white stems & large dark green crinkly leaves. Has a clear light taste.	Refrigerate in vegetable crisper or perforated plastic bag. Will keep up to 1 week.	Requires little cooking. Can be stir-fried with any meat, poultry or seafood. Can be quick cooked in soups. Use all the vegetable.
Sui Choy (lettuce)	April through October	Crisp tightly packed vegetable about 25-30 cm long. Has firm vertical, yellow white leaves tinged at top with pale green. Has a distinctive but not strong taste, somewhere between lettuce & cabbage.	Refrigerate in vegetable bin or perforated plastic bag. Will keep more than 1 week.	Can be eaten raw in salads Western-style. Delicious stir-fried. Quick-cook in soups.
Choy Sum (greens)	April through October	Slim white stem vegetable with yellow flower. Smaller variety of Bok Choy and more tender.	Refrigerate in vegetable crisper or perforated plastic bag. Keeps up to 1 week.	Same as Bok Choy.
Yau Choy Sum (greens)	April through October	Chinese green vegetable with small leaves, tender stock similar to Choy Sum but without flower.	Refrigerate in vegetable crisper or perforated plastic bag. Keeps up to 1 week.	Same as Bok Choy.
Gai Choy (mustard greens)	April through October	Dark green vegetable with tightly packed leaves that are curved, fluted and fanlike. Is slightly cool and bitter in taste.	Refrigerate in vegetable crisper or perforated plastic bag. Will keep approx. 1 week.	Use in soups also as a sweet and sour vegetable dish.
Gai Lan (Chinese broccoli)	April through October	Similar in colour to the familiar broccoli, but more leafy and longer, 30-35 cm. Has irregular shaped stalks, large flowerets with yellow and white blossoms. Its taste is fresh and delicate.	Refrigerate in vegetable bin or perforated plastic bag. Will keep approx. 1 week.	Stir-fry as a vegetable or with meat.

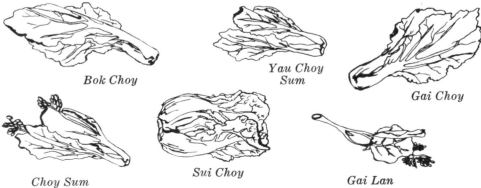

Bok Choy

Yau Choy Sum

Gai Choy

Choy Sum

Sui Choy

Gai Lan

CHINESE VEGETABLES ... HOW TO BUY, STORE AND PREPARE

NAME	SEASON	LOOK FOR ...	STORE	PREPARE
Lo Bak (Chinese radish)	May through October	White, crisp-textured radish about 5-10 cm in diameter and 15-25 cm long. Very subtle in taste.	Refrigerate in vegetable bin or perforated plastic bag. Will keep 1 week.	Can be stir-fried or braised. Also slow-cooked in soup and marinated for cold dishes. To cook: Peel and slice.
Ngah Choi (bean sprouts)	Year round	Tiny white shoots with pale green hoods; not actually the sprouts of beans but of tiny mung peas. Have a crunchy texture and sweet delicate flavour.	Wash well. Place in jar of water to cover and refrigerate. Change water daily. Will keep 4-5 days. Bean sprouts can be quick frozen. Wash. Par-boil 1 to 2 minutes. Drain well. Place in freezer bag or carton. Freeze. Thaw fully before using.	Cook briefly to retain crunchiness. Add to omelets, shellfish, salads, soups and other vegetable dishes.
Ho Long Dow (snow or sugar peas)	May through September	Special variety of green pea pods, picked before maturity. They add crispness, subtle taste and colour to meat. Very tender.	Refrigerate in perforated plastic bag. Use preferably the same day.	Require little cooking. Stir-fry to retain delicate colour, flavour and vitamin content. To use: Break off tips and remove strings.
Fu Qua (bitter melon balsam pear)	June through October	Cucumber-like vegetable with clear, green shiny and very wrinkled skin.	Refrigerate in vegetable bin or perforated plastic bag. Will keep up to 1 week.	Stir-fry with meats, etc. Simmer in soup, steam or braise. To use: Slice off stem end. Cut length-wise in half. Scoop out spongy pulp, pinkish seeds: then slice and parboil 3 minutes. (It will be too bitter otherwise.)
Mow Qua (fuzzy melon)	July through October	Cylindrical green vegetable about 6-15 cm long and covered with a fine hair-like fuzz.	Refrigerate in vegetable bin. Use within 1 week.	Used primarily as a soup ingredient. May be stir-fried or braised. To use: Peel and slice.
Si Young Choy (watercress)	May through November	A medium green cluster of small round leaves with willowy stem.	Wash well. Place in a jar of water to cover and refrigerate. Change water daily. Will keep 4 to 5 days.	Use as a garnish.

Fu Qua

Ngah Choi

Lo Bak

Ho Long Dow

Mow Qua

Si Young Choy

Vegetable Cookery

PRINCIPLES OF VEGETABLE COOKERY

If raw vegetables have superior nutritive value to cooked ones and if most vegetables are palatable raw, why then do we cook vegetables? The answer lies in the changes which occur when a vegetable is cooked:

1.   The softening of the cellulose structure of the vegetable reduces its bulk and makes it more easily digested.

2.   Starch granules absorb water and swell, called gelatinization. This makes the starch in vegetables more appetizing and digestible.

3.   In many cases the flavour is altered so as to be more acceptable.

4.   Colour or appearance changes may occur and in some cases this is desirable.

5.   Any active micro-organisms present are destroyed. Longer cooking sterilizes vegetables, an important consideration when feeding infants and small children.

6.   Dried and freeze-dried vegetables must have the moisture content replaced by cooking in order for them to be edible.

7.   Cooking adds variety and interest to vegetables.

A well cooked vegetable has a tender, firm texture and has retained its nutritive value and its natural form, colour and flavour. The principles of vegetable cookery are designed to protect and preserve all of these natural qualities. The amount of water used and the length of cooking time are the most important considerations to achieve this result. Some vegetable nutrients are water soluble and seep out into the cooking liquid. This is why it is so important that the cooking water be used in some way, not discarded.

Some vegetable vitamins are easily destroyed by heat and overcooking. Cooking vegetables only until fork tender but still slightly crisp will help prevent nutrient loss. Overcooking also causes colours to become unattractive and unpleasant flavours and odours to develop in some vegetables. Mushy vegetables that have lost their pleasing texture and taste are also the result of overcooking.

METHODS OF COOKING VEGETABLES

1. Boil

This method is by far the most often used and the least often done in a way that will preserve maximum nutrients. Place the prepared vegetables in a saucepan containing a small amount of boiling water. Add salt. Cover the pan and return the water quickly to the boil. Reduce the heat so that the water simmers gently and cook the vegetable until only fork tender. Drain well, saving the cooking water. Add garnish, seasoning or butter sauce as desired and serve immediately.

Place frozen vegetables in the boiling water while still frozen. They will take less time to cook because they were blanched (scalded) in preparation for freezing.

Use vegetable water for gravy or sauce or save and use in soup.

2. Steam

This method is especially suited to mild flavoured vegetables, particularly leafy ones and those of the squash family. Because the vegetable is not submerged in the water there is good retention of water soluble nutrients.

Place a small amount of boiling water in the bottom of the steamer (1-1.5 cm). Prepare vegetables, sprinkle with salt and place on the rack or basket in the steamer or saucepan. (Put squash cut side down.) Cover with a tight lid and cook only until fork tender. (Leafy vegetables will be just wilted.)

3. Pressure Cook

Because the cooking time is so short, vegetables cooked in a pressure cooker usually have good colour and flavour. Nutrient losses are low since so little water is required. However, there is great danger of overcooking, especially of those vegetables which require a short cooking time by other methods. For best results, follow manufacturer's directions supplied with the pressure cooker. Use as a time and energy saving method for vegetables that take fairly long to cook, for example, dried beans and lentils.

4. Bake

This method is an excellent way of preserving water soluble nutrients. However, because of the high temperature used, vitamin C losses are great. Baked vegetables retain much of their delicate flavour and colour and can be served at the table directly from the baking dish.

Vegetables such as potatoes and squash are best baked dry in their skins. Simply wash thoroughly (prick potatoes), place directly on the oven rack or in a shallow pan and bake until tender.

Other vegetables are more acceptable when pared and cut. Place the prepared vegetables in a greased baking dish, sprinkle with salt, dot with butter and in the case of vegetables with a low moisture content, sprinkle with 10-25 ml water. Cover and bake until just tender. Stir or turn the vegetables several times during cooking. Aluminum foil can be used in place of a covered baking dish.

Various temperatures can be used and many vegetables can be baked along with another part of the meal. For example, 160°C with meat or poultry, 190°C with a casserole or cookies or 220°C with pastry. Not all vegetables can be baked at any of these three temperatures. Green vegetables discolour, unless baked quickly at a high temperature; others such as squash become dry and scorched if cooked at the high temperatures.

5.   Broil

This is a good way to cook some vegetables as tomato halves, egg plant slices, zucchini squash halves, and mushroom caps. In addition to the nutrients which they provide, vegetables cooked this way are an attractive garnish to the dinner plate.

Brush melted butter on the vegetable, season and if desired add a coating or topping. Place on the broiler rack 6-8 cm from the heating unit. Broil until vegetables are just tender and lightly browned.

6.   Pan

This method is a simple way of cooking vegetables on top of the range. It is a slight variation of the "stir-fry" method employed in Oriental recipes. Rapid cooking preserves the natural colour and flavour of the vegetable and nutrient losses are minimal since any water used is evaporated. Panned vegetables are especially attractive when interesting shapes are used and contrasting colours and flavours are combined.

To prepare vegetables for cooking, pare if necessary, and slice, chop or shred, as desired. For four servings melt 30-50 ml butter in a large heavy skillet or fry pan having a good fitting lid. Add vegetables, then sprinkle with salt. If a combination of vegetables is being used, start those that require longest cooking first. Add 30 ml water only if needed to prevent scorching. Cover fry pan, heat quickly to form steam, then reduce heat and cook gently until vegetables are crisp-tender. Shake the pan or stir frequently to avoid sticking. Serve vegetables immediately.

PREPARING AND COOKING VEGETABLES FOR MAXIMUM FOOD VALUE

1. Purchase, or pick from the garden, only the amount of fresh vegetables that can be properly stored and used in a short time. See chart page 151.

2. Cook only enough for one meal. Reheated vegetables lose their food value. Cooked vegetables improperly stored for more than a day or two can cause food poisoning.

3. Avoid paring vegetables whenever possible since it removes much of the mineral matter and vitamins. If you are going to pare vegetables, use a utensil that makes a very thin peeling.

4. If necessary to cut vegetables, cut with the grain. Cutting across the grain exposes a greater area to cooking water that dissolves out vitamins and minerals. Chopped, minced or shredded vegetables lose vitamin C rapidly.

5. Avoid soaking vegetables because it dissolves out vitamins and minerals. If vegetables must be prepared in advance, cover them from the air and light and store in a plastic bag in the refrigerator.

6. Use the shortest cooking time possible. Have water boiling first and use a tight lid unless otherwise directed.

7. Stir as little as possible. Air worked into the vegetables increases loss of vitamin C. Mashing or whipping is particularly destructive.

8. Do not overcook. Cook only until tender-crisp, no more. The longer the cooking time the greater the vitamin loss.

9. Don't throw away liquid in which foods have been cooked. Refrigerate in a covered jar and use for gravies, sauces, soups, stews or combine with vegetable juice to make appetizer cocktails.

10. Reheat canned foods in the liquid in which they were canned. Save extra liquid and use as in No. 9.

11. Serve vegetables as soon as they are cooked. Keeping them hot for a long time reduces vitamin content.

12. Avoid using baking soda in cooking vegetables. Although it helps bring out green colour and will tenderize old vegetables, it usually makes texture and flavour less desirable and destroys vitamins.

SERVING CANNED VEGETABLES

Since the time allowed for processing the vegetable in canning has cooked it, commercially canned vegetables require only heating before they are served. (See note below.) Unfortunately, water soluble nutrients dissolve out into the canning water and, unless used, will be lost. This liquid can be drained from the can and heated in an uncovered pan to evaporate it. When only about one-third of the liquid remains, add the vegetable, heat and serve the liquid with the vegetable.

Usually canned vegetables are more appetizing if presented with a sauce made from the liquid or if the vegetable is drained and the juices are used in gravy or soup.

IMPORTANT

To avoid the possibility of food poisoning all home canned vegetables must be boiled in an open saucepan for fifteen minutes before they are used. Firmly packed vegetables such as creamed corn and spinach require twenty minutes. Do not taste before boiling time is completed and carefully dispose of, without tasting, any food which has a bad odour.

COOKING DRIED VEGETABLES

Beans and peas are the vegetables most commonly used in the dried form. Both nutritionally and in cost they are good value. In addition to B vitamins they provide iron and calcium. When combined with even small amounts of meat, fish, eggs or dairy products the vegetable dish becomes complete. Refer to Nutrition, page 55.

Dried vegetables must be soaked before cooking. To preserve the vitamins and minerals dissolved in the soaking water, it is important to cook the vegetables in the water in which they were soaked. Whenever possible, use this water as part of the liquid in the final dish.

To prepare dried beans, for example, wash thoroughly first and remove any foreign material. There are two effective ways of soaking the beans:
1. Cover with cold water using 650-750 ml water for each 250 ml beans. Soak overnight.
2. Using 650-750 ml water for each 250 ml beans, place water and beans in saucepan, bring to a boil and boil for 2 minutes. Remove them from heat and let stand, covered, for 1 to 2 hours.

Cooking times, after soaking, vary considerably for different varieties. If the beans are to be cooked further after boiling, continue only until they can be pierced with a toothpick. Because they make the cooking time longer when added at the beginning, salt and other seasonings are best added after the beans have started to become tender. To avoid the foaming that occurs during boiling, add 15 ml of fat to the cooking water for each cup of beans. Approximate cooking times that will serve as a guide are as follows:

VEGETABLE	BOILING	PRESSURE COOKING 105 kPa
White beans (large)	1 - 1½ hours	20 minutes
Navy beans (small white)	1½ - 2 hours	25 minutes
Lima beans (large)	1 hour	15 minutes
Lima beans (small)	45 minutes	10 minutes
Kidney beans	2 hours	30 minutes
Pinto beans	1½ - 2 hours	25 minutes
Soy beans	3 hours	45 minutes

When calculating the amount of dried beans needed, allow 250 ml beans for 500-750 ml cooked beans or 1 500-1 750 ml cooked beans from 500 grams of dried beans.

To prepare dehydrated or instant dried vegetables, best results are assured by following the directions on the package.

Fruit

Food Value of Fruit

Fruits are essential to good health because they supply so many important nutrients. Nutritionists encourage two servings of fruit, or their juices, daily with one of them an excellent source of vitamin C.

In addition to their nutritive contribution, fruits stimulate the appetite with their appealng flavour, texture, aroma and colour. The fibrous material furnishes bulk and acts as a valuable natural laxative. Fibrous fruits, also play an important role in dental hygiene by helping to remove plaque from the teeth.

Here is an outline of the food elements found in fruit with some examples of the fruits in which they are found:

1. **VITAMINS**

C – Rich sources of vitamin C are: all citrus fruits (oranges, mandarins, grapefruit, lemons, limes) cantaloup, fresh strawberries, vitaminized apple juice and tomatoes. Because the body does not store vitamin C, it is important to have the required amount each day.

A – The vitamin A found in fruit is directly proportional to the brightness of the yellow or orange pigment. Rich sources of vitamin A are cantaloup, apricots and peaches.

Folic Acid – found in lemons, bananas. strawberries, cantaloup.

2. MINERALS

Iron is found in good amounts in dried fruits such as prunes, apricots, raisins and dates. It is also found in strawberries, raspberries, plums and cantaloup. Although iron is stored in the body, a daily food intake of iron is essential to maintain body reserves.

3. CARBOHYDRATES

Most fruits are relatively low in their energy value but some have considerable amounts. As the fruit ripens, the starch content is changed to sugar. Since more than half the water is removed during drying, dried fruits are high in carbohydrate. So are all canned fruit and bananas and plums.

4. CELLULOSE

This important element is found in most fruits. Because it cannot be digested it provides bulk to prevent constipation.

5. WATER

Most fruits have a high water content which also helps to regulate the body.

Classification, Selection and Storage of Fruit

Fruit can be classified into several main groups. Each group has a distinctive shape and structure. It is a real help to know the characteristics to expect in good fresh fruit as well as something about the varieties that are available.

1.   CITRUS FRUIT

This group includes all varieties of oranges, mandarins, grapefruit, lemons, limes, citron and kumquats. Navel oranges are seedless and have a rich, sweet taste with deep yellow, thick skins. Avoid oranges that have cracks, soft spots or spongy or shrivelled skins. Choose grapefruit that are a bit springy to touch, heavy, and thin skinned; reject any with a puffy appearance, very coarse skin or soft decayed areas near the stem end. Examine lemons at the stem end for decay. Limes should be green or yellow in colour.

Citrus fruits keep best in a cool place. Refrigeration temperatures are also desirable for the most usual ways of serving them.

Oranges　　　　　　　　　　*Mandarins*

Grapefruits　　　　　　　　　*Limes*

Kumquats　　　　　　　　　　*Lemons*

2.   TREE FRUIT

Tree fruits are of two types, the pomes and the drupes. Pomes are characterized by a smooth skin covering a fleshy area which surrounds a core. Examples are apples and pears. Drupes contain a single seed or pit. The fleshy, juicy edible portion surrounds this and is covered by a skin. Examples of drupes are apricots, peaches, nectarines, cherries, plums.

Red Delicious Apples

Golden Delicious Apples

McIntosh Apples

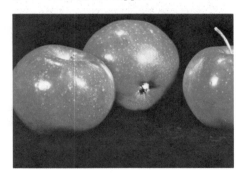

Rome Beauty Apples

Newtown Apples

Winesap Apples

All tree fruits should be firm but not hard, plump in order to give a natural fruit flavour, well shaped, smooth surfaced and free of insect bites and decay or wood spots. Medium sized apples are generally a cheaper buy than large ones. Purchase them according to what is currently in season (see chart on page 177) and the use you expect to make of them, either for eating or cooking.

Peaches

Apricots

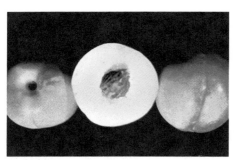

Nectarines

Bing Cherries

Peaches are available in either clingstone, freestone or semi-freestone types. Freestone are easier to use for home canning peach halves since the pits separate from the fruit readily. Semi-freestone are suitable for quarters or peach slices. Clingstone are grown for commercial processing. Choose peaches that are mature and free from cracks, bruises, shrivelled or soft spots. Those that ripen on the tree have superior flavour to those picked and allowed to ripen in storage. Nectarines are similar in flavour and shape to peaches but have a smooth skin. Apricots have a smooth skin and are smaller.

Sweet cherries include Bing and Lambert, red to rich purple; Queen Ann, pale yellow with a red blush. Avoid those bruised or having brown spots. Split cherries should be eaten or cooked soon after purchase. Removing stems speeds decay. Sour cherries for cooking are red with a soft flesh.

Choose plums that have slightly soft, plump, unblemished skins. Plums with brownish colour on the side are sunburned and have poor flavour.

Blue Plums

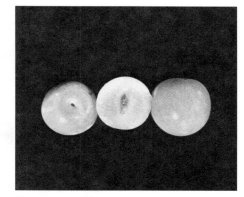

Greengage Plums

Pears are best when ripened in storage but they must be sorted frequently to remove the ripe ones before they begin to spoil. Choose pears that have smooth skin free from bruises or decay.

D'Anjou Pear

Bartlett Pear

All tree fruits must be carefully washed to remove the residue from insect sprays. Frequent sorting is needed to remove and use the ripened ones. Most keep well and ripen better without home refrigeration.

3.   VINE FRUITS

Cantaloups, honeydews, muskmelons, watermelons and other melons all have a characteristic aroma. The fully ripe ones have the richest smell and yield slightly to pressure at the stem end. Avoid melons with bruised surfaces and shrivelled or flabby fruit.

Cantaloup

Persian Melon

Grapes are usually classified as a vine fruit also. They should be purchased for immediate use having full coloured, fresh appearing fruit that is tightly attached to the stems. Reject those that have a whitish or shrivelled appearance or that are mouldy or decayed at the stem end.

All vine fruits need to be stored in the refrigerator. Strong smelling melons such as cantaloup should be wrapped to prevent other foods from absorbing their flavour.

Perlette Grapes

Concord Grapes

4.   TROPICAL FRUITS

Fruits that are grown in the tropics include bananas, pineapple, avocados, pomegranates, papayas and mangos. Bananas are purchased by mass and if necessary ripened in a cool place. They are fully ripe and best for eating when the peel is yellow flecked with brown. Green tips indicate they contain starch which has not yet turned to sugar. They should not be refrigerated as this causes them to darken without ripening.

Pineapples should be heavy for their size and have a spicy fragrance with good orange-yellow colour and flat eyes when fully ripened. They are most plentiful in March through June.

Avocado fruit has a yellow-green meat with dark green skin and a large nutlike pit. Light skin markings like scabs do not affect quality. For salads, select firm but not hard fruit. For a spread, select fruit that has ripened to a softer stage.

Bananas

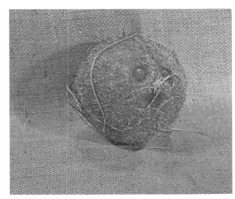

Coconut

Pineapple

Avocado

Mango

Papaya

Pomegranate

5. BERRIES

All types of berries should be plump, solid, fragrant, bright, full coloured and free from dirt. When the caps cling tightly the berries are underripe. Avoid choosing berries that are overripe, dull coloured, soft or capped (except strawberries which should have caps still on.) Carefully tip the basket to check for mouldy or decayed fruit at the bottom.

Berries must be handled gently and used as soon after picking as possible. They should be washed carefully in a sieve just before serving. Do not let stand in water. Refrigeration is essential to retard the spoilage which occurs so quickly.

Blueberries

Blackberries

Strawberries

Red Currants

Raspberries

Gooseberries

Principles of Fruit Cookery

The first step in preparation of a fresh fruit is to wash it thoroughly, removing spray residue, dust, bacteria and any other contamination. For fruits eaten with the skin on this is particularly important. Since the highest mineral concentration is directly under the skin those fruits that can be eaten unpeeled are best used this way.

Any cutting utensils used must be sharp to prevent a bruised, ragged appearance and loss of valuable juices. A stainless steel or silver knife will prevent darkening of the surface when peeling and slicing fruit. Fruits should be prepared just before serving since they lose vitamins and flavour on exposure to air.

Exposing cut surfaces to the air causes discolouration of pale coloured fruits. This browning can usually be prevented by sprinkling with a little lemon or other citrus fruit juice or with pineapple juice. Immersing in water containing a little salt or ascorbic acid, or cooking the fruit will also prevent browning.

It is well known that fresh fruit supplies more nutrients than cooked fruit. If this is so, why then is fruit so often served in the cooked form? Here are some of the reasons for cooking fruit.

1.   A more interesting variety is possible.

2.   Cellulose is softened and the fruit becomes easier to digest.

3.   **In some instances, the flavour and texture are improved over that of the raw fruit.**

4.   Cooking helps to prevent food spoilage since the enzymes are inactivated.

5.   Cooking is essential to home canning of fruit, a principal method of preserving seasonal fruits for future use. (Since freezing does not involve cooking the product which results more closely resembles fresh fruit. However, freezer storage space is needed for this and is not always readily available.)

A basic principle of all fruit preparation, including cookery, is the protection of the nutrients found in the fruit. Vitamin C, one of the most important elements contained in fruit, is the most easily destroyed of all vitamins. Exposure to the oxygen in air, heating, and placing in water, are all factors which reduce the amount of vitamin C present.

Other nutrients contained in fruit can also be easily lost. Here are some factors to consider when preparing fruit for maximum nutrient retention:

1.   Vitamin loss due to air is minimized by preparing fruit and juices just before serving.

2.   Cut fruits have more surface exposed to air and vitamin loss will be greater.

3. Vitamins and minerals concentrated just under the skin are retained when fruit is served unpeeled or peeled thinly.
4. Straining fruit juices results in greater destruction of vitamin C because the juice is in greater contact with air.
5. Opened canned fruits and cooked fruits should be stored in a covered container in the refrigerator. Oxygen will have less chance to destroy vitamins if the proper size container is used.
6. As little water as possible should be used when cooking fruit. The cooking liquid containing dissolved vitamins and minerals should be served with the fruit.

The method used to cook fruit depends upon the end result desired. When a softened texture is wanted as with applesauce and cooked dried fruit, the fruit should be simmered first in water. The cellulose structure is broken down as water passes through the fruit cells and bursts them. Then after cooking is completed, sugar can be added without any danger of it toughening the cellulose of the product. Puréed fruit is prepared by forcing fruit cooked this way through a sieve or food mill.

When fruit having a full well rounded shape is desired, as with peeled fruits and fruit compote, a sugar-water syrup is prepared first. Then the fruit is added and a higher temperature can be used to cook the fruit. The cells absorb the sugar and the fruit becomes translucent. If too much sugar is used in the syrup, water will pass from the fruit into the syrup and the fruit will shrink and become tough. With either method a short cooking period will keep nutrient and flavour loss to a minimum.

Cooking dried fruit is slightly different from cooking fresh fruit. Whole dried fruits are best when soaked first. Cut dried fruit will plump during the cooking time and does not require soaking. However, a short soaking period will reduce the cooking time.

Soaking can be done by leaving the fruit in cold water for several hours or overnight. Because dried fruits take up moisture more rapidly in hot water than in cold, 30-60 minutes will be long enough if hot water is used. The fruit should be cooked covered, in the water it was soaked in. To allow full plumping, a simmering temperature is required. When the fruit is lustrous and plump it can be removed from the heat and the appropriate amount of sugar added.

Most fruits can be cooked in many ways. When the same fruit is served often, using different cooking methods helps to provide variety. Apples, pears and peaches are favourites for baking. Varying the seasonings gives an additional change. Broiled fruit is quick to fix and attractive on the plate. Try grapefruit, bananas, pineapple, peaches and pears. Fruits that are suitable for frying or sautéing in butter include bananas and apple or pineapple slices. Many desserts are based on fruits. See page 346, Desserts and the recipe section of this book for ideas.

Orange Cups

Grating Rind

Peeling Oranges

Slices

Sections

Pieces

FRESH PINEAPPLE CUTS

QUARTERS

THE OUTRIGGER

Frozen Fruit

Commercial freezing makes available all year many different kinds of perishable fruits and their juices. The cost is usually higher than the cost of canned or in-season fresh fruits but there is no waste as there is in fresh fruits and preparation time is minimal. Although storage is convenient the use of frozen fruit requires having access to a home freezer.

Frozen fruits are available in Canada Fancy and Canada Choice grades. Choose packages that are solid and show no signs of leaking or a broken seal. Frozen packages should be taken from a well filled, deep freezer having a temperature between $-15°C$ and $-20°C$. They should be double wrapped and quickly transported home before thawing occurs.

Thaw frozen fruit just before serving. A few remaining ice crystals are usually desirable to help retain the shape of the fruit. Completely thawed fruit has a characteristic fresh flavour but a slightly softer texture than in the fresh form. It is important to remember that freezing merely retards the ripening process. It does not destroy enzymes. Ripening continues as soon as the fruit thaws. Thawed fruit must be refrigerated in the same way as fresh in order to prevent spoilage.

Canned Fruit

Canned fruits offer a great variety to the homemaker. Some are canned whole, in halves, sliced, cubed, as a sauce or as a juice. Processed during the peak of the season when at their ripest and most flavourful, canned fruits provide a convenient alternative to the fresh and frozen forms.

All commercially canned fruits in Canada are packed under government inspection and graded as one of the following:

Canada Fancy is preferred where uniformity of size and colour is
    desired.
Canada Choice is used when flavour and tenderness is desired but perfect
    appearance is not important.
Canada Standard is used where appearance is not important.

It is well to remember that these grades are based on colour, uniformity of size and maturity, clearness of syrup and absence of defects but that all grades are good wholesome food with similar nutritional value. The grade you choose will depend upon the price and how the fruit is to be used. Also, a dented can or rust on the can is not a sign of spoilage unless either of these has caused a leak.

In addition to government grading, canning companies are required by law to use informative labels which indicate:

1.   The grade of the fruit.

2.   The contents by volume.

3.   The sweetness of the sugar syrup.

4.   The style of pack (whole, halves, slices, etc.).

Other information which may voluntarily be added includes:

1.   Maturity or size of the fruit.

2.   Method of processing used.

3.   Number of average servings.

4.   Suggested recipes or ways of serving.

   Canned fruits should be stored in a cool, dry place. After the can has been opened, the fruit should be stored in a covered dish in the refrigerator.

Dried Fruit

During the drying process a large portion of the water is removed and the keeping quality of the fruit is extended. The drying process destroys the vitamin C but due to concentration, dried fruits are a richer source of iron and sugar. Most loose dried fruit is cheaper than the packaged kind. Dried fruit sealed in packages is kept clean but the food value is not different from that which is sold loose.

   Dried fruits should be stored in a cool dry place in the original carton or bag. Bulk fruit can be placed in a plastic bag. Cooked dried fruit should be covered and refrigerated.

GENERAL FACTORS THAT INFLUENCE FRUIT SELECTION

The skill of the consumer in selecting suitable, good quality food that has the desired keeping characteristics and satisfies the family's nutritional needs is important in all food areas. Selection of fruit which falls within budget limitations will take into account these factors:

1.   Market forms available are increasingly varied; e.g., fresh, canned, frozen, dried or frozen juice forms.

2.   Quality of the fruit you select varies with:
     the season of the year,
     the standards of goods maintained by the merchant,
     the day of the week the wholesaler delivers,
     transportation and refrigeration facilities available,
     your ability to recognize a good quality fruit of desired ripeness.

3.   End use of the fruit will determine the quality and market form which you choose. Apples for a pie need not be uniform in size; they should be a variety that will cook well. Apples for lunches should be free of blemishes and of a variety suitable for eating.

4. Amount of fruit you purchase will depend on the storage space available as well as your immediate need. Consider the keeping qualities of a fruit. Very perishable ones should be bought in smaller quantities.

5. Price of fruit will depend upon:
    the season of the year,
    the supply and demand.

PEAK SEASONS FOR BRITISH COLUMBIA GROWN FRUITS

Apples	
Yellow Transparent, Lodi	Mid-July to mid-August
Duchess	August
Wealthy, Taydemans Red, Rob Roy	Mid-August to mid-September
McIntosh Red, Red Spartan, Red Delicious, Golden Delicious	**Available the year round in Controlled Atmosphere Storage**
Rome Beauty, Newton, Winesap	November to June — Long keeping if kept in cold storage
Apricots	Mid-July to August
Blackberries	Mid-August to September
Blueberries	Mid-July to September
Cherries	Mid-June to July
Crabapple	Late July to mid-August
Cranberries	October
Currants	July
Grapes	August to November
Gooseberries	Mid-July
Loganberries	July to mid-August
Peaches	
Rochester, Red Haven, Spotlight	Late July to mid-August
Vees	August to early September
Eberts, J. H. Hole	August to September
Pears	
Bartletts	August to September
Flemish	September to November
Anjou	October to February
Plums and Prunes	August to September
Raspberries	July
Rhubarb	Mid-March to June
Strawberries	Late May to mid-July
Watermelon	August to mid-September

Eggs

Structure of an Egg

An egg has four distinct parts, namely: the yolk, the egg white (or albumen), the shell membrane and the shell. The *shell* is composed mainly of calcium. Because it is porous it permits the escape of moisture and the absorption of gases. The outside of the shell is covered by a thin transparent coating called the *bloom.* Its function is to assist in maintaining the freshness of the egg by sealing the porous shell. Inside the shell lie two *membranes,* one of which is firmly attached to the shell and another which lies next to it.

There is no *air cell* in an egg when it is laid. The contents completely fill the shell. As soon as the egg cools, the contents contract and air is drawn in through the porous shell to form an air space between the two shell membranes. Because the shell is generally more porous at the large end of the egg, the air space usually forms there. It may, however, occur at some other point, depending upon where the shell membranes separate most readily. As the egg contents evaporate, the egg cell size increases. This change occurs most rapidly under storage conditions of low humidity and high temperature.

The *albumen,* or white of the egg, is of two kinds. That next to the yolk is very thick, that next to the shell is thinner and becomes more liquid with age.

The *yolk* of a fresh egg is round and upstanding but as the egg deteriorates the yolk absorbs water from the white, making the yolk swell and flatten. The colour of the yolk may vary from a pale light yellow to a deep orange, according to the feed and the individual characteristics of the hen. The germ of an unfertilized egg appears as a small, irregular-shaped, light-coloured spot on the surface of the yolk.

The yolk is anchored to the centre of the egg by two *chalazas* which are part of the thick albumen. They look like twisted, whitish, rope-like cords. In addition to serving as an anchor to keep the yolk in the centre and as a sort of shock absorber to prevent it moving toward the shell, the chalazas form an axis which enables the fertilized germ spot always to be nearest the body of the hen as she sits on the egg for hatching.

COMPOSITION OF AN EGG

Although eggs are a good protein food containing many other valuable nutrients, they have a surprisingly high proportion of water. This chart shows the composition of the edible part of an egg. Notice how the white differs from the yolk in its makeup.

	WHITE	YOLK	WHOLE EGG
Water	87.77%	49.0%	73.7%
Protein	10.00	16.7	13.4
Fat	.05	31.6	10.5
Mineral matter	.82	1.5	1.0

An insignificant amount of carbohydrates, differing slightly with breed, age and diet of the bird, and with the seasons, makes up the remainder.

FOOD VALUE OF EGGS

Eggs provide excellent food value at a reasonable cost to the consumer. Their high nutritive value is proven when we remember that a chick, before hatching, can be nourished from the contents of only an egg.

Protein

Egg protein contains all the essential amino acids of a complete protein food. When a complete protein food is served with foods containing incomplete protein the body is able to make use of both proteins. Served as a meat substitute, two eggs contain about the same amount of complete protein as an average serving of meat.

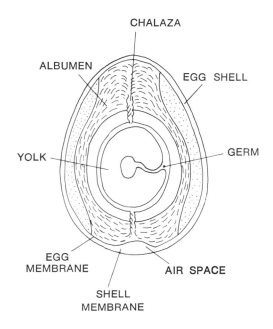

Fat

Because the fat content of the egg yolk is highly emulsified, it is easily digested, making eggs a good food for patients, convalescents, young children and elderly people. The fat, together with the protein, makes up the kilojoule count of an egg. This is low in relation to its high nutritive value.

About half of the fat in an egg is of the saturated kind and half is unsaturated. Consumption of saturated fats, (which are largely from animal sources), tends to cause a rise in blood cholesterol. Consumption of the soft or liquid unsaturated fats from plant sources tends to lower blood cholesterol. Although the exact implications of these changes in the blood cholesterol level are not fully understood, high blood cholesterol and heart attacks have been statistically correlated. However, coronary attacks do occur in persons having normal or low blood cholesterol, even amongst vegetarians. Many other factors besides diet are involved. Research is continuing.

Vitamins

The fat soluble vitamins A, D, E and K and the water soluble vitamins of the B complex, (mainly riboflavin), are all found in worthwhile amounts. The actual quantity of vitamin A in an egg is determined by the feed which the chicken has received. The intensity of the yellow or orange colour of the yolk and vitamin A content are related – the brighter the colour the more vitamin A. The amount of vitamin D varies with the content of the feed and also with the season of the year.

Minerals

The yolk is recognized as an important source of iron which is in a form that is readily used by the body. Eggs also contain phosphorus and a number of trace minerals.

There are a few nutrients lacking in the eggs we eat. These are: calcium, which is present in the shell; carbohydrate, an insignificant amount of which is present; and vitamin C. The lack of these nutrients is satisfied by a breakfast of milk, cereal or bread, and a citrus fruit.

STANDARDS FOR GRADING EGGS

All eggs offered for sale in commercial outlets have been graded according to federal government regulations. This is for the consumer's protection, but also ensures that egg producers are paid for their eggs on the basis of quality.

Most modern egg grading stations are mechanized. Small grading stations and some producers who grade their own eggs may use a combined system of mechanized sizing and manual candling and packaging. A farmer with a few hens and a few egg customers to whom he sells directly does not usually grade his eggs. There are three factors involved in the grading of eggs.

1. **Shell Condition**

    Shells are graded on the basis of their cleanliness, shape and soundness. As a hen becomes older the shells of the eggs she lays are larger and thinner. Since deterioration occurs so rapidly, a shell with large pores is less desirable than one with fine pores. Shell colour is dependent on the breed of hen and has no effect on food value, flavour, or quality of the egg.

2. **Interior Quality**

    Candling is the commercial method of checking the internal quality of eggs before they are marketed. Eggs are rotated in front of a candling light to reveal the position, movement, and shape of the yolk; the size of the air cell; and the presence or absence of any imperfections such as blood spots. On the basis of interior quality shown by a candling, eggs are divided into the following grades:

    A1: These are eggs of superior quality and are not readily available because of their limited quantities. Grade A1 eggs are produced from registered flocks on farms having a special permit from the Department of Agriculture.

CANADA GRADE A1 — Yolk round, compact and erect, surrounded by very thick, dense albumen.

 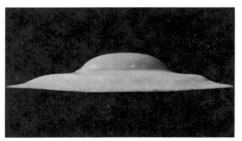

CANADA GRADE A — Yolk fairly well rounded and erect, surrounded by thick albumen.

 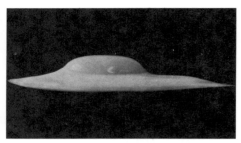

CANADA GRADE B — Yolk moderately oblong, slightly flattened and enlarged, surrounded by albumen covering a large area through thinning.

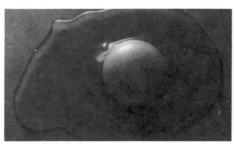 

CANADA GRADE C — Yolk oblong, enlarged or flattened, surrounded by weak, watery albumen.

A: These eggs are the top quality most generally found. They are sold in greater numbers than any other grade and are always available in the stores. Only Grades A and A1 are sized.

B: Grade B eggs are rarely sold on the retail market. They are not sized but must be of minimum allowed mass. These are usually eggs that are less fresh when graded or that have deteriorated in interior quality due to improper refrigeration during the marketing process. Other factors include heredity, bird management, and feed.

C: Grade C eggs are broken from the shell, as are some Grades B and A eggs, and sold in the frozen and dried forms. Originally used by bakeries and large food industries, these are now available in retail stores.

3.   Mass Measurement

At the grading station egg size is determined by manual or automatic scales. Although the sizes are called extra large, large, medium, small and peewee, they are based on mass. There is a minimum allowable mass per egg and a minimum allowable mass per multiple unit.

BUYING EGGS

The size of the eggs you buy should depend upon the price and the way you plan to use them. The price will vary since it depends upon the season and supplies available. When the new flocks start laying, small eggs are usually in heavy supply. There is a period when the medium size is plentiful and finally the large eggs are in greatest supply.

Since eggs are actually sold by mass it is possible to work out which size is most economical at any one time. Medium eggs at ⅛ less in price than large are equal in cost by mass. Small eggs which are ¼ less in price than large are equal in cost when masses are compared.

When the best value has been determined by price, the use to be made of the eggs should also be considered. Sometimes it is sensible to have more than one size on hand. Large eggs may be prepared for serving individually either poached, fried or in the shell. However, infants and young children may well prefer a small sized egg. Similarly, if the eggs are to be scrambled or used in an omelet, salad or sandwich, the size of the egg is unimportant. The quantity can be adjusted.

Most recipes are developed using medium size eggs. Recipes in this book indicate where another size is more suitable. The size of the egg will make a great difference in some special recipes. For example, a chiffon cake which requires 3 eggs would not have the desired characteristics if small eggs were used. However, 4 small eggs might successfully be substituted.

Consider using Grade B eggs when they are available. The cost will be much less than Grade A and they may be used for cooking in the shell, scrambling, in omelets and for other general cooking. Grade A eggs are best for attractive poached or fried eggs. In making meringues and sponge type cakes best results are achieved with Grade A eggs which are fresher and will hold the air that is beaten into them much better.

STORING EGGS

Because eggs lose quality rapidly at warm temperatures, refrigeration is essential during the entire shipping and marketing process, as well as in the home. If temperatures are not maintained below the maximum of 15°C at all times the consumer will be getting eggs of a quality less than the grade label indicates. Unfortunately, the consumer has no way of knowing to what temperature the eggs have been subjected before they are selected from refrigerated cases in the store.

At home, eggs should be stored away from strong smelling foods. Door racks or egg cartons are preferable since eggs should always be stored with the large end up. The length of time eggs may be satisfactorily stored depends upon the temperature maintained. No more than one week storage is recommended at home refrigerator temperatures. Under controlled conditions it is possible to store eggs for six months. Temperature between 0°C and −1°C are optimum and the shells must be dry to prevent mould and bacterial growth.

The shelf life of eggs is extended by coating the shell with a substance that will prevent moisture from getting out and contaminants from getting in. Before refrigerators were plentiful waterglass was widely used to dip eggs for this purpose. Eggs are now sprayed within a few hours after they are laid, with an edible mineral oil. The oil covers the pores of the egg thus reducing mould penetration and retarding spoilage.

PROPERTIES OF EGGS AND USE IN COOKERY

1. **Thickening**

   Eggs stiffen or coagulate when heated. Hence they can be used for thickening custards and sauces.

2. **Leavening**

   When eggs are beaten they form a foam which holds air. On heating the protein coagulates to retain the foam structure. This principle is involved in the making of sponge type cakes, meringue, soufflés and puffy omelet.

3. **Binding**

   As the protein of egg coagulates it helps to bind food mixtures. Eggs hold together the ingredients in flour mixtures, croquettes, meat loaf and other mixtures.

4. **Coating**

   Crumb mixtures of bread, crackers or cereal adhere well to foods that have first been dipped in slightly beaten egg. This is again due to the coagulating of egg protein. This is useful when the coated foods are to be fried in fat or baked in the oven for the protein coating protects the food against the intense heat of the fat or the dry heat of the oven.

5. **Emulsifying**

   An emulsifying agent causes a liquid to mix with fat. Egg yolk surrounds the droplets of oil and prevents them from joining together to form larger droplets which can settle out. The method of making mayonnaise and Hollandaise sauce is based on this principle.

6. **Clarifying**

   Eggs have the ability to take up particles that make a liquid cloudy. Examples of where this fact may be useful are soup broth and boiled coffee.

7. **Retarding Crystallization**

   Beaten eggs act as interfering substances and help to produce small ice crystals in frozen mixtures such as ice cream and sherbets. They trap tiny bubbles of air which prevent ice crystals from coming together to form large masses of the frozen mixture. Egg white is important in preventing the formation of sugar crystals in some frostings and candies.

PRINCIPLES OF EGG COOKERY

Whether eggs are being cooked alone or in combination with other foods, correct temperature is essential to a successful product. The protein of the egg coagulates at a temperature well below the boiling point of water which is 100°C. Egg whites coagulate at a slightly lower temperature than egg yolks. When they are together a temperature of 65°C is adequate.

Remember that eggs are a protein food and that all protein foods are more tender when cooked at a low temperature. Eggs cooked at boiling temperatures or in very hot fat will be toughened and more difficult to digest.

EGGS AS EGGS

1. Eggs-in-the-Shell should be cooked in water that is at simmering temperature or just below. Do not boil. Hard cooked eggs should be placed in cold water to prevent a brown sulphur ring forming around the yolk. Eggs cooked in boiling water cook less evenly, become tough and are less appetizing.

2. Poached eggs should be cooked in water that is just below simmering. Cooking eggs this way will also help them to retain their shape in the water when an egg poacher is not used. A jar ring will keep the egg in position.

3. Fried Eggs should be cooked in a thin layer of fat with a 150°C setting on the frypan. A lid can be used to help firm the top of the yolk. Cooking in fat that is too hot makes the white tough, crisp and difficult to digest.

4.   Scrambled Eggs may be cooked at 160°C setting of the frypan. Using a higher temperature makes the eggs watery, especially if they are cooked longer than is necessary.

5.   Baked Eggs – Eggs reach the proper coagulation temperature when baked in the oven at 160°C. This has been found by careful testing and is explained by the principle of heat transfer.

6.   Omelets – There are two kinds of omelets. Plain or French omelet is a light, rolled egg pancake with a flavour similar to scrambled egg. Puffy or foamy omelet is a step short of a soufflé and the final cooking is done in the oven.

EGGS AS LEAVENERS

1.   Soufflés – A soufflé is made from a thick, seasoned white sauce, containing egg yolks, that has been folded into stiffly beaten egg whites and baked in the oven. The baking dish is set in a pan of hot water to help maintain an even temperature (this is called oven poaching) and the soufflé is baked until a knife inserted in the centre comes out clean (like custard). Hot soufflés do not remain in the puffy risen shape for very long after they are removed from the oven. They should be served immediately they are ready.

2.   Sponge-type cakes – Sponge cakes and angel cakes are included in this classification. Their only leavening agent is the air which is beaten into the egg white and which expands when heated in the oven. The

same principle applies in chiffon cake and jelly roll, although some baking powder is also used.

3.   Meringue – Both soft and hard meringues are made from beaten egg whites and sugar.

EGGS AS THICKENERS

Many recipes use egg as a thickener. Sometimes the eggs are in combination with other thickeners such as cornstarch, flour and gelatin. Hollandaise sauce, custard, and custard sauce have egg as the only thickener. See page 348, Desserts, for details on custards. Here are some principles to remember when using eggs as a thickener in puddings and sauces:

1.   When adding egg to hot liquid, add only small amounts of the hot liquid to the egg, with continuous stirring, to prevent lumping of the egg.

2.   When using egg whites only, remember that they begin to cook at a lower temperature than do the yolks. Therefore, reduce the temperature.

3.   Since eggs will continue cooking after the pan has been removed from the heat, stop the cooking process before thickening is complete.

MERINGUES

Types of Meringues

There are three types of meringues which can be made from beaten egg whites and sugar in some form. These differ in the ingredients added to the basic egg white foam and the way the egg protein is treated to coagulate it.

1.   Soft Meringue – This is the kind that is used for a topping for one-crust pies. Basic proportions are 30 ml sugar and 1 ml cream of tartar for each egg white used. Baking temperatures can be adjusted according to the type of product desired. A low oven temperature (150°C) will eventually give a crisp meringue; a higher temperature (200°C) will give a well browned meringue with a soft centre, in a very few minutes. Preparation of a soft meringue is frequently involved as a step in dessert recipes. Examples are Spanish cream, snow pudding, chiffon.

   Soft meringue can be coagulated by dropping spoonfuls of the mixture on the surface of hot water in a shallow pan and cooking over medium heat until firm. This method is employed in preparation of an old-time favourite dessert, Floating Island, which is essentially a soft custard decorated with meringue.

2. Hard Meringue – This kind has a higher proportion of sugar and is baked slowly until dry to give a crisp crunchy texture. Pie shells, individual meringue shells and macaroons are examples.

3. Cake Icing – A seven-minute frosting is made with egg whites and sugar which are beaten over boiling water until the soft foam coagulates. Corn syrup, brown sugar or cream of tartar help to prevent the formation of sugar crystals.

VOLUME AND STABILITY OF BEATEN EGG WHITES

A number of factors affect the volume and stability of egg white foams:

1. Age of the egg – Fresh eggs form a foam slowly; the volume is not as great but the stability of the foam is good.

2. Temperature of the egg white – At room temperature eggs foam more readily and give a greater volume than those just removed from the refrigerator.

3. Equipment – Cleanliness of the equipment used is very important. Beaters and bowl must be free of any other materials, especially fat, because fat reduces the amount of air that can be incorporated into the egg white. Even the smallest amount of egg yolk will interfere with the foaming quality. Deep, narrow sided bowls are most suitable for beating and they must be large enough to allow for the increase of volume. Some cooks prefer a whisk to a rotary type beater.

4. Other ingredients – An acid in the form of cream of tartar or lemon juice helps to stabilize the foam since these substances coagulate the egg white slightly and give strength to the foam. A fine sugar such as berry sugar or powdered sugar will dissolve more readily and give a finer textured product.

5. Rate of beating and adding sugar – Before any other ingredients are added the whites are beaten to the *frothy stage*. Acid, if being used, may be added at this time. As beating continues the sugar is added very gradually. Slow addition of sugar insures that the sugar is completely dissolved and a fine grained meringue is produced. Amber coloured droplets on the surface of a pie meringue will form during baking if any undissolved sugar crystals remain. If the egg white foam is part of a cake, the texture of the baked product will be coarse. Slow addition of the sugar also increases the strength of the foam so that less air is lost.

6. Extent of beating – As beating continues, the air bubbles become increasingly smaller. When the peaks will just bend over as the beater is removed, egg whites are suitable for folding into a batter. This *soft peak stage* is right for soft meringues.

More beating will result in peaks that stand up straight as the beater is withdrawn – the *stiff peak stage*. At this point, the foam is more difficult to fold in with other ingredients. Care must be taken at any stage to prevent loss of air which has been beaten into the foam.

Overbeating is possible and produces a dry foam having little use since the air escapes as the foam breaks into pieces.

PREPARING PIE MERINGUE

Beat whites until frothy. Add cream of tartar.

Beat to soft peak stage and add sugar gradually.

Place carefully on cooled pie filling.

Milk and Milk Products

Milk is the liquid formed by all female mammals for feeding their young. Although the milk of cows is used in this country with few exceptions, the milk of other animals is also used as human food in other parts of the world. The milks of different animals are very similar and contain the same nutrients, but there are slight differences in the proportions of these food elements.

Since cow's milk is the only food of the young calf it must contain all the food elements needed for its life and growth. Milk is the most complete single food we know. It does not, however, contain sufficient amounts of vitamin C, vitamin D and iron for even a young child. For this reason, these elements are added to the child's diet during the first few months. While not a complete food for human beings, cow's milk is an important food.

NUTRITIVE VALUE OF MILK

The exact composition of milk depends upon the particular breed of cow, the type of feed, and other seasonable variables. This diagram shows an approximate composition of whole milk.

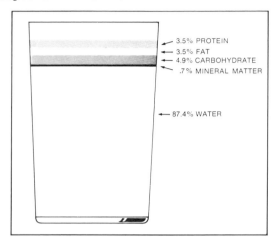

Protein

Milk is a protein food and it is important that we understand how this nutrient contributes to good health. Skin, muscles, bone, and all the soft body tissues are made mostly of protein. It is commonly called the building nutrient. When young bodies are growing, foods having plenty of high quality protein are needed to make sure parts of the body are properly formed. When growth is complete, a daily supply of protein continues to be needed to keep tissues repaired so they can function effectively. Throughout life milk can supply much of the high quality protein that is needed.

Amino acids are the building blocks of all proteins. High quality proteins are those which contain the essential amino acids which must be provided in food, as the body is unable to synthesize them for itself. They are sometimes called complete proteins. The principal complete proteins in milk are *casein,* that protein which forms the curd from which most cheeses are made. *Lactalbumin* and *lactoglobulin* are found in the whey which remains after the removal of the curd. Cheese is also an excellent source of complete protein, but since it does not contain the whey proteins, its amino acid contribution differs from that of milk. When combinations of foods are eaten at the same meal, milk's high quality protein complements the incomplete proteins found in cereals and vegetables.

Fat

The fat in milk is referred to as milk fat or butterfat. Because it is highly emulsified, milk fat is more easily digested than any other food fat except that of eggs. Fat supplies energy to our bodies and in the case of whole milk, accounts for about half of its kilojoule count. Skim milk is suggested when a lower kilojoule intake is desired but the fat soluble vitamins will not be present unless the milk has been fortified.

Carbohydrate

Milk is the only food source of *lactose,* (called milk sugar), the carbohydrate found in milk. Milk sugar, like all carbohydrates, provides energy to the body and accounts for about 30% of the kilojoule count of whole milk.

MINERALS

Calcium

From the nutrition point of view, calcium is one of milk's main attractions. It is almost impossible for young people to get enough calcium to build and maintain the bones and teeth without plenty of milk in their meals every day. If the food eaten does not supply the needed calcium, the body is able to draw calcium from the bones which are a storehouse for this mineral. Calcium strengthens the bones and a continuous loss of calcium from them will affect the soundness of both the bones and teeth. In addition to causing fragile bones and teeth, a calcium deficiency can interfere with normal nerve function, blood clotting, muscle contraction and heart beat. If the amount of milk recommended by nutritionists is taken daily, nearly all of the body's calcium requirement will be met.

Phosphorus

There is an interdependence between calcium, phosphorus, and vitamin D for normal bones and tooth formation. All three must be supplied simultaneously. Milk, which satisfies this requirement, is an especially important food. In addition to its role in building and maintaining the bones and teeth, phosphorus is needed for every body cell. It influences the oxidation of foods in the cells to release energy to the body.

VITAMINS

Vitamin D

Another nutrient the body needs to work along with calcium and phosphorus when the bones and teeth are being formed. Since milk contains a small and unpredictable amount of vitamin D naturally, government agencies have encouraged its controlled addition so that the needed amount may be easily obtained. See page 195, Fortify.

RIBOFLAVIN

Few other foods are such a good source of this nutrient which is one of the B vitamins. The riboflavin content of milk is fairly constant although it is easily destroyed by ultraviolet light. The amount of milk suggested in government endorsed food guides will provide the body with nearly all of its total recommended daily intake of this vitamin. Riboflavin is essential to the healthy condition and function of the skin, eyes, tongue, nerves and digestive tract. It also assists the body cells to use oxygen, so that the other foods eaten can release energy for all daily activities.

WORDS TO UNDERSTAND

Pasteurize

Pasteurized milk is milk that has been heated to kill any harmful bacteria. Unpasteurized milk may contain harmful micro-organisms which can cause several diseases. Pasteurization destroys these without significantly reducing the nutritive value of the milk, and ensures a safe food. Pasteurization also kills a great many of the milk-souring bacteria and therefore extends the storage time of the milk. Many dairy foods are made from pasteurized milk including buttermilk, butter, cream, cottage cheese, chocolate milk, skim milk, two percent milk, ice cream, half and half, sour cream and yogurt.

There are two methods of pasteurization used in dairies across Canada. One, the old Vat Method, which is used in small plant operations, heats and holds the milk at a temperature of 62°C for 30 minutes. It is then rapidly cooled to between 5°C to 10°C. The newer, most commonly used method, is called the High Temperature Short Time (H.T.S.T.) system of pasteurization. This method heats and holds the milk at a temperature of 71°C for 16 seconds; then the milk is rapidly cooled to 5°C. The cold, pasteurized milk then flows along sanitary pipes to the filling and sealing machines.

Sterilize

Sterilization is the heating of a food or utensil until all living micro-organisms are destroyed. Evaporated milk is sterilized after it is canned, by heating for 10 to 15 minutes at 100°C to 120°C. This process extends its storage life indefinitely. Sterilized milk is milk that is heated to and held at 75°C for 5 seconds, increased to 135°C and held under pressure for 2 seconds, then cooled rapidly to 15°C. After the pressure is released the milk is homogenized, cooled and packaged aseptically. This milk, though not commonly available, will keep at room temperature for up to eight weeks. It must be refrigerated once the package is opened.

Homogenize

Homogenized milk is whole milk that has been treated mechanically to break up the milk fat into smaller particles which will not rise to the top as cream but remain uniformly dispersed. Homogenization involves pumping the pasteurized milk, under pressure, through very small holes. The fat is broken into minute globules which are immediately surrounded by a film of protein that prevents them from reuniting. Because the new emulsion is more stable, a cream layer does not form upon standing. Other foods that may be homogenized are: cream, half and half, dairy sour cream, ice cream, two percent milk.

Fortify

Fortification refers to the addition of nutrients to a food. The availability of vitamin enriched milk products varies across Canada since provincial regulations differ and the program is not mandatory. The label on the package will indicate if and to what extent any milk product has been enriched.

The addition of vitamin D to milk ensures an adequate daily supply of this vitamin for all growing persons, and pregnant and lactating women, provided they consume the amounts recommended by provincial health authorities. The small amount of vitamin D occurring naturally in milk is affected by the feed and sunlight available to the animal from which the milk has come. Vitamin D occurs in very few natural foods and its synthesis in the body from the sun's ultraviolet rays is severely limited in urban, smog or fog prevalent areas. Hence, the chief source of this essential nutrient, other than milk, has been vitamin supplements or fish liver oils. Most important, vitamin D is primarily associated with calcium utilization. Since milk is the most significant source of calcium for Canadians, adequate consumption of milk, with added vitamin D ensures sufficient supplies of both calcium and vitamin D.

Vitamin A enriched milk is found in some areas of Canada. Because vitamin A is fat soluble, the valuable amount of this nutrient is reduced when the fat is removed as in skim and partly skimmed milk. Thus the addition of vitamin A to these forms of milk is a protective measure for the many persons who choose them instead of whole milk.

The addition of vitamin C to evaporated milk has been permitted for a number of years. This is primarily to meet the needs of infants on formulae made from evaporated milk and who do not receive citrus juice or vitamin supplements.

FORMS OF MILK

Fresh Fluid Products

WHOLE MILK — is defined in Canada as milk that contains at least 3.25% milk fat and at least 8% non-fat milk solids. Milk fat and butterfat are synonomous terms. Most communities require that milk sold to the consumer be pasteurized. Most of the fluid whole milk marketed and all of the fluid partially skimmed milk is homogenized. Whole milk that is not homogenized is referred to as standard or cream-line milk because the lighter fat globules rise and form a distinct cream layer.

SKIM MILK – is milk from which most of the fat has been removed. Some provinces have established a maximum milk fat content and some have set minimum standards for non-fat milk solids. These standards vary between provinces. Skim milk has the same nutritional value as whole milk with two minor exceptions. It has a lower kilojoule count because of the reduced milk fat and a lower vitamin A content, unless fortified, because this vitamin is found in the fat.

PARTLY SKIMMED MILK – is milk that has had part of the milk fat removed. Standards for fat content vary from 0.17% to 3.2% milk fat but the most common product contains 2% fat and is called two percent milk.

CREAM – is made by separating standard milk into skim milk and cream. This concentrated cream having about 40% milk fat is diluted with milk to obtain the different cream products:

WHIPPING CREAM – contains 35% fat. When packaged in aerosol cans it may range from 18-26% fat.

TABLE CREAM (cream) – contains no less than 18% fat and up to 32% fat.

HALF AND HALF – contains 8-16% fat and has 8-16% non-fat solids.

CEREAL CREAM (light cream) – contains 8-16% fat but is usually 10% fat by weight.

Concentrated Milks

POWDERED WHOLE MILK AND POWDERED SKIM MILK – are whole milk and skim milk respectively from which all but 3% of the water content has been removed. Most powdered milk is made by spraying it into a heated chamber where it dries almost instantly and falls as a powder ready for cooling, sifting and packaging. To produce instant skim milk powder that dissolves more readily, the milk powder is blown into a steam chamber where the minute particles form larger particles containing many tiny air spaces. Powdered whole milk has a short shelf life because the milk fat which it contains will become rancid. Powdered skim milk is more widely used because it is convenient, inexpensive, and stores well at room temperatures. Dried buttermilk is also available.

EVAPORATED MILK – is a canned milk product produced by removing about 60% of the water from homogenized whole, partly skimmed or skim milk. All evaporated milk has darker colour than the original milk because the high temperatures required for evaporation of the water and sterilization of the canned product cause a browning reaction between the milk protein and the lactose.

SWEETENED CONDENSED MILK – is a canned milk product prepared from whole milk which has been condensed to one third of its original volume.

It is thick, cream coloured and contains about 40% sugar. High temperatures of evaporation pasteurize the milk and the high sugar content acts as a preservative, making sterilization unnecessary.

Cultured Dairy Products

These products are prepared by adding bacterial cultures to pasteurized or sterilized milk. As a result the lactose is converted into lactic acid, and the casein is coagulated.

BUTTERMILK was originally a by-product of buttermaking. Today buttermilk is made by the culture method – the controlled fermentation of lactic acid and flavour-producing bacteria. The milk, a partly skimmed form, is inoculated with the culture, incubated under controlled conditions until a certain acidity is reached and then cooled quickly to 10°C. The resulting product has a characteristic tangy flavour, a smooth rich body and contains less than 2% milk fat.

SOUR CREAM is a cultured milk product containing from 10-18% milk fat by weight. It is made by the same process as buttermilk, by ripening pasteurized cream with a lactic acid culture.

YOGURT is a delicate, tangy product made from whole, partly skimmed or skim milk, with skim milk powder sometimes added to make about 16% total milk solids. Milk fat content varies but it is usually about 2%. Yogurt is made by heating the pasteurized, homogenized milk and inoculating it with acid producing bacterial cultures. If a set custard type, having a semi-solid consistency, is being made, the warm inoculated milk is put directly into consumer containers, incubated under controlled conditions and then cooled to less than 5°C.

In making the stirred type, called Swiss style, the vats of warm inoculated milk are incubated, cooled to less than 5°C and stored for up to 48 hours. It is then stirred to a smooth, cream-like consistency before being placed in consumer-sized containers. If properly refrigerated, yogurt has a storage life of 2-4 weeks. Yogurt is available plain, with flavourings, and with fruit or fruit juice added.

COTTAGE CHEESE is an uncured, soft, mild, white cheese made by adding a lactic acid producing starter, and a coagulator such as rennet, to pasteurized skim milk. The resulting curd is cut and heated to develop texture and body; the whey is removed; the curd is washed; and salt may be added. Small curd, called country or farmer's, and large curd cottage cheese are both sold either dry or creamed. The creamed contains at least 4% milk fat by mass.

Frozen Dairy Products

ICE CREAM is a popular frozen dairy product containing at least 36% total solids of which 10% is milk fat. It is made from a combination of basic ingredients including cream, whole and/or condensed milk, and/or milk solids, sugar and flavouring. A stabilizer and an emulsifier are also added to the mix which is then pasteurized, homogenized and rapidly frozen to obtain a smooth creamy product. To provide an increase in volume that is essential for a light, desirable product, air is incorporated by whipping during freezing. The packaged product is hardened at −32°C and held at −23°C to −30°C during storage and distribution.

SOFT ICE CREAM is a smooth, compact product having at least 10% milk fat, slightly more non-fat solids and less sugar than hard ice cream. The additional stabilizers and emulsifiers used, extra milk solids, whipping, and a lower serving temperature (about −8°C) all contribute to its characteristic soft texture.

ICE MILK is a frozen milk product containing at least 3% milk fat, added milk solids to a total of 33%, sugar and flavouring.

SHERBET is a tart flavoured frozen product made from a syrup and fruit juice base with fresh or dried skim milk and milk fat added to a maximum of 5% total milk solids.

Other Dairy Products
BUTTER is a dairy product made from cream which may be sweet, sour or more frequently, mildly sour. When cream is churned the fat particles cluster together and form larger masses of fat globules. These break away from the surrounding liquid, called buttermilk and form the semi-solid material, butter. Carefully controlled modern procedures of churning, washing, salting and testing preserve the distinctive flavour of butter and ensure a uniform product having minimum of 80% by mass of milk fat. Because fat soluble vitamin A remains in the milk fat when it is removed from milk, butter is an important source of this vitamin. It contains only small amounts of other vitamins and minerals.

CHEESE is a concentrated form of milk made from the solid portion of the milk, called the curd, after it is separated from the liquid portion, called whey. See page 201 for Cheese.

HOME CARE OF FLUID MILK PRODUCTS
All fluid dairy foods can be properly cared for by following these precautions:

1. Keep containers clean, covered and cold.

2. Use within a reasonable length of time.

3. Protect from sunlight and fluorescent light.

4. Once removed, do not return the unused portion to the original container.

This guide is based on these facts:

1. As the temperature of a milk product rises, bacterial growth increases rapidly forming lactic acid which characterizes souring.

2. Pasteurized milk has a longer shelf life than unpasteurized milk because the enzymes that promote fat rancidity have been inactivated and potentially dangerous bacteria destroyed.

3. Ultraviolet light destroys riboflavin which explains the use of darkened milk boxes and refrigerators.

Unopened cans of evaporated or sweetened condensed milk may be stored at room temperature but once opened, should be refrigerated. Unopened packages or envelopes of dry milk may be stored at room temperature but once reconstituted, it should be refrigerated. Dried whole milk should be kept in a moisture proof, air tight container, preferably in the refrigerator to prevent fat turning rancid.

PRINCIPLES OF MILK COOKERY

1. When milk is heated, a scum forms on the top. This milk scum consists of coagulated protein. It may be removed by skimming with a spoon but the surface will soon be covered again. A better way is to prevent its formation.

    Many recipes use scalded milk. This means that the milk has been heated to just below the boiling point, about 82°C, as indicated by bubbles which form around the edge of the pan. Past the scalding point, the tough scum which forms will hold in the steam and cause a pressure to build up. Unless the pan is carefully watched the milk will eventually break through this film and boil over the sides of the pan.

    a. Recommended procedure for scalding milk, therefore, is to use a double boiler to maintain a low heat and to cover the pan to prevent evaporation. This method also prevents scorching of the proteins which settle to the bottom, stick and scorch.

    b. If a regular saucepan is used the milk should be heated over very low heat. This method will take longer than the double boiler method but if the temperature is low enough, scorching can be avoided. The milk may be stirred occasionally. Beating with an egg beater will produce a foamy layer on top which will retard evaporation and scum formation.

    c. All cooked milk sauces should have a cover placed over the completed product until it is served.

    d. Milk pudding should be tightly covered as soon as it is removed from the heat. Individual servings will not form a scum if covered with wax paper or plastic film while they are cooling.

Summarizing: *a.* use a double boiler to scald milk.

　　　　　　b. use low heat to cook milk products.

　　　　　　c. cover thickened milk products until serving time.

2. Milk is easily curdled.

　　a. Acid foods cause milk to curdle. If an acid vegetable, such as tomatoes, is to be combined with milk it is necessary to first thicken either the milk or the tomato before combining them. In making tomato soup, the casein will be held in suspension by the flour used to thicken the white sauce and curdling will be prevented when the tomato is added later.

　　b. The tendency of milk to curdle is also reduced by the use of a low temperature for cooking the food. Scalloped potatoes cooked at a high temperature will be more likely to curdle than if a low temperature is used for a longer cooking period.

　　c. As milk becomes less fresh it is more likely to curdle when heated. The lactic acid bacteria normally found in milk can change the milk sugar into lactic acid. Milk with the higher acid content will curdle more readily.

Summarizing:

　　　　a. use fresh milk.

　　　　b. use a low temperature.

　　　　c. thicken either the milk or the acid food before combining them.

Cheese

PRODUCTION OF CHEESE

The first step in the commercial production of cheese is curd formation. A pure culture of lactic acid producing bacteria is added to the warm milk as a starter. These bacteria are allowed to grow until the milk reaches the acidity desired and the action of the coagulant *rennin*, which is used in the production of most varieties of cheese, has begun.

The soft *curd* which is separated from the *whey* and not treated any further is known as unripened cheese. Both cottage cheese and cream cheese are examples. Ripened cheeses are produced by further treatment of the curd with varying degrees of heat and pressure and also by adding special cultures of bacteria or mould. The cheese is permitted to ripen or cure under controlled conditions and will change from a tough rubbery mass to a soft, sometimes crumbly product having the desired characteristics. Factors which determine the distinctive flavour, texture, aroma and appearance of a cheese include:

1. the kind of milk used – cow, goat, sheep or other.

2. the method used to coagulate the milk – either by lactic acid, by rennin or a combination of both.

3. the way the curd is cut, cooked and formed. Most cheeses have a well known shape – round or block, large or small.

4. the type of bacteria or mould used in ripening – holes that are characteristic of some cheeses are formed by the bacteria which produce gas during the early stages of ripening while the cheese is still soft and elastic. The bluish veined appearance of certain cheese is produced by a penicillin mould which is injected into the cheese.

5. the temperature and humidity during ripening – ripening is slower at lower temperatures.

6. the length of time the cheese is aged – mild cheeses are ripened for a shorter time than sharp cheeses.

7. the amount of salt or other seasonings added – as well as affecting flavour, salt affects the rate of ripening by controlling bacterial growth.

Classification of Cheese

Cheeses are frequently classified according to their firmness and method of ripening used:

1. Soft
   unripened – cottage cheese, cream cheese
   mould-ripened – Brie, Camembert
   bacteria-ripened – Limburger

2. Semi-hard
   mould-ripened – blue cheese, Gorganzola, Roquefort, Stilton
   bacteria-ripened – Brick, Gouda, Jack, Muenster

3. Hard
   bacteria-ripened – Cheddar, Edam, Emmenthal, Gruyère, Parmesan, Provalone, Romano, Swiss

Processed Cheese is made by blending one or more natural cheeses with an emulsifier, such as sodium citrate or disodium phosphate, to make a cheese that is pliable and melts easily without becoming stringy or tough as do the cheeses from which it is made. During the manufacturing process, the selected cheese or cheeses are grated or ground, melted, pasteurized and blended with milk, water or milk solids to which may be added food colouring and seasonings or flavourings. The mixture is poured into moulds, jars or packages and is marketed in slice, block or spread form. Because the bacterial and enzyme action has been halted by heating, ripening does not continue. Processed cheese has excellent keeping qualities and usually a bland flavour.

HOME CARE OF CHEESE

Cheese is packaged in a moisture-proof material which protects the prdouct from moisture losses and limits mould growth on the surface. Once the package is opened, the cheese should be kept in a tightly covered container or wrapped in heavy waxed paper, aluminum foil or transparent plastic wrap. If left uncovered it will dry out as the water in it evaporates. The mould which may form in time is in no way harmful and may be cut off without changing the quality of the remaining cheese. Scraps of cheese may be grated and kept in a covered jar for cooking purposes. 250 grams of cheese makes approximately 500 ml of grated cheese.

Cheese should be kept in a cool place since warm temperatures cause some of the fat to melt and escape from the cheese. Soft cheese such as cream cheese or cottage cheese is more perishable than the firmer varieties. Therefore, these should be stored covered, in the refrigerator, and eaten while fresh. Ripened cheese should never be served chilled. A better flavour is evident when the cheese is neither cold or over-warm.

Cheese may be frozen successfully provided it is cut in small pieces of approximately 500 grams and measuring not more than 3 cm thick. Larger pieces take too long to freeze and tend to crumble when thawed. Wrap the cheese in aluminum foil or a heavy plastic bag, excluding as much air as possible. Cheese sold in heavy plastic wrap or a cardboard container does not need additional wrapping. Always thaw cheese in the refrigerator. If the cheese does become crumbly or mealy after freezing it can be used in salads or in cooking where texture is not important. Cream cheese and cottage cheese do not freeze well because they become watery and mealy.

PRINCIPLES OF CHEESE COOKERY

1. Use a low heat. Cheese is a protein food and like all other proteins, it is toughened by high heat. Tough proteins are more difficult to digest. All cheese dishes should be cooked at low temperatures, whether the dish is a simple cheese sauce, a soufflé or a cheesecake. Cheese should be melted in a double boiler or chafing dish, rather than over direct heat. To oven poach means to place the cheese dish in a pan of hot water and bake it in a moderate oven until a knife, inserted in the centre, comes out clean. This method is recommended for any uncooked mixture of eggs, cheese and milk.

2. Do not overcook. When cheese is melted it is cooked. Overcooking will produce the same toughening effect as cooking with too high a heat. Cheese will mix more evenly and quickly with other ingredients if it is first grated or as with cottage or cream cheese, sieved. Cheese dishes made with cooked foods should be baked in a moderate oven only long enough to thoroughly heat the mixture.

Home Production of Yogurt

Yogurt is produced commercially, as defined on page 197, by introducing a bacterial culture to the milk. Although buttermilk was originally a by-product of churning butter it is today a skim milk product fermented by the streptococcus lactic bacteria. Yogurt can be prepared at home from milk in a similar way by introduction of a yogurt culture which contains the suitable bacteria.

An explanation of the yogurt recipe on page 486 follows. Yogurt is usually made from 2% milk from which small amounts of moisture have been evaporated. This reduction process is achieved by gently boiling the milk. This also ensures sterilization of the milk in preparation for the addition of the culture or "maya" as it is called in Greece and Turkey where yogurt is consumed in considerable amounts and frequently as a breakfast food.

During fermentation yogurt acquires an acidic tangy flavour and becomes custard-like in consistency. The extent of acidity of the yogurt is directly related to the incubation period. For a more delicate, less acid yogurt the incubation period could be reduced to 4 or 5 hours, followed immediately by refrigeration. For a more piquant tangy yogurt an incubation period of up to 10 hours is allowed.

The thickness of the yogurt can also be controlled. If a thick yogurt is desired, skimmed milk powder can be added to the milk before it is heated, then simmering, with constant stirring, can be continued for 5-10 minutes to evaporate more water.

Despite the claims of historians through the ages, and health enthusiasts of today, yogurt is not a cure for all ills nor is it the long sought after fountain of youth. Being a milk product it contains the original nutrients of that food, namely calcium, riboflavin, and protein. Its kilojoule count increases with the addition of milk solids, sweeteners and fruit.

Yogurt is an exciting and different means of introducing milk to the diets of people of all ages. It can be used as a substitute for sour cream or buttermilk in almost all recipes, and in addition there is enormous scope for its use as a food unique in itself. Here are some suggested uses:

1. Yogurt with baked potato – Mix together 50 ml crumbled blue cheese, 15 ml chopped chives and 125 ml yogurt. This topping is a good protein source and has a much lower kilojoule count than sour cream.
2. Yogurt French Dressing – Combine 250 ml plain yogurt with 125 ml French dressing and serve over lettuce wedges.
3. Fruit Shake – Combine in a blender 175 ml of fruit yogurt, 175 ml milk and 500 ml vanilla ice cream.
4. Onion Dip – Combine 500 ml yogurt with 1 envelope onion soup mix. Serve with potato chips or raw vegetables.
5. Yogurt Popsicle – Combine 375 ml yogurt with 200 ml frozen orange juice concentrate. Pour into containers, insert sticks and freeze.

Meat

The term meat refers to the flesh and some of the internal organs of animals and birds. Birds, called poultry, have been separated from this section and are discussed in Poultry. Poultry includes chickens, turkeys, ducks and geese. Game meat (deer, moose, elk, bear, wild sheep, mountain goat) and game birds (grouse, pheasant, partridge and ducks) are included in Game. Fish and Shellfish are another section.

Domestic meats used in this country are beef, veal, pork, lamb and mutton. Here is a description of each kind:

1. Beef is the flesh of mature cattle that are raised for meat. The lean is a rich red colour varying from light to dark. Darker red meat may result from a longer hanging time or may have come from an older animal. Extended counter life of packaged meat can also result in darker coloured meat. The meat will be firm, velvety and fine grained with streaks of fat through it. The outside fat is firm and white or creamy white. Bones are hard with very little hollow portions. They will be greyish white in older animals, red in young animals. Baby beef, although not in great supply, is produced from calves specially fed to produce finished beef at ten to twelve months. Its colour is bright pink, lighter than the typical beef colour, with a light covering of fat.

2. Veal is the flesh of young cattle of the dairy or beef type three to twelve weeks old. Since veal comes from animals of different maturity and weight, cuts vary in size and the meat varies in colour. The younger animals yield greyish pink flesh; the older ones a pinkish brown meat. There is very little fat in the meat and what little covers the surface may be white, creamy white or tinged with pink. Bones are soft and porous and of a reddish colour since they are not fully developed.

3. Pork is the flesh of hogs which is sold fresh, cured or smoked. The lean varies in colour from light grey pink to a deeper rose in the older animals and is well marbled with fat. The outer fat covering should be firm and white. Bones will be porous and slightly pink in colour.

4. Lamb is the flesh of young sheep up to 14 months of age. The colour of the lean meat varies with age from light to dark pink. Lamb fat is firm, smooth and creamy white or slightly pink in colour. Bones are small and porous with a reddish tinge. Although available throughout

the year, Canadian lamb is most plentiful and reasonably priced from September to December. "Spring lamb" is a term referring to meat from young lambs slaughtered at ages ranging from three to five months.

5.   Mutton is the flesh of sheep more than 14 months old. The meat varies from light to dark red and has more fat than lamb. Mutton fat is also more brittle and is white in colour.

STRUCTURE OF MEAT

Most cuts of meat consist of three easily identified parts; the bone, the fat and the lean. The lean part is the most complicated in its structure but a thorough understanding of its makeup will simplify learning how to cook meat.

Bone

Bones are the framework of the animal and have a considerable bearing on the grading of meat. The shape of the bone found in a cut of meat indicates from which part of the animal the meat was taken, its size indicates the age and the size of the animal and in some cases the type of animal. The characteristics of the bone, such as the degree of ossification making it soft or hard and the colour, white or pink, help to determine the age of the animal.

Fat

Good quality meat animals are covered with a thick layer of fat just under the skin referred to as the *finish*. Some animals, pork for example, have more external fat than others; older animals (beef) have more finish than younger ones (veal). Certain cuts of meat also have visible fat distributed between the muscles.

In addition to this visible fat the meat contains fat cells which can be seen only with a microscope. These cells are entangled in the network of the tissues which make up the lean. Meat with a good even distribution of fat throughout the lean is said to be well *marbled*. Marbling is desirable for the contribution it makes to the juiciness, tenderness and flavour of the meat.

The amount of fat contributed to the diet by a serving of meat depends not only on the kind of meat it is but also on the amount of trimming done and the method of cooking used. Fat contributes to the kilojoule count of meat and therefore provides energy. Pure fat yields twice the kilojoules as does the same weight of carbohydrate or protein. The body digests fat slowly which explains why fatty foods have a good "staying power" and keep a person from being hungry for a longer time than a carbohydrate food such as candy.

Lean

This part is the muscle of meat. Muscle is composed of bundles of *muscle fibres* that are held together by *connective tissue*. Each bundle of muscle fibres is made up of hollow spindle-shaped cells which contain the *extractives* that give meat its characteristic flavour. *Fat cells* are distributed throughout.

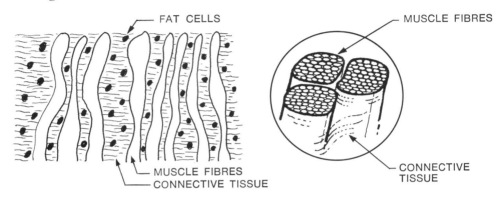

FAT CELLS

MUSCLE FIBRES

MUSCLE FIBRES
CONNECTIVE TISSUE

CONNECTIVE TISSUE

Longitudinal Section of a Muscle Bundle

Structure of Meat

When meat is cooked, fat melts and the protein of the muscle tissue coagulates. However, connective tissue is made up of a different protein than muscle tissue. There are actually two kinds of connective tissue fibres. The amount and kind of connective tissue determines the tenderness of the meat.

1. Elastin is a yellow coloured protein fibre which is tough and strong. It is found mainly in the tendons of the muscles. Since elastin is extremely resistant to application of heat or acids, no significant changes occur when the meat is cooked. Most of it is therefore cut away when the meat is trimmed before cooking.

2. Collagen is white coloured. These fibres are tough and elastic but will be converted into gelatin given the right conditions which are: low temperature, long cooking and the presence of water. The time required for conversion to gelatin to take place depends upon the thickness of the tissue, acidity of the liquid, temperature of cooking and the size of the piece of meat. Eventually, heating softens the collagen allowing the bundles of muscle fibres to fall apart. At this point, the meat will be tender.

From this description of elastin and collagen an understanding of tough and tender meat is possible. The relative proportions of these two proteins in meat cuts have significance in the tenderizing accomplished during the cooking process.

Cuts of meat in which collagen predominates over elastin become tender upon cooking.

Cuts containing much elastin can only be made palatable by grinding into hamburger or by careful trimming. Only meat that has little of either connective tissue is suitable for hot temperatures and dry cooking methods.

FOOD VALUE OF MEAT

All meat is classed as a protein food but among the various types of meat there are differences in the amounts of other nutrients present. These are the most important contributions meat makes:

1. **Protein**

   Meat contains several kinds of protein including actin and myosin which are of a high quality since they contain all of the essential amino acids. They are called complete proteins and are essential to the growth and repair of body tissues. Collagen of the connective tissue which is converted to gelatin upon cooking, becomes available to the body as an incomplete protein because it lacks some of the essential amino acids. Refer to the Nutrition unit for details on the importance and different kinds of protein.

2. **Fat**

   The marbling fat of meat varies with the type, cut, location and age of the animal. It is this fat which contains the fat soluble vitamin A. Much of the visible exterior fat is generally removed from the cut before it is cooked, especially if the extra kilojoules are not wanted. In addition to its energy value, fat contributes to the flavour, palatibility and tenderness of the meat.

3. **Vitamins**

   The vitamins in lean meat are chiefly those of the B group, particularly riboflavin. Lean pork, bacon and ham are rich sources of thiamine, probably due to a difference in the feed given pigs, which is not the same as that of cows and sheep who feed on grass. Similarly the marbling fat contains traces of vitamin A, especially where grass is part of the animal's diet. Liver usually contains a useful amount of vitamin A. Other organ meats contain valuable amounts of B vitamins.

4. **Minerals**

   The minerals obtained from meat in significant amounts are phosphorus, copper and iron. Liver is an especially good concentrated source of iron. Other organ meats are valuable for the minerals they supply. Together with copper, iron helps produce and maintain the red blood cells. The importance of phosphorus is related to the oxidation of foods in the body cells and to the building of bones and teeth.

MEAT INSPECTION

Meat inspection is a service provided by the Health of Animals Branch, Canada Department of Agriculture. Any meat plant in Canada that applies and meets the requirements may receive inspection service. Meat destined for interprovincial, foreign or import trade must be inspected by Federal Government inspectors. Meat sold within the province in which it is produced may, or may not, be federally inspected. This depends on whether the area is one included by the Meat Inspection Act or, if not, by a local by-law under the Municipal Act. Persons buying meat which has not been health inspected take a calculated health risk.

All animals entering inspected plants are examined by Federal veterinarians before and after slaughter to determine whether or not the animal is fit for human consumption. Diseased or otherwise unwholesome meat is condemned. Once the carcass has been inspected and passed, it is stamped, usually on each wholesale section, with a health inspection stamp. The stamp does not indicate quality or grade of the meat but indicates only that it is fit for human consumption.

The stamp is brown in colour and made of a harmless vegetable dye so that it need not be cut off before cooking. Round shaped, it bears a crown in the centre and around the crown, the words "Canada Approved" or "Canada", plus the registered number of the plant.

Meat inspection is also carried out in the processing departments of the meat packing plants. Meat used in the making of sausage, wieners, prepared canned meat, etc., is also inspected. The same official Inspection Legend is stamped, tagged or labelled on these foods.

Standards have been established and are administered by the Health Protection Branch, Health and Welfare Canada, as to what spices, preservatives and stabilizers are permitted in prepared meat products such as sausage and bologna. The amount of meat binder and moisture content is specified and, in the case of hamburger, the kind of meat and the fat content as well.

MEAT GRADING

Beef was the first meat to be generally purchased by grade in Canada. A discussion of these grades follows this section. Beef grading is compulsory if the product is to be shipped between provinces, or exported. Each province establishes whether or not grading will be compulsory within its boundaries.

The national grades established for veal are little used. Lamb and mutton carcasses may be officially graded and ribbon branded upon request. This grading service is primarily used as a basis of settlement between packer and producer.

Hog standards are based on the mass and amount of fat on the carcass. Age of the animal is not a factor. Hog grades are used as a basis of settlement between the producer and packer but no attempt has been made to carry these grades through to the consumer. Hog carcasses are not suited to branding for consumer identification as are beef, veal and lamb for these reasons:

a. The grade identification brands, which must be placed on the outside surface of the carcass, are removed when the carcass is broken down into pork cuts since most of the external surface (skin and fat) is then removed.
b. Many pork cuts are processed and during this step (for example, curing) the grade brand would be removed or made unrecognizable.
c. All cuts from a top grade hog do not make top grade pork products.

BEEF GRADING

Once the Health Inspector has determined that the beef animal was healthy and the meat wholesome, the Federal Grader from the Livestock Division of Agriculture Canada makes an assessment. In determining the grade to be assigned to the beef carcass three factors are considered:

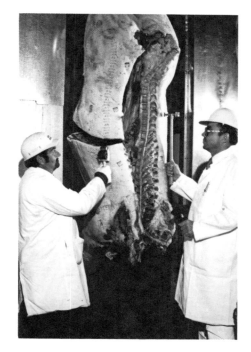

a. Age – The age of the animal affects the quality of the beef – the older the animal, the less likely the carcass will produce tender cuts of beef. By observing the degree of hardening of the cartilage the grader determines the maturity of the animal.
b. Quality – Based on potential for cooking and eating satisfaction, an ideal carcass has lean meat that is bright red, firm and fine grained in texture with some marbling and a firm, white fat

cover. The grader checks the colour, texture and firmness of the fat and the lean and assigns a grade which indicates how close the carcass comes to the ideal.

c.   Meat Yield — The grader takes a fat measurement between the 11th and 12th ribs. Research has shown that there is a relationship between the amount of fat covering on the carcass and the meat yield. The fat measurement, then, indicates the proportion of lean meat in the carcass and, therefore, the yield of the saleable beef.

When the grader from Canada Department of Agriculture has assessed the carcass on the basis of age, quality and meat yield, a brown square mark is placed indicating the grade on the main wholesale cuts. Then under supervision, a ribbon-like mark is applied so that the ribbon brand appears on each wholesale cut. The colour of the marking indicates the grade: Canada A is red; Canada B is blue; Canada C is brown; and Canada D and E are black. Look for this ribbon brand when you buy beef. It is the consumer's guide to quality.

GRADES OF BEEF

Canada Grade A (red)

Highest quality young beef and accounts for about 70% of all beef produced in Canada. The meat is bright red, firm and fine grained with at least slight marbling. The external fat layer is firm and white and extends well over the carcass but may be thinner on the hips and chucks. Depending on the amount of fat covering, this grade is subdivided into four categories: A-1, having the least amount of fat to A-4, having the greatest fat content. A-1 and A-2 are most commonly sold over retail counters since they have a higher retail yield.

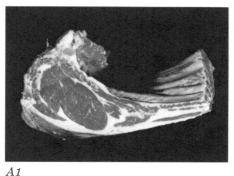

A1

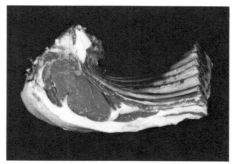

A2

FAT LEVELS

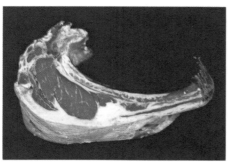

A3

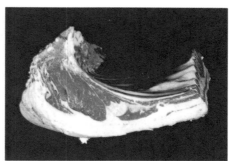

A4

Canada Grade B (blue)

Lower quality beef from young animals and accounts for only about 4% of all beef graded. The lean meat ranges from bright red to medium-dark red. It is moderately firm and slightly coarse with marbling not necessary. The white to pale yellow fat may be slightly soft and somewhat lacking on the exterior surface. B-grade is also subdivided into four levels depending on the fat cover.

Canada Grade C (brown)

Beef from intermediate aged animals or young animals not meeting the quality standards for Grade A or B. Usually processed or sold to butcher trade this grade accounts for about 4.5% of the beef graded. It is subdivided into Class 1 and 2, depending upon quality characteristics, muscling standards and fat levels.

Canada Grade D (black)

Beef from mature females and steers and accounts for about 20% of all beef graded. It is usually processed into canned meat or hamburger. Grade D is divided into Class 1 to 4 on basis of muscling and fat level.

Canada Grade E (black)

From mature male animals. It is processed and accounts for 1.5% of all graded beef.

AGING OR RIPENING OF MEAT

After the animal is butchered and skinned, inspected and graded it is allowed to age to produce a tender meat. This process involves holding the carcass or certain cuts in cold storage at constant temperatures of 1°C to 3°C. The period of aging depends on the type, age and weight of the animal and may extend for as little as 3 days or up to 2 weeks. Special beef cuts may be held longer.

To be aged successfully, the meat must have a good fat covering to prevent evaporation and deterioration. Aged meat commands a higher price because of the extra time and handling necessary and the shrinkage involved. Fresh pork does not improve with aging since the fat of pork has a tendency to become rancid. Veal is unsuitable for aging because it does not have enough external fat.

When the animal is slaughtered a condition of rigor mortis sets in during which the muscle proteins coagulate and the fat solidifies. In this condition the carcass is stiff and the meat is very tough. After about 24 hours rigor passes and the muscles begin to soften. Aging is the softening of the muscle fibres caused by the enzymes present naturally in the meat. Acids are formed which improve the flavour and help to break down the connective tissue. In this way, the meat becomes more tender. During the aging period evaporation of moisture occurs so that there is less shrinkage when the meat is cooked.

Another method of achieving tender meat has been developed. A few minutes before slaughter a selected enzyme, usually *papain*, is injected into the jugular vein of the animal. The enzyme is distributed throughout the animal's body by its circulatory system causing tenderizing of all cuts. Meat tenderized in this way is usually sold under special brand names.

METHODS FOR TENDERIZING MEAT

1. Cooking by a moist heat method. Moisture is needed with the heat to soften the large proportion of collagen in tough meat.
2. Pressure cooking. This is also a moist heat method but with the application of pressure the cooking time needed for the collagen to convert to gelatin is greatly reduced.
3. Pounding. This breaks up the connective tissue thereby changing the character of the cut of the meat before it is cooked.
4. Cutting in some way; for example: chopping, dicing, scoring and grinding. These methods cut the connective tissue to change the nature of the meat. Grinding is the only effective way to make elastin edible.

5. Adding a meat tenderizer. This is sprinkled on the surface of the meat before it is cooked. The surface should be moistened and pricked with a fork to allow deeper penetration of the tenderizer. Meat tenderizer contains a protein splitting enzyme. The one most commonly used, *papain,* is extracted from a tropical tree, the papaya.

6. Adding an acid substance, for example: vinegar, lemon, tomatoes, sour cream. Acids assist in softening the collagen.

OBJECTIVES OF COOKING MEAT

1. To make it more palatable. Meat is made more flavourful and juicy by cooking. (Steak Tartare is minced beef mixed with egg and seasonings and served raw.)

2. To make its appearance more appetizing. Colour changes that occur during cooking and the sauces and garnishes used accomplish this objective.

3. To tenderize it, especially the less tender cuts. See above for methods used.

4. To make it easier to digest.

5. To destroy harmful organisms. It is important that the parasite, *trichinae,* that may be found in pork, be destroyed.

FACTORS INFLUENCING THE TENDERNESS OF MEAT

1. Location of the cut on the carcass

Some parts of the animal are exercised more than others. The muscles in these well exercised areas are stronger and tougher and have more connective tissue than muscles from the other parts of the body which have less work to do. The cuts taken from the more heavily exercised parts are more flavourful due to a heavier concentration of extractives.

2. Age of the animal

A young animal has little connective tissue since its muscles have not been used for long. The flesh of older animals is made up of thick, long muscle fibres having a large amount of connective tissue and gristle. The tenderest meat is from young animals with thinner, shorter fibres, less connective tissue and less gristle.

3. Period of Aging of the Meat

During aging the connective tissues are softened by the action of the enzymes found in the meat. The length of time usually depends upon the type and age of the animal but especially in the case of beef, long aging time produces a more tender meat which shrinks less when cooked.

PRINCIPLES OF MEAT COOKERY

If the objectives of cooking meat are to be met, certain changes in the structure of the meat must occur. All meat cookery is based upon the changes which take place as the meat progresses from the raw to the cooked state.

1. **Colour**

    Heat changes the haemoglobin, which accounts for the red colour of raw meat, to hemin, which is brown. The interior of the meat changes colour according to the extent of heat penetration. A brown colour is reached between 70°C and 85°C depending upon the type of meat being cooked. Hence, a meat thermometer will register "rare" when the interior of the beef roast reachs 60°C and "medium" when it registers 70°C. Pork requires an internal temperature of 85°C to be well cooked.

2. **Tenderness**

    The principal protein of tender meat is that found in the muscle fibre and called myosin. Small amounts of collagen associated with the connective tissue may also be present. Because myosin requires only a little cooking to make it palatable, these cuts may be cooked by dry heat methods in a comparatively short time. When cooked too long, the muscle fibre becomes toughened. This explains why rib or loin steaks containing only small amounts of connective tissue are less tender when broiled to the well done stage than if broiled to the rare stage.

    Tougher cuts of meat contain large amounts of the collagen found in fully developed muscle fibre. This type of protein is softened by moisture or one of the other methods of tenderizing meat just listed.

3. **Flavour**

    The outside layers of meat cooked by dry heat methods are more flavourful because the juices which are squeezed out of the meat evaporate on the surface. These extractives are also found as brown particles on the roasting pan or broiler. Hence, gravy making involves stirring down these bits into the gravy liquid in order to obtain full flavour.

    The tenderness obtained by moist heat methods is achieved with some sacrifice of flavour extractives lost in the liquid. Therefore, some of these methods employ a browning or searing step (which improves the flavour) before the moisture is added. Lost juices are utilized in the gravy or sauce.

4. **Shrinkage**

    As the proteins of the muscle fibres and its connective tissue coagulate, meat juices are squeezed out of the muscle cells. Heating of the meat also causes the fat to melt and this collects in the roasting pan or cooking water. Much research and testing has shown that two factors are important in controlling cooking losses:

a. The higher the cooking temperature, the greater the shrinkage. The best temperature for oven roasting has been found to be 150°C to 160°C.

b. The higher the internal temperature when the meat is taken from the heat, the greater the shrinkage. Therefore, a "well" done roast registering 75°C on a meat thermometer will be more shrunken than a "medium" one with internal temperature of 70°C.

5. **Food Value**

The nutritive value of meat is affected to some extent by cooking. Ways to retain maximum food value may be summarized:

a. As previously stated, less juices are lost at a low temperature.

b. Since the B-vitamins are water soluble, loss of these nutrients from the meat is greater in moist heat than in dry heat. If, however, the cooking liquid is used in some way a large percentage of this loss will be salvaged.

c. When some of the extractives dry on the surface of the meat, as in broiling or other dry heat methods, the thiamine found in these extractives will be destroyed by the high heat. Some thiamine will be retained if the meat is cooked slowly in liquid.

Methods of Cooking Meat

A. DRY HEAT METHODS

1. Oven Roasting

Meat is cooked in an uncovered pan in the oven with no water added during cooking. Meat should be placed fat side up. A piece of fat or several bacon strips may be added if the roast is a lean one. Greasing of the pan and the rack will simplify later cleanup.

A meat thermometer, when used, should be inserted to the centre of the thickest part of the roast. It should not rest on bone nor should the tip touch a fatty seam in the meat.

The time required for roasting depends upon:

a. Temperature of the meat at beginning of the cooking period. A roast at refrigerator temperature takes more time than one at room temperature. A roast that goes into the oven frozen takes half again as long as a thawed one.

b. Cooking temperature used. The least shrinkage results from an oven temperature between 150°C to 160°C.

c. Stage of cooking desired. Personal preference dictates whether the roast is "medium" or "rare". A meat thermometer is the best indicator of internal temperature.

d. Size of the roast. The shape will be important, too; i.e., the distance from the surface of the thickest part.

e. Composition of the meat; i.e., amount of fat, bone and lean. A fat roast takes more time; a bony one less time.

Pork Loin Roast

Broiled Shish-kabob

2. Broiling

The meat is cooked by placing it on a rack and exposing it to some type of direct heat. With the regulator at "broil" setting, the meat is adjusted so that it is 5-15 cm from the heat source which would be the electric element or gas flame.

The distance from the heat will vary with the type of meat, its thickness and the amount of cooking desired. A "rare" steak would be cooked close to the heat for a short time, well cooked lamb chops would be placed farther from the heat and cooked longer, unthawed steaks would be first placed a distance from the heat until thawed, then moved closer for completion of the cooking.

After one side has browned, it should be seasoned, then turned and the other side browned. Excess fat should be trimmed to prevent burning and oven spattering. Pork and veal do not broil well. The instruction book that comes with every range should be consulted but as a general rule when using an electric range the oven is left partly opened; with a gas range the oven door is closed.

3.   Barbecuing

The meat is cooked over hot coals instead of using a gas or electric heat source. This method gives a characteristic flavour of the wood or charcoal used and often also of the coating or basting sauce placed on the meat to prevent it from drying or burning.

4.   Pan Broiling

The meat is cooked in a heavy pan or griddle using a surface element and no moisture or added fat. As the meat cooks, the accumulated fat must be poured off for if it is left the meat will fry, not broil.

B. MOIST HEAT METHODS

1.   Pot Roasting

The meat is first browned or "seared" on all sides in a hot pan or hot fat. Then about 250 ml water or other liquid and seasonings are added. The pan is covered and the meat allowed to simmer until tender. Vegetables may be added to the liquid, allowing only enough time to cook them before the meat is served. A pot roast may also be cooked in the oven in a heavy covered pan or Dutch oven.

2.   Braising

The meat is first browned in hot fat, then seasonings are added and a small amount of liquid. The pan is covered and the temperature turned low. Meat simmers for several hours until tender, then juices are thickened before serving.

3. Pressure Cooking

This method is comparable to braising. Meat, often with vegetables and a sauce, are cooked in the pressure cooker according to manufacturer's instructions. Meats are all cooked at 105 kilopascals pressure. This is a much quicker method than braising since the steam is under pressure.

4. Boiling

Meat is usually not browned first but a large amount of water is added and meat, usually with bones, is allowed to simmer until tender.

5. Stewing

Meat is cut in uniform pieces, dredged in flour, browned in hot fat and seasoned. Then only enough liquid is added to cover meat, the pan is covered and meat simmers until tender (2-3 hours). Vegetables are usually added before end of cooking period and gravy is thickened further with a flour and water paste.

6. Clay Pot Cooking

The moist cooking of food by this method is dependent upon water being absorbed into the pores of the clay pot before any food is added. This moisture, in the form of steam, is gradually released to the food as cooking proceeds. For this reason partially glazed pots require the addition of slightly more water to the food than unglazed ones. In either case, only a little water need be added to the food after it is arranged in the pot and then the tight-fitting lid is set in place. Cooking temperatures, whether from an oven or a separate thermostatically controlled element, are very low (below simmer) and cooking times are correspondingly lengthy. Since there are several different kinds of clay pots available, follow the manufacturer's instructions carefully.

C. FRYING METHODS

1. Pan Frying

Meat is cooked in a small amount of fat or the fat from the meat is allowed to accumulate. The pan is not covered; meat is cooked until both sides are browned and meat is cooked through.

2. Sautéing

Meat and/or vegetables are cooked in a small amount of fat or oil in a covered pan which allows steam to form.

3. Deep Fat Frying

Meat is completely immersed in hot fat, 150°C to 180°C. Usually some coating agents such as egg and crumbs or batter is used to cover meat first and prevent penetration of fat into meat. This coating will protect a protein rich food from the toughening effect of the intense heat.

D. OTHER METHODS

1. Rotisserie Cooking

This method is suitable for cooking tender meat that is of a size and shape that can be placed on a spit and rotated. Meats cooked this way are more moist than when oven roasted for the juices are held within the meat by the rotating motion. Follow instructions provided with the rotisserie equipment which may be a separate appliance, or a spit attachment for the oven or barbecue.

2. Microwave Cooking

The principle involved in microwave cooking is different from any other method. The electronic oven uses high frequency electric waves produced by a magnetron. These microwaves are radiated to the centre of the oven where they agitate the molecules of the food and cause them to heat. Unlike conventional methods where the food reaches the highest temperature on the outside first and turns brown, in microwave cooking the food cooks from within and the time is too short for the outside surfaces to brown. Browning may be achieved by a brief exposure to a conventional broiling element.

The principal advantage of microwave cooking is its speed. Because the magnetron gives off a fixed amount of energy the amount of food cooked is an important factor to the time required. Where one item might require three minutes to cook, two items of the same size would require six minutes. Hence, an electronic oven is most valuable in cooking individual servings, to defrost small items or to reheat foods.

There are disadvantages of using this method to cook meat. The cooking tends to be uneven because the microwave energy does not penetrate very deeply. Also, the different materials within a food absorb microwave energy at vastly different rates. For example, fat is heated four times faster than lean meat; marrow heats faster than the bone surrounding it.

Certain precautions are important to use of the electronic oven. These will be outlined in the manual which accompanies the appliance.

FORMS OF MEAT AVAILABLE

1.   Fresh

This includes meat from all the different types of meat animals as well as the organ meats. Fresh meat has undergone no special treatment except for a period of aging in cooling rooms as required to make that particular type of meat tender.

2.   Cured

This is fresh meat that has been treated with a mixture of salt, sugar, spices and other chemicals. Originally used as a preservative, the curing solution, called the pickle, is now used chiefly to change the flavour and colour of the meat with improvement of keeping qualities a secondary result. Surface treatments where the chemicals are rubbed on dry are for thin cuts such as bacon. Larger cuts may be immersed in the solution but more often hams and other large pieces are injected with solution so that it reaches all parts of the meat rapidly before spoilage can occur.

3.   Smoked

Either fresh or cured meat may be smoked by exposing the surface to a heavy concentration of wood smoke. The smoke dries out the surface of the meat and deposits various chemicals that contribute flavour and kill bacteria. If the smokehouse is kept hot, the meat may become partially or wholly cooked during the process. The smoked surface layer helps protect against spoilage until the meat is cut.

4.   Frozen

Frozen meat is available either in the uncooked or cooked form, often in combination with other foods as partially prepared and ready-to-eat foods. Frozen meat should be kept frozen until ready to be thawed for use. It may be cooked from the frozen state but will require additional time. Thawed meat should never be refrozen but it may be cooked and then frozen. This becomes especially important to the consumer buying meat for the freezer since it is not uncommon to find on many counters meat which has been frozen and thawed. See Food Preservation section for freezing meat and cooking frozen meat.

5.   Freeze-Dried

A number of products now on the market use freeze drying to preserve meat. The chicken or beef pieces in dehydrated soups and meat bits in sauce mixes are kinds with which the homemaker is familiar. Other products are available to the commercial food establishments. Large pieces of meat, such as roasts and whole chickens cannot be satisfactorily freeze dried.

SELECTION OF MEAT BY BONE SHAPE

The shape of the bone in a cut of meat can be used as a guide to indicate a tender or less tender cut. Pictured below are familiar bone shapes. These can help you identify a cut of meat and predict how tender or tough it is likely to be.

Name of Bone

| T-bone | rib bone | wedge bone | round bone | blade bone |

BEEF CUTS

| Porterhouse Steak | Club Steak | Sirloin Steak | Round Steak | Chuck Roast |

T-bone steak	rib steak	sirloin steak	round steak	chuck steak
Porterhouse steak	rib roast	sirloin roast	shoulder steak	chuck roast
	club steak	top sirloin steak	chuck steak	
			chuck roast	

PORK CUTS

| Loin Chop | Rib Chop | Loin End Roast | Centre Ham Slice | Boston Butt |

loin chop	rib chop		shoulder steak	boston butt roast
centre cut loin roast	centre cut loin roast		fresh picnic	shoulder steak
			fresh ham	blade loin roast
			shoulder roast	
			smoked ham	
			ham slice	
			smoked picnic	

LAMB CUTS

| Loin Chop | Rib Chop | Sirloin Chop | Leg of Lamb | Blade Chop |

loin chop	rib chop		leg roast	blade bone chop
loin roast	rib roast		leg steak	shoulder roast
	"rack of lamb"		round bone chop	saratoga chop
			shoulder roast	

BUYING OF MEAT

Several factors contribute to the price of various cuts of meat.

1. Supply and demand — If all beef was the same price most people would choose steak leaving the tough cuts behind.

2. Approximately two thirds of the beef carcass consists of tougher cuts. In order to sell hamburger at a lower price, a butcher who pays by the kilogram for the whole carcass must charge more for the tender cuts.

3. Considerable amounts of the carcass which a butcher buys are waste (bone, fat, gristle).

AMOUNT OF MEAT TO BUY

The number of servings you can obtain from the package of meat you bring home depends upon the amount of bone, fat and gristle in it. The size of servings expected and any cooking losses need to be taken into account. Your skill in cooking and any meat extenders used will also have an effect. For the *average* serving allow the following:

Ground meat	100-150 g
Stew meat (boneless)	150 g
Braising meat (bone in)	250 g
Chops	150-250 g
Steaks	150-250 g
Roasts (bone in)	150-250 g
Roasts (boneless)	100-150 g

CHOOSING MEAT CUTS

An understanding of the structure of the meat animal is helpful when determining the part from which the cut came. You will remember that cuts from seldom exercised areas such as the rib and loin sections will be naturally tender. Cuts from the heavily exercised areas will be tough and require slow cooking in moist heat to soften the connective tissues.

Always compare prices and use the less expensive tough cuts frequently. They have the same nutritive value and sometimes have superior flavour to the expensive, more tender cuts. The secret to serving tender meat is in using the proper cooking method for the meat you have selected.

A careful study of the meat charts shows that there are many more tough cuts than tender cuts from any meat animal. This is a contributing factor to the higher cost of tender cuts. The greater demand for tender cuts also increases their price. Therefore, one can expect to pay more for a standing rib roast than for the same weight of blade roast.

EXTENDING THE MEAT PURCHASED

A family that spends one quarter of its food dollar on meat alone, not including the amount spent on fish, poultry and eggs, runs the risk of spending too little on milk, fruit, vegetables and other essential foods. Such a high expenditure on meat may be justified if there is a generous food allowance but when the income is low, nutritional deficiencies can develop.

When the money available for meat is limited, cuts must of necessity be carefully selected, the meat used sparingly and its flavour extended by combining it with other foods. Here are some suggestions for using some of the more common meat extenders:

1. **Dressing**
   Stuffed flank steak, rolled round steak, stuffed pork roast.

2. **Cereal**
   This can be used in any ground meat mixture in place of bread crumbs and provide greater food value. Rolled oats in meat loaf, wheat germ in meatballs, cereal crumbs to coat croquettes.

3. **Dough**
   Pie crust, bread dough, pizza, biscuit meat roll, meat pies, dumplings with stew, biscuits.

4. **Beans**
   Many good casserole recipes are developed using a small amount of meat for flavour and complete protein, with the beans or other legumes to supply incomplete protein, and bulk. Examples are chili con carne, baked beans.

APPROXIMATE YIELD FROM CANADA A1 SIDE (135 kilograms)

FRONT QUARTER   PERCENT OF SIDE

RIB	prime rib roast, rolled rib roast braising ribs	8.5
PLATE	rolled plate or rolled brisket ground beef, stew meat	3.8
CHUCK	short rib roast, cross rib roast chuck roast, stew meat, ground beef	20.4
SHANK	shank meat, ground beef stewing meat	5.0

TOTAL USABLE MEAT CUTS FROM FRONT   37.7 ⎫
Fat Waste   6.6 ⎬ 51.1%
Bone Waste   6.2 ⎪
Shrinkage   .6 ⎭

HIND QUARTER

HIP	rump roasts, round steak stew meat, ground beef	15.7
LOIN	sirloin tip, sirloin steaks porterhouse steaks, T-bone steaks wing or club steaks, stewing beef ground beef	15.8
FLANK		3.6

TOTAL USABLE MEAT CUTS FROM HIND   35.1 ⎫
Fat Waste   7.0 ⎬ 48.9%
Bone Waste   6.3 ⎪
Shrinkage   .5 ⎭

                                                                    ————
                                                                    100%

BUYING BEEF FOR THE FREEZER

Based on an average side weighing 135 kilograms, the saleable meat of a Canada A or A2 side of beef is approximately 99 kilograms or about 73 percent of the total side mass. The other 36 kilograms, which is about 27 percent, is lost in fat, bones and cutting shrinkage.

The front quarter yields some good roasts but has a higher proportion of less tender cuts. The cost per kilogram will be less than that quoted for a side. A hind quarter contains a higher proportion of the more tender cuts and is therefore priced higher than a whole side. Study the beef chart on page 229 and the following table to know what to expect in meat yield from a side or a front or hind quarter of beef.

Before deciding to purchase a side of beef or a quarter of beef for the freezer, consider these points:

1. The family unit. How many persons are being served? How much beef will they eat in six months, the optimum storage time? Do they like all cuts of beef or do they insist upon steaks and tender roasts? Is there time and cooking skill available to supervise proper cooking of the less tender cuts?

2. Freezer space. Approximately 0.3 cubic metres is required to hold a 135 kilogram side of beef. Consider also the cost of freezer purchase and/or maintenance or the cost of locker rental.

3. The price of meat. You will pay for the mass of the side or the quarter before it is cut and the bone and fat is trimmed away. This means that the actual price per kilogram of meat you put in the freezer is higher than the price you were quoted. The cost of cutting, wrapping and freezing may or may not be included in the quoted price. Also remember that this final price is calculated after waste and handling has been considered, includes all the cuts, both tender and less tender. Hamburger and steak cost the same when you buy this way!

Principal advantages are these:

1. You can take advantage of price fluctuations caused by the amount of meat available and consumer demand.

2. You can get good, consistent quality beef.

3. The cuts are tailored to the family unit if you give the butcher appropriate specifications: how big the roasts, how thick the steaks, how much ground beef in a package, how much fat to trim, bone in or out.

4. If you find there is no money saved, remember you are probably eating more and better beef.

HOME STORAGE OF MEAT

Meat is highly perishable and should be refrigerated or frozen immediately when it is brought home from the store. Different types of meat require specialized care.

1. **Fresh Meat**

    Should be removed from the store wrappings and wrapped loosely in waxed paper for refrigerator storage. Never leave the original wrapper on fresh meat. Because they have proportionately less surface area, larger cuts of meat are less perishable than smaller ones. Here is a guide for storing meats at normal refrigerator temperatures (2°C to 5°C).

CUT OF MEAT	MAXIMUM STORAGE TIME
Beef — roasts	5 days
steaks	4
ground beef, stew meat	2
Pork — roasts	4 days
hams	7
chops, spareribs	3
sausage	2
Veal — chops	4 days
Lamb— roasts	5 days
chops	3
ground lamb	2
Variety Meats —	1 day

2. **Cooked Meats**

    Should be tightly wrapped using waxed paper, plastic wrap, aluminum foil or a plastic bag before it is refrigerated. A covered container is also suitable. For maximum flavour use cooked meat within two days.

3. **Cured and Smoked Meats**

    Store wrapped in the refrigerator. Original wrapping may be used.

4. **Frozen Meat**

    Store at −15°C or lower. Overwrap store frozen meat if it is to be kept for an extended time. Temperatures of a home freezer are lower than those of the freezer part of a refrigerator and therefore are more suitable for retaining best flavour and texture in meat stored for a long period. Cook meat as soon as possible after thawing and do not refreeze. See Food Preservation section for storage times.

BEEF

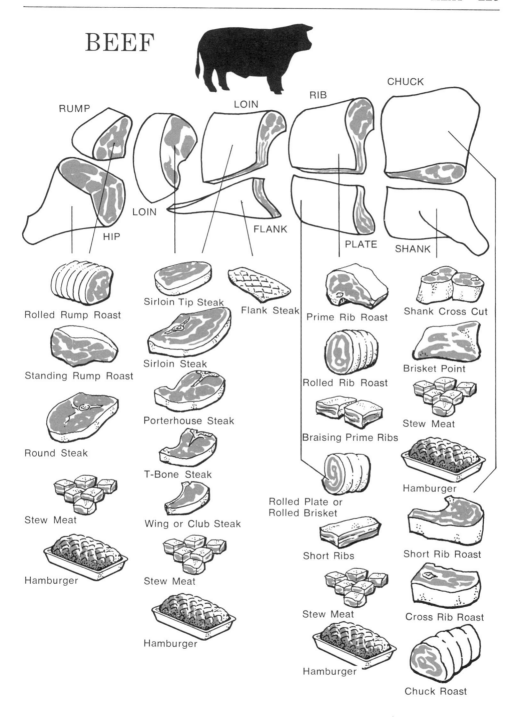

RUMP

LOIN

RIB

CHUCK

LOIN

FLANK

HIP

PLATE

SHANK

Rolled Rump Roast

Standing Rump Roast

Round Steak

Stew Meat

Hamburger

Sirloin Tip Steak

Sirloin Steak

Porterhouse Steak

T-Bone Steak

Wing or Club Steak

Stew Meat

Hamburger

Flank Steak

Prime Rib Roast

Rolled Rib Roast

Braising Prime Ribs

Rolled Plate or
Rolled Brisket

Short Ribs

Stew Meat

Hamburger

Shank Cross Cut

Brisket Point

Stew Meat

Hamburger

Short Rib Roast

Cross Rib Roast

Chuck Roast

PORK

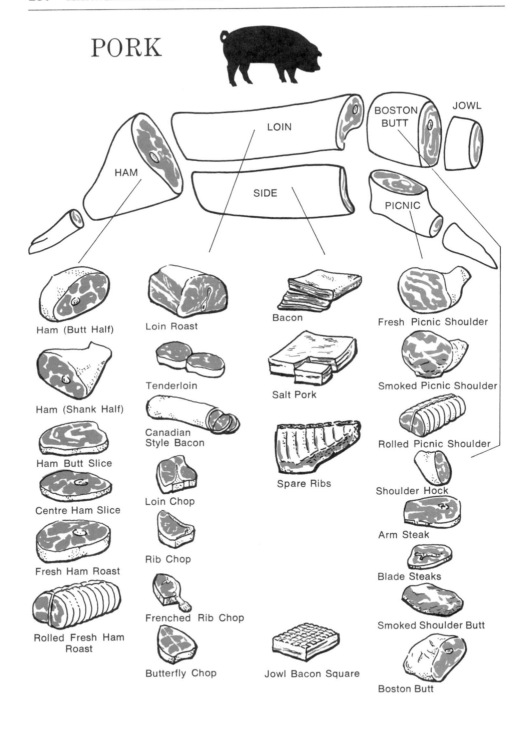

HAM

LOIN

SIDE

BOSTON BUTT

JOWL

PICNIC

Ham (Butt Half)

Ham (Shank Half)

Ham Butt Slice

Centre Ham Slice

Fresh Ham Roast

Rolled Fresh Ham Roast

Loin Roast

Tenderloin

Canadian Style Bacon

Loin Chop

Rib Chop

Frenched Rib Chop

Butterfly Chop

Bacon

Salt Pork

Spare Ribs

Jowl Bacon Square

Fresh Picnic Shoulder

Smoked Picnic Shoulder

Rolled Picnic Shoulder

Shoulder Hock

Arm Steak

Blade Steaks

Smoked Shoulder Butt

Boston Butt

LAMB

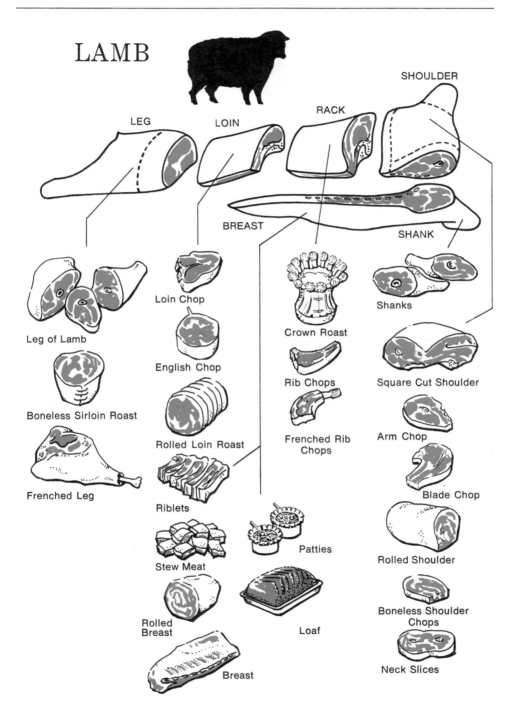

SHOULDER

RACK

LEG

LOIN

BREAST

SHANK

Leg of Lamb

Loin Chop

Crown Roast

Shanks

Boneless Sirloin Roast

English Chop

Rib Chops

Square Cut Shoulder

Frenched Leg

Rolled Loin Roast

Frenched Rib Chops

Arm Chop

Riblets

Blade Chop

Stew Meat

Patties

Rolled Shoulder

Rolled Breast

Loaf

Boneless Shoulder Chops

Breast

Neck Slices

VEAL

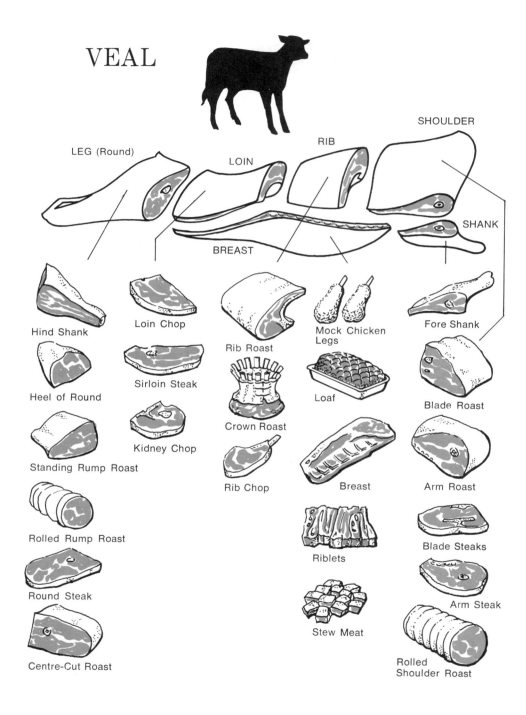

LEG (Round)

LOIN

RIB

SHOULDER

BREAST

SHANK

Hind Shank

Loin Chop

Rib Roast

Mock Chicken Legs

Fore Shank

Heel of Round

Sirloin Steak

Crown Roast

Loaf

Blade Roast

Standing Rump Roast

Kidney Chop

Rib Chop

Breast

Arm Roast

Rolled Rump Roast

Riblets

Blade Steaks

Round Steak

Stew Meat

Arm Steak

Centre-Cut Roast

Rolled Shoulder Roast

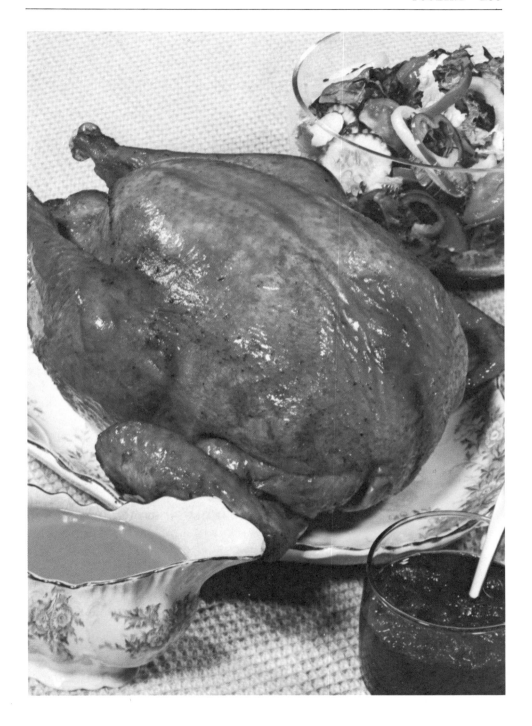

Poultry

POULTRY INSPECTION

In most areas poultry and poultry products are slaughtered and processed in poultry plants operating under federal inspection. These are administered by the Canada Department of Agriculture according to regulations of the Canada Meat Inspection Act and Regulations.

In these plants all live birds are examined by veterinary inspectors. Birds showing signs of disease are removed and only birds that appear healthy may be slaughtered. After slaughter, each part of the bird, including the head, feet, skin, muscles and all internal organs, is subjected to rigid inspection. Only those carcasses and portions that are wholly safe and fit for human consumption may bear the Canada Approved stamp. Since undrawn poultry cannot be completely health inspected, only eviscerated poultry is eligible to carry this mark. The Canada Approved stamp on the tag, bag or label of a poultry product is your assurance that the product is safe and wholesome.

The same system of inspection is provided for a wide range of poultry products such as baby foods, soups, TV dinners, frozen pies, and canned poultry. These products all carry the Canada Approved stamp on their labels.

Further, the spices, seasonings and other condiments used in the preparation of poultry products are limited to the kinds and amounts permitted in the Food and Drugs Act and Regulations. Labelling is also strictly controlled to ensure a true and correct description of the products.

GRADING OF POULTRY

Chickens, capons, fowl, turkeys, ducks and geese must be graded for interprovincial and export trade. This law also applies to poultry sold in retail stores in most major cities. Imported poultry must conform to Canadian grade standards although it does not bear the word "Canada" on the grade mark.

Poultry grades are usually printed on a metal breast tag, transparent bag or label insert. In addition to displaying the grade on turkeys, ducks and geese, these must also be marked "young" or "mature".

The grading and colour system for poultry is as follows:

Canada Grade Special – purple
These are not generally available in retail outlets but are the finest quality produced. They are commercially perfect specimens.

Canada Grade A – red
These are the best quality commonly available on the retail market. Grade A chickens have fat showing over breast and thighs. Turkeys measuring more than five kilograms have breast and thighs reasonably well covered with fat and a moderate covering of fat over the back. Less fat is required on birds over eight kilograms. Fowl, ducks and geese have the breast, thighs and back covered with fat. A slightly crooked keel bone, a few small tears, minor discolourations and a small number of pinfeathers are allowed.

Canada Grade B – blue
These birds are normally formed but may have a slightly crooked keel bone. Moderate sized tears, minor discolourations and pinfeathers that do not seriously detract from the appearance of the bird are allowed. They are not as well fleshed and fatted as Canada Grade A birds.

Canada Grade Utility – blue
These are grade A or B quality birds but one or more parts of the bird may be missing, or there may be large skin tears.

Canada Grade C – yellow
This includes birds that may be poorly fleshed or may have large tears, pinfeathers and prominent discolouration. They are generally not available on the retail market.

These grading standards are carefully maintained by federal inspectors of the Canada Department of Agriculture who check at the plants and at wholesale and retail levels. The grades which are assigned are determined according to these factors:

Conformation – proportion of flesh to bone, absence or presence of deformities of the carcass that affect its appearance or the normal distribution of flesh, for example, a crooked keel bone.

Flesh – the covering of meat on the carcass, its distribution and the amounts on the breast and thighs.

Fat – the covering of fat, its distribution and the amounts in specific areas of the carcass.

Dressing – the condition of the carcass as to feathers, discolouration, tears or other blemishes.

BUYING POULTRY

Poultry is available to the consumer in many different forms: fresh, frozen, whole, pieces, cooked, canned and in a wide range of convenience foods. Whole poultry is classified and marketed according to this classification:

Chicken

Broilers and Fryers – are young birds, 6 to 10 weeks old, measuring up to 2 kilograms.

Roasters – are 10 weeks to 7 months old and over 2 kilograms in mass. High quality birds are well fatted and fleshed.

Capons – are desexed male birds, 5 to 9 months old, measuring from 2.5 to 4 kilograms. They have excellent flavour, are very tender and have a high percentage of white meat.

Fowl – are mature hens that have served their purpose for egg production. They are over 7 months old and are 1.5 kilograms and over. (These birds require careful cooking to make the meat tender and moist.)

Turkey

Broilers – are young birds, usually under 15 weeks of age, weighing up to and including 5 kilograms.

Young turkeys – are usually marketed when they are 4 to 8 months old, 5 kilograms and over in mass. The majority of turkeys on the market are young turkeys. These birds have a flexible cartilage at the posterior end of the keel or breastbone and soft pliable skin of smooth texture.

Mature turkeys – are over 8 months old, 5 kilograms or over in mass. They have hardened breast bones and coarser skin than young birds.

Ducks

These are usually 2-3 kilograms in mass and less than a year old when marketed. The meat of these birds is all dark and there is a larger proportion of fat than in chickens or turkeys. (Because the bones are large, at least 500 grams of duck is needed for one serving.)

Geese

These also are less than a year old when marketed but from 4.5 to 6 kilograms in mass. As in ducks, the meat of these birds is all dark and is fatter than that of chickens or turkeys.

Other Birds

Cornish Hens — These small birds of up to 500 grams, have dark meat.

Guineas — These can be broiled, barbecued, rotisseried or roasted.

Squabs — Young pigeons, measuring from 375 to 750 grams. They should be broiled or barbecued.

BUYING GUIDE FOR POULTRY

TYPE OF POULTRY	EVISCERATED WEIGHT	AMOUNT TO BUY (per serving)*	COOKING METHOD
Chicken broilers & fryers [1]	up to 2 kilograms	400-500 grams	fry, barbecue
Chicken roasters	over 2 kilograms	400-500 grams	roast
Chicken capons	2.5-4 kilograms	400 grams	roast
Fowl	over 1.5 kilograms	400 grams	braise, stew pressure cook
Turkey broilers [1]	over 5 kilograms	400-500 grams	broil, bake, roast, barbecue
Young turkeys	5-6 kilograms over 6 kilograms	400-500 grams 250-400 grams	roast roast
Mature turkeys	5-6 kilograms over 6 kilograms	400-500 grams 250-400 grams	roast or braise
Young ducks [2]	2-3 kilograms	500-650 grams	roast
Young geese [2]	4.5-6 kilograms	400-500 grams	roast
Cornish hens	up to 500 grams	½-1 bird	broil, barbecue, roast
Squab broilers	up to 575 grams	½-1 bird	broil, barbecue

[1] Chicken and turkey broilers can be marked as "chicken" or "young turkey" respectively.

[2] When sold on the retail market, mature ducks and geese are marked "mature" on the grade label or tag.

AMOUNT TO BUY

Because poultry is usually about half meat and half bone, how much poultry to buy is often a difficult question. Estimated amounts shown in "Buying Guide for Poultry" are based on servings – each serving amounting to approximately 100 grams of cooked meat without bone, skin or juices. In most cases, large turkeys are more economical and leftovers can be used in future meals. When buying chicken, too, compare prices on the basis of cost per serving rather than cost per kilogram. A whole chicken usually sells for less per kilogram than the parts. Allow 400-500 grams of cut up parts for one serving but 500 grams of breast will make two servings and 500 grams of chicken livers will make four servings.

In addition, in order to estimate amounts realistically, consider the method of cooking and the foods to be served with the poultry including any meat extenders such as dressing or dumplings. Also take into account the appetites of those being served. If it is a popular dish many may want second servings. Food habits are a personal thing and serving sizes are only intended as a guide.

FORMS OF POULTRY AND POULTRY PRODUCTS

Turkey is sold fresh and frozen. Sizes of birds vary widely from 2 to 12 kilograms and larger. Turkey parts are also frequently available. These are usually from young broiler turkeys. In some areas, halves and quarters may be available. These are a good alternative to a whole bird, especially when fewer servings are wanted. Boneless turkey made by boning and rolling mature birds is marketed both uncooked and cooked.

Chicken is available fresh or frozen, whole, in pieces or in packages of parts such as all drumsticks or all breasts. Cooked chicken is available in many forms also. Some supermarkets and specialty shops operate rotisseries and offer for sale ready-cooked barbecued chicken. These products require careful handling for their moisture and warm temperatures makes them subject to Salmonella, and other bacteria that can cause food poisoning. To be sure of avoiding health hazards when buying and serving barbecued chicken follow these procedures:

1. Buy hot products "hot" from the warming cabinet or "piping hot" right off the spit.

2. Buy cold products "cold" from a refrigerator or cooler.

3. Avoid leaving the chicken at room temperature any longer than necessary – either in the store or on the way home.

4. If serving the chicken within 1½ hours after purchase, place it in a preheated oven at 65°C to keep it hot.

5. If serving later than this, remove the chicken from the foil bag, refrigerate it as soon as possible and then reheat for 20-30 minutes before serving, in an oven preheated to 160°C. Follow this same procedure to serve leftover chicken hot.

Canned poultry is available in a wide variety of forms and can sizes. A large can containing a whole chicken is a good addition to the emergency shelf of any kitchen. Pieces and boneless meat in small size cans have long been popular grocery items. Other specialty items include turkey à la king, chicken chow mein and poultry sandwich spreads. Many convenience foods containing poultry meat are to be found in the freezer section of most supermarkets.

STORING POULTRY

If properly cared for, fresh poultry may be stored in the refrigerator for two or three days before it is cooked. The outer wrapping should first be removed and the giblets (heart, gizzard and liver) if present, should also be removed and stored separately. The bird should be covered loosely with waxed paper or aluminum foil.

Because the giblets are highly perishable they should be cooked promptly. Any liquid used to cook them can be saved for use in gravies or soups.

Store cooked poultry in a covered container, plastic bag or aluminum foil. It may be kept refrigerated for 3 or 4 days or frozen for one to two months.

A frozen bird should be kept frozen until time to thaw it for cooking. If properly wrapped, fresh whole chicken or turkey may be stored in a freezer at −20°C for 12 months; cut up poultry may be stored for 6 months; geese and ducks store well for 3 months.

For thawing poultry in the refrigerator allow 10 hours per kilogram. This is the ideal place for thawing since it keeps the meat cold until it is completely thawed. To thaw entirely at room temperature allow 3 hours per kilogram. Leave the bird in its original wrapper but make a small slit in the wrapper along the back or underside and place on a rack to allow the moisture to drain out.

Another way is to place the bird, still in its original sealed wrapper, in cold water and allow 2 hours per kilogram for thawing. This method is not recommended because greater moisture losses will occur. The slower the thawing method used for poultry, the less the moisture loss will be and the more juicy and flavourful the cooked meat which results.

Thawed poultry should be cooked within 24 hours after defrosting. Do not thaw and then refreeze uncooked poultry. It must be cooked before it can be safely refrozen. See chart page 431. Care must be taken when purchasing poultry for freezing that it has not been frozen and thawed before purchase.

METHODS OF COOKING POULTRY

The same principles as apply in cooking meat also apply to cooking poultry. Tender young birds may be cooked by dry heat methods; less tender parts and older birds require a moist heat. The time required to tenderize the more fully developed connective tissues will depend upon the type of bird and its age.

Before cooking the poultry selected, you should inspect it and remove all remaining pinfeathers and hairs. If it is a whole bird, run cold water into the body cavity and remove any remaining viscera. Dry inside and out with paper towelling. Chicken pieces should also be blotted dry with paper towelling.

There are many good recipes for cooking all the different kinds of poultry. Most of these are simply variations of the basic methods which follow:

Dry Heat Methods

Barbecuing applies the same principles as broiling except that the direct heat source is below the meat and is from charcoal instead of the gas or electric heat of the oven.

Broiling is a direct heat method of cooking poultry pieces, halves or quarters. Because the upper surface of the meat is subjected to intense drying while the lower surface keeps moist, it is usually advisable to turn the pieces for more even cooking. Brushing with oil or other fat will help prevent over-drying and a specially flavoured basting sauce is often used instead. Overbrowning may be prevented by rearranging the pieces as they cook or by adjusting the distance from the heat.

Roasting is a dry heat method of cooking the whole bird on a rack in an uncovered, shallow pan. Recommended oven temperature is 160°C although some recipes differ from this. The bird may be stuffed or not. If a dressing is used, it should be made and placed inside the bird just before roasting. Dressing is a good growth medium for a bacteria that causes food poisoning so it should not be allowed to stand uncooked in the bird. As the bird cooks it may need to be protected from over-browning by a loose layer of aluminum foil. Basting prevents drying.

Rotisserie – Whole birds are placed on the metal spit and tied well to prevent slipping. They must be well balanced in order to turn easily. Then the heat is applied, either from the oven element or from charcoal in the barbecue. See page 243, Preparing Birds for the Rotisserie.

Pan Frying is only suitable for small pieces. Cooking is done in a fry pan containing about 0.5 cm fat. Usually the meat is coated first with seasoned flour or dipped in egg mixture and rolled in crumbs. The kind of fat used will determine the cooking temperature. Vegetable oil is the most suitable at high temperatures, butter and margarine contribute more flavour and sometimes a mixture is preferred. True frying is done without a lid but sometimes one is used to speed the cooking process. It should be removed at least for the last 15 minutes to achieve a crisp product. Tongs are recommended to turn the pieces since they do not puncture the meat and cause juice losses. Paprika improves browning in less fat birds.

Deep Frying is a popular method for cooking smaller chicken. The pieces are first breaded or dipped in a batter and then fried in deep fat at about 180°C. The degree of browning is a good indication of how far along the cooking has progressed.

Moist Heat Methods

Stewing – Older, mature poultry is tenderized by stewing or *simmering* in liquid. The water should not be boiling but merely simmering as shown by occasional bubbles rising to the surface. When the meat is cooked and tender it can be removed from the bones and used in a variety of ways. The broth also is used for preparing soup, gravy or sauce.

Fricassee – This is a stew-like dish made with white or pale fleshed meats. Chicken fricassee is prepared by cutting chicken into sections as for frying and then stewing it in simmering water until just tender. When the liquid has been properly seasoned and evaporated to a concentrated broth it is used with equal quantities of milk or cream to prepare a cream sauce. A colourful variety of cooked vegetables is added to the creamed sauce which is then served over the platter of cooked chicken.

Braising — The poultry pieces are started in fat in a similar way to frying. When slightly browned a small amount of water is added, the pan covered and the meat cooked slowly on the surface element or in the oven. Other ingredients as vegetables and seasonings are added at some point during the cooking process and before serving the juices are thickened to make a gravy.

Pressure Cooking — This is a much faster way of tenderizing older, mature birds by moist heat. The product will be similar to braised poultry. An instruction manual that comes with the cooker will provide recipes and times for the various types of poultry.

SPECIAL PROCEDURES FOR POULTRY

Dressing a Bird

Bread for stuffing can be prepared by cutting in small cubes with a knife or breaking into coarse crumbs with the fingers. Whichever method is used, the bread should not be too fresh. Dry crumbs also are not as suitable. Toss bread lightly with dry seasonings before adding any moist ingredients. This way is easier for the beginner to assure all flavours are thoroughly mixed. Then add sautéed vegetables and melted fat.

If a light, fluffy dressing is desired, care should be taken not to add too much liquid to the dressing. During cooking additional juices will seep into the dressing from the bird and could result in a heavier dressing than was wanted.

When stuffing is ready place it in the body cavity. This can be done with a spoon but clean hands are more efficient. If a new type of special dressing is being tried, it is a good idea to use the family favourite in the body cavity and the new recipe in the neck cavity. If you do not want your dressing to be heavy, pile it into the cavity lightly because during cooking it expands as it absorbs juices from the bird. If your family prefers a heavy dressing that can be sliced, pack it firmly. Stuffing recipes for duck and goose can have less fat and moisture added because these birds have more fat to cook out.

All poultry should be cooked as soon as it is stuffed. Bacteria causing food borne illnesses can grow and multiply rapidly at temperatures between 5°C and 60°C. Therefore, it is unsafe to stuff the bird and then refrigerate it until cooking time because the stuffing cools slowly and it is a superb food for the bacteria to grow in. For additional safety, use a meat thermometer when cooking to determine the temperature in the centre of the stuffing. Allow it to reach 75°C. When cooking some or all of the stuffing in a separate container cook until the thermometer registers 75°C in the centre also.

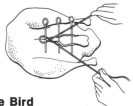 

Trussing the Bird

This is the process of tying, pinning and/or sewing the legs and wings of the bird to its body to make it more compact and to prevent it from falling apart in the oven. It also reduces the danger of overcooking its extremities. A layer of foil to cover the extremities later in cooking can also help this problem.

There are several ways of doing this — use whatever method works for you. The wing tips are turned back on the shoulder so that they come across the neck skin and hold it in place. Once you have seen how this is done it will be easy. Tie the legs and the tail securely together with string. This is an easier way than using the "natural" truss which involves pushing the tips of the legs through the natural band of skin formed above the tail and large opening into the body cavity. When the "natural truss" method is used the band of skin should be cut during the final hour so that the thick meated joints can be completely cooked.

In addition, many cooks use skewers and/or string to close the body cavity and prevent loss of any dressing. Several skewers inserted across the body cavity can be laced with string or the whole opening sewed shut with needle and thread or string.

Preparing Birds for the Rotisserie

Whole chickens (one or more) and whole turkeys are suitable for rotisserie cooking provided the mass does not exceed the manufacturer's specifications and the birds are properly placed on the spit.

First tie the drumsticks tightly to the tail. Fasten the neck skin to the back with a skewer. Flatten the wings against the breast and then tie with string around the breast to hold the wings securely.

Insert the spit rod through the centre of the bird lengthwise from tail end toward the front to ensure a balanced load on the spit. Put the skewers firmly into the bird and screw tightly. Test the balance and re-adjust if necessary to ensure a balanced load on the spit so that the bird will rotate smoothly throughout the cooking period. This is especially important when more than one bird is being cooked. As cooking progresses the bird shrinks and if it slips in the skewers it will not go around properly.

The bird can be brushed with oil or melted butter as it cooks. Most barbecue sauces are best added during the last few minutes of the cooking time since they often contain sugar or other ingredients that promote browning and can cause burning of the surface.

Fish and Shellfish

SELECTING GOOD FRESH FISH

Fish is a highly perishable food and care must be taken to choose it wisely, store it carefully and use it quickly, preferably on the day it is bought. Fresh fish in season is available whole (in the round) or dressed. Here are the points to look for to ensure freshness:

Odour
Fish should smell fresh with a mildly characteristic odour but no strong "fishy" or other objectionable odour.

Eyes
They should be bright, clear, full and slightly bulging.

Gills
They will be bright reddish pink and free from slime.

Scales

Fresh fish scales adhere tightly to the skin, are a bright colour with characteristic sheen but no slime.

Flesh

It will be firm and elastic, retaining no imprint when pressed and not separating easily from the bones.

When choosing fish fillets and steaks look for these characteristics:

Odour

A mild characteristic odour will be present but no strong or "fishy" odour.

Flesh

Look for a firm elastic flesh that does not separate easily from the bones or retain an imprint of the fingers when handled.

Appearance

Fish should look fresh, with no trace of browning or drying out of the flesh.

SELECTING FROZEN FISH

In recent years fish and shellfish have become more readily available in the frozen form. There has been a growing tendency to freeze some species almost immediately after they are caught; sometimes there are freezing facilities on the fishing boats.

Any fish or shellfish that is freshly caught may be frozen but no fish should ever be thawed and then refrozen. Fish that is bought at the market may also be frozen provided it has not been frozen before. However, this is difficult to determine. The best way is to inquire if you intend to freeze the fish you buy. Much of the fish displayed in large supermarkets has been frozen for storage even though it is defrosted when you buy it. Here are some considerations in selecting frozen fish:

Packaging

Packages should be solidly frozen. The wrapping material must be moisture and vapour-proof and the packages wrapped tightly with little or no air space between fish and package. A glaze of ice over the whole fish is a good alternative.

Flesh

The fish should be firm and glossy with no discolouration or fading of flesh, no evidence of drying out, and no parched white areas indicating freezer burn.

Opening

There should be no evidence of frost or ice crystals when the package is opened.

FORMS IN WHICH FISH MAY BE BOUGHT

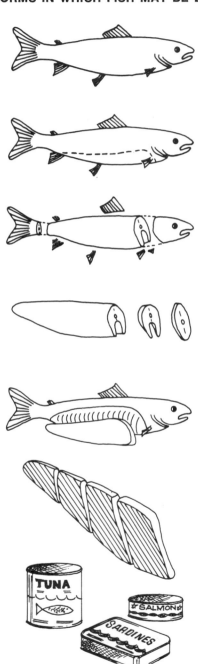

Whole Fish or Fish *"in the round"*

Those that are marketed just as they come from the water. Before cooking, they must be eviscerated and scaled or skinned. Usually the head, tail and fins are also removed.

Drawn Fish

Sold with only the entrails removed. Before cooking, the head, scales and fins are usually removed.

Dressed or Pan-dressed Fish

Eviscerated and scaled. Usually they have had the head, tail and fins removed. This form is ready for cooking as purchased.

Steaks

Cross-section cuts from larger dressed fish. They are ready to cook as purchased.

Fillets

The meaty sides of the fish, cut lengthwise away from the backbone. They should be free of bones and are usually skinned. Ready to cook as purchased, they are often sold packaged and frozen.

Sticks and Portions

Pieces of fish cut in uniform size from blocks of frozen fillets. These are also ready to use as purchased and are most frequently sold in the frozen state.

Canned Fish

Includes a wide range of both fish and shellfish that can be used as purchased in many different ways.

CANNED FISH – SALMON

Generally speaking, the five varieties of salmon can be used interchangeably in recipes. As a basis for selection, however, choose the deeper coloured varieties for dishes in which the colour of the salmon is an important consideration. Choose the light coloured and lower priced varieties for casserole dishes and cooked mixtures in which the colour of the salmon is of minor importance.

Sockeye Salmon

An attractive red coloured flesh which is rich in oil. Considered the choicest of all the varieties, sockeye is recommended for use in salads and for eating just as it comes from the can.

Coho Salmon

A medium red coloured flesh which is lower in oil content than the sockeye. It is a good general purpose salmon for use in salads, sandwiches and cooked dishes.

Pink Salmon

A delicate pink coloured, fine textured flesh. In some years more pink salmon is canned than any other single variety. Pink salmon is a good choice for fish cakes, chowders and casserole dishes.

Chum or Keta Salmon

A pale fleshed variety having a low oil content. It is relatively low in price and especially suitable for use in many cooked dishes.

Spring Salmon

A flesh which is rich in oil and which will separate into large flakes. There are three classifications of spring salmon, based on the colour of the flesh which varies from deep red to white. Spring salmon is especially suitable for use in salads. Only a relatively small quantity of it is canned in Canada.

CANNED FISH – TUNA

Several species of fish are marketed as tuna, all of which are equally desirable. Varieties of tuna include albacore, bluefin, skipjack, yellowfin, and little tuna. Albacore as a rule has lighter meat than the other species and is usually labelled as "white meat." The other species are labelled as "light" or "dark meat" tuna, according to colour.

Canned tuna is available in three different styles of pack. The pack does not indicate a quality difference. It refers to the size of the pieces in the can.

Regular Solid Pack

This pack is ideal for cold plates or for recipes where appearance is important. Usually three or four large oil packed pieces are found in each can. It is the most expensive pack.

Chunk Style
This pack is especially adaptable to salads and other dishes where chunks of tuna are desirable. Each can contains conveniently sized pieces packed in oil. It is a moderately priced style of pack.

Flake Style
This is excellent for sandwiches or other recipes where the tuna is blended into a paste. The cans contain mechanically sized oil packed pieces that are smaller than the chunk style pieces. It is generally lower priced than the other packs.

HOW MUCH FISH TO BUY
Servings of fish are generally based on 150 g to 225 g of the edible flesh per person. Here is a chart which will help in determining the amount to purchase. Remember always, that appetites and eating habits vary between families.

	2 servings	4 servings
Fillets, sticks, meaty pieces with bones removed.	300 g	600 g
Steaks – cross sectional slices, some bones.	500 g	1 kg
Pan Dressed, ready to be cooked head, tail and fins removed	500 g	1 kg
Drawn, eviscerated only.	600 g	1.5 kg
Whole or Round, just as taken from the water.	1 kg	2 kg

STORING FRESH AND FROZEN FISH
Both fish and shellfish are highly perishable foods. In order to preserve the quality, freshness and flavour of the fish you have secured it must be promptly and properly handled. Any fish is best used the day it is bought from the market or better yet, on the day it is caught. It should be wrapped tightly in moisture proof paper or placed in a tightly covered container and stored immediately in the coldest part of the refrigerator. Stored this way the odour of fish will not penetrate other foods.

If it is not possible to use your fish within a day, then it should be stored in the freezer. Commercially frozen fish may be stored in its original package. Tray pack frozen fish will keep better longer if overwrapped before storing in the freezer.

Frozen fish should be kept solidly frozen in the unopened package. A constant temperature of −20°C or lower is recommended. Since this low temperature is hard to maintain in a household freezer it is advisable to keep supplies of frozen fish for a relatively short time. Satisfactory flavour in lean fish can be expected for three months, in fatty fish for only two months. Examples of fish high in fat content are salmon, herring, sardines, black cod, tuna, and lake trout. Those classed as lean fish include cod, sole, haddock, halibut, perch, and pike.

THAWING FROZEN FISH

Although thawed fish is necessary for success with certain cooking methods, all fish is juicier when cooked from the frozen state. A good principle to guide your decision is to thaw fish before cooking only when it is necessary for handling and then to thaw only sufficiently to permit ease of preparation. Fillets and steaks can be cooked frozen as if they were fresh if additional time is allowed. Fish that is to be breaded or stuffed must first be thawed.

Thawing of frozen fish is best done at refrigerator temperature which is about 0°C. The preferred method is to leave the fish in the refrigerator overnight. If room temperature thawing is necessary, great care must be taken so the fish remains chilled at all times. Whole or drawn fish can be more readily thawed by immersing in cold running water. Once fish is thawed it should be cooked immediately and not refrozen. Good results cannot be obtained using fish that has been thawed and then frozen again.

Fish and shellfish are available in many different forms: fresh, frozen, canned, smoked, salted, dried and pickled. As fresh fish is sold ready for the pan most of the time, homemakers seldom need to clean and dress a fish for cooking.

However, at times freshly caught fish may be available, especially to families that enjoy the sport fishing for which much of British Columbia is famous. Therefore, information on cleaning and preparing fish for cooking is presented here.

STEPS IN CLEANING FISH

Lay the fish on the table and with one hand hold the fish firmly by the tail. Holding a knife almost vertical, scrape the scales off in the opposite direction to the way they lie and work from the tail toward the head. Since scales are more easily removed from a wet fish it is advisable to soak the fish in cold water for a few minutes before scaling.  (Keeping the fish submerged in cold water as the scaling proceeds will prevent scales from scattering over work surfaces.)

Cleaning

1. Begin by cutting the entire length of the belly from the vent (anal opening) to the head. Remove the entrails.

2. Cut around the pelvic fins and remove them. Remove the head by cutting just back of the collarbone next to the gills. If it is a large fish, cut down on each side of the fish and then snap the backbone by bending it over the edge of the cutting board or counter.

3. Next cut off the tail by cutting through the flesh and snapping the backbone, as with the head.

4. Remove the dorsal or large backfin by cutting the flesh along both sides of the fin. Then, giving a quick pull forward toward the head of the fish, remove the fin with the root bones attached. (Trimming the fins off with the knife or shears will leave the bones at the base of the fin in the fish.)

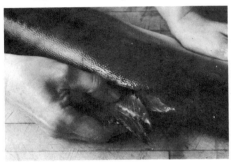 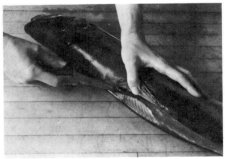

5. Wash the fish in cold running water, removing the blood, any remaining viscera and membranes. The fish is now dressed or, if small enough, pan dressed, and is ready for cooking. Small fish, such as trout, can be cooked whole. Larger fish may be cut crosswise into steaks or lengthwise into fillets.

Filleting

With a sharp knife, cut through the flesh along the back from the tail to just behind the head. Then cut down to the backbone just above the collarbone. Turn the knife flat and cut the flesh along the backbone to the tail allowing the knife to run over the rib bones. Lift off the entire side of the fish in one piece. Turn the fish over and repeat the operation on the other side.

Skinning

Lay the fillets flat on the cutting board, skin side down. Hold the tail end with your fingers and with a knife cut through the flesh to the skin about one half inch from the end of the fillet. Flatten the knife on the skin and cut the flesh away from the skin by pushing the knife forward while holding the free end of the skin firmly between your fingers.

NUTRITIVE VALUE OF FISH

The edible portion of fish contains many elements the body needs. No matter what type of fish is available or what the market price, these nutrients, with variations noted, are present:

Protein

Fish contains from 15-20 percent protein which is about the same proportion as in other protein foods such as meat and poultry. Like those of meat, eggs, milk and cheese, fish proteins supply all of the essential amino acids. This means that when eaten as the only protein food at a meal, it can supply the body's protein needs for health and growth. In addition, fish protein is easily digested by humans.

Fat

Except for a particularly high concentration just below the skin, the fat in fish is not localized as it is in meat. Instead, it is distributed throughout the flesh. The proportion of fat found in fish varies with the species. This explains why the kilojoule count of certain fish is greater than others. Those which contain a small amount of fat have a relatively larger proportion of water so that the proportion of protein remains nearly constant. Fish fat is also easily digested.

Vitamins

The proportion of the different vitamins found in fish also varies with the species. Fatty fish contain vitamins A and D. Lean fish have almost none of these fat-soluble vitamins. However, the oils from fish livers, especially those of the fatty species, provide a reliable source of both vitamins A and D.

Fish is also a good source of niacin with less significant amounts of riboflavin present as well.

Minerals

All varieties of fish are good sources of phosphorus, iodine, copper and fluorine. The bones contain most of the calcium. Therefore, it is nutritionally sound practice to include the softened bones when preparing canned fish. With the exception of shellfish such as oysters and clams, that are eaten whole, the iron content of most fish is low.

COOKING FISH

Unlike most meat, the flesh of fish contains very little connective tissue. For this reason fish requires only a short cooking period and a high temperature is recommended. Use of a low temperature dries and toughens fish, as does overcooking. In addition, nutrients are lost in the juices which cook out of the fish during the extended time. Therefore, cook fish at a high temperature only until done. The time required will depend on the thickness of the piece you are cooking. To determine if your fish is cooked look for these characteristics:

1. The flesh loses its translucent appearance and becomes opaque.

2. Juices that in the raw fish were clear, now have become milky.

3. The flesh separates into flakes readily.

4. The flesh is easily pierced by a fork.

Do not thaw frozen fish before cooking except when necessary for ease in handling. Once cooked, fish should be served immediately while it is still piping hot, tender and juicy. If it is to be used for salads, casseroles or other combinations, it should be cooked without browning. Suitable methods are those which employ boiling water or steam.

METHODS OF COOKING FISH

In the Frying Pan

This is a popular method for cooking fish steaks, fillets, and small whole fish. For easier handling, some frozen fish, such as whole trout, may be partially thawed and then cooked immediately.

1. Have fish in serving-size pieces, cut if necessary. Season with salt and pepper.

2. Dip fish in liquid (milk, beaten egg, or a mixture of both) and then in breading mixture (flour, fine crumbs, cornmeal).

3. Heat fat or oil in frying pan. Have it hot, but not smoking.

4. Fry fish until golden brown on one side, turn and brown the other side. The complete cooking time will be approximately 5 minutes for each centimetre thickness. Drain fat and serve piping hot.

In Deep Fat

Fillets, smelts, fish cakes and some shellfish such as oysters are delicious when fried in deep hot fat. If frozen fish is used, partial thawing is suggested to allow even cooking throughout.

1. Cut fillets into uniform size not thicker than 1.5 centimetre. If too thick, make several slits in the sides. This will help the fish to cook more evenly and quickly. Frozen fish should be thawed just before cooking. Wipe dry before using.

2. Sprinkle fish with salt. Dip in liquid (milk, beaten eggs or a mixture of both) and then in breading mixture (flour, fine crumbs, cornmeal) or use a batter coating.

3. Place one layer of fish in frying basket. Do not atempt to fry more than one layer at a time as this lowers the temperature of the fat below the proper cooking temperature.

4. Fry in hot deep fat at 190°C until golden brown, about 3 or 4 minutes. Drain on paper towels and serve piping hot.

In Boiling Water

Fish for salads, casseroles, fish cakes or creamed fish dishes may be cooked in water or court bouillon.

1. Wipe fresh fish with a damp cloth or rinse quickly in cold water. Leave frozen fish frozen.

2. Measure the thickness of the fish at its thickest part and place it on a piece of greased aluminum foil.

3. Season with salt and pepper. If desired, add 15 ml each of chopped celery and chopped onion.

4. Wrap fish in aluminum foil. Make double folds on top and on the ends and pinch the folds to make the package water tight, (drug store wrap).

5. Plunge packaged fish into rapidly boiling water. Cover container. When water returns to boiling point reduce heat to maintain a simmer and begin timing. For fresh fish allow 5 minutes and for frozen fish about 10 minutes for each centimetre of thickness. Save the fish juices in the foil package for use in fish sauces.

In Court Bouillon

This method is essentially the same as cooking in boiling water except that the boiling water is seasoned and the fish is not first wrapped in a water-proof package.

1. Prepare court bouillon liquid using the water, vinegar, vegetables and seasonings as your recipe directs.

2. Wipe fresh fish with a damp cloth or rinse quickly in cold water. Leave frozen fish frozen.

3. Measure the thickness of the fish at its thickest part. Place the fish in a wire basket or on a plate wrapped in cheesecloth with long ends to serve as handles when lifting the fish in or out of the liquid.

4. Plunge fish into boiling liquid. Cover container. When the liquid returns to the boiling point begin timing. Adjust heat to maintain a

simmer. For fresh fish allow 5 minutes for each centimetre of thickness and for frozen fish allow about 10 minutes for each centimetre thickness.

5. Remove fish carefully to a hot platter, garnish colourfully and serve with a sauce.

In Steam

This method is especially suitable for fish that is to be used in casseroles, salads or other combinations with cooked fish. It is a favourite of people on low kilojoule diets.

1. Wipe fresh fish with a damp cloth or rinse quickly in cold water. Leave frozen fish frozen.

2. Measure the thickness of the fish at the thickest part.

3. Use a steamer or improvise one using a sieve or a colander that will fit into a deep saucepan or soup kettle. Partially fill the bottom of the steamer or kettle with water and bring it to a rapid boil.

4. Place the fish on the upper part of the steamer or in a sieve or colander and place over the boiling water. For ease in handling, tie the fish in cheesecloth. Water should not touch the fish. Cover with a tight lid.

5. For fresh fish allow 5 minutes for each centimetre thickness; for frozen fish allow 10 minutes for each centimetre thickness.

In Milk

Fish may also be poached, either in milk or in a small amount of water. Smoked fish is especially good when cooked this way.

1. Measure thickness of fish at its thickest part.

2. Place fish in milk in a covered pan and simmer until the fish flakes easily when tested with a fork. Allow the usual 5 minutes for each centimetre of fresh fish and 10 minutes for each centimetre of frozen fish. The fish may be poached in milk on top of the stove or baked in a hot oven at 230°C. Do not overcook or milk will curdle.

3. Dot with butter and sprinkle with pepper. Serve with milk poured over the fish or make a cream sauce with the milk.

In the Oven

Baking is a suitable method for cooking whole fish, steaks and fillets, both fresh and frozen.

1. Wipe fish with a damp cloth. Leave frozen fish frozen unless a dressing is to be used.

2. Measure the thickness of the fish or pieces of fish at the thickest part.

3. Season fish, place it in a greased baking pan and brush with melted fat. Or instead the fish can be dipped in seasoned milk and rolled in coating.

4. Bake in a very hot oven 230°C to 260°C. Allow 5 minutes for each centimetre thickness of fresh fish, 10 minutes for each centimetre of frozen fish.

In the Oven, Steamed in Aluminum Foil

With this method the flavour and juices are sealed in by aluminum foil and the fish steams in its own liquid.

1. Wipe fish with a damp cloth or wash quickly in cold water. Leave frozen fish frozen.

2. Measure thickness of fish at its thickest part and place in a piece of greased aluminum foil. Season with salt and pepper.

3. Fold foil over fish with double folds on top and edges and pinching folds to make the package steam-tight, (drug store wrap).

4. Place package on a baking sheet or in a shallow pan and bake in a very hot oven 230°C to 260°C. Allow the standard cooking time of 5 minutes for each centimetre thickness of fresh fish and 10 minutes for each centimetre of frozen fish. Then add an additional 5 minutes and 10 minutes respectively to the total estimated time to allow for heat to penetrate the foil and fish.

In the Oven, Stuffed

Baked stuffed fish is a festive dish to serve family and guests alike. It is simpler to prepare and takes much less time to cook than roast beef or a roast turkey.

1. Clean the fish, remove scales and any viscera clinging to the backbone. Rinse and dry the fish.

2. Sprinkle the inside with salt. Stuff fish loosely with a bread stuffing of your choice allowing about 200 ml stuffing for each half kilogram dressed fish. If the backbone is removed, allow about 250 ml stuffing for each half kilogram dressed fish.

3. Fasten the opening with small skewers or toothpicks and loop string about them as you would lace shoes. An alternate method is to sew the opening with a large needle and coarse thread. Place the stuffed fish on a greased baking pan and brush skin with melted fat or oil.

4. Measure the stuffed fish at the thickest part. Bake in a hot oven 230°C. Allow 5 minutes cooking time for each centimetre thickness of stuffed fish.

5. Lift fish carefully onto a heated serving platter using two wide spatulas. Remove skewers or toothpicks and string, then garnish with parsley and lemon slices.

Under the Broiler

Broiling is one of the best and easiest methods of cooking fish steaks, fillets or small whole fish. While being cooked the fish is basted with melted butter or a basting sauce.

1. Have fish in serving-sized pieces or whole if small. Wipe with damp cloth. Measure thickness of widest piece of fish. Cuts of 2-3 cm have less tendency to dry out during broiling than thin cuts. Frozen fillets or steaks need not be thawed.

2. Preheat the broiler.

3. Season fish with salt and pepper. Place on a greased broiler pan. Baste with melted fat or a basting sauce.

4. Place the fish in the oven 5-10 cm from the heating unit. Frozen fish should be placed lower yet to prevent overcooking the surface before the inside is cooked. Leave the door ajar unless manufacturer's directions state otherwise.

5. When fish is browned on one side, season and turn. Brush with melted fat or sauce and complete cooking. Thin cuts of fish may be broiled without turning. For fresh fish allow about 5 minutes cooking time for each centimetre thickness; for frozen fish allow about 10 minutes for each centimetre thickness of fish.

Over the Barbecue

Moderately fat and full-flavoured fish such as salmon and trout are best for the barbecue because the smoke enhances their flavour, while smoke might overpower a delicately flavoured fish. Instructions here are for barbecuing serving-sized fish steaks or fillets and small whole fish.

1. Have steaks or fillets in serving-sized pieces at least 1.5 cm thick. Wipe small whole fish with a damp cloth.

2. Place fish over moderately hot coals. Fairly thick fish steaks or fillets may be placed directly on the greased grill of the barbecue. Smaller pieces are easier to handle and turn if held inside a hinged wire broiler. Baste with melted butter or basting sauce.

3. Grill until the fish is browned and flakes when tested with a fork. Turn once only and baste often.

4. Use a wide spatula to remove the fish to a warm plate. Serve at once.

Shellfish

CLAMS

Several varieties of clams are to be found along the rocky shores of the Pacific coast. All of them are edible. They are sold alive in the shell and as shucked meat in fresh, frozen and canned forms.

Cleaning Clams

Begin to care for clams after digging by washing the surface with sea water to remove the sand. Cover the clams with clean sea water and let them stand to allow them to cleanse themselves. Provided salt water is used, they will open and discharge sand which will settle to the bottom of the container. If possible, the sea water should be changed.

Clams may be left overnight in salt water with a few handfuls of rolled oats or cornmeal thrown on top. This will help the cleansing process, especially important if clams are to be steamed open or eaten from the shell.

Shucking Clams

To open the clam, hold it in the palm of one hand with the shell's hinge against the palm. Insert a slender, strong, sharp knife between the halves of the shell and cut around the clam, twisting the knife slightly to pry open the shell. The knife will sever the muscle allowing the shell to open. Save the clam liquor.

Another way is to place the cleaned shell clams in a small quantity of boiling water. Cover and steam them for 5-10 minutes or until they are partly opened. Drain liquid, reserving it for use in flavouring chowders.

Clams are served most often in chowder. This is a thick soup containing cubed potatoes and various other vegetables and either milk or tomatoes depending on the type. A favourite way of serving the smaller sized clams is to steam them open and serve dipped in melted butter to which has been added lemon juice, salt and pepper. Sometimes Worcestershire sauce and a dash of Tabasco is added for a special zip.

There are a variety of other good ways to serve clams. They can be served chilled in the half shell with cocktail sauce. In the ground form they make a delicious appetizer dip and quick-to-fix patties or fritters. Deep fat fried clams, clam casserole and clam scallop are among the other possibilities.

OYSTERS

Oysters are sold alive in the shell, shucked and packed in 500 grams or 1 litre waxed cartons, or canned, either plain or smoked. They are generally sold by the dozen when in the shell and must be alive when purchased. The shell should be tightly closed. A gaping shell that does not close when handled indicates that the oyster is dead and no longer usable. Shucked fresh oysters should be plump and have a natural creamy colour with clear liquor and be free from shell particles. They must be refrigerated or surrounded by ice to retain freshness.

Shucking Oysters

Rinse the shells thoroughly in cold water. To open or shuck the oyster place it on a table with the flat shell up and holding it with the left hand. With the right hand, force an oyster knife between the shells at or near the thin end. Now cut the large abductor muscle close to the flat upper shell in which it is attached and remove the shell. Cut the lower end of the same muscle, which is attached to the deep half of the shell and drop the oyster into a container. Reserve the oyster liquor which drains out. It is used to cover oysters which are to be frozen and is good for flavouring seafood chowders.

After shucking, examine the oysters for bits of shell. It may be necessary to drain them in a sieve or colander, reserving the liquor, and then rinse them under cold water to remove any sand or shell particles.

Aside from their delicious flavour, the special appeal of oysters lies in the lack of waste from trimmings and the ease with which they can be prepared and served. Oysters are entirely edible and can be served raw on the half shell as a cocktail or cooked in a variety of ways. They may be baked, broiled, fried, creamed or scalloped or used in combination with other foods for stew, chowder or as a stuffing for poultry.

In order to retain the delicate, distinctive flavour of oysters they should not be cooked too long. Serve them while still plump and tender. Overcooking will make them tough and dry.

SHRIMP

The shrimp caught off the coast of British Columbia vary in size from tiny members of the species to good-sized prawns. Although raw shrimp range in colour from greenish grey to brownish red, cooked shrimp differ little in appearance and flavour. Regardless of the initial hue, all turn the distinctive shrimp pink colour on cooking. Raw shrimp are often referred to as "green shrimp".

In a few markets close to the fishing grounds, raw or cooked whole shrimp, called "heads-on shrimp", may be purchased. Unless otherwise stated, the term "shrimp" refers to the tail section only, which may or may not have the shell removed.

Cooked shrimp in the shell is available either fresh or frozen; shelled shrimp is also available canned. Cooked or canned shrimp may be used in any recipe calling for shrimp.

Shrimp are customarily sold according to size or grade. This is based on the number of heads-off shrimp to the kilogram. The count or number designation may also be described by such general terms as jumbo, large, medium and small. Jumbo or large shrimp generally cost the most but take less time to peel and de-vein; small shrimp cost less but take longer to prepare. One kilogram of headless shrimp will yield approximately 500 grams of shelled meat.

Cooking Shrimp

Immerse the green or raw shrimp in boiling salted water. Work with small quantities and use only enough water to cover the shrimp. The recommended proportion is 50 ml salt for 1 litre of water. Cover the saucepan and begin timing as soon as the water returns to the boiling point.

Suitable boiling times vary according to the size of the shrimp being cooked and whether or not they are in the frozen state. Both frozen shrimp, which need not be thawed first, and large prawns, require 3-5 minutes cooking time. Small thawed or fresh shrimp require only 1-3 minutes cooking time.

Because the shells become difficult to remove and the meat undesirably soft, it is important that shrimp not be overcooked. To prevent this happening, chill the cooked shrimp immediately in running cold water or ice water. Once they are cooked, drain shrimp and remove shells. Larger shrimp will have a noticeable sand vein to be removed. Because shellfish deteriorate rapidly, store in the refrigerator until ready to use.

CRABS

Pacific or Dungeness crabs are fished off the Queen Charlotte Islands, on the west coast of Vancouver Island, and in less significant numbers along the British Columbia coastline. King crabs come from the North Pacific off Alaska.

Crabs are available alive in the shell, cooked in the shell, either fresh or frozen, and as shelled crabmeat, which is sold fresh, frozen or canned. Live crabs are generally sold within a comparatively short distance of the point of capture as it is difficult to ship them long distances. Fresh crabs should be alive at the time of cooking. Once cooked, they must be kept refrigerated, iced or frozen until they are used.

Cooking Live Crab

Plunge the live crab, head first, into actively boiling salted water. The proportion of salt to use is about 50 ml salt for each litre of water. Cover and simmer for 15-20 minutes. Cool quickly under cold water.

Shelling and Cleaning Crab

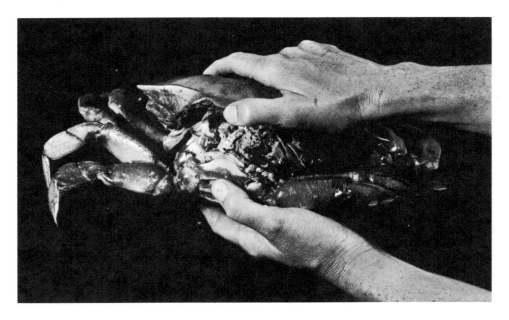

1. Holding the crab with the left hand, lift the top shell from the rear and pull off. Discard the shell and the yellow fat which clings to it.

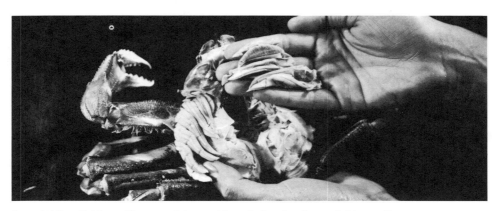

2. Lift off the gills on either side of the back and discard.
3. Turn the crab on its back and break off the mouth parts and the tail piece or apron.
4. Turn the crab over again and scrape out the centre fat and entrails and flush the cavity under cold running water.

5. Holding the crab with both hands, crack the body shell in half over the edge of a sink or other convenient projection.
6. Shake out the body meat from each half shell (to which the legs are still attached) by crushing the shell and knocking it against the edge of a bowl. Remove any bits of meat that cling to the shell with a small fork or pick.
7. Break off the legs. Pull out the movable small claw or pincer claws and the sharp inside shell pulls out, too. Holding the legs curved side down to avoid crushing the meat, hit sharply with a loosely held mallet. Extract meat from the shell.
8. Rinse meat in salted water and drain.

SCALLOPS

Although scallops have been found off the coast of British Columbia, commercial fishery is confined to deep water areas off the coast of the Atlantic provinces. Like oysters and clams, scallops are two-shelled. They are shelled or "shucked" as soon as they are caught. Only the tender cube of white meat which functions as a muscle to control the movement of the shells, is kept. This meat is packaged and marketed by weight in both fresh and frozen form.

Scallops require a very short cooking time at a moderate temperature. The delicately flavoured meat resembles the white meat of chicken or turkey and will dry out and become tough if overcooked.

LOBSTER

Lobster is marketed live, cooked in the shell (either fresh or frozen), or as canned lobster meat. Although seldom available in Western Canada, a live lobster shows movement of the legs and a tail which curls under the body when handled. The tail of a cooked lobster should spring back quickly after it has been straightened out showing that the lobster was alive and healthy when immersed in the boiling water. It should have been alive until the moment of cooking.

There are two distinct types of lobster, the Northern or Maine lobster and the related rock or spiny lobster. The Northern lobster is most plentiful along the Atlantic coast. The southern variety imported principally from Australia is the one with which Westerners are most familiar. The Maine lobster is valued partly for its big, meaty claws and ranges in mass from 500 g to 1 500 g. Rock lobster has most of the meat in the tail. Tails, with the shell on, usually range from 120 g to 250 g each. A serving may consist of one large tail or two smaller ones. They are usually available frozen.

The back or upper side of the rock lobster tail is covered by fairly heavy, jointed shell and the underside by a thin, flexible membrane. In order to remove the meat, this membrane can be cut with kitchen shears or a sharp heavy knife along both edges and then pulled away. To broil the tail, remove the membrane, bend the tail backwards, brush with butter and broil about 8 cm below the heat for about 5 minutes.

PARALYTIC SHELLFISH POISONING

("Red Tide")

The so-called "red tide" is a phenomenon caused by the presence of a tiny marine organism in such large numbers as to impart a red colour to the sea water. This organism ordinarily lives far out at sea. Occasionally during July and August it moves into shellfish beds through the effects of ocean currents, tides or winds and makes the shellfish which feed upon them unsafe to eat.

The organism contains a specific substance which is very toxic to man and yet it has no effect upon the host shellfish after accumulating in the digestive tract of the clam, oyster, mussel or other shellfish.

No amount of cooking will make such shellfish fit for human consumption because the toxin is of a chemical nature. Therefore, unlike bacterially affected shellfish, which may be made safe by adequate cooking, the shellfish picked up during a red tide retain the toxic materials at all times. Therefore, during summer months, May to October, check with local fishery officers regarding the shellfish condition.

Wild Game and Game Birds

Big Game

Venison is the meat of antlered animals (antelope, caribou, deer, elk, moose, and reindeer). In general usage, the word venison is taken to refer to the meat of the deer. The procedure for field dressing, skinning and cutting are similar for all of these animals although the meat of each has its own characteristic flavour.

No matter which animal the meat comes from, the enjoyment of venison depends on the care it has received in the field. Many hunters, once they have shot their game, give little thought to its handling from then on until it appears on the dinner table. The strong or gamey flavour to which some people object when they say they "don't care for venison" is actually that of meat improperly cared for. If a prime steer were to be similarly mishandled, it too would have a tainted flavour, quite different from the flavour of good beef. When people react unfavourably to wild meat it is not necessarily the fault of the cook. It is more likely that the animal was not dressed properly and that the meat wasn't handled afterwards as it should have been.

STEPS FOR THE HUNTER

1. **Bleeding**

   The bleeding procedure is of prime importance no matter what type of ammunition is used and this step in game preparation should be given careful attention.

2. **Field Dressing**

   Musk glands of deer, identified by oval tufts of bristly hair on both the inside and outside of the hind legs, should be carefully removed before field dressing is begun. The hands should not touch these or the meat may become tainted when it is handled later on.

   Veteran hunters vary in their preferred steps in field dressing. The important points, however, are to remove the internal organs immediately after the kill, without contaminating the body cavity with dirt, hair, or the contents of the digestive tract; and to drain all excess blood from the body cavity. The carcass should be cooled quickly, using a stick to prop it open so that the air can circulate. Any part of the meat which has been badly shot up can be cut away.

3.   Skinning

The animal may be skinned in camp or it may be taken home for this step. It should be skinned as soon as is reasonably practical, generally within the first 24 hours after shooting. A large animal will not cool quickly in temperate weather with the skin on. In a cold climate the skinning is completed more easily before the hide freezes on.

A properly skinned animal will have no nicks on the surface of the skin and the hide will be free of flesh and of knife cuts.

4.   Transportation

Great care should be taken to get the carcass home in as clean a condition as possible. If the animal has been skinned in the field it can be quartered and wrapped in cheesecloth or the butchers' tubing used in packing houses for easy, clean transportation.

The practice of bringing the animal home draped over a car fender is to be discouraged, as the heat of the car motor will start meat spoilage. It is better to carry the carcass on the car roof. Depending upon outside temperature, the trunk of the car may be preferable.

STEPS BEFORE COOKING

1.   Handling the Meat

Before cutting up the carcass it is best to age or ripen it as is done for good beef. A temperature of $0°C$ to $5°C$ is ideal. The meat should be allowed to hang in a well ventilated area at this temperature for 5-7 days. Very large animals such as moose may be aged up to 10 days and smaller deer, perhaps only 2 or 3 days. If the recommended low temperature cannot be maintained, the time should be reduced.

2.   Cutting the Meat

Skilful butchering of game ensures maximum yield in good cuts of meat with minimum waste. It is generally most convenient to use the locker service of an experienced butcher for the cutting, wrapping and freezing of the meat. A butcher will usually also have facilities for hanging the meat.

Whether it is to be stored in a locker or a home freezer, the meat should be properly wrapped and quick-frozen at $-20°C$ or lower. Slow freezing, which results if a large amount of fresh wrapped meat is placed in the home freezer all at once, causes large crystals to form. These rupture the cells of the meat and result in loss, upon thawing, of the vital meat juices.

If locker service is not available, a satisfactory job of cutting and wrapping can be done in the home. A good sharp knife, a common handsaw or meat saw, and a meat cleaver or hatchet are basic tools.

Protecting the table or counter top with cutting boards or a large piece of plywood is important.

Cutting venison is very similar to cutting beef or veal. Antlered animals vary in size and, therefore, in meat yield. The dressed yield of game animals works out to about 50 to 60 per cent of live weight.

The first step in butchering is to saw the hanging carcass in half down the backbone. Then each half can be worked with separately. Some knowledge of the location of the large bones in the carcass is a definite advantage in cutting meat. The diagram included here locates and names the major bones.

Bone Structure

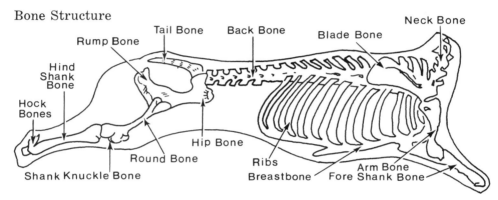

The next step is to divide the carcass into pieces systematically as indicated by the cutting lines on the diagram below:

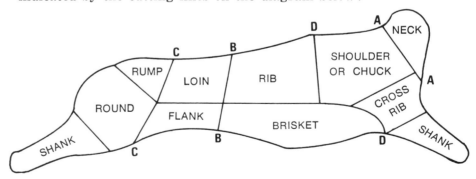

Begin by removing the neck along line A-A. Then separate the animal into quarters, front and hind, by cutting through on line B-B, which is between the second and third rib. Next, remove the hind leg by cutting close to and in front of the hip bone along C-C. To cut off the foreleg, start between the fourth and fifth or the fifth and sixth ribs and continue along the line of D-D.

When the carcass has been broken down in this manner, the large cuts can be divided into smaller pieces as illustrated on the diagram. The number and size of each type of small cut will depend upon the size and species of animal and the size (mass) of cut most suitable for the family for which the meat is being cut. Here is a list of the cuts obtained from antlered animals:

CUTS OF VENISON

Loin and Rib
This is the most tender meat and is generally cut into steaks or chops. It may be boned and rolled for choice roasts or may be boned entirely, leaving a tenderloin strip and prime boneless steaks.

Rump
Depending upon the age and condition of the animal, this part may be used for oven roasts or pot roasts.

Round
This is normally tender and may be cut into steaks. When the leg of the animal is small it may be oven-roasted whole. Some of the round may be tough and more suitable for braising, stewing or cooking in the minced form.

Shank
Both hind and fore shank yield good stew meat. This meat is frequently ground and the bones used for soup.

Shoulder or Chuck
This part may be tough but will make good pot roasts or ground meat. If the animal was young, some steaks can be cut here, too.

Neck, Flank and Brisket
After the tendons have been removed from the neck, the meat is suitable for stew or ground meat. The flank and brisket are best ground, but can also be used for soup or stew meat.

3.   Wrapping and Freezing
As the meat is cut up it should be wrapped, sealed, labelled and placed so as to freeze quickly. Stewing and hamburger meat is wrapped in recipe-size packages; roasts wrapped individually, and steaks or chops wrapped individually or according to the number suitable for a meal. A close airtight wrapping, free of air pockets, is necessary for fine quality and freshness in any frozen meat. This is particularly true of venison, which is lean and coarse and tends to dry out quickly.

Tough, heavy moisture and vapour-proof wrapping, intended for freezing purposes, is the best choice. Plastic bags which are heavy-duty, leak-proof and large enough to be secured with a twister, are especially suitable for minced meat and stew meat. A quick dip in hot (not boiling) water before sealing will collapse the bag to the contours of its contents, allowing it to be sealed air-free. Remember, the thinner the package, the faster it freezes. (For more information on wrapping and freezing meat, refer to the Freezing section in this book).

If a home freezer is the only method available for quick-freezing, an effort should be made to place the packages well spread out along the sides and bottom of the freezer, allowing air circulation to speed the freezing process. Do not pile the packages. If necessary, some packages can be held in the refrigerator until the first lot has completely frozen. Remember that the amount of fresh meat which a home freezer can efficiently freeze at one time is directly related to the total capacity of that freezer. Properly frozen venison will keep at −20°C for up to a year.

Some cooks who specialize in game cookery advise removing all traces of fat and others insist that the fat is essential to the flavour of the meat and the fatter the animal, the better. The fat layer is the main source of any "gamey" taste. If a strong characteristic flavour is preferred, let the meat cook in its own fat. However, there are times when it is advisable to trim away the fat as butchering continues:

1. The meat flavour is influenced by feeding habits of the animal and diet flavours settle in the fat. Certain vegetation results in an objectionable flavour.

2. Any "off" flavours the game may have picked up between the field and the kitchen tend to concentrate in the fat.

3. Removing all the fat from meat which is to be frozen and kept will allow maximum length of storage time. As with pork, it is the fat which deteriorates first.

COOKING GAME MEAT

There is little difference between cooking wild meat and range-fed beef. The cuts and methods of cooking used are similar. There are, however, some basic differences in the characteristics of the meats of domestic stock and most game meats. Skilful cooking of the wild varieties must make allowance for these differences:

1. Even a fat deer has very little intermuscular fat. Especially if the

covering layer of fat has been removed, fat in some form must be added. There are many ways of replacing fat:

(*a*) Fat may simply be added to the meat. Examples:
- beef fat on top of a roast during cooking.
- steaks basted with table fat while broiling.
- butter, margarine, ground pork or sausage meat mixed with minced meat before cooking.

(*b*) The meat may be wrapped with strips of bacon or salt pork and toothpicks or string used to fasten them in place.

(*c*) A common way is by *larding* the meat. A tubular needle is used to draw chilled pork fat or salt pork through the meat at intervals about 5 cm apart. If asked, a butcher will usually do this.

(*d*) The meat can be pierced with a long thin knife and then chilled strips of pork pushed into the holes.

2. Because the meat tends to dry easily, a special effort is needed to keep it moist.

(*a*) When cooking by dry heat methods, addition of bacon drippings, butter or oil will help prevent drying.

(*b*) Less tender cuts should be cooked by moist heat methods.

(*c*) Avoid overcooking, especially with venison. If possible, serve steaks and chops rare. If well done meat is wanted, stop the cooking immediately when the juices stop flowing. The zestful flavour of the meat is derived from its natural juices. Meat cooked too long will quickly become dry and tough.

(*d*) A good habit when serving a meat like venison is to pour a little gravy or pan juice over the meat on the serving platter. In this way the meat arrives at the table moist and flavourful.

3. The age of the animal, the type of feed available and the season of the year all affect the tenderness of the meat. If you are not sure of the cut or the age and condition of the animal from which it came, some tenderizing procedure may be advisable to ensure tender meat:

(*a*) Use an unseasoned meat tenderizer.

(*b*) Use a moist heat cooking method such as pot roasting, braising or stewing .

(*c*) Include an acid ingredient in the recipe. Substances such as lemon juice, vinegar, sour cream or tomatoes help to tenderize the meat.

(*d*) Pounding is one way of breaking up the connective tissue of tough meat; mincing also makes meat tender to eat.

(*e*) Use a *marinade*. This is a combination of vinegar, oil and season-ings, in which the meat is soaked for several hours to make it more tender and give it additional flavour.

4. Do not attempt to conceal the excellent flavour of good game meat. Proper cooking is simple and will bring out the taste of the meat and not camouflage it. If you want to modify the flavour, spices, herbs and sauces may be used sparingly. Bouillon cubes, beef extracts and similar preparations are a good alternative. Marinades will tenderize as well as flavour the meat.

COOKING BEAR MEAT

The main difference between cooking bear meat and the meat from any of the cloven hoofed animals previously discussed is that it should always be cooked until well done. The same parasite infection, called trichinosis, which can occur in domestic pork is a danger in bear meat if it is served rare and pink. There is usually quite a thick layer of fat on the animal but the meat itself is not marbled, so fat must be added, as with venison. As bear meat has a rather strong flavour for which a taste must be culti-vated by most people, the seasoning is important. Here are some sugges-tions for cooking bear meat:

1. Cut off any fat that has not been removed during butchering.

2. Use a tenderizer, following the directions on the label.

3. Use a marinade over the meat, cover and place in the refrigerator for 48 hours.

4. Choose a recipe that is quite highly spiced or add seasonings to suit your taste.

5. Cook until well done in order to kill any trichinae parasite that may be present. There is a danger of trichinosis if the meat is served pink and rare. See page 456 for trichinae in pork.

GAME BIRDS

As with game animals, prompt care of freshly shot birds is essential. To prevent intestinal waste from seeping through the shot holes into the flesh, all game birds should be cleaned immediately after shooting. Cut off the oil sac at the tail base. An effort should be made to allow the flesh to cool before packing birds for the trip home. They should be transported in such a manner that air can circulate.

Plucking of the bird is best done as soon as possible. Plucking wild birds is preferable to skinning them since the skin adds much to the flavour and appearance of the meat, and prevents the meat from drying out. Birds that are skinned are best cooked with moist heat as they dry out quickly.

To avoid tearing the skin, dry pluck birds while still warm. Pull the feathers downward and in the direction that they grow. The feathers can be loosened by dipping the bird in boiling water for a few seconds. Remove the pinfeathers with tweezers. Then singe the down feathers with a lighted, twisted newspaper, being careful not to burn the skin.

If birds are to be frozen for later use they are more tender if allowed to hang for 1-2 days or to age in the refrigerator for 2-3 days. Preparation for freezing is outlined in the section on Freezing, page 449.

Cooking of game birds is basically the same as for any poultry. Some varieties are a bit tough unless cooked by a moist heat method. See Cooking Tough Poultry. Game birds sometimes have a gamey flavour. This is not to be confused with the really rank odour of ducks that have dined on decayed fish before shooting. Such birds are better destroyed than attempting to cook and eat them.

The gamey or fishy taste of wild birds can be reduced or improved in a number of ways. Here are some methods that have proven successful:

1. Place raw onion and carrot in body cavity of bird. These can remain overnight and during roasting, then remove and discard vegetables after meat is cooked.

2. Soak overnight in cold water to which baking soda, to draw the strong flavour, and salt, to draw out blood, has been added.

3. Soak overnight in milk or in a marinade.

Introduction to Flour Mixtures

A flour mixture is a product which obtains its structure from gluten, the elastic-like protein substance in flour that forms when a liquid is mixed with flour. It is usually, though not always, baked in the oven. Examples of exceptions are pancakes which are cooked on a griddle, waffles in a waffle iron, doughnuts in deep fat. Flour mixtures vary widely as to ingredients, the proportions of the basic ones determining the structure which results. Also important is the method of combining these ingredients, the type of cooking utensil chosen and method of preparing it, and the temperature used to cook batter or dough. It is important to first understand the function of the ingredients which are common to most flour mixtures.

THE INGREDIENTS

A. Flour

Gluten is the protein substance in flour which forms strong elastic strands when mixed or kneaded with liquid. Heat hardens this protein and the flour mixture is held in its risen state.

All purpose flour has a good amount of gluten to provide the framework for most baked products.

Cake flour or cake and pastry flour contains less gluten than all purpose flour and, therefore, results in a tender, fine-textured product.

Most recipes specify the kind of flour that should be used. If a recipe does not, take it for granted that enriched all purpose flour is intended. For accuracy, sift flour once before measuring. If you must substitute all purpose flour in a recipe which calls for cake or pastry flour, use 10% less of the all purpose kind to reduce the amount of gluten in the flour mixture. You may make up the difference with cornstarch, which has no gluten.

See page 113, Cereals and Cereal Products for a more complete explanation of the types of flour.

B. Leavening Agent

A leavening agent is an ingredient or combination of ingredients which will make the flour mixture rise and become light and porous. *Carbon dioxide* is usually the gas which leavens a baked product, but air and steam, where they exist or are formed in the batter, are very important, too. Tiny bubbles of air, steam or carbon dioxide permeate the gluten framework and the oven heat causes them to expand. The heat of cooking finally hardens the protein and in so doing, traps the small bubbles into the mixture. There are three principal ways of producing carbon dioxide in a flour mixture:

1. BAKING POWDER is the leavening agent most frequently used. It is a commercially prepared complete leavener made from an acid in salt form, soda and starch.

    The acid salt determines the nature of the baking powder and whether it is single acting or double acting.

    The soda (sodium bicarbonate) is an alkali substance similar to baking soda used in the home.

    The starch is usually cornstarch. Its function is to absorb any moisture which may be in the air and which would release the carbon dioxide prematurely when the lid is off the tin.

    There are two types of baking powder, single acting and double acting. *Single-acting* baking powders have one acid ingredient, either phosphate or tartrate, which acts as soon as it is combined with a liquid and continues to give off carbon dioxide until it is no longer able to do so. This kind is sometimes called *fast acting.*

    Double-acting baking powder, sometimes termed *slow acting,* has two active acid ingredients. One of these acids reacts as soon as liquid is added but the second, sodium aluminum sulphate or SAS as it is usually called, has a delayed action. It forms carbon dioxide only when the batter or dough containing it is subjected to heat for cooking.

    Both of these kinds give satisfactory results and the type is usually indicated on the label. Unskilled cooks might find the double acting baking powder helps them produce a lighter product since some of the carbon dioxide is released after the batter or dough is in the oven. Double acting baking powder is also preferable in quick-mix recipes where the baking powder is added at the beginning of the recipe and in recipes where baking is delayed for some time after the mixture is prepared. Usually less of the double acting than single acting kind is required in recipes. To substitute a double for a single-acting baking powder use two thirds as much.

2. BAKING SODA acts as a leavening agent when combined with a suitable acid substance such as sour milk or buttermilk. Other acid ingredients which when they are included in the recipe, will produce the desired carbon dioxide are: cream of tartar, sour cream, yogurt, vinegar, lemon juice, molasses or any acid fruit. Some recipes which utilize the action of soda call for baking powder as well.

3. YEAST is a single-celled microscopic plant which produces carbon dioxide gas as a by-product of its growth. In order to grow, it must

have sugar for food, warmth and moisture. Its growth and carbon dioxide production can be controlled by temperature as well as available sugar. The yeast becomes active at about 10°C and multiplies rapidly at temperatures of 25° - 30°C. Cooler temperatures are less effective. The rising temperatures of the yeast dough as it warms in the oven accelerates the release of carbon dioxide until eventually the yeast plants are killed. Continued baking firms the strong gluten framework that was formed by kneading and a porous yeast bread product results. (See section on Yeast breads.)

Air contributes leavening to all batters and doughs. Its importance to the total amount of leavening of the finished product varies considerably. The amount of air contained in the batter is determined by the amount and kind of mixing done, the thickness or thinness of the batter, the ingredients used, and the length of time between mixing and baking. Whatever air is present in the mixture will expand as it is warmed in the oven and cause an increase in the volume of the baked product. Air is incorporated when the flour is sifted, when the batter is beaten, when eggs – especially the whites – are whipped. The most outstanding example of the value of air as a leavener is in foam-type cakes such as angel or sponge cake. These contain no additional leavener. Air and a small amount of steam formed, provide the total leavening power in these products.

Steam contributes some leavening power in all flour mixtures since they all contain liquid in some form. Even a product such as angel cake, which contains no milk or juice and a very small proportion of flour, will be leavened in part by formation of steam when the water content of the egg whites is heated in the oven.

Because the volume of water expands as much as 1600 times when it converts to steam, even a small amount of water in a batter or dough causes considerable leavening action. A stiff dough as is used for rolled or pressed cookies will expand slightly when the little moisture it contains converts to steam. A spectacular increase in volume is achieved when popover batter is baked. The intense heat of the oven very quickly converts the high proportion of fluid to steam. This accounts for the rising action which can easily be observed. Similar reactions occur when Yorkshire pudding and cream puff batter are baked.

C. Liquid

Liquid is essential to all flour mixtures since the gluten cannot be formed until a liquid is added to the flour. Liquid also functions as a solvent for certain dry ingredients such as sugar and salt. In particular, it is a solvent for a chemical leavening agent, such a baking powder, so that the carbon dioxide can be released. As mentioned in the preceeding section, any fluids present contribute to the leavening action by their conversion to steam during baking.

The liquid ingredient used in a recipe might be milk, water, juice, sour milk, sour cream or some other fluid. Each contributes a characteristic flavour and texture to the product. Water and juices give a coarse texture. Milk in any of its forms contributes better food value than the others and gives the product a finer texture and better flavour.

D. Fat

Fat performs several functions in a flour mixture:

1. It has a tenderizing effect because it interferes with the development of gluten. A batter or dough having a high proportion of fat can be manipulated more than one containing a minimum amount. If manipulated too much when there is little fat present in the mixture, the gluten strands become long and fully developed and a tough product is the result. For example, muffin batter is stirred only slightly to ensure tenderness but a butter cake batter is mixed or beaten until all the ingredients are well combined.

2. The appearance of the baked product is affected by the type of fat used. The difference in colour of products made with butter or margarine and those made with vegetable oil, shortening or lard is obvious. However, the firmness of the fat, where it is not creamed or melted, has an effect, too. Pastry or biscuits made with a firm fat produces a flaky product whereas liquid fat (oil) produces a more compact, though tender, product.

3. Depending upon the type used, the fat ingredient chosen may or may not improve the flavour. A vegetable shortening would not be substituted for butter or margarine in a shortbread cookie recipe but a similar substitution in a chocolate cake recipe would not impair the flavour of the cake.

4. Although not as important a factor in the browning process, as for example, sugar, certain fats do affect the colour of the product, especially when they are used to prepare the baking pans. Butter and margarine brown easily and may cause unwanted browning if used to grease a cake or cookie pan. A vegetable oil or lard would be a safer choice.

E. Eggs

The functions of eggs in flour mixtures are numerous. The extent of their importance to the finished product depends upon the number used and the way they are handled before they are added to the batter.

1. Eggs contribute valuable nutrients to the mixture.

2. Eggs contribute to the structure of the product in direct proportion to the volume of egg present. For example, egg protein in a standard

muffin recipe contributes little to the protein framework whereas the larger amounts of egg used in a butter cake made with low gluten flour are more significant. As the cooking heat coagulates these proteins, the final structure becomes fixed.

3. When the yolk of the egg is used it contributes colour.

4. Flavour is contributed by yolks and whites.

5. The leavening effect of eggs due to the ability of both yolks and white to form foams, has been discussed under "B", Leavening Agents.

6. Egg yolks are an important emulsifying agent especially in cake batters which contain a high proportion of fat. This emulsifying ability is best seen in the preparation of cream puffs.

F. Sugar

Properties of sugar determine its function in the flour mixture.

1. Sugar is sweet. Therefore, it contributes to the flavour.

2. Sugar caramelizes when subjected to heat. In a baked product this causes the browning which occurs. If one compares the ingredients used to make biscuits with those used to make muffins, it becomes evident that, aside from the egg also present in muffins, sugar is the main variable. This explains why muffins are a browner colour than biscuits.

3. Sugar has a high affinity for water. Some of the liquid in a batter or dough is attracted to the sugar present. Therefore, less liquid is available for gluten development. This means that more manipulation is necessary to develop the gluten framework of flour mixtures having a high proportion of sugar. Adequate mixing is possible without unwanted toughening.

4. Sugar has a number of other functions related to the volume of the finished product. It weakens the gluten network, allowing stretching to occur more readily as the gases expand. Presence of sugar in a flour mixture raises the coagulation temperature of the proteins present. This allows a longer baking time, before the structure is finally set, in which maximum leavening can take place.

G. Salt

The principal reason for adding salt to any flour mixture is that it improves the flavour of the other ingredients. In yeast products it also assists in regulating the rate at which the yeast grows.

H. Flavourings

Some flour mixtures contain special flavouring ingredients which enhance the natural flavours of the other ingredients present.

CLASSIFICATION OF FLOUR MIXTURES

Flour mixtures are often divided into batters and doughs. A batter is of a consistency to be poured or dropped on to the baking pan. During preparation a batter is beaten, more or less vigorously, depending upon the proportions of the ingredients used in the recipe. A dough is too thick to be beaten. It requires handling or kneading in order for the ingredients to be properly combined.

Batters are sometimes divided into drop batters and pour batters. Those with a high proportion of liquid to dry ingredients pour readily and are included in the thin or pour batter group. Although most cake batters contain much less liquid than other pour batters, they do, however, pour because of the effects of the high level of sugar and are usually grouped with the pour batters. A drop batter usually contains about half as much liquid as a pour batter. Doughs are similarly classified as soft and stiff doughs, also on the basis of the proportion of liquid to dry ingredients.

PROPORTIONS OF LIQUID TO DRY INGREDIENTS IN FLOUR MIXTURES

CLASSIFICATION	LIQUIDS	FLOUR	EXAMPLES
Thin or pour batter	1 part	1 part	pancakes, waffles, popovers, Yorkshire pudding.
Thick or drop batter	1 part	2 parts	muffins, cakes, coffee-cake, gingerbread, fruit-nut loaf, corn-bread, drop biscuits.
Soft dough	1 part	3 parts	biscuits, bread, dumplings, dough-nuts, fritters.
Stiff dough	1 part	4 parts	pastry, cookies.

Liquid ingredients include any that are in liquid form when added to the dry ingredients such as: milk, water, juice, melted fat or oil, egg.

STEPS IN PREPARATION OF ANY FLOUR MIXTURE *(Except when flour mixture is to be cooked by some method other than baking)*

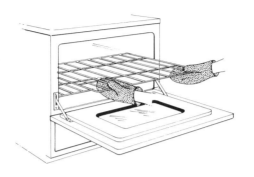

1. **Adjust Oven Racks**

   The rack on which the pan is to be placed should be in the centre of the oven. A rack for yeast bread can be placed closer to the bottom of the oven. Cakes having a large volume such as chiffon, sponge and angel cakes are better on a lower rack also so that the product will bake evenly on all sides. Foods should not be placed on two racks unless absolutely necessary. When using two racks, arrange them so the oven is divided into thirds. Then it is important to place the pans so that heat can circulate freely.

2. **Preheat Oven**

   The two oven elements may both be used for preheating. The signal light which glows when the oven is turned on will usually go off when the desired temperature is reached. It then goes on and off during baking to indicate the temperature is being maintained. If the flour mixture is placed in the oven while the top element is still on to preheat the oven, the top of the product will burn.

   A preheated oven is important so that the product can be baked at a constant temperature. Timing can be accurately estimated and the product will not dry out or burn.

3. Prepare the Pan

Use the pan size specified in the recipe and prepare it as instructed. Use the right type of pan for the mixture being prepared. Aluminum pans are best for all cakes, cookies, breads and biscuits. Black, discoloured, warped or glass pans concentrate the heat so that baked foods overcook. Glassware is best for pastry since it concentrates the heat and helps to bake the bottom crust quickly before it can become soggy. Cookie sheets should be absolutely flat with no sides. A jelly roll pan, having shallow sides, will prevent proper browning of thin cookies.

Remember that butter and margarine brown easily at most oven temperatures. This may give the product an undesirably darkened crust. In addition to oil, shortening and lard, various spray coatings are available which prevent sticking of the product. Pans for most products are greased. Examples: muffins, cookies, pancakes.

Cake pans are greased and dusted with flour or lined with waxed paper.

Pans for foam type cakes are never greased and should be spotlessly clean.

Paper liners may be used for cupcakes or muffins.

Pans coated during manufacture may not need to be greased.

4. Assemble and Measure Ingredients

Preparation time is reduced when all the ingredients are ready before mixing is begun. This is important to success when ingredients should be combined quickly as in making muffins. Some flour mixtures lose part of their leavening power when allowed to stand. Egg white foams lose air, baking powder releases carbon dioxide.

In addition, certain ingredients serve their function better when they are at room temperature. For example: eggs beat to a better volume, firm fats combine with sugar more readily.

Measuring ingredients correctly is essential to good results. In no type of cooking is it more critical than in preparing flour mixtures. See Appendix for detailed instruction.

5. **Prepare the Flour Mixture**

    Careful attention to the details of the recipe is the best assurance of a good product. It is a wise cook who reads the recipe through first and then attempts to understand not only how, but why, each step is taken.

6. **Place the Mixture in the Prepared Pan**

    Allow for expansion during baking. Place a cake in the correct sized pan so that it will not be too flat or will not overflow the sides. Fill cupcake pans ½ - ⅔ full; separate cookies so they will not join together on the pan; adjust the amount of batter used for each pancake to the size of the pan and the diameter of pancake you desire; allow room for bread dough to double in bulk.

    Beginning cooks are often disappointed with the contour of cakes and loaves they make using a thick batter. The simple practice of pushing the batter up the sides of the pan will produce a more level surface on the baked loaf.

    Cleanup will be simplified if drips of batter or dough falling on the pan where they are not intended, are prevented or are wiped up before they burn in the oven.

7. **Bake the Flour Mixture** *(This step is meant to include cooking of flour mixtures which are not baked; for example, pancakes, waffles, doughnuts, fritters.)*

    The circulation of heat in the oven is essential to good baking results. To keep the heat circulating freely the pans must be properly placed in the oven. Assuming the racks were adjusted (step 1) before the oven was preheated, pans can be placed so that they do not touch each other, the oven walls or the door. If heat cannot circulate, products will not be evenly browned and will also rise unevenly. If two racks are being used, "stagger" the pans so one is not directly over the other.

    Oven racks are intended to glide out easily. If they are pulled out for loading and unloading the oven, burnt arms and fingers can be prevented. Check the time when your flour mixture goes into the oven.

    If you are using a "minute minder", set it for the shortest baking time stated in the recipe. Most cake recipes will have a 10-15 minute deviation in suggested cooking time, cookies may allow only 2-5 minutes. The variations allowed will depend upon the total cooking time and the product. A product which has a lengthy baking time will have a greater time flexibility than one which is baked for only a few minutes.

    When the minimum suggested time has elapsed, check the product to determine if it is "done". (Do not open the oven before this time since maintaining a constant oven temperature is important to time and baking results.) Have a toothpick ready if the test requires it. Use oven mitts or potholders to pull out racks. Be ready to remove the product if it is cooked. If the product is not completely cooked, replace it quickly and close the oven door to prevent unnecessary escape of heat.

8. **Cool the Product**

Some flour mixtures are at their best when served immediately, while hot from the oven. Others must be cooled carefully to retain the best quality characteristics and may require further treatment, for example, addition of an icing or glaze. Details of care of the product after it is baked will be dealt with when specific flour mixtures are discussed in the sections which follow.

Quickbreads

A quickbread is a flour mixture that can be prepared quickly and easily, without the aid of yeast for leavening, and is usually served hot in place of bread at a meal. Examples include muffins, biscuits, pancakes, waffles, popovers and some coffeecakes and fruit or nut loaves.

All quickbreads differ from yeast breads in the time required for preparation and the leavener used. Quickbreads can be mixed and baked in an hour or less; most yeast bread recipes require 4-6 hours. Quickbreads are leavened by air, steam and carbon dioxide, while yeast breads, as their name indicates, are leavened by the carbon dioxide produced by yeast.

This section deals separately with the preparation of muffins, pancakes, waffles and biscuits. The principles involved can be applied to the preparation of any other quickbread and also to many other flour mixtures. For example, most fruit and nut loaf recipes are essentially a muffin batter baked in a loaf pan. Popover batter is very similar to pancake batter although it contains a higher proportion of eggs and no baking powder. The same steam leavened mixture is used to make Yorkshire pudding, a quickbread traditionally served with roast beef and gravy. In Yorkshire pudding the melted fat is beef drippings rather than oil or melted butter.

A coffeecake is a flour mixture that can be classified as a quickbread. It is mixed by either biscuit method, muffin method or a combination of the two and is usually served hot, with a beverage, for a snack. A coffeecake is not iced but usually has a topping of spices, fruit, nuts, cereal, sugar.

For a more complete explanation of the ingredients used for flour mixtures in general refer to page 274, Introduction to Flour Mixtures. Also included in that section is a classification of all flour mixtures with the basic step by step procedure for their preparation. Page 294 begins a section on the preparation of yeast breads while following sections deal with other specific types of flour mixtures.

Muffins

Muffins are an easy-to-prepare quickbread and often the first flour mixture attempted by beginning cooks. The ingredients are few in number but each aptly demonstrates its characteristic function where it occurs in any flour mixture. Refer to page 274 for the functions of ingredients used in flour mixtures. The method used to combine these ingredients, called muffin method, is used in the preparation of many other flour mixtures. Proficiency with this mixing method will, therefore, contribute to success with other recipes.

A good muffin has these characteristics

EXTERIOR   A golden brown colour.
A gently rounded top without a peak or knob-like projections.
A pebbly surface, not smooth.
A light weight in relation to its size.

INTERIOR   A uniform texture free from tunnels.
A tender crumb which allows the muffin to break easily without crumbling.
A delicate flavour characteristic of the ingredients used but with no trace of bitterness.

Preparation

Muffins are mixed by "muffin method". To do this the dry ingredients are first measured and sifted altogther into the mixing bowl. The liquid ingredients, which include the beaten egg, milk and melted fat, are combined separately in a small bowl. The recommended sequence is to beat the egg well, then beat in the milk and add the fat. A well beaten egg reduces later mixing, and dilution of the egg with milk avoids possibility of the egg cooking in lumps from the addition of hot fat. Cooling of the fat before it is added is a further precaution.

The mixing step is the critical one in preparing light tender muffins. Because the batter contains a high proportion of flour which produces strong gluten, and has little fat or sugar to exert a tenderizing effect, it can easily be overmixed. Recipes all advise to stir gently, preferably with a fork, only until the dry ingredients are moistened. The batter should still be quite lumpy. A smooth batter indicates overmixing and will result in muffins with a smooth exterior surface and a peaked top, and long vertical tunnels inside.

Speed in mixing the dry and liquid ingredients together once they have come in contact with each other, and avoiding delay in getting the muffins into the oven, will prevent loss of carbon dioxide gas which accounts for the principal leavening. Use of a double acting baking powder would be especially helpful to a beginner in obtaining a good muffin product.

Baking

To prevent the product from sticking, muffin pans usually need to be greased with vegetable shortening or oil. Butter or margarine will cause unwanted additional browning, and will contribute to eventual discolouration of the pans. Dark or discoloured pans produce a darkened product; shiny pans are more desirable.

Specially treated muffin pans requiring no pre-treatment are available. These pans should be carefully handled to prevent scratching the non-stick surface.

To save time, sometimes paper baking cups are used in regular pans. Then the paper liners are removed as the muffins are eaten.

Pans should be ready before the liquid and dry ingredients are combined. Then once the batter is ready it can quickly be spooned into the pans. Extra mixing is to be avoided as this is being done. Better muffins are obtained when the spoon holds just enough batter to fill the pan two-thirds full without adding or removing further small portions. Any batter drops or spills should be wiped from the pan or these will burn during baking.

The temperature for baking muffins is usually relatively high ranging from 190°C to 220°C depending upon the proportions of ingredients in the recipe. A hot oven causes very rapid conversion of the moisture in the batter to steam which then expands and contributes to the leavening action of the carbon dioxide which is being produced at the same time.

Serving

Muffins are usually at their best when served hot although many varieties, especially the richer ones, are good when eaten cold. They may easily be reheated in an oven or a covered electric fry pan or other suitable appliance. As are all quickbreads, muffins are most often served with butter or margarine to replace bread at a meal.

Pancakes

Pancakes are a type of quickbread made from a pour batter which is cooked quickly on a griddle, skillet or electric frypan. A good pancake will be golden brown on both sides without crusty edges and will be light, fine grained and tender. It should be cooked through to the center and served piping hot.

Depending upon personal preference, pancakes can be thick or thin. The consistency of the batter determines thickness of the pancake. A thin batter tends to give a thin, crisp, pancake which cooks quickly. A thick batter gives a thick pancake with a texture more like that of cake or bread. Thick batters cook more slowly and the pancake will have a tendency to be soggy in the centre.

Preparation

The ingredients and method for pancakes are the same as for muffins but different proportions are used. Because the batter for pancakes is much thinner it can be mixed until there are fewer flour lumps in the batter. Pancakes can be made from flour, milk, baking powder and salt but their quality is much improved by adding eggs. Fat added to the batter in melted form helps to make a tender product and relieves sticking to the pan. When sugar is present it assists the browning process.

Cooking

Unless the pan is thermostatically controlled it should be heated slowly. This will help achieve an evenly heated pan and give an evenly browned pancake. The griddle is ready if a drop of water bounces when dropped in the pan.

If the recipe contains a high proportion of fat the griddle may not need to be oiled. Avoid using margarine or butter to grease the skillet for it burns easily and gives a darkened product.

When placing the batter on the griddle remember that a thin batter spreads out readily. Use a small amount for the first pancake to determine how much space to allow. The batter can be spooned onto the pan but pouring it from a jug is easier.

Pancakes should be turned only once during the baking. They will become heavy otherwise. The pancake is ready to be turned when the bubbles that have formed on the surface begin to break. A thick batter does not form air bubbles that are noticeable, therefore care must be taken not to overcook. Turn them and brown the other side.

Serving

Pancakes should be served as soon as they are cooked, while piping hot. When stacked and held in the oven they very quickly become soggy. They can be placed on a rack on a cookie sheet and held for a short time. Breakfast pancakes are usually served with syrup, a fruit sauce, or some other favourite spread which is usually sweet. Tiny plain pancakes are sometimes served cold, spread with butter to accompany a hot beverage.

French pancakes, called "crêpes suzettes" are served as dessert. They are made from a batter which contains more eggs, sugar and milk than the standard pancake recipe. These pancakes may have a crisp crust and are thin. To serve, they are rolled and filled with fresh fruit and whipped cream. When placed on individual serving dishes they are dusted lightly with icing sugar.

Waffles

Waffles are made from a pour batter similar in composition to pancake batter. However, more fat and eggs are normally used and make for a richer quickbread. It is necessary to have a waffle iron to make waffles.

This piece of equipment consists of two halves which fit together to form the pattern and are hinged at one side. Because a large surface of the batter is exposed to the heat the waffle becomes crisp. Modern waffle irons are thermostatically controlled while older models are heated on the surface of the range.

A good waffle will be well formed to the shape of the waffle iron used. It will be a uniform golden-brown colour, light, porous, tender and crisp and will be served piping hot.

Preparation

Many waffle recipes follow the muffin method for combining ingredients as do most pancake recipes. Usually the egg yolks and whites are beaten separately and the whites folded in last. This is a slight variation of the muffin method and gives a better texture. (See recipe page 505.)

Using a flour which has a low gluten content, such as pastry flour, gives a crisper waffle. Most waffle batter is of a medium consistency, a bit thicker than the usual pancake mixture. The thicker the batter the less it should be mixed, to prevent toughness.

Cooking

The waffle iron must be at the correct temperature or the waffles will stick. When using a non-automatic iron, put 5 ml water inside the iron and close it. When steaming stops, the iron is ready. Follow manufacturer's directions for an automatic iron. A pre-treated iron need not be greased.

When filling the waffle iron allow room for expansion of the batter during cooking. To prevent overflowing use 50-75 ml batter for each waffle.

Waffles rich in fat and sugar require 2-3 minutes additional baking time. Rich waffles may seem limp when first removed but they will become crisp in a short time.

Serving

Waffles are usually a breakfast quickbread although they may also be served as a luncheon dish or for a light supper meal. Serve them alone with butter and syrup, a fruit sauce or other preferred condiment, or to accompany some protein dish. Adding a protein food such as grated cheese, bacon bits, or chopped ham or luncheon meat to the batter provides a more substantial quickbread.

Biscuits

Biscuits are made from a soft dough of flour, salt, fat, milk and baking powder. Sometimes sour milk or buttermilk is used, in which case baking soda instead of baking powder produces the carbon dioxide gas which helps them raise. Other ingredients may be included in the recipe to give special flavour or texture effects.

Biscuit making requires a minimum of ingredients and demonstrates very well the "cutting in" of firm fat as well as the manipulation skills required to make similar products. Learning to make good biscuits, therefore, is an important first step in the progressive sequence of learning to handle other stiff flour mixtures and more difficult techniques.

A good biscuit has these characteristics:

EXTERIOR   Well shaped and symmetrical with straight sides and a level top.

          A delicate golden brown top with lighter coloured sides.

          A light weight in relation to its size.

INTERIOR   A creamy white colour.

          A crisp crust, free of excess flour.

          A tender, slightly moist crumb.

          A delicate flavour with no trace of bitterness.

Preparing the Dough

To prepare a biscuit dough the dry ingredients are sifted together into a mixing bowl. Then the cold fat is cut in until the mixture resembles coarse meal. This cutting step characterizes what is referred to as "biscuit method." A pastry blender is an efficient tool. Otherwise, two table knives held one in each hand and worked in a criss-cross motion are suitable. Some cooks use the tips of their fingers. This method is not recommended for beginners since the warmth of the hands may soften the fat and produce a sticky, overworked crumb mixture.

When the flour-fat mixture is ready the measured milk is added all at once. A fork is the best utensil for stirring since a lighter stroke is possible and overstirring is less likely. Usually about 30 strokes are required to thoroughly combine the ingredients. When the mixture is stiff, with no traces of dry flour, the dough can be turned onto a lightly floured board or wax paper and kneaded gently. Care is required to prevent overworking the dough — usually 10-15 strokes are sufficient.

Forming Biscuits

Next the dough is rolled or patted on a lightly floured board or pastry cloth until it is 1.5-2 cm thick. A floured cutter is used to cut the round shapes. If the cutter is pressed down without twisting the product will be more symmetrically shaped. Scraps are combined (without using more flour), re-rolled and cut. Shapes should be placed on the pan to allow 2 cm space between them for heat circulation. When placed close together, biscuits with soft sides similar to pan yeast rolls will result.

Preparation time can be reduced by simply cutting the biscuit dough, once it is the right thickness, with a sharp knife.

Another variation produces biscuits with an irregular shape and a more crumbly texture. To make these the milk is increased to give a thick drop batter and this is spooned directly onto a greased baking pan. Thus the kneading, rolling and cutting steps are eliminated and the cleanup required is reduced. Although much easier for beginners, drop biscuits do not provide practice in the important manipulation skills.

Baking

The baking pan used for rolled biscuits need not be greased. It should have low sides, preferably none at all, so that the oven heat will move evenly around each biscuit. A shiny-surfaced pan is desirable so that an even pale colour can be obtained.

Baking temperature for biscuits is hot, usually 220°C. This insures that the biscuits will rise quickly, forming layers which are characteristic of a good product.

Yeast Bread

Breadmaking is an art as old as history. It has always been an exciting experience, perhaps because yeast is a living plant and the baker can see evidence of this while watching the bread rise. Manipulation of the bread dough by a special technique called kneading has been credited with relaxing muscles and releasing built up tensions and frustrations. Each person has his or her own mental associations of the techniques and smells of bread making — usually they are happy ones.

METHODS OF MAKING YEAST BREAD

In recent years "convenience" methods of breadmaking have been perfected to the point where a homemaker who does not normally devote much time or effort to baking can prepare a quality product quickly and easily. Careful selection of an appropriate recipe is important. Although the basic principles are the same for each, certain aspects are quite different. Therefore, a wise cook will attempt to understand the method being used and the part that each ingredient plays in achieving satisfactory results. Here is an outline of the common methods of making yeast bread:

1. **Straight Dough Method**

   This is the standard method of making bread or buns with yeast. The kneaded dough is allowed to rise, is shaped into loaves or rolls, and allowed to rise again, and then baked. The entire sequence takes approximately four hours.

2. **Refrigerator Method**

   This method is the same as for the straight dough method except that the dough is allowed to rise overnight in the refrigerator. Because the rate of yeast development must be so carefully controlled in this method, the proportion of ingredients varies from the straight dough type breads. Specific refrigerator bread recipes must, therefore, be used.

3. **Cool Rise Method**

   The first steps for this method are the same as for straight dough. However, it is used only in recipes which have been developed specifically and should not be applied to any other yeast bread recipe. Cool rise method requires specially balanced formulas. After kneading, the dough is covered on the board and allowed to rest for about 20 minutes. It is then divided, shaped into loaves, and placed into greased pans.

After covering with oiled waxed paper and plastic wrap, it may be stored in the refrigerator for 2 to 24 hours. At baking time, raised loaves stand at room temperature for 10 minutes before baking.

4. **Rapid Mix Method**

The dry yeast is not dissolved first in warm water, but is instead mixed with some of the dry ingredients. This method should only be used with a finer grind of active dry yeast identified on the package label as Rapid Mix yeast. It does not work well with the more generally used pellet-type active dry yeast. Rapid mix makes it easier to blend the ingredients and there is no chance of lumps. The dough feels lighter and springier when it is being kneaded and it rises faster because the liquids are warmer (50°C to 55C°) when added. Rapid mix method can be applied to both the cool rise and the conventional (straight dough) methods of yeast baking.

5. **Batter Method**

This method is mainly used for rolls. It does not involve kneading, shaping and the second rising. The mixed batter is allowed to rise once, then is poured into muffin tins and baked. The texture is much more porous and no elaborate shapes can be made.

6. **Sponge Method**

This method is a combination of the batter and straight dough method and is used for bread rather than for rolls. In the soft batter stage it is allowed to rise, then more flour is added and the recipe is completed by the straight dough method.

7. **Brown and Serve Method**

The ingredients are mixed together, kneaded, allowed to rise, shaped, allowed to rise again and then baked only until almost done. The cooled buns then are put into plastic bags and kept in the refrigerator for up to a week. They are browned in the oven just before serving, allowing fresh-from-the-oven bread to be served for any occasion.

8. **Freezer Bread Method**

The dough is mixed, kneaded, and shaped right away without being allowed to rise. It is then covered and placed in the freezer. When frozen, it can be stored in plastic bags in the freezer for up to four weeks. Before baking, it must be allowed to thaw and to rise fully until doubled in bulk.

INGREDIENTS USED FOR YEAST BREADS

When following any recipe, the cook who understands the "why" of the reaction between the ingredients as well as the "how" of handling them will have a much better chance of consistently good results. A thorough knowledge of the ingredients used and the way each affects the basic structure of the yeast product is important to achieving success.

Flour

The flour chosen for breadmaking must contain a high proportion of the proteins *gliadin* and *glutenin* which, when moistened, form gluten, an elastic substance that develops during the kneading process. All purpose flour is most suitable; cake-and-pastry flour does not form enough gluten to make bread. Other types of flour may be included in a recipe but they are usually mixed with a strong wheat flour.

Flours also vary in the amount of natural moisture they contain. This can affect the total amount of flour actually required in bread recipes. For this reason, except for unkneaded bread recipes, only approximate amounts of flour are suggested.

Yeast

Yeast is a living plant which, given the right conditions, grows quickly. It produces the carbon dioxide gas that acts as a leavening agent in all yeast products. It may be bought in two forms – active dry yeast which is granular, and compressed fresh yeast in the cake from. Fresh yeast is usually available only from bakeries. It requires refrigeration and has a "life" of less than one week.

Active dry yeast resembles dry brown seeds. This is the dormant state. To activate it, the yeast is sprinkled over a mixture of warm water and sugar. The usual proportions are 125 ml water and 5 ml sugar. Throughout the breadmaking process, optimum conditions for yeast growth must be maintained. For the conventional method they are as follows:

1. Temperature   Optimum temperature is about 25°C. Higher temperatures kill the yeast; lower temperatures slow its growth. This fact is used to advantage in the "refrigerator" and "cool rise" methods.

2. Food   Sugar is combined with the water to activate the yeast. Accurate measurement is essential, for too much sugar can retard yeast action.

3. Moisture   Milk and water are used. Both must be at the correct temperature before they are combined with the yeast. Liquids are the right temperature when they feel slightly warm when dropped on the wrist.

$$\text{YEAST} + \text{SUGAR} \xrightarrow[\text{moisture}]{\text{warmth}} CO_2 + H_2O + \text{ALCOHOL} \uparrow$$

Liquid

In the initial step, water is always used to penetrate the yeast covering because milk solids retard the dissolving and dispersing action of the water. Milk is ordinarily used in the latter steps. It produces a velvety grained bread that keeps fresh longer, has a richer flavour, a darker brown colour and a higher nutritive value than bread made only with water. The milk used may be whole, skim, evaporated or dried but it must always be scalded to destroy unwanted bacteria. All-water dough produces bread with a wheaty flavour and a crisp crust. Occasionally, other liquids such as fruit juices are added for special flavour.

Sugar

Sugar works with the yeast to form the carbon dioxide gas which causes the bread to rise. Accurate measurement of sugar is essential because too little or too much will retard yeast development. Other sweeteners, such as honey, molasses or corn syrup, are sometimes used in making whole wheat or other special breads. Sugar also helps to brown the product when it is baked in the oven.

Salt

Salt improves the flavour of the product. Without it, any flour mixture tastes flat. Because it also regulates the action of the yeast, it should not be added until some of the flour is in the dough. Accurate measurement of salt is important so that the yeast action is not slowed too much.

Fat

Some type of fat or oil is included in nearly all yeast products. It can be shortening, butter, margarine, lard or vegetable oil. Fat lubricates the ingredients, making the dough or batter stretch more easily as the carbon dioxide gas bubbles expand. Fat also adds characteristic flavour, depending on the type chosen; makes the crust tender, and gives it an attractive sheen. It also improves the keeping quality. Some types of bread such as French bread and hard rolls are made without any fatty ingredient. These products are hard-crusted and chewy.

Eggs

Eggs are sometimes used, especially in sweet dough and other variety recipes. They add food value, colour and flavour while contributing to a fine crumb and a tender crust.

Other Ingredients

Seasoning, herbs and spices, nuts and fruits add flavour to breads, rolls and coffee cakes. Care must be taken when adding fruits. Certain recipes will not tolerate their addition for the balance of ingredients is upset when sugar from the fruit comes in contact with the growing yeast. Recipes which specifically include fruit will have calculated for the additional sugar to balance the formula.

The gluten framework will be strong enough to support only the amount of fruit and/or nuts suggested in the recipe. Using more will result in a heavy, sticky dough.

PREPARATION OF A YEAST BREAD

No matter which method of mixing is chosen for making the yeast product, the two main considerations are correct formation of the gluten and controlled production of the carbon dioxide gas. Temperature control throughout the process is of prime importance. Simply stated, the steps in preparing bread or rolls by the conventional method are:

1. Preparing the dough.   This includes the mixing and kneading to develop the gluten.

2. Fermenting the dough.   Carbon dioxide is produced during the rising stages.

3. Shaping the dough.   This involves forming of the loaf or rolls. The mixture is cooked to expand the gases and harden the gluten structure.

Assembling the Ingredients

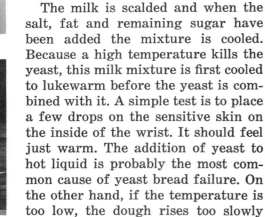

To prepare a yeast dough by the straight dough method, the yeast is first added to a small amount of sugar in warm water. These ingredients are set aside for approximately 10 minutes. During this period the yeast begins to grow and carbon dioxide bubbles are formed.

The milk is scalded and when the salt, fat and remaining sugar have been added the mixture is cooled. Because a high temperature kills the yeast, this milk mixture is first cooled to lukewarm before the yeast is combined with it. A simple test is to place a few drops on the sensitive skin on the inside of the wrist. It should feel just warm. The addition of yeast to hot liquid is probably the most common cause of yeast bread failure. On the other hand, if the temperature is too low, the dough rises too slowly and other organisms and off-flavours may develop; for example, "yeasty" flavour.

When it is evident that the milk mixture is cooled enough the activated yeast is stirred in. Flour addition begins when this process is complete.

Mixing

The flour is stirred into the liquids until about one-third of the flour is added. A vigourous beating is recommended at this point because it is easy to beat the mixture thoroughly either by hand or with a good electric mixer. Thorough mixing improves the structure of the bread and develops a good network of gluten.

It is at this stage flour particles containing the proteins gliadin and glutenin become well moistened and together form the elastic-like gluten. This framework later stretches with release of the carbon dioxide gas and eventually is hardened by the oven heat.

More flour is added until the dough forms an irregular ball which comes away from the bowl leaving only a small amount on the sides. At this point the dough is ready for kneading.

Kneading

The dough can be kneaded in several ways. If the bread is being mixed in a large institutional mixer or in a heavy-duty household electric mixer equipped with a dough hook, it probably will not require any further mixing. However, for dough mixed by hand or in a regular household mixer, the elastic network of the gluten will require further development.

To start, the dough is placed on a floured board. At first it will be very soft and sticky and will tend to cling

to the board. As more flour is worked in, the gluten and starch granules will take up water and the dough will become stiffer. Adding too much flour causes the dough to be hard and the finished bread heavy and tough and poorly flavoured.

As compared to the kneading of biscuits, which is a gentle movement of short duration, kneading of bread dough is quite a vigourous process. The dough is folded in half and given a firm push with the heels of both hands. The dough can then be rotated a quarter of a turn and folded and pushed again. If the kneading is done with a light motion and tearing of the dough is avoided, the dough will not stick to the board after the first few motions. As soon as the correct amount of flour has been incorporated, only a light dusting of flour on the board is needed for the remainder of the kneading process.

It is difficult to give a definite time required for kneading because it depends upon the experience of the person making the bread and upon other conditions such as the type of ingredients used and their temperature. Dough which has been sufficiently kneaded will be satiny and smooth, with blisters of gas showing just under the surface when the dough is folded over. It should still feel soft and pliable. It is possible to knead dough too much but this is unlikely to happen unless the dough has been mixed with a heavy-duty mechanical mixer. It is much more likely that the dough will be underkneaded than overkneaded.

Rising

When the kneading stage is completed, the dough is formed into a round ball and the surface and container oiled. This may be accomplished by placing the dough, smooth side down, in a greased bowl and then turning it over immediately — leaving a light coating on the surface. If the surface of the dough is allowed to dry out during rising, a crust forms that shows up as a streak in the finished loaf. To prevent this, the bowl can be covered with plastic wrap or it can be put in a cabinet or unlighted oven together with a pan of hot water.

Optimum temperature for rising or fermentation is between 27°C and 29°C. The dough is allowed to ferment until it has about doubled its original bulk. Thus, the size of the bowl chosen must be large enough to allow for this expansion. When doubled in size, the gluten of the dough will begin to lose some of its

elasticity and a deep depression made in the dough will remain. To test the risen dough, insert two fingers deeply into the dough. If holes remain when the fingers are withdrawn, the dough has probably doubled in volume.

During the fermentation period, carbon dioxide is formed by the yeast only for as long as there is sugar available in the dough. Omitting or reducing the amount of sugar from that indicated in the recipe, therefore, has serious consequences in obtaining a light product. Too large an increase of sugar should also be avoided since beyond a certain amount, the activity tends to be inhibited and the time required for fermentation is longer rather than shorter.

If the dough is allowed to rise to more than double in bulk, the cell walls become so stretched and thin that they will break and cause an uneven texture. Allowed to rise too long, so many cells will rupture that the bread will fall and be compact. In extreme over-fermentation the yeast will use up all of the sugar before the structure of the product is set during baking.

When the dough is fully risen (doubled in bulk) it is ready to be "punched down". This is done by putting a fist into the centre of the dough, folding the edges of the dough to the centre and turning it over to form a new ball. This step breaks up any big air pockets that may have formed and helps to ensure a fine, even-textured finished product. Depending upon the recipe used, the dough will then be allowed to rise a second time or it will be shaped into loaves or buns. If required, a second rising will not take as long as the first rising; the dough will again be allowed to rise until the impression of a finger remains in the dough.

Shaping

Before the dough is shaped, it should be punched down to give a fine, even texture with no air holes. Then with a large, sharp knife, the dough can be divided into equal portions according to the number of loaves the recipe makes. The dough will be easier to handle if it is allowed to "rest" for 10-15 minutes before the shapes are formed.

There are several methods of forming the dough into a loaf. The objective is to obtain a shape with a smooth surface and no large air holes. One way is to roll the dough into a rectangle slightly less wide than the length of the baking pan. Then by rolling or folding and sealing the edges by pinching, a shape can be formed that is approximately the same as the pan but which fills it only half full.

Because butter and margarine cause the product to darken, the pans should be greased with non-salted fat or vegetable oil. The dough is placed in the pan with sealed edges down.

Rolls and fancy breads are formed in a similar manner. All types of dough should be handled with a light touch. Melted fat or vegetable oil can be used to grease the top slightly, then the shaped dough is covered and placed to rise under similar conditions as were used for the first rise.

Bakers speak of "proofing" for the final rise when the dough is in the pan. Proofing continues until the dough has doubled in bulk. To test, press a finger very gently into one end of the dough near the edge of the pan. When the finger indentation remains, the bread product is ready to be baked. Dough that has not risen long enough makes a small compact loaf. Dough that has risen too long, however, may rise and then fall, causing the bread to have an open crumbly texture.

Baking

A preheated oven is essential to successful results in bread making. The temperature recommended by the recipe being used will range from 190°C to 220°C. Before the oven is set to preheat, it is good practice to adjust the racks so that the bread can be placed in the centre of the oven, to allow maximum heat circulation. Avoid having the pans touch each other or the sides of the oven.

The time required for baking will depend on the oven temperature selected, the loaf size, the composition of the dough, and the type of crust desired. Long baking thickens the crust. It also will decrease the thiamine content of the product since this B-vitamin is heat-sensitive.

When the fully risen dough is first placed in the heated oven, there will be a sudden increase in volume called "oven spring." Two factors play a role in this characteristic expansion. During the early baking period carbon dioxide is produced more rapidly as the temperature throughout the loaf rises. Eventually, the dough reaches the temperature at which the yeast is destroyed and fermentation ceases.

By this time all the gases (carbon dioxide, and to a lesser extent, air, and water vapour) held captive by the gluten framework become heated and expand, carrying the bread mixture upward. This expansion continues until the proteins coagulate, and the gluten eventually loses its stretching ability.

The bread will be ready to remove from the oven when it is a deep golden brown, shrinks from the sides of the pan, and produces a hollow sound when tapped on the crust. Underbaked bread will fall because the protein framework will not have been completely hardened by the oven heat.

To prevent steaming and softening of the bottom crust, loaves and rolls should be removed from their pans immediately. They can be placed on a wire rack or crosswise on the top edges of the pans. If a soft crust is desired, a light brushing of fat may be used on the top.

Fresh bread should never be covered while warm. As soon as it is thoroughly cooled, it should be placed in a covered container. A moisture-vapour-proof bag may be used to store bread products in the freezer.

CHARACTERISTICS OF A GOOD YEAST BREAD AND REASONS FOR VARIATIONS

EXTERIOR APPEARANCE

COLOUR — an even golden brown with the top slightly darker than the sides.	DARK CRUST — Too high an oven temperature. Oven heating unevenly. Placing pans higher than centre of oven.
	PALE CRUST — Too low an oven temperature. Drying of dough during rising period. Too much salt, too little sugar. Too high a temperature during rising.
SHAPE — a plump, well rounded, symmetrical form that has no cracks, lumps or bulges.	CRACKED CRUST — Too rapid cooling in draft.
	UNEVEN SHAPE — Improper shaping of dough for pan. Too much dough for pan. Insufficient rising.
	BULGES AND CRACKS — Too stiff dough. Insufficient rising. Uneven oven heat.

SIZE — a large volume for the mass.	TOO SMALL — Insufficient rising (too short a time or too cool a temperature). Insufficient kneading. Too high an oven temperature. Too much salt.
	TOO LARGE — Too much rising. Too low an oven temperature.

INTERIOR APPEARANCE

COLOUR — a uniform creamy white with a silky sheen (not grey, darkened, streaky or dull).	STREAKY INTERIOR — Drying of top of dough during first rise. Addition of flour during formation of shapes. Insufficient mixing of ingredients.
	DARK CRUMB — Characteristic of liquid or flour use. Old or stale yeast. Too much rising or insufficient rising. Unfavourable rising temperature. Too low an oven temperature.
CRUST — tender and relatively thin.	THICK CRUST — Too low an oven temperature. Too long baking time. Insufficient greasing of crust before rising period.
	TOUGH CRUST — Insufficient rising. Too much handling of risen dough.
TEXTURE — a fine even grain with small thin walled cells and no large air-bubbles. — a crumb that is tender, smooth and elastic but with no doughiness. — should not crumble enough to make cutting difficult.	COARSE GRAIN — Too long a rising period. Failure to "punch down" dough. Too low an oven temperature.
	CRUMBLY — Too long a rising period, at too high a temperature. Too low an oven temperature. Insufficient hard wheat flour combined with specialty flours.

TASTE QUALITY

FLAVOUR — wholesome, sweet, nutlike, with no unpleasant, flat or sour taste.	POOR FLAVOUR — Incorrect measurement of ingredients. Inferior ingredients. Incorrect temperature of rising or baking.
AROMA — excellent and appetizing, delicately yeasty.	STRONG YEASTY ODOUR — Too low temperature during rising, allowing growth of unwanted organisms. Too much yeast.

Pan Rolls — Plain buns are placed together on a cookie pan so they will stick together when they rise.

Cloverleafs — These round balls of dough are placed in a muffin pan so that they are touching but will have enough room to rise.

Fan-Tans — Layers of thin dough with butter spread between them are baked in muffin pans.

Parker House Rolls — A round piece of flat dough is folded in half with butter between to form a half circle.

Crescent Bars — A flat triangular shape of dough is rolled from wide end to small end and placed on a cookie pan in a semi-circle.

Coffee Ring — Dough is rolled out flat and spread with butter, sugar, cinnamon and raisins, then rolled up and sliced with scissors.

DANISH PASTRIES

SOURDOUGH

In the days when prospectors and the first settlers were opening up the interior and northern parts of British Columbia and moving into the Yukon, essential food supplies could be taken in only once or twice a year. Heavy winds and seas delayed ships, ports-of-call and inland waters were often ice-bound, and goods had to be transferred from ships to coastal boats, river steamers, dog sleds and backpacks to be carried to the isolated areas where they were needed.

All these difficulties made it important that the foods ordered should have good keeping qualities to survive the long, slow delivery route. Yeast plants, for instance, would become inactive and, sensitive to extreme cold, would not grow. Pioneers learned that sourdough starter brought from the communities to the south would survive in the climate and was tough and practical in the rugged circumstances in which they lived.

Sourdough Breads

Sourdough bread is leavened by "starter" containing a special strain of fermentation-causing bacteria. The gas given off during fermentation makes the product rise. The bacteria in the starter contributes a characteristic tangy or sour flavour to any baked product made with it.

To make the starter, naturally soured milk which contains the desired bacteria is used. Flour is added to the sour milk forming a glue-like white paste which, left at room temperature, forms bubbles during the fermentation process. To make the flour mixture, fresh milk, flour and varying other ingredients are added to some of the starter. If the product is bread, the mixing and kneading steps are much the same as for yeast bread although the rising period will usually be longer due to the slower action of the gas-forming bacteria. Temperature control is essential and baking is the same as for other breads.

The Starter

Starter can be obtained in a number of ways. The most usual is to get a portion of the active starter from a friend. Then it can be "fed" and stored in your own container in the refrigerator. Commercial sourdough starters are marketed in a dried and powdered form. The addition of water brings it to life. Or you may wish to make your starter from milk in the traditional manner. Place about 250 ml fresh milk in a glass or crockery container. Allow it to stand at room temperature for 24 hours, then stir in 250 ml flour. Leave in a warm place, about 25°C, for 2 to 5 days. It will be ready to use when it is full of bubbles and has a good sour smell. If the first attempt is not successful it may be because the necessary bacteria were not present in the milk. Therefore, a second try should begin with milk from another source.

Once you have a cup of starter it may be kept indefinitely provided it is used every week and stored in the refrigerator for the rest of the time. The storage container must be non-metallic (glass, crockery or plastic).

If the starter has not been used for two or three weeks it can be replenished by discarding about half the starter and stirring in equal amounts of flour and milk. When it is again full of bubbles, return it to the refrigerator until next use. If you do not plan to use the starter for some longer time it may be frozen. To use again allow it to thaw. Then, because the bacterial action will be slowed down, allow it to stand at room temperature for about 24 hours before you begin the recipe.

Using the Starter

Recipe books vary in their instructions for using and replenishing the starter. In all, the principle is the same: flour and milk mixed with the starter will allow it to continue fermenting. We speak of "feeding" the starter. Here is a suggested method.

Prepare a *primary batter* first by mixing together until smooth 250 ml of the cold starter, 500 ml warm water (30°C to 32°C), and 625 ml flour. This could be done in the evening of the day before the bread or other flour mixture is to be made and should sit, covered, in a warm place for 12 hours. At the end of this time, 250 ml of the mixture is placed in the starter container for refrigeration and is the starter for the next time. This step is most important. The primary batter which remains is the basis for the recipe to which other chosen ingredients are added. It is important that all utensils including bowls and mixing implements be non-metallic.

Because space in this book does not allow inclusion of a variety of sourdough recipes, one only has been chosen. Sourdough Muffins, page 514, is typical of sourdough recipes and has the advantage to the beginner of requiring a minimum of time. Sourdough recipes for pancakes, waffles, biscuits, bread (including white, whole wheat, French, casserole and many others), are readily available.

310

Cakes and Frostings

The infinite variety of cakes offers a delightful, although non-essential, addition to the daily food of many people. Whether selected in a supermarket, ordered from a bakery, prepared from a quantity recipe in an institution, or baked with loving care in a home kitchen, nearly all cakes contribute little more than kilojoules to the daily food intake. For a young person obtaining the required amounts of vital nutrients from quality foods, additional food energy for an active life may pleasantly be obtained in cake and similar products. For an adult struggling to maintain a correct weight level, for a child having an unpredictable appetite, or for an elderly person with a sweet tooth, cake and its accompanying frosting can have a disastrous nutritional effect.

Provided the nutritional deficiencies of this type of food are recognized, the study of cake making can be an interesting and often highly satisfying topic. To be able to prepare, bake, ice and serve a light delicious cake has long been a highly prized skill among cooks. In some European countries where cake making is regarded as an art, bakers renowned for their creations enter their best in national competitions. Recipes are highly prized and carefully guarded.

TYPES OF CAKE

The two principal kinds of cake are those containing fat and those containing no fat. For simplicity these will be referred to respectively as butter cakes and foam cakes.

Butter Cake

Cakes made with fat are sometimes called shortened cakes. They include such favourites as white, chocolate, spice, one-bowl, pound and fruit cakes. These and many other varieties can be baked as a loaf, in layers or as cupcakes. Standard ingredients for all butter cakes are a fat (not necessarily butter), sugar, flour, egg, liquid and flavouring and leavening ingredients. The method of mixing described in the recipe will be a conventional cake method, sometimes called "creaming method," or perhaps a quick-mix or one-bowl method.

Foam Cake

Cakes made without fat are sponge cake and angel food cake. They are made from eggs, sugar, flour, flavouring and an acid ingredient such as cream of tartar or lemon juice. No leavening agent is used and air beaten into the eggs is the principal leavener. Foam cakes are light with a very large volume. They are usually baked in a tube pan but other shapes such as sheet, muffin or loaf pans are sometimes used. A jelly roll is a sponge cake baked in a flat pan and then rolled.

Chiffon cakes are frequently grouped with the foam cakes since they have the same large volume as angel and sponge cake. However, a chiffon cake does contain fat, in the form of vegetable oil, and baking powder is used for additional leavening. Therefore, a chiffon cake having the richness of a butter cake and the lightness and volume of a sponge cake, combines the characteristics of both types. The chart on page 314 compares the ingredients, mixing method, baking pan and oven temperatures of the basic types of cake. For more information on the function of ingredients used in each refer to "Introduction to Flour Mixtures", page 274.

In no other type of food preparation than in baking is it more important to understand why certain procedures are used. To obtain a product of excellence the method of preparation outlined by the recipe must be carefully followed. In addition, a successful cook will have more detailed information to draw upon which will supplement the recipe's necessarily abbreviated instructions. The recipe section of this book contains basic recipes for each type of cake. Included in this section are more complete instructions for mixing and baking these cakes.

BUTTER CAKES
Preliminary Preparation
1. For best volume and texture and for easier mixing have all ingredients at room temperature.
2. Adjust oven racks so that cake will bake in the centre of the oven.
3. Preheat oven at 180°C to 190°C depending on the recipe and the type of pan being used. A loaf cake that requires a long time to bake will need a lower temperature than cup cakes or layer cakes. When a glass pan is used the temperature should be reduced about 10°C.

4. Prepare the pan as indicated. Be sure to choose the correct size pan. Vegetable oil or shortening are most satisfactory for greasing the pan since they do not promote browning. A light dusting of flour after greasing is sometimes preferred. Shake out any excess. If waxed paper is to be used cut it carefully to size. When a rectangular pan is used the waxed paper can be cut to the corners with scissors so that a smooth fit is obtained.

Conventional Cake Method
1. Cream fat well until soft.
2. Gradually add sugar a little at a time creaming well after each addition to allow the sugar to dissolve. Sugar not dissolved before baking will contribute to a coarse texture in the finished product.

Many air bubbles are beaten into the mixture during this process and it should not be rushed. This is probably the most important step. The mixture should be light and fluffy and there should be no gritty sound when a spatula is pressed against the side of the bowl. At this point the mixture has been well "creamed"; hence the term "creaming method."
3. Add eggs one at a time, beating well after each addition. Beat until fluffy; add flavouring and beat.

4. Sift flour, measure. Sift together with other dry ingredients, usually baking powder and salt. Measure liquid, usually milk, and have ready.

5. Add about one-quarter of the dry ingredients to the creamed mixture and mix until combined. Then add about one-third of the liquids and mix in. Continue adding dry and liquid ingredients alternately so that a portion of dry ingredients is the last to be added. This will prevent the final mixture from becoming curdled in appearance. Stir until smooth after each addition but do not mix more than necessary. When the batter is overmixed the gluten of  the flour becomes fully developed and a tough cake can result. This is less likely to happen when cake flour has been used than when all purpose flour is used.

Baking Butter Cakes

1. Place batter in prepared pan and spread evenly. If layer cake pans are used divide batter equally to make cakes the same size. Wipe edges free of any drips. A level top on the baked cake is more easily obtained if the batter is pushed gently up the sides of the pan. This is the part of the batter which heats first and will be first to harden. Then as the batter in the centre of the pan continues to rise it usually rises higher  than the sides. This means the cake has a rounded top. By pushing the sides higher to begin with, a humped centre is prevented.

2. Place pan in the centre of the preheated oven. If more than one pan is used arrange them on one rack so that heat can circulate. If two racks are needed "stagger" the pans.

COMPARISON OF BASIC TYPES OF CAKE

CAKE	LEAVENING	EGG	FAT	SUGAR
Conventional	carbon dioxide (from baking powder) air (from beating) steam (from liquids)	1 or 2 whole unseparated	butter margarine or shortening	creamed with fat
Chiffon	carbon dioxide (from baking powder) air (from beaten whites) steam (from liquids)	3 or 4 whole separated	vegetable oil	mixed with oil, yolks and liquid
Sponge	air (beaten into whites) steam (from liquids)	4 or more separated	none	beaten into egg whites
Angel	air (beaten into whites) steam (from liquid in eggs)	8 or more whites only	none	part beaten into egg whites part folded in with flour

3. Bake until the batter begins to pull away from the side of the pan. The cake will spring back when touched with a finger, and a toothpick when inserted should come out clean.

4. Remove from oven and allow to sit in the pan for about 5 minutes before inverting on a cake rack. A damp cloth under the pan is suggested. Steam will form at the bottom of the cake and make it easier to remove the cake in one piece. If waxed paper was used alone to line the pan, invert immediately, lift off the pan and peel away the paper. The paper will stick if there is any delay.

COMPARISON OF BASIC TYPES OF CAKE *(continued)*

LIQUID	MIXING METHODS	PAN	OVEN TEMPERATURE
milk	creaming fat and sugar stirring liquids and flour	grease, flour or paper lined round layer square rectangular	180°C to 190°C
water or juice	beating egg whites, stirring liquids and flour, folding in whites	ungreased tube	180°C
water or juice	beating separated whites and yolks, folding in whites and flour	ungreased tube	180°C
none	beating whites folding in dry ingredients	ungreased tube	190°C

Other Methods for Butter Cakes

A number of one-bowl or quick mix methods have been developed. They are much faster than the conventional cake method and in many cases give equally good results. However, the ingredients are in slightly different proportions and the two methods cannot be used interchangeably for the same recipe. Recipes for a one-bowl cake usually contain a higher proportion of sugar and liquid than recipes for the conventional method.

The dry ingredients are measured into a mixing bowl first. Then the shortening, which must be soft, is added, then the flavourings, part of the milk and in some recipes the egg. These ingredients are mixed for a specified time, then the remaining ingredients are added, followed by a final mixing

period. Preliminary preparation and baking steps are the same as for all butter cakes. Two recipes of this type have been included: Quick Mix Cake on page 517, (a layer cake) and One-Bowl White Cake on page 517, (a large slab cake.)

FOAM CAKES

Preliminary Preparation

1. To obtain the best volume have eggs at room temperature.

2. The baking pan should be free of any traces of grease which would prevent the cake from rising to its full volume while in the oven.

3. Adjust oven rack placing it in the lower one-third of the oven. Foam cakes have a large volume and may darken on top if placed on a centre rack.

4. Preheat oven to 180°C to 190°C, depending upon the recipe. A lower temperature than this has long been recommended for angel cake because it was thought that higher temperatures would toughen the protein of the egg white. However, 190°C has been found to produce a more moist, tender cake having good volume.

5. Separate eggs carefully so as not to get even the smallest amount of yolk in the white portion. Egg yolk or fat of any kind on the utensils will prevent the whites from beating to a good volume. See page 189 for more on egg white foams.

6. Sift flour, then measure. Use of cake flour is especially important to obtain a tender foam cake (see page 274). If cake flour is not available use all purpose flour and reduce the amount by 10%.

7. Sift sugar to remove lumps, then measure. Because it is ground finer, berry sugar will dissolve more readily and the cake will have a finer grain.

Mixing Angel Food Cake

1. Sift part of the measured sugar, usually about one-third, together with the flour. A mixture of flour and sugar blends more readily with the beaten egg whites than flour only does.

2. Beat whites with a rotary beater until they are foamy, then add cream of tartar and beat until soft peaks will form. The cream of tartar is an acid which helps to stabilize the egg white foam. It coagulates part of the egg protein thus preventing the foam from collapsing before coagulation temperature is reached in the oven.

3. Sprinkle remaining sugar over the beaten whites a small amount at a time beating well after each addition, to dissolve sugar. When all the sugar has been added beat in flavourings.

4. Sift about one-quarter of the flour over the egg white mixture. Combine carefully by "cutting and folding." To do this use a rubber or metal spatula. Cut through the mixture to the bottom of the bowl, turn the spatula and move it across the bottom, up the side and over the top. At the same time, the bowl should be turned slightly with the left hand so that the spatula will cut through the batter in a different place each time. At no time when folding should the mixture be stirred or beaten as the entrapped air will quickly escape and the cake will lose volume.

Mixing Sponge Cakes

1. Beat egg whites until they are foamy. Gradually add half the measured sugar, beating well after each addition, to dissolve the sugar. Continue beating until stiff and the peaks hold their shape when the beater is withdrawn. The mixture should remain glossy, not dry.

2. Beat egg yolks until thick and lemon coloured. Add lemon or other flavouring. Gradually beat in the other half of the sugar and continue beating until mixture is foamy and light.

3. Gently fold yolk mixture into beaten whites. See step 4, "Mixing Angel Food Cake", above.

4. Sift about one-quarter of the flour over the egg mixture. Combine carefully by cutting through the mixture to the bottom and folding over the top. Continue adding flour in three more portions, combining with the same folding motion after each addition.

   A jelly roll is a sponge cake. It is baked, filled and rolled as shown.

Baking Foam Cakes

1. Pour or spoon the batter carefully into an ungreased pan. The shape and volume of the cake will be best if the size of pan indicated by the recipe is used. The hollow centre of a tube pan allows the heat to penetrate to all parts of the mixture evenly. One with a removable bottom and centre section allows easier removal of the cake than a pan made in one piece.

2. Once in the pan, large air bubbles should be removed by gently moving the spatula through the batter. The cake will have a more level top if the batter is pushed slightly up the sides of the pan at the same time.

3. Place on a rack low in the oven and bake until the cake springs back when touched with the finger. At this time it will begin to pull away from the sides of the pan. Overbaking will toughen the cake.

4. Remove from the oven and invert to cool. If the cake has risen above the pan, place the centre

of the tube on a jar, glass or bottle to hold it above the counter surface.

5. Be sure the cake has completely cooled before attempting to remove it from the pan. If removed while hot it may collapse. Loosen cake around the edge of the pan and ease it out.

6. Since foam cakes are delicate and light they are usually not heavily frosted. They may be served with a thin layer of icing or dusted with sifted icing sugar.

Method for Chiffon Cake

Although the ingredients for chiffon cake are not the same as those for angel or sponge cake the procedures used are similar. Preliminary preparation and baking routines are the same as just described for foam cakes. The mixing method is an adaptation of muffin method.

1. Sift flour, sugar, baking powder and salt into a large bowl and make a well in the centre.

2. To the dry ingredients add egg yolks, vegetable oil, flavourings and liquid. Beat until smooth.

3. Beat egg whites until foamy, then add cream of tartar and continue beating until stiff peaks are formed.

4. Carefully and gently fold the egg yolk mixture into the beaten whites. This can best be done if the liquid mixture is poured over the whites in about three portions and folded after each addition. Unless thoroughly combined the yolk portion will separate to the bottom and a layered effect will be evident in the baked cake.

FROSTING A LAYER CAKE

Place bottom layer upside down on a cake plate. Spread with frosting to form the filling. Cover with top layer right side up.

Protect cake plate with strips of wax paper. Ice the sides first, spreading from the bottom up using a pliable knife or spatula.

Cover the top with frosting in a few simple swirls.

Characteristics of a Good Butter Cake

EXTERIOR   A good volume.
A flat or slightly rounded top.
Smooth surfaces and a uniform thickness. (Layer cakes should be of equal size.)
A uniform golden brown on all surfaces.

INTERIOR   An even, fine-textured grain.
A velvety moist crumb.
A good flavour of well blended ingredients.

Characteristics of a Good Foam Cake

EXTERIOR   A large volume which fills the baking pan.
A flat or slightly rounded surface. (Angel cake may have shallow cracks on the top.)
A uniform delicate brown on all surfaces.

INTERIOR   A fine texture of uniformly small cells.
A very light, slightly moist crumb.
A pleasing delicate flavour.

FRUIT CAKES

General Characteristics

Fruit cakes are served traditionally in our country on special holidays and on important occasions (e.g., weddings, anniversaries, receptions.) The reason for their popularity may be that they:

1. have good keeping qualities
2. are rich with fruit and nuts
3. have good flavour and aroma
4. can be served without a rich frosting
5. make an attractive and welcome gift.

There are two main types of fruit cakes with many possible variations of ingredients:

1. LIGHT FRUIT CAKE has a butter cake base with light-coloured raisins and colourful fruits and almonds. It has a delicate flavour.

2. DARK FRUIT CAKE has a similar base but is generally made with brown sugar or has molasses added to darken the batter. Fruit jam or jelly or grape juice is added sometimes. Usually walnuts and pecans are used with dark raisins and other fruits. More spices give a heavier aroma and flavour.

Planning the Cake

Plan to make the cake well in advance of the time it is to be used. Storing it for one month or more before use:

1. allows the fruit to moisten the cake
2. improves the texture and cutting qualities
3. allows the flavours to penetrate and become blended.

Some people prefer to make their Christmas cakes one year and use them the next Christmas. Proper wrapping and storage precautions are essential. The top layer of a wedding cake is often saved to be served at the naming of the first-born child. Light fruit cakes do not keep as well as dark fruit cakes, especially if they contain only a small amount of fruit.

Preliminary Preparations

1. Blanch the almonds in boiling water to remove the skins. Then dry on a tray in the oven set at a low temperature until golden brown. Split in half if desired.

2. Wash, drain and dry raisins and currants and check for seeds and stems.

3. Cut peel into thin strips, halve cherries, slice pineapple thinly, with the grain.

4. Pour fruit juice over fruit if recipe so directs. Mix fruits, cover, and allow to stand overnight.

5. Prepare the pans:
   a. Line with three layers of heavy brown paper; grease the last layer. Be sure that corners are square but closed to prevent batter dripping through bottom of springform pan or,
   b. Line with aluminum foil, being sure that corners are well overlapped and squared.

Mixing Ingredients

1. Have all ingredients at room temperature for best results. This gives better volume, better texture and makes mixing much easier.

2. Mix nuts with the prepared fruit. *Dredge* with some of the measured flour. This prevents fruits from sticking together in lumps and also prevents all the fruit from settling onto the bottom of the pan.

3. Conventional cake method is used. Butter must be soft and well creamed before sugar is added. Add only a little sugar at a time; use berry sugar for a finer texture and easier creaming. The most important step in mixing the cake is thorough creaming of butter and sugar *before* adding the egg.

4. Continue as recipe directs, adding the dredged fruit and nuts last. Mix only to combine.

5. Place in pan pressing firmly into the bottom and corners. Drop filled pans on table top to remove any remaining air pockets.

Baking the Cake

1. Use a low temperature for a long time. Never raise oven temperature above 150°C. A small cake bakes well at 150°C; a large cake bakes better at 120°C to 130°C for 3½ - 5 hours, depending upon recipe used.

2. If the cake appears to be browning too quickly on the top, place a piece of foil or heavy brown paper over top of the baking pan.

3. To keep the cake moist while cooking, place a pan of water in the oven to give moisture to the air inside.

Storing the Cake

1. Cool on rack; remove from pan.

2. Wrap securely in aluminum foil or use plastic wrap and a tightly sealed plastic bag.

3. Store in an airtight container.

4. If desired, wrap for freezer and freeze. Good for periods of longer than a year. May be frozen iced.

Decorating Methods

1. Shortly before baking is completed, remove from the oven, brush with slightly beaten egg white, and arrange bits of candied fruit and halved nuts on the surface. Work quickly or the egg will cook before the design has been stuck in place.

2. Reserve some of the cake batter (before fruit and nuts are added) and spread over the rest of the cake when it is in the pan. Arrange the nuts on the surface.

3. Cover the surface with a coating of almond paste after baking and cooling. Decorate with fruit and appropriate written greetings.

4. When cool, cover the sides and top with almond paste. Allow to stand one day. Spread with icing (Decorative Icing is soft, Royal Icing is very hard and has more egg white). Decorate as desired using varying colours and tube tips to make designs.

Cookies and Slices

Served as an accompaniment to a beverage or light dessert, cookies have become a popular part of the food patterns of Canadians. Many varieties, notably those associated with festive occasions and family celebrations, originated in the countries of our ancestors. Although they may be fun to make and good to eat, unless a special effort is made to enrich them, most cookies have a high kilojoule count and contribute little to our daily food needs.

Types of Cookies

Cookies are classified according to the way they are formed.

1. Bar or Slice cookies are made in a rectangular cake pan and sliced into pieces after they are baked. Some bar cookies, for example brownies, are simply a soft dough spread evenly in the pan and baked. Others, such as raspberry bar or matrimonial cake, consist of several layers.

2. Drop cookies are made of dough soft enough to be placed by spoonfuls on the cookie pan. This kind will usually spread during baking so space must be allowed to prevent them from touching. Popular varieties are chocolate chip, rolled oat, raisin-nut.

3. Moulded cookies are made of dough that is a little stiffer than either bar or drop cookies. The dough is moulded with the fingers to produce the desired shape and then placed on the pan for baking. Small round balls are easy to form and they can later be

flattened with a fork or other utensil. Examples of cookies that are sometimes moulded are peanut butter, rolled oat and thumbprint cookies (sometimes called thimble cookies or birds' nests).

4. Refrigerator cookies are a stiff dough cookie. Once mixed the dough is formed into a long roll or bar and thoroughly chilled. Cooling firms the fat in the dough making it easy to cut thin slices with a sharp knife. A refrigerator cookie recipe is a good kind to use when it is more convenient to bake the cookies at a later time. This can be several hours or several days later.

5. Rolled cookies are formed by rolling the chilled stiff dough on a lightly floured surface. When an even 0.5 cm thickness is obtained the dough is cut with variously shaped cookie cutters and the shapes baked. Rolled cookies are sometimes decorated, either before or after baking. Some decorative bits of fruit, nuts, etc., can be baked on. Others, such as a thin layer of icing, are added after the cookies are cooled.

6. Pressed cookies are made from a rich stiff dough using a special cookie press. The chilled dough is packed into the press, then forced through the shaping disks onto an ungreased cookie pan. Shapes and sizes can be varied by changing the disk and pressing out more or less dough to form each cookie.

Preparing the Dough

With few exceptions cookie recipes are a variation of a conventional butter cake. See page 312 for the steps. The method requires creaming of the fat and sugar with subsequent addition of other ingredients. The ingredients used vary with the kind of cookie being made. Basic to all of them are fat, sugar and flour, usually with egg or other liquid, and a leavener. Usually there is a higher proportion of fat and less sugar than in a cake recipe. Only a small amount of liquid is needed to produce the thick batter or stiff dough required to form a cookie. Egg, where used as liquid, also helps to hold the fat-sugar-flour mixture together. Additional ingredients such as nuts, fruit, chocolate or cereal contribute to the flavour and texture.

It is often possible to add or substitute ingredients for a standard recipe in order to obtain a product with greater nutritive value. For example, wheat germ can be added to a favourite recipe or raisins can be used in place of all or some of the chocolate chips indicated. In addition some recipes have been developed which incorporate nutritious ingredients. One such recipe, Cereal Drop Cookies, is found on page 522.

Forming the Cookies

The proportion of ingredients and, therefore, the stiffness of the dough determines how it must be handled. A drop cookie batter having too much liquid will spread on the pan during baking and make very flat cookies that run together. A mixture having more flour or other dry ingredients can be stiff enough to be rolled or moulded with the fingers.

Each recipe will indicate how the cookie is to be formed. It may be done by dropping batter from a spoon, by pressing dough from a cookie press, by rolling and cutting dough into shapes, or by forming individual shapes with the fingers, or it may be cut into bars later.

Baking Cookies

The cookie pan may or may not require greasing — the recipe will usually indicate. The high proportion of fat in most cookies, especially the stiff dough ones, makes it relatively easy to remove the cookies from an ungreased pan when they are baked. Soft dough cookies are less likely to stick if the pan is first greased. Except for bar or slice type cookies, prompt removal from the pan will also discourage sticking.

The oven temperature used to bake cookies varies from 180°C to 200°C, depending upon the kind. A more moist drop cookie batter needs a moderate temperature while thin cookies bake quickly at a higher temperature. Regardless of the temperature used and any pre-treatment given the pan, individual cookies bake best on a flat, shiny pan having no sides.

Cooling and Storing

Bar and slice type cookies are cooled in the baking pan, then sliced and served or stored. Other kinds are better when removed from the pan and cooled on a rack in a single layer. Cookies placed on top of each other will usually stick together but once cooled they can be layered in airtight containers. A tin box, plastic container, or crockery cookie jar are popular choices. Most types of cookies freeze well. See page 452 for freezing baked goods.

Pastry

The term "pastry" refers to baked goods having a flaky consistency which results from a relatively high proportion of fat to flour. This family of products is made from a basic mixture of flour, fat and water, with milk, sugar, egg or cream added, depending upon the kind of baked goods. The main differences are dependent upon the kind and amount of fat used and the method of mixing and rolling.

"Pastry" may refer only to the cooked-dough portion, as the crust of a pie, or to its combination with fillings or toppings. Many other baked products not falling strictly into the definition may be referred to from time to time as "pastries"; for example, Danish pastries, sweet rolls, little cakes, cream puffs. Puff pastry (examples: Napoleons, patty shells) is the flakiest type of pastry but its preparation is difficult and use rather limited. This book will consider only the "plain" pastry ordinarily used for pies. Pastry in this context will refer to the crust used for pies of all kinds, tarts, turnovers, cheese sticks and other types prepared by the creative cook.

QUALITIES OF GOOD PASTRY

1. **Appearance**
   - a delicate brown colour.
   - surface blisters visible.

2. **Texture**
   - "short" – product is tender, cuts easily with a fork and offers little resistance to breaking yet will hold its shape when the filling is added.
   - flaky – product is layered throughout with tiny air pockets.

3. **Flavour**
   - pleasant, characteristic of the ingredients used.

Although pastry which is both tender and flaky is usually preferred to a product having only one of these characteristics, tenderness is probably the most important feature to most people. A short pastry which is not flaky is crumbly and unattractive in appearance. A pastry which is flaky but not short is attractive in appearance but tougher in texture.

INGREDIENTS USED FOR PASTRY

Flour

Plain pastry can be made successfully from all purpose flour or from cake and pastry flour. Because all purpose flour produces a dough which is easier to work with, it is probably the best choice for persons making a first attempt at pie making. Experienced cooks find that to produce pastry of equal tenderness, less fat is required with flour of a lower protein content, such as cake and pastry flour, than with all purpose flour. The gluten strands formed from all purpose flour are longer and stronger than those formed from pastry flour. This means more fat is required to "shorten" or break the gluten strands to make the product tender. Pastry dough made from a soft flour which produces less gluten will be more crumbly and difficult to roll and will result in a product that is tender but more mealy than one made from a hard flour. Some cooks find a suitable compromise in using a combination of both types of flour.

Fat

The type of fat chosen will depend upon the characteristics desired in the product and, to some degree, the recipe and method being used. The amount of fat necessary to produce a tender product is governed by the ability of the fat selected to coat the flour particles. Oils, which are liquid in nature, will give a very tender but mealy pastry that is not at all flaky. Lard and hydrogenated shortening are most frequently used because they will produce a flaky pastry. Lard usually makes a more tender pastry than vegetable shortening, perhaps because it is softer over a wide temperature range. Both are plastic and become soft while being incorporated into the dough. This allows them to be mixed readily with and coat the flour.

Butter and margarine produce less tender pastry than hydrogenated shortening, largely because of their water content. Whereas hydrogenated vegetable oil, lard, and non-hydrogenated oil contain 100% fat, butter and margarine contain only 80% fat. They do, however, contribute a characteristic flavour and colour to the product and this may be desired, as in making fruit tarts.

As would be expected, the tenderness of pastry increases with the proportion of fat used. However, an excessive amount makes a product that is too tender to remove from the pan and one that has an unpleasant fatty consistency. For home use, 60-75 ml of fat for 250 ml flour is the standard amount. With hydrogenated fat, the higher level, 75 ml, may be safer for the beginner because the differences in technique are less likely to result in a tough pastry than when smaller amounts of fat are used. With lard or vegetable oil, 60 ml of fat for 250 ml flour is usually adequate.

The proportion of fat needed also depends on the type of flour chosen. Because of the larger amount of gluten formed with all purpose flour, about 75 ml of fat for 250 ml flour may be required to produce a tender crust. With pastry flour, 60 ml of fat for 250 ml of flour is usually ample.

Liquid

Because it provides the moisture to develop the gluten structure, water is an important ingredient. Only enough to barely form a dough should be added; for most recipes this means about 30 ml of water for each 250 ml of flour. Since flour is more moist at one time than another depending upon storage conditions, the amount of liquid which is needed will vary. Other variables include the type of fat used, the room temperature and the mixing technique. Flour soaks up moisture so if the liquid is added a little at a time less will be needed and a more tender pastry will result than if the liquid is added all at once. Adding too much water will make the pastry tough as more gluten is developed and the dough becomes more elastic. Also, the baked crust will shrink in the pan from its original size. Insufficient water makes the dough crumbly and difficult to roll.

Some recipes use milk or fruit juice. Each would contribute a characteristic flavour. When milk is used rather than water it helps in the browning process. The substitution of milk for water should be avoided except where the recipe permits, because increasing the protein content of the mixture will result in a corresponding hardening or toughening of the product.

Salt

Salt has no effect on the flakiness or tenderness of the pastry. It is present only to contribute flavour, for without salt pastry is flat and tasteless. One ml for each 250 ml of flour is the standard amount.

METHODS OF MAKING PASTRY

1. Conventional Method

This is the most commonly used method. The solid fat is first cut into the measured flour and salt. When the fat has been evenly distributed, cold water is added to the mixture a little at a time until the dough will form a ball that can be rolled. If a suitable fat is used and the dough is handled carefully, a tender flaky product usually results.

2. Paste Method

This is a variation of the conventional method, considered to be especially well suited to beginners. The ingredients used are the same. The only difference is in the way the water is added. A measured amount of cold water is added to a small part of the measured flour and mixed to form a paste. Most recipes suggest 30 ml of flour be removed for each 250 ml of flour used in the recipe. After the fat and the remaining flour have been combined, the paste is added all at once and stirred in thoroughly to form a ball of stiff dough.

Because the water is an exact amount for this method there is no possibility of adding too much water – a mistake frequently made by beginners. Also, as the paste is stirred, the flour absorbs the water and forms an elastic gluten network. Then when the paste is added to the flour-fat mixture, there is less water available to form more gluten and the resulting product is suitably tender even if it has been handled more than an experienced cook would do.

The paste method produces a tender, yet crisp pastry particularly suitable for small tarts which will be eaten in the hand instead of from a plate.

3. Hot Water Method

Measured boiling water is first beaten together with the solid fat. The resulting creamy mixture is then added all at once to the flour and salt. All of the ingredients are stirred together until they are blended, in much the same way as muffins are mixed. A stiff dough results and is generally chilled for about 2 hours before it is rolled, so that it can be handled easily.

Pastry made this way is usually more uniformly tender than pastry made by the conventional or paste methods. It does tend to be very crumbly, a characteristic that is considered to be less desirable than the flaky textured product resulting from either of the other two procedures. When beaten with hot water the fat is broken up into tiny globules which are then distributed evenly throughout the dough so reducing the formation of gluten strands.

4. Oil Method

Oil pastry is mealy and crumbly rather than flaky. It is similar to hot water pastry since the fat is so evenly distributed throughout the dough. Some recipes suggest the oil be stirred into the flour, then the water added, but more often the oil and water are shaken or stirred together first and then combined with the flour and salt. Either way the dough is mixed lightly with a fork until it holds together. It will be moist but not sticky. Although oil appears to moisten the flour in making pastry, the addition of water or milk is essential for proper development of the gluten.

PREPARATION OF CONVENTIONAL PASTRY

1. Blending Flour and Fat

When making pastry by the conventional method, the flour and salt are first sifted together and the lard or hydrogenated shortening is "cut in" until the particles are no larger than peas. A pastry blender is most commonly used for this but cutting with two table knives in a crossed position works equally well. Some experi-

enced cooks use their fingertips for blending but novices overmix when using this method and tend to allow the warmth of their hands to soften the fat too much.

A reasonably even blending of the fat with the flour produces a more uniformly tender crust since the gluten strands which are formed in the next step will be shorter. A paste-like consistency is to be avoided, partly because with such a mixture the addition of a necessary amount of water to form the gluten becomes difficult, and without sufficient water the baked crust will be too short and crumbly. In any case, the larger fat particles will eventually be rolled into thin layers and may contribute to the flakiness of the product.

There is much contradiction about what temperature pastry ingredients should be for best results. Most available evidence shows that ingredients at room temperature produce more tender pastry than cold ingredients. This is a logical finding since during mixing warm fat coats the flour while cold fat is broken into separate particles. The fat should be cold enough to be firm rather than oily or pastry, but plastic enough to be measured accurately and to blend with flour easily. In warm weather or in a very warm room, some chilling of the fat may be necessary. There seems to be no need to use ice water as some recipes suggest; water and fat at room temperature will give good results.

2.   Adding Water

When the fat and flour have been suitably combined, water is sprinkled over the mixture a little at a time and mixed lightly with a fork. An effort should be made to distribute the water evenly by sprinkling it on dry portions and by pushing aside any moist lumps as they form. Only enough water should be added to allow the dough to stick together in a loose ball. The entire mixture can then be picked up in the hands and quickly but gently worked into a ball. It may still appear a little dry. Over-mixing should be avoided after the water is added since mixing develops the gluten and toughens the pastry. Although a similarity in appearance and method exists between biscuit and pastry dough, the latter is never kneaded as the former is.

3.   Preparing for Rolling

1.   ALLOW THE PASTRY TO "REST". Pastry may be rolled as soon as it

has been mixed but allowing the pastry to "rest" for a few minutes results in more even distribution of water. This makes the rolling step easier and discourages shrinkage.

Dough which is rolled immediately feels soft and is easily broken whereas dough that has stood is firmer, more elastic and holds together better. This is not to suggest that rolling the dough should be postponed for an extended period, for some toughening of the product has been noticed even after storage periods of only 30 minutes.

2. PREPARE THE BOARD. To prepare the pastry board for rolling, place a damp cloth under it. This prevents slipping of the board while rolling. A very light dusting of flour should be used on the board and on the rolling pin, to prevent sticking. Excessive flour on the board is to be avoided since it upsets the balance of ingredients in the recipe.

A lightly floured pastry cloth may be used, if preferred, in which case the rolling pin may be covered with stockinette and also lightly floured. Sanitary practices which insure that these cloths are kept clean will be especially important if this method is used.

Oil pastry can best be rolled between two pieces of waxed paper, without any flour. The bottom paper can be prevented from sliding by first wiping the counter with a damp cloth and placing the paper on the moistened spot. (This is the same principle as placing a damp cloth under the pastry board.) This method can be used for other types of pastry as well and has the advantage of keeping cleanup time to a minimum.

3. DIVIDE THE DOUGH. A standard pastry recipe using 500 ml of flour yields enough pastry for a two-crust pie or two pie shells. This means that the ball of dough must first be cut in half so that only enough dough for one crust is rolled at a time. To prepare it for rolling into a uniform circular shape, each division of the dough is then flattened out into a smooth-edged round patty.

4. Rolling the Dough

1. SHAPING THE CIRCLE. The actual rolling of the dough is often the most difficult technique for beginners to master. The most effective way is to start in the centre of the patty of dough and roll outward to stop just short of the edge of the dough. Rolling

too far causes the edges to become thin and to crack readily. If the edges do break they can be pinched together with the fingers.

A uniform thickness can more easily be achieved if a rather firm pressure is applied at the centre and a lighter pressure used as the rolling pin approaches the far edge of the dough. Short, light strokes should be used and the rolling pin lifted between strokes. "Heavy handed" rolling increases gluten development. A circle will form as the dough is rolled from the centre outwards in all directions. Frequent loosening of the dough from the board, using the side of a metal spatula, is suggested. Additional light flouring of the board may be necessary if the pastry tends to stick.

2.   PLACING THE PASTRY IN THE PAN. When the circle of dough is approximately 0.5 cm thick and at least 3 cm larger than the pie pan it is ready to be placed in the pan. The most usual way to make the transfer is to fold the dough in half and then in half again, with the aid of a metal spatula for loosening and lifting. After it is in the pan the full circle can be unfolded. Some people have good success by rolling the dough lightly around the rolling pin and then unrolling it on the pie pan. If the dough has been rolled between waxed paper the top piece of paper can be peeled off gently, then the dough placed paper side up in the pan, and the second paper carefully removed.

Some shrinkage may normally occur when the pastry is baked. Especially susceptible to shrinkage are pie shells, since they are baked without any filling to help hold the shape. Excessive shrinkage may be prevented by fitting the pastry into the pan without stretching it. Any other procedure, such as re-rolling, which develops more gluten, may result in greater shrinkage. If shrinking persists the circle may be rolled a little larger to give enough dough to permit building up a rim or frilled edge.

5.   Preparing One-Crust Pies

1.   PREVENTING AIR POCKETS. A pie shell to be used with a cooked filling is commonly the first kind attempted by beginners. When the dough is being fitted into the pan special care needs to be taken

to avoid leaving pockets of air between the pie pan and the dough. Air left beneath the dough expands in the oven heat and raises the pastry forming blisters. The dough can be unfolded in such a way as to push the air out of that part of the plate, ahead of the dough. Then the pastry which lies up the sides of the pan can be gently pressed into place from the bottom upward again to exclude as much air as possible.

2. FLUTING THE EDGE. The next step is to trim the pastry hanging over the edge of the pie pan to a uniform width with knife or scissors. For a fluted edge, 1-2 cm of pastry shell should overhang. Turn this under to fit the rim of the pan. The object of fluting is to establish an edge which will help retain the filling when it is added and which will be attractive in appearance. Many methods have been successfully employed. It can be done by pinching the thumb between the first two fingers of the same hand while turning the pan with the other hand. Some people use two fingers of one hand with the tip of a spoon held in the other hand while others use the index finger of one hand and the thumb and index finger of the other hand.

3. PRICKING. Finally, the entire surface of the pie dough is pricked with a fork to further prevent formation of large blisters and air pockets. Crusts that are to have fillings cooked in them are never pricked because the small holes made would permit the filling to flow under the crust and make it soggy.

Single crust pies which have the filling cooked in them are known as custard pies. They are made of a milk and egg mixture which thickens when the oven heat coagulates the eggs. Popular variations are pumpkin and pecan pie.

Most cream-type pies are topped with a meringue after the cooked filling has been added. See page 190, Eggs, for preparation of meringues.

6. Preparing Two-Crust Pies

1. TRIMMING THE EDGES. To prepare a two-crust pie the procedure for rolling and placing the bottom crust in the pan is the same as for a single crust pie except that the overhanging pastry will be trimmed off, even with the edge of the pie pan. The filling is then placed in the pastry lined pan. The top crust can be rolled a little larger than the lower crust and then trimmed so that there is about 2 cm of dough extending past the edge of the plate.

2. SEALING THE EDGES. To ensure a good seal between the top and bottom crusts along the rim of the pie plate, water or milk may be used to moisten the edges before the layers are pressed together. Then the extending top crust can be turned under the edge of the lower crust and the three layers fluted together as described for a single crust pie.

3. STEAM VENTS. Top crusts for fruit pies will break under the pressure of steam if vent holes are not provided. Most cooks prefer to cut short slashes in the folded pastry before it is removed from the rolling surface and placed on the filling. Large holes should be avoided as they are not as attractive, and permit the loss of juices.

7. Baking the Pie

When the pastry is rolled, the gluten and fat particles are flattened to form layers of gluten, fat and entrapped air. The entrapped air and the steam which is formed from the water in the dough, both expand rapidly when subjected to oven heat. Further baking in the oven causes coagulation of the protein network which retains its extended form after the steam is gone. A flaky tender pastry results where there are many small air pockets surrounded by thin sheets of gluten encased in very thin layers of fat.

Temperatures suitable for baking the pastry depend upon the type of pie and the kind of filling used. As a general rule, a high baking temperature of 230°C to 250°C is recommended at least for the first part of the baking period. Products baked at a high temperature will be browner and have a richer, more desirable flavour while also having less chance of a soggy undercrust.

1. SINGLE CRUST: For a pie shell or tart shells the high temperature may remain constant and the time can be judged by the colour desired. Delicate fillings containing eggs and milk need a cooler oven (160°C) but the dough may first be seared at 230°C for 10-15 minutes. Time of baking will depend upon the size and depth of the pie or tarts, and the recipe used.

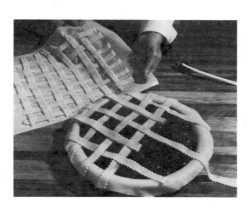

2. DOUBLE CRUST: For two-crust fruit pies a high temperature to sear the pastry has proved most successful. Before the high heat penetrates the filling, the oven temperature can be reduced to 180° - 190°C. Baking continues until the fruit is tender and the thickener, if used, has lost its characteristic starchy taste. When the filling has bubbled for about three minutes the fruit is usually tender and thickening of the juices has taken place. If the edge of the crust becomes too browned, it can be covered with a strip of aluminum foil pie tape.

Meringue Pies

Most cream-type pies are topped with a meringue. Information on meringues, the types and their preparation, is included in the section on Eggs, see page 188. The comments found here are intended to assist the cook in producing an attractive pie meringue.

1. Spreading Meringue on Pie

A suggested method for spreading the surface of a cooked filling with meringue is as follows:

1. Place spoonfuls of meringue around the outside edge first.

2. Secure the edge of the meringue to the edge of the pastry shell. This procedure prevents shrinkage of the meringue during baking.

3. Place spoonfuls of meringue over the centre of the pie and then join them by spreading with a spatula or the back of a spoon.

4. The most attractive meringue pies have an uneven surface with interesting peaks and hollows. Too much spreading will produce a smooth surface which looks "over worked".

2. **Preventing Moisture on the Surface**

Beads of moisture sometimes form on top of the meringue after it has been browned in the oven. This is known as a "weeping" meringue and the condition can usually be prevented if the following precautions are taken:

1. Use no more than 30 ml of sugar for each egg white in the recipe.

2. Bake at temperatures not higher than 220°C; a lower temperature is much better.

3. Cool the meringue carefully. Avoid placing the pie in a draft or in the refrigerator until it has been cooled completely.

4. Be sure the meringue is not undercooked. This may mean that at a high temperature the peaks of the meringue become very dark. A better procedure is to use a lower temperature for a longer time.

Fruit Pies

Fruit pies are frequently a source of frustration to cooks who find they are left with a very messy oven after some of the fruit juice has boiled out of the pie. Many methods have been tried to prevent this. Here are some precautions which have been found to be successful:

1. Follow a tested recipe carefully, using a thickener, and do not overfill the pan with fruit.
2. Be sure that the top and bottom crusts are firmly sealed together:
    *   moisten the edge of the bottom crust with water or milk before the top crust is put on.
    *   fold the top crust over and under the bottom crust and then press together.
    *   flute the three thicknesses firmly together.
3. Cut slits in the centre of the upper crust to allow the steam to escape as the filling is cooking and prevent the juice from being forced out around the edges.
4. Place a paper cone or straws in the steam vents for the juices to expand up into. As the pie cools the juices will retreat into the pie.
5. Place a sheet of foil with upturned edges, or a cookie tin, on the oven bottom or on a lower rack. If this is at least four inches below the pie and there are several inches space for heat circulation around the edges of the foil or tin, there will not be any interference with the cooking. However, there should be nothing resting directly on the electric heating unit.
6. Use a high temperature, 230°C, for 10-15 minutes and then reduce the heat for the remaining time until the fruit is cooked.

Another problem that plagues cooks is how to prevent the juice of the filling from soaking into the crust. Raw crust is almost waterproof but as it cooks it tends to become porous. Here are some suggestions for preventing soaked crusts in fruit pies:

1. Scatter part of the thickener and sugar mixture over the bottom crust so that it will be right where it is needed to reduce juice penetration.
2. Coat the surface of the bottom crust with melted butter.
3. Use a hot oven temperature for the first 15 minutes of baking.
4. Thicken the filling before placing it in the pastry-lined pan. Pre-cooked fillings lessen the chance of the filling boiling over while the pastry is baking and the problem of a soggy bottom crust is virtually eliminated. An additional advantage is that flavouring and sweetness can be controlled.

Custard Pies

Custard-type pies are made by combining an uncooked pastry shell and an uncooked egg thickened filling. The principles for preparing and cooking baked custard apply. See page 349.

Preventing the soaking of crusts of the custard-type of pie is even more difficult than with fruit pies because the lower baking temperature used for egg mixtures prolongs the baking time and permits soaking before the pie is cooked. Here are some methods that have been found to improve the crusts of custard pies:

1. Use a drier pastry by slightly reducing the water in the recipe.
2. Chill the pastry for an hour before adding the filling.
3. Use a high oven temperature for the first 10 minutes of baking.
4. Partly bake the pie shell in a hot oven for 10 minutes, then pull out the oven rack and pour the custard filling into the shell and continue baking at a lower temperature until the filling is cooked.
5. Partly cook the filling as a boiled custard, then pour into a cooked pie shell and bake until the custard is done.
6. Increase the rate of coagulation of the eggs in the filling by:
   - increasing the percentage of egg in the mixture (at least 3 eggs for 500 ml of milk).
   - scalding the milk used for the filling. This shortens coagulation time.
7. Do not overcook the custard. Insert a knife about one-third of the way out from the centre and when it comes out clean, remove the pie. The centre may still be liquid but heat from the rest of the pie should finish cooking it outside the oven. An overcooked custard exudes water which makes a very wet crust.
8. Use a glass pan because the crust receives the maximum amount of direct (radiant) heat through glass. A second choice is a dull aluminum pan rather than one of shiny metal.
9. Bake custard-type pie on a shelf near the bottom of the oven so that the crust will receive more heat than the filling.

Types of Pies

SINGLE CRUST PIE

Cream Pie
A cooked filling thickened with starch and egg is placed in a baked pie shell and topped with a meringue or whipped cream.
Examples: banana cream, coconut cream, lemon, chocolate, butterscotch.

Custard Pie

The uncooked filling is poured into an unbaked pastry shell and both are baked until the filling (which is thickened by the eggs) is cooked (a knife inserted comes out clean.)
Examples: pumpkin, pecan, custard.

Chiffon Pie

Gelatin type – A gelatin pudding mixture containing egg yolk is cooled until nearly set, then beaten egg whites are folded in. The filling is spooned into a baked shell and the pie chilled before serving.
Starch-thickened type – Stiffly beaten egg whites are folded into a warm starch-thickened pudding mixture. This filling is placed in a cooked shell and may be cooked further in the oven or simply chilled.

DOUBLE CRUST PIE

Fresh Fruit Pie

At least three cups of fruit, either fresh or frozen, are needed. Sugar and a thickening agent such as flour, cornstarch or tapioca are combined with the fruit and often butter and seasonings are added. A solid or lattice top may be used. The pie is baked until the pastry is cooked, the fruit is tender and the juices are thickened.

Cooked Fruit Pie

Juice of the fruit and/or added water, is thickened and the fruit cooked before the filling is placed in the pastry. Ready-to-use canned filling may be used or a filling prepared from fresh or canned fruit. Dried fruit may be cooked and the liquid thickened, or mincemeat may be used.

OTHERS

Meat Pie

A stew-like mixture of meat, gravy and vegetables is placed between two layers of crust or put in a baking dish and covered with a single crust only.
Examples: chicken, beef, steak and kidney, pork.

Deep Dish Pie

The fruit is placed in a casserole or other baking pan, the sugar and any flavourings or other ingredients are added and a single crust is fitted over the top. A standard top crust with vents is most common but a lattice top may be used instead.

Open Face Pie

An open face pie has a bottom crust only and is prepared in the same way as a two-crust pie except that the top crust is omitted. If canned fruit is used or the filling is cooked separately, a pre-cooked shell can be used and further baking limited to whatever time is needed to heat the crust and filling together. One popular variation is made using a cooked shell and fresh berries. These are placed in the shell and covered with a gelatin or cornstarch-thickened glaze.

Tarts

These are individual pies made with any filling commonly used in a regular sized pie, as well as many other specialties. Some kinds are cooked as a shell and then filled (examples: lemon, glazed strawberry). Others are cooked with the filling in them (examples: mincemeat, raisin, butter). Tarts cooked with the filling inside sometimes have a top crust. The pre-baked variety are frequently topped with meringue or whipped cream before serving.

Turnovers

Pastry rounds or rectangles have filling placed on one half and the other half folded over. Techniques of a two-crust pie are followed. Pastry edges are moistened and pressed together carefully; vents are cut in the top crust to allow steam to escape. Turnovers are baked on a cookie pan until they are browned, the filling has bubbled and steam escapes through the vents.

Desserts

The term dessert refers to any food served at the end of a meal. Most desserts are sweet and provide a welcome contrast to the other flavours of the meal. Natural sugar is present in fruit, which is often used for a dessert. Fruit, especially when served fresh, is more tart than sweet in flavour. Various types of puddings and baked products served for dessert are sweetened by the addition of sugar in the recipe. The one type of dessert that is not sweet at all is cheese. To complete a meal many people prefer a highly flavoured cheese served with crisp crackers.

There is a variety of sweetened desserts ranging from gelatins and custards made with very little sugar to puddings which have a very high sugar content. Similarly, there is a variation in the richness of desserts, from the simple jelly dessert to a very filling bread pudding, strawberry shortcake or mince pie.

The richness and sweetness of the dessert you choose to serve is primarily a matter of individual and family taste. Many families, finding their lives less active than those of their forefathers, are restricting the serving of desserts to very special occasions. Others use dessert as an extender to a light meal or serve dessert only to those of the family who are active, such as teenagers who will utilize the extra food energy without undesirable side effects.

Carefully planned desserts can provide food values needed to balance a meal and can contrast and complement it without repeating either texture or flavour. A simple principle to follow is to serve a light dessert after a heavy, nourishing meal and to serve the rich, nutritious kind of dessert after a light meal.

Most desserts contain sugar and many include fat as well. Since both of these are rich in kilojoules, desserts in general will contribute kilojoules to satisfy energy needs but will add little to protein, vitamin and mineral needs. Desserts that will provide significant nutrients other than kilojoules are mainly limited to those containing a high proportion of milk or fruit. Fresh fruit is probably the best choice when food value is a primary concern. Because there are many convenience dessert items available it is easy to serve desserts often and as a result daily meals can quickly become overloaded with extra kilojoules.

Desserts are classified according to the ingredients from which they are made and the method of preparation used. Nutritive value of any dessert depends, of course, on the ingredients used. It is customary to group cake, pie and cookie desserts in separate sections of a cookbook. The dessert section of this book is limited to a discussion of types of desserts other than these three. It includes a variety of puddings and prepared fruits. All of these can be conveniently classified as: fruit desserts, milk desserts, gelatin desserts, frozen desserts, baked desserts (other batter and dough based desserts) and dessert sauces.

Fruit Desserts

Fruit desserts are a very suitable finish to a heavy meal. Served fresh, they are the simplest of all desserts to prepare, are low in calories and rich in vitamins and minerals. One has merely to wash the fruit to remove residue sprays and dust, drain or dry it and, depending on the specific fruit, chill it for a most appetizing presentation. Frozen, canned or dried fruits prepared in a simple manner are a good substitute where a variety of fresh fruits is not available. Interesting colour and flavour combinations are possible by mixing or arranging fruits together.

Examples of Simple Fruit Desserts
1. Fruit compote (fruit cooked in sugar syrup) of fresh or dried fruits.
2. Fruit cup of mixed fresh and canned fruit.
3. Fruit ambrosia, made by dusting fresh fruit slices with confectioners sugar, then sprinkling with shredded coconut.
4. Baked whole fruit, such as baked apple.
5. Fruit sauce, made by simmering rhubarb, apples, dried fruit or soft tree fruit.
6. Broiled fruit such as grapefruit, pineapple, banana.

Fruit whips are another kind of simple fruit dessert. They are made from soft cooked fruit such as peaches, apricots, or prunes that have been put through a sieve. Egg whites are beaten until foamy, sugar is added, and then the fruit pulp is beaten in gradually until the mixture mounds nicely. Uncooked fruit whips must be served immediately since the egg whites do not hold their volume well.

Baked fruit whips are known as soufflés. The fruit pulp and sugar are heated together until the sugar dissolves. This hot syrup is poured slowly over stiffly beaten egg whites while beating continues. The mixture is piled lightly into an ovenproof dish and baked. It, too, should be served at once. Both uncooked and baked fruit whips are often served with a custard sauce made with the remaining egg yolks.

Baked fruit puddings are popular desserts. The more common varieties are made from fresh or canned fruit covered with a batter, dough, or crumb topping and baked in the oven. Fruit Betty is made with buttered bread crumbs layered with fruit and a syrup of fruit juice and sugar poured over all. Fruit Crumble topping is usually made with flour, brown sugar, butter or margarine and rolled oats. These ingredients are mixed together and sprinkled over prepared fruit. A Fruit Crisp topping is made from the same ingredients although proportions are different and the rolled oats are omitted. A Fruit Cobbler is fruit, often canned, with a sauce of sweetened thickened juice topped with spoonfuls of a rich drop biscuit batter. It is baked until the biscuit dough is cooked and resembles dumplings on the fruit and sauce.

Milk and Egg Desserts

Milk desserts have good nutritive value because they contribute significantly to the daily milk intake. Because of their food value and generally bland flavour they are a particularly suitable dessert for young children, the aged, and all sick and convalescent persons.

The ingredients used to make them are few and steps in preparation simple, but attention to details is important to ensure a good product. Observing the principles of milk cookery which are detailed in the section, Milk and Milk Products, is essential. A low cooking temperature is used to prevent scorching. When scalded milk is required, it is heated over low direct heat or boiling water only until a film of bubbles begins to form.

Many desserts classed as milk desserts also contain eggs. Therefore, the principles of egg cookery discussed in the section, Eggs, are important. To avoid over-coagulation of egg protein use a low temperature and do not overcook the pudding.

Milk puddings are usually named by the ingredient used to thicken them. The basic ingredients are milk, sugar, flavouring and a thickening agent. Starch puddings are thickened with a starch from a cereal product such as cornstarch, flour, tapioca or rice. Custards are thickened with eggs.

CUSTARD

A custard is a cooked mixture of milk and egg, usually with sugar and flavouring. True custards are thickened by the eggs alone although some desserts having an additional starch thickener are incorrectly called custard puddings.

The eggs may be whole, or only the yolks may be used. Either way, a characteristic colour and texture results. Similarly the method of cooking affects the characteristic of the custard. If the ingredients are stirred during cooking the egg combines with the milk to form a thickened liquid. If allowed to bake undisturbed, the same ingredients form a weak, delicate gel that will hold its shape when turned out from the baking dish.

Custard is a simple dessert but timing and temperature are very important in preparing it. Both egg and milk require a low-to-moderate cooking temperature. Overcooking the mixture quickly spoils the texture of the product.

PREPARATION OF CUSTARD

Both types of custard are made with the same ingredients but the method of cooking determines the consistency.

1. To make either type, first scald the milk over boiling water or low direct heat. This heating prevents the milk from curdling and shortens the cooking period.

2. Next, beat the eggs slightly, only enough to break the structure and blend yolk and white together. Overbeating results in a porous baked custard and may produce a foam on the top of a soft custard. Sugar, salt, and in some cases, flavourings, are blended into the eggs now.

3. The scalded milk is slowly added to the eggs and other ingredients, with constant stirring. At this point in the preparation the method differs for each type of custard.

For Baked Custard

- Pour the mixed ingredients into individual custard cups or a single baking dish. Sprinkle the surface with spices such as nutmeg, as desired. Set the dish or dishes in a pan of sufficient hot water to come at least halfway up the side. (An easy way is to place the custard dishes in a pan, set in on the oven rack, and then pour hot water from the kettle to a level that can be safely handled without getting the water into the pudding!) Surrounding the dish with water prevents the outside of the custard from becoming overcooked while the heat is penetrating to the centre.

- Bake the custard at a moderate oven temperature of 180°C or lower, until a knife inserted comes out clean and free of custard particles. Test first when the skin which forms on the surface begins to turn yellow or brown. A sharp knife will be least likely to make a scar in the surface of the pudding.

An individual custard is tested at the centre and removed immediately when it is done. A large dish of custard will remain slightly undercooked in the centre but done when tested halfway between the centre and the outside edge. Cooking will continue for a short time after removal from the oven. Place on a rack to cool, then into the refrigerator to chill until serving time. If you suspect the custard is overcooked, set it immediately in a pan of ice water to stop further cooking.

If baked custard is overcooked, or cooked at too high a temperature the protein is toughened and the custard tends to shrink. You will notice the custard is filled with air holes and will "weep" or exude whey. The separation of liquid from baked custard is called *syneresis*.

For Soft Custard

- Place the ingredients in the top of a double boiler set over simmering water which does not touch the bottom of the pan. Cook the custard, stirring it constantly, only until the mixture begins to make a smooth coating on a metal spoon. This will take about 12-15 minutes. Remove the upper pan from the heat immediately and stir in the vanilla. If you suspect that you have overcooked it, set the pan in cold water.

  Overcooked soft custard will curdle, separating into fine lumps or grains. If this happens, chill it in cold water and beat it vigourously with a whisk or rotary beater. Unless very much overdone, this should smooth it to an acceptable consistency and texture.

A soft (stirred) custard is often incorrectly called "boiled" custard. After reading these preparation principles it is easy to understand the false impression this error would give. Heating a custard to boiling temperature would cause it to curdle.

Coagulation temperatures of an egg mixture vary. The thickening agent in custard is egg. When coagulated the egg holds all of the ingredients together. This happens somewhere between 60°C and 71°C, depending on the proportions of other ingredients:

- the more egg, the lower the temperature required.

- the more sugar, the higher the temperature needed.

Custards can be used in many ways. They can be made with a variety of flavours such as chocolate, vanilla, other extracts and instant coffee. A caramel custard is made by placing caramelized sugar in the bottom of the custard cup before the custard mixture is added. Baked custards may also be unmoulded from the baking dish and served garnished or with a fruit sauce. Custard forms the filling for custard pie.

Soft custard may be served alone or with cake, fruits, or gelatin. A variety of attractive garnishes is possible including fruit, nuts, jelly or jam, coconut and whipped cream. Spoonfuls of meringue on a soft custard makes a dessert known as Floating Island.

Custard sauce is similar to soft custard but of thinner consistency. It is served over fruit and puddings.

Starch Thickened Milk Desserts

TYPES OF STARCHES USED FOR THICKENING

All starches are distributed in plants in the form of tiny grains or packages called granules. These differ in size and shape according to the plants from which they were taken. The chief commercial source of starch is the seed of grains but important amounts are also obtained from roots, tubers and the fleshy stems of a number of plants. Here are basic facts about the most common thickeners found on our grocers' shelves:

1. **Cornstarch**
   - derived from corn.
   - strongest thickening agent; has thickening power of twice the amount of flour.
   - produces a translucent gel.

2. **Wheat Flour**
   - less thickening power than cornstarch.
   - makes opaque rather than clear gel.

3. **Tapioca**
   - derived from the root of the cassava plant in the tropical regions of the world.
   - thickening power lies somewhere between that of cornstarch and wheat flour.

4. **Arrowroot**
   - comes from the fleshy underground stems of the maranta plant in the West Indies.
   - used chiefly in desserts.
   - has a more delicate flavour than tapioca or sago.

5. **Sago**
   - extracted from the pith of the stems of the sago palm grown in the tropics.

6. **Potato Starch**
   - an extract from potato.

7. **Rice Flour**
   - increasing in importance, particularly in preventing curdling of frozen sauces.
   - gives a slightly grainy texture, not as smooth as cornstarch.

Each thickening agent has a different thickening power and is used for certain dishes although one may be substituted for another in many instances. The proportion necessary depends upon the use for which the sauce is intended or the type of product desired. The resulting texture varies with the nature of the thickening agent used.

PROPERTIES AND PROPORTIONS OF THICKENING AGENTS COMMONLY USED

THICKENING AGENT	USES AND PROPORTIONS	MIXING PRE-CAUTIONS	TEMPERA-TURE EFFECTS	THICKENING FACTORS	QUALITIES OF GEL
Flour	Thin sauce — 15 ml for each 250 ml liquid Medium sauce — 30 ml for each 250 ml liquid Thick sauce — 45 ml for each 250 ml liquid Very thick sauce — 60 ml for each 250 ml liquid	Separate starch granules in cold liquid or in fat or mix with sugar before adding hot liquid. Stir while cooking.	Heat to 90°C or above to obtain maximum thickening. Viscosity increases on cooling.	Heating with acid causes thinning. High sugar concentrations retard gelatinization and reduce thickening power.	Opaque paste results.
Corn-starch	15 ml corn-starch can be substituted for 30 ml flour	Same as flour.	Same as flour.	Same as flour.	Paste more translucent than flour paste.
Tapioca	Puddings — 50 ml for 500 ml liquid Fruit pies — 25 ml for 20-22 cm pie Soup — 25-50 ml for 1 litre liquid Substitute equal amount of tapioca for flour	None	Heat below boiling point for gelatinization and maximum viscosity. Thins when boiled.	Thickens as it cools.	Tendency to become gummy.
Eggs	Custard pudding, Custard sauce, Custard pies 2-3 eggs or 4-6 yolks thickens 500 ml milk	Blend well with sugar and milk. Coagulate by slow heating.	Overcooking causes syneresis (weeping) and curdling.	Sugar and dilution raise coagulation temperature; acid lowers it. Use of water instead of milk not satisfactory.	quite translucent. Baked custard forms a firm continuous clot. Stirred custard is soft and thickened but not set.
Gelatin	Moulded desserts and salads One envelope sets 450-500 ml liquid	Soak in 3-6 times weight of cold liquid. Dissolve by heating to 40°C or by adding hot liquid.	Gel forms after a few hours of chilling Softens at 26°C or higher.	Heating with acid reduces gel strength. Raw pineapple prevents setting because of enzyme action.	Gel firm but springy and quivery. Transparent in appearance.

PRINCIPLES OF STARCH COOKERY

The thickening action of starch is due to the ability of the numerous granules to swell to many times their original size when in hot liquid. In so doing they crowd each other and more or less fill the space throughout the dispersion. This swelling of starch granules in hot water is called *gelatinization*. It takes place gradually as the temperature of the dispersion is raised, and it is made evident by the gradual thickening of the product.

To ensure even cooking, the granules must be separated before the hot liquid is added. Separating agents are cold liquid, sugar as used in sweet sauces or desserts, and melted fat, used in non-sweet mixtures, such as white sauce and gravy.

During the thickening process the mixture should be stirred constantly as it is heated in order to keep the starch grains separate and to establish an even distribution of the granules as they gelatinize.

Flavour is generally improved with long cooking periods when using cornstarch and flour. However, overcooking of the coarser thickeners is undesirable. Tapioca becomes glue-like and rice may cook to a uniform mass.

Flavouring extracts are added last to prevent evaporation during the cooking period. In the case of lemon juice, as in lemon pie or pudding, or the addition of any other acid substance, it must be added after the thickening and cooking is completed. Acid added to a starch-thickened mixture causes some *hydrolysis* of the starch changing it to a form of sugar which reduces the viscosity of the product. If acid is added too soon the mixture will not thicken but will become thin instead.

Sucrose affects the consistency of mixtures thickened with starch. If the concentration of this kind of sugar is great it may even cause a mixture which would otherwise have formed a gel to become syrupy.

If the recipe includes eggs they are beaten slightly and must have some of the hot liquid stirred in first so that the egg will not cook in lumps when it comes in contact with the main portion of the hot liquid.

CORNSTARCH PUDDING

Cornstarch is widely used for thickening food of all types, including puddings. When properly cooked to a jelly-like consistency which allows it to keep its shape when unmoulded, cornstarch pudding has a smooth texture and a delicate flavour. In its simplest form, flavoured with vanilla, this is commonly called *blancmange*. Cornstarch-thickened puddings can be made in several flavours such as chocolate, coconut, caramel or butterscotch. They can be served alone as a dessert or may be the basis of other desserts such as pies and soufflés. Cornstarch puddings may not be as popular now as in the past, perhaps because of the competition of ready-to-mix packaged desserts that are somewhat similar.

For a number of reasons cornstarch is more suitable than flour for thickening most milk desserts as it is a strong thickener. To obtain the same consistency, twice as much flour would have to be used. A flour thickened mixture is opaque rather than clear. Cornstarch thickened mixtures are semi-transparent adding no colour to the liquid being thickened. Hence, it is possible to obtain an appetizing looking product in any colour or flavour. Although for some products the characteristic flavour of flour is preferred, cornstarch has very little flavour so added flavours do not clash.

Preparation of Cornstarch Pudding

1. Mix the cornstarch (or flour) with the sugar and salt to separate the starch granules of the thickener.

2. Add some of the cold liquid and stir to make a smooth paste. This will further separate the starch grains. Then, stir in the remaining liquid. In some cases this liquid is added hot (boiling water or scalded milk) to cut down on the cooking time required.

3. Cook the pudding until thickened and no flavour of raw starch remains. There are two common methods:

    a. Over direct heat, medium to low temperature. Stir constantly until mixture boils. Then allow the pudding to boil for one minute to completely cook the starch.

    b. Over boiling water in a double boiler. This method requires a longer cooking time but does not require such constant attention. After the initial thickening takes place the pudding needs stirring only at 5 minute intervals. (Over-stirring results in a heavy, pasty pudding.)

4. When the pudding is cooked, remove it from the heat, stir in the flavouring extract, and cool. So that a skin will not form on top as the pudding cools, cover the dish or individual dishes with wax paper or transparent wrap.

5. Blancmange is usually poured into custard cups or other moulds to set until firm, and then turned out on to dessert plates or dishes. It is often served with fruit. Other flavoured cornstarch puddings are poured into a bowl or into individual dessert dishes. They may be served with cream, whipped or plain, or garnished with coconut, nuts or sliced fruit.

TAPIOCA

Tapioca consists of balls of starch granules made from cassava root. The root is grated and washed to remove poisonous juices, then heated so as to burst starch grains. "Pearl" tapioca is made by forcing the moist starch through sieves. "Minute" tapioca is made by grinding the pearl tapioca.

Tapioca is frequently used to thicken fruit pies, especially juicy berry pies, but is best known in connection with the pudding which bears its name.

Of the two sizes, minute tapioca cooks more quickly, producing a smoother product that is so generally superior that the large pearls are seldom found in stores anymore. The recipe section of this book includes a pudding recipe using minute tapioca which has been found to give a most desirable product. Many other recipes exist, however. Tapioca goes well with fruit and served this way it would provide additional food value to the milk and egg of the basic recipe.

RICE PUDDING

Rice pudding can have a custard base or it can be prepared without any egg at all. If prepared well it will have a distinctive taste with soft rice grains that have retained their shape. It is an economical dessert with many variations possible such as those derived by the addition of maple sugar, chocolate or fruit flavours. It may be served hot or cold and is easy for an inexperienced cook to prepare.

Regular rice, either the long, short or pearl type, should be used for pudding. Although recipes exist which require quick cooking rice, this type may not be used in other recipes since it will not soften and expand enough to give the accepted consistency. Converted rice may also react differently enough to need special treatment.

Custard rice pudding is of two types — baked and stirred. These correspond to the kinds of plain custard pudding. For baked rice pudding a standard custard recipe is used increasing the sugar and flavouring slightly and mixing this with about half its bulk of cooked rice. Baking is done in the same manner as for plain custard; cooking time is similar and the test for correct cooking is the same. Especially at the beginning of the cooking period, the rice tends to settle to the bottom of the dish, giving a layered effect. This is less noticeable if the amount of rice is increased. When it is about half cooked the mixture can be stirred, to prevent layering. Slide a spoon in near the edge and stir the bottom without breaking through to the top and disturbing the surface film which has formed.

Stirred rice custard is made from a standard custard recipe with cooked rice added. One cup of cooked rice to each 500 ml milk is suitable. Raisins may be added as well in amounts of 75-125 ml for each 250 ml of cooked rice. As with a basic soft custard, the ingredients are cooked in a double boiler with constant stirring. When cooked, the mixture will be thickened by some starch from the rice which the custard picks up, as well as by the eggs. Because of the starch thickening this pudding is less likely to curdle than a plain stirred custard.

Old fashioned rice pudding uses no eggs. It depends upon long oven cooking to move the starch from the rice grains into the milk, causing it to thicken. Raw rice is used for this type. As baking continues, the pudding is stirred occasionally to allow even thickening and to prevent lumping. If it is thick and hard then too much rice or too little milk has been used or the mixture may have been cooked too long.

Gelatin Desserts

Desserts which are thickened with gelatin are a popular choice for the cook who likes to experiment, and are especially suitable when a spectacular effect is desired. Attractive desserts low in kilojoules can be made easily using gelatin but very rich desserts with a wide range of possibilities can also be made.

Gelatin is a colourless, tasteless, odourless product extracted from the bones, ligaments, tendons and cartilage of beef animals. It is an incomplete protein whose main property is the ability to change liquids into a solid.

Gelatin is easily digested. For this reason it is frequently included in menus for the elderly, infants, invalids and convalescents. The food value of the gelatin itself, though protein, is not significant since one spoonful of gelatin in a recipe is diluted by the addition of up to 500 ml of liquid. The food value of a gelatin dessert is derived from the ingredients which are added, very often highly nutritious foods such as milk, eggs, cheese and fruit. Similarly the kilojoule count can be maintained at a low level by restricting the added ingredients to egg white, skim milk solids, and unsweetened fruit and by increasing volume by beating the mixture until light and fluffy.

Gelatin is available to the homemaker in two forms — flavoured and unflavoured. Unflavoured gelatin is marketed in small packages containing 15 ml gelatin. This is enough to solidify up to 500 ml liquid which could be water, milk, broth or fruit or vegetable juices. If solid ingredients are to be added later less liquid should be used. If an acid fruit juice is included even less liquid would be used.

The gelatin is first mixed with a small amount of cold liquid to soften it.

It is then dissolved in hot liquid or heated slowly and stirred until the gelatin dissolves. If the recipe contains more than 15 ml sugar the dry granular gelatin may simply be mixed with the sugar and then added directly to the hot liquid without first being softened.

Flavoured gelatin, called jelly powder, is a convenient alternate form. In addition to the gelatin, this dessert mix contains sugar and artificial colour and flavourings. It can be dissolved directly in hot liquid. One package of flavoured gelatin will gel 500 ml water or other mixed liquids. The first 250ml hot liquid is sufficient for dissolving the jelly powder; the second is usually added cold to speed the gelling process.

Either form is easy to use when basic principles are understood. Here are some factors to consider to ensure a good product.

1. Soften unflavoured gelatin in cold liquid or mix with sugar before dissolving in hot liquid.

2. If solid ingredients are to be added, chill the gelatin mixture to unbeaten egg white consistency first. If added too soon, when the mixture is too thin, the solids will sink to the bottom or rise to the top.

3. Beaten eggs or whipped cream blend in best if added as the gelatin begins to congeal.

4. When combining beaten egg whites and a gelatin mixture, always fold the gelatin mixture into the egg whites. The final mixture will stand up and be more fluffy.

5. If fresh pineapple is to be used in a gelatin mixture it must first be cooked. This inactivates the enzymes found in fresh pineapple which would otherwise prevent the gelatin from congealing.

6. Layered effects may be obtained by partially filling a mould with some of the gelatin, allowing it to congeal in the refrigerator, then adding a layer of fruit, nuts or other foods, followed by another layer of gelatin. Return the mould to the refrigerator until the new layer sets and continue adding layers as desired.

7. To chill gelatin dishes quickly, set the container of gelatin mixture in a bowl of ice and water and stir until it thickens, or, the container may be placed in the freezer for about 10 minutes. Stir occasionally so that it will chill evenly throughout. If the mixture becomes too solid, melt it over boiling water.

8. An alternate quick set method used when preparing flavoured gelatin is to add ice to the gelatin mixture as part of the cold liquid and stir slowly until the gelatin begins to set. The addition of ice in this manner is the most rapid way of obtaining a jelly but on certain occasions may be a disadvantage since the gel will soften more quickly than a comparable mixture that has been allowed to set slowly at a more moderate temperature.

9.   The most stable gelatin mixture is one which has been allowed to set at room temperature. This method will take longer than setting at cooler temperatures but the result may be worth the waiting if a firm moulded product is important. Mixtures chilled quickly in the freezer or over ice will soften quickly when served and may prove disappointing in appearance. Care must be taken to refrigerate any gelatin mixtures containing ingredients susceptible to bacterial food spoilage, such as milk, cream and cheese.

Steps for using moulds

a.   Rinse mould in clear water or grease *very* lightly with vegetable oil. Usable containers are as varied as the sizes and shapes of the pans, bowls, cups and dishes in your kitchen.

b.   Pour gelatin mixture into mould and allow to set until really firm. This may take 3-4 hours. If the dessert is to be served on a warm day, chilling overnight is highly desirable.

c.   Dip mould for 5 seconds in warm, not hot, water, to the depth of the gelatin.

d.   Loosen around the edge of mould with the tip of a paring knife.

e.   Place serving dish on top of mould and turn upside down. Shake gently, holding serving dish tightly to the mould. If gelatin does not unmould readily, dip again and repeat.

UNMOULDING GELATIN DISHES

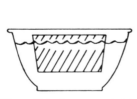

1. Dip mould in warm water (not hot) to depth of gelatin.

2. Loosen around edge with the tip of a paring knife.

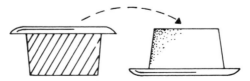

3. Place serving dish on top of mould and turn upside down. Shake, holding serving dish tightly to the mould. If gelatin does not unmould readily, repeat.

TYPES OF GELATIN DESSERTS

1. **Jelly**

   Plain gelatin desserts, called simple gels, are made from a clear liquid, sugar and gelatin. There are two ways to prepare a jelly:

   a.   A basic jelly is made with unflavoured gelatin, sugar, fruit juice and flavouring as required.

   b.   A quicker jelly is made with jelly powder which contains sugar and flavouring. It is mixed with hot water and/or juice.

2. **Fruit Jelly**

   This is a simple jelly to which fruit has been added. So that the fruit will not all sink to the bottom, the basic gel must first be chilled to the consistency of unbeaten egg whites.

3. **Whip**

   A whip contains the same ingredients as a basic jelly and can be made with unflavoured gelatin or jelly powder. When partially set, it is whipped until light, fluffy and double in volume, then it is chilled until set before serving.

4. **Sponge or Snow**

   A snow pudding is a basic gelatin to which egg whites have been added. The egg white can be added after the gel has partly set and the mixture beaten until stiff, or the basic gelatin and the egg whites can be beaten separately, then beaten together. This dessert is often served with a fruit or custard sauce.

5. **Chiffon**

   A chiffon dessert is made from a basic gelatin cooked with egg yolks. When partially set, this mixture is folded into a stiff meringue of egg whites and sugar. Chiffons are usually served as a pie filling.

6. **Gelatin Creams**

   These are made with milk and/or cream and sometimes with eggs and/or fruit. There are two types:

   BAVARIAN CREAM is a clear basic gelatin which has been chilled to un-beaten egg white consistency and then had whipped cream folded into it.

   SPANISH CREAM is made by dissolving gelatin in a custard-like mixture (egg yolk and milk), chilling it to the unbeaten egg white stage, then folding it into stiffly beaten egg whites.

7. **Mousse**

   A mousse is a rich mixture which can be served as ice cream when frozen or as a pudding when served at room temperature or chilled. Because of the high proportion of cream it usually does not crystallize during freezing.

8. **Charlotte**

    Another elaborate gelatin dessert containing a high proportion of cream. The ingredients and method for a charlotte are similar to those for a Spanish cream or a mousse. To make a charlotte russe, the mould is first lined with lady fingers, cake or soft cookies, then filled with the chilled pudding mixture.

Frozen Desserts

Depending upon the ingredients from which they are made, frozen desserts can be a light refreshing conclusion to the meal or a rich addition suitable to a less substantial meal.

Ice cream is undoubtedly the most popular type of frozen dessert. It may be served alone or as an accompaniment to fruit, pudding, pie or cake, or it may be served with one of a wide range of sauces. Sundaes and parfaits are arrangements of ice cream and sauces, nuts and fruit. Peach Melba is a combination of fruit, sauce and ice cream arranged in a special dish. Baked Alaska is cake-wrapped ice cream which has been spread carefully with meringue and browned in the oven. The possibilities for frozen desserts are unlimited.

Ice cream can be made in the home. An ice cream freezer in which the ingredients are stirred or beaten together during freezing may be used but this is not a common practice in the modern home. More frequently a refrigerator freezer method is used. The mixed ice cream ingredients are poured into the refrigerator tray but because they cannot be stirred as freezing continues, the mixture must be removed and whipped after it is partially frozen. Air is incorporated by the beating and the ice crystals are broken up to give a smoother texture.

Then the beaten ice cream mixture is returned to the freezer tray to freeze again. Acceptable ice cream can be made this way but its texture will not be as smooth as that made in an ice cream freezer.

For those who find preparing and freezing homemade ice cream too time consuming there is a large selection of commercial products available. The cost of these is often less than the cost of homemade ice cream. You may judge the ice cream you buy or make by these qualities:

1. Texture or fine grain is influenced by the amount of sugar, fat, stabilizers and emulsifiers used. The size, shape and arrangement of ice crystals also affects texture.

2. Flavour is determined by high quality ingredients and the addition of fresh fruits, artificial flavourings and other flavouring ingredients.

3. Body depends upon the amount of air beaten into the mixture. Ice cream should be firm but not solid and it should melt slowly.

Commercial ice cream is sold in various quantities from amounts suitable for one or two servings to a several weeks' supply in a plastic bucket. There are also specialties such as ice cream bars, cones, cups, and cakes.

TYPES OF FROZEN DESSERTS

Frozen desserts are grouped here on the basis of the ingredients used to make them. Many variations are possible but these are the common classifications:

1. **Ice**

   This type of frozen dessert is made from fruit juices to which sugar and water have been added. (Ice cream was developed by perfecting this.) Crystals of ice are prevented from forming if gelatin or egg white is included.

2. **Ice Cream**

   The basic ingredients of ice cream are sugar, milk, cream and flavouring. Commercial ice cream contains a stabilizer such as cornstarch, gelatin, or other thickener. It may contain chocolate, fruits or nuts as well. There are three types:

   PHILADELPHIA ice cream is an uncooked mixture made by freezing the basic ingredients while stirring to break down ice crystals.

   FRENCH ice cream is richer than Philadelphia since it also contains eggs in a cooked custard base and additional cream. This is the richest type.

   AMERICAN ice cream is similar in composition to French but it contains less cream and may also contain cornstarch, flour or gelatin instead of eggs as a thickening agent.

3.   **Ice Milk**

Ice milk is similar to ice cream but there is less butterfat, from cream, and more non-fat dry milk solids contained in it.

4.   **Sherbet**

A sherbet is an ice to which beaten egg whites have been added or in which milk or cream is used in place of all or part of the water content. Because of their high sugar content, sherbets melt quickly. They are not as smooth and creamy as ice cream but the addition of gelatin will improve the smoothness. A sherbet is a light, refreshing, dessert to end any meal.

5.   **Mousse**

A mousse is a very rich dessert containing large amounts of whipped cream with fruit flavouring and gelatin. It may be served frozen or chilled. When frozen, the cream gives a very smooth texture and the gelatin adds firmness to the mixture. This mixture is frozen without stirring.

Sugar and Sugar Cookery

Sugar is a carbohydrate, as is starch, and both are composed of the elements carbon, hydrogen and oxygen. The two differ only in their complexity of molecular structure, which becomes manifest in their individual physical properties.

The simplest of all carbohydrates are *monosaccharides,* glucose, fructose and galactose. The chemical formula for monosaccharides is $C_6H_{12}O_6$, meaning that one molecule of glucose, for example, consists of 6 atoms of carbon, 12 atoms of hydrogen and 6 atoms of oxygen. Its chemical structure looks like this:

The carbon chain structure for fructose and galactose is similar except for a slightly different rearrangement of the hydrogen and oxygen atoms attached to it.

The *disaccharides,* sucrose, maltose and lactose, consist of two carbon chain molecules of simple sugars that are linked together to form one molecule, the complex sugar. Starches are *polysaccharides.* Their molecular structure would be composed of many simple carbon chain units.

SUGAR CLASSIFICATION

1. Monosaccharides

Glucose, also known as dextrose, is the sugar from which plants manufacture starch. It is found particularly in grapes and in vegetables such as sweet corn, and is also present in corn syrup along with other more complex sugars. *Fructose* occurs with glucose in ripe fruits. It is also found in honey. It is sweeter and more soluble than glucose. *Galactose,* the third of the simple sugars, is produced when lactose, the sugar in milk, is hydrolized.

2. Disaccharides

Sucrose is the most common and most available of this group, and is used widely in food production both commercially and in the home. It is manufactured from beet sugar, sugar cane and sugar maple sap. This sugar is extremely soluble. It is, therefore, able to produce a super-saturated solution which crystallizes easily. See page 367.

Lactose is the disaccharide found in milk. It is less sweet and less soluble than all other sugars. *Maltose* is found in cereals and malt products and is rarely used in its true form.

3. Polysaccharides

These include all starches, and also cellulose, the roughage in plant matter, and in pectin, which is present in varying amounts in most fruits.

SUGAR PRODUCTION

Sugar cane and sugar beet are the two plants yielding most of the sugar we eat. The sugar which results from both of these is chemically identical but the production processes are different.

Production from Sugar Cane

Sugar cane is grown in the warm moist tropical climate of the West Indies, Hawaii, Fiji, Philippines, North Eastern Australia, South Africa and India. These countries provide two-thirds of the world's sugar supply. The sugar cane plant is a heavy bamboo-like grass which stores sugar in its thick stalk. The sugar cane crop, which takes about two years to reach maturity, is still cut by hand in some countries. In other areas harvesting is done with huge machines which dig up the entire plant and deposit it in waiting trucks.

The raw sugar juice is extracted from the washed stalks by squeezing them through a series of rollers. The juice is then heated in the presence of lime. Many of the impurities present in this raw sugar juice settle out of the mixture with the lime, to which they adhere. The brown juice that remains is evaporated to a mixture of viscous syrup and raw sugar crystals. The crystals are isolated from the mixture and become the starting material for the sugar refining process. This raw sugar is then shipped to Canada and other countries around the world for final refinement and distribution.

During the refining process the coarse, yellow, sticky, raw sugar is transformed into fine white sugar crystals by a successive filtering process. A syrup is made of the raw sugar with water, and this is filtered through charcoal beds. The charcoal removes further impurities and has a decolourizing effect on the syrup. The sugar in the syrup is then recrystallized and dried to separate the crystals.

Production from Sugar Beets

The sugar beet grows best in a temperate climate. Large quantities are harvested every year on the Canadian prairies. Part of this crop is refined into sugar and the remainder is used to feed domestic animals.

The sugar beet crop takes about nine months to reach maturity and is then uprooted by a spiked wheel device. The beets are sliced into long strips and then soaked in hot water which, by a process of diffusion, releases the sugar. The resultant juice, which is blue-black in colour, contains the beet sugar. This is given a lime and carbon dioxide treatment, a process that is comparable to the lime and charcoal clarification of cane sugar. The clear juice is then processed in a series of steps involving evaporation, crystallization under carefully controlled conditions, isolation of the sugar crystals from the mother liquor, air drying, screening and packaging.

FORMS OF SUGAR

In food preparation we can take advantage of the particular properties of the various forms of sugar available to us and achieve desirable variations in flavour and texture.

1. **Granulated Sugar**

    Over half of factory sugar production is granulated sugar because its sweetness, colour and solubility are well suited for wide use in food production and in food preparation. Granulated sugar is crystalline sucrose. The size of the crystals will vary from larger crystals as are present in standard granulated sugar, to those smaller in size as in berry or fruit sugar. This fine sugar is passed through additional sifting screens. It dissolves more readily and is ideal for sprinkling over fruit, pies, cookies and doughnuts, for cold beverages and in the making of meringue.

2. **Cube Sugar**

    This is also called loaf sugar. This sugar is obtained by pressing sugar that has been moistened with a white syrup into moulds, then dried in that shape. This type of sugar is usually served as a beverage accompaniment and in this respect is excellent for use in restaurants.

3. **Powdered Sugar**

    Powdered sugar, confectioner's sugar or icing sugar is made by pulverizing granulated sugar. A small amount of cornstarch is added to absorb moisture, even that of moist air, thus preventing its powdery texture from caking. This sugar is used for uncooked frostings, fondants and for dusting the surface of certain cookies, cakes and slices.

4.   Brown Sugar

Partial refinement of raw sugar gives brown sugar, which indicates the presence of some molasses which coats and colours the sugar crystals. The lightness or darkness of the sugar depends on the degree of refinement reached. A dark, strong flavoured brown sugar as demerara has undergone less purification than has yellow sugar, the most refined brown sugar, or medium brown sugar. Brown sugars contain significant amounts of iron compounds, have a greater moisture content than white sugar and tend to pack more. Because of their pleasing distinctive flavour, brown sugars are frequently used in baked products and in the making of pickles, ketchup and chili-like sauces.

5.   Molasses

This is the by-product of sugar refinery. It contains sucrose and the monosaccharides fructose and glucose. Also present are the minerals iron and calcium. The flavour of molasses varies considerably, depending on its order of removal from the centrifuged sugar or sucrose crystals. The mother liquor from which these crystals are separated becomes molasses. In the three successive centrifuging processes table molasses, cooking molasses and blackstrap molasses are produced. Choice in food preparation will depend on the strength of flavour desired.

6.   Maple Syrup

Maple syrup is produced by boiling the sap from the sugar maple tree. Moisture loss through evaporation concentrates the syrup. Continued evaporation produces maple sugar. This can be reconstituted to give maple syrup. Maple sugar is a mixture of sucrose and small amounts of invert sugar. This type of syrup is most frequently used for serving with pancakes and waffles. Syrups with artificial maple flavouring are considerably less expensive than the natural product.

7.   Corn Syrup

This is a mixture of simple glucose and complex maltose and dextrin, produced by heating corn starch with an acid until the starch has hydrolized. The syrup is clear, almost colourless, with a bland, slightly sweet flavour.

8.   Honey

Honey is made by bees from the nectar of flowers. The colour and flavour of the honey will depend on the kinds of plant or plants from which the honey has been produced. Common honey flowers are clover and alfalfa and, more recently, orange blossom and sage. All honey is composed of equal parts of glucose and fructose. It is the glucose molecules that tend to crystallize upon long storage. The fructose, on the other hand, is hygroscopic in that it has the ability to attract and retain moisture. It is for this reason that products such as muffins and breads baked with honey do not dry out as quickly.

PROPERTIES OF SUGAR

1. Sweetening and Flavouring Ability

Sugar has a number of valuable properties which explains its extensive use in food preparation. Foremost is its ability to sweeten food, but it also affects other flavours. It will, for example, in small amounts, counteract the salty flavour of over-salted soup, and it affects the sourness of very acid foods such as grapefruit. It is frequently added to the cooking water of fresh vegetables to help restore their fresh flavour. The natural sugars which vegetables contain tend to change to starches very rapidly after they are picked. The enzymes in the vegetables cause this change.

2. Crystallization

In candy making the crystallizing properties of sugar are valuable. In order for crystallization to occur the sugar solution one is dealing with must become super-saturated. To be super-saturated suggests that some sugar is actually in solution that should not be held in solution, and this is made possible by heating it to a higher temperature. This means that the excess sugar which is held in solution at those high temperatures will precipitate as the mixture cools, and form sugar crystals.

3. Caramelization

When sugar is heated by itself the sugar changes from a solid granular state to a colourless liquid. With further heating this physical change is accompanied by a chemical change in the nature of the sugar, as it begins to change from golden to amber to dark brown in colour. This burnt sugar, as it is often called, has a pleasing characteristic aroma and distinctive flavour. Caramelized sugar should be diluted with water before blending into other foods as the sugar alone becomes very hard and brittle as it cools.

Caramelization in jam and jelly making is undesirable since it produces a dark colour and flavour that makes the natural fresh flavour of the jelly. This problem can be avoided by rapid heating or preparation of the jelly, in small quantities.

It appears that some organic acids are formed as breakdown products of caramelization. The presence of some acid is evident when baking soda is added to hot peanut brittle. The addition of the alkaline soda causes the caramelized candy mixture to effervesce abruptly with the release of the gas carbon dioxide. The result of this reaction is a porous textured brittle.

4. Hydrolysis

Hot acid solutions cause the disaccharide sucrose molecule to split into the two monosaccharides glucose and fructose. This chemical reaction is termed *hydrolysis* and the combination of the two simple sugars produced is known as invert sugar. (This same split occurs physiologically in the digestive tract, but there, it is brought about by an enzyme found in the intestinal juices.) See page 75.

Hydrolysis of sucrose is also of relevance in candy making. Extensive hydrolysis tends to produce a softer candy.

5. Preservation

High sugar concentrations preserve certain foods. Microorganism activity is stopped by a process of cell dehydration. In a concentrated sugar solution water is withdrawn from the cells of yeast and bacteria by the process of osmosis. *Osmosis* in this instance refers to the passage of water from within the cells of the microorganisms through the cell membrane in an attempt to reach a state of equilibrium or a free flow of water back and forth between the interior of the cells and the surrounding sugar concentration. This equalization, of course, can never be achieved and the yeast and bacteria cells become totally dehydrated. See page 385, Food Preservation.

This same principle applies to the cooking of fruit in a strong sugar solution where retention of shape is desired.

Candy

Candies are of two basic types: crystalline and non-crystalline, or amorphous.

Crystalline candies have an organized or uniform structure and are characterized by their soft, smooth creamy texture which also makes them easy to bite. Examples are fondant, fudge, panocha (or vanilla fudge), divinity, mints and the cream centres in chocolate creams.

The non-crystalline candies contain more moisture and are cooked to a higher final temperature than the crystalline candies. Crystallization is interfered with by the presence of such ingredients as corn syrup, or honey, or some other invert sugar or cream of tartar, lemon juice and vinegar. Additional ingredients as milk solids, fats such a butter or cream, egg white and in commercially produced candies, starch or pectin. Examples of non-crystalline candies are caramels, butterscotch, taffy, brittles, and marshmallows. The texture and consistency of these candies vary considerably from the chewy consistency of caramel, to the extremely hard, glass-like texture of brittle and taffy, to the soft, airy sponge-like mass of marshmallow.

Crystalline Candies

1. Fondant is a white crystalline candy which illustrates very well the principles of sugar cookery. It is used as the foundation for many cream candies and is the centre for a wide range of coated candies.

   Fondant can be made from sucrose and water, although corn syrup and other invert sugars are frequently added. Cream of tartar is the acid generally used to hydrolyse the sucrose and produce invert sugar. Cream of tartar is generally preferred because it produces a less sweet fondant than that made with corn syrup, and a much whiter fondant than that made by other acid ingredients. (Lemon juice or vinegar can be used almost as effectively but their degree of acidity is less constant and this has a bearing on the degree of hydrolysis.)

   Agitation of the fondant must begin at the correct cooling temperature (40°C to 43°C) in order to achieve a fine textured product. See page 371, Crystallization.

   Fondant has many uses. When kneaded it is a suitable centre for stuffed prunes, or it can be pressed in small amounts between two halved nuts. Fondant candies can be made by adding coarsely chopped nuts or candied fruits or a mixture of the two into the cooked fondant. This is then pressed into a pan or shaped into a cylinder of about 2-3 cm in width, rolled in chopped nuts and sliced as needed.

   Melted fondant can be used for making cream mints. The fondant is melted in the top of a double boiler with flavourings and colourings stirred in. If the fondant does not soften easily, 5 ml of hot water can be added. The mint can then be shaped by dropping spoonfuls of the mixture from the tip of the spoon onto a flat surface covered with waxed paper. Suggested flavourings are oil of peppermint, wintergreen, spearmint, clove or lemon.

   Melted fondant can also be used for dipping nuts, grapes, unhulled strawberries, maraschino cherries and chocolates.

2. Fudge is a popular crystalline candy made from sucrose and water with milk solids, fat and usually corn syrup added. Chocolate in some form is usually present but maple or molasses can be used instead for flavouring. Ingredients used to interfere with crystalline formation are the milk, fat and syrup. Nuts, coconut or marshmallows are often included to add interest and variety.

3. Panocha is similar to fudge, but is made with brown sugar. Brown sugar already contains some invert sugar, therefore, corn syrup can

be omitted or smaller quantities required to produce a fine textured candy. Vanilla is the flavouring commonly used and coarsely chopped nuts added for additional variety.

4. Divinity is a candy mixture which is prepared in a similar way to fondant. After the syrup has been cooked to the proper temperature it is poured over stiffly beaten egg white while constant beating continues. This step incorporates air into the mixture, producing a candy with a light fluffy texture. Since the egg white contains a considerable amount of water which has a diluting effect on the cooked syrup, it is necessary to cook the syrup until it reaches a highly concentrated state. See temperature chart, page 544.

Non-Crystalline Candies

1. Caramels are prepared from sugar (often brown and white mixed), corn syrup, butter and large quantities of concentrated milk products such as evaporated milk, sweetened condensed milk or non-fat dry milk powder. They contain a large proportion of non-sugar ingredients which contribute a "softening effect". With such large proportions of milk present and with such high temperatures involved, care must be taken to prevent scorching of the caramel mixture during cooking. This problem may be overcome by selecting a heavy weight aluminum pan and by stirring constantly throughout the cooking period to prevent the candy from sticking to the bottom of the saucepan.

    Some of the flavour and colouring of caramels results from sugar caramelization. However, it is essentially the reaction between the protein in the milk and the milk sugar, lactose, that produces the characteristic brown colour, flavour and aroma of caramels. Additional ingredients for flavouring caramels include chocolate, toasted coconut, chopped dried fruits (raisins, figs, or dates), and nuts, particularly almonds and Brazil nuts. Well made caramels are chewy in texture but easily bitten.

2. Butterscotch is similar to caramel but is made with brown sugar instead of white sugar and the amount of butter is increased. The cooled mixture is poured into a shallow buttered pan to a thickness of about 1 cm. The squares should be creased with a blunt knife while the mixture is still warm, and then broken into pieces when cold and hard.

3. Brittles are made by caramelizing sucrose. Corn syrup or invert sugar may be added. After cooking, the candy is poured onto a greased tray and allowed to cool undisturbed. Crystallization is prevented in this kind of candy by the rigidity which the mass assumes on cooling, giving it its glass-like texture, and by the presence of corn syrup.

Peanuts or a mixture of coarsely chopped nuts or shredded coconut can be added to the mixture before cooling is allowed to begin. Good brittles are fairly easy to bite.

4. Taffy is made by adding cream of tartar to a mixture of sugar and water or sugar, corn syrup and water. The flavourings are added before cooling. Colouring can be added to white taffy just before pulling. Molasses taffy is made from a mixture of brown and white sugar and molasses. The brown sugar and molasses contain the invert sugar which would be provided by the corn syrup and cream of tartar in white taffy. The candy is pulled as soon as the mixture is cool enough to handle. Cooling can be assisted by using a spatula to turn the edges of the cooler candy towards the centre. This will also help it cool evenly. The hands should be well greased and care should be taken not to burn the hands. The pulling process incorporates air bubbles into the taffy and the candy becomes smooth, satiny and opaque. Its porous texture is due to the entrapped air. This candy should be difficult to bite but not brittle. Each taffy or candy cane should be wrapped individually in waxed paper.

5. After-dinner mints can be made from white taffy by the addition of a few drops of oil of peppermint instead of vanilla. The candy is pulled without twisting and then cut into 5 cm pieces. The mint should be dropped onto a shallow pan containing a mixture of 250 ml of confectioner's sugar and 250 ml of cornstarch. Stir candies well until they are thoroughly cooled. The candy and sugar mixture should then be stored in a tightly sealed container and allowed to stand for at least one week in a warm room. After that time the sugar is sifted from the mints.

CONTROL OF CRYSTAL FORMATION

Both the time at which crystallization occurs and the size of the crystals formed can be controlled in the making of crystalline candies. Careful and adequate cooling is of utmost importance if a fine grained candy is to result. The size of the crystals is mainly controlled by the choice of ingredients added to the candy and by sufficient beating that has been initiated at the correct cooling temperature and continued through until crystallization has completed.

1. Ingredients Chosen

The size of the crystals in crystalline candies can be partially controlled by the addition of substances that inhibit crystal growth.

a.   SUGAR TYPE

The presence of more than one type of sugar, for example white sugar with brown sugar, corn syrup or molasses, interferes with crystal formation. The brown sugar and syrups contain invert sugar which do not crystallize out of solution as readily as sucrose crystals.

b.   ACID INGREDIENT

The hydrolysis of sucrose into invert sugar by the addition of an acid ingredient such as cream of tartar, lemon juice or vinegar, causes crystallization to occur less readily and a fine grained candy results.

c.   FAT SUBSTANCE

Fats, generally butter or cream, inhibit crystallization by coating the sugar crystals, making it more difficult for the sugar to precipitate onto existing crystals. This factor is important in making velvety smooth crystalline candies. When butter, (also the flavouring vanilla), is to be added to the mixture, it should not be stirred in. The butter should be allowed to melt and spread across the surface of the cooling mixture. It is then adequately blended during the beating process.

2.   Extent of Cooling

The size of the crystals formed can be controlled by controlling the extent of cooling that is permitted to take place before beginning the agitation of the mixture. A creamy smooth product will be obtained by allowing considerable cooling before beating. The temperature which ideally should be reached before beating begins is 40-43°C.

This temperature can be determined in two ways. The candy can be cooled in the saucepan in which it was cooked, leaving the thermometer clipped to the side of the pan. This is perfectly satisfactory provided that the candy is deep enough to cover the bulb of the thermometer completely, to give an accurate reading. The thermometer should not in any way be wiggled during the cooling process. See page 373, Premature Crystallization. The second way of determining the temperature is by feeling the bottom of the dish containing the candy, the cooked candy having been poured immediately from the saucepan onto a cold wet platter large enough to hold the mixture. Any mixture adhering to the pan should not be scraped off and mixed with that which has been poured off. This could encourage premature crystallization. The candy mixture will cool more quickly in this shallow dish and the cooling temperature can be determined by very carefully raising and touching the bottom of the platter with your hand. It should feel lukewarm. Beating should be done with a spatula or knife.

3. Mixing and Beating

Agitation of the candy mixture aids in developing small crystals by preventing the formation of larger crystal aggregates. Beating should be continued until crystallization is completed to ensure a fine-textured product. At the moment of crystallization, and this occurs very suddenly, the candy loses some of its sheen and becomes duller in appearance.

4. Premature Crystallization

Crystallization may be started prematurely in a number of ways and every precaution should be taken to prevent this. Disturbing the candy in any way by movement of a thermometer within it, or by causing rippling of its surface, will initiate crystallization. The thermometer, if used, should be clipped firmly to the side of the pan and the mixture left totally undisturbed during cooling. If particles of lint or dust or undissolved sugar crystals clinging to the side of the pan enter the cooling solution, they will behave as nuclei around which other crystals will cluster, producing large crystals rather than fine, small ones.

These possibilities can be prevented by ensuring that all the sugar goes into solution during the cooking period, and by keeping the candy covered during cooling. Also slow stirring of the mixture during heating will help all the sugar to go into solution, but it is advisable to discontinue stirring several degrees below the final temperature. Any crystals that remain on the sides of the pan can be wiped away with a clean, damp cloth. An alternate method would be to bring the mixture to the boil in a tightly covered pan. The condensed steam will wash the crystals from the sides of the pan.

5. Effect of Storing

A ripening period of about 24 hours in a tightly covered container slightly softens crystalline candy and gives extra smoothness. Crystal formation during long storage of candy requires as much consideration as is given to candy preparation. The structure of prepared candy is constantly undergoing change. There exists between the crystals a liquid medium known as the mother liquor. During storage small crystals dissolve into the mother liquor and re-crystallize from the liquor onto existing nuclei. Since the small crystals are more soluble than the larger ones, there is a gradual change from the fine crystals of the freshly made candy to the larger crystals formed during prolonged storage. The presence of the crystal interfering or inhibiting agents mentioned earlier is useful in maintaining a fine-grained candy during storage.

Beverages

Historians mainly agree that coffee was first prepared and drunk as a beverage by the Arabians. By the end of the 15th century Arabia had become a nation of coffee drinkers who were vainly attempting to keep the plant a national monopoly. Trade in coffee spread to Turkey, Egypt, Syria and eventually to Italy, France, England and China. By 1700, coffee-houses or cafés were the centres of cultural life in England and France. The French introduced coffee plants to the West Indies and today 80% of the world's coffee is grown in Latin America.

Although coffee is the favourite in this country, tea is the most popular beverage in the world. The origin of tea is not certain but it was probably first cultivated in China as early as 2000 B.C. Introduced into Japan in the thirteenth century, it was not a common beverage in Europe before the seventeenth century. English settlers brought it to this country. Tea is traditionally served with most meals in India, China and Japan. In some areas its service is a matter of tradition. An example is the Japanese tea ceremony which is a ritual performed in a special part of the house with utensils reserved for the occasion. Other countries also have traditional procedures associated with the preparation and service of tea.

Tea is made from the leaves of a plant called "thea". The leaves from the top shoots are gathered for making tea. The best tea results from the bud and the top two leaves. The third and fourth leaves are used as well but produce tea of a poorer quality. There are three different types of tea made from the same shrub but each is treated differently:

1. Black tea is prepared from leaves that are allowed to ferment after picking. The leaves first wilt and wither, then turn a dark green before they are dried and rolled. During fermentation the enzymes of the tea cause this colour change and the development of the characteristic flavour.

2. Green tea is made from leaves that have not been allowed to ferment. This is done by drying the leaves at a high temperature which causes them to curl up but allows them to keep their green colour.

3. Oolong tea is semi-fermented then dried to produce a tea which falls somewhere between the green and black teas in flavour and colour.

Like tea and coffee, cocoa has a long history. The Indians of the American equatorial region used cocoa not only as a beverage but also as a form of currency. While in South America, Cortez tasted cocoa made from the cacao bean. French, Dutch and Austrians soon began to experiment with the bean and eventually chocolate houses became a favourite social gathering place in Europe. From there the use of chocolate spread to the English colonies in America.

The bean is the fruit of the cacao tree, which grows near the equator. There are two main harvests a year. The bean is dried and partly fermented before the meat of the bean is passed through rollers to form a "chocolate liquor". Bitter chocolate or baker's chocolate is made from this liquor. Semi-sweet chocolate has added sugar. Milk chocolate has added sugar and milk.

STORAGE

Ground coffee loses flavour and aroma very quickly – in a few weeks – if exposed to the air. Therefore, keep coffee tightly covered at all times. Coffee may be frozen in the sealed package in which it was bought from the store.

Since freshly roasted and ground coffee is necessary for the best possible beverage, purchase only small quantities at a time.

As tea also absorbs moisture it should be stored in an air-tight container in a cool dry place. Purchasing only small quantities at a time is also a good policy for tea. Both cocoa and chocolate lose flavour when exposed to air. As with tea and coffee, chocolate products should be purchased in quantities which can be used within a reasonable period.

FOOD VALUE

Coffee and tea have no appreciable food value except that contained in the cream and sugar that may be added. Persons on a reducing diet need to consider the energy value of cream and/or sugar taken in their beverages when calculating their daily kilojoule count.

Caffein, a mild stimulant found in coffee, affects the heart, kidneys and nervous system and produces sleeplessness in some people. Decaffeinated coffee is available. Theine, the equivalent substance to caffein, is present in tea.

Tannin is the substance which contributes a bitter taste and is present in both beverages. The longer the coffee is infused, or water is left on the tea leaves, the more tannin will be extracted into the solution.

Coffee and tea are not recommended for growing children because:

1. They can grow and develop better without such stimulants.

2. When they drink these beverages it is usually instead of milk, which they need for physical development.

Cocoa and chocolate contain small amounts of protein, starch and minerals but larger amounts of fat. This fat is called cocoa butter. As a result, chocolate is a rich source of energy. Since cocoa has much of the fat removed it is much lower in energy value.

By combining chocolate or cocoa with milk the resultant beverage is a good source of protein and preferable to tea or coffee for young people. Flavoured milk drinks like milk shakes, malted milk and cocoa offer pleasing ways of including milk in the diet. Cocoa and chocolate may also be used in a variety of ways to add flavour to cakes, pastries, puddings, desserts and candies.

PERCOLATED   STEEPED COFFEE   DRIP   VACUUM
COFFEE   METHOD   METHOD

METHODS OF MAKING COFFEE

A. General Directions for Good Coffee

1. Use a spotlessly clean coffee maker as coffee leaves an oil residue.
2. Use fresh ground coffee that has been properly stored.
3. Use fresh cold water, preferably soft water.
4. After you have experimented to decide the proportions of coffee to water that you prefer, measure the same amount accurately each time.

NOTE: *Most coffee recipes suggest 30 ml for each 200 ml of water; unless you like extremely strong coffee, this may be too much coffee. Try 20 ml for each 250 ml cup and adjust to your taste.*

5. Be consistent in your timing after you have reached the desired result once.
6. If possible, use coffee maker at full capacity, never less than $3/4$ full.
7. Never allow coffee to reach boiling temperature.
8. Serve coffee as soon as possible after it is made.

B. Specific Methods of Making Coffee

1. PERCOLATED COFFEE
   - Rinse percolator with boiling water.
   - Put cold water in percolator, place regular grind coffee in basket, cover.
   - Place over heat until percolation begins.
   - Reduce heat to allow gentle percolation for 6-8 minutes.

NOTE: Percolated coffee can be made with freshly boiled water if desired.

2. STEEPED COFFEE
   - Rinse coffee pot with boiling water.
   - Place coarse grind coffee in pot, add boiling water.
   - Place on heat, bring slowly to the boiling point, reduce heat and allow to brew below the boiling point for 4-5 minutes.

NOTE: Clarify, using cold water, egg shell, egg yolk or white, added to the finished pot of coffee.

3. DRIP METHOD
   - Rinse dripolator with boiling water.
   - Measure fine or drip grind coffee into filter section.
   - Measure freshly boiled water into upper container and put in place.
   - When dripping is completed, remove upper section.
   - Stir coffee before serving.

4. VACUUM METHOD
   - Measure fresh cold water into lower bowl of heat resistant glass pot.
   - Place on heat.
   - Place filter in upper bowl and measured amount of fine or drip grind coffee. When water boils, reduce heat and insert upper bowl into lower bowl with a slight twist to insure a tight seal.
   - Let most of water rise into upper bowl, stir water and coffee thoroughly.
   - Remove from heat in 1-3 minutes depending on strength desired.
   - When brew returns to lower bowl remove the upper bowl and serve.

5. INSTANT COFFEE – DRIED OR FREEZE-DRIED
   - Follow manufacturer's directions for these.

C.   Variations

1.   CAFÉ AU LAIT
   - A French specialty. Use a pot of strong, hot coffee and a pot of hot rich milk; pour simultaneously equal amounts of coffee and milk into a cup.

2.   MOCHA JAVA
   - From the Orient. Use a pot of strong, hot coffee and a pot of hot cocoa; pour equal amounts of both into a cup.

3.   DEMITASSE
   - After dinner coffee. Brew coffee by any method but make it nearly double the usual strength. Serve black (without cream) with or without sugar in very small (demitasse) coffee cups.

4.   ICED COFFEE
   - Brew coffee by any method making it double strength. Pour hot coffee over ice in glasses. (A metal spoon in glass prevents breakages.)

GENERAL DIRECTIONS FOR MAKING GOOD TEA

The tea pot may be china, pottery, silver or heat resistant glass. The tea pot should be washed with soap and hot water after each use, and rinsed with boiling water to remove any oils.

First heat the tea pot by rinsing it with boiling water. Then place in the pot 1-1.5 ml loose tea or 1 tea bag for each cup of boiling water. A variety of tea balls are available to use when using loose tea to make removal of the leaves easier.

Pour fresh bubbling boiling water over the tea or tea bags. Cover the pot and infuse (steep) for 3-5 minutes. Strain or remove tea bags and serve immediately. Serve hot with sugar, cream, thin slices of lemon or orange. Tea should have a rich flavour with no bitterness and a tempting aroma. It should not be cloudy and should be served when piping hot.

Introduction to Food Preservation

Food preservation is the procedure by which a food is processed to ensure its keeping quality for a more or less indefinite period of time. Nature has provided conditions to improve the keeping quality of some foods. For example, certain fruits have skins which prevent the penetration of bacteria. Grain seeds are thoroughly dried during ripening and this makes them resistant to spoilage agents. In this way, the next grain crop is assured.

In the early years when every family unit was also a food producing unit, the "root cellar" or "root house" was used for extended storage of root vegetables. Traditionally fish and thin strips of meat have been placed in the sun and air to dry where other preservation methods are not available. This food could be kept for later use. People living in the North may place game meat and fish deep in the snow, a simple method of freezing and refrigeration.

Our modern society employs various techniques to hold food from season to season. These methods allow food to be transported from places of abundant production to places of little or no production. In this way food supplies can be equalized in all parts of the country at all times of the year and can provide a wider variety of foods to be available at moderate cost. It may be noted that this same principle operates in world trade of food items.

Principles of Food Preservation

All methods of food preservation are an effort to stabilize the condition of the food and prevent it from spoiling. Knowledge of why foods spoil, therefore, is essential to an understanding of the principles of food preservation. Deterioration in food is the result of:
1. activity of the *enzymes* within the living cells,
2. destructive action of *micro-organisms* (moulds, yeast, bacteria),
3. oxidation of the food.

1. ENZYMES
It is important to remember that all living cells contain enzymes. *Enzymes* are chemical substances produced within the living tissues of plants and animals. They behave as catalysts in helping along and speeding up the chemical changes which eventually occur within plant and animal tissue cells.

In meat, enzyme activity breaks down the muscle tissues and makes it more tender.

In the case of fruits and vegetables, the enzymes bring about normal ripening or maturation. The starch within the food is converted to a sugar which sweetens fruit and some vegetables. This chemical change is accompanied by such physical changes in the food as softening of the tissues and development of the full characteristic shape and colour. If enzymic action is allowed to continue the tissues can become excessively softened and eventual putrefaction or rotting will result. Enzyme activities continue even after the harvesting of fruits and vegetables — a good reason for reducing as much as possible the time between gathering and preservation.

Enzymes can easily be inactivated by the simple application of heat as in blanching, sterilizing or cooking. During refrigeration or freezing, enzyme activity is inhibited but the enzymes themselves are not destroyed. Enzyme activity continues whenever warmer temperatures are again attained, and the normal ripening process proceeds.

2. MICRO-ORGANISMS

If enzymatic action is not checked in food the softened tissues of the food become an ideal environment for *micro-organisms*. As the name implies, micro-organisms are microscopic in size and they are always present in the soil, in the air, and in water. Therefore, any method of preservation must include a treatment which either completely destroys the micro-organisms present or inhibits their activity to such an extent that they cannot cause spoilage.

Micro-organisms include *mould, yeast* and *bacteria,* of which there are many varieties and strains. Some are perfectly harmless, others very hazardous and yet others extremely useful both in food production and for medicinal purposes.
Examples are:

MOULDS
- used to obtain blue veins in certain cheeses such as Gorgonzola, Roquefort
- making of penicillin

YEAST
- breadmaking
- making of vinegar

BACTERIA
- milk souring to make yogurt, sour cream
- making of vinegar
- making sauerkraut
- making of some ripened cheeses, e.g., Swiss and Gruyère

1. Moulds

Since moulds frequently begin their growth on the surface of food this type of spoilage is familiar to everyone. They are widely distributed in nature and reproduce by means of *spores,* which are easily scattered throughout the air.

Moulds usually require some oxygen (air) and considerable moisture for growth. They feed readily on sugars, starches, and protein foods. Since they grow well in the presence of acid, all fruits and tomatoes are susceptible.

Moulds and their spores can be destroyed by heating food at boiling temperature for a few minutes. When this micro-organism grows freely on canned food it is a good indication the jar is not sealed properly.

2. Yeasts

Yeasts too, are widely distributed in nature but are not difficult to control in canning. They also form spores which have thick, resistant cell walls allowing them to remain dormant until conditions are favourable for them to germinate into actively growing cells.

In order to grow, yeasts require food (in the form of sugar), some warmth (optimum temperature is 25°C) and moisture. Most yeasts break down the sugar to alcohol, producing a gas which bubbles and makes the spoilage easily recognized. Since they obtain their oxygen from this reaction, yeasts can grow in a sealed jar. They can also grow readily in the presence of acids. Therefore, they are active in the spoilage of canned fruits and fruit products.

Yeasts are readily destroyed by heating the food to a boiling temperature for a short time. Fermentation will not occur if the product is sufficiently processed and the containers are air-tight.

3. Bacteria

Of all micro-organisms, bacteria are the most dangerous type because they are the most difficult to destroy. Ideal temperatures for their growth are 20°C to 40°C. Some grow in the refrigerator and certain of them do not even require oxygen. In the actively growing stage, which continues by cell division, bacteria can be destroyed by subjecting them to boiling temperatures for a suitable length of time.

However, whenever the environment becomes unfavourable many bacteria, as do yeasts and mould, produce spores which are so highly resistant to heat they are able to survive until conditions again become favourable. Applied to home canning this means that if the jar of food does not receive enough heat the spores may survive. Later, during storage, they may grow in the sealed jar and cause a most dangerous type of food spoilage. Herein lies the danger – bacteria form *toxins* which are odourless, tasteless and which cause no visible texture changes in the food.

When attempting to destroy bacterial spores which may be present in the food to be canned, time and temperature of processing have a direct relationship. Also, the time needed is in part determined by the acidity of the food being canned. The natural acid in fruits helps in retarding bacterial growth. For these reasons, it is recommended that all non-acid foods such as meat and vegetables should be processed in a pressure canner.

All micro-organisms can be destroyed by heat. Yeasts and moulds are readily killed but bacteria is more difficult to destroy because some spore-forming types are more heat resistant than others. Even after destruction their harmful toxins, which are often unaffected by heat, may remain to infect the food. Proper sealing of canned foods is important to prevent contamination of the canned product by any of these micro-organisms which could re-enter the container.

3.   OXIDATION

When the flesh of light coloured fruits and vegetables is exposed to air, the action of the enzymes, coupled with oxidation, results in brown discolouration on the surface. The enzymes in the presence of oxygen aid in oxidation of the chemical substance, *tannin*, on the fruit to produce a brownish compound. A noticeable change in the texture of the food accompanies this discolouration, for example, the softened texture of apples and pears.

The exposure of food to air will cause dehydration of the food but more important is the destructive effect of oxygen on the texture and flavour of the food and on its vitamin content, particularly that of vitamin C. See page 402 for methods of preventing discolouration of light coloured fruits during canning and freezing.

In summary, then, stabilization or the preservation of food can be achieved by these methods:

1.   by inactivating or destroying food enzymes.

2.   by preventing or delaying decomposition caused by micro-organisms

   • by removing these micro-organisms, e.g. water filtration

   • by excluding air – obtaining a tight seal

   • by hindering their growth – low temperature, drying

   • by destroying them – using heat, applying radiation

   • by using a preservative, e.g. vinegar in pickles.

3. by preventing oxidation
   * by filling containers and allowing only the headspace recommended when freezing or canning
   * by using a vacuum seal as is achieved in canning
   * by minimum cutting to reduce the surface area exposed to air
   * by processing immediately after harvesting fruits or vegetables.

4. by preventing damage or contamination that may be caused by insects, animals or humans.

Food Preservation Methods

The methods which are used to halt or retard the decomposition of food can be grouped into the following categories:
1. Applying a low temperature.
2. Applying a high temperature.
3. Removing moisture.
4. Excluding air.
5. Adding preservatives.

Very often two or more methods are used together to achieve stabilization of the food. For example, canned fruit is subjected to a high temperature and then is stored in an air-tight vacuum sealed container. The addition of sugar may or may not have a preservative effect, depending upon the concentration used. Freeze drying involves subjecting the food to both low temperature and drying conditions. This process results in a product which can be stored at room temperature if the container used protects it from moisture, oxygen and light.

1. Preservation by Low Temperature

Low temperatures inhibit the activities of both enzymes and microorganisms. Examples include household refrigeration, refrigeration during commercial transport or warehouse storage, quick freezing, freeze drying, dehydro-freezing.

It is well to remember that freezing does not destroy all the microorganisms present in the food but it prevents their growth because of the cold temperature and the unavailability of water which is present in the form of ice crystals only. Enzyme activity is also retarded but the maturation process resumes when temperatures are again warm enough to allow it to proceed.

Freeze drying is a process which involves two preservation methods. The food is first frozen and then the water totally extracted by placing the food in a vacuum chamber. Under pressure, the moisture present in the food as ice crystals is able to pass directly from a solid state to a gaseous form. This physical conversion of water from ice to gas is called *sublimation*. The freeze dried food is then vacuum sealed in packages or containers. Foods processed by this method have the advantage of being extremely light, compact and requiring no refrigeration.

Dehydro-freezing is a process of food preservation which first requires partial dehydration of the food, thereby reducing it to about half its original weight, followed by freezing. Because of its reduced weight dehydro-frozen food costs less to package, freeze, store and transport.

2. Preservation by High Temperature

The enzymes present in food are very readily destroyed by heat. Yeasts and moulds are also destroyed by heat. Most bacteria require higher temperatures and those which are able to form spores which resist heat, are very difficult to kill.

Canning is a good example of preserving with heat. The exclusion of air is, however, vital to sucessful canning. Blanching of fruits and vegetables involves a heat treatment with boiling water or steam which inactivates the surface enzymes and other spoilage agents until freezing is complete.

Sterilization is heat treatment which destroys both enzymes and micro-organisms, including spores, which are present in the food or in the utensils and jars which are to be used. This is the principle which is applied in home canning.

Pasteurization refers to application of heat to a degree which stops short of sterilization. Some other means of preservation should be used as well. For example, pasteurized milk is refrigerated to induce a low temperature unfavourable to the growth of undestroyed spoilage agents. Pasteurized fruit juices have such a high acidity as to be unsuitable for the growth of any remaining spoilage agents.

3. Preservation by Removing Moisture

The water content of dried foods is so low that micro-organisms will not grow on them. Vegetable enzymes are usually first inactivated by blanching before the drying process begins. Enzymes in light coloured fruits may instead be inactivated by a sulphite.

Sun drying is one of the oldest methods of food preservation. Foods which have at some time been dried this way are dates, figs, raisins, apricots, apple slices, fish and meat. Light coloured fruits were first protected from browning by being exposed to burning sulphur fumes before they were placed to dry. Sulphites were later found to be an effective substitute for sulphur dioxide to prevent browning.

In many climates and other situations where sun drying is not a reliable method, forced hot air is widely used. A greater variety of fruits and vegetables can be dried this way and the method is much quicker.

Liquid foods such as milk, eggs and coffee are dehydrated by a method called *spray drying*. The liquid is sprayed into a heated cylinder. If the particles are clustered after drying the powdered dry food will disperse in water more readily. This method, sometimes called instantizing, is used to make dried skim milk. The milk powder is moistened enough to agglomerate the particles and then dried again to produce a light dehydrated milk that reconstitutes quickly.

4.   Preservation by Excluding Air

The exclusion of air from a food is important to its stability because it prevents oxidation, (see page 382). Vacuum packaged foods are an application of this principle. Canned foods when properly processed have a vacuum seal. Wax is used in various ways to prevent contact of the food with air. Examples are jellies, jams, some pickles, and the surface of certain cheeses. Water-glass, which is sodium silicate, has been used for many years to close the pores of the egg shell and prevent the exchange of air for water in the egg. More recently, tasteless and odourless mineral oil has been introduced to coat the surface of eggs.

5.   Preservation by Adding Preservatives

The preservatives most commonly used in the home are sugar, salt and vinegar. Some spices help in preserving food. Wood smoke has long been used as a preservative.

The concentration of the preservative determines the chemical reaction which takes place and whether any additional methods of preservation need to be used. For example, when the sugar solution is sufficiently concentrated (as in jam or jelly) the osmotic pressure exerted upon any micro-organisms present will destroy them. Foods preserved in this manner must be sealed from contact with air so that air-borne yeasts and moulds are unable to enter.

Less concentrated sugar solutions such as are used for preserving fruit will improve the flavour, colour and texture but will not have an appreciable effect in preserving the food. Adequate processing to destroy micro-organisms and a vacuum seal is more important in canning than the sugar used.

In the making of sauerkraut from cabbage a small amount of salt is added not for preservation but for initiating a fermentation process.

The osmosis between the cabbage and surrounding salt and solution causes water and some sugar to be removed from the food into the salt solution. When this happens, bacteria feed upon the sugar and acids are made.

Food Additives

Food additives are substances added to foods in an attempt to preserve their flavour, colour, texture and quality. The use of spices to camouflage or improve the flavour of foods has been practised for many years. More recently, monosodium glutamate has become widely used to enhance the natural flavours of commercially prepared foods such as meat pies, soups and sauces. Home cooks make use of both these additives also.

Use of a specific food additive is justified if it satisfies one or more of the following criterion; i.e., if it:

1. maintains the nutritional quality of a food
2. enhances the keeping quality or stability of a food
3. makes the food attractive to the consumer without being deceptive
4. provides an essential aid in food processing.

Without the use of food additives many food products could not be offered for sale in their present form and those that might be available, would be more expensive due to marketing problems. The use of food additives accounts for much of the variety in our food supply.

Consumers are sometimes disturbed to learn that all additives, whether of natural origin or synthetically produced, are chemicals. The fact is that all foods have a chemical composition. Some common kitchen ingredients that are used as chemical additives include: vinegar (acetic acid), baking soda (sodium bicarbonate), meat tenderizer (papain), sugar (sucrose) and salt (sodium chloride). It is possible that much of the controversy over the use of food additives has been exaggerated when consumers read or hear the chemical name of the additive used. Usually these terms are unfamiliar to a person who has not studied chemistry. Any possible danger in the use of food additives lies in the use of untested substances and/or addition of unsafe amounts of a particular additive. Protection against this happening is the role of the Health Protection Branch of Health and Welfare Canada. This Branch also reviews and monitors the latest scientific information on food additives already in use to ensure that potential hazards are eliminated as soon as they become recognized.

The Canadian Food and Drug Regulations define a food additive as "any substance, including any source of radiation, the use of which results or may reasonably be expected to result in it or its byproducts becoming a part of, or affecting the characteristics of a food." Materials such as salt, sugar and starch are not included in this definition since they are recognized under most circumstances to be an ingredient in food. Certain other ingredients which might be added to foods, such as vitamins, minerals, flavourings are also excluded or they are covered separately in the Food and Drug Regulations.

Food additives then, are used for a variety of purposes. The permitted additives are classified by function. Here are some of them:

1. Preservatives are used to maintain the appearance, palatability and wholesomeness of food by retarding or eliminating food spoilage. In this way they play an important role in reducing food waste caused by food spoilage. Foods can be transported over vast distances, stored for extended lengths of time and still be consumed safely.

   There are two important categories. *Antimycotics* prevent the formation of moulds. Sodium diacetate and calcium propionate are two chemicals used to prevent mould in bread. *Antioxidants* are added to fatty foods (cooking oil, potato chips) to prevent rancidity. They are also used to keep fruit from darkening (browning caused by enzymes, pages 379 and 402). Some commonly used antioxidants are butylated hydroxyanisole (BHA), butylated hydroxtoluene (BHT) and ascorbic acid.

2. Texturizing agents impart and maintain the desired consistency in foods. Three categories are recognized.

   Emulsifiers permit the dispersion of tiny globules of one liquid in another (oil and vinegar dressing, mayonnaise) and they also improve the volume, uniformity and fineness of grain in bread and rolls.

   Stabilizers are used to keep particles from separating and settling to the bottom (chocolate in chocolate milk) and to prevent the formation of ice crystals (ice cream).

   Thickeners regulate the consistency of some foods (jams and jellies) and thicken others (ice cream, frozen desserts, confections).

3. pH adjusting agents control the acidity or alkalinity of foods. They are used extensively for technological purposes in the manufacture of many foods (baked goods, soft drinks, chocolate). They may sometimes modify the taste of a food slightly, i.e., citric acid intensifies fruit flavour, sodium carbonate reduces acidity of canned vegetables.

4. Colours, both natural and synthetic, are added to food mainly to give it an appetizing appearance because the way a food looks has a definite effect on its palatability. Colouring agents are permitted in products such as soft drinks, frozen desserts, gelatin desserts, puddings.

5. Bleaching and maturing agents are used by the baking industry. Freshly milled wheat flour is yellowish in colour. If left alone it will gradually whiten. Bleaching agents hasten this process making it possible to have high quality flour quickly and consistently.

6. Leavening agents such as yeast, baking powder, and baking soda are also widely used in baked goods because they react chemically and release carbon dioxide into the product to give a light texture.

7. Anti-caking agents are used in many salts and dried powdered mixes to keep them free-running. For example, calcium aluminum silicate is permitted to be used in salt.

8. Food enzymes act as catalysts to trigger desired chemical reactions in certain foods. Rennet is an enzyme used to curdle milk in the making of cheese.

9. Glazing agents make certain food surfaces shiny and in some cases protect the product from spoiling. An example is candy.

10. Non-nutritive sweeteners are used to sweeten dietetic foods without contributing any food value or calories.

The oldest methods of preserving foods are smoking, pickling, salting and sun drying. These methods are still being used today. As well as these, many other methods have been developed. Chemical preservatives are being used to control the growth of yeast, bacteria and moulds, to retard enzyme action, to prevent rancidity, to increase shelf life and to enable foods to hold their flavour and quality during long periods of transportation and storage. It is the responsibility of the Health Protection Branch of Health and Welfare Canada to control the use of food additives by deciding what additives can be used, in what foods, for what purpose and in what amount.

Home Canning

Canning is a method of processing food using heat to destroy the agents which cause food spoilage. In addition, the container must have an air tight seal so that no micro-organisms can enter it after the food in the container has been sterilized. Before undertaking any canning project the following factors should first be considered:

1. THE FOOD TO BE CANNED

Almost any food can be canned successfully. However, for purposes of discussion it is usual to divide them into two categories: acid foods and low acid foods.

Acid foods are all of the fruits. Pickle mixtures containing vinegar might be included here as well. Tomatoes present a special problem. Many varieties are acid and can be treated as an acid food but strains of low acid tomatoes have been developed and the home canner will not know which are being used. This is the recommended procedure: *Add 5 ml lemon juice to each litre size jar of tomatoes before processing to ensure a correct acid level without affecting the flavour.* (Add 3 ml to each 500 ml size jar.) Acid foods can be safely processed in a boiling water bath canner.

Low acid foods are all the other foods including vegetables, meats, poultry, meat and vegetable mixtures, fish. The only way to obtain a safe product from this group is to process in a pressure canner. See page 403.

2. METHOD OF PROCESSING TO BE USED

Processing is the application of heat to the filled container which sterilizes both food and container.

A. Boiling Water Bath

This method is used for all fruits and acid-treated tomatoes. Filled containers are placed in the canner and water to come 2-3 cm over the top of the containers is added. With the lid on the canner, water is brought to a boil and maintained at a full boil.

B. Pressure Canner

A pressure canner is used to process all non-acid foods. It is especially designed to heat foods to a higher temperature than the boiling water bath will ever reach. This higher temperature is required to destroy the spores of harmful bacteria which may be present in the low acid foods. These foods should not be canned without a pressure canner.

C. Other Methods

The oven method for processing has been used by some people in the past. This method is not recommended for any product. There is a danger of too little processing because of the slow rate of heat transfer from the air and the uneven heat distribution in ovens. Danger of explosions of jars while in the oven or while being removed is always present.

Open kettle method of canning can be used for jams, jellies and pickles. The food is cooked with preservatives in an open saucepan and then packed into sterilized jars and sealed at once. This method is not recommended for any other product as food spoilage agents may enter the jar while the food is being transferred from the kettle to the jar and, also, the heat treatment is not sufficient to prevent spoilage and possible food poisoning, especially in non-acid foods.

3. Utensils Required

The few essential pieces of equipment should be checked in advance. This includes having the correct canner for the job. Jars or cans need to be made ready and lids to fit must be on hand. It is important that needless time not be spent assembling utensils once the food to be canned is obtained.

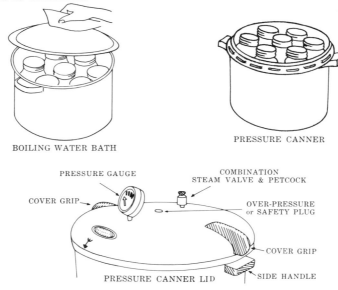

BOILING WATER BATH

PRESSURE CANNER

PRESSURE GAUGE   COMBINATION
                    STEAM VALVE & PETCOCK
COVER GRIP   OVER-PRESSURE
                                       or SAFETY PLUG

                                       COVER GRIP

PRESSURE CANNER LID   SIDE HANDLE

Home Canning Steps

The steps to follow when canning different foods at home are essentially the same. Methods of pack may vary, the liquid added to the container may be juice, water, or syrup, depending upon the product, and one of two main processing methods will be chosen. However, whether the food to be canned is peaches, tomatoes, beans or fish, a logical sequence of assembling, packing, processing, checking and storing is followed. These steps will be described as they relate to canning fruit. Later in the chapter the methods for vegetables and fish are outlined.

1.   ASSEMBLE EQUIPMENT

Essential equipment for successful home canning consists of comparatively few articles. Most of these items are found in the average kitchen. It is important, however, to see that the necessary equipment is on hand and in good working order.

Basic utensils are sharp paring and French knives, colander or steamer, bowls, measuring utensil, towels, wooden spoons, small brush, tongs. Other useful utensils include a wide-mouthed funnel, strawberry huller, cherry pitter, wire basket, jar lifter.

For canning in tin cans, there are several types of sealing machines available. When buying a machine, choose one that is guaranteed to seal satisfactorily. The machine should be well made, durable and easy to operate. Carefully follow specific directions for use supplied by the manufacturer.

One of these types of canners will be needed for processing:

A.   Boiling Water Bath Canner

This is the least expensive type of canner and may be used for all fruits. It is a large, deep kettle fitted with a rack and a lid. One especially made for canning may be bought or any large container deep enough to allow water to cover the containers by at least 3 cm may be used. If the water does not cover the containers the food will not cook evenly and the portion above the water may become discoloured. The canner must be fitted with a rack which will allow the circulation of water under the containers. If the rack has dividers, containers will not touch each other or fall against the sides of the canner during processing. Method for using this canner is described on page 396.

B.   Pressure Canner

This is an expensive piece of equipment which is necessary for canning any low acid foods. At 105 kilopascals temperatures inside the canner reach 120°C because the steam is under pressure as compared to boiling temperature of 100°C in the boiling water bath. The pressure canner is equipped with a gauge which indicates the amount of steam pressure reached and a safety valve or petcock which can be opened or closed to permit exhausting the air. The lid will lock tightly into place so that no steam can escape. Method for using a pressure canner is outlined on page 403.

C.   Pressure Cooker

Pressure cookers or pressure saucepans are sometimes suitable for processing small amounts of canned food. They are intended primarily for cooking but are normally deep enough for small (500 ml) jars to be placed in them. If the pressure saucepan has a rack to hold the jar off the bottom of the pan and allow steam to circulate and if it has an accurate pressure gauge which will indicate clearly the pressure inside, it can be used. However, additional processing times will be required to compensate for the short time needed to heat up and cool down the smaller sized cooker. Increase times allowed for small (500 ml) jars by 20 minutes.

2.   PREPARE CONTAINERS AND LIDS

Choose containers to suit your needs. Use of tin cans eliminates any possibility of breakage but the metal is expensive and special equipment for making a seal is required. Cans can be re-used for 2-3 times with new covers each time. Glass jars are more commonly used in the home.

A.   Glass Canning Jars

Use standard glass sealers that are manufactured for home preservation, and lids designed to fit them. They are tempered to withstand heat and pressure and below zero cold. (Many of the glass jars in which commercial products are packed will not withstand high temperatures, especially the temperatures reached in a pressure canner.) The jar has a threaded mouth top so that either a zinc cap and rubber ring or a flat metal lid with a screw band will make an air-tight closure.

Check to be sure there are no cracks and that the rim of the sealer is not chipped. Even a very small nick will prevent the seal from forming. Check the metal screw bands and discard any that have become bent, stretched or corroded. Metal lids having the edges lined with sealing compound cannot be used a second time. Check to be sure you have an adequate supply of new lids to fit the jars being used.

Wash jars thoroughly in hot, soapy water and rinse well with clear hot water. To prevent cracking, jars should be heated before hot food is placed in them. To heat, half fill the jars with water and stand in a pan of water. Bring water to the boiling point and leave the jars in the water until ready to fill them.

B. Cans

There are three types of tin cans sold for home canning. Be sure to use the correct kind.

1. PLAIN CAN:

    This is a general purpose can which may be used for all foods except red-coloured fruits and beets. If plain cans are used by mistake, the red fruit or beets will fade in colour and lose much of their flavour. However, use only plain cans for tomatoes and tomato juice.

2. R OR STANDARD ENAMEL CAN:

    This can has a bright reddish gold lining and should be used for reddish fruits, such as red berries, red and purple plums, red and black cherries, rhubarb and for beets. The special enamel lining prevents the fading of the colour. DO NOT use "R" or "Standard" enamel cans for tomatoes, tomato juice, light coloured fruits or for any vegetable except beets. If this type of can is used for any of these foods, they will turn dark and lose flavour.

3. C-ENAMEL CAN:

    This can has a dull gold lining. Although this special lining helps to prevent discolouration in corn, a "Plain" can may also be used for corn. DO NOT use "C-Enamel" cans for fruit, tomatoes or vegetables other than corn since they will turn dark, and lose flavour. Use C-Enamel cans for fish.

    Both Plain and R or Standard Enamel cans are sold in two sizes: medium (about 550 ml) and large (about 800 ml). The C-Enamel cans are sold in medium (550 ml) size only.

    Choose can covers – Plain, R or Standard Enamel and C-Enamel – to correspond with the three types of tin cans. The inside edge of the cover is lined with a rubber compound.

    Check to see that the rim of each can to be used is in good condition. Do not use any cans that are badly dented. Wash cans thoroughly in hot soapy water, rinse with boiling water and invert to drain.

3. PREPARE THE SYRUP

If the food being canned is fruit, a syrup of water and sugar is normally used either to pour over the fruit, if Cool Pack method is being used, or to pre-cook the fruit in, if Hot Pack method is used. This syrup must be ready before the fruit is prepared. See "Syrups for Canning and Freezing", page 401 and "Special Methods of Canning Fruit", page 402.

4. PREPARE THE FRUIT

When equipment, containers and syrup are ready the fruit can be prepared. No matter what food is being canned a minimum time lapse from this stage to processing is essential.

(1) Sorting

Sort fruit or vegetables for size and maturity. Immature or over-mature fruits and vegetables should not be canned. Unripe fruits and tomatoes should be allowed to ripen before canning. Bruised or spotted fruit should not be canned. If bruises are cut out, the good portion of the fruit may be used for jam or fruit juices.

(2) Washing

Fruits and vegetables must be thoroughly washed. Wash only a small quantity at a time. To remove all sand, lift fruits or vege-tables from the water instead of draining the water off. A wire basket is excellent for this purpose. Greens should be washed in several waters. Strawberries should be washed before hulling.

(3) Blanching

Blanching consists of placing peaches or tomatoes in boiling water for 15 to 60 seconds, depending on maturity or variety, and then dipping immediately in cold water. The peaches or tomatoes should be removed from the water as soon as cool enough to handle. Blanching loosens the skins so that they slip off easily. Only sufficient fruit for two or three containers should be blanched at one time. A wire basket, large strainer or a square of cheesecloth can be used for blanching.

(4) Peeling

Some fruits and vegetables need peeling or scraping with a knife, in which case the thinnest possible portion should be removed.

5. PACK THE CONTAINERS

Work quickly when packing food into containers. To prevent sealers cracking, place the hot empty sealers on a dry cloth or folded paper. If necessary, reheat jars by immersing in kettle of hot water. Fill containers, one at a time, with raw or partly cooked food to within 3 cm of the top. Then add liquid, leaving headspace.

Headspace is the space between the surface of the liquid and the rim of the container. When proper headspace is not left, liquid will be lost from sealers and cans may burst.

For glass sealers, allow 1.5-2 cm headspace except for corn and peas. For these allow 2.5-3 cm headspace.

For cans, allow 1 cm headspace except for corn and peas. For these allow 1.5-2 cm headspace.

For meat, fish, shellfish, allow 2.5-3 cm headspace.

After filling, work out air bubbles by running the blade of a knife down the sides of the container. With large fruits, tilt the container to allow any trapped air to escape. Do not fill more containers than your boiling water bath or pressure canner will hold at one time.

A.   Cold Pack Method

The food is packed raw into the containers, then hot liquid, syrup, water or fruit juice is added. Processing follows. This method is commonly used for fruits and sometimes for meat and fish but not for vegetables.

B.   Hot Pack Method

The prepared food is pre-cooked first for a short time. Then the product with some of the juice or syrup is packed into containers and processed immediately.

This method is used for all vegetables, fruit, meat and fish. This method of packing helps to prevent discolouration and allows a more solid pack.

FRUITS – Prepare the desired type and necessary amount of syrup. Simmer the fruit for the required time in a small amount of the syrup in a large kettle. Pack into containers, add syrup, allowing headspace. Pre-cook at one time only sufficient fruit to fill 3 or 4 containers, otherwise it may be unevenly cooked.

VEGETABLES – Partially cook prepared raw vegetables with water in a covered kettle for time indicated on chart. Place in containers while hot and cover with cooking water allowing headspace. Add salt allowing:

5 ml salt for each medium (litre) sealer or can.

2 ml salt for each small (500 ml) sealer or can.

6.   CLOSE THE CONTAINERS

To soften sealing compound and ensure a good seal, metal lids should be placed in a saucepan with water to cover and brought to the boil. They should be kept in the hot water until used. Check the instructions on the lid package as recommended times will vary.

After filling each container, carefully wipe the jar rim with a clean, damp cloth. Seeds, food particles or syrup on the rim may prevent sealing. As each rim is wiped, put a hot lid in place and screw the metal band on by hand as tightly as possible without using force. For tin cans, place lid on top of can and close with sealing machine according to manufacturer's instructions.

7.   PROCESS THE FILLED CONTAINERS

Processing is the heating of filled containers to a sufficiently high temperature for a sufficient length of time to destroy any bacteria, yeasts or moulds that might cause the foods to spoil.

Never allow filled containers to stand and cool before processing. The processing container should be ready with hot (not boiling) water in it so that the sealers or cans may be placed in it immediately they are closed.

Steps for Processing with a Boiling Water Bath

(1)   Place filled sealers on a rack in the canning kettle so they are not touching (2 cm apart). Cans may be stacked, but they must be arranged so that there is sufficient space for circulation of the water around, over and under them.

(2)   Add boiling water to cover tops of sealers or cans by at least 3 cm.

(3)   Cover boiling water bath. Bring water to the boiling point.

(4)   Start to count processing time from the moment water is actually boiling vigourously, not just beginning to show bubbles. Keep water boiling until the end of processing time. If necessary, add boiling water to keep at least 3 cm of water over containers.

8.   COOL THE CONTAINERS

To prevent breakage of sealers, avoid sudden changes of temperature. Never put hot sealers down on a porcelain or cold surface or let them stand in a draught. Remove the lid of a canner or pressure cooker by tilting it away from you to prevent a steam burn.

A.   Glass Jars

1.   Cool sealers in an upright position. Turning sealers upside down may break the seal that has already formed.

2.   Cool sealers away from draughts which may cause cracking. Place them on a towel or newspaper but do not cover with a cloth as this will retard cooling.

3.   Older style sealers required additional attention to complete the seal. Vacuum type sealers require no further tightening

since the seal is formed as the jars cool. Any further tightening may break the seal.

B. Cans

1. Cool tin cans by plunging them immediately into cold water after removing them from the processer.
2. To cool cans rapidly, keep water cold by changing it or by leaving the tap running slowly. Gently turn cans over in the water allowing the food at the centre of the can to cool.
3. Leave the cans in the water until cold.

9. CHECK THE SEAL

The metal lids of vacuum type sealers snap down while the jars are cooling. You can count the number of "ping" sounds as each lid snaps into place and then check to be sure that all of the lids are curved slightly inward. When the jars are cooled and the screw band is removed it should not be possible to lift the metal lid off because the sealing compound holds it tight. After the jars are completely cold, the lid should give a clear ringing sound when tapped lightly with a spoon.

If the seal is not air-tight the food can be eaten but it must be refrigerated immediately and used before it spoils. Reprocessing is not recommended since the food would be badly overcooked.

10. STORING HOME CANNED FOODS

Before storing home canned foods, wipe the containers or wash and rinse if necessary, and dry them thoroughly. Glass sealers can then be labelled on the lid with a wax marking pencil or a gummed label. Include the name of the produce and the date so that preserved supplies can be used in the correct order. Always label tin cans to avoid confusion. A wax marking pencil may be used or a narrow strip of paper long enough to circle the can and fastened at the ends with gummed tape. After one week, each container should be examined. Any sign of leakage from glass sealers or bulging of tin cans indicates spoilage.

IMPORTANT

To avoid the possibility of food poisoning, all home canned vegetables must be boiled in an open saucepan for 15 minutes before they are used. Firmly-packed vegetables such as creamed corn and spinach require 20 minutes. Do not taste before boiling time is completed and carefully dispose of, without tasting, any food which has a bad odour.

BOILING WATER BATH FOR PROCESSING FRUIT

PRODUCT	PREPARATION AND PACKING	PROCESSING TIME	
		Small 500 ml	Medium litre
APPLES	Wash, peel, core and slice or quarter. Drop in brine bath. HOT PACK: Drain off brine. Bring to boil in syrup and simmer 3 minutes. Pack hot with some syrup, leaving headspace.	15 min	15 min
APPLESAUCE	Wash, peel, core and slice apples. Cook until tender with water, if needed. Add sugar to taste. OR Wash, remove stems and blossom ends. Slice. Cook until tender with water, if needed. Press through sieve. Add sugar to taste. Bring to boil after either preparation method. HOT PACK: Pack hot sauce into jars, leaving headspace.	15 min	15 min
APRICOTS	Wash, halve and pit or leave whole. COLD PACK: Pack. If halved, put cut side down. Cover with boiling syrup, leaving headspace.	20 min	25 min
	HOT PACK: Bring to boil in syrup and simmer 2-3 minutes. Pack hot with some syrup, leaving headspace.	15 min	15 min
BERRIES (except Strawberries)	Wash, remove stems. COLD PACK: Pack. Cover with boiling syrup, leaving headspace.	15 min	20 min
CHERRIES	Wash, stem, pit if desired. COLD PACK: Pack. Cover with boiling syrup, leaving headspace.	20 min	25 min
	HOT PACK: Bring to boil in syrup; simmer 3 minutes. Pack hot leaving headspace.	15 min	15 min
FRUIT JUICES	Wash, pick over, cut if necessary. Add water in approximately equal amounts to the fruit used. Bring to boil and simmer covered until softened and crushed (5-15 minutes.) Strain through moistened jelly bag. Add sugar if desired. Reheat to boiling point. Pour into hot containers, leaving headspace.	10 min	10 min

BOILING WATER BATH FOR PROCESSING FRUIT *(continued)*

| PRODUCT | PREPARATION AND PACKING | PROCESSING TIME | |
		Small 500 ml	Medium litre
PEACHES	Blanch 15-60 seconds, cold dip, peel and pit. Drop in brine bath.		
	COLD PACK: Pack in halves, cut side down or slice into jars. Cover with boiling syrup, leaving headspace.	20 min	25 min
	HOT PACK: Leave in halves or slice. Bring to boil in syrup, simmer 3 minutes. Pack hot with syrup, leaving headspace.	15 min	15 min
PEARS	Wash, peel, halve or quarter, core. Drop in brine bath.		
	COLD PACK: Pack, cut side down. Cover with boiling syrup, leaving headspace.	20 min	25 min
	HOT PACK: Bring to boil in syrup and simmer 3-5 minutes, depending on firmness. Pack hot, leaving headspace.	15 min	15 min
PLUMS	Wash, halve and pit, or leave whole and prick skins.		
	COLD PACK: Pack, cover with boiling syrup, leaving headspace.	20 min	25 min
	HOT PACK: Bring to boil in syrup and simmer 2 minutes. Pack hot, leaving headspace.	15 min	15 min
RHUBARB	Wash, cut in 1-2 cm pieces. COLD PACK: Pack, cover with boiling syrup, leaving headspace.	10 min	15 min
	HOT PACK: Oven bake in covered casserole with 250 ml sugar for each 1 500 ml fruit. When tender, pack hot, leaving headspace.	10 min	10 min
STRAWBERRIES	Wash and hull berries; prepare medium or heavy syrup.		
	COLD PACK: Place berries in syrup, bring slowly to boil. Cover, remove from heat, let stand 1 hour. Pack leaving headspace.	15 min	20 min
	HOT PACK: Bring syrup to boil in kettle; add berries. Cover, remove from heat and let stand 1 hour. Bring to boil. Pack hot, leaving headspace.	10 min	10 min

BOILING WATER BATH FOR PROCESSING FRUIT *(continued)*

PRODUCT	PREPARATION AND PACKING	PROCESSING TIME	
		Small 500 ml	Medium litre
TOMATOES	Blanch 15-60 seconds, cold dip, remove stem end, peel.		
	COLD PACK: Pack whole, adding 5 ml salt per medium (litre) sealer. Cover with hot tomato juice leaving headspace.	25 min	30 min
	OR:		
	Pack whole or quartered, pressing down until tomatoes are covered in their own juice. Leave headspace and add 5 ml salt per medium (litre) sealer.	30 min	35 min
	HOT PACK: Quarter or leave whole. Heat to boiling point. Pack hot leaving headspace. Add 5 ml salt per medium (litre) sealer.	15 min	15 min
TOMATO JUICE	Wash tomatoes, remove core and any damaged areas.		
	HOT PACK: (1) Cut into pieces. Bring to boil and simmer, covered, 5 minutes. Press through sieve or food mill. Bring juice to boil. Pour into containers, leaving headspace. Add 2 ml salt per small sealer.	15 min	15 min
	(2) Extract juice using juice extractor. Heat juice to boiling. Pour into containers, leaving headspace. Add 2 ml salt per small sealer.	15 min	15 min

CHART VARIATIONS:

1. Headspace: When using glass sealers allow 1.5-2 cm headspace. When using cans allow 1 cm headspace.

2. Pressure Canner: Boiling Water Bath is recommended for processing all acid foods. If a pressure canner is used for these foods, pack by the Cold Pack Method and allow: 5 minutes at 35 kilopascals (kPa) pressure for fruits; 8 minutes at 35 kPa pressure for tomatoes.

3. Altitude: The processing times given here for Boiling Water Bath are for altitudes under 600 metres. At 600 metres, increase the processing time by 1/5 for every additional 300 metres. For example, if processing time stated is 20 minutes then:
   - at 600 metres add 1/5 more processing time or 1/5 of 20 minutes=4 minutes.
   - at 900 metres add 2/5 more processing time or 2/5 of 20 minutes=8 minutes. Therefore, total processing time at 900 metres is 28 minutes.

SYRUPS FOR CANNING AND FREEZING

PERCENT-AGE SUGAR	SUGAR*	WATER	APPROX. YIELD	TYPE OF SYRUP	SUGGESTED FRUITS
20%	250 ml	1 000 ml	1 125 ml	very light	pears, blueberries
30%	500 ml	1 000 ml	1 250 ml	light	apples, sweet cherries, prune plums, black-berries, saskatoons
40%	750 ml	1 000 ml	1 375 ml	medium	apricots, peaches, plums, raspberries
50%	1 000 ml	1 000 ml	1 500 ml	heavy	sour cherries, goose-berries, loganberries, rhubarb
60%	1 500 ml	1 000 ml	1 750 ml	very heavy	strawberries

* When any of these syrups are made, up to ¼ of the sugar may be replaced with an equal volume of honey or corn syrup. So that the fruit flavour is not masked, a mild-flavoured honey or white corn syrup is suggested, especially for bland-flavoured or light-coloured fruits. There is a definite flavour change when this substitute is used.

PREPARING SYRUP:

1. First estimate the amount of syrup required for the fruit to be canned. For each medium (litre) sealer allow approximately these amounts depending upon the density of the pack.
   350 ml - 450 ml for large fruits such as peaches, pears, apricots, plums.
   250 ml - 350 ml for medium fruits such as cherries, rhubarb, raspberries, strawberries, gooseberries, loganberries.
   150 ml - 250 ml for small berries such as blackberries, blueberries, saskatoons.
   When Cold Pack Method is used, the amount of syrup needed will depend upon the size of the fruit and the care taken when packing it.
   When Hot Pack Method is used, allow the minimum amounts of syrups suggested above.

2. Choose the type of syrup according to how sweet you want the fruit and, to some extent, upon how you plan to use the fruit. Those with the highest proportions of sugar will usually make the most attractive product but the lighter syrups give a truer fruit flavour and do not contain as many kilojoules. Fruits listed for the types of syrups in the chart are suggestions only.

3. Place measured sugar and water in kettle or large saucepan. Stir, bring to boil and boil until all the sugar is dissolved.

4. To use for canning, keep syrup hot but do not boil, as some of the water will evaporate and change the proportions. To use for freezing fruit, cool syrup thoroughly and store in refrigerator until needed.

Special Methods of Canning Fruits

DRY SUGAR METHOD

Half fill sealer or can with fruit then add sugar and fruit in alternate layers. Cover with boiling water leaving headspace. Process as for Cold Pack (see Table pages 398-400).

QUANTITIES OF SUGAR TO USE FOR DRY SUGAR METHOD:

Percentage Sugar	Equivalent Type of Syrup	Sugar for one Medium (Litre) Sealer	
		Large Fruit	Small Fruit
20%	very light	125 ml	80 ml
30%	light	165 ml	125 ml
40%	medium	185 ml	165 ml
50%	heavy	250 ml	185 ml
60%	very heavy	310 ml	250 ml

SOLID PACK METHOD

This method is especially recommended for rhubarb, blueberries and cherries to be used in making pies or puddings. It may also be used for other fruits.

Wash, prepare fruit and crush part of it in the bottom of a preserving kettle. Add remaining fruit and heat for a few minutes. Stir occasionally and, if necessary, add a little water to prevent scorching. Pack in sealers or cans, crushing fruit down slightly so that it is covered with its own juice. Sprinkle between layers of fruit the amount of sugar recommended for dry sugar canning. Leave headspace and process as for Cold Pack (see Tables, Pages 398-400).

SUGARLESS METHOD

Follow Solid Pack method but omit sugar. The keeping quality of canned fruit does not depend on the addition of sugar but rather on sufficient processing and the use of air-tight containers. However, the colour of most fruits is retained better when some sugar is added.

PREVENTING DISCOLOURATION OF LIGHT COLOURED FRUITS

The brown discolouration on the peeled and cut surface of light coloured fruits such as apples, pears, bananas, peaches, apricots is caused by the action of enzymes in the presence of oxygen (see page 382). A number of methods can be used to prevent or reduce this discolouration. Citrus juices or ascorbic acid solutions inhibit enzyme activity by lowering the pH of the fruit. Salt and sugar solutions also have a retarding effect on these enzymes. By immersing larger quantities of prepared fruit for canning or freezing into salt solutions this discolouration can be prevented. The fruit should be drained thoroughly before packaging or pre-cooking. This brine should be changed as it becomes discoloured. Long standing in brine gives a definite salty taste.

Suggested amounts for enzyme inhibitive solutions for 1 litre of cold water are:

    5 ml salt

  15 ml vinegar or lemon juice

    5 ml ascorbic acid

500 ml sugar will give a light 30% sugar solution.

Heating the fruit will prevent discolouration by destroying the enzymes. This may be undesirable for some purposes; for example, frozen apple slices, because it softens and partially cooks the fruit. This could, however, be done with fruit to be canned by the hot pack method. It would only require simmering for 2-3 minutes in the hot syrup before packing.

There are commercial anti-oxidants also available that are especially suitable when the prepared food is to be frozen.

Other suggestions which will help to prevent discolouration of light coloured fruits are:

1. Do not use underripe or overripe fruit.
2. Work quickly with small amounts of fruit.
3. Simmer fruit for 2-3 minutes in hot syrup before packing in jars.
4. Entirely cover fruit in containers.

Processing Using a Pressure Canner

A pressure canner is absolutely necessary for processing foods that are naturally low in acid. These foods include corn, beans of all kinds, carrots, beets, greens and almost all other garden vegetables, and all meats, poultry and fish. It takes more than boiling water temperature to destroy spore forming organisms when they are present in low acid foods. Follow the exact processing time specified for each food to ensure adequate heat penetration.

Proper care of the pressure canner is important for its effective use. Keep the pressure canner clean, particularly the openings to the petcock, safety valve and pressure gauge. A metal wire may be used to remove any particles from these openings. Make sure the gasket is clean and fits perfectly. Replace when necessary. Never immerse the pressure gauge in water. Be sure that your canner is in perfect order and that each step of the canning process, including time and temperature directions, is followed exactly. As a supplement to manufacturer's directions provided with the canner here are general directions:

1. Pour hot water into canner to a depth of 5 cm. This is sufficient water for processing any number of tin cans or for a capacity load of jars. If, however, the canner is not filled to capacity with jars, add 500 ml extra water for each one missing. This helps to prevent liquid being drawn from the jars.

2. Place filled jars or cans on rack in canner with space between so the jars do not touch. Tin cans may be stacked if they are arranged so that there is good circulation of steam around, over and under them. Use a rack between layers of glass jars.

3. Adjust lid of canner and fasten securely. Leave petcock open to allow steam to escape through the vent. Heat cooker. When steam pours steadily from the vent with a hissing sound, begin counting the time needed to exhaust cooker, i.e. remove all the air. This takes 5-10 minutes depending upon the size of the canner.

4. Close petcock and allow pressure to rise slowly until the gauge indicates the required pressure.

5. Start to count processing time when correct pressure has been reached. Regulate heat under canner to keep pressure constant. Do not lower pressure by opening petcock. If pressure fluctuates, liquid will be drawn out of the jars. Process for the required time. See Table, page 405.

6. At the end of the processing time, remove canner from the heat and place on heat proof surface. Make no attempt to lower pressure but allow pressure to drop gradually to zero of its own accord. Sudden cooling will cause loss of liquid from jars.

7. When gauge reaches zero, let canner stand 1-2 minutes, then slowly open petcock. With tin cans, the petcock may be opened as soon as the gauge registers zero. Let canner cool 2-3 minutes before removing lid.

8. Unfasten lid and tilt the far side up so that steam escapes away from you. Remove containers using tongs or thick potholders.

Serving Precautions

Unless you are absolutely sure of the accuracy of the pressure canner gauge being used and canning methods, all home canned vegetables and meat should be boiled after opening and *before* tasting. Heating usually makes any odour of spoilage more noticeable.

Bring home-canned vegetables to a rolling boil and boil uncovered for at least 10 minutes. Boil leafy vegetables and corn 20 minutes. If the food looks spoiled, foams, or has an off-odour, destroy it.

Boil home-canned meat or poultry 20 minutes in an open pan before tasting. If there is any indication of spoilage, destroy without tasting.

Canning Vegetables

The procedure for canning vegetables is essentially the same as that for canning fruit which has been described on pages 391 to 397. Hot Pack is used for all vegetables and a pressure canner is required for processing. Here are the steps with variations from the procedure for fruit noted:

1. Assemble equipment as outlined on page 391.
2. Prepare container and lids as outlined on page 392.
3. Prepare the vegetable as outlined on page 394.
4. Precook the vegetable.
   Precooking the vegetable before packing it into containers softens the tissues so that a more compact product results. It also halts enzyme action. Add the amount of water recommended in the chart below, cover and boil for the stated time.
5. Fill the containers as outlined on page 394.
6. Close the containers as outlined on page 395.
7. Process in a pressure canner.
   The chart "Pressure Canner for Processing Vegetables", below, gives details of time and pressure. General dirctions for use of the pressure canner are found on page 403.
8. Cool the containers.
9. Check the seal.
10. Label and store.

PRESSURE CANNER FOR PROCESSING VEGETABLES

VEGETABLE	PREPARATION AND PACKING	PROCESSING TIME Small 500 ml	Medium litre
Asparagus	Wash well. Cut into lengths to fit containers. Tie in uniform bundles. Stand upright in sufficient boiling water to come halfway up stalks. Cover; bring to boil and cook 3 minutes. Pack hot, tips up, except for a few in centre to keep stalks upright. Add boiling water or cooking water allowing 1.5 cm headspace.	30 min	35 min
Beans, Green or Yellow Wax	Wash, trim ends, and string if necessary. Leave whole or cut in pieces. Pre-cook covered for 3 minutes in enough boiling salted water to cover the vegetables. Pack hot. Add salt. Cover with hot cooking liquid leaving 1.5 cm headspace.	30 min	35 min

VEGETABLE	PREPARATION AND PACKING	PROCESSING TIME	
		Small 500 ml	Medium litre
Beans, Broad or Lima	Pre-cook in boiling water for 3 minutes. Pack hot. Cover with boiling water or cooking water to within 2.5 cm of top.	50 min	60 min
Beets	Wash small young beets. Trim tops leaving 5 cm stem. Boil, covered, until skins slip off easily, about 20 minutes. Remove skins and roots. Pack hot. Add salt. Cover with boiling water leaving 1.5 cm headspace.	30 min	35 min
Carrots	Wash and scrape young, tender carrots. Pre-cook, covered in boiling water for 5 minutes. Pack hot in upright position, alternating stem and root ends. Add salt. Add boiling water leaving 1.5 cm headspace.	30 min	35 min
Corn, kernel	Remove husk from fresh corn. Cut kernels from cob. Add boiling water using half as much water as corn. Bring to boil and boil 5 minutes. Pack loosely. Add salt. Add juice and boiling water allowing 2.5 cm headspace.	60 min	70 min
Corn, cream style	Remove husk and silk from corn. Wash cobs. Slice a thin layer from kernels of cob. Next, slice remainder of the kernels from the cob to remove any cream or juice. Add boiling water, using half as much water as corn. Bring to boil, stirring to prevent scorching. Pack hot, very loosely, leaving 2.5 cm headspace. Add salt.	75 min	not advisable
Greens, Beet Tops, Chard, Kale, Spinach	Wash thoroughly. Cook, covered, in very little water until completely wilted, about 5-8 minutes, turning several times during cooking. Pack loosely while hot. Cut greens crosswise with a sharp knife to bottom of container. Add salt. Cover with boiling water, leaving 1.5 cm headspace.	50 min	60 min

PRESSURE CANNER FOR PROCESSING VEGETABLES

VEGETABLE	PREPARATION AND PACKING	PROCESSING TIME	
		Small 500 ml	Medium litre
Peas	Shell and wash young, tender peas. Cover with boiling water. Bring to boil and boil, covered for 1 minute. Pack loosely, while hot. Add salt. Cover with hot cooking liquid from peas, leaving 2.5 cm headspace.	40 min	45 min
Mushrooms	Wash and peel. Drop into water containing 15 ml vinegar per litre water. Drain. Boil 3 minutes in fresh water to which salt and vinegar have been added in the proportion of 5 ml salt and 15 ml vinegar for litre of water. Pack hot. Add boiling water leaving 1.5 cm headspace.	30 min	35 min
Pumpkin and Squash	Cut into pieces. Remove seeds and stringy fibres. Steam, bake or boil in a small amount of water until tender. Scrape vegetables from skins and mash or sieve. Bring to boiling point, adding a little water if necessary, to prevent scorching. Pack hot, leaving 1.5 cm headspace.	70 min	80 min

CHART VARIATIONS:

1. HEADSPACE: For glass sealers allow 1.5-2 cm headspace for all vegetables except corn and peas.
   For corn and peas allow 2.5-3 cm headspace. For cans allow 1 cm headspace for all vegetables except corn and peas. For corn and peas in cans allow 1.5-2 cm headspace.

2. SALT: Add 2-3 ml salt to each small (500 ml) sealer or 640 ml can.
   Add 5 ml salt to each medium (litre) sealer or 800 ml can.

3. CANNING PRESSURE: All vegetables listed are processed at 70 kilopascals (kPa) pressure with these exceptions:
   At sea level and up to 600 metres use 70 kPa pressure.
   At 600 metres altitude add 7 kPa pressure. For each 600 metres altitude more add a further 7 kPa pressure.

4. USING HOME CANNED VEGETABLES: Home canned vegetables should be heated to the boiling point in an uncovered saucepan and boiled for 10-15 minutes before serving. *Discard, without tasting, any vegetable that has a bad odour or looks spoiled.*
   PROCESSING IN A BOILING WATER BATH IS NOT RECOMMENDED FOR VEGETABLES OR ANY OTHER LOW ACID FOOD.

Home Canning of Fish

IMPORTANT

Since we have no control over the various factors affecting the canning process, we cannot guarantee the adequacy of the processing information given herein and we will not be responsible for any damage resulting from its use.

Use Correct Procedures

The reason for concern is that several deaths occur each year from botulism, contracted through consumption of improperly home canned fish and other food. Because botulism spores are killed by heat, the culprit in home canning is under-cooking either by not using a high enough temperature, or by cooking for too short a time, or a combination of these conditions.

It is important to note that the WATER BATH method is definitely unsafe, because a high enough internal temperature cannot be reached to kill botulism spores, should they be present. By increasing the pressure, higher temperatures can be reached and so it is essential that a pressure canner be used. General guidelines for canning are given here and on page 403. It is, however, imperative to follow accurately the manufacturer's instructions for using a pressure canner and also for the particular jars or cans used and for the can sealer as well.

Use Good Equipment

1. THE CANNER: You must have proper canning equipment. A pressure canner should be used but an ordinary pressure cooker, in good working condition, that is fitted with a canning (non-automatic) gauge measuring up to 70 kilopascals pressure may be substituted. If a regular pressure cooker is used, always add 20 minutes to the processing time prescribed for use with a pressure canner.

2. THE CONTAINERS: Either cans or glass sealers may be used. Cans should be of the C-enamel type. They are available in several shapes and sizes. Sealers having a capacity of 250 ml or 500 ml are suitable. Wide-mouthed jars are better than those with narrow tops as the tender cooked fish is less likely to break when being removed for serving. They may have glass or metal lids.

    Always wash glass jars or cans in hot soapy water and rinse them in boiling water just before using them. Pour boiling water over the can lids and leave them in the water until ready to slip them on the cans. Gloves will be needed to handle the hot cans or jars.

STEPS FOR CANNING FISH

1. Preparing the Fish

Only fish that is of good quality, and absolutely fresh, should be canned. If the fish must be kept for canning for more than 3 hours after it is caught, it should be cleaned and packed in ice, or stored in a refrigerator. Smoked fish must be canned as soon as it has been cooled after the smoking process, following the same procedure as for fresh fish as far as processing time is concerned.

Clean the fish thoroughly by removing viscera, head, tail, and fins. See section on Fish, for how to clean a fish. Then either remove the scales from the fish, or fillet it completely. Filleting results in a more attractive product, especially if served in a salad. The bones need not be removed as they will soften during processing and become thoroughly edible. They contain valuable calcium and other nutrients that would otherwise be lost. The backbone, however, is sometimes best removed if a fancy pack is desired or if small containers are being used which would have too high a proportion of bone to fish.

2. Packing

IN SEALERS: Cut the cleaned fish into lengths suitable for the size of jars you are using. Pack the fish firmly as you cut, being careful not to break or crush the flesh. A good procedure is to lay the length of the strip of fish along the side of the jar in an upright position so that the last space to be filled is the centre. Allow 2 cm headspace as overfilling will result in leakage from the sealers during processing.

IN CANS: Pack the fish firmly, filling the cans only to a level slightly below the flare used in sealing. Overfilling can result in a poor vacuum and possibly bulged cans which would be dangerous to use.

To each sealer or can add salt in the following proportions:

250 ml container – add 2 ml salt
500 ml container – add 5 ml salt

Carefully wipe the edges of the jars or lips of the cans to remove any remaining fish or salt.

3. Processing

Before beginning this step read general directions for processing with a pressure canner, page 405. Refer also to manufacturer's instructions for the canner being used.

IN SEALERS:
    a.   Heat the fish in jars set in boiling water until the fish in the centre of each jar reaches a temperature of 77°C. Use a meat thermometer to test.

    b.   Prepare the lids. To soften the sealing compound, boiling of metal lids for 5 minutes is recommended.

    c.   Seal jars. Metal-lidded jars are screwed down tightly, glass-lidded jars are sealed loosely.

    d.   Pack jars into canner and follow general instructions for canner use. Process at correct pressure for required time. See chart which follows.

    e.   Remove jars and cool upright, well separated from each other and out of drafts. Label, date and store.

IN CANS:
    a.   Heat the fish in cans set in boiling water, until the fish in the centre of each can reaches a temperature of 77°C. Use a meat thermometer to test.

    b.   Slip the heated lids on the cans and seat the cans.

    c.   Pack cans into canner and follow general instructions for canner use. Process at correct pressure for required time. See chart which follows.

    d.   Cool the cans in the open pressure canner under cold running water or remove the cans and lower them gently into cold water, changing the water frequently. The ends of the cans should bulge at first and then retract as they cool. Press the ends of the cans in, gently, if necessary. Always check cans for leakage.

    e.   When the cans are cold to the touch, dry them. Label, date and store cans in a cool, dry place.

PROCESSING TIMES FOR SALMON AND TROUT

CONTAINER	PROCESSING TIME	TEMPERATURE	PRESSURE
Glass Sealers:			
500 ml	110 min	115°C	70 kPa
250 ml	110 min	115°C	70 kPa
Cans:			
650 ml	135 min	115°C	70 kPa
500 ml flat	120 min	115°C	70 kPa
500 ml tall	100 min	115°C	70 kPa
250 ml flat	90 min	115°C	70 kPa

DETECTING SPOILAGE IN CANNED FOODS

1.   Food Canned at Home in Jars

Each jar of home canned food should be carefully inspected before serving. To detect spoilage in these foods check for any visible signs of spoilage and smell the product.

Visible signs include patches of mould, a foamy or murky appearance, evidence of leakage from the jar or a bulging or corroded lid. Food in jars showing any of these characteristics should be disposed of *without tasting*.

The food should have a pleasant odour characteristic of the food. If it has a disagreeable odour, do not taste it. Any low acid food should be boiled, uncovered, for at least 10 minutes before it is served. Closely packaged foods like corn and leafy vegetables should be boiled for 20 minutes. (More water may be added to prevent scorching.)

2.   Commercially Canned Food

Commercial canning is one of the safest methods of food processing. However, an occasional can becomes spoiled and a few of these may even be dangerous. If a can's contents do not look, sound or smell right, the can may be trying to tell you something, *so when in doubt – throw it out!*

Look at the can. A can may safely be used when corroded or rusty *provided* it is not rusted through. Discard if in any doubt. A bulging can should never be used. If you find one on the grocery shelf, ask the clerk to dispose of it and report it to the manager. When the contents of an opened can appears bubbly or mouldy, do not use. This is probably the result of bacterial or mould growth. If the can has a broken seam there will often be a small amount of dried food at that spot. *Throw it out!*

Listen when you open the can. If a can's contents spurt out when the can is opened this could be the result of a pressure building up in the can by gas produced by bacteria. Beware – *do not taste!*

Smell the food. If a can's contents smell putrid, musty or sulphurous (like rotten eggs) in all likelihood the food has gone bad. Rather than taste the food, *throw it out!*

Any food which shows no other signs of spoilage except that it tastes off flavour, rancid or bitter *do not use!*

3.   Food Canned at Home in Tin Cans

The same precautions noted for Commercially Canned Food (above) apply. Look, listen and smell in case the can is trying to tell you something.

Any low acid food should be boiled before tasting as described in Food Canned at Home in Jars, above.

DETERMINING THE CAUSE OF UNSATISFACTORY RESULTS

Food Floats in Liquid

1. Syrup was too heavy for the fruit (i.e., too high a proportion of sugar to water).
2. There was too much liquid in proportion to the food.
3. Foods packed raw may float after they have been cooked by the processing step. They may have been packed too loosely.

Liquid is Lower than Before Processing

1. Food was packed too tightly.
2. Jar was packed too full. If insufficient head space is allowed the product will boil out during processing.
3. Jar was sealed too tightly to allow expanding air to escape during processing. Liquid is then forced out.
4. Air bubbles were not removed.
5. Boiling water bath canning. Liquid may be lost when there is less than 3 cm water over the tops of the jars.
6. Pressure canning. Liquid is forced from the jar when pressure in the canner is allowed to fluctuate.

Undesirable Colour Change Occurred

1. Enzymes were not destroyed quickly enough or completely (i.e., too long between harvest and canning; underprocessing.)
2. Oxidation occurred because air bubbles were not removed.
3. Insufficient liquid to completely cover food.
4. Food was overprocessed.
5. Poor storage conditions (i.e., too hot or too light.)
6. Light coloured fruits were not treated with enzyme inhibitive solution (see page 402).
7. The bright colour of some fruits or vegetables will cook into the syrup or liquid.

Jar Did Not Seal

1. Rim of the jar was chipped.
2. Rim of the jar was not wiped free of particles of food.
3. Sealing compound on lid was scratched or damaged before use. New lids must be used each time.
4. Lids were not correctly pre-treated according to manufacturer's instructions. Some require boiling, others need only be dipped in hot water.
5. Screw band was rusted or bent.
6. Screw band was removed or tampered with before firm seal was made on processed jar.

Jellies, Jams and Pickles

Jelly Making

Jellies are made from the juice extracted from fruits. They can be made from one kind of fruit or from a combination of fruits. Sometimes commercially canned juice or frozen juice is used. Generally, however, the juice is extracted from fresh fruit. The method used to extract the juice depends upon the fruit being used. The recipe section of this book has in it specific instructions for making jelly from a variety of fruits using a variety of methods.

A perfect jelly has a clear, bright colour and a fresh flavour characteristic of the fruit used. It should hold its shape when unmoulded and quiver when the plate is moved. It should spread easily without being thin or syrupy and should have a smooth, tender texture.

In order to make perfect jelly these elements must be in the right proportions:

PECTIN

Pectin is a substance found naturally in all fruits which, when heated with sugar, causes the juice to congeal ("gel", set, harden). The amount of pectin varies greatly in fruits as well as in varieties of the same fruit. Even growing conditions will affect pectin content from year to year. Pectin content decreases as the fruit ripens. This is why sometimes slightly under-ripe fruit, having the most pectin, is combined with fully ripe fruit, which has better flavour, to make jelly or jam.

ACID

All fruits contain some natural acid. Fruits such as sour apples, sour plums, currants and gooseberries have plenty of acid for jelly making. Others such as peaches, pears and blueberries usually have such a small amount of acid that lemon juice or some other acid fruit must be added. As the fruit ripens the acid content decreases.

SUGAR

As the pectin content of a fruit decreases with the ripening of the fruit, the amount of sugar needed is decreased also. Fruits with little natural pectin require little sugar. Use of commercial pectin increases sugar requirement.

CHART OF ACID AND PECTIN CONTENT IN FRUIT

Fruit	Rich in Acid & Pectin	Deficient in Acid	Deficient in Pectin	Will jelly if slightly under-ripe
Sour apples	X			
Crabapples	X			
Currants	X			
Sour gooseberries	X			
Sour plums	X			
Grapes	X			
Cranberries	X			
Blueberries		X		
Sweet apples		X		
Quince		X		
Blackberries		X		
Rhubarb			X	
Strawberries			X	
Pineapple			X	
Peaches			X	
Cantaloup			X	
Melon				X
Blueberries				X
Blackberries				X
Raspberries				X
Sour Cherries				X
Sweet Plums				X
Loganberries				X

To make a good jelly, the pectin, acid, sugar and water must be in the right proportions. This chart shows the acid and pectin content of some common fruits. The sugar and water content varies with the type of fruit, its maturity and growing conditions, but these levels can be balanced during the jelly-making process.

1. If a fruit to be used is low in either pectin or acid it may be combined with one or more fruits rich in the needed element.

2. Both pectin and acid content of a fruit decreases as the fruit matures. Therefore, never use over-ripe fruit for making jelly. For best results, use a mixture of fully ripe and slightly under-ripe fruit.

3. If the fruit to be used is low in pectin a commercial fruit pectin may be used economically. The preparation steps will vary from those followed when no commercial fruit pectin is used. Therefore, follow manufacturer's directions carefully.

COMMERCIAL PECTIN

Commercial fruit pectin is a product which is prepared from extracts of pectin-rich fruits. Available in both liquid and crystal form, it is used to best advantage with fruits which are low in pectin and would otherwise be difficult to make into jelly or jam. Whichever form of pectin is used, the manufacturer's directions must be followed carefully. Methods for crystals and for liquid are different and the products cannot be used interchangeably.

Because the boiling time is very short, the fruit juice is not evaporated and up to twice as much jelly or jam results as in recipes not using commercial pectin. Also, the amount of sugar required is increased considerably. This amount may seem great but it is necessary in order to make the correct balance of pectin and sugar to produce a good product.

Advantages:

1.	A faster method	• Boiling time is reduced to one minute only. • Fuel needs are reduced.
2.	Greater yield	• Up to twice as much jelly or jam from the same amount of fruit. • More sugar used to balance the added pectin. • Reduced boiling time results in less evaporation.
3.	Product has good colour	• Less high heat which darkens fruit and caramelizes sugar.
4.	Product has good flavour	• Fully ripe fruit is used, no under-ripe fruit needed. • No long cooking which changes flavour.

5. A good product can be made from almost any fruit, even those containing very little natural pectin.

PREPARING JUICE FOR JELLY

1. Select sound fruit. Use a mixture of ripe and slightly under-ripe fruit, about equal parts of each. Two or more kinds of fruit may be combined provided both acid and pectin are present in the mixture. Choose combinations using Chart of Acid and Pectin Content in Fruit, page 414.

2. Wash thoroughly and discard any damaged spots. Cut hard fruits into quarters or smaller; berries may be crushed.

3. Place in heavy kettle with cold water. Use proportions as noted on chart below:

FRUIT	PREPARATION	AMOUNT OF COLD WATER
Apple	Wash, remove stems and blossom ends, cut into eighths, or slice.	To completely cover prepared fruit.
Chokecherry and Apple	Wash and stem chokecherries, crush in bottom of kettle. Wash apples, stem, cut into eighths. Prepare equal quantities of both fruits.	To come just below top layer of prepared fruit.
Crabapple	Wash, stem, cut into quarters.	To completely cover prepared fruit.
Currant, Red	Wash, stem.	125 ml water for 250 ml prepared fruit.
Currant, Black	Wash, stem.	250 ml water for each 250 ml prepared fruit.
Gooseberry (Green)	Wash, stem.	200 ml water for 250 ml prepared fruit.
Grape	Wash, stem.	To come just below top layer of prepared fruit.
Plum, Sour	**Wash, stem, cut into halves or quarters, leave pits in.**	To come just below top layer of prepared fruit.
Quince and Apple	Wash quinces and apples thoroughly, remove stems and blossom ends, cut into quarters. Prepare equal quantities of both fruits.	To completely cover prepared fruit.
Quince and Grape	Wash quinces, remove stems and blossom ends, cut into quarters. Wash and stem grapes. Prepare equal quantities of both fruits.	To come just below top layer of prepared fruit.
Raspberry and Currant (Red)	Wash raspberries. Wash and stem currants. Prepare equal quantities of both fruits.	75 ml water for 250 ml prepared fruit.

4. Follow either A, Conventional Method or B, Cellulose Method of extracting juice from the fruit:

A. CONVENTIONAL METHOD

a. Simmer fruit in covered kettle until it is soft and mushy. Crush fruit as it cooks.

b. Pour hot cooked fruit into moistened jelly bag made of unbleached cotton or several thicknesses of fine cheesecloth.

c. Hang over a bowl and drain until dripping stops. This may be left overnight. For clear jelly, do not squeeze the bag.

B. CELLULOSE METHOD

a. Place 10 sheets of unscented and untinted facial tissue in a saucepan. Pour about 2 litres of boiling water over them and stir to break up the tissues. Turn mass into a sieve and shake gently. Do not press out the excess water as this will prevent tissues from absorbing fruit juice.

b. Put the tissue mass into a heavy saucepan with prepared fruit (1.5-2 litres for 10 sheets of tissue) and cold water. Boil until fruit is tender, stirring constantly.

c. Pour fruit and tissue mixture into scalded jelly bag made of unbleached cotton or several thicknesses of fine cheesecloth. As soon as bag is cool enough to handle, force all the juice out by squeezing. It is not necessary to let the bag hang to drip overnight.

NOTE: *Because the facial tissues are composed of cellulose or wood fibre, they break down the cell walls of the fruit and allow the juice to escape during cooking. The tissues filter the juice making it clear even when squeezed. This method yields at least 1½ to 2 times as much juice as the Conventional Method above.*

STERILIZING JARS

1. Wash jars in soapy water. Rinse.

2. Place inverted on a rack or cloth in a large saucepan. Add sufficient water to come about half way up the sides of jars. Cover and boil for 15 minutes. OR,

3. Place in a cloth or rack in a large saucepan and cover with water. Bring to boil and boil 15 minutes.

4. Leave in hot water until ready to use.

NOTE: *If food is to be processed in a boiling water bath or pressure cooker after it is packed, it is not necessary to sterilize the jars before packing them. If no further cooking is to take place after jars are packed, as with jams, jellies, pickles, etc., then jars must be sterilized first.*

JELLY MAKING STEPS

1. Sterilize jelly glasses or jars. See page 417.

2. Measure juice. Work with small amounts at a time, not more than two litres.

3. Place measured juice in a large saucepan. (Pan should hold 4-6 times as much as juice being used.) Boil, uncovered, for 3 minutes.

4. Remove pan from heat and test for pectin using the Epsom Salts or the Alcohol Test. If clot does not form, continue boiling, testing frequently until pectin test is satisfactory.

    A. EPSOM SALTS TEST: Place 30 ml cooked juice in a cup or small dish. Add 10 ml sugar and 15 ml Epsom Salts. Stir until salts are dissolved; let stand 20 minutes. If mixture forms into a semi-solid mass, the juice contains sufficient pectin to proceed.

    B. ALCOHOL TEST: Place 5 ml juice in a cup or small dish. Add 5 ml alcohol and blend together. DO NOT TASTE THIS MIXTURE – RUBBING ALCOHOL IS POISONOUS.
    If a jelly-like mass or clot is formed, the juice contains sufficient pectin for jelly making.

5. Measure sugar. If a heavy clot formed when pectin test was made at the end of the three minute boiling period, allow 250 ml of sugar for each 250 ml of extracted juice used. If boiling was continued after the first pectin test, allow 175 ml for each 250 ml juice measured in step number 1.

6. Add measured sugar slowly to juice. To ensure a clear jelly, warm the sugar first. Boil rapidly, uncovered, removing scum as it forms. Test boiling juice for jelly stage by one of these methods:

    A. SHEET TEST: Dip a metal spoon into the boiling hot syrup. Hold spoon well above the kettle and allow syrup to run off the side. Jelly stage has been reached when the syrup no longer runs off the spoon in a steady stream but separates into two distinct lines of drops which finally flow or "sheet" together.

    B. SAUCER TEST: Put a little of the cooked fruit on a chilled saucer. If the liquid jellies, it is cooked sufficiently.

7. Remove pan from heat immediately when the jelly point is reached. Longer boiling will give a stiff, tough jelly. Skim hot juice as it stands for about 1 minute.

8. Pour into hot sterilized jelly glasses or jars. Fill each to within 0.5 cm of the top. Using a moistened clean cloth, carefully remove any trace of jelly clinging to the inside of the glass above the jelly level. Then wipe dry with a clean cloth. This step ensures a better seal with the paraffin.

9. When jelly is partially set, cover surface with a thin layer of hot melted paraffin. Allow wax to harden, then add a second layer, rotating jar so that wax adheres to inside of glass.

10. Cover jars with paper or a metal lid and store in a cool, dry place.

CHARACTERISTICS OF A GOOD JELLY

1. Appearance
   • Clear and sparkling with no cloudiness, bubbles or sugar crystals.
   • Colour characteristic of the fruit, not artificial.

2. Consistency
   • Holds its shape when turned out of the jar, when shaken it quivers.
   • Tender enough to cut easily, not tough or gummy; the cut surface retains the angle of the cut.

3. Flavour
   • Good fruit flavour characteristic of the fruit.
   • Not scorched or too sweet.

JAM MAKING

Jams are made from whole, sliced, chopped or crushed fruit mixed with sugar and cooked until thick. Jams differ from jellies mostly in consistency and texture. A good jam should be thick but not stiff or gummy, with pieces of fruit evenly distributed throughout. It should have a flavour characteristic of the fruit and there should be no separated fruit or sugar crystals.

There are many ways of making a good jam. Examples are included in the recipe section of the book. Some recipes call for the cleaned, washed fruit to be crushed, while others require grinding, slicing or chopping. If the fruit is not very juicy it is pre-cooked with water before the sugar is added. Pectin, acid, sugar and water must be in the correct proportions for the jam to set to the characteristic consistency. The principles of making jam are the same as for jelly except that the entire fruit is used instead of only the juice.

JAM MAKING STEPS

1. Sterilized jars to be used for jam. See page 417.

2. Select firm ripe fruit and prepare as outlined in Chart for Jam Preparation. If fruit being used is deficient in pectin add a pectin-rich fruit. See chart of Acid and Pectin Content in Fruit, Page 414.

3. Place fruit in large kettle, add water if required. As indicated, most

fruits are cooked before sugar is added. Bring to the boil and count time for pre-cooking from when fruit begins to boil vigourously.

4. Add sugar. Bring to boil again and boil, uncovered, with frequent stirring for the minimum time noted. Count time from when mixture begins to boil vigourously.

5. Test the jam for consistency. Remove kettle from heat. Place a small spoonful of jam on a chilled saucer and cool quickly. If jam does not set to desired thickness, cook a few minutes longer and test again.

NOTE: Depending upon the fruit used, final temperature of the jam varies considerably. Therefore, recommended boiling time can only be approximate and testing is necessary. However, this method must not be confused with the method for making jam using commercial fruit pectin where total cooking time is very short and is accurately timed.

6. Pour hot jam into hot sterilized jars. Fill to within 0.5 cm of the top. Using a moistened clean cloth, carefully remove any trace of jam clinging to the inside of the glass above the level of the jam. Wipe dry with a clean cloth. This step ensures a better seal with the paraffin.

7. When jam is partially set, cover surface with a thin layer of hot melted paraffin. Allow wax to harden, then add a second layer, rotating the jar so that wax adheres to the inside of the glass.

8. Cover jars with paper or a metal lid and store in a cool, dry place.

CHART FOR JAM PREPARATION

FRUIT	AMOUNT TO BUY	PREPARED FRUIT	WATER	PRE-COOK TIME	SUGAR	BOILING TIME
Apricot	2.5-3 kg 40-60 medium	3 000 ml (quartered)			1 750 ml	10-12 min
Black Currant		1 500 ml	1 250 ml	15 min	1 625 ml	5- 8 min
Gooseberry (Green)		2 000 ml	750 ml	15 min	1 875 ml	5- 7 min
Peach	3-3.5 kg 12-15 medium	3 000 ml (chopped)			1 500 ml	15-20 min
Plum (except Damson)	3-3.5 kg	3 000 ml (quartered)	125 ml	10 min	1 750 ml	6- 8 min
Plum, Damson	2-2.5 kg	2 000 ml	750 ml	15 min	1 750 ml	6- 8 min
Raspberry		2 000 ml (crushed)	—	15 min	1 500 ml	12-15 min
Strawberry	2-2.25 kg 1 large basket		—	—	2 000 ml	5 min and 5-7 min

Marmalades, Butters, Conserves and Preserves

Because their consistency and method of preparation is similar, other kinds of preserved fruits are often called jams.

MARMALADES

Made from fruits or a combination of fruits which most often includes one or more citrus fruits. A marmalade should be clear and sparkling with thin slices of fruit suspended in a jelly-like syrup. It is similar to jam in texture but is set a little firmer. Citrus fruit marmalades always contain finely chopped or shredded peel as well as the pulp of the fruit. With the exception of the fruit preparation, the method of making marmalades is the same as that used for jams.

BUTTERS

Made by pressing fruit pulp through a sieve or colander and cooking it with sugar and sometimes spices until the mixture has a smooth consistency.

PREPARATION STEPS FOR JAM	APPROXIMATE YIELD
Wash, remove pits and cut into quarters or smaller pieces. Add sugar; let stand 1 hour. Add 30 ml vinegar or lemon juice. Bring to boil and boil uncovered, to jam stage.	2 250 ml
Wash, remove tops and tails. Add water; bring to boil and pre-cook uncovered. Add sugar, bring to boil and boil uncovered to jam stage.	1 750 ml
Wash, remove tops and tails. Add water, bring to boil and pre-cook uncovered. Add sugar, bring to boil and boil uncovered to jam stage.	2 250 ml
Wash, blanch in hot, dip in cold water to remove skins. Remove pits and chop in small pieces. Add sugar and let stand 1 hour. Add 30 ml vinegar or lemon juice. Bring to boil and boil uncovered to jam stage.	2 250 ml
Wash, remove pits and cut into quarters. Add water, bring to boil and pre-cook uncovered. Add sugar, bring to boil, and boil uncovered, to jam stage.	1 750 ml
Wash. Add water, bring to boil and pre-cook, uncovered. Add sugar, bring to boil, uncovered, to jam stage. Remove as many pits as possible as they rise to the surface.	1 750 ml
Wash, crush and measure. Bring to boil and pre-cook, uncovered. Add sugar, bring to boil and boil uncovered, to jam stage.	1 750 ml
Wash and hull berries. Place in large bowl or kettle layered alternately with sugar. Let stand 2-3 hours. Bring to boil and boil, uncovered for 5 minutes. Add 125 ml lemon juice and boil to jam stage.	1 750 ml

JAM PREPARATION USING COMMERCIAL PECTIN

INGREDIENT	STRAW-BERRY		BLACK-BERRY		RASP-BERRY		BLUE-BERRY		HUCKLE-BERRY	
Fruit to buy	1.25 kg		1.25 kg		1.25 kg		1.25 kg		1.25 kg	
Prepared fruit	1 000	ml	1 000	ml	1 000	ml	1 125	ml	1 125	ml
Sugar	1 625	ml	1 625	ml	1 500	ml	1 625	ml	1 625	ml
Lemon juice	60	ml	—		—		30	ml	30	ml
Fruit Pectin	½ bottle		½ bottle		½ bottle		1 bottle		1 bottle	
Other										

Note: Liquid fruit pectin is generally sold in 175 ml bottles.

FRUIT PREPARATION

Strawberry, Blackberry, Raspberry, Blueberry, Huckleberry.
Wash only if necessary; remove stems and pick over. Crush thoroughly, then measure required amount.

Plum
Wash, pit but do not peel. Cut in small pieces and chop. Place in saucepan with 125 ml water and bring to boil. Simmer, covered 5 minutes. Measure required amount. *Substitute 125 ml lemon juice for that amount of prepared fruit where sweet plums or freestone prune plums are used.

Peach, Pear
Peel and pit or core fruit. Grind or chop very fine, then measure.

Cherry
Wash, stem and pit cherries. Chop fine, then measure.

Apricot
Wash, pit, do not peel. Cut in small pieces or grind, then measure.

Rhubarb
Wash, slice thin or chop but do not peel rhubarb. Add 200 ml water and simmer covered, until soft, about 1 minute. Measure.

A butter should be soft enough to spread easily when cold. Less sugar is used for a butter than for jams or marmalades and the mixture must be cooked slowly with frequent stirring to prevent scorching.

CONSERVES

Made of a mixture of several fresh and/or dried fruits often combined with nuts. They are similar in sweetness to jams and marmalades but are usually of a slightly different consistency.

PRESERVES

Made of whole small fruit or pieces of larger fruit which are combined with sugar and cooked until the syrup is quite thick and the fruit clear, shiny and transparent and tender. The fruit should keep its form and plumpness and be somewhat crisp and tender rather than tough and soft.

PLUM	PEACH	PEAR	SWEET CHERRY	SOUR CHERRY	APRICOT	RHUBARB
1.5 kg	1.5 kg	1.5 kg	1.5 kg	1.5 kg	1.25 kg	0.75 kg
1 125 ml	1 000 ml	1 000 ml	825 ml	1 000 ml	750 ml	750 ml
1 750 ml	1 750 ml	1 750 ml	1 625 ml	1 625 ml	1 500 ml	1 250 ml
* 125 ml	60 ml	60 ml	60 ml	—	60 ml	—
½ bottle	1 bottle	1 bottle	1 bottle	1 bottle	½ bottle	½ bottle
	cinnamon, cloves, allspice		1.25 ml almond extract, after cooking	1.25 ml almond extract after cooking		

JAM PREPARATION

1. Prepare fruit. Measure required amount. Add lemon juice, if desired.
2. Place measured prepared fruit in a very large saucepan. Add measured sugar and stir. (Pan should be large enough to be less than half filled with fruit and sugar.)
3. Place saucepan over high heat; bring to a boil; boil hard for 1 minute, stirring constantly. Maintain a full rolling boil that cannot be stirred down for this time.
4. Remove from heat and at once stir in fruit pectin.
5. Skim off foam with a metal spoon. Stir and skim for 5 minutes and cool slightly to prevent floating fruit.
6. Ladle into sterilized jars and cover immediately with 0.5 cm hot paraffin wax.

Pickles

Pickles are fruits and vegetables preserved by the addition of two or more of these preservatives: salt, vinegar, sugar, spices. There are many different kinds of pickles, including those made with fruits and vegetables that are left whole or cut into chunks or slices, and mixtures that are ground or chopped and cooked to a sauce consistency. The name of the kind of pickle is usually derived from the predominating flavour of one of the preservatives used; either sour, salty, sweet or spicy. Pickles are served as an addition to the meal, not as a main part of the meal and are usually included for their interesting flavour and texture which adds zest to the other foods being served.

SUCCESS IN MAKING PICKLES

1.   Vegetables and Fruits

Use only firm, fresh vegetables and fruits that are free from bruises or decay. Best success, especially in recipes using whole vegetables (e.g., dill pickles) is achieved when there is a minimum time lapse between the garden and the jar. Over-mature or stale vegetables will shrivel during the pickling process; over-ripe fruits will not hold their shape.

2.   Utensils for Pickling

Containers and utensils used for pickling should be carefully selected. Stainless steel or unchipped enamel are best for cooking pickles. Glass and crockery make good containers. Plastic bowls may also be used. Stir with a wooden spoon. Since vinegar and salt react with iron, copper and brass, causing discolouration, utensils made of these metals should not be used (e.g., copper pan, galvanized pail).

3.   Containers for Storage

Containers for storing pickles include glass jars, sealers and crocks. Glass or enamelled lids are recommended as metal tops will corrode in a short time. Pickles kept in crocks should be stored in a cool place and should be well covered with vinegar solution to prevent moulding. A plate or board fitted inside the crock and weighted down with a heavy object will hold the pickles under the solution. Relishes and sauces should be packed in hot, sterilized jars and properly sealed with lids or paraffin.

4.   Salt

Vegetables such as cucumbers are frequently soaked in a brine of salt and water before they are placed in the vinegar pickling solution. The purpose of this brine is to draw water from the tissues of the vegetables. Preparing them to absorb the pickling solution helps to keep them firm and crisp during the succeeding pickling process. It also reduces bitterness.

a.   Coarse or pickling salt should be used for pickling. Free running table salt is treated with chemicals, to prevent caking, which may interfere with the pickling process and cause cloudiness in the solution.

b.   When making brine, use the proportions indicated in the recipe. A brine commonly used for preliminary soaking uses 375 ml coarse salt (or 250 ml fine salt) with 2.5 litres water. If not enough salt is used, the pickles will be soft or slippery; if too much salt is used they may shrivel or become tough.

5. Vinegar

Good quality vinegar, used full strength and measured according to the recipe, will give best results. If vinegar is weak or diluted too much, pickles will be soft and may not keep. There are several kinds of vinegar sold; the recipe usually specifies which to use for the desired flavour. Substituting one for another should be done only with caution.

a.   White vinegar gives a better colour where light coloured foods, such as onions, ripe cucumbers, cauliflower or pears are used. Its acid flavour seems to be stronger or more harsh.

b.   Cider vinegar, made from apple juice, is most commonly used for pickles. It is amber coloured and has a mild fruit flavour that is more mellow than that of white vinegar.

c.   Malt vinegar is preferred in some recipes for its distinctive flavour. It is dark amber in colour.

6. Spices

Spices should be fresh, carefully measured and cautiously used. Because they tend to lose flavour if stored too long, buying spices fresh each year is recommended. Some spices such as allspice, cloves and red chili peppers have exceptionally strong flavours and if too much is used or they are boiled too long in the vinegar, a pickle with bitter flavour or dark colour may result.

Whole spices give better colour and flavour than ground spices. They should be tied loosely in a cheesecloth bag large enough to allow the vinegar to boil through the spices. Then they can be cooked with the vinegar or pickle and removed when the desired flavour is developed.

7. Sugar

Sugar is used in many pickle recipes. White cane or beet sugar is generally used but brown sugar may be specified where a special flavour or colour is desired.

PICKLE MAKING PROBLEMS

Here are some common problems encountered when making pickles, with possible reasons for the failure:

1. Hollow Pickle

Faulty development of the cucumbers.

Too long a time lapse between gathering and pickling.

NOTE: Cucumbers to be used for dill pickles should be soaked in ice water as soon as they are picked; cucumbers for gherkins are placed in brine. Holding them for even a few hours at room temperature may result in hollow centres.

2. **Soft Pickle**

Brine used for soaking was too weak.

Vinegar solution not strong enough.

Pickles stored in an open container (crock) with some of them exposed above the solution.

Pickles heated too long in vinegar, causing their crispness to be lost by over-cooking.

3. **Shriveling and Toughness**

Too heavy a syrup.

Too strong a brine.

Too strong a vinegar solution.

NOTE: *Some pickles, especially certain sweet ones, should have a preliminary treatment in a weaker solution and then the density of the syrup may be raised gradually until finished pickle is the desired sweetness.*

Freezing

THE FREEZER APPLIANCE

There are three distinct types of freezers and each has special features which may or may not be suitable to your needs. Choosing a home freezer will be easier if the features of each are assessed in relation to the situation for which it is intended. Consideration should be given to the people who will use the food – how many, the way they entertain, their life style, the foods they like.

All home freezers, of whatever type, can be adjusted to maintain an even temperature of −20°C. At this temperature frozen food can be stored for the times indicated on page 430.

Most home refrigerators have a *frozen food storage compartment*. Here frozen foods can be stored for brief periods. However, a temperature low enough to preserve the quality of the frozen food for an extended time is not maintained. Temperatures usually fluctuate between −5°C and −10°C. This is not cold enough to produce small ice crystals and foods frozen this way will not be of optimum quality.

TYPES OF FREEZERS

Chest

Chest style freezers are available in a wide size range (0.25 m³ to 0.75 m³) and the floor space required varies also. Because of the floor space needed, especially for the larger models, chest freezers are often installed in a basement or utility room. Large and awkward shaped articles store well in this kind.

Because it takes up less floor space the upright style fits more easily into a kitchen, giving easy access to the food stored there. Capacity varies also. Bulky shaped items may require adjustment of the shelves.

Combination Freezer-Refrigerator

Two separate appliances are incorporated into one. The floor space required will be greater than for an upright freezer, but will not be as much as for a refrigerator and upright freezer standing side by side. The combination freezer-refrigerator is available with the freezer at the top, at the bottom, or beside the refrigerator section. It must, of course, have a separate door for each section or it cannot be classified as a freezer. (See comment about home refrigerator frozen food storage compartments.)

Installation and Operation of Home Freezer

1. Locate the freezer away from direct sunlight and heat and where it will be convenient to use.

2. A fully loaded freezer is heavy. Be sure the floor where it will sit is firm and strong.

3. The surrounding temperature is important to efficient operation of the home freezer. Do not locate it in an open carport or unheated porch. An ambient temperature of between 5°C and 30°C is most efficient.

4. Be sure the freezer is level. If it is not it may be noisy and there may be cold lost from the lid or door.

5. Proper air circulation around the freezer is necessary. For an upright model allow 5 cm between the top of the freezer and upper cabinets. For a chest freezer allow 5 to 7 cm at the sides and back.

6. Read the manufacturer's instruction book. Then remove any packing tape marks and rinse the interior. Dry thoroughly. Insert plug into a single circuit outlet where it can be left permanently. Do not use a divided circuit. Set the control and run the freezer at coldest setting for at least 8 hours before placing any food in it. This step is especially important to cool the freezer thoroughly before it is used. Remember to fill out and send the guarantee or warranty to the manufacturer.

HOME FREEZER MANAGEMENT

To get the best out of a home freezer, it is important to:

1. Follow the directions of the manufacturer about the care of the freezer, setting the controls (if this is necessary), and where to place the food in the freezer.

2. Freeze food rapidly and in small quantities. To freeze food quickly:

   a. in a chest freezer, place the unfrozen food close to the outside walls.

   b. in an upright regular-defrost model place unfrozen food on the shelves having cooling coils.

   c. in upright, frost-free models place unfrozen food directly on shelves.

   Allow space for the cold air to circulate between the packages. Leave in this position for 24 hours, then rearrange for long-term storage. The amount of food you can freeze properly in 24 hours is directly proportionate to the size of your freezer. If you find it necessary to freeze more than your freezer can handle at one time, have the food quick frozen in the locker plant. If this is not possible, keep the extra amount in the refrigerator until it can be put into the freezer.

3. Have a system for budgeting freezer space so that a variety of frozen foods can be stored. Choose foods because the family likes them, not simply because they are plentiful or cheap. Avoid filling too great a portion of the space with the first products of the season.

4. Have an orderly arrangement of foods in the freezer, storing frozen fruits and vegetables in one part, meat in another, baked goods in another, etc. A freezer in which the foods are systematically arranged will generally hold many more packages than one poorly organized.

5. Label all packages with the name of the food, the date frozen and any other details that will be helpful when the food is to be thawed or cooked. To aid in finding foods stored in the freezer, use labels or strings of different colours on the different kinds of meat, etc., and store small parcels together in stockinet or large plastic bags.

6. Keep an up-to-date inventory or stock sheet of the contents of the freezer, making sure to record foods as they are put in and taken out.

7. Keep the freezer full; empty space is wasteful.

8. Use, do not save, the food in the freezer — the more rapid the turnover of food the greater the economy.

9. Defrost regularly and keep the freezer clean so that undesirable "cold storage" odours will not develop.

10. Plan ahead, using imagination and ingenuity, watching for new ideas and developments and remembering that almost anything commercially frozen can be frozen in a home freezer.

11. Remember the basic steps to success in freezing food.

With thoughtful planning, selective buying and good management, a home freezer filled with frozen foods can mean more convenience in meal preparation; nutritious, delicious, attractive and varied meals all year round; and a greater saving of time, effort and money.

Foods Not Suitable for Freezing

1. Uncooked cake batters.
2. Cream fillings, puddings and custards.
3. Boiled potatoes (as in stews or casseroles).
4. Salad greens and garnishes.
5. White of hard cooked eggs (unless put through a grinder).
6. Creamed cottage cheese.
7. Cream other than whipping cream.

FREEZER STORAGE CHART

	FROZEN FOOD	OPTIMUM TIME AT −20°C
BAKED GOODS	BREAD — Quick Breads	2- 3 months
	— Yeast Breads	1- 2 months
	CAKES — Not iced, Iced	4- 6 months
	— Spice Cake	6 weeks
	— Fruit Cake	12 months
	COOKIES AND SLICES — Baked	9-12 months
	— Unbaked	4- 6 months
	CREAM PUFFS AND ECLAIRS	1 month
	DESSERTS — Steamed Pudding	6-12 months
	— Dessert Toppings	9-12 months
	PASTRY — Baked	6 months
	— Unbaked	3 months
	PIES — Baked	1- 6 months
	— Unbaked, fruit, berry and mince freeze best.	1- 3 months
	— Chiffon Pie	2- 3 weeks
	SAUSAGE ROLLS	2- 4 weeks
FISH	OILY FISH — Salmon, Trout, Mackerel	4- 6 weeks
	LEAN FISH — Halibut, Sole, Cod	4- 6 months
FRUIT	All kinds	9-12 months
GAME	GAME ANIMALS	8-10 months
	GAME BIRDS	6- 9 months
JAM	JAMS, JELLY, MARMALADE	12 months
MEAT	BEEF	8-10 months
	LAMB	6- 9 months
	VEAL	6- 9 months
	PORK, Fresh	3- 6 months
	CURED AND SMOKED MEATS	1- 2 months
	GROUND MEAT	1- 3 months
	COOKED BEEF, PORK, VEAL	2- 3 months
	COOKED HAM	4- 6 weeks
PREPARED MEALS	CASSEROLES OF HAM	4- 6 weeks
	CASSEROLES	1- 2 months
	STEW, MEAT PIE, T.V. DINNER	1- 2 months
	BAKED BEANS, CHILI CON CARNE, SPAGHETTI SAUCE	3- 4 months
	SOUPS	2 months
	SAUCE, GRAVY	2 weeks
POULTRY	UNCOOKED — Whole	6- 9 months
	— Pieces	3- 4 months
	COOKED — Sliced or cubed in broth or gravy	2- 3 months
	— Casserole	1- 2 months
	DRESSING — Packaged separately	1 month
SHELLFISH	SHRIMP, OYSTERS, CLAMS	Up to 3 months
	LOBSTER, CRAB	Up to 2 months
VEGETABLES	Most kinds	9-12 months
	Onions	2 months
	Potatoes	1 month

IF THE POWER IS INTERRUPTED

In case of a power interruption or mechanical breakdown, if the freezer is almost fully loaded and the door is not opened, the food will stay frozen for one or two days. A fully loaded freezer will likely keep food frozen two to four days if it is *not* opened.

Dry ice may be used to keep the food frozen. Wear gloves when handling dry ice, and do not allow it to touch the contents. In an upright model place the dry ice on the top shelf. In a chest type, cover packages with cardboard and set dry ice on this. Refreezing itself is not harmful, but the texture and colour will likely deteriorate. The danger is in refreezing thawed food that has already begun to spoil. If the food becomes thawed, cook immediately or discard. Meat can sometimes be cooked and then refrozen. Check the chart pages 431-432 for details. Note the differences between treatment of commercially frozen and home frozen foods.

SAFETY GUIDELINES FOR REFREEZING *HOME FROZEN* FOOD

Condition of Commercially Frozen Foods	Partially Thawed (ice crystals still present)	Completely Thawed but still VERY COLD to touch (5°C)	Completely thawed at room temperature (20°C) for NOT longer than 2 hours
FROZEN UNCOOKED PRODUCTS			
Fruit and Fruit Juices	Safe	Safe	Questionable. May ferment.
Meats	Safe	Questionable — safer to cook and eat or refreeze once cooked.	DO NOT REFREEZE. Cook immediately. Discard if there is a bad odour.
Poultry	Safe	Questionable	DO NOT REFREEZE. Cook immediately. Discard if there is a bad odour.
Fish and Shellfish	Safe	Questionable	DO NOT REFREEZE. Discard.
Variety Meats, liver, kidney	Safe	Questionable	DO NOT REFREEZE. Discard.
Vegetables	Safe	Questionable	Questionable — safer to cook immediately or discard
FROZEN PREPARED AND PRECOOKED FOODS			
TV Dinners and casseroles	Safe	Questionable	DO NOT REFREEZE. Heat and serve immediately or discard.
Ice cream and sherbets	Safe	Safe. Beat or stir during refreezing to improve texture.	DO NOT REFREEZE. Discard.
Baked Goods	Safe	Safe	Safe. Product will become more stale each time refrozen.

CHART NOTES:

1. *Any frozen food which is completely thawed and held at room temperature for an unknown period of time should be discarded.*

2. *Refreezing foods always causes some deterioration in texture, flavour and colour. When in doubt, do not refreeze.*

3. *The advisability of refreezing will depend on the original quality of the fresh food and the care with which it was handled in preparation for the freezer.*

SAFETY GUIDELINES FOR
REFREEZING *COMMERCIALLY FROZEN* FOOD

Condition of Commercially Frozen Foods	Partially Thawed (ice crystals still present)	Completely Thawed but still VERY COLD to touch (5°C)	Completely thawed at room temperature (20°C) for NOT longer than 2 hours
FROZEN UNCOOKED FOODS			
Fruit, Fruit Pies, Fruit Juice Concentrates	Safe	Safe	Safe
Meat, Poultry	Safe	Safe	Do not refreeze. Cook immediately and eat OR cook and refreeze.
Fish & Fish Products	Safe	Cook and eat immediately.	Do not refreeze. Cook and eat.
Vacuum packaged meat — lightly smoked or cured; bacon, ham, wieners	Safe	Safe	Do not refreeze. Cook and eat.
Vegetables	Safe	Safe	Do not refreeze. Cook immediately and eat OR cook and refreeze.
Vacuum packaged "boil in bag" vegetables	Safe	Remove from package — cook and eat immediately, OR remove from package, cook and refreeze.	Discard.
Bake 'n' Serve Bread, Rolls	Safe. Some rising power will be lost.	Safe. Bake, refreeze with minimum loss of quality.	Safe. At this stage over-proofing occurs. Punch down and knead, reshape and bake.
FROZEN PREPARED AND PRECOOKED FOODS			
Ready-to-eat frozen soups.	Safe	Discard.	Discard.
	Safe	Serve and eat immediately.	Discard.
Bakery Goods	Safe	Safe	Safe. Product becomes more stale if refrozen.
Meat Pies, TV Dinners, Ready-to-Eat Dishes	Safe	Safe	Do not refreeze. Heat immediately and eat.
Vacuum packaged meats e.g. Bologna, Luncheon Meats.	Safe	Do not refreeze. Use as quickly as possible.	Discard.
Vacuum packaged Main Dishes "Boil in bag"	Safe	Heat thoroughly without delay and eat.	Discard.

CHART NOTES:

1. *Any frozen food which is completely thawed and held at room temperature for an unknown period of time should be discarded.*

2. *The general rule "Do not refreeze" appears on most commercially frozen food packages and is the best advice since the safety of the food may be affected.*

3. *Take special care with vacuum-packaged foods. Any vacuum-packaged food product which has been improperly thawed should be discarded.*

BASIC STEPS FOR FREEZING FOOD

With thoughtful planning, selective buying and good management, a home freezer filled with frozen foods can mean more convenience in meal preparation; nutritious, delicious, attractive and varied meals all year round; and a greater saving of time, effort, and money. Here are the seven basic steps to successfully freezing food:

1. Select top quality foods.
2. Prepare quickly and work with small amounts.
3. Package with moisture-vapour-proof freezer wrappings and containers and be sure as much air as possible is excluded.
4. Label and date outside of package and include special instructions for thawing and cooking.
5. Freeze quickly and store at –20°C with as little temperature variation as possible. Use within recommended storage time.
6. Thaw properly and use as soon after thawing as possible.
7. Cook frozen foods carefully according to directions.

PACKAGING MATERIALS

Good packaging of the food to be frozen is essential to successful results. Because of the low temperature and low humidity in a freezer, foods will dry out if they are not well protected. Containers and wraps must be moisture-vapour-proof, odourless and tasteless. Most wraps may be re-used if washed and dried carefully.

Freezer Wrappings

Freezer wraps must be sufficiently flexible to withstand freezing temperatures without cracking. To prevent puncturing thin wrappings, an outer covering of plastic bag or heavy paper could be used.

FREEZER FOIL – This is especially good for irregular-shaped packages. Save odd-shaped pieces for padding bones and separating steaks, chops, and patties that are to be wrapped with freezer paper or stored in plastic bags. Lightweight household aluminum foil is not adequate as a freezer storage wrapping. Heavyweight freezer foil can be used successfully for the suggested storage times.

FREEZER PAPER – Suitable freezer paper has a plastic or wax coating. Ordinary uncoated brown paper and household waxed paper are not satisfactory. Freezer tape is used to seal the package.

PLASTIC WRAP – Household plastic films have not proven successful for storage for longer than a few days.

Freezer Containers

RIGID CONTAINERS – Many shapes and sizes are available. Square and rectangular containers take up less space than round ones. Those that are flat on both top and bottom are easier to stack. All should have wide tops so that the food can be removed while still frozen. Most common sizes are 250 ml and 500 ml. Choose sizes which will hold only enough of a fruit or vegetable for one meal for the family.

Plastic containers, waxed cardboard cartons and glass jars are all suitable for liquid or dry pack. Special care must be taken when using glass jars as there is always danger of breaking them. Leave room for expansion as liquid freezes, allowing 3 cm headspace in glass jars and 1-2 cm headspace in the other containers. Seal any loose fitting tops with freezer tape.

CARDBOARD BOXES – Boxes designed especially for freezer use are sold in several sizes. They usually come with inner liners or bags that are moisture-vapour resistant.

OTHER CONTAINERS – Many household containers are suitable for freezing. Cans with a shiny interior and a lid, ovenware dishes, clean milk cartons, biscuit tins, and other carefully washed reusable containers from the supermarket are all usable. Lids should be sealed on with freezer tape or masking tape. When a large size tin is being used, layers of the food such as cookies, slices, fudge, may be separated with foil or waxed or brown paper so that the desired amount can be taken out at a time.

Freezer Bags

Various sizes of bags made from plastic material are available. They may be purchased ready to use or accumulated by washing and saving reusable plastic bags. Freezer bags are good for packaging dry pack fruits and vegetables, prepared foods such as bread, cakes and cookies, and some cuts of meat. They are especially suitable for irregular shaped foods such as poultry.

As much air as possible should first be pressed out of the bag, then the top should be twisted several times, folded over into a loop and secured tightly with a metal closure. To prevent puncturing of the bag during long storage a protective covering of heavy paper may be used. For delicate items such as iced cakes, a cardboard box gives protection but must be overwrapped to make the package moisture- and vapour-proof.

WRAPPING FOODS FOR FREEZING

1. Use moisture-vapour-proof wrap or containers that can be sealed. The moisture-proof property protects the food from moisture loss while it is being frozen and allows the food to retain its natural moisture when subjected to the drying effects of a very low temperature. The vapour-proof property protects the flavour of the food and prevents other flavours and odours from mingling while in the freezer.

2. Wrap so as to exclude as much air as possible. Any air that is locked in the package when it is sealed dries the product and makes meat, for example, grey in colour. This is known as *freezer burn*. The section of meat that is freezer burnt, when cooked, will be tough and stringy and will have less flavour.

3. Label each package clearly with the name of the food and the date packaged. Include also where applicable, the cut, weight, method of preparation, type of pack and any details for cooking. Write on the freezer tape with pencil or crayon. Do not use felt tip marker pens as many of them use a kerosene or gasoline based ink which can penetrate the wrapping and cause "off" flavours during long term storage. Label see-through wrappings or containers because frost covers the package in time and prevents one seeing what is in it.

4. Wrapped packages should be compactly shaped in order to use freezer space to best advantage and tightly sealed with freezer tape or masking tape. These are the two best methods of wrapping for freezing:

Butcher Wrap

Be sure that packages wrapped this way, sometimes called flat-fold wrappings, are completely sealed with freezer tape and are moisture- and vapour-proof.

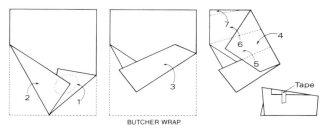

BUTCHER WRAP

Drug Store Wrap

The drugstore method of wrapping foods for freezing is best to use as it ensures the tightest possible closing. The food is placed in the centre of the wrapping paper and the two edges are brought together over the top of the food. The edges are folded over two or three times until the wrapping fits closely around the food, forming a tight seal and leaving as little air space as possible. The air should be forced out of the ends of the parcel by pressing the hand outward to the edges of the paper and folding the ends under it.

Metal foil need not be drugstore wrapped but simply shaped around the food.

DRUG STORE WRAP

FREEZING TIPS

1. When freezing cooked meat or poultry be sure to cover the product with gravy, broth or other liquid so that peak flavour and freshness will be retained. Remember storage life for these products is shorter than for the uncooked food.

2. For emergency meals that can be frozen quickly, use serving size casseroles or foil pans for freezing. Cover with plastic film or foil. Small or shallow ones can go right into the oven without thawing.

3. Freeze leftover chopped green pepper, onion, pimento, grated orange or lemon rind, etc., in labelled plastic film or foil pouches. These packages, being small and easily lost, could be stored in plastic containers or plastic bags.

4. When freezing large quantity casseroles it is better to put them in several smaller containers (1 litre - 2 litre) rather than one large one. Also, it is better if these containers are shallow. The finished casserole retains better flavour and consistency if you prepare and freeze it unbaked, then defrost and follow recipe instructions for baking. Print directions (oven temperature, time, etc.) on outside of frozen package.

5. Food that is bought for freezing (small amounts of meat, commercially prepared frozen food, bread, etc.) should be over wrapped or repackaged with moisture-vapour-proof wrappings as the commercial wrapping does not give it lasting protection.

6. When making freezer jam, freeze in small wax-coated drinking cups and seal with plastic film and freezer tape. After opening, storage time even in the refrigerator is limited.

FREEZING FRUIT

1.   Selection

Some varieties of fruit freeze better than others. Select mature, firm textured, unblemished fruit. Use a small amount at one time, work as quickly as possible, and handle carefully.

2.   Preparation

Blanch fruit only if necessary to remove skins of peaches and apricots. Washing fruit in ice water is preferred as it firms the fruit flesh.

3.   Packaging

There are three different types of pack. The method chosen will depend upon the type of fruit being frozen and the use planned for it.

DRY PACK – Freeze the dry fruit on a tray, then loose pack in plastic bags.

DRY SUGAR PACK – Mix fruit with dry sugar and pack in rigid containers leaving 2 cm headspace. Use approximately 500 ml sugar for 2 kilograms fruit.

SYRUP PACK — Pack fruit in rigid containers and cover with desired syrup leaving 2-4 cm headspace. Press light coloured fruit under syrup with crumpled wax paper, freezer wrap or aluminum foil. See Chart page 401 for preparation of syrup.

4.   Thawing and Serving

Thaw fruit in unopened container, inverting container several times to redistribute the juice. For best texture, serve while a few ice crystals remain. Allow these times for thawing:

- In the refrigerator, allow 6 hours per 500 millilitres.
- At room temperature, allow 3 hours per 500 millilitres.
- In warm tap water, allow one-half hour per 500 millilitres.

CHART FOR FREEZING FRUIT

FRUIT	PREPARATION	METHOD OF PACKING
Apple slices	Wash, peel and core firm, mature apples.	DRY PACK — * see directions in chart notes. SYRUP PACK — Place cold ascorbic acid treated syrup into rigid containers. Peel and core apples and slice directly into syrup. Press down, add syrup to cover and hold under with crumpled paper or foil.
Applesauce	Prepare and sweeten as desired.	Pack in rigid containers.
Apricots	Use firm, mature fruit. Wash. Blanch 30 seconds only to remove skins. Cut in halves or quarters and remove pit.	SYRUP PACK — Pack in rigid containers. Cover with ascorbic acid treated syrup. Crumple paper on top to hold fruit under syrup. DRY SUGAR PACK — Mix 2.5 ml ascorbic acid with 125 ml sugar. Sprinkle over 1 litre prepared fruit. Mix and pack.
Berries: Blueberries Raspberries Gooseberries	Use only ripe berries. Discard green or over-ripe berries. Wash in ice water.	DRY PACK — Suitable for pies. DRY SUGAR PACK — Use 125-200 ml sugar per litre of berries. SYRUP PACK — Pack in rigid containers, cover with desired syrup.
Berries: Strawberries	Use firm, fully ripe berries. Wash quickly in ice water, sort and hull. Slice, quarter or leave berries whole.	DRY SUGAR PACK — Use 125-250 ml sugar per litre berries. Pack in rigid containers. DRY PACK — Freeze single layer on tray then pack in plastic bags. Use for garnishes. SYRUP PACK — Pack in rigid containers, cover with desired syrup.
Berries: Currants Cranberries Saskatoons	Sort, stem and wash. Dry well.	DRY PACK — Freeze single layer on tray, then pack in plastic bags. DRY SUGAR PACK — Use 125-200 ml sugar per litre of berries.
Cherries, Sour (preferred)	Use firm, ripe cherries. Wash, stem and pit.	DRY SUGAR PACK — Use 250 ml sugar per litre fruit. Suitable for pies. SYRUP PACK — Use heavy syrup.
Cherries Sweet	Use firm, ripe cherries. Wash and stem. Pit if desired. (Pits add flavour).	SYRUP PACK — Use rigid containers and cover with ascorbic acid treated syrup. DRY SUGAR PACK; DRY PACK — Both suitable, depending upon use.
Fruit Juices	Choose firm, mature fruit. Extract juice as for jelly making.	Pack without sugar or sweeten to taste.
Fruit Purée and Sauces	If necessary, cook or steam fruits until soft in small amounts of water. Wash fruit, press through sieve or use blender.	Add sugar and/or lemon juice to taste. Chill. Pack into rigid containers.
Fruit Salad or Fruit Cocktail	Choose and prepare firm, fully ripe fruits; e.g., peaches, apples, cantaloup, red and green grapes.	SYRUP PACK — Use ascorbic acid treated light syrup to cover. Crumple paper on top to hold fruit under syrup.
Melon: Canteloup Honeydew Watermelon	Use only firm, fully ripe fruit. Cut in half; remove seeds and peel. Cut into slices, cubes or balls.	SYRUP PACK — Use light syrup adding 5 ml lemon juice to each 250 ml syrup OR Pack in fresh orange juice, pineapple juice or ginger ale.

CHART FOR FREEZING FRUIT *(continued)*

FRUIT	PREPARATION	METHOD OF PACKING
Pears	Canning pears is generally preferred. For freezing, wash, peel, halve and core. Work quickly to prevent discolouration.	SYRUP PACK — Quarter or slice into boiling heavy syrup. Simmer 1-2 minutes. Chill, then pack.
Peaches	Use firm, ripe peaches. Blanch 30-60 seconds in boiling water; cool in ice water. Remove skins and pits. Work quickly to prevent discolouration.	SYRUP PACK — Place cold ascorbic acid treated syrup into rigid containers. Cut halves or slices directly into syrup. Crumple paper on top to hold fruit under syrup. DRY SUGAR PACK — Mix 2 ml ascorbic acid with 150-200 ml sugar. Sprinkle over 1 litre sliced peaches.
Plums	Wash, cut in halves or cut fruit away from pit in quarters.	SYRUP PACK — Pack in rigid containers and cover with ascorbic acid treated syrup. Crumple paper on top to hold fruit under syrup.
Rhubarb	Use only early, tender stalks. Wash, trim and cut in 2-3 cm lengths OR make rhubarb sauce.	DRY PACK — good for pies. DRY SUGAR PACK — Use about 250 ml sugar per litre fruit. Sweeten sauce to taste and pack in rigid containers.

CHART NOTES:

1. FREEZING APPLE SLICES — *Drop peeled slices into a weak brine solution of 10 ml salt for 4 litres water. When 15-20 apples have been sliced, remove from brine and place in freshly prepared sulphite solution for 5 minutes.*

    Sulphite solution: Dissolve 5 ml sodium sulphite or sodium bisulphite in 4 litres water using an earthenware, stainless steel, glass or plastic container. Keep apples under solution with glass or china plate. This solution can be used to treat 4-5 lots of apples.

    After 5 minutes (carefully timed), remove slices to earthenware, stainless steel, glass or plastic bowl. Place bowl in refrigerator for 4-5 hours before packaging apples. Pack dry, using no sugar or syrup.

2. *Syrup for Canning and Freezing Fruit — See Chart page 401.*

3. ASCORBIC ACID TREATED SYRUP — *To the chosen syrup add 1 ml pure ascorbic acid for 250 ml syrup. This will help prevent darkening of light coloured fruits such as apples, apricots, cherries, peaches, pears and plums. Refer to page 402. in Home Canning for other suggestions for preventing discolouration.*

FREEZING VEGETABLES

There are several important steps, outlined below, which MUST BE FOLLOWED for the satisfactory home freezing of vegetables. Some varieties are better for freezing than others but all may be frozen safely.

1.   Selection

Use only tender, young unblemished vegetables. Pick early in the day and freeze as soon as possible after picking.

2. Preparation

Wash vegetables in cold water, then proceed as outlined in the chart. To remove insects that may be present in broccoli, brussels sprouts or cauliflower, soak prepared vegetable for 15 minutes in brine made of 10 ml salt per litre of water.

3. Blanching

Blanch all vegetables except peppers, onions and herbs to inactivate the enzymes. If this is not done the vegetables will develop "off" flavours and toughen in storage. Work with small quantities – no more than 500 grams at a time.

a.   WATER BLANCHING is the most common method although a few vegetables are better when blanched in steam. Place vegetables in a wire basket, colander or loose cheesecloth bag and submerge in a large kettle of rapidly boiling, unsalted water – at least 2 litres. Cover and time accurately from the time the vegetables are added. Keep heat on high so that water will quickly return to the boil. Underblanching or overblanching by a minute or two can make a serious difference in the quality of the frozen vegetable. Keep vegetables moving to ensure even blanching.

b.   STEAM BLANCHING. Extreme care should be used to ensure even penetration of steam. Steam blanching is preferred for French cut green beans, finely chopped or diced vegetables. DO NOT use this method for spinach or other greens. Times should be increased $1\frac{1}{2}$ times over water blanching.

Place 3 cm unsalted water in a large kettle and bring to rolling boil. Place a thin layer of vegetables in a wire basket, colander or loose cheesecloth bag and suspend over water. Cover and time accurately from the time vegetables are added.

4. Chilling

Chill vegetables immediately and thoroughly by placing them in a large container of ice water or cold running water. Cool to centre – break one open to test. Chilling time should be at **least as long** as blanching time but vegetables should not remain in cooling water any longer than necessary. Drain thoroughly.

5. Packaging

Place in a rigid container or moisture-vapour proof bag and seal. Label packages and place in freezer as soon as possible after packaging. Do not allow to stand at room temperature. For loose pack – pat vegetables dry, spread on a tray and freeze 1-2 hours. When solid, remove from freezer and package quickly.

COOKING AND SERVING FROZEN VEGETABLES

The secret of cooking and serving frozen vegetables successfully is to cook the vegetables until they are just tender and to serve them as soon as they are done. This not only saves the vitamins but also helps the vegetables to keep their bright colour and fresh flavour. Almost all frozen vegetables have been partially precooked during blanching and the freezing process softens the tissues still further, so care must be taken to avoid overcooking.

In general, frozen vegetables are cooked by the same methods as fresh vegetables except that the frozen require only one-third to one-half the time.

Serve cooked frozen vegetables in the same ways as fresh vegetables. Season them with butter, herbs, or spices; put two or three together; use them in soufflés, fritters, timbales, casserole dishes, soups and salads.

Thawing

Cook most vegetables without thawing. Thawed vegetables should be cooked immediately. Vegetables requiring partial or complete thawing should be thawed in the original sealed package. Frozen asparagus and broccoli may be thawed just enough to break the stalks apart. Thaw spinach sufficiently to break apart or cut frozen block in 2.5 cm cubes; for ease in handling, thaw peppers for stuffing and baking.

Cooking Methods

1. PAN SAUTÉ – This method is especially suited to loose pack or partially thawed solid pack vegetables. For each cup of vegetables to be cooked, melt 15 ml butter or margarine in a heavy skillet or saucepan having a tight fitting lid. Add 1 ml each of salt, sugar and monosodium glutamate. Add frozen vegetables and toss until coated with butter. Cover tightly – DO NOT add water. Cook over medium heat a few minutes, reduce heat and cook slowly until vegetable is just tender.

2. BOIL – Use a saucepan with tight fitting lid. Use only enough water to supply steam and prevent scorching, adding extra boiling water if necessary. For 500 ml of vegetable use 50 to 125 ml boiling water and 2 ml salt. Add vegetables, cover saucepan and bring to boil. As soon as vegetables are partially thawed, break apart with a fork to allow all parts to cook evenly. As soon as water returns to the boil begin counting cooking time, then reduce heat and cook gently until vegetables are just tender.

3. BAKE – Place frozen vegetables in buttered casserole. Season and dot with butter. Add no water or only enough to prevent sticking. Cover tightly and bake in a moderate oven until vegetables are just tender.

4. PRESSURE COOK – Partially thaw vegetables, if necessary, to separate pieces, then follow directions in cook book supplied with pressure saucepan. Even with careful timing it is difficult to pressure cook frozen vegetables without overcooking.

CHART FOR FREEZING VEGETABLES

VEGETABLE	PREPARATION	BLANCHING AND CHILLING	COOKING
Asparagus	Use only young, tender stalks. Break off woody ends.	Water blanch: 3-4 minutes Chill: 3-4 minutes	3-5 minutes
Beans (wax or green)	Trim ends, string if necessary. French cut or cut in 3 cm lengths.	Water Blanch: 3 minutes Chill: 3 minutes	5-7 minutes or 3-4 minutes if French cut.
Beans (lima)	Use well filled, bright green pods. Shell, discarding white or cracked beans.	Water blanch: 2-4 minutes Chill: 2-4 minutes	7-15 minutes
Beans (broad)	Use only plump, fresh pods. Shell.	Water blanch: 2-3 minutes Chill: 2-3 minutes	3-5 minutes
Beets	Cook until tender. Chill. Rub off skins. Slice or dice.	Steam blanch: 4-6 minutes Chill: 4-6 minutes	3-5 minutes or until heated.
Broccoli	Use only tender head and stalk. Cut in pieces not thicker than 2 cm. Soak 30 minutes in salted water Drain and rinse.	Water blanch: 4 minutes Chill: 4 minutes	Thaw slightly, then 1-3 minutes
Brussels Sprouts	Use only firm, dark green sprouts. Soak 30 minutes in salted water. Drain and rinse.	Water blanch: 4 minutes Chill: 4 minutes	4-6 minutes
Carrots	Use only young, small carrots. Remove tops and scrape. Cut in slices, strips or leave whole.	Water blanch: 3-5 minutes Chill: 3-5 minutes	6-8 minutes
Cauliflower	Break into flowerets 3 cm in diameter. Wash thoroughly. Soak 30 minutes in salted water. Drain and rinse.	Water blanch: 3 minutes (add 5 ml lemon juice to 1 litre blanching water) Chill: 3 minutes. Freeze loose pack.	3-4 minutes or until tender.
Corn (on cob)	Pick in early morning. Husk and process as soon as possible. Work with only 6-12 cobs at once. Test for maturity: press thumbnail into kernel — milk should spurt freely.	Water blanch: 5-11 minutes Chill: 10-15 minutes or until cob is chilled through.	Cover frozen cobs with cold water. Bring to boil rapidly. Boil 3-5 minutes.
Corn (kernel)	Pick and test as for corn on cob.	Blanch and chill on cob. Cut off kernels with sharp knife and scrape cob to remove remainder.	Use a small amount of water or pan sauté 4-5 minutes.
Herbs — chives, parsley, dill, marjoram, mint, and thyme.	Pick before plant blooms. Wash and shake or pat dry. Chop chives, mint and parsley.	Do not blanch. Spread on trays and freeze 1-2 hours. Use loose pack.	Add frozen herbs to soups, sauces, meat during cooking.
Mixed vegetables	Prepare according to instructions for individual vegetables.	Blanch and chill each vegetable separately. Spread on trays, freeze 1-2 hours. Mix and use loose pack.	6-8 minutes

CHART FOR FREEZING VEGETABLES *(continued)*

VEGETABLE	PREPARATION	BLANCHING AND CHILLING	COOKING
Mushrooms	Wash, cut off base of stem. Slice if large, leave small ones whole. Sauté in butter for 4 minutes. Chill quickly, package with any remaining butter and freeze.	—	Sauté — no more butter needed — or thaw and use in cooked dishes.
Onions	Peel and chop.	Do not blanch. Package in small amounts or loose pack.	Add to stews, sauces and casseroles. Keeps well 2 months.
Parsnips	Use only firm, straight small parsnips. Trim off stem and root ends. Wash. Cut in slices or fingers.	Water blanch: 1 minute	6-8 minutes
Peas	Use only young, tender peas. Shell. Discard old or immature peas.	Water blanch: 2-3 minutes Chill 2-3 minutes	3-5 minutes
Peppers — red, green or pimento	Wash, remove seeds and pulp. Slice or dice. Freeze extra canned pimento also.	Do not blanch. Package in small amounts or loose pack.	Add to dishes which will be cooked.
Potatoes	See separate chart.		
Pumpkin, Squash — winter varieties	Use only mature pumpkin with dry pulp. Cut and remove seeds.	Bake or steam until tender. Chill: Remove pulp and mash or sieve.	Reheat in double boiler or over low heat. For pies — thaw and use as fresh or canned.
Squash — summer varieties	These are acceptable after freezing but difficult to prepare without overcooking. Use only small squash with tender rind and small seeds. Cut into slices 2-4 cm thick.	Water blanch: 3-6 minutes Chill: 3-6 minutes	Reheat in butter or in double boiler.
Spinach, Beet Greens, Chard	Use only young, tender leaves. Pick over well, remove tough ends. Wash thoroughly.	Water blanch ONLY: 2 minutes. Chill: 2-3 minutes. Agitate basket constantly so leaves will not mat.	Thaw slightly, then 3-4 minutes.
Tomatoes	Peel and stew. (Uncooked tomato pulp may be frozen and stored for a few months.)	Chill: Season if desired.	Thaw and use in cooked dishes.

CHART NOTES:

1. *These vegetables do not freeze well: whole beets, cucumbers, celery, eggplant, lettuce, whole onions, whole tomatoes, unpeeled Hubbard squash.*
2. *Blanching times vary with the size and maturity of vegetables. Use shortest time for smallest size vegetable of that type; longest time for larger or more mature one; e.g., small corn cobs, 5 minutes; large or mature cobs, 11 minutes; medium ones, 8 minutes.*
3. *Cooking times are approximate and counted from the moment the water returns to the boil after the vegetable is added. The time needed will be affected by the variety, maturity, method of preparation, size of pieces, etc. Pan sautéing is a good method for many frozen vegetables.*

FREEZING POTATOES

POTATOES	PREPARATION	THAWING AND SERVING
Baked and Stuffed*	Bake, stuff and cool. Freeze on tray, then package in plastic freezer bags or wrap individually in foil.	Open foil, bake unthawed at 200°C for 30-45 minutes or until heated and brown.
Mashed*	Pack into foil lined casserole or form into patties; freeze on a tray, then package.	Reheat foil liner in original container in oven. Broil or bake patties.
Sweet	Bake and mash. Shape into logs or patties, freeze on tray then package.	Broil or bake.
French Fries, Cooked	Peel, cut and scald for 1-2 minutes. Pat dry, deep fry at 160°C until tender, but not brown. Drain and cool. Freeze loose.	Heat and brown from frozen state in the broiler; in the oven at 200°C; in a single layer in electric frypan or deep fry.

*NOTE: * The addition of a fat source such as butter, cream or cheese will improve the quality of the finished products.*

FREEZING MEAT

Selection

Beef, pork, lamb and veal can all be frozen successfully. All meat for freezing should be of good quality. No food will improve with freezing. Most meat cuts selected in the supermarket can be frozen, provided they are fresh and a suitable wrapping is used.

Careful slaughtering and handling of the meat is especially important when it is to be frozen. Home raised meat should be thoroughly chilled in the carcass for at least 24 hours before freezing. Unless you are experienced at butchering, it is best to have it cut by an expert.

Preparation

Boneless meat requires less space in the freezer and takes less freezer wrap. Therefore, it is good procedure to have as many bones as possible removed before wrapping. The bones can be frozen in plastic bags to use later for soup or they can be made into soup stock which can then be frozen in rigid containers.

Prepare the meat in cuts of a size and weight to suit the needs of your family. When buying a large portion of meat to store in the freezer (side, quarter, freezer pack) be sure to tell the butcher exactly how you want it cut and wrapped. Only if this is done can you expect to get the cuts you want and the size of packages that are most suitable. The butcher will want to know:

- thickness to cut steaks
- number of steaks or chops per package (wrapping steaks individually is preferred)
- mass per package of ground meat

- mass per package of stew meat
- size to cut oven roasts
- size and number of pot roasts

Some parts of the animal can be cut several different ways and your preferences should be stated. For example, the rib section of a side of beef can be cut into rib steaks, standing rib roasts, or can be boned and rolled into a roast suitable for the rotisserie. Short ribs can be boned and the meat ground if your family does not enjoy them braised. Brisket meat can be rolled to form a pot roast, cut into stew meat, or ground. There are many other alternatives.

Packaging

Use recommended freezer wrap only and package carefully to exclude as much air as possible. Drug store or butcher's method of wrapping are both suitable if packages are taped securely.

Package steaks, chops and meat patties in freezer wrap or plastic bags with folded pieces of freezer wrap placed between the layers so that they can be separated easily while still frozen. For short term storage hamburger patties can be placed on a tray, frozen, and then packaged in plastic freezer bags. Thin or small pieces of meat have a tendency to dry out when stored for several months.

When packaging meat with bones, cover sharp bones with small pieces of crumpled aluminum foil to prevent puncturing the outer wrap. Omit salt when packaging all ground meat as it tends to hasten rancidity. Leftover meat should be sliced and covered with gravy or made into a casserole to retain its natural moisture and flavour.

It is important to mark on each package the kind of meat, name of cut, weight and date so that no meat will be kept longer than the recommended storage time. See chart page 430 for freezer life of meat.

Thawing

Most meats can be cooked frozen or thawed depending upon the cut, time available, and the end result desired. Cooking time is easier to judge for defrosted meat. Steaks and chops that have been thawed first will brown more readily than those cooked from the frozen state. When meats such as liver or cutlets are to be breaded or floured, the coating will adhere more easily if the meat is at least partially thawed. Meat to be stuffed or deep fried must also be thawed. Variety meats, cured and smoked pork, sausages and bacon may be partially or completely thawed before cooking.

Roasts can easily be cooked from the frozen state. The cooking time will be longer and the meat may be less evenly cooked. In the case of roast beef, which many people prefer rare, cooking from the frozen state works very well.

For best results and the least juice loss, defrost all meat in the original wrap, in the refrigerator. Thawing times vary with the size, thickness and shape of package. For a 5 kg package allow approximately 12 hours in the refrigerator OR 2-3 hours at room temperature.

To reduce thawing time at room temperature, direct the air current of an electric fan onto the package of frozen meat. Steaks and chops can be thawed quickly in an oven heated to 65°C but they must be cooked immediately after thawing. Frozen cooked meat can be thawed and heated over hot water. It is important to remember that any method which reduces the time required to thaw meat also interferes with the quality of the meat when cooked.

Do not refreeze meat that has been completely thawed. Cook it promptly to prevent spoilage. Fresh or thawed meat, may be frozen after cooking and stored for a short period in the same way as other leftover cooked meats. If meat has only partly thawed, it can be refrozen without risk. See charts pages 431 and 432.

Cooking

Thawed meat can be cooked in the same way and for the same time as fresh meat taken from the refrigerator.

For frozen meat the cooking time must be increased to allow for thawing. The amount of time to increase will depend upon the thickness, size and shape of the meat being cooked.

Frozen roasts require approximately one and one half times the time required for fresh roasts. A meat thermometer is recommended as a sure way of determining the cooking stage reached. It can be inserted as soon as the meat has thawed sufficiently.

FREEZING POULTRY

1. **Wrapping**

    NEVER FREEZE STUFFED POULTRY — store stuffing separately. Commercially stuffed frozen poultry is prepared by experts under strict sanitary conditions that cannot be duplicated in the home. Prepare poultry and package it so it will be ready to cook when removed from freezer. Package giblets and freeze separately. Cut up poultry is easier to wrap and takes up less space in the freezer.

    Put a whole bird in a freezer plastic bag and lower it 3/4 way into hot, *not boiling* water. The water will collapse the plastic firmly around the bird and expel the air — don't let any water get into the bag. Twist top and make tight closure.

    Place whole bird or pieces on freezer wrap — pad bony and protruding parts if using foil. Use drug store fold to wrap and gently press wrap down to expel air. Seal by folding ends tightly, using freezer tape if necessary.

Always check the wrap on commercially frozen birds. Overwrap if torn or ripped.

2. Thawing

Broilers and poultry for frying, braising or stewing can be cooked when defrosted enough to separate the pieces. Frozen food research has suggested that a good way to defrost a whole bird is in the unopened freezer wrap, immersed in cold water. Allow approximately 2 hours per kilogram. The approved method of thawing poultry is in the refrigerator, allowing 10-12 hours per kilogram. Slit the freezer wrap over the vent.

NOTE: Darkened bones — young birds from the freezer may have this discolouration, which is caused by seepage of haemoglobin from the marrow during freezing and thawing. It has absolutely no effect on the flavour and quality.

3. Cooking

Cook thawed poultry immediately, or hold in the refrigerator and cook within 24 hours. Whole birds should be completely thawed for uniform cooking. Cook as you would fresh poultry, allowing more time for poultry still frozen.

FREEZING GAME ANIMALS

Spoilage of game animals occurs rapidly, especially in the muscles torn and bruised by bullets. Warm temperatures during transportation and storage will speed this process. Prompt cleaning and thorough chilling is essential to preserve the good flavour of game meat. The section on Game has specific details on how to care for this meat.

Small game such as rabbits and squirrels are first eviscerated, then chilled, washed and cut into serving sized pieces. Generally only the thick back and hind quarters are frozen. Suitable packaging is the same as for cut-up poultry.

Larger game such as deer, elk, moose and bear should be prepared, cut and packaged in the same way as beef or veal. Careful trimming and removal of excess fat is recommended.

FREEZING GAME BIRDS

Prompt attention by the hunter to important details will ensure a tasty meal. These are the steps:

1. Bleed the birds immediately.
2. Allow to chill quickly in the open air before placing together in a hunting bag.

3. Pluck and draw game birds as you would domestic poultry. (Because they feed on strongly flavoured water plants, ducks especially require immediate care.)

4. Remove all the shot that can be located.

5. After most of the feathers are off, dip or roll the birds in melted paraffin to remove pinfeathers and down.

6. Wrap game birds in moisture-vapour-proof materials in the same way as domestic poultry.

7. Label and freeze promptly.

FREEZING FISH

1. **Selection**
    Freeze only freshly caught fish, keep fish chilled and work quickly.

2. **Preparation**
    Fish should be prepared and ready to cook before freezing. To reduce leakage when thawed, immerse steaks and fillets of lean fish in a cold salt solution for 20 seconds, (125 ml salt in 1 litre water). Oily fish (trout, salmon and mackerel) can be kept in frozen storage longer if dipped for 1 minute into a solution of 7 ml ascorbic acid in 1 litre cold water. Smoked fish should be frozen and stored as fresh.

3. **Packaging**
    Fish tends to dry out quickly in frozen storage so protect it with the best moisture-vapour-proof containers and wraps. Place a double thickness of freezer paper between each fillet or steak so they can be separated before being completely thawed. Pack small whole fish in fully waxed or plasticized containers or milk cartons, fill container with water, freeze and seal. Glaze a whole fish with water by first freezing it unwrapped, then dipping quickly in water chilled to just about the freezing point (or spoon water over), to form a film of ice. Repeat as many times as necessary to make glaze 0.25 cm thick. Seal in a plastic bag or moisture-vapour-proof paper. Label and date packages — use within 4 weeks to 6 months.

4. **Thawing**
    The most satisfactory way is to defrost the unopened package slowly in the refrigerator. A glazed fish should be defrosted under a slow stream of cold water.
    A 500 g package of frozen fish will thaw in:
    8-10 hours in the refrigerator.
    4 hours at room temperature.
    3 hours in front of a fan.

5. Cooking

Cook while frozen or as soon as defrosted.

Use a high oven temperature for baking (250°C) allowing:

5 minutes for 1 cm thickness of thawed fish.

10 minutes for 1 cm thickness of frozen fish.

Allow same times for frying, broiling or steaming.

FREEZING SHELLFISH

Selection

Freeze only strictly fresh shellfish.

Preparation

For preparation steps refer to section on Shellfish.

Packaging

CLAMS	Pack rinsed shucked clams in rigid containers and cover with clam liquid (or brine made with 15 ml salt each litre water). Allow 2 cm headspace. Freeze immediately.
CRAB	After crab is cooked, crack and pick meat from shells. Package immediately in amounts to be used at one time. Allow 2 cm headspace. Add 0.5 cm cold water or brine (15 ml salt each litre water). Put container top on securely, turn upside down and freeze at once. The water will form a seal. When the crab is frozen the container can be turned right side up.
LOBSTER	Proceed as for crab.
OYSTERS	Pack rinsed oysters in rigid containers and cover with strained oyster liquid or brine (15 ml salt each litre water). Freeze immediately.
SHRIMP AND PRAWNS	After cooking, rinse, drain and package in freezer containers as you would crab. Shrimp and prawns can be frozen raw as well. Leave whole or remove heads, package in heavy, shallow cardboard boxes that have been lined with freezer paper to prevent leaking.

Thawing

Thaw completely for use in seafood cocktails or salads, but only enough to separate the pieces for use in cooked dishes. Turn container over several times during thawing, to distribute moisture. To thaw a 500 g package allow approximately:

8 hours in the refrigerator.

3 hours at room temperature.

½ hour in cold water.

Cooking

Cook or use shellfish as soon as defrosted in the same way as you would fresh shellfish.

FREEZING BAKED GOODS

Baked products in the freezer provide real convenience and often both time and money can be saved by advance preparation. For most efficient use of the freezer, baked goods should be kept moving. Refer to the Optimum Freezer Storage Chart for recommended storage times. Those kept longer will lose colour and flavour but will not necessarily become dangerous.

1. **Preparation**

   Bake yeast breads, rolls, biscuits, muffins, cakes, cookies in the usual way. Cool thoroughly before wrapping. Macaroons and meringues do not freeze well. Freeze cakes uniced unless the icing is one that will freeze well. Pies are most successfully frozen unbaked. Do not make slits in crust before freezing a two crust pie. For fruit pies to be frozen, add 1/3 more thickener. Cornstarch or tapioca thickened pies freeze successfully. Pastry may be frozen in bulk, rolled into circles, or as a pie shell, cooked or uncooked.

2. **Wrapping**

   To prevent damage during storage, cakes and cookies may be placed in a cardboard box, then over-wrapped with freezer paper. Pies can be protected by an inverted pie plate or a cardboard collar before wrapping. An iced cake can be frozen on a tray before wrapping. Small baked goods may be separated with foil or wax paper where applicable.

3. **Thawing**

   Unless baked goods are to be heated for serving ALWAYS THAW IN FREEZER WRAPPING to avoid moisture condensing on the surface. Waffles, pancakes, and sliced bread may be thawed in a toaster. To give freshness to bread, rolls, muffins or biscuits thawed at room temperature, heat them on a baking sheet for 5-15 minutes at 150°C just before serving. Do not heat waxed or plastic wrappings or bags, as they will melt.

APPROXIMATE THAWING TIMES

FOOD	AT ROOM TEMPERATURE	IN 150°C OVEN
Yeast Breads, Rolls	1-2 hours	15-30 minutes
Muffins, Biscuits	1 hour	15-20 minutes
Cakes, not iced (depending on size)	1-3 hours	15-20 minutes
Cakes, iced	2-3 hours	—
Cookies	15-30 minutes	—
Cookie and Pastry Dough	1 hour	—
Waffles, Pancakes	—	5-10 minutes

CHART FOR FREEZING BAKED GOODS

BAKED GOODS	PREPARATION	THAWING & SERVING
Quick Breads — Biscuits, Muffins, Pancakes, Waffles, Fruit & Nut Bread	Do not overbrown. Cool.	Thaw wrapped loaves at room temperature. Place unwrapped frozen waffles, biscuits, etc., in toaster or 150°C oven.
Yeast Breads — Bread, Rolls, Doughnuts	Always overwrap commercially wrapped bread and rolls.	Thaw wrapped at room temperature. Frozen bread slices may be toasted.
"Brown 'n Serve" Rolls	Bake at 150°C for 25 minutes until partially baked but not brown. Cool. Overwrap commercial Brown 'n Serve" rolls.	Thaw in wrapping at room temperature. Unwrap, heat and brown in 200°C oven 7-10 minutes.
Cakes — not iced — iced	Let fruit cakes ripen 6 weeks. Use a butter or fudge frosting only. Almond paste freezes — Royal icing doesn't. Freeze on a tray 1-2 hours, then wrap.	Thaw wrapped. 1-2 hours for most cakes. 6-8 hours for fruit cake. Thaw wrapped 1-2 hours.
Cookies — Baked (also squares and bars) Unbaked	Form into roll or leave in bulk.	Thaw wrapped 30-60 minutes. Thaw just enough to slice or shape.
Cream Puffs — Éclairs	Package unfilled.	Thaw while wrapped, or recrisp in 160°C oven for 15 minutes. Cool before filling.
Desserts — Baked Alaska Tortes	Freeze on serving plate or foil covered board. Note: Store 1 day only!	Remove from freezer 10-20 minutes before serving.
Steamed	Steam as usual. Cool	Thaw wrapped for 6 hours then steam to heat through.
Toppings, Oatmeal, etc. Hard sauce	Freeze in rigid containers.	Spread unfrozen over prepared fruit. Bake. Thaw covered in the refrigerator.
Pastry — Unbaked	Leave in bulk or roll, shape and cut. Separate crusts with wax paper, and freeze flat or roll around foil covered tube before wrapping.	Thaw wrapped, until pliable.
— Baked		Thaw covered 20-30 minutes before filling.
Pies — Fruit — unbaked	Use cornstarch or tapioca for thickening. Increase thickening by ⅓ to absorb extra juice created by freezing.	Remove wrapping. Cut vents in top crust. Bake unthawed at 200°C 45-60 minutes.
— baked		Thaw completely in wrapping or unwrap and heat frozen pie in 160°C oven 30-40 minutes.
Cream and Custard Chiffon	Freezing not recommended. Use a recipe calling for beaten egg white or whipping cream.	Thaw unwrapped at room temperature 1 hour.
Sausage Rolls	Bake as usual and cool.	Leave wrapped until thawed, then heat. Or place frozen rolls in slow oven to thaw and heat.

HOW TO FREEZE DAIRY PRODUCTS

DAIRY PRODUCT	PREPARATION AND SERVING	STORAGE TIME AT −20°C
Butter —		
Salted	Over-wrap in foil or place in freezer bag.	1-3 months
Unsalted	Over-wrap in foil or place in freezer bag.	3-6 months (Does not keep long after thawing.)
Buttermilk	Freeze in original carton or rigid container, leaving 3 cm headspace. Use only for cooking.	3-4 weeks
Cheese —		
Blue or Roquefort	Package in small quantities. May be crumbly when thawed.	6 months
Cottage (creamed)	Do not freeze — becomes watery and grainy.	
Cottage (dry curd)	Add cream when serving.	6 months
Camembert, Cheddar, Mozarella, Parmesan, Swiss	Freeze in small quantities — 250 g pieces not more than 3 cm thick.	6 months
Cream —		
Whipping	Freeze in small quantities in rigid containers leaving headspace. Thaw in refrigerator. It will whip very quickly and may be slightly grainy.	1-2 months
Sweetened — Whipped	Place small mounds on tray in freezer. When frozen, package in rigid container, separating layers with waxed paper.	2 weeks
Commercial Sour	Becomes grainy when frozen but can be whipped smooth when defrosted and used in cooking.	1-2 months
Eggs —		
Whole	Mix yolks and whites together thoroughly but without beating in any air. To each 500 ml of eggs add 15 ml sugar or light corn syrup or 5 ml salt, depending on end use. Package in recipe quantities.	6-8 months
Whites	Do not need special treatment. Package in recipe quantities.	8-11 months
Yolks	Prepare as whole eggs.	6-8 months
Ice Cream and Sherbet	Over-wrap in foil. After opening package fit a piece of freezer paper snugly over remaining ice cream.	1-3 months
Milk Homogenized	Freeze in original carton or rigid container, leaving 3 cm headspace. Use for cooking.	3-4 weeks

Sanitation

Food-Borne Illnesses

People involved in the preparation and service of food need to be aware of the factors which contribute to the wholesomeness of the foods they are offering for consumption. Food-borne illness, more commonly known as food poisoning, affects thousands of Canadians each year. Occasionally it results in death but most often symptoms range from mild nausea and discomfort to violent fits of vomiting, cramps and diarrhoea.

Good sanitary practices on the part of any persons handling or preparing food will greatly minimize the incidence of food spoilage or contamination. Personal cleanliness, frequent washing of hands with soap and hot water, thorough washing of equipment and work surfaces are essential.

Bacterial food poisoning agents multiply most rapidly in temperatures between 5°C and 40°C. Temperatures between 5°C and 60°C are considered to be the DANGER ZONE. Therefore, it is extremely important to keep foods out of this range to prevent bacterial growth. Here is a temperature guideline for food handlers:

Home canning	115°C to 137°C
Cooking	75°C
Warm Holding	60°C
DANGER ZONE	5°C to 60°C
Refrigeration	2°C to 5°C
Frozen Storage	−15°C to −20°C

TYPES OF FOOD-BORNE ILLNESSES

The chart "Bacterial Food Poisoning" summarizes the most prevalent types of food poisoning. While most of the bacteria of our environment are beneficial or harmless, these few strains can cause food poisoning and other illnesses. The bacteria which cause food-borne illness are frequently divided into two categories; those which produce toxins and those which do not.

1. Toxinogenic organisms are themselves quite harmless when eaten in moderate amounts. Their danger lies in the toxins which they produce. Some toxins can be destroyed by adequate cooking while others are stable even over extended periods of high temperature.

2. Infectious food poisoning organisms cause illness when the live bacteria enter the digestive system in contaminated food. Usually the organism multiplies rapidly in the ideal conditions which explains the explosive nature of the illness. Most of the infectious type of food poison organisms can be controlled by adequate cooking and refrigeration.

Other causes of food-borne illnesses should also be mentioned. Some foods are contaminated by coughing or sneezing of food handlers. Diphtheria can be passed this way. Rats, mice, roaches and flies are frequently carriers of disease and germs and they must, therefore, be carefully controlled. Some diseases such as dysentery and typhoid fever can be traced to water which was contaminated at the source. Improper washing of hands and/or work surfaces and implements are found so often to be the cause of illness that it deserves frequent repeating.

Animal parasites or "worms" sometimes cause diseases of which the most familiar one is Trichinella spiralis. The larvae of this parasite, when consumed in meat (principally pork) can cause a disease known as trichinosis in humans. Government inspection does not involve a method of detecting the trichinae parasite so that pork cannot be assumed to be free of it. Practically speaking, trichinosis presents less of a problem than would be expected.

1. Hogs can contract this disease by eating uncooked garbage. New methods of feeding to produce a leaner high grade pork have discouraged this practice. However, "home grown pork" from hogs fed scraps presents a definite possibility of the disease.

2. Humans can contract the disease by eating raw, inadequately cooked, or improperly cooked meat. Improved production techniques for pork have reduced its incidence.

3. The trichinae parasite is killed by freezing as well as by adequate cooking. (An internal temperature of 85°C is recommended for fresh pork.)

Another type of poisoning has been discussed in the section on Fish and Shellfish. See page 265 for Paralytic Shellfish Poisoning.

Certain chemicals can be harmful to humans and much research is continuing in this field, especially in the area of pesticides and insecticides. The Health Protection Branch of Health and Welfare Canada can provide up-to-date information.

BACTERIAL FOOD POISONING

DISEASE[1]	FOOD POISONING AGENT	TOXICITY FREQUENCY	SYMPTOMS AND DURATION	NATURAL HABITAT FOODS INVOLVED
Botulism	Clostridium botulinum (an anaerobic bacteria which produces a heat labile toxin) [2]	rarest; death is frequent mortality rate: at least 50%	Symptoms appear 12-72 hours after eating food. Nervous system is affected, double vision occurs, then paralysis and/ or death. Recovery is slow.	Found in most soils. Foods affected are home canned or commercial canned vegetables, fish, shellfish and meats, that have been insufficiently processed.
Staphylococcal [1] food poisoning	Staphylococcus aureus (produces a heat stable toxin) [2]	most common; death is rare	Symptoms appear 1-6 hours after eating and last for 1 day. Symptoms include cramps, nausea, vomiting, diarrhoea.	Found in the nose and throat of most people. Foods affected are baked ham, roast, poultry, meat or potato salads, fish and cream desserts.
Perfringens food poisoning	Clostridium perfringens	very common; death is rare	Symptoms of diarrhoea and cramps begin 8-24 hours after eating and last for 8 hours.	Found everywhere especially in gut of animals. Foods affected are meats, gravies.
Salmonellosis	Salmonella	very common; occasional death among aged, infants, infirm	Symptoms of cramps, chills, fever, vomiting, diarrhoea may begin 5-72 hours after eating. They usually continue 2-3 days but may last for weeks.	Found in the gut of domestic animals especially chickens. Foods affected are poultry, meat, eggs and egg products.
Shigella poisoning	Shigella	uncommon; death unknown	Cramps and diarrhoea may begin 7-72 hours after eating and last for 12 hours to 1 week.	Found in sewage-contaminated water. Foods affected are milk, ice cream.
E. coli poisoning	Esherichia coli	uncommon; death unknown	Cramps, diarrhoea and vomiting may begin 6-48 hours after eating and last for 12 hours to 1 week.	Found in sewage-contaminated water. Foods include shellfish.

CHART NOTES

1. *Botulism and Staphylococcal food poisoning are caused by the toxins produced by the respective bacteria. The other types of food poisoning listed are caused by the bacteria which grow in the affected food and are able to infect the person eating it.*

2. *Heat labile means that the toxin will be destroyed by adequate cooking. Heat stable toxins are especially dangerous because once formed, even extended cooking at high temperature will not destroy them.*

CONTROLLING FOOD-BORNE ILLNESSES

Sanitary handling practices and carefully controlled temperatures are the most important safeguards against food-borne illness. (See page 455 for more information.) To understand the principles of prevention the following points are also recommended:

1. Bacteria that can cause food poisoning or other food-borne illness are everywhere – in the house, on raw foods, on counter tops and on your hands, your nose or in your hair.
2. To produce food-borne illness, bacteria must be given the opportunity to multiply to a great number.
3. Given the right food (milk, meat, eggs) and the right temperature (see page 455) bacteria will grow very rapidly and within a few hours reach a dangerous level.

Ways to Prevent Food Poisoning

1. Buy from reputable dealers. Patronize only clean stores.
2. Keep hot food hot (60°C or higher), cold food cold (5°C or lower.)
3. Remember that vacuum-packaged meat is perishable and must be kept refrigerated. Check expiry date stamped on the package.
4. Do not buy foods which ought to be frozen but which are thawed.
5. After marketing, place frozen foods in the freezer compartment of your refrigerator or in a deep freeze unit until ready for use.
6. Frozen foods that are completely thawed or have been held at refrigerator temperature more than 1 or 2 days should not be refrozen.
7. Heat pre-cooked commercially frozen foods for the time and temperature recommended on the labels. Read the labels.
8. Foods as salads with dressing, milk products, gravy and all proteins, are an ideal growth medium for bacteria and must be refrigerated.
9. Refrigerate "left-overs" within an hour and keep refrigerated until re-serving or re-heating. Store left-over poultry and stuffing separately.
10. Do not prepare foods to be served cold (sandwiches, picnic dishes, buffet luncheons) more than four hours ahead unless you refrigerate the foods.
11. Avoid handling food if you have an infected cut, a cold or a cough.
12. Ready-to-eat barbecue chicken should be bought piping hot and kept hot or refrigerated until serving time.
13. If canning foods at home: always use a pressure-canner with accurate gauge for non-acid foods such as meat, fish, meat-vegetable mixtures, soups and vegetables.
14. Do not taste foods from bulging or leaking cans, or cans whose contents spurt out or are bubbly, off-colour or bad-smelling. Do not eat foods that have an "off" flavour.
15. Keep everything about your kitchen clean.

Part 4

Recipes

Sauces

PROPORTIONS FOR WHITE SAUCE

TYPE	FAT	FLOUR	LIQUID	SALT	USES
Thin	15 ml	15 ml	250 ml	1 ml	cream soups cheese sauce
Medium	30 ml	30 ml	250 ml	1 ml	creamed vegetables pudding sauces egg sauce mushroom sauce gravy
Thick	45 ml	45 ml	250 ml	1 ml	salad dressings
Very Thick	60 ml	60 ml	250 ml	1 ml	soufflés croquettes

Method for White Sauce:

1. Melt measured fat in heavy saucepan (top of double boiler preferred).
2. Remove from heat and stir in flour and salt. Stir over heat until smooth. Do not allow mixture to burn.
3. Add cold liquid slowly, stirring constantly.
4. Cook over boiling water or on low, direct heat. Stir constantly until sauce is thickened, smooth and all the taste of raw starch is gone. This takes about 10 minutes in double boiler; 5 to 7 minutes over direct heat.

VARIATIONS OF WHITE SAUCE

1. Cheese Sauce

250 ml medium to thin white sauce
125 ml grated cheese

1 ml paprika
2 ml Worcestershire sauce

To the thickened white sauce add grated cheese and seasonings. Stir until smooth. Serve as soon as cheese melts. The preferred cheese is sharp Cheddar — other kinds are suitable. Each gives its distinctive flavour. More or less cheese may be used — 250 g cheese yields 500 ml when grated.

2. Egg Sauce

250 ml medium white sauce
2 hard cooked eggs, diced

3 ml chives, chopped finely
3 ml parsley, chopped finely

To the thickened white sauce, stir in other ingredients. Adjust seasonings. Egg sauce is particularly good with fish.

3. Mornay Sauce

To 250 ml thin white sauce made with milk, cream or half and half, add 30 ml grated Parmesan cheese and 50 ml of grated Swiss, Gruyere or Samsoe cheese. Stir and heat until cheese melts.

4. Mock Hollandaise Sauce

250 ml medium white sauce
2 egg yolks

15 ml lemon juice
15 ml margarine

1. Beat egg yolks in a small bowl. Stir a little of the thickened sauce into the yolks. Blend well; add more hot sauce until egg is warmed.
2. Pour egg yolk mixture into the hot sauce. Cook and stir for 2 minutes.
3. Remove from the heat and beat in margarine and lemon juice. Serve hot over eggs, fish or vegetables such as asparagus, broccoli, brussels sprouts and cauliflower.

HOLLANDAISE SAUCE

461

3 eggs
125 ml melted butter
15 ml lemon juice

1. Place eggs in top of double boiler or use a small bowl that will just fit over a saucepan.
2. Beat eggs well. Beat in melted butter, a little at a time. Then beat in lemon juice.
3. Place hot water in bottom of double boiler or saucepan and put top part over it. The bottom of double boiler should not touch water and the water should not boil.
4. With continued stirring, cook over simmering or very hot water until thick (4 to 6 minutes). Remove from heat immediately.
5. Serve with vegetables, eggs, fish; refrigerate any leftovers and reheat while stirring over hot water.

Note: If the water touches the pot or is too hot or the sauce is cooked too long it will curdle. It can usually be brought back to a smooth consistency by adding 15-30 ml of hot water, 5 ml at a time, with continued stirring.

BÉARNAISE SAUCE

Yield: about 125 ml

3 green onions, cut finely
1 large sprig parsley, chopped
3 ml dry tarragon leaves
3 ml dry chervil leaves
50 ml wine vinegar
30 ml water
4 egg yolks
60 ml soft butter
2 ml salt
f.g. cayenne

1. Combine onions, parsley, tarragon, chervil, vinegar and water in a saucepan. Simmer over low heat 5 minutes. Strain, reserving liquid.
2. Put egg yolks in top of double boiler. Add vinegar a little at a time, beating constantly with a wire whip or rotary beater.
3. Set over simmering water and cook, stirring constantly until the mixture thickens.
4. Add butter a little at a time, stirring after each addition until butter is blended.
5. Season with salt and cayenne. Serve slightly warm.

NIPPY COCKTAIL SAUCE

Yield: 300 ml, 6-8 servings

125 ml chili sauce
100 ml ketchup
100 ml prepared horseradish
7 ml Worcestershire sauce
dash Tabasco sauce (optional)

Mix all ingredients; chill and serve.

SEAFOOD COCKTAIL SAUCE

Yield: 200 ml, 6 servings

125 ml ketchup
30 ml lemon juice
15 ml chopped onion
30 ml mayonnaise
15 ml Worcestershire sauce
1 ml salt
f.g. pepper

Combine all ingredients. Chill.

TOMATO SPAGHETTI SAUCE

Yield: 1.75 to 2 litres

20 ml garlic, minced
150 ml oil
350 ml onions, chopped
250 ml celery, chopped
30 ml green peppers, chopped
1 500 ml Italian tomatoes
750 ml tomato purée
5 ml crushed sweet basil leaves
5 ml crushed oregano leaves
1 small bay leaf

1. Sauté onions, celery and green peppers in oil about 5 to 6 minutes, stirring frequently.
2. Add garlic and cook a minute longer.
3. Add tomatoes, purée and seasonings.
4. Simmer uncovered 1½ hours.
5. Remove from heat and strain.
6. Season with salt.

Note: To make a meat sauce, add 500 g ground beef after step No. 1.

MEAT SPAGHETTI SAUCE

125 ml salad oil
  5 medium onions, chopped
  1 green pepper, coarsely chopped
5 or 6 stalks of celery, coarsely cut
  4 small cloves garlic, crushed
500 g ground chuck steak
 10 ml oregano
 10 ml thyme
 10 ml Italian seasoning (optional)

  3 whole chilies, broken (optional)
15 ml salt
15 ml pepper
 5 whole bay leaves
400 ml tomato paste
650 ml tomato juice
650 ml tomatoes
500 g fresh mushrooms, coarsely cut
   (optional)

1. Place oil in a large heavy pot. Add onions, green pepper and celery and sauté until tender but not browned.
2. Add garlic and ground meat. Stir in spices and brown mixture.
3. Add paste, juice, tomatoes and mushrooms. Simmer about 2 hours.
4. Refrigerate overnight to develop flavour fully. Heat slowly with frequent stirring to prevent scorching. Serve on spaghetti, sprinkled with Parmesan cheese.

CURRY SAUCE
Yield: 400 ml

250 ml chopped onion
250 ml chopped tart apple
 50 ml margarine
  1 clove garlic crushed
30-45 ml curry powder

 50 ml ketchup
500 ml meat stock (chicken, veal)
 30 ml lemon juice
  1 ml salt

1. Cook onion and apple in margarine until onion is transparent.
2. Add garlic, curry powder, ketchup, stock and lemon juice. Salt to taste.
3. Heat slowly.

Variations

One of the following may be added before serving, if desired:
250 ml cooked chopped chicken, cooked chopped beef, cooked seafood or 3-5 hard cooked eggs.

BARBECUE SAUCE
Yield: 500 ml

200 ml chopped onions
125 ml salad oil
200 ml tomato ketchup
200 ml water
 75 ml lemon juice

45 ml sugar
45 ml Worcestershire sauce
30 ml prepared mustard
10 ml salt
 3 ml pepper

1. Sauté onions in salad oil until soft.
2. Add tomato ketchup, water, lemon juice, sugar, Worcestershire sauce, prepared mustard, salt and pepper. Stir.
3. Simmer 15 minutes.

SMOKY BARBECUE SAUCE

 60 ml salad oil
125 ml chili sauce
 60 ml vinegar
 10 ml chopped onion
 ½ clove garlic

10 ml Worcestershire sauce
 1 ml salt
30 ml brown sugar
30 ml hickory liquid smoke

Combine sauce ingredients until blended. Season salmon steaks with salt and pepper. Marinate in sauce before barbecuing for one hour or longer, turning occasionally. Serve barbecued fish with additional barbecue sauce, preferably heated.

TARTAR SAUCE
Yield: 300 ml

250 ml mayonnaise
 15 ml chopped capers (optional)
 15 ml chopped olives

15 ml chopped sweet pickles
15 ml chopped parsley

Combine all ingredients. Chill.

LEMON, ORANGE OR LIME SAUCE

100 ml sugar, granulated
20 ml cornstarch
250 ml water
30 ml butter

2 ml grated lemon or orange rind
25 ml lemon or lime juice or 50 ml orange
juice
f.g. salt

1. Combine sugar, cornstarch, water in top of double boiler. Cook over hot water until thick and clear, stirring constantly. Remove from heat.
2. Stir in butter, rind, juice and salt.

Variations

1. VANILLA SAUCE — Omit lemon rind and lemon juice and use 5 ml vanilla instead. Prepare as for Lemon Sauce.
2. CARAMEL SAUCE — Omit fruit rind and juice. Use instead 50 ml of caramel. Reduce water by 15 ml. (Recipe for Caramel follows.)

CARAMEL

Yield: 250 ml

250 ml granulated sugar

250 ml hot water

1. Place sugar in a heavy pan (preferably heavy aluminum). Heat pan gradually until sugar melts. Stir constantly to prevent the sugar burning. Use a long handled spoon for safety.
2. When liquid is slightly golden in colour, add water a drop at a time, stirring continually. Sugar is very hot and quick addition of the water could be explosive.
3. Boil for 5 minutes. Then remove from heat and cool. Store covered.

CHOCOLATE SAUCE

Yield: 200 ml

2 squares semi-sweet chocolate
125 ml sugar

125 ml water
50 ml vanilla

1. Melt chocolate over hot water.
2. Add half the sugar gradually. Stir only to combine.
3. Add boiling water slowly, then remaining sugar.
4. Cook until sugar is dissolved and sauce has thickened slightly.
5. Add vanilla.
6. Serve hot.

BUTTERSCOTCH SAUCE

Yield: 200 ml

75 ml white corn syrup
160 ml packed light brown sugar
30 ml butter

f.g. salt
80 ml evaporated milk or cream

1. Boil syrup, light brown sugar, butter and salt in a heavy saucepan until consistency of heavy syrup. Cool.
2. Add evaporated milk or cream. Stir to combine.
3. Serve hot or cold.

HARD SAUCE

Yield: 250 ml

250 ml powdered sugar
75 ml butter
f.g. salt

5 ml vanilla or 15 ml rum extract, coffee,
or lemon juice
50 ml heavy cream

1. Sift the sugar.
2. Soften the butter and gradually add the sugar. Beat until smooth.
3. Add salt and flavouring.
4. Beat in cream until sauce is smooth and fluffy. Chill.

MOCK MAPLE SYRUP

Yield: 250 ml

250 ml brown sugar
60 ml water

15 ml butter
2 ml vanilla

1. Boil sugar and water in a saucepan for 5 minutes.
2. Remove from heat. Add butter and vanilla.

CUSTARD SAUCE

Yield: 225 ml

175 ml milk
1 egg yolk
25 ml sugar

f.g. salt
1 ml vanilla

1. Scald milk.
2. Beat egg yolk lightly. Add sugar, salt and vanilla.
3. Add hot milk to egg mixture slowly, stirring constantly.

4. Cook over hot, not boiling, water until mixture thickens slightly and will coat a metal spoon.
5. Remove from heat. Cool.

Note: Custard Sauce is similar to Soft Custard but of thinner consistency. It is served over fruit and puddings.

HOT FUDGE SAUCE

Yield: 250 ml

2 squares unsweetened chocolate
15 ml butter
75 ml boiling water

250 ml granulated sugar
30 ml corn syrup
5 ml vanilla

1. Melt chocolate in a double boiler.
2. Add butter to melted chocolate.
3. Blend in boiling water.
4. Add sugar and corn syrup. Stir well.
5. Place pan over direct heat and allow

sauce to boil gently. Do not stir.
6. Boil 5 minutes or 8 minutes for a thick sauce to use on ice cream.
7. Add vanilla. Serve hot. This sauce can be reheated over boiling water.

Soups

VEGETABLE SOUP

Yield: 8-10 servings

2 kg beef soup bone
30 ml fat
2 ml salt
2 litres cold water
1 onion

500 ml tomatoes
6 sprigs parsley
6 carrots, medium sliced
125 ml chopped celery
60 ml barley

1. Cut the meat from soup bone and brown in 30 ml fat.
2. Add 2 ml salt and 2 litres cold water.
3. Saw bone in several pieces. Add to above and let stand 30 minutes.
4. Add onion and simmer for 2 hours.

5. Add tomatoes, parsley, carrots, celery, barley and simmer 1 hour.
6. Skim the surplus fat from the surface.
7. Serve steaming hot.

CHICKEN RICE SOUP

Yield: 1.5 litres

carcass of roasted chicken, or small boiling fowl
2 litres cold water
125 ml rice, uncooked

4 stalks of celery
7 ml salt
30 ml parsley, chopped

1. Break or chop chicken carcass into pieces. Place in heavy skillet with water. Simmer for 1 hour. Strain.
2. Remove meat from bones, chop and

return to liquid.
3. Add rice, celery, salt.
4. Cook for 35 minutes over low heat.
5. Adjust seasoning. Add parsley.

VOYAGEUR BEAN SOUP (a potato and legume soup)

Yield: 6-8 servings

3 litres cold water
1 ham bone
500 ml navy beans or split peas
250 ml celery, chopped
500 ml raw potatoes, diced

1 large onion, finely chopped
3 carrots, sliced
15 ml salt
1 ml pepper
2 ml sage

1. Place beans or peas in a soup kettle with the ham bone and cold water.
2. Bring to a boil, cover and boil slowly for 2 hours.

3. Add the rest of the ingredients. Bring to boil. Cover and simmer over low heat for 2 hours. Stir occasionally.
4. Serve hot with croutons.

CREAM OF CELERY SOUP

375 ml celery, chopped
750 ml water
500 ml thin white sauce

salt
onion juice

1. Cook celery in boiling water until soft. Press through a coarse sieve (should be 500 ml).
2. Add celery mixture to thin white sauce gradually.

3. Place over low heat and bring to serving temperature.
4. Adjust seasonings.
5. Serve hot.

Variations

Add to 500 ml thin white sauce one of the following:
375 ml puréed green peas
375 ml cream-style corn
375 ml puréed asparagus
or an equivalent amount of other vegetables.

BOSTON CLAM CHOWDER (New England Clam Chowder)   Yield: 1.5 litres

250 g salt pork
2 medium onions, sliced
750 ml cubed potatoes
10 ml salt
1 ml pepper
24 shucked clams, finely chopped

500 ml boiling water
1 litre milk
40 ml butter
15 ml flour
clam liquor

1. Cube salt pork; sauté in large heavy saucepan until crisp and golden. Remove pork bits from pan and reserve.
2. Place onion in the pan and cook until tender.
3. Add potatoes, salt and pepper. Cook slightly.
4. Add butter, melt and stir in the flour.

5. Add milk slowly. Heat over low heat, stirring until mixture is slightly thickened.
6. In a separate saucepan bring clams, water and clam liquor to a boil.
7. Add clams and clam stock to first mixture. Heat slowly. Adjust seasoning. Add pork bits.

MANHATTAN CLAM CHOWDER   Yield: 2 litres

3 slices bacon, diced
5 ml thyme
250 ml thinly sliced onions
125 ml diced celery
375 ml diced carrots
750 ml cubed potatoes
1 500 ml hot water

10 ml salt
f.g. pepper
800 ml canned tomatoes
24 shucked clams
15 ml parsley
2 ml thyme

1. Sauté bacon until crisp; add onions and 5 ml thyme and cook until tender.
2. Add celery, carrots, potatoes, tomatoes, hot water, clam liquid and salt and pepper. Simmer uncovered over

low heat for one hour.
3. Cut clams into small pieces. Add clams, parsley and remaining 2 ml thyme. Simmer for 10 minutes before serving.

FRENCH ONION SOUP   Yield: 6-8 servings

50 ml butter
4 large onions, sliced thinly
15 ml flour
2 litres brown beef stock
salt

pepper
French bread cut in 2 cm thick slices and toasted
grated Parmesan cheese

1. Melt butter in heavy skillet. Add onions, and cook gently until soft but not brown.
2. Add flour and stir to blend.
3. Stir in beef stock; simmer 10 min.
4. Adjust seasoning to taste.

5. Pour soup into individual ovenproof soup bowls. Top with toasted French bread sprinkled thickly with Parmesan cheese.
6. Place under broiler until cheese is brown and bubbly.

Sandwiches

BROILED TUNA AND CHEESE SANDWICH

Yield: 4-5 sandwiches

    200 ml canned tuna, drained
     30 ml onion, finely chopped
     30 ml sweet pickle relish
30-45 ml salad dressing

    salt and pepper to taste
  4-5 slices cheddar or processed cheese
      sliced bread
      butter

1. Combine tuna, onion, salt and pepper and relish. Moisten with salad dressing.
2. Butter 4-5 slices of bread and spread with tuna mixture.
3. Open Faced — Top tuna with cheese slices and broil about 4 minutes or

until cheese melts. Serve open.
OR
Closed — Butter 4-5 more bread slices and place cheese slices on them. Broil both the tuna and cheese covered slices. Put layers together to serve.

Variations
Use hamburger buns.

DEVILLED EGG SANDWICH

Yield: filling for 3-4 sandwiches

     3 hard cooked eggs
    30 ml finely chopped celery
    30 ml finely sliced green onion

     3 ml salt
  f.g. pepper
    50 ml salad dressing

1. Dice and mash cooled, peeled eggs.
2. Add prepared celery, green onion. Add salt and pepper to taste.

3. Combine with sufficient salad dressing to moisten.
4. Spread between buttered slices of bread.

LUNCHEON MEAT AND PICKLE SANDWICH

     1 tin luncheon meat, OR
   375 g cold roast beef or cold ham
    30 ml pickle relish

     5 ml prepared mustard
       salt and pepper to taste
 30-45 ml salad dressing

1. Grind meat, add pickle relish, mustard, salt and pepper and sufficient salad dressing to moisten. Combine well.

2. Spread between buttered slices of bread.

POOR BOY SANDWICH

Loaf of French bread or small individual French loaves sliced in half lengthwise
salad dressing
few slices of salami, summer sausage, etc.

thin sharp cheese slices
thinly sliced tomato
thinly sliced dill pickle
folded thin slices of bologna or ham

1. Butter both halves of bread and spread thinly with salad dressing.
2. Cover bottom layer of bread with layers of salami or summer sausage, cheese, tomato, pickle and bologna or ham.

3. Cover with top of loaf end and slice vertically to make individual sandwiches.

CLUB HOUSE SANDWICH

     3 slices sandwich bread, toasted
    15 ml salad dressing
       tomato slices
     3 slices of crisp bacon

       lettuce leaf
       cold cooked chicken slices
    15 ml salad dressing

1. Spread first piece of toast with salad dressing.
2. Add tomato slices, salt and pepper to taste, drained bacon and a lettuce leaf torn to size.
3. Place second piece of buttered toast

on lettuce leaf and cover it with cold chicken slices.
4. Spread third piece of toast with salad dressing. Cover chicken slices.
5. Slice sandwich diagonally; garnish and serve immediately.

GRILLED CHEESE SANDWICH

467

2 slices bread
    cheddar or processed cheese slices
    salt and pepper to taste

1. Butter 2 slices bread.
2. Place sliced cheese on unbuttered side of bread. Salt and pepper to taste.
3. Top with unbuttered side of second piece of bread.

4. Grill closed sandwich in small skillet turning to brown on opposite side. Press down with spatula to "mould" sandwich together during cooking.

Variations
1. Cold thin ham slices or cooked crisp bacon may be placed on top of cheese slices.

SANDWICH SHAPES

1. Cutting the Closed Sandwich. Cut the crusts from sandwich and cut into illustrated shapes.

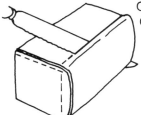 OPEN FACE FROM COOKIE CUTTERS

2. Shapes for Open Face Sandwiches. Cut slices as shown above; for variety use cookie cutters.

PINWHEEL

3. Pinwheel Sandwiches. Slice lengthwise, spread with mixture. Place centre on one end, roll as jelly roll. Chill before slicing.

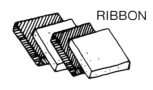 RIBBON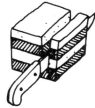

4. Ribbon Sandwiches. Alternate 2 lengthwise white slices with 2 brown slices. Chill and slice crosswise.

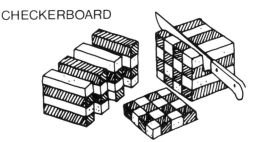

5. Checkerboard Sandwiches. Alternate 2 lengthwise white slices with 2 brown slices. Place 3 or 4 together with spread. Chill before slicing.

SANDWICH LOAF

6. Sandwich Loaf. Remove crusts from loaf. Cut lengthwise in 1.25 cm slices. Spread and stack slices. "Frost" top and sides with cream cheese mixture. Garnish, chill and slice.

Cereals

GRANOLA

1 250 ml rolled oats (or a mixture of rye flakes, wheat flakes and oats)
250 ml sesame seeds
250 ml sunflower seeds
250 ml wheat germ
250 ml instant powdered milk

250 ml vegetable oil (not olive)
250 ml honey
250 ml chopped nuts
250 ml shredded coconut
250 ml raisins, currants (optional)

1. Mix dry ingredients except nuts, coconut and raisins.
2. Combine and warm vegetable oil and honey; mix with dry ingredients.
3. Spread on 2 or 3 cookie sheets; bake in low oven 130°C about 30 minutes, stirring frequently until slightly browned.
4. Add nuts, coconut and raisins during last 10 minutes.
5. Store in airtight containers in refrigerator. Use as cereal.

Note: For snacking purposes, add 250 ml roasted soy-nuts or peanuts. Dried fruits such as apricots, prunes, etc., may be added if desired.

RISOTTO

Yield: 6-8 servings

50 ml butter, margarine or oil
250 ml chopped onion
250 ml sliced celery

250 ml rice
750 ml chicken stock
3 ml salt

1. Sauté onions and celery in fat until onions are golden.
2. Add rice, stirring constantly until browned.
3. Add the chicken stock. Pour into a buttered baking dish.
4. Cover and bake at 180°C for 45 minutes.

Variations
1. Add 250 ml sliced mushrooms to mixture. Season with garlic if desired.
2. Cook a fresh, seeded, chopped tomato in the mixture. Stir in cooked fresh or frozen green peas when the rice is cooked.
3. Serve risotto with a generous sprinkling of grated Parmesan cheese.

SPANISH RICE

250 ml rice
40 ml shortening
125 ml onions, chopped
¼ green pepper, chopped

10 ml salt
10 ml chili powder
500 ml tomatoes
250 ml water

1. Brown rice in shortening.
2. Add onions, pepper, salt, chili powder and tomatoes. Mix well. Add water.
3. Cover and simmer 30 minutes or until rice is tender. Do not stir.

4. Remove lid and allow mixture to dry for 5 minutes before serving.

WILD RICE STUFFING

250 ml wild rice (or mixture of 50-100 ml wild rice and remainder white rice)
1 large onion, chopped
125 ml chopped celery with leaves
75 ml butter or margarine

500 ml chicken broth
125 ml chopped nuts
125 ml chopped canned mushrooms
poultry seasoning
salt and pepper

1. Sauté rice or mixed rices, with onion and celery in butter for 5 minutes.
2. Add broth and bring to a boil. Cover and simmer 30-45 minutes, or until rice is tender.

3. Add nuts, mushrooms and desired amount of seasonings. Use to stuff 4-6 Cornish hens; duck or goose.

Casseroles

MACARONI AND CHEESE

Yield: 2 servings

125 ml uncooked macaroni
30 ml butter or margarine
30 ml flour
2 ml salt
250 ml milk

125 ml grated cheese
30 ml bread crumbs
10 ml butter or margarine, melted (for crumbs)

1. Set oven at 180°C. Grease baking dish.
2. Boil large saucepan of water, salt; add uncooked macaroni and simmer gently until tender — about 8 minutes. Drain.
3. Melt 30 ml butter or margarine in top of double boiler. Add flour and salt.
4. Remove from heat. Add milk gradually, stirring constantly.
5. Place over boiling water and cook for 10 minutes.

6. Add cooked macaroni and cheese to white sauce. Heat until the cheese is melted.
7. Turn into a greased baking dish or two individual casseroles.
8. Mix bread crumbs with 30 ml melted butter or margarine; sprinkle on top of macaroni and cheese.
9. Bake at 180°C for 15 minutes until bubbly and lightly browned on top.

TUNA CHOW MEIN CASSEROLE

Yield: 4 servings

250 ml celery, chopped
50 ml onion, chopped
30 ml green pepper, diced
15 ml margarine
320 ml canned mushroom soup
50 ml milk

75 ml water
200 ml canned flaked tuna, drained
400 ml chow mein noodles, divided
175 ml cashew nuts or peanuts
1 ml monosodium glutamate
1 ml pepper

1. Preheat oven to 180°C.
2. Prepare vegetables. Sauté in margarine.
3. Dilute soup with milk and water.
4. Combine vegetables, tuna, 325 ml noodles, nuts, seasonings and soup.

5. Pour into greased casserole dish.
6. Sprinkle with remaining 75 ml chow mein noodles.
7. Bake 30 minutes until heated through.

Protein Food	Sauce	Vegetables	Starchy Food	Topping
350-500 ml	1 can condensed soup and 75-100 ml liquid	350 ml	350-500 ml	25-50 ml
Cooked ham, cubed or slivered	Cream of celery	Sautéed green pepper and onions	Cooked noodles	Crushed potato chips
Cooked or canned chicken or turkey	Cream of chicken and buttermilk	Cooked or canned green beans	Cooked macaroni	Fresh bread crumbs
Canned lunch meat	Cream of mushroom and cream	Cooked or canned peas	Cooked spaghetti	Fried onion rings
Cooked beef, veal, lamb, pork	Cream of potato and sour cream	Cooked or canned carrots	Cooked rice	Crushed corn flakes
Hard cooked eggs	Green pea and tomato juice	Cooked or canned asparagus	Cooked potatoes	Potato sticks
Weiners	Cheddar cheese and vegetable juice		Cooked sweet potatoes	Slivered almonds
Cheese	Tomato and water		Cooked corn	Cracker crumbs
Canned tuna or salmon	Cream of celery	Cooked or canned peas	Cooked noodles or rice	Crushed stuffing mix
Cooked hamburger	Tomato and water	Sautéed green pepper and onions	Cooked macaroni or cooked rice	Crushed corn chips

1. Choose a food from each column with consideration as to flavour, colour and texture combinations.
2. Mix and heat soup and liquid to make sauce. Add protein food.
3. Place in casserole dish with vegetable and starchy food.
4. Sprinkle topping over all and bake at 180°C until hot and bubbling.

LASAGNE
Yield: 4 servings

250 g ground beef	3 ml oregano
50 ml onion, chopped	1 ml pepper
30 ml celery, diced	2 ml salt
250 ml canned tomatoes	125 g lasagne noodles
50 ml tomato paste	180 g Mozarella cheese
45 ml water	175 ml cottage cheese
½ garlic clove, minced	50 ml Parmesan cheese

1. Brown the meat in a frypan; drain the fat.
2. Add onion and celery and cook until tender.
3. Stir in the tomatoes, tomato paste, water, garlic and seasonings. Cover and simmer 30 minutes.
4. Cook noodles in a large amount of boiling salted water. Drain and rinse when tender.
5. In a 20 cm x 20 cm pan layer ⅓ of the noodles, then thirds of the Mozarella, meat sauce, cottage cheese and Parmesan cheese. Repeat layers.
6. Bake at 180°C for approximately 30 minutes. Let stand 10 minutes for easy serving.

CABBAGE ROLLS

500 g   ground beef
125 ml instant or precooked rice
½   medium onion, chopped fine
1   small egg
1 ml garlic powder
1 ml pepper
5 ml salt
1   medium green cabbage

Sauce Ingredients
125 ml tomato sauce
75 ml ketchup
30 ml brown sugar
30 ml vinegar
    salt and pepper

1. Remove core from the cabbage and cover with boiling water. Return to boil and simmer for 10-15 minutes until leaves are tender. Separate the leaves and remove the tough centre stalk from each. If leaves are too brittle for rolling, return to boiling water for 1-2 minutes.
2. Mix together the meat, rice, onion, slightly beaten egg, garlic powder, salt and pepper. Combine well.
3. Place 15-30 ml of the meat mixture on each cabbage leaf. Roll toward the stalk, tucking in the sides of the leaves.
4. Pack the rolls "seam" side down into a large pan or casserole which has been lined with extra cabbage leaves or veins cut from centre stalk.
5. Combine the tomato sauce, ketchup, brown sugar, vinegar and salt and pepper to taste. Pour sauce over the rolls. Seal pan well with foil. Bake 180°C for 1½-2 hours.

PORK AND BEANS

250 g   dried navy beans
3 ml salt
½   large onion, sliced
15 ml oil
30 ml vinegar
75 ml ketchup
125 ml salt pork

250 ml canned tomatoes
15 ml molasses
15 ml brown sugar
2 ml salt
1 ml pepper
1 ml dry mustard

1. Wash beans thoroughly and drain well.
2. Cover with water and soak overnight.
3. Next day, add first quantity of salt to beans, cover with water and simmer over low heat until they can be pierced with a toothpick.
4. Heat oil in a heavy pot — add thinly sliced onion and sauté 3 minutes.
5. Add vinegar, ketchup, tomatoes, mo- lasses, brown sugar, second quantity of salt, pepper and mustard to heavy pot. Bring to boil. Reduce heat and simmer 5 minutes.
6. Drain beans (save liquid). Place in bean pot in layers with diced salt pork.
7. Add all of sauce and enough bean liquid to cover.
8. Cover and bake at 150°C for 6-8 hours adding more liquid as needed. Refrigerate when cool.

Note: A superior flavour is obtained upon reheating the beans the next day.

CHICKEN TETRAZZINI

Yield: 4 servings

250 g   spaghetti
250 ml cooked chicken, diced
30 ml margarine
60 ml flour
325 ml chicken broth
125 ml milk
30 ml apple juice

2 ml salt
1 ml monosodium glutamate
f.g.   pepper
125 ml canned mushrooms
30 ml green pepper, chopped
60 ml Parmesan cheese, grated

1. Cook spaghetti in a large amount of boiling salted water until just tender; drain and rinse.
2. In a heavy saucepan, melt margarine and blend in flour. Gradually stir broth into flour mixture. Add milk. Cook and stir over medium heat until mixture thickens.
3. Add the apple juice and seasonings. Divide sauce in half.
4. To one-half of sauce add spaghetti, mushrooms and green pepper. Place in a shallow baking dish.
5. Add chicken to remaining sauce. Make a well in the centre of the spaghetti mixture and pour in chicken mixture.
6. Sprinkle Parmesan cheese over all.
7. Bake uncovered at 180°C for approximately 25 minutes until heated.

CHILI CON CARNE

Yield: 4 servings

500 g ground beef
250 ml onion, chopped
  1 green pepper, chopped
500 ml canned tomatoes
  1 bay leaf

250 ml tomato sauce
500 ml cooked kidney beans
  5 ml salt
5-10 ml chili powder

1. In a heavy skillet cook hamburger, onion and green pepper until meat is crumbly and browned and vegetables are tender. Drain excess fat.
2. Add canned tomatoes and juice, bay leaf and tomato sauce, drained kidney beans, salt and chili powder. Mix well.
3. Cover and simmer 1 hour stirring frequently. Remove bay leaf before serving.

SUNNY SOYBEAN SCALLOP

Yield: 4 servings

250 ml cooked soybeans
250 ml kernel corn
250 ml stewed tomatoes

  2 ml salt
125 ml grated cheese

Note: Soybeans must be soaked, then cooked, before proceeding with recipe. (125 ml uncooked beans will yield approximately 250 ml cooked.)

1. Preheat oven 180°C.
2. Grease casserole dish.
3. Layer half drained soybeans, half the corn, half the tomatoes in the casserole salting each layer. Repeat.
4. Sprinkle with grated cheese. Bake 30 minutes uncovered.

SALMON RICE CASSEROLE

Yield: 4 servings

125 ml uncooked rice
  2 eggs
125 ml milk
 50 ml margarine, melted
125 ml bread crumbs

200 ml canned salmon
 30 ml parsley
  7 ml salt
 30 ml lemon juice

1. Preheat oven to 180°C.
2. Cook rice as directed.
3. Beat eggs and combine with milk and rice.
4. Fold in drained salmon, salt, parsley and lemon juice. Melt margarine and mix with breadcrumbs.
5. Toss mixture with buttered crumbs.
6. Bake uncovered 30 minutes.

Salads, Salad Dressings

SEAFOOD COCKTAIL

Yield: 4 servings

160 ml crab or shrimp
      chopped lettuce
      cocktail sauce

1. Place chopped lettuce in a chilled cocktail glass.
2. Arrange crab pieces or whole shrimp on top allowing about 40 ml per serving.
3. Top with cocktail sauce. (See page 461, Sauces.) Garnish with parsley.

FRUIT CUP

Yield: 6 servings

  1 grapefruit, sectioned
  2 oranges, sectioned
  2 bananas

125 ml diced pineapple
  1 apple
125 ml green grapes

1. Wash and prepare fruit.
2. Arrange fruit in serving dishes having a variety in the size of the pieces; bananas should be added just before serving.
3. Cover fruits with their own juices or with juice of one lemon.
4. Serve with tangy fruit dressing garnished with maraschino cherry.

Variations
1. Add canned peaches or pears or fresh berries or other fruit in season.
2. Add 15 ml preserved ginger and pour gingerale over the cut fruit.
3. Add 6 after-dinner mints, which will dissolve in the juice.

TOSSED SALAD

Suitable Salad Ingredients:
Greens:
> lettuce, head or leaf; spinach, endive, watercress, nasturtium leaves, dandelion leaves, parsley.

Others:
> celery, green pepper, cucumber, green onions, tomatoes, carrots, turnip, raw cauliflower, radishes.

Seasoning:
> chives, mint, basil, tarragon, oregano.

1. Wash and dry salad greens.
2. Rub inside of salad bowl with a slice of onion or cut clove of garlic.
3. Tear greens into bite-size pieces. Cut other vegetables as desired.
4. Just before serving, add French dressing. Toss lightly until ingredients are coated with dressing. Serve immediately.

COLE SLAW

500 ml finely chopped or medium shredded cabbage
125 ml shredded carrot
125 ml finely chopped celery
50 ml finely chopped green onion or mild cooking onion
f.g. salt and pepper
125 ml salad dressing or mayonnaise

Combine vegetables and toss with salad dressing.

Variations

Any of the following may be used with cabbage in place of the other vegetables in the basic recipe: green pepper, pimento, radishes, olives, raisins, diced pineapple.

WALDORF SALAD

250 ml diced unpeeled, cored apple
15 ml lemon juice
250 ml diced celery
50 ml mayonnaise or salad dressing
50 ml raisins
50 ml walnuts, chopped

1. Sprinkle chopped apples with lemon juice.
2. Toss apples, celery, raisins and walnuts with dressing.
3. Serve in lettuce cups.

Variations

1. Add 2 small tins tuna chunks to make a main course salad.
2. Use seedless green grapes in place of apple.
3. Use toasted almonds in place of walnuts.

CAESAR SALAD
Yield: 6 servings

60 ml salad oil or olive oil
45 ml wine vinegar or cider vinegar
30 ml lemon juice
1 clove garlic, minced
5 ml salt
1 ml coarse pepper
5 ml Worcestershire sauce
1 large head romaine lettuce
250 ml croutons
50-75 ml anchovy fillets (optional)
1 egg
75-125 ml Parmesan cheese

1. Combine the first seven ingredients in the bottom of a large salad bowl.
2. Prepare lettuce (wash, dry and chill to crisp). Just before serving, break into bite-sized pieces in the bowl. Do not mix with dressing yet.
3. Sprinkle Parmesan cheese over top and add anchovies if desired.
4. Break raw egg over all. Toss salad, spooning from the bottom of the bowl each time until greens are evenly coated with dressing.
5. Sprinkle with crisp croutons; toss well to coat. Serve at once.

STUFFED TOMATO SALAD
Yield: 4 servings

4 medium tomatoes
2 hard cooked eggs
40 ml salad dressing or mayonnaise
40 ml cooked luncheon meat or cooked ham, finely diced
30 ml finely chopped celery
salt and pepper to taste

1. Wash tomatoes and cut in half crosswise, making a saw tooth edge for a more decorative tomato half.
2. Remove pulp from tomato halves.
3. Combine chopped pulp, finely chopped eggs, meat and celery. Toss together with dressing and salt and pepper.
4. Fill tomato halves with stuffing and garnish with paprika.

FOUR BEAN SALAD

Yield: 6-8 servings

400 ml kidney beans, drained and rinsed
400 ml garbanzo beans (chick-peas),
    drained
400 ml cut green beans, drained
400 ml cut wax (yellow) beans, drained
  1 green pepper, diced

1 medium sweet onion, sliced or cut in
    rings
175 ml sugar
150 ml vinegar
 75 ml salad oil
  5 ml salt
  5 ml pepper

1. Prepare green pepper and onion.
2. Combine canned beans with green pepper and onion. Toss lightly to mix.
3. Combine the sugar, vinegar and oil. Pour over vegetables; add salt and pepper. Toss lightly.

4. Cover and chill vegetables in marinade overnight.
5. Before serving, toss the vegetables again to coat with marinade. Drain before serving.

POTATO SALAD

Yield: 6 servings

1.5 litres cooked, diced potatoes
  5 ml salt
  1 ml pepper
  3 hard cooked eggs
125 ml mayonnaise or salad dressing

Additional Ingredients:
 30 ml chopped onion or chives or pickles
 50 ml sliced or diced radishes, celery,
    pepper or cucumber, carrots, peas
250 ml cubed cheese or diced cooked
    meat or poultry or flaked fish

1. Combine potatoes with your choice of additional ingredients.
2. Sprinkle with salt and pepper.

3. Add salad dressing and toss lightly.
4. Chill before serving and keep any leftovers refrigerated.

TOMATO ASPIC

Yield: 4-6 servings

  1 envelope gelatin
375 ml tomato juice
  5 ml sugar
  3 ml salt

3 ml onion juice
3 ml Worcestershire sauce
15 ml vinegar

1. Soak gelatin in 40 ml cold tomato juice until liquid is absorbed.
2. Mix remaining ingredients with the rest of the tomato juice and heat just to boiling point.
3. Add soaked gelatin and stir until dissolved.

4. Pour mixture into 750 ml mould or small loaf pan or individual moulds.
5. Chill until firm; about 3 hours.
6. Unmould and serve on lettuce. Garnish with mayonnaise or salad dressing.

LIME JELLIED SALAD

Yield: 6-8 servings

  1 package lime flavoured jelly powder
200 ml boiling water
200 ml evaporated milk, undiluted
  1 can crushed pineapple, drained
250 ml cottage cheese

125 ml chopped nuts
 15 ml lemon juice
125 ml chopped celery
125 ml mayonnaise

1. Dissolve jelly powder in boiling water. Cool slightly.
2. Stir in evaporated milk. Chill until partially set.
3. Add drained pineapple and all of the other ingredients. Mix well.

4. Pour into 1 litre mould and refrigerate until set. Unmould to serve or pour into square cake pan and refrigerate until set. Cut in squares and place individual servings on salad plates garnished with lettuce leaves.

CHICKEN OR TURKEY SALAD

Yield: 6 servings

750 ml diced cooked chicken or turkey
250 ml diced celery
250 ml diced cucumber
 50 ml chopped green onion or cooking
    onion

 50 ml chopped green or ripe olives
  2 ml salt
125 ml slivered blanched almonds
125 ml salad dressing or mayonnaise

1. Combine chicken or turkey, celery, cucumber, onion and olives and toss.

2. Sprinkle with salt; add almonds and salad dressing and toss to coat pieces.

FRENCH DRESSING

125 ml salad oil
30 ml vinegar
30 ml lemon juice
10 ml sugar

3 ml salt
2 ml dry mustard
2 ml paprika
dash cayenne

Combine all ingredients in screw-top jar; cover and shake.

Chill. Shake again just before serving.

CREAMY FRENCH DRESSING

Yield: 275 ml

5 ml salt
2 ml dry mustard
50 ml sugar
50 ml ketchup

125 ml salad oil
60 ml undiluted evaporated milk
50 ml vinegar

1. Measure all of the ingredients except the vinegar into a small bowl. Beat with a rotary beater until thick and smooth.
2. Add the vinegar all at once and beat until thoroughly mixed. Refrigerate.

COOKED SALAD DRESSING

Yield: 700 ml

3 eggs
175 ml sugar
5 ml salt
10 ml dry mustard

30 ml flour
250 ml vinegar
50 ml water
15 ml butter

1. Beat eggs in top of double boiler. Add sugar, salt, mustard and flour. Continue beating until mixture is well blended.
2. Add water and vinegar to egg mixture in top of a double boiler.
3. Cook over boiling water, stirring constantly until mixture thickens.
4. Remove from heat and stir in butter. Cool.
5. Store in covered jar in the refrigerator.

MAYONNAISE

Yield: 500 ml

5 ml salt
2 ml dry mustard
1 ml paprika
dash cayenne
3 egg yolks

30 ml vinegar
500 ml salad oil
30 ml lemon juice
15 ml hot water

1. Mix dry ingredients in a bowl or blender.
2. Add egg yolks and blend.
3. Add vinegar and mix well.
4. Add salad oil, 5 ml at a time, beating with electric beater or at medium speed in a blender, until 60 ml has been added.
4. Add remaining oil in increasing amounts, alternating last 125 ml with lemon juice.
5. Add water to cut oil appearance.

LEMON BLUE CHEESE DRESSING

Yield: 500 ml

50 ml Blue cheese
175 ml salad oil
250 ml dairy sour cream
75 ml lemon juice

5 ml grated lemon rind
5 ml seasoning salt
f.g. garlic powder

1. Mash cheese well.
2. Blend in oil, adding a little at a time and beating until smooth.
3. Add remaining ingredients and beat until smooth.
4. Cover and chill several hours to blend flavours.
5. Bring to room temperature for serving.

THOUSAND ISLAND DRESSING

Yield: 400 ml

250 ml mayonnaise
75 ml chili sauce or ketchup
30 ml minced olives

15 ml chopped green pepper
15 ml minced onion
10 ml chopped parsley

Blend all of the ingredients together in a bowl.

Vegetables

HARVARD BEETS

Yield: 4 servings

400 ml canned beets, sliced or diced
   (500 g fresh cooked)
250 ml beet liquid
 50 ml sugar

20 ml cornstarch
 5 ml salt
f.g. pepper
75 ml vinegar

1. In a medium-size saucepan combine sugar with cornstarch, salt and pepper.
2. Gradually stir in cool reserved beet liquid (adding water to make 250 ml)

and vinegar. Stir until smooth.
3. Cook over medium heat stirring constantly until thickened and clear.
4. Add beets and heat through.

To Prepare Fresh Beets:
Cut the tops from the beets leaving 3 cm of stem. Wash beets well. Cover with boiling water. Cover pot and cook until tender. Cooking time will vary with size and age of beets. Add more boiling water if needed. When done, cool beets to remove skins (they should slip off like a blanched peach). Remove stem and root.

BAKED SQUASH

Yield: 4 servings

  2 acorn squash or
1-1.5 kg Hubbard squash
     salt, pepper and margarine

1. Preheat oven to 200°C.
2. Wash and halve acorn squash or cut Hubbard squash into 6 serving pieces. Remove seeds and stringy parts.
3. Place pieces soft part down in a baking pan; add a few drops of water

to the bottom of the pan (or place in a covered pan with soft parts up).
4. Bake for 20 minutes then turn pieces (or remove cover). Continue baking 20-40 minutes longer or until tender.

Variations
1. About ten minutes before serving time, put butter or margarine in each piece. Add salt, pepper and f.g. thyme.
2. When turning or uncovering the squash, place a slice of uncooked bacon in each cavity. Sprinkle lightly with salt, pepper and paprika and bake until tender.
3. Place applesauce in the squash cavity when squash is turned. Sprinkle with cinnamon and nutmeg. Continue baking until tender.

SCALLOPED POTATOES

Yield: 4 servings

  4 medium potatoes, pared and thinly
     sliced
 45 ml flour (approximately)
  5 ml salt
  2 ml pepper

 30 ml margarine
 15 ml parsley flakes
  1 medium onion, finely chopped
375 ml milk (approximately)

1. Rinse potatoes in cold water and drain well.
2. Place ⅓ of the potatoes in a buttered casserole dish.
3. Sprinkle with 15 ml flour, 2 ml salt, 1 ml pepper, 5 ml parsley and approxi-

mately ⅓ of the chopped onions. Repeat the layers.
4. Pour enough milk over the potatoes to just cover. Dot butter over the top.
5. **Bake uncovered at 160°C for approximately 1½ hours or until tender.**

Cream Sauce Method:
1. Prepare a cream sauce: melt the margarine, stir in 30 ml flour, the salt, pepper and parsley flakes. Add the milk all at once and stir well over a moderate heat until the sauce thickens.
2. Add the potatoes and onion to the sauce and cook over a low heat until the sauce comes to a boil.
3. Turn into a greased baking dish. Bake covered at 180°C for 30 minutes. Uncover and continue baking until potatoes are tender, (approximately 30 minutes).

Lemon Butter

50 ml butter, melted

30 ml lemon juice

1. Add lemon juice to melted butter. Simmer 1 minute to blend flavours.

2. Serve over cooked, drained vegetables.

Suggested Vegetables: Artichoke, asparagus, broccoli, carrots, parsnips, spinach.

Parmesan Buttered Crumbs

15 ml margarine
50 ml dry breadcrumbs

30 ml Parmesan cheese

1. Melt margarine.
2. Combine with breadcrumbs.

3. Stir in Parmesan cheese.
4. Sprinkle over cooked vegetables.

Herb Butter

50 ml margarine
 3 ml thyme (or rosemary or parsley or savory or tarragon)

1. Melt margarine.
2. Stir in crushed herb.
3. Simmer 1 minute to blend flavours.

4. Serve over cooked, drained vegetables.

SPEEDY CORN FRITTERS
Yield: 4-6 servings

250 ml buttermilk pancake mix
 2 ml baking powder

200 ml milk
250 ml canned kernel corn, drained

1. Combine pancake mix and baking powder.
2. Add drained kernel corn and milk. Stir until just blended.

3. Drop by spoonfuls into deep hot fat (190°C) and cook until golden brown (about 2 minutes).
4. Drain on paper towelling. Serve hot.

BROCCOLI AND CAULIFLOWER
Yield: 4-6 servings

½ head cauliflower broken in flowerets
375 g broccoli broken in flowerets, stem cut in even size chunks
 ½ green pepper, sliced in strips
250 g mushrooms, quartered
 1 small onion, diced coarsely

15 ml oil
 salt and pepper to taste
75 ml boiling water
 1 chicken bouillon cube
 dash soy sauce
10 ml cornstarch

1. Heat oil in pan and prepare vegetables.
2. Sauté mushrooms, onion and green pepper.
3. Add cauliflower and broccoli and stir fry. Add salt and pepper to taste.
4. Dissolve bouillon cube in boiling water and add to vegetable mixture. Cover

and steam approximately 5 minutes. (Vegetables should not be over-cooked. The secret of success is crispness.)
5. Combine soy sauce, 30 ml *cold* water and cornstarch to make a smooth paste.
6. Pour paste over vegetables and stir about 1 minute to allow starch to clear and thicken. Serve immediately.

SWEET AND SOUR RED CABBAGE
Yield: 3-4 servings

750 ml coarsely shredded cabbage, cooked
 6 strips bacon, diced
15 ml brown sugar
15 ml water

45 ml vinegar
 2 ml salt
 1 ml paprika
 1 ml dry mustard

1. Cook bacon until crisp. Do not drain.
2. Combine dry ingredients and add to bacon.

3. Add vinegar and water; stir well.
4. Heat to boiling and pour over hot cooked cabbage.

To Cook Red Cabbage:

Cut head in half and place flat side down on a board. Hold the cabbage and slice into long shreds with a sharp knife. Place in 2 cm of rapidly boiling salted water to which has been added 30 ml vinegar or lemon juice. Cover and simmer 5-7 minutes until tender crisp.

FRENCH FRIED POTATOES

1. Cut pared potatoes lengthwise in even strips.
2. Soak 1 hour in cold water. Drain and dry well between towels.
3. Fry a small amount at a time in deep hot fat (185°C) until just light brown. Drain on paper towels. Cool thoroughly. Cover and refrigerate until serving time.
4. Return potatoes to hot fat (190°C) for 3-5 minutes until crisp and golden. Drain on paper towels. Serve immediately.

BAKED POTATOES

1. Select potatoes of uniform size. Scrub thoroughly.
2. For crisp skin, pierce once with a fork and bake as is.
   For soft skin, rub skin with butter and wrap each pricked potato in a small square of foil.
3. Bake medium potatoes in a 220°C oven for 45-60 minutes.

Potato is done when it feels soft if squeezed gently with a pot holder. When removed from oven, roll potato back and forth on counter top with a pot holder to soften. Make a criss-cross in the top with a knife. Squeeze potato gently at both ends to make the inside pop up.

To decrease cooking time:

1. Cut potato in half lengthwise and butter cut half before baking.
2. Wrap in foil and pierce through with a skewer before baking.
3. Parboil before baking.

Suggested potato toppings:

chopped parsley	sour cream
paprika or chives	Parmesan cheese
sautéed chopped onion	grated cheddar cheese
chopped green onion	crumbled bacon

CHART FOR COOKING VEGETABLES

VEGETABLE	PREPARATION FOR COOKING	AMOUNT FOR FOUR	AMOUNT OF BOILING WATER	TIME TO BOIL
Artichoke	whole	4 medium	cover	35-45 min
Asparagus	break off woody ends	4-6 spears per person 500-750 g	150 ml	10-20 min (spears)
Beans (wax and green)	whole or broken; strings removed	375-500 g	125 ml	14-18 min (2 cm slices)
Beets	whole; skin, root and 3 cm stem left on.	500-750 g	cover	small whole 15-25 min medium whole 20-35 min
Broccoli	slice stalks; separate flowerets	750 g	200 ml	7-10 min
Brussels Sprouts	Remove outer leaves; split stalk	500 g	200 ml	10-15 min
Green Cabbage	remove outer leaves and stalk	1 small head	125 ml	wedges 10-15 min shredded 5-7 min
Red Cabbage	remove outer leaves and stalk.	1 small head	125 ml plus 30 ml vinegar	wedges 10-15 min shredded 5-7 min

HASH BROWNED POTATOES

1. Chop cooked potatoes in small pieces.
2. Melt about 30 ml bacon fat or drippings in a frypan. Add potatoes, sprinkle with salt and pepper; add a little minced onion if desired.
3. Pack the potatoes into the pan; if they are too dry to stick together, pour in a little milk.
4. Cook over low heat until brown crust forms on the bottom.
5. Add more fat if the potatoes appear to stick.
6. Fold and serve like an omelet.

PEA MEDLEY

30 ml margarine
125 ml onion, chopped
1 small stalk celery, chopped
50 ml boiling water

250 ml frozen peas
2 ml salt
1 ml pepper
f.g. ground marjoram

1. Sauté onion and celery in margarine until tender in a saucepan.
2. Add the remaining ingredients and cover. Bring back to the boiling point.

3. Reduce heat and simmer, stirring occasionally, about 10 minutes. Serve immediately.

BATTER FRENCH FRIED ONION RINGS

1-2 large onions, sliced crosswise 1 cm thick
1 egg, slightly beaten

50 ml flour
hot fat

1. Separate the onion into rings.
2. Dip each ring into slightly beaten egg, then into flour.

3. Fry in 1 cm hot fat until delicate brown. Drain.
4. Salt lightly. Serve immediately.

TIME TO STEAM	TIME TO PAN SAUTÉ	TIME TO BAKE	SERVING SUGGESTIONS
—	—	—	1. dip in lemon butter, drawn butter, mayonnaise, Caesar salad dressing. 2. fill with chicken, crab, shrimp or turkey salad and chill.
12-25 min	10-12 min	—	1. lemon butter, mushroom soup, white sauce, cheese sauce, Hollandaise sauce.
20-25 min	—	—	1. top with toasted almonds, crumbled cooked bacon, sautéed mushrooms, celery and pimento. 2. cheese or Hollandaise sauce.
30-35 min	—	—	1. pickled beets. 2. Harvard sauce.
15-20 min	5-7 min	—	1. lemon butter or clear French dressing. 2. sour cream, cheese sauce, Hollandaise sauce. 3. Parmesan-buttered crumbs.
10-20 min	—	—	1. crumbled bacon. 2. white sauce, cheese sauce or Hollandaise.
—	—	—	1. grated cheese. 2. sweet and sour sauce. 3. white or cheese sauce.
—	—	—	1. sweet and sour sauce.

VEGETABLE	PREPARATION FOR COOKING	AMOUNT FOR FOUR	AMOUNT OF BOILING WATER	TIME TO BOIL
Carrots	scrub, scrape or pare, cut if large	500 g	125 ml	whole small 10-15 min lengthwise slices, 14-18 min
Cauliflower	remove outer leaves and stalk; separate into flowerets	1 med. head	whole — 375 ml flowerets 200 ml	15-25 min 8-12 min
Celery	slices	500 g	75 ml	10 min
Corn on Cob	remove husk and silk break off stalk	1-2 ears per person	cover ears	3-5 min
Eggplant	slice	1 med.	—	—
Mushrooms	—	500 g	—	—
Onions	small whole peeled	500 g	just cover	20 min
Parsnips	scrape or pare; quarter lengthwise	4 medium	just cover	12-15 min
Peas	shell	500 g	fresh — 125 ml frozen — 30-45 ml	8-12 min 2-3 min
Green peppers	remove stem, seeds and membrane	4 medium	cover and fill peppers	10 min
Potatoes	new, scrubbed; old, pared	4 medium 500 g - 750 g	200 ml	15-20 min
Sweet Potatoes	scrub; peel after cooking	4 medium	—	—
Spinach	remove coarse stems and roots; wash well	500 g	drops of water on leaves	3 min
Squash — acorn	cut in half; remove seeds	750 g	200 ml	15-20 min
Squash — butternut Hubbard	remove seeds and membrane; cut in serving pieces; remove skins if boiled or steamed	750 g	250 ml	10 min
Squash — marrow	—	750 g	125 ml	5-8 min
zucchini	—	2-3 small	—	—
Swiss Chard	wash well	500 g	125 ml	10-12 min
Tomatoes	—	4 medium	in own juice	7-10 min
Turnips	pare and dice	500 g	125 ml	10-15 min

TIME TO STEAM	TIME TO PAN SAUTÉ	TIME TO BAKE	SERVING SUGGESTIONS
20-25 min	—	30 min	1. honey or brown sugar glaze. 2. lemon or parsley butter.
10-15 min	—	—	1. cream of celery or mushroom soup. 2. cheese or Hollandaise sauce. 3. herbed butter.
10-20 min	3-5 min	—	1. cheese sauce.
—	—	—	1. buttered with sprinkling of salt and pepper.
—	2 min each side	20-30 min	**1. sprinkle with Parmesan cheese or herbs.**
—	3-5 min	—	1. sauté to a golden brown. 2. sauté with onions. 3. broil or stuff caps.
20-25 min	until tender but not brown	45 min	1. white or cheese sauce. 2. mix with cooked peas.
15-20 min	—	—	1. parsley or lemon butter. 2. glazed.
—	—	—	1. cook with celery, carrots, tiny onions or corn kernels. 2. top with sautéed mushroom or crumbled bacon. 3. white sauce, rosemary or thyme butter.
—	—	—	1. corn stuffed or meat stuffed.
20-25 min	—	45-60 min 200°C	1. may be mashed, topped with sour cream, chives, crumbled bacon, mint or parsley.
30-35 min	—	30-45 min. 200°C	1. candied.
—	—	—	1. cream or scallop. 2. lemon, nutmeg, basil or dill butter.
—	—	45-50 min 200°C	1. mashed and herbed. 2. oven baked and stuffed with dressing, sausage, applesauce or bacon.
20-25 min	—	50-60 min 200°C	**1. crumbled bacon or Parmesan cheese.** 2. stuffed.
20-25 min	—	20 min	1. panned with peppers, onions and tomatoes.
—	10 min (cover and steam)	—	
—	—	—	1. cheese sauce. 3. crumbled bacon. 2. green onions. 4. sieved egg.
—	—	15-20 min	1. whole — broiled or stuffed. 2. canned — casseroles and scallops.
20-25 min	—	—	1. mash with brown sugar, carrots or potatoes. 2. fry cooked cubes with onions. 3. with ginger, nutmeg or parsley butter.

Fruit

STEWED DRIED FRUIT

250 g dried prunes, figs, apricots, peaches, apples, raisins

500 ml water
50-125 ml sugar (optional)

1. Wash dried fruit.
2. Place in saucepan. Add cold water and soak for several hours or overnight or add hot water and soak for 30-60 minutes.
3. Cover and cook over low heat in the same water for 10-20 minutes or until the fruit is tender.
4. Add sugar only if desired and return to heat only until sugar dissolves. (Prunes usually require little or no sugar; apricots are more acceptable if sweetened.)
5. Serve warm or cold.

Variations
1. Add 15 ml lemon juice or 2 slices of lemon just before removing from the heat.
2. To prunes add several slices of orange with peel a few minutes before the end of cooking time.

STEWED FRESH FRUIT

1. Wash the fruit thoroughly.
2. Peel if desired (apples, peaches, pears). Remove pits or stems if present. If slicing, slice uniformly. Plums and apricots may be cut or left whole and pricked.
3. Place in a shallow sauce pan. Add water to half the depth of the fruits.
4. Cover and simmer until the fruit is tender when tested with a fork.
5. Remove from heat and add sugar to taste. Stir and heat if necessary until the sugar dissolves.
6. Serve warm or cold.

Note: Early addition of sugar produces a tougher product but the fruit will retain more of its original shape.

BROILED FRUIT HALVES

2 fruit halves (grapefruit, orange, peach or pear)

25 ml sugar or honey
10 ml butter or margarine

1. Preheat broiler. Prepare fruit.
2. Place fruit halves in a small shallow pan. Sprinkle with sugar and dot with butter.
3. Place pan so that fruit is 8-10 cm from heating element. Broil 3-5 minutes or until sugar melts and fruit is a light brown.
4. Garnish with maraschino cherries, raisins or chopped nuts and serve hot as an appetizer, meat accompaniment or dessert.

APPLE SAUCE

4-5 tart apples (medium-large)
125 ml water

75-125 ml sugar
2 ml cinnamon or nutmeg

1. Wash, peel, quarter and core apples. Slice into saucepan.
2. Add water. Cover and simmer 15-20 minutes or until apples are fork tender. Stir occasionnally to prevent sticking.
3. If necessary, evaporate water by cooking without a lid or, if needed to prevent scorching, add more water.
4. Remove from heat and stir in sugar until dissolved. The amount will depend on natural sweetness of the apples.
5. Stir in desired seasoning and cool before serving.

Variations
1. If apples are sweet add 15 ml lemon juice or a slice of lemon after cooking.
2. Sieved applesauce – slice but do not peel apples. When cooked, press fruit through a sieve or food mill. Then stir in sugar, seasoning if desired and cool before serving. (This is a quick method especially suited to infants and persons with stomach disorders.)

BAKED APPLES

4 large apples
60-75 ml sugar, white or brown
2 ml cinnamon

25 ml butter or margarine
125 ml hot water, approximately

1. Wash apples, remove core but do not peel. Slash peel around centre of apples.
2. Place apples in baking dish. Fill centres with a mixture of sugar, cinnamon and butter. Pour hot water around apples, about 2 cm deep.

3. Bake at 180°C for 30-45 minutes or until fork tender. Baste every 10 minutes.
4. Serve hot or cold with juice poured on the apples. Cream or ice cream are tasty accompaniments.

Variations
1. Add raisins, chopped dates, nuts to filling mixture.
2. Stuff apples with peanut butter.

Eggs

EGGS AS EGGS

Soft-cooked eggs:

Cover eggs with lukewarm water, at least 5 cm above top of eggs. Cover, heat rapidly to boiling point, then remove from heat. Let stand 3-6 minutes depending on individual taste. If more than 2 eggs are cooked at one time increase the time to 5-8 minutes.

Hard-cooked eggs:

Cover with lukewarm water, at least 5 cm above top of eggs. Bring water to the boil rapidly. Remove from heat, cover tightly. Let stand where water will keep hot for 30 minutes. Plunge immediately into cold water.
OR
   Put eggs in cold water, cover tightly. Heat slowly to the boiling point. Remove from heat and let stand where water will keep hot for 20 minutes. Plunge immediately into cold water.

Devilled eggs:

1. Hard cook 6 eggs as directed. Chill. Remove the shells and cut the eggs in half.
2. Gently separate the yolks from the whites placing the yolks in a bowl and the whites on a large plate.
3. Mash the yolks with a fork.
4. Add 1 ml salt
      f.g. pepper
      mayonnaise (about 25 ml)
   Blend well. (Additional seasonings may be added to taste; finely chopped onion, chives, celery, sweet pickle, walnuts.)
5. Refill egg whites with yolk mixture piling it lightly into the hollow.
6. Garnish with parsley, stuffed olive or pimiento.

Poached eggs:

1. Have boiling salted water in a shallow pan (at least 4 cm deep).
2. Break eggs, one at a time, into a saucer or shallow cup. Quickly slip each egg into the water. Reduce heat and hold just below simmering. Cover.
3. Cook about 3 to 5 minutes. White should be firm and a film formed over the yolk.
4. Remove from water with a slotted spoon. Serve immediately.

Fried eggs:

1. Heat 20 ml of margarine or butter in a heavy skillet. Do not allow margarine or butter to darken in colour.
2. Break eggs one at a time into a saucer or shallow cup.
3. Carefully slip egg into skillet.
4. Reduce heat, cook gently, basting eggs with the margarine or butter.
5. Cook about 3 or 4 minutes or to desired firmness.   Season and serve.

Scrambled eggs:

1. Heat 20 ml margarine or butter in a heavy skillet. Do not allow fat to darken.
2. For each egg add 20 ml milk or water, salt and pepper to taste.
3. Beat lightly with fork.
4. Pour egg mixture into skillet. Reduce heat.
5. Cook slowly lifting from the bottom and sides to allow uncooked part to flow to the bottom. Stir occasionally.
6. Cook about 5 to 8 minutes or until mixture is thickened but still moist.
7. Serve immediately.

Baked eggs:

1. Grease individual shallow baking dishes.
2. Break eggs into the dish.
3. Pour a little melted margarine or butter over the eggs.
4. Sprinkle lightly with salt.
5. Bake uncovered, 180°C for 12 to 18 minutes, depending on firmness desired.
6. Lift from pan gently and serve immediately.

Creamy eggs:

1. Allow 15 ml milk for each egg, and 1 ml salt.
2. Beat eggs, milk, salt, and pepper to taste, slightly.
3. Cook over hot, not boiling, water.
4. As mixture cooks, gently draw it away from the sides until all mixture is cooked but not dry. Do not overcook.
5. Serve immediately on toast.

FRENCH OMELET
Yield: 1 serving

2 eggs
30 ml water or 30 ml milk
f.g. salt

1. Break eggs into a bowl. Add water and salt.
2. Beat lightly.
3. Heat omelet pan. Grease lightly.
4. Pour in egg mixture.
5. While shaking pan gently back and forth, stir eggs with flat back of fork using circular clockwise motion, scraping eggs from bottom of pan.
6. Just before eggs are completely set and while still creamy, spread evenly in the pan. Allow a few seconds for eggs to set.
7. Roll omelet away from handle. Slip out of pan onto a plate.
8. Garnish with parsley.
Cheese Omelet:
At Stage 7 sprinkle over eggs 50 ml grated cheese.

PUFFY (Foamy) OMELET
Yield: 1 serving

2 eggs
1 ml salt
30 ml milk or water
15 ml margarine or butter
f.g. pepper

1. Heat oven to 180°C.
2. Separate eggs. Beat yolks in medium sized bowl until thick and lemon coloured. Add seasonings and milk.
3. Using a clear, dry, egg beater, beat egg whites in a small bowl until stiff but not dry.
4. Heat an omelet pan, 20 cm diameter. Put in butter and be sure sides and bottom of pan are well buttered.
5. Cut and fold egg white into yolk mixture.
6. Turn omelet into the pan when it is quite hot. Spread evenly and reduce heat.
7. Cook slowly until omelet is set, about 5 minutes. Place in the oven to dry slightly on top, about 10 minutes.
8. Fold one side of omelet over the other. Slide out onto plate. Garnish and serve immediately.

FRENCH TOAST

     2 eggs
     2 ml salt
   175 ml milk
     2 ml vanilla

     8 slices bread
    30 ml butter or margarine
       confectioners sugar and cinnamon

1. Melt butter or margarine in heavy skillet. Fat should be hot but not darkened.
2. Beat eggs slightly. Add salt, vanilla and milk. Blend well.
3. Dip each slice of bread in egg mixture. Put immediately into skillet. Brown on both sides.
4. Serve sprinkled with sugar and cinnamon.

CHEESE SOUFFLÉ

Yield: 3 servings

    45 ml margarine or butter
     2 ml salt
    45 ml flour
       cayenne

   250 ml milk
     3 eggs
   125 ml grated cheese

1. Make a thick white sauce of the first three ingredients.
2. Add cayenne and grated cheese stirring until smooth.
3. Separate eggs.
4. Beat egg yolks until thick and lemon coloured.
5. Add the slightly cooled sauce to the egg yolks. Blend carefully.
6. Beat the egg whites until stiff but not dry. Gently fold the egg whites into the sauce mixture.
7. Turn the mixture into three custard cups.
8. Place custard cups in a pan of hot water. Bake in a slow oven, 150°C for 25 minutes or until a knife inserted in the centre comes out clean.

BAKED CUSTARD

Yield: 6 servings

   500 ml milk
    50 ml sugar
     1 ml salt

     2 eggs
     2 ml vanilla

1. Heat milk to scalding.
2. Add sugar, salt to the hot milk.
3. Beat eggs slightly. Add vanilla.
4. Slowly add the hot milk to egg mixture, stirring constantly. Add vanilla.
5. Pour into individual moulds or 1 litre mould.
6. Place on rack in shallow pan. Pour hot water in pan to depth of 3 cm from top of moulds.
7. Bake in moderate oven 180°C about 35 minutes for individual mould, 60 minutes for 1 litre mould.
8. Test by inserting a knife in mixture. When it comes out clean custard is done.
9. Remove from water immediately and cool.

SOFT CUSTARD

Yield: 4 servings

   500 ml milk
     4 yolks of eggs
    50 ml sugar

     1 ml salt
     2 ml vanilla

1. Scald milk.
2. Beat egg yolks lightly. Add sugar, salt and vanilla.
3. Add milk slowly to egg mixture, stirring constantly.
*4. Cook over hot, not boiling, water, stirring constantly until mixture is thick enough to coat a metal spoon.
5. Remove from heat. Cool.

* Do not allow water to get too hot or eggs will separate and cause curdling.

EGG FOO YUNG

Yield: 3 servings

     3 eggs
   125 g cooked pork or chicken, thinly sliced
     1 small green pepper. diced
   125 ml shrimp (optional)

    15 ml soya sauce
     1 ml salt
     1 medium onion, diced
   125 ml celery, diced

1. Beat eggs and add 60 ml water and soya sauce and salt.
2. Sauté meat, pepper, shrimp, onion and celery in margarine.
3. Add egg mixture.
4. Panfry as an omelet.

Milk, Milk Products

HOMEMADE YOGURT

1 000 ml 2% milk
50 ml skim milk powder
15 ml plain yogurt

Mixing Instructions:

1. Combine fresh milk and milk powder in a heavy pot and bring to a boil, stirring constantly. For yogurt of a thicker consistency, reduce heat and simmer milk for 5 minutes, stirring continually.
2. Remove milk from the heat and allow it to cool to 45°C, stirring occasionally to prevent scum formation. This temperature can be tested with your finger; you should be able to keep your little finger in the milk, comfortably, for 20 seconds. If still unsure use a clinical thermometer.
3. Blend a little of the warm milk with the yogurt, then stir this into the milk in the saucepan. Mix completely.
4. Incubate, using one of the five methods which follow. Do not move the yogurt any more than is absolutely necessary during incubation as this might interfere with thickening processes. Avoid jarring.
5. After incubation, gently transfer the yogurt containers to the refrigerator and chill well.

Note: Experience in yogurt making will increase your sensitivity to the correct temperatures for incubation.

Incubation Procedure:

METHOD 1.

1. Warm 250-300 ml jars (preserving jars are ideal) or 200-250 ml drinking glasses (for individual servings) by rinsing in hot water. Shake dry. Pour in the yogurt mixture and cover with lids or plastic wrap.
2. Place jars or glasses on a low trivet or on jar rings in an electric fry pan. Add sufficient warm water to cover trivet, about 2 cm. Cover fry pan or sucepan with lid.
3. Set thermostat of fry pan between OFF and lowest possible setting. The temperature setting will vary with different fry pans. The water temperature at all times must be bearable to the finger. Check frequently and adjust thermostat accordingly.
4. Incubation period will be 6 to 8 hours depending on the acidity desired. Check by tasting.

METHOD 2.

1. Same as method 1.
2. Place jars or glasses on a trivet in a large, heavy-based saucepan. Add water to come to the top of the trivet and cover the saucepan with a tight lid.
3. Set saucepan on range burner at a minimum temperature. Check the water frequently to be sure it is not too cool or too hot. Again, the finger test, or 110°C.
4. Incubation time will be 6 to 8 hours, depending on the acidity desired. Check by tasting.

METHOD 3.

1. Same as method 1.
2. Place jars or glasses in a warm cupboard, for example, a furnace room or space around a hot water tank. Some homes will have a space just the right temperature, others will be too cool or too hot.
3. If the temperature is found to be suitable, the incubation period will be about 8 to 10 hours. Overnight is suggested.

METHOD 4.

1. Preheat a wide-mouthed vacuum bottle by pouring hot water into it and allowing it to stand until ready to use.
2. Drain bottle and pour yogurt mixture into it. Place lid on carefully.
3. Wrap vacuum bottle in a towel and set in a warm place.
4. Incubation period will be 5 to 7 hours.

METHOD 5.

Electric yogurt makers are available. Follow manufacturer's directions.

BLENDER YOGURT

175 ml skim milk powder
200 ml evaporated milk
250 ml boiling water
500 ml 2% milk
30 ml plain yogurt

1. Pour all ingredients into blender and blend at low speed for 15-30 seconds. Incubate as for "Homemade Yogurt".

Note: This recipe gives a smooth, thick, rich yogurt which appeals to babies and toddlers.

COCOA
Yield: 2 servings

15 ml cocoa
25 ml sugar or honey
f.g. salt
250 ml boiling water
250 ml milk
1 ml vanilla
2 marshmallows

1. Using the top of the double boiler, mix cocoa, sugar or honey and salt. Gradually add boiling water and mix thoroughly.
2. Boil gently for 5 minutes to cook the starch.
3. Add cold milk and heat over boiling water.
4. Beat until a thick froth forms to prevent a scum forming. Add vanilla.
5. Pour over marshmallows.
6. Serve hot.

ORANGE BANANA SHAKE
Yield: 2 servings

250 ml orange juice
1 egg
1 banana, cut up
125 ml ice cream

1. Place all ingredients in the blender in the order given.
2. Blend and serve.

CHOCOLATE EGG NOG
Yield: 2 servings

1 egg
50 ml chocolate syrup
250 ml cold milk

1. Beat egg until light and foamy.
2. Mix in chocolate syrup.
3. Add milk. Mix well.
4. Serve cold.

INSTANT LIQUID BREAKFAST
Yield: 1 serving

150 ml cold water
125 ml skim milk powder
f.g. salt
1 egg
5 ml vanilla
30 ml corn syrup

Place all ingredients in a blender and set at low setting for 20 seconds.

Variations

CHOCOLATE — Omit vanilla and corn syrup. Add instead 15 ml instant chocolate powder.

POWDERED MILK WHIPPED TOPPING
Yield: about 750 ml

125 ml cold water
15 ml lemon juice
150 ml skim milk powder
f.g. salt
50 ml sugar
1 ml vanilla

1. In a medium or large bowl, combine water, lemon juice, milk powder and salt. Blend well.
2. Beat with a rotary beater until mixture stands in firm peaks. This will take about 5 minutes.
3. Gradually beat in sugar, then vanilla. Chill.

Meat

OVEN ROASTING AND ROTISSERIE CHART
(Oven temperature all 160°C)

TYPE OF ROAST	APPROXIMATE TIME PER 500 GRAMS	INTERNAL TEMPERATURE
BEEF		°C
Boneless or boned and rolled		
Rare	25-35 min	60
Medium	30-40	70
Well-done	35-45	75
Bone-in		
Rare	20-25	60
Medium	25-30	70
Well-done	30-35	75
VEAL		
Leg	35-45	80
Boneless or boned and rolled	45-55	80
PORK		
Leg or loin	40-45	85
Boneless or boned and rolled	55-60	80
HAM		
Cook-before-eating		
Bone-in	25-35	70
Bone-out	35-40	70
Fully-cooked ham	10-15	55
Cottage roll	30	70
LAMB		
Bone-in (leg, rack, shoulder)		
Rare	25-30	70
Medium	30-35	75
Well-done	35-40	80
Boneless or boned and rolled		
Rare	25-30	70
Medium	30-35	75
Well-done	35-45	80

Using the Chart

1. Times are based on the temperature of meat when taken from the refrigerator (about 5°C). Reduce time if meat is at room temperature. To cook a frozen roast increase time by half that required for fresh or thawed meat.

2. Oven temperature is the same for all meats, 160°C.

3. Allow the longer times given for small roasts (i.e., 2-3 kilograms) and the shorter times for larger, heavier roasts (3-4 kilograms).

4. The approximate time required is merely a guide to know when to put the roast in the oven. An accurate meat thermometer is the only certain way to obtain meat cooked the way you want it. If the meat is being cooked from the frozen state, insert the meat thermometer part way through the cooking time.

5. Allow 10-15 minutes "resting time" after the roast is removed from the oven and before it is carved. This helps to make the roast easier to carve since the protein tissues are set and less juice will escape.

PAN GRAVY

1. Remove the meat from the pan and place it where it will remain hot. Pour off all but 60 ml of drippings, keeping the brown pieces also.
2. Stir 60 ml flour into these drippings using a wire whisk. Stir until flour has thickened, is well combined and smooth.
3. Over low heat continue to cook and slowly add 500 ml of liquid, water, stock, vegetable juices, milk or cream.
4. Season the gravy with salt, pepper, herbs.
5. You may serve gravy without straining or strain and reheat before serving.

POT ROAST GRAVY
Yield: 4-5 servings

1. Remove roast from pan.
2. Skim off excess fat.
3. Using 30 to 40 ml of fat and juice remaining in pan thicken this with a mixture of 30 ml flour mixed with 60 ml cold water. Be sure flour and water are thoroughly combined, add slowly, stirring constantly over low heat.
4. If necessary, add additional water, meat stock or vegetable water to make gravy the consistency of a medium white sauce.

BROILING MEAT

TYPE OF MEAT	APPROXIMATE THICKNESS	TIME-ON EACH SIDE
BEEF STEAK		
Rare	2-3 cm	5- 8 min
Medium	2-3 cm	8-10
Well-done	2-3 cm	10-12
LAMB CHOPS		
Rare	2-3 cm	6- 8
Medium	2-3 cm	8-10
Well-done	2-3 cm	8-12
HAM SLICES		
Ready-to-eat	2 cm	4- 5
Cook-before-eating	2 cm	8-10
PORK CHOPS		
Well-done	2-3 cm	10-12

SWISS STEAK

500 g cut 2.5 cm thick round steak
flour, salt and pepper
15 ml fat
1 small onion, diced
125 ml celery, diced
½ green pepper, diced
150 ml tomato soup
50 ml water
2 ml cornstarch or
5 ml flour to thicken gravy

1. Cut meat in serving pieces. Season with salt and pepper.
2. Sprinkle flour over meat and pound with the back edge of a French knife or with a meat hammer. Pound both sides.
3. Heat pressure cooker and add fat. Sear the meat until golden brown on both sides.
4. Add onion, celery, pepper, tomato soup and water.
5. Close cover securely. Place pressure regulator on vent pipe and cook 15 minutes at 105 kPa.
6. Let pressure drop of its own accord. If desired, gravy may be thickened with cornstarch or flour which has been mixed to a thin smooth paste with 15-30 ml cold water.

Optional Method:
After meat has been pounded, it may be seared slowly on both sides in a heavy iron skillet. Add vegetables and liquids and cover and bake at 150°C for 1½ hours or more until the steak is fork tender.

POT ROASTED BRISKET   Yield 4-5 servings

1.5-2 kg rolled brisket
   50 ml flour
    5 ml salt
    1 ml pepper

250 ml water
250 ml sliced mushrooms
  1 medium onion, coarsely chopped

1. Preheat oven to 150°C.
2. Combine flour, salt and pepper. Roll roast in seasoned flour mixture until thoroughly coated. Save remaining seasoned flour.
3. Heat a small amount of fat in a heavy pan or cast-iron Dutch oven and brown meat *slowly* and well on all sides.
4. Remove the meat. In the pan in which you browned the meat, lightly brown the onion, then the mushrooms, adding more fat if necessary.
5. Place the browned meat in a roasting pan or oven-proof Dutch oven with a close fitting lid.
6. Add the vegetables to the meat and 250 ml of very hot or boiling water.* If most of the fat is drained out of the pan, heat the water in the same pan in which you browned the meat and vegetables — this will give the pot roast extra flavour.
7. Cover the roasting pan and place in oven for 2½-3 hours until meat is fork tender. More water may be added during cooking but too much will weaken flavour and colour.
8. Once the roast is done, remove it to a warm platter. The liquid may be thickened with 15 ml of the reserved seasoned flour stirred to a smooth paste in 30 ml of cold water. This paste may then be added to the roasting pan and stirred over a medium heat until thick and bubbly.

Note: Potatoes or other vegetables may be baked in the oven during the last hour of roasting time.

STUFFED FLANK STEAK   Yield: 2 servings

500 g flank steak
      tomato juice, beef stock or water
      flour for coating and for thickening
      fat for browning
Dressing:
250 ml soft bread crumbs
   1 ml salt

f.g. pepper or paprika
   1 egg, slightly beaten
  50 ml margarine or bacon drippings
  30 ml onion, chopped
  50 ml celery, diced fine
  30 ml fresh parsley, chopped
   1 ml poultry seasoning (optional)

1. Melt margarine. Sauté vegetables until soft. Mix dry bread crumbs with seasonings; add vegetables and beaten egg and toss to combine.
2. Score a flank steak by slashing diagonally across the grain every 2 cm. Make a second set of slashes at right angles to the first set.
3. Spread steak with dressing. Tuck in the ends and roll the steak parallel with the grain. Tie into shape with string or fasten with metal skewers.
4. Roll steak in flour and brown in a small amount of fat in a heavy fry pan.
5. Place meat in a suitable sized pan or baking dish. Pour in tomato juice, stock or water to come half way up the side of the meat. Cover and bake at 180°C for about 2 hours or until the meat can be pierced easily with a fork.
6. Place the steak roll on a heated platter and carefully remove string or skewers. Slice.
7. Thicken the juices by stirring in a thin paste made with 15 ml flour and a small amount of cold water. (If your baking dish cannot be heated on the range burner, pour the broth into a saucepan. Be careful to retain the flavourful brown particles clinging to the sides of the dish). Serve the thickened juices in a separate gravy dish, or pour around the steak.

Note: This flank steak may be pressure cooked successfully. Place the meat and juice or water in the pressure cooker. Close the cover securely and place the pressure regulator on the vent pipe. Cook for 20 minutes at 105 kPa. Let pressure drop of its own accord, remove the meat and proceed with steps 6 and 7.

LIVER AND ONION CASSEROLE

125 ml fresh onion, minced
375 ml chicken or beef broth
15 ml Worcestershire sauce
125 ml tomato ketchup
500-750 g beef liver, sliced

5 ml paprika
3 ml salt
50 ml flour
45 ml shortening

1. Preheat oven to 190°C.
2. Combine onion, broth, Worcestershire and ketchup. Allow to stand while rest is prepared.
3. Mix paprika, salt and flour.
4. Dredge liver in flour mixture and brown both sides in hot shortening.

5. Remove meat to casserole or shallow baking pan.
6. Stir the broth mixture into the pan drippings. Bring to boiling point, then pour over liver.
7. Cover and bake for 30-45 minutes until tender.

STUFFED BEEF HEART

1 baby beef heart (about 750 g)
  salt and pepper to taste

Dressing:

3 slices soft bread torn or cut into cubes
1 small egg
5 ml sage
2 ml salt

1 onion, chopped
125 ml water

1 ml pepper
½ onion, finely minced
30 ml margarine, melted

1. Have butcher cut a pocket in the heart. Soak heart in cold, salted water for 15 minutes. Wipe dry.
2. Prepare stuffing by combining all ingredients and tossing lightly.
3. Stuff heart with dressing, fasten with skewers and string.
4. Brown and place in heavy roasting

pan with water and chopped onion. Cover and bake at 180°C for about 2 hours or until tender. Additional water may need to be added during cooking.
5. Remove heart from pan and slice to serve. Thicken pan juices and serve as gravy.

Alternate Methods:

1. Stuffed beef heart pressure cooks successfully. After step No. 3, place heart in pressure cooker. Add water and cover cooker securely. Place pressure regulator on the vent pipe and cook for 45 minutes at 105 kPa. Allow

pressure to drop of its own accord. Then proceed with step No. 5.
2. Heart can also be simmered slowly on the top of the range instead of in the oven.

BEEFSTEAK AND KIDNEY PIE

1 small beef kidney
500 g round steak
  flour for coating
  fat or oil for browning
1 medium onion, sliced

*750 ml hot water
75 ml flour
50 ml cold water
  salt and pepper to taste
  pastry for 1 crust

1. Soak kidney in lukewarm salt water (15 ml salt to 1 litre water) for 1 hour. Drain; remove skin and tubes. Cut into small (1-1.5 cm) cubes.
2. Cut steak into 2 cm pieces. Sprinkle with salt and pepper. Roll in flour and brown in a little hot fat.
3. Add kidney pieces and brown with beef.
4. Add onion when meat is partially browned.

5. Add hot water. Cover and simmer until meat is tender (1 hour or more).
6. Thicken stock with flour blended with cold water. Season to taste. Place in a greased baking dish.
7. Prepare pastry. Roll 2 cm larger than baking dish. Place pastry over meat mixture. Slit top, turn under pastry edge and flute.
8. Bake 225°C for 15 minutes.

* For beefier flavour, substitute 1 can beef bouillon for 250 ml of hot water.

BEEF STROGANOFF

500 g sirloin steak
5 ml monosodium glutamate
1 ml salt
f.g. pepper
50 ml butter or margarine

125 ml mushrooms, sliced
30 ml onion, finely chopped
30 ml flour
100 ml canned beef bouillon, undiluted
125 ml dairy sour cream

Suggest use of electric fry pan or very carefully regulated temperature if using cast iron fry pan.

1. Trim fat from meat.

2. Cut meat in long, thin strips (5 cm x 1.5 cm). Sprinkle with monosodium glutamate, salt and pepper.

3. Heat butter and brown meat strips. Remove meat from pan. Place on platter to catch drippings.

4. Sauté onion and mushrooms slowly.

Remove from pan.

5. Blend 15 ml flour into pan drippings well; add undiluted bouillon and simmer and stir until thick.

6. Return meat, mushrooms, onion and remaining juices to fry pan. Heat to serving temperature.

7. Blend remaining 15 ml flour with sour cream. Stir into meat mixture. Heat but DO NOT BOIL.

Note: Serve over egg noodles and garnish with parsley.

BEEF STEW Yield: 3 or 4 servings

250 g stewing beef
50 ml flour
2 ml salt
1 ml pepper
2 ml paprika
15 ml fat
1 carrot, cut in chunks or thick strips

1 stalk celery, sliced
½ medium onion, coarsely chopped
375 ml boiling water
2 ml salt
1 ml sugar
1 small bay leaf

1. Trim meat; cube in even-sized pieces.

2. Combine flour, salt, pepper and paprika. Dredge meat cubes in seasoned flour.

3. Brown the meat slowly in hot fat in a heavy pan. Add onion and cook until yellow.

4. When the meat is well browned add boiling water, salt, sugar and bay leaf.

5. Cover and simmer for 1 hour, stirring occasionally. Add more water if necessary.

6. Remove bay leaf and add celery and carrot. Continue simmering until vegetables are tender (approximately ½ hour).

7. Skim fat from meat stock, remove meat and vegetables from stock. Combine 15 ml flour with 30 ml of cold water to make a smooth thin paste. Add paste slowly to meat stock and stir constantly over moderate heat until gravy bubbles and thickens. Adjust the seasoning. Pour over meat and vegetables.

Note: Beef stew will bake well at 180°C. Cooking times are the same as in steps 5 and 6.

BROILED LAMB CHOPS

1. Loin, rib, or shoulder chops are suggested. Choose or have them cut 2-3 cm thick. Unless very large or very thick, allow 2 chops per serving.

2. Slash the edges of chops to prevent them from curling.

3. Place chops on broiler pan and adjust rack so that meat is 10-12 cm from the heat. (Broiler should be preheated for 5 minutes.)

4. Broil chops 6-8 minutes on each side, longer if the chops are thicker.

5. Before broiling, one of the following variations may be tried for additional flavour:

- Brush chops with French dressing.
- Rub surface of meat with cut garlic clove.
- Rub meat with a little rosemary (or other herb of your choice).
- Marinate overnight in equal amounts of soya sauce and water to which a minced garlic clove has been added.

BOILED BEEF DINNER

1.2 kg lean boneless chuck roast
7 ml salt
2 peppercorns
1 bay leaf
1 litre water

6 small potatoes, scrubbed
6 yellow onions, peeled
6 medium carrots, scraped and quartered
1 medium cabbage

1. Place meat in large kettle. Add salt, peppercorns, bay leaf and water. Cover and simmer 1½ hours.
2. Remove meat. Let fat rise to the top and skim off.
3. Replace meat. Place potatoes, onions and carrots around meat. Simmer 1 hour longer until meat is fork tender.
4. Cut cabbage into 6 wedges. Arrange on top of meat and vegetables. Cover and cook until cabbage is just tender (15 minutes). Serve.

LAMB SHISH-KABOB

Marinade:

125 ml salad oil
60 ml wine vinegar or lemon juice
5 ml salt
15 ml fresh parsley

1 garlic clove, minced
60 ml sliced onion
5 ml rosemary or thyme

1. Combine above ingredients in a non-metal container. When meat is soaked overnight in refrigerator in a mixture such as this it gains flavour and becomes more tender.
2. Lamb leg or shoulder cut into 2-3 cm cubes is recommended. 1 kg boneless lamb will serve 6 people amply.
3. The term "shish-kabob" is applied to meat cooked on a wooden or metal skewer. "En brochette" and "shashlik" and "souvlaki" are other words used to describe this method of cooking. For best results the skewers should be 15-25 cm long.
4. Usually meat cubes are alternated with vegetables on skewers. Each skewer is then turned often and broiled for about 10 minutes over hot coals or in an oven 10-12 cm from heat.
5. It is best to combine vegetables which require about the same cooking time.

Some suggested foods suitable for Shish-kabobing:

• canned whole onions, parboiled small onions • mushroom caps (parboiled for 1 minute) • large squares of green or sweet red peppers • pineapple cubes or chunks • cherry tomatoes • canned potatoes • stuffed olives • bacon squares • apricot halves

Serving suggestions:

1. Shish-kabobs are traditionally served on a bed of hot rice.
2. It is quite acceptable to serve the kabob with the skewer left in.
3. If the skewer is removed before serving, use care so that pieces stay in the same order.

PORK CUTLETS

Yield: 2-3 servings

500 g pork cutlets*
125 ml dry bread crumbs or crushed salted crackers
1 small egg, beaten slightly

3 ml soya sauce
1 ml salt
f.g. pepper

*Pork cutlets can be made by pounding pork steak or slices of pork butt.

1. TO BREAD CUTLETS: Dip each piece of meat into a mixture of beaten egg and soya sauce. Pat each cutlet onto a pile of bread crumbs or cracker crumbs, turning to coat both sides.
2. TO COOK CUTLETS: Place breaded cutlets in a hot frying pan in which a small amount of fat or oil has been placed. Brown on one side for 2-3 minutes. Turn cutlets, reduce heat, cover and cook for 8-9 minutes. Remove lid and allow steam to escape 2 minutes before serving time.

Note: Cooking time will vary with thickness of cutlets — time given is for 1-1.5 cm cutlets.

SAUSAGE

METHOD I.
TO PAN FRY SAUSAGE:
1. Place sausage links in a cold frypan; add a little water (0.5 cm deep), simmer for 5 minutes. Do not let sausages boil and do not prick links.
2. Drain water or allow to evaporate. Pan fry links slowly. Continue to cook until sausage is brown and cooked throughout, (approximately 15 minutes).

METHOD 2.
1. Place pricked sausages in a cold slightly greased frypan. This prevents sausages from bursting or sticking.
2. Cook slowly over low heat turning frequently. Drain on paper towels. Cooking time is approximately 20 minutes.

TO BAKE SAUSAGE:
1. Spread a single layer of sausages in a shallow oiled pan.
2. Bake at 190°C for approximately 30 minutes. Turn to brown evenly. Baking sausages may be pricked once near the end of the cooking time to allow fat to escape.

HAM STEAK
OVEN BAKED – this method is recommended for a thick slice of ham (2 cm or thicker).
1. Place ham in a baking dish after slashing the fatty edges to prevent curling.
2. Ham may be topped with a mixture of:
   3 ml prepared mustard, 15 ml brown sugar, 10 ml vinegar.
3. Approximately 125 ml of liquid (milk, pineapple juice, orange juice) will improve flavour, tenderness and moistness. Do not cover.
4. Bake 180°C for approximately 1 hour.
5. Ham steak may be garnished with pineapple rings, orange slices, peach slices or apricot halves 15 minutes before end of baking time. Fruit will brown nicely if brushed with a little fat.

BROILED HAM – this method is recommended for thinner slices of ham (0.5-1.5 cm) cut into individual serving pieces.
1. Preheat broiler. Slash edges of ham to prevent curling. Place ham on broiler pan.
2. Broil 12 cm from heat – 5 minutes on each side for ready-to-eat or fully cooked ham, 10 minutes on each side for uncooked ham.
3. Suggested garnish: pineapple rings (may be buttered and broiled for 1-2 minutes on top of ham slice), or crushed pineapple.

BACON
TO PAN FRY:
1. Place bacon slices in an unheated skillet.
2. Fry over a moderately low heat for 6-8 minutes.
3. Bacon may be turned more than once during cooking.
4. Drain bacon on paper towelling to remove excess fat.
Note: For crisper bacon, spoon off fat during cooking.

TO BROIL:
1. Preheat broiler.
2. Place separated slices on broiler pan.
3. Broil 8-12 cm from heat.
4. Turn only once.
Note: Bacon must be watched closely as it cooks very quickly.

TO BAKE:
1. **Preheat oven to 190°C.**
2. Place separated bacon slices on a rack in a shallow pan.
3. Bake for 10 minutes.
Note: Bacon need not be turned or drained.

OVER BARBECUE RIBS

Yield: 4 servings

2 kg spareribs or loin back ribs (500 g per serving is suggested)

1. Steam or parboil the ribs for 15-20 minutes before cooking. This will produce a more moist finished product.
   OR
2. Place ribs on a rack over a pan. Bake at 200°C for 30 minutes. This will produce a drier finished product.

Barbecue Sauce:

60 ml ketchup	**10 ml prepared mustard**
30 ml chili sauce	**5 ml Worcestershire sauce**
15 ml brown sugar	**f.g. garlic salt**
15 ml margarine	**2 thin lemon slices**
15 ml onion, finely chopped	

Combine sauce ingredients in a pan. Bring mixture to a boil, stirring often.

TO BAKE RIBS:
1. Place in shallow roasting pan. Spoon sauce over ribs.
2. Bake uncovered at 180°C for 20-25 minutes. Baste once or twice with sauce during baking.

BAKED STUFFED SPARERIBS

2 kg spareribs

1. Have butcher cut ribs into individual serving pieces. Allow 2 pieces per person.
2. Parboil the ribs for 5 minutes while preparing stuffing.
3. Preheat oven to 250°C.

Stuffing:

250 ml bread crumbs or cubes	**2 ml salt**
1 apple, cored, chopped but unpared	**3 ml poultry seasoning**
30 ml raisins	**1 ml pepper**
50 ml celery, sliced	**125 ml boiling water**
50 ml onion, diced finely	**1 chicken bouillon cube**

4. Toss together crumbs, apple, raisins, celery, onion, salt, poultry seasoning and pepper. Dilute bouillon cube in boiling water. Add bouillon to crumb mixture and toss to moisten.
5. Spread stuffing on one piece of rib, top with a second piece and tie the two pieces together. Repeat for remaining pieces.
6. Rub the outside of the meat with a little flour, salt and pepper.
7. Place on rack in roasting pan in very hot oven. Reduce heat immediately to 170°C. Bake for 1 hour. Baste meat with fat in pan.

PORK PIE

Yield: 4-6 servings

750 g lean pork, cut in 2 cm pieces	**125 ml milk**
15 ml oil or shortening	**50 ml flour**
250 ml water	**750 ml thinly sliced, pared, cored apples**
125 ml chopped onion	**(2 large cooking apples)**
5 ml ground sage	**15 ml sugar**
5 ml salt	**1 recipe pastry***

1. Brown pork cubes well in fat over medium-high heat in heavy saucepan.
2. Add water, onion, sage and salt. Cover and simmer until meat is tender. (The time will depend upon the tenderness of the pork cut used.)
3. Combine milk and flour to make a thin paste. Stir into pork mixture. Cook and stir until the mixture is thickened and bubbly.
4. Line a 1.5 litre casserole with pastry. Turn half the hot pork mixture into the casserole. Place apple slices over meat; sprinkle with sugar. Cover with remaining pork mixture. Place pastry wedges atop meat or cover with full topping.
5. Bake at 230°C for 10 minutes; reduce heat to 180°C and bake 25 minutes more.

*Cheese pastry made with sharp cheddar cheese is good for this recipe. Use 250 ml flour, 1 ml salt, 150 ml grated cheese, 75 ml shortening and 45 ml cold water.

SWEET AND SOUR PORK

Yield: 4 servings

375 g pork butt, cut into 2.5 cm cubes
  1 egg
  2 ml monosodium glutamate
  2 ml salt
  5 ml soya sauce
 30 ml cornstarch
125 ml cornflake crumbs
 90 ml sugar
 60 ml ketchup

 60 ml vinegar
 10 ml Worcestershire sauce
 30 ml cornstarch
    drained pineapple juice from 250 ml tin
    pineapple chunks
  1 small green pepper, cut in strips
  1 large or 2 small tomatoes, cut in
    wedges
    drained pineapple chunks

Electric fry pan is recommended.

1. Prepare pork.

2. Beat egg, monosodium glutamate, salt, soya sauce, and cornstarch together.

3. Dip meat cubes into egg mixture and roll in cornflake crumbs. Let stand 15 to 20 minutes on plate.

5. While meat is cooking, prepare rice, if desired.

6. Mix together sugar, ketchup, vinegar, Worcestershire sauce, cornstarch and pineapple juice to make sweet and sour sauce.

7. Prepare vegetables.

8. When meat is cooked, add vegetables, cover and steam 1 minute.

9. Reduce heat and add sweet and sour sauce. Stir gently until sauce has cleared and thickened.

ORIENTAL BEEF WITH VEGETABLES

250 g stewing beef
125 ml water
  2 stalks celery
  ⅓ large green pepper
  ½ medium onion
 15 ml vegetable oil
175 ml pineapple chunks, drained

 80 ml pineapple juice, divided
 15 ml sugar
 15 ml soy sauce
  2 ml ginger
  3 ml monosodium glutamate
 15 ml cornstarch
  1 tomato

1. Cut stew meat into small pieces. Sear in the bottom of a pressure cooker with a small amount of oil.

2. Add water and pressure cook at 105 kPa for 15 minutes.

3. Cut celery and green peppers slanted across the grain. Cut onion in rings. Sauté in 15 ml of oil for approximately 5 min. Add pineapple chunks, 50 ml of drained pineapple juice, sugar, soy sauce, ginger and monosodium glutamate. Add meat, simmer for 5 minutes.

5. Combine remaining 30 ml pineapple juice with the cornstarch to make a smooth paste. Stir into meat mixture and cook to thicken for 2-3 minutes.

6. Slice tomato into wedges and place on top for colour just before serving.

Serving Suggestion: Serve on hot fluffy rice with cooked broccoli.

Note: Stewing meat may be browned, then covered and simmered gently in water for 1½-2 hours or until tender, before proceeding with vegetable and sauce preparation. Add extra water as it evaporates.

STUFFED GREEN PEPPERS

Yield: 2 servings

  1 large or 2 small green peppers
250 g ground beef
 60 ml uncooked "instant" rice
  2 ml salt
  1 ml pepper

  3 ml Worcestershire sauce
 15 ml onion, chopped
  1 small egg
250 ml tomato sauce

1. Halve a large pepper or cut the tops off 2 small ones. Remove membranes and seeds.

2. Precook peppers in boiling salted water for 5 minutes; drain.

3. Combine uncooked rice, ground beef, salt, pepper, Worcestershire sauce, onion, egg and 75 ml tomato sauce.

4. Stuff peppers with meat mixture. Place in small casserole so peppers won't fall over.

5. Pour remaining tomato sauce over peppers.

6. Cover peppers and bake at 180°C for 45-50 minutes.

Note: Baste peppers once or twice during baking with sauce.

CHINESE BEEF DINNER

250 g mushrooms, sliced
50 ml butter or margarine
250 g lean ground beef
1 stalk celery, sliced thinly
1 large onion, diced
1 tomato, sectioned
½ green pepper diced

1 clove garlic, minced
30 ml soya sauce
500 ml cooked rice — long grain, short grain or brown
5 ml salt
2 raw eggs
250 ml shredded lettuce

1. Sauté mushrooms in fat, add meat and salt, brown well.
2. Add all other ingredients except the eggs and lettuce. Mix well. Heat thoroughly.

3. Just before serving add eggs and stir quickly. Stir in shredded lettuce. Serve immediately.

HAMBURGER PIE

320 ml cream of mushroom soup
500 g ground beef
60 ml onion, finely chopped
1 egg, slightly beaten
60 ml dry bread crumbs

15 ml parsley flakes
2 ml salt
1 ml pepper
500 ml seasoned mashed potatoes
60 ml grated cheddar cheese

1. Preheat oven to 180°C.
2. Combine 250 ml undiluted soup, the beef, onion, egg, bread crumbs, parsley, salt and pepper.
3. Press meat mixture into a 22 cm pie plate.

4. Bake for 30 minutes, spoon off excess fat.
5. Spoon potatoes over meat pie, spoon over remaining soup, and sprinkle the cheese over the top.
6. Return to oven for 10-15 minutes until potatoes are heated through.

Variation:
Pie may be topped with biscuit topping instead of potatoes. At step No. 6 return to a 200°C oven to bake biscuits.

SWEDISH MEAT BALLS

30 ml onion, finely chopped
15 ml butter
250 g ground beef
2 ml salt
1 ml pepper

15 ml flour
1 small egg
30 ml light cream
100 ml canned consommé, undiluted

1. Cook onion in butter until tender but not brown.
2. Combine meat and seasonings thoroughly.
3. Beat in flour and egg with a wooden spoon. Gradually beat in cream. Add onion. Mix well.

4. Form 12, 2.5 cm meatballs.
5. Brown meat balls lightly in a little additional butter.
6. Remove excess fat. Add consommé. Simmer uncovered 12-15 minutes.
7. If desired, thicken gravy.

PORCUPINE MEAT BALLS

375 g ground beef
60 ml rice
2 ml salt
1 ml pepper

15 ml onion, minced
125 ml water
150 ml tomato soup

1. Wash rice in cold water and drain.
2. Combine meat, rice, salt, pepper and onion well. Shape into small balls.
3. Heat tomato soup and water in pressure cooker.
4. Place meatballs in soup mixture.

5. Close cover securely. Place pressure regulator on vent pipe and cook 10 minutes at 105 kPa.
6. Let pressure drop of its own accord before opening to serve.

Optional Method:
After meat balls are made, they may be simmered in a covered pan on top of the stove for one hour.

MEAT	500 g ground beef	250 g ground beef plus 250 g ground pork or bulk pork sausage	250 g ground veal plus 250 g ground pork	250 g ground beef plus 250 g ground veal	
LIQUID	1 egg	1 egg	1 egg	1 egg	1 egg
	250 ml tomato sauce or juice	125 ml milk plus 125 ml tomato soup	250 ml milk or broth	250 ml diluted gravy	125 ml barbecue sauce, ketchup or chili sauce diluted with 125 ml water
DRY INGRE-DIENTS	75 ml breadcrumbs (soft or dry)	75 ml cornflake crumbs	100 ml whole grain cereal or oatmeal	*50 ml wheatgerm may be substituted for part of crumbs or cereal	
VEGETABLE	75 ml chopped onion	40 ml chopped onion and 40 ml chopped celery	½ green pepper cubed and sautéed in 15 ml margarine	125 ml grated carrot	250 ml thawed drained frozen vegetables or leftover vegetables
SEASONINGS	5 ml brown sugar 5 ml vinegar 5 ml mustard combined with tomato sauce, juice or soup	15 ml Worcestershire 5 ml dry mustard	125 ml cheddar cheese cubes	bacon strips to line the pan or to top the meat loaf	
SPICES	5 ml salt f.g. pepper	5 ml garlic salt f.g. pepper	3 ml mixed Italian herbs 5 ml salt	2 ml sage 3 ml thyme 5 ml salt f.g. pepper	3 ml poultry seasoning 5 ml salt f.g. monosodium glutamate

a. With consideration to flavour combinations and texture, choose one item or group (food or foods) from each line (i.e., meat, liquid, etc.)

b. Combine ingredients chosen by the method for meat loaf which follows:

1. Beat egg slightly in a large bowl.
2. Add the meat and break up with a fork.
3. Combine spices and dry ingredients separately.
4. Combine the dry ingredients with the meat mixture.
5. Combine any liquid flavourings with the liquid chosen.
6. Stir the vegetables and liquid into the meat mixture. Mix well.
7. Pack meat into pan and bake according to method chosen:
    a. Loaf pan, 180°C for 1 hour or until done.
    b. Mini loaves (4), 200°C for approximately 20 minutes.
    c. Muffin pans for individual servings, 200°C for 15 minutes.

MARINADE FOR BEAR ROAST

500 ml water
15 ml salt
50 ml vinegar
30 ml pickling spices
dash chili powder

1 lemon, juice of
1 orange, juice of
herbs to taste (rosemary, sweet basil, sage, thyme)

Mix ingredients well and pour over the meat. Turn occasionally during the 48 hour period if marinade does not cover the entire roast or steak.

MARINADE FOR VENISON STEAK

30 ml vegetable oil
125 ml wine vinegar
15 ml oregano
1 ml salt

1 ml black pepper
dash cayenne pepper
1 onion, sliced thin

1. Mix all ingredients except the onion and pour into a flat dish.
2. Place the steak, cut 3-4 cm thick, into the dish. Top with thinly sliced onion.
3. Turn meat at least once in the 12-24 hour period before cooking.

MEAT BALL SUPPER

Yield: 2 servings

250 g ground beef
1 egg
½ small onion, finely chopped
50 ml bread crumbs
7 ml prepared mustard
15 ml vegetable oil

2 ml salt
2 ml oregano
1 ml pepper
125 ml tomato sauce plus 100 ml water
125 ml celery, sliced
125 ml frozen peas

1. Combine beef, beaten egg, onion, crumbs, mustard, salt, oregano, pepper and 15 ml tomato sauce well.
2. Shape into 10 meat balls.
3. Roll meat balls in seasoned flour and brown in hot oil at medium temperature.
4. Pour off excess fat.

5. Add celery and cook lightly.
6. Add the remaining sauce which has been mixed with water. Simmer tightly covered for 15 minutes.
7. Add peas and cover and continue cooking for about 5 more minutes, until peas are cooked.

Serving suggestions:
May be served on pasta, rice or mashed potatoes or with baked potato.

SHAKE AND BAKE

500 ml very fine, dry, sifted, toasted bread crumbs
125 ml all purpose flour
5 ml salt

10 ml monosodium glutamate
3 ml berry sugar
2 ml garlic salt
3 ml seasoned salt

1. Prepare crumbs in a blender.
2. Mix remaining ingredients with crumbs, blending well.
3. Store in covered container.
4. To use: • Moisten meat with water or milk.
   • Pour needed amount of shake and bake into plastic bag and add meat one piece at a time and shake until evenly coated.
   • Place on ungreased baking sheet. Bake at 200°C until tender, the time depending upon the meat used.

Chicken

CHICKEN CROQUETTES

375 ml minced cooked chicken
125 ml minced celery or sautéed mushrooms (or combination of these)

1 ml celery salt
5 ml lemon juice
5 ml chopped parsley
salt and pepper to taste

1. Combine these ingredients with a thick hot velouté sauce, about 200 ml.
2. Cool and shape into slightly oval shaped balls about 75 ml in each.
3. Roll each ball in flour and then coat with seasoned fine bread crumbs to which salt and pepper have been added, also any seasonings to taste; (e.g., dried parsley, thyme, sage). Allow to stand for about 1 hour.
4. Fry in deep fat preheated to 190°C for about 2 to 4 minutes. Drain on absorbent towel.
6. Serve with a sauce, tomato, mushroom or egg.

CHICKEN POT PIE

Yield: 6 servings

375 ml cold stock or water
150 ml skim milk powder
50 ml flour
3 ml salt
1 ml dry tarragon, crushed fine
f.g. pepper

1. Mix together the milk powder, flour and seasonings.
2. Gradually add the cold water. Cook slowly, stirring constantly to make a smooth sauce.
3. Remove from heat; add chicken, onions and vegetables. Taste and season if necessary.
4. Put this mixture into 1.5 litre casserole.

750 ml chopped cooked chicken or turkey
6 medium pre-cooked onions
500 ml cooked vegetables (peas, lima beans, celery, carrots, green beans are all suitable)

5. Prepare pastry for the top:
125 ml flour
50 ml margarine
1 ml salt
15-20 ml cold water

Make a soft dough, shape into a ball and roll on a lightly floured board to 1.5 cm thickness. Prick with a fork and arrange pastry over casserole, pinching down edges firmly to casserole. Bake in a preheated oven at 230°C until bubbling hot and the crust lightly browned and cooked through, about 20 minutes.

CHICKEN CACCIATORE

Yield: 4-6 servings

50 ml vegetable oil
1.25-1.5 kg frying chicken, cut up
2 medium onion, sliced thick
2 cloves garlic, minced
400 ml canned tomatoes

1. Heat oil in a large skillet until hot enough to sizzle a drop of water. Add chicken pieces and brown slowly, turning once with tongs.
2. Remove chicken from skillet. Add onions and garlic and cook until tender but not brown.
3. For sauce — combine the remaining ingredients. Taste sauce and season if necessary. Return browned chicken to

250 ml tomato sauce
2 ml pepper
5 ml salt
3 ml celery seed
5 ml crushed oregano or basil
1 bay leaf

skillet and pour the sauce over.
4. Cover and simmer for 45 minutes being careful not to let the sauce bubble hard. Remove cover and cook, with occasional stirring, for 20 minutes more or until chicken is fork tender and the sauce looks like chili sauce.
5. Remove bay leaf, skim off excess fat. Serve with hot noodles or spaghetti sprinkled with Parmesan cheese.

CHICKEN STEW WITH DUMPLINGS

3 kg stewing chicken cut into serving sized pieces
5 ml salt
50 ml flour
1 bay leaf

1. Rinse chicken pieces in cold water, pat dry.
2. Place in a heavy kettle and cover with cold water to which salt and bay leaf have been added.
3. Bring to a boil and simmer until tender; about 3 hours.
4. Pour off some of the broth for later use leaving just enough to come to the top of the chicken pieces.
5. Mix 50 ml of flour with 150 ml of cooled broth and add to chicken and broth in kettle. Cook slowly, stirring

until slightly thickened. Taste and season if necessary.

6. Prepare dumplings:
250 ml flour
10 ml baking powder
150 ml cold milk

1. Sift together the flour, salt and baking powder into a bowl.
2. Add milk all at once. Stir lightly.
3. Bring chicken to a full boil. Drop dumplings onto liquid in 4 or 5 equal parts.
4. Cook for 20 minutes without lifting the lid.
5. Serve a serving of chicken, a dumpling and some of the gravy.

(Oven temperature 160°C)

TYPE OF POULTRY	EVISCERATED WEIGHT	ROASTING TIME
Chicken	2-2.5 kilograms	2¾-3½ hours
	2.5-3 kilograms	3½-4½ hours
	3-3.5 kilograms	4½-5 hours
Turkey		
Whole	4 kilograms	3¾-4½ hours
	6 kilograms	4¾-5½ hours
	8 kilograms	5¼-6 hours
	10 kilograms	5¾-6½ hours
	12 kilograms	6¼-7 hours
Halves	2 kilograms	2½-3 hours
	4 kilograms	4-4½ hours
	6 kilograms	4½-5 hours
Quarters	2 kilograms	3-3½ hours
	3 kilograms	3½-4 hours
Turkey Rolls	1.5-2.5 kilograms	3½-5 hours
	2.5-3.5 kilograms	5-6 hours
	3.5-5 kilograms	6-6½ hours
Goose	4-5 kilograms	1½-2 hours
	5-6 kilograms	2-2½ hours

Notes about Roasting Poultry:

1. Stuffed and unstuffed poultry require the same time to cook.

2. Begin testing to determine if the bird is cooked when it has been in the oven the shorter of the two times. To do this press the thick muscle of the drumstick, protecting your fingers with a pot holder or towel, to see if it feels soft. Then check how easily the leg moves. The bird is cooked when the drumstick muscle feels soft and the leg moves readily in the joint when you lift or twist it. When pricked with a fork between the body and the heaviest part of the thigh the juices will run clear.

3. If using a meat thermometer, insert it before cooking, into the thickest part of the thigh muscle or into the centre of the stuffing. Be sure that it is not touching on bone. Cooked chicken will register 85°C on the thermometer placed in the thigh, in the stuffing it will register 75°C. Roast stuffed turkey to 75°C in the stuffing and to 85°C in the thigh.

4. Because geese vary in shape their cooking times may differ. Therefore, allow an extra half hour before serving time in case more cooking time is needed.

5. Because duck has more fat it should be roasted at a higher temperature than chicken or turkey.

6. Overbrowning may become evident as cooking proceeds. To prevent this happening cover the bird loosely with aluminum foil, shiny side out.

7. To prevent drying of the meat, baste the surfaces occasionally with fat and/or juices as they cook out of the bird.

Fish, Shellfish

CRISPY FRIED TROUT

Yield: 6 servings

6 pan-dressed fresh or frozen trout or other small fish
50 ml evaporated milk
7 ml salt
   dash pepper

125 ml flour
50 ml yellow cornmeal
5 ml paprika
12 slices bacon

1. Thaw frozen fish. Clean, wash and dry fish.
2. Combine milk, salt and pepper. Combine flour, cornmeal and paprika.
3. Dip each fish in milk mixture and then roll in flour mixture.
4. Fry bacon in a large heavy fry pan until crisp. Remove and drain on absorbent paper. Reserve fat for frying.
5. Fry fish in hot fat for 4 minutes. Then turn carefully and fry for 4-6 minutes longer or until fish is brown and flakes easily when tested with a fork. Drain on absorbent paper. Serve hot with bacon.

Variation:
This recipe can be used to cook 1 kg fish fillets. Fat or oil may be used for frying and bacon omitted.

BATTER FOR DEEP FRIED FISH

375 ml all purpose flour
15 ml baking powder
5 ml salt

   dash pepper
2 eggs
250 ml milk

1. Measure and sift dry ingredients together.
2. Beat eggs, add milk and beat.
3. Add liquid ingredients to dry ingredients and stir or beat gently until smooth.
4. Dip prepared pieces of fish in batter and cook following general instructions for deep fat frying of fish found in Fish section.

BAKED FISH FILLETS

Yield: 6 servings

1 kg fish fillets
125 ml milk
5 ml salt

175 ml fine bread crumbs
30 ml butter or other fat

1. Wipe fish with a damp cloth and cut into individual portions. If fillets are frozen, do not thaw before cooking.
2. Soak in milk to which salt has been added for about 3 minutes. Drain and roll in bread crumbs.
3. Place on a greased baking dish and dot with butter.
4. Measure the thickness of the pieces. Bake in very hot oven 230°C to 260°C allowing approximately 15 minutes for 3 cm thickness of fresh fish and 30 minutes for 3 cm of frozen fish.

BREAD DRESSING FOR FISH

75 ml chopped onion
75 ml diced celery
50 ml butter or other fat
2-5 ml salt

   dash pepper
3 ml seasoning (poultry seasoning, savoury, thyme, sage, mint, tarragon)
750 ml soft bread crumbs

1. Cook onion and celery in fat until tender (about 5 minutes).
2. Put bread in a bowl, add seasonings, toss lightly.
3. Add cooked vegetables and mix.
4. This should make enough dressing for a 2 kg fish. It can also be used between two layers of fillets or fish steaks.

BARBECUED WHOLE SALMON

Preparing:

Clean and remove scales from a 2-4 kilogram salmon. Trim off head just back of the collarbone. Sprinkle salt and pepper inside body cavity. Tuck inside cavity one whole lemon (sliced) and 1 small onion (sliced) and a handful of parsley sprigs.

Cut 2 pieces of foil, one to fit exactly each side of the fish to the tail; press smoothly against fish on each side. To overwrap, tear off a 60 cm long sheet of 45 cm wide heavy foil. Centre fish on foil sheet, folding back one edge to expose fish tail. Bring lengthwise edges of foil to meet in the centre, crease a 2 cm seam, then fold over and over to seal tightly against the side of the fish, (drug store wrap). Seal foil at head end and press tightly against fish near exposed tail.

Barbecuing:

Adjust the barbecue so that grill will be about 15 cm above the firebed. Ignite pile of 30 long-burning briquets. When glowing coals form, in about 30 minutes, spread evenly directly under where the fish will be (not under tail — for best appearance it must be kept cool). Place fish on grill with foil seam up. Arrange a wad of foil under the tail to support it and shield it from the heat.

Carefully turn the fish over every 10 minutes. Brush tail with water from time to time. After 30 minutes, open seam on top and test by cutting a narrow slit into the thickest part of the fish with a sharp knife. When cooked, the meat is firm, looks lighter in colour and is less translucent. If necessary, reseal the foil and continue cooking, turning and checking stage of cooking every five minutes.

Serving:

Remove some of the coals from the barbecue leaving just enough to keep the fish warm. Open foil seam and fold back to keep the juices from dripping. Lift off foil piece on top of fish. If you wish, also lift off a layer of skin. To serve, cut directly to bone, slide a wide spatula between meat and bone, and lift off each serving.

BARBECUED SALMON FILLETS

Preparing:

Clean and scale and fillet salmon. Set each fillet skin side down on foil, then cut foil to just fit under fillet.

Barbecuing:

Ignite a pile of about 20 long-burning briquets. When glowing coals form, spread evenly beneath where fillets will cook. Grill should be 12-15 cm above heat. Place fillets on grill, foil side down. If barbecue has a hood, use it to enclose the smoke. Baste fish frequently with marinade. Cook without turning until fish flakes readily when tested with a fork, about 40 minutes (about 20 minutes on a covered barbecue).

Serving:

Cut down to skin and lift off fish. Serve on heated plates. Allow 250 g fillet for each serving.

CLAM FRITTERS

Yield: 12-15 fritters   (8 cm diameter)

350 ml ground or minced clams (2 dozen drained)
2 eggs
125 ml milk

30 ml melted shortening or vegetable oil
250 ml all purpose flour
10 ml baking powder
5 ml salt

1. Prepare clams by grinding or mincing finely.
2. Beat eggs in bowl. Add milk and beat. Add melted fat. Stir in clams.
3. Mix dry ingredients. Stir into liquid ingredients.

4. Drop batter by spoonfuls into hot fat that is 0.5 cm deep. Fry until golden brown on both sides. Drain on paper towels and keep warm until all fritters are cooked. Serve with lemon wedges.

1. Lemon Butter

50 ml melted butter or margarine   50 ml lemon juice

2. Herb Butter

50 ml melted butter or margarine
50 ml lemon juice
5 ml grated lemon rind
2 ml salt

dash pepper
15 ml finely chopped onion
2 ml marjoram

Combine all ingredients. Marinate fish in this sauce for 10-15 minutes turning once. Then broil, using sauce as a basting liquid.

3. Herb Basting Sauce

125 ml lemon juice
125 ml melted butter or oil
4 green onions, thinly sliced
50 ml minced parsley

3 ml salt
2 ml rosemary leaves
dash pepper

Combine all ingredients and mix well. Generously brush the fish (good for salmon steaks or fillets) with some of the basting sauce. Let stand about 30 minutes before barbequing. This makes enough to baste the two fillets from a salmon weighing up to 4 kilograms.

SALMON LOAF   Yield: 4-6 servings

1 can (500 ml) salmon
500 ml soft bread crumbs
30 ml chopped parsley
30 ml onion, grated or chopped fine
30 ml lemon juice
5 ml salt

2 ml celery salt
dash pepper
50 ml melted butter or margarine
2 eggs
250 ml liquid (liquid from canned salmon plus milk to make up the volume)

1. Drain salmon, reserving liquid.
2. Mix together all ingredients except the eggs and liquid.
3. Place the salmon mixture in a well greased loaf pan.
4. Beat eggs, add salmon liquid and milk and beat. Pour over the salmon mixture in the loaf pan.
5. Bake at 180°C for 45 minutes or until firm in the centre and lightly browned.
6. Unmould on heated platter. Serve plain or with desired sauce.

SALMON BURGERS   Yield: 8 salmonburgers

400 ml canned salmon or cooked fresh salmon
250 ml soft bread crumbs
2 ml salt
1 ml pepper

15 ml finely chopped onion
1 egg, well beaten
8 slices raw tomatoes
8 cooked bacon strips
8 hamburger buns, heated

1. Place salmon in a bowl, mash the bones, flake the flesh and mix with salmon liquid.
2. Add bread crumbs, salt, pepper and onion and mix lightly.
3. Add egg and mix well.
4. Shape into eight patties. Pan fry until browned, on one side. Turn and brown the other side.
5. To assemble place a cooked patty on a heated bun. Top with a tomato slice and a strip of bacon.

Quickbreads

MUFFINS

Yield: 12 medium muffins

500 ml all purpose flour
20 ml baking powder
2 ml salt
75 ml sugar

1 egg
75 ml melted fat or salad oil
250 ml milk

1. Set oven to 200°C, grease muffin tins.
2. Sift and measure flour. Add other dry ingredients and sift into bowl.
3. Melt fat, beat egg, then add the milk. Mix.
4. Make a well in the centre of the dry ingredients. Add egg and milk, then the cooled fat. Stir lightly with a fork just until dry ingredients are all moistened. Batter will be lumpy.
5. Spoon into muffin tins filling ⅔ full. Bake at 200°C for about 20 minutes until muffins pull away from the sides of the pan and are a golden brown colour.
6. Turn out on a cake rack and serve warm.

BRAN MUFFINS

Yield: 12-16 medium muffins

1 egg, beaten
225 ml milk
50 ml vegetable oil
30 ml molasses
375 ml all-bran or bran flakes

250 ml all purpose flour
15 ml baking soda
2 ml salt
60 ml brown sugar
100 ml raisins (optional)

1. Combine beaten egg, milk, vegetable oil and molasses.
2. Stir in the bran and let stand five minutes.
3. Sift together flour, baking powder and salt. Blend in brown sugar.
4. Add bran mixture and raisins to dry ingredients, stirring until just combined. Do not overmix.
5. Bake in preheated 200°C oven for 25 minutes.

WAFFLES

Yield: 6 servings

375 ml sifted flour
30 ml sugar
10 ml baking powder
2 ml salt

2 eggs, separated
250 ml milk
100 ml melted butter or margarine

1. Heat waffle iron. Melt fat.
2. Sift flour, sugar, baking powder and salt together in a large bowl.
3. Beat egg whites to form softly rounded peaks.
4. Beat yolks until thick. Add milk and cooled fat. Blend with a rotary beater.
5. Make a well in flour mixture, pour in yolk mixture, stirring quickly until flour is just moistened.
6. Fold whites into batter using 8-10 light strokes.
7. Pour 50-75 ml of batter into centre of iron (or divide amount and pour about 15 ml in the centre of each of the four compartments.)
8. Bake waffles without opening the lid for 3-5 minutes or until steam no longer escapes. At this time the waffle should be crisp and golden brown.

Variations
Use the same recipe but fold in one of the following additional ingredients to make the desired variation:

200-250 ml grated cheese
250 ml finely diced apple
125-200 ml chopped nuts
125-200 ml shredded coconut
125-200 ml drained, crushed pineapple

125 ml drained kernel corn with 2 ml salt
5 strips bacon, chopped, cooked and drained

BISCUITS   Yield: 12 medium biscuits

500 ml flour   75 ml shortening
  20 ml baking powder   200 ml milk
   2 ml salt

1. Sift flour, baking powder and salt into mixing bowl.
2. Cut fat into dry ingredients until particles resemble coarse crumbs.
3. Add milk a little at a time, stirring lightly with a fork until the soft dough forms a ball.
4. Turn onto lightly floured surface and knead for a few seconds, about 10 times.
5. Pat or roll dough until it is 1.5-2 cm thick. Cut with floured biscuit cutter or knife.
6. Place on ungreased baking pan and bake in hot oven 220°C for 12-15 minutes.

Biscuit Variations

DROP BISCUITS: Use an additional 75 ml milk to make a very soft dough, then drop by spoonfuls onto a baking sheet.
CHEESE BISCUITS: Add 200-250 ml grated cheddar cheese to the dry mixture before adding milk. 2 ml celery seed may be added as well, if desired.

FRUIT PINWHEELS:
1. Add 10 ml sugar to basic biscuit recipe.
2. Roll dough into a rectangle not more than 1 cm thick. Spread with 30 ml softened table fat to within 1 cm of *one* of the long edges.
3. Sprinkle 45 ml brown sugar and 3 ml cinnamon evenly over the fat. Add raisins and/or chopped nuts.
4. Beginning on the long side, roll dough towards unbuttered strip. Seal edge.
5. Cut in 1.5 cm slices. Bake cut side down on a greased baking pan or in a greased muffin pan.

TUNA ROLL-UPS

500 ml biscuit mix   30 ml chopped onion
200 ml milk   30 ml chopped celery
  30 ml softened butter   15 ml chopped green pepper
200 ml can tuna, drained   1 egg
   2 ml salt

1. Mix biscuit mix and milk; knead slightly, (or prepare one recipe of biscuit dough). Roll into a rectangular shape 1 cm thick.
2. Mix remaining ingredients together. Spread over biscuit dough.
3. Roll up and pinch edge to hold in filling. Cut into slices 2 cm thick.
4. Place on a greased cookie sheet or in greased muffin pans and bake at 220°C for 10-15 minutes.
5. Serve hot with cheese or vegetable sauce.

PANCAKES   Yield: 12 pancakes

250 ml flour   1 egg
  15 ml baking powder   200 ml milk
  30 ml sugar   50 ml fat, melted
   2 ml salt

1. Heat griddle slowly. Melt fat, set aside to cool.
2. Prepare dry ingredients. Sift into bowl.
3. Beat egg until thick, add the milk, then the fat.
4. Make a well in the dry ingredients and pour in egg mixture. Stir quickly until all ingredients are well moistened.
5. Test griddle: When a drop of water rolls around on it the griddle is ready. Pour batter on hot griddle making pancakes of 8-10 cm diameter.
6. Cook until bubbles begin to burst on top, then turn with a pancake turner and brown the other side.

POPOVERS

3 eggs
250 ml milk
250 ml all purpose flour

2 ml salt
20 ml melted table fat or shortening

1. Beat eggs until very thick and pale yellow, add milk and cooled fat; beat until combined.
2. Place a dot of fat in each popover cup, heat in the oven until very hot.
3. Sift flour and salt into liquids. Beat with rotary beater until smooth. Pour

batter into sizzling pans, fill ⅓ full.
4. Bake at 220°C for 20 minutes. Reduce heat to 160°C and continue baking for 15 minutes or until firm. Turn off heat, leave popovers in oven 10 minutes or until crisp.

Variation
YORKSHIRE PUDDING: Substitute table fat or shortening with fat drippings from beef roast. Heat pan as for popovers. When roast is cooked, remove it from oven and keep hot. Turn oven to 220°C. Pour batter into hot pans and bake as for popovers. Serve with beef and gravy.

BRAN DATE BREAD

175 ml hot water
250 ml all-bran or bran flakes
250 ml chopped dates
375 ml sifted flour
15 ml baking powder

5 ml salt
5 ml cinnamon
30 ml shortening
200 ml sugar
2 eggs

1. Pour hot water over dates and bran and let stand.
2. Sift flour, baking powder, salt and cinnamon.
3. Cream sugar and shortening until

fluffy. Add eggs and beat.
4. Add flour mixture and date mixture alternately, stirring until combined.
5. Bake at 180°C for 1 hour.

BANANA BREAD

500 ml all purpose flour
10 ml baking powder
2 ml salt
2 ml baking soda
2 ml nutmeg
2 eggs

125 ml melted table fat
30 ml sour milk
250 ml white sugar
375 ml mashed ripe bananas (3 medium)
250 ml chopped nuts (optional)

1. Grease a large loaf tin.
2. Combine first five ingredients and set aside.
3. In another bowl combine egg, melted fat, sour milk, sugar and mashed bananas, and nuts.

4. Combine liquid ingredients with dry ingredients stirring until mixture is just moistened.
5. Pour into pan and bake for 40-50 minutes at 160°C or until a toothpick comes out clean.

MASTER MIX

2 250 ml sifted all purpose flour
75 ml baking powder
15 ml salt
10 ml cream of tartar

50 ml sugar
250 ml powdered skim milk
500 ml shortening

1. Sift together several times the flour, baking powder, salt, cream of tartar and powdered milk.
2. Cut in the shortening with pastry

blender or two knives until the mixture looks like coarse cornmeal.
3. Store in covered containers at room temperature. See page 508 for recipes.

PRODUCT	YIELD	TEMP.	TIME	MIX	SUGAR	WATER	EGGS	ADDITIONAL INGREDIENT	MIXING
Biscuits	18 5 cm	220°C	10-15 min	750 ml		200 ml			Stir until blended; knead 10-15 times. Pat or roll to 1 cm thick.
Muffins	12 7 cm	220°C	20 min	750 ml	30 ml	250 ml	1		Mix eggs & water, stir all ingredients until moist.
Pancakes or Waffles	12 med. pancakes 3-4 waffles			375 ml	30 ml	200 ml	1		Stir until blended.
Dumplings			12 min	500 ml		125 ml			Stir until blended; drop spoonfuls on hot stew, soup, fruit sauce. Cover and steam without lifting cover.
Gingerbread	20 x 20 cm	180°C	40 min	500 ml	75 ml	125 ml	1	125 ml molasses 5 ml ginger 5 ml cinnamon 2 ml cloves f.g. nutmeg	Add half liq. beat 2 min. Add remaining liquid; beat 2 min.
Coffeecake	22 x 22 cm	200°C	25 min	750 ml	125 ml	175 ml	1	TOPPING: 125 ml brown sugar 45 ml table fat 5 ml cinnamon	Stir until well blended; place in pan. Combine topping ingredients and sprinkle over cake.
Oatmeal Cookies	3 doz.	190°C	10-12 min	750 ml	125 ml	85 ml	2	125 ml brown sugar 5 ml cinnamon 250 ml rolled oats	Stir until well blended. Drop by spoonfuls onto greased cookie sheet.
Drop Cookies	3 doz.	190°C	10-12 min	750 ml	250 ml	85 ml	1	5 ml vanilla *Variations:* 125 ml nuts or 125 ml choc. chips or 125 ml raisins or 250 ml dates or coconut	Stir until well blended. Drop by spoonfuls onto greased cookie sheet.
Orange-Raisin Cake	20 x 20 cm	180°C	30 min	500 ml	250 ml		2	juice of one orange plus water to make 250 ml 125 ml chopped raisins grated peel of one orange	Add sugar & 250 ml liquid; beat 2 min. Add remaining water, raisins and peel. Beat 1 min.

QUICK COFFEE CAKE

250 ml sifted all purpose flour
 10 ml baking powder
  2 ml salt
  3 ml cinnamon
  1 egg
125 ml sugar
125 ml milk
 15 ml grated orange rind
 30 ml melted shortening

TOPPING:
 15 ml melted butter
125 ml brown sugar
 30 ml grated orange rind
125 ml broken nuts

1. Sift flour, baking powder, salt and cinnamon together in large bowl.
2. Beat egg until thick, add sugar, milk, fat and rind and blend with beater.
3. Pour egg mixture over flour mixture and stir quickly until just moistened.
4. Place in greased 20 or 22 cm square pan and bake at 190°C for 25 minutes.
5. Combine ingredients for the topping and spread over hot cake.

QUICK APPLE COFFEE CAKE

625 ml pastry flour
    OR
550 ml all purpose flour
 25 ml baking powder
  5 ml salt
 30 ml sugar (optional)

 75 ml shortening
  2 eggs
250 ml milk
  2 red apples, sliced
 50 ml sugar, mixed with 5 ml cinnamon

1. Sift the dry ingredients several times. Cut in the shortening with a pastry blender.
2. Add beaten eggs and milk all at once. Mix only until the flour is dampened. The dough should have a slightly lumpy appearance.
3. Pour into a greased 25 cm x 30-35 cm pan.
4. Press unpeeled apple slices into the top of the batter. Sprinkle with sugar and cinnamon mixture.
5. Bake at 200°C for 20 minutes. Serve hot.

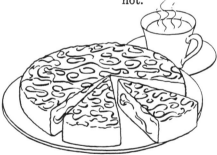

DUMPLINGS

Yield: 10-12 dumplings

450 ml sifted all purpose flour
  5 ml salt
 20 ml baking powder

50-75 ml fat
175 ml milk

1. Sift the flour, salt and baking powder together.
2. Cut in the fat until it is the texture of cornmeal.
3. Stir in the milk all at once to make a sticky dough.
4. Form the dumplings with a metal spoon, placing them on a flour-sprinkled plate.
5. Place dumplings onto the unthick-ened stew, spacing them evenly. Cover the pan with a tightly fitting lid.
6. Keep the stew simmering and do not lift the lid for 15 minutes.
7. Lift the dumplings onto a heated plate and keep warm until serving time while you thicken the stew and place it in a serving dish. Arrange dumplings on top.

Yeast Breads

WHITE BREAD

Preparation Time:	4 hours
Baking Temperature:	200°C
Baking Time:	25-30 minutes
Yield:	1 loaf

Yeast Liquid
- 85 ml warm water
- 5 ml sugar
- 5 ml yeast

Additional Ingredients
- 675 ml flour
- 20 ml sugar
- 5 ml salt
- 60 ml milk powder
- 20 ml melted shortening
- 160 ml warm water

1. Reconstitute yeast by dissolving 5 ml sugar in 85 ml lukewarm water (40°C) from the tap. Sprinkle yeast on top and allow to stand until frothy — about 8-10 minutes.
2. Combine dry ingredients to form a mix.
3. Add yeast liquid, 160 ml warm water and melted shortening all at once to dry mix. Stir with a wooden spoon to form a soft dough.
4. Turn dough onto a lightly floured board and knead until dough is smooth and springy — about 10 minutes.
5. Cover with oiled plastic and allow to rise until double in size — about 1½ hours.
6. Punch dough down to remove all air bubbles.
7. Form into a loaf shape. Place in pan. Cover with oiled plastic and allow to rise until a dent remains when the dough is pressed lightly with a floured finger — about 30 minutes.
8. Bake at 200°C for 25-30 minutes.

BROWN BREAD

Preparation Time:	2 hours
Baking Temperature:	180°C
Baking Time:	30-35 minutes
Yield:	1 loaf

Yeast Liquid
- 10 ml dried yeast
- 5 ml sugar
- 125 ml warm water

Additional Ingredients
- 500 ml all purpose flour
- 500 ml whole wheat flour
- 20 ml sugar
- 10 ml salt
- 250 ml water

1. Prepare yeast liquid by dissolving 5 ml of the sugar in 125 ml lukewarm water (40°C) from the tap. Sprinkle dry yeast on top. Allow to stand 8-10 minutes until frothy.
2. Prepare dry mix, stirring all dry ingredients together.
3. Make a soft dough stirring the yeast liquid and extra water into the flour mixture all at once.
4. Knead dough until it is smooth — about 2-3 minutes.
*5. Cover with oiled plastic and allow to rise until double in size. Punch down.
6. Shape dough and place in small loaf pan.
7. Cover with oiled plastic and allow to rise until double in size.
8. Bake at 180°C for 30-35 minutes.

* This step can be missed out if bread is made in one lab period.

Note: This recipe is specially designed as an introduction to yeast baking. The product tends to be close textured with the single rise but gives a very adequate result. The use of a well greased flower pot as a baking utensil also provides an interesting variation in shape!

WHOLE WHEAT BREAD

Preparation Time:	3 hours
Baking Temperature:	180°C
Baking Time:	40-45 minutes
Yield:	1 medium loaf

Yeast Liquid
15 ml yeast
175 ml warm water
5 ml sugar

Additional Ingredients
750 ml whole wheat flour
7 ml salt
30 ml brown sugar
30 ml melted shortening
150 ml warm milk

1. Reconstitute yeast by dissolving 5 ml sugar in 175 ml lukewarm water (40°C.) Sprinkle yeast on top and let stand until frothy—about 8-10 minutes.
2. Mix together remaining dry ingredients.
3. Add above to yeast liquid, milk and melted shortening. Combine with a wooden spoon to form a soft dough.
4. Turn onto lightly floured board and knead until smooth — about 5 minutes.
5. Cover with oiled plastic and allow to rise until double in size — about 1 hour.
6. Punch dough down to remove all air bubbles.
7. Shape to fit medium loaf pan. Cover with oiled plastic and allow to rise until a dent remains when the dough is pressed lightly with a floured finger.
8. Bake at 180°C for 40-45 minutes.

YEAST DOUGHNUTS

Preparation Time:	3 hours
Frying Temperature:	190°C for 2-3 minutes
Yield:	18 doughnuts

190 ml milk
7 ml yeast
1 000-
1 250 ml flour
75 ml sugar

2 ml salt
2 ml grated lemon rind
f.g. nutmeg
40 ml shortening (melted)
1 egg, beaten

1. Warm milk; then sprinkle yeast on top and allow to stand until frothy — about 8-10 minutes.
2. Combine 1 000 ml flour and dry ingredients. Add with beaten egg and melted shortening to yeast liquid.
3. Add enough flour to make a soft dough and knead until smooth.
4. Cover with oiled plastic and let rise until double in size.
5. Roll dough 1 cm-1.5 cm thick.
6. Cut with doughnut cutter. Let rise covered, until a slight dent remains when the dough is pressed lightly with a floured finger.
7. Drop gently into the fat at 190°C. Brown lightly on both sides.
8. Drain and roll in icing or berry sugar.

SWEET DOUGH

Preparation Time: 2½-3 hours

Yeast Liquid
10 ml yeast
2 ml sugar
50 ml water

Additional Ingredients
450-
500 ml flour
2 ml salt
35 ml sugar
40 ml margarine, melted
90 ml milk
1 egg, beaten

1. Dissolve sugar in lukewarm water (40°C). Sprinkle yeast on top and allow to stand until frothy — about 8-10 minutes.
2. With a wooden spoon, stir in additional ingredients and enough flour to form a soft dough.
3. Knead until smooth and elastic (8-10 minutes.)
4. Cover with oiled plastic and allow to rise until double in size.
5. Punch dough down and use as desired for rolls, cinnamon buns, Cranberry Tea Ring, etc.

CINNAMON BUNS

Baking Temperature: 190°C
Baking Time: 20-25 minutes
Yield: 12 buns

1 recipe Sweet Dough
75 ml margarine, melted
125 ml brown sugar

20 ml cinnamon
75 ml raisins

1. Roll dough into rectangle about .5 cm thick. Brush dough with melted margarine.
2. Sprinkle dough with sugar, cinnamon and raisin mixture.
3. Roll up dough from long side like a jelly roll. Seal edges well.

4. Cut into 12 equal sized portions. Place in a greased 28 cm x 18 cm pan.
5. Cover and allow to rise until a slight dent remains when dough is lightly pressed with a floured finger.
6. Bake at 190°C for 20-25 minutes.

RAISIN CASSEROLE BREAD

Preparation Time: 3 hours
Baking Temperature: 180°C
Baking Time: 45 minutes
Yield: 1 loaf

500 ml flour
20 ml rapid mix yeast
5 ml salt
175 ml milk
60 ml honey

40 ml margarine
1 egg
125 ml raisins
60 ml mixed peel
6 glazed cherries, halved

1. Combine 125 ml flour and yeast.
2. Mix milk, honey and margarine in saucepan over low heat until liquid is warm to the touch.
3. Stir liquid into dry mix.
4. Beat egg into mixture.
5. Stir remaining flour and salt into the batter.

6. Cover and let rise 1 hour or until double in size.
7. Stir in the fruit mixture.
8. Pour into a greased 1.5 litre casserole.
9. Bake at 180°C for 30 minutes. Then at 160°C for 10-15 minutes.

COOLRISE RAPIDMIX WHITE BREAD

Baking Temperature: 200°C
Baking Time: 35-40 minutes
Yield: 2 loaves

1 500 ml all purpose flour (approximate)[1]
2 packages rapidmix yeast
30 ml sugar

15 ml salt
50 ml soft margarine
550 ml very hot tap water[2]

1. Measure flour onto wax paper. In a large bowl combine 500 ml flour, the dry yeast, sugar and salt. Stir well to blend.
2. Add soft margarine. Pour hot water into bowl all at once. Beat with electric mixer at medium speed for 2 minutes, scraping the sides of the bowl often. Add 250 ml more flour and beat at high speed for 1 minute. Dough will be thick and elastic.
3. Stir in remaining flour gradually, using a wooden spoon. Use just enough flour to make a soft dough which leaves the sides of the bowl.
4. Turn dough out on a board floured with part of the measured flour. Shape into a ball[3]. Knead dough for 5-10 minutes adding more flour as needed until dough is smooth and elastic. Cover with greased plastic wrap and a towel.
5. Allow to rise in a warm place free from drafts for 15-20 minutes. Punch down, divide the dough and shape each half into a loaf. Place in greased bread pans and brush surface of dough with oil. Cover loosely with oiled wax paper then plastic wrap. Refrigerate for 4-48 hours[4].
6. Uncover loaf and allow to stand at room temperature for 10 minutes. Puncture any surface bubbles with an oiled toothpick.
7. Bake at 220°C for 40-45 minutes. Bake on lower oven rack for best results.

— Cont'd.

1. *Amount of flour used will vary from person to person depending on technique. Atmospheric conditions also affect amount needed.*
2. *Hot water is required to dissolve the rapidmix yeast. This is not to be confused with the lukewarm temperature required by conventional granular yeast.*
3. *If two students are working together, the ball may be divided so that each can practise the kneading technique.*
4. *This recipe must be refrigerated for a minimum of 4 hours to allow for rising. There is a volume decrease after 24 hours of refrigeration but the texture is acceptable up to 48 hours.*

DANISH PASTRIES

Preparation Time: 2 hours
Baking Temperature: 190°C
Baking Time: 10-15 minutes
Yield: 8 large pastries

Yeast Liquid
115 ml warm water
  3 ml sugar
  5 ml dried yeast

Additional Ingredients
500 ml all purpose flour
f.g. salt
  30 ml shortening
  50 ml milk powder
   2 eggs
  20 ml sugar
   1 ml ground cardamom
125 ml margarine

1. Dissolve 3 ml sugar in the warm water (40°C). Sprinkle yeast on top and allow to stand until frothy — about 10 minutes.
2. Sift flour and salt and cardamom. Rub in shortening.
3. Add milk powder, sugar, egg and yeast liquid and mix to a soft dough.
4. Turn onto a lightly floured board and knead very lightly until the dough is smooth.
5. Place dough inside a lightly oiled plastic bag and allow to rest in refrigerator 10 minutes.
6. Beat margarine until soft.
7. Roll dough out to a 25 cm square.

Spread margarine on two thirds of the dough (as illustrated) leaving a 2 cm border at the edge.
8. Fold the unbuttered side over first, then place the buttered third over top. Seal the bottom and top very carefully by pressing firmly with the rolling pin.
9. Roll to an oblong strip about three times as long as it is wide, approximately 15 cm x 45 cm. Fold evenly in three. Place in a plastic bag to rest in a cool place 10 minutes.
10. Repeat the rolling and folding twice more. Finally rest dough for 10 minutes more. Then roll out and use as required.

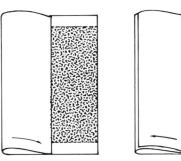

SHAPING DANISH PASTRIES: See page 307, Yeast Breads.

CLASSIC PIZZA CRUST Yield: 2-30 cm pizza crusts

1 package active dry yeast
625 ml sifted all purpose flour
5 ml salt
250 ml warm water
15 ml cooking oil

1. In a large bowl combine yeast, 250 ml of the flour, and the salt. Add warm water and oil. Beat at low speed of electric mixer for ½ minute, scraping sides of bowl. Beat 3 minutes at high speed.
2. By hand, stir in enough of the remaining flour to make a stiff dough. Knead till smooth — 8 to 10 minutes.
3. Place in greased bowl, turning once to grease surface. Cover and let rise until more than double. About 1½ hours.
5. Punch down. Cover and chill until cold, about 2 hours.
5. Cut dough in half.
6. On floured board, roll each half to 30 cm circle, about 0.3 cm thick.
7. Place in 2 greased 30 cm pizza pans. Crimp edges.
8. Brush each with an additional 15 ml cooking oil.

SOURDOUGH MUFFINS Yield: 12 large muffins or 20 small muffins

750 ml primary batter (see page 309)
375 ml whole wheat flour
125 ml sugar
5 ml salt
75 ml skim milk powder
5 ml baking soda
250 ml raisins (optional)
125 ml melted fat

Note: Remember to return 250 ml of primary batter to starter container, leaving the needed 750 ml.

1. Preheat oven to 190°C.
2. Grease muffin pans.
3. Sift dry ingredients into a bowl. Make a well in the centre.
4. Mix egg and fat thoroughly with the primary batter. Add this to the dry ingredients.
5. Stir only enough to moisten dry ingredients.
6. Fill greased muffin pans ¾ full. Bake at 190°C for 30-35 minutes.

Cakes, Frostings

ANGEL FOOD CAKE

FULL SIZE	HALF SIZE	FULL SIZE	HALF SIZE
(20-22 cm cake)	(22 cm x 10 cm loaf)	2 ml salt	1 ml
250 ml sifted cake flour	125 ml	6 ml cream of tartar	3 ml
350 ml berry sugar or sifted sugar	175 ml	6 ml vanilla	3 ml
300 ml egg whites (4-5 large or	150 ml	2 ml almond extract (optional)	1 ml
5-6 medium makes 150 ml)			

1. Preheat oven to 190°C. For full size cake, rinse 22 cm tube pan, invert. For half size cake use well scrubbed loaf pan.
2. Sift flour and 75 (35) ml sugar four times.
3. Beat the egg whites and salt until foamy. Add cream of tartar and beat until stiff enough to form soft peaks.
4. Sprinkle remaining sugar over egg whites 25 ml at a time, beating after each addition. Beat in flavourings.
5. Sift about one-quarter of the flour over the mixture and fold in gently (15 strokes) turning bowl gradually. Add remaining flour in three portions.
6. Place in ungreased tube pan. Cut through batter to remove air bubbles. Bake at 190°C for approximately one hour (25-30 minutes for half size).
7. Invert pan for one hour until cooled. Then loosen to remove from pan.

TRUE SPONGE CAKE

200 ml sifted cake flour
  1 ml salt
  5 large eggs (or 6 medium), separated

200 ml berry sugar or sifted granulated
    sugar
  grated rind of ½ lemon
 15 ml lemon juice

1. Preheat oven to 180°C. Rinse 22 cm tube cake pan and invert. Have eggs at room temperature.
2. Sift flour and salt. Grate lemon rind and extract juice.
3. Beat egg whites in large bowl until they form soft peaks. Gradually add half the sugar, 25 ml at a time, beating well after each addition.
4. Beat egg yolks until light coloured. Add the other half of the sugar gradually and beat until very foamy and light.
5. Beat lemon juice and rind into yolks.

Fold yolk mixture into egg whites.
6. Sift about ¼ of the flour over the egg mixture. Cut and fold in lightly. Add remaining flour in three portions folding gently to combine, after each addition.
7. Spoon batter into ungreased pan. Cut through the batter gently with a knife or spatula to break up any large air bubbles.
8. Bake at 180°C for 35-40 minutes or until cake springs back when pressed lightly with a finger. Invert pan over a funnel or bottle until cold.

CHIFFON CAKE

LARGE CAKE	SMALL CAKE	LARGE CAKE	SMALL CAKE
450 ml cake flour, sifted	225 ml	10 ml vanilla	5 ml
350 ml granulated sugar	175 ml	175 ml water	85 ml
15 ml baking powder	7 ml	10 ml lemon rind	5 ml
5 ml salt	2 ml	6-7 large egg whites	3
125 ml vegetable oil	60 ml	2 ml cream of tartar	1 ml
6 egg yolks	3		

1. Preheat oven to 160°C.
2. For small recipe use pan 22 cm x 8 cm. For large recipe use pan 25 cm x 11 cm.
3. Sift first 4 ingredients together into a mixing bowl and make a well in the centre.
4. Add the vegetable oil, egg yolks, rind, vanilla and water. Beat mixture with a spoon until smooth.
5. Pour egg whites into a large clean bowl and sprinkle with cream of tartar. Beat until very stiff peaks are formed.

6. Pour egg yolk mixture over beaten egg whites and fold gently until combined. Do not stir.
7. Turn into an ungreased tube pan of a size required for the size of cake prepared.
8. Bake at 160°C for 55 minutes. The surface should spring back when pressed lightly with a finger.
9. Immediately invert pan over bottle or funnel to cool. When cooled, loosen sides of the cake with a knife or metal spatula before removing from the pan.

Variations

ORANGE CHIFFON CAKE — Omit vanilla and lemon rind from the basic recipe. Use instead 15 ml (30 ml) orange rind. Substitute orange juice for the water (or use some orange juice with water to make the right volume). A good choice for frosting is Orange Butter Icing.

SPICE CHIFFON CAKE — Omit vanilla and lemon rind from the basic recipe. To the dry ingredients add 3 ml (5 ml) cinnamon, 1 ml (2 ml) each of nutmeg, allspice and cloves.

BUTTERSCOTCH CHIFFON CAKE — Omit sugar and lemon rind from the basic recipe. To the sifted dry ingredients add 225 ml (450 ml) packed brown sugar.

CHOCOLATE CHIP CHIFFON CAKE — Omit lemon rind from the basic recipe and increase the sugar to 200 ml (400 ml). At the last, gently fold in 1½ (3) squares grated unsweetened or sweetened chocolate.

MAPLE PECAN CHIFFON CAKE — Omit vanilla and lemon rind from the basic recipe. Sift only 90 ml (175 ml) granulated sugar with the dry ingredients. Add 90 ml (175 ml) packed brown sugar to the sifted dry ingredients. Use 5 ml (10 ml) maple flavouring. At the last, gently fold in 125 ml (250 ml) very finely chopped pecans.

JELLY ROLL

4 egg whites (large) (150 ml)	4 egg yolks
1 ml salt	2 ml vanilla or lemon flavouring
175 ml berry sugar or sifted granulated sugar	175 ml sifted cake flour
	2 ml baking powder

1. Preheat oven to 200°C. Line bottom of pan 25 cm x 40 cm with heavy waxed paper. Have eggs at room temperature.
2. Place egg whites in a large bowl. Add salt. Beat until foamy.
3. Sprinkle baking powder over the surface and continue beating until soft peaks form when the beater is withdrawn.
4. Beat in the sugar gradually. Beat until stiff peaks form.
5. Add the unbeaten egg yolks one at a time, beating after each addition. Beat in the vanilla.
6. Sift the flour over egg mixture in three portions and fold gently to combine.
7. Spread batter evenly into prepared pan. Bake at 200°C for 10-13 minutes.
8. Remove from oven. Turn out on a towel that has been liberally dusted with icing sugar. Remove paper immediately. If the edges are very crusty, trim them off to prevent cracking when rolling.
9. Spread with jelly or jam. Beginning on the short side, roll, using towel to guide the cake. Roll onto serving plate or cooling rack with the seam edge down, to retain the shape. Cool thoroughly before slicing to serve.

Variation
Roll cake without adding jelly. Cool thoroughly. Then open and spread generously with cream pie filling, chocolate pudding, lemon butter or sweetened whipped cream. Roll and refrigerate until serving time. Or spread with softened ice cream, roll and store in freezer until serving time. Refreeze any remaining ice cream roll.

QUICK HOT MILK CAKE

FULL SIZE	HALF SIZE	FULL SIZE	HALF SIZE
(22 cm x 22 cm)	(20-22 cm x 10 cm)	1 ml salt	pinch
2 eggs	1	60 ml skim milk powder	30 ml
250 ml sugar	125 ml	125 ml hot water	60 ml
250 ml all purpose flour	125 ml	30 ml vegetable oil	15 ml
5 ml baking powder	2 ml	5 ml vanilla	2 ml

1. Preheat oven to 180°C. Prepare pan by lining with wax paper.
2. In a deep bowl beat egg until thick and lemon coloured.
3. Add sugar gradually with continued beating.
4. Sift flour, baking powder, salt and skim milk together. Stir into first mixture until smooth.
5. Add oil and hot water and mix well. Stir in vanilla.
6. Pour into wax paper lined pan and bake at 180°C for 30-35 minutes (20-25 minutes for half size cake.)
7. When baked, invert on cake rack and remove paper immediately.

Note: This is a very moist fine-grained cake similar in appearance to a sponge cake. Instead of using an icing, try it spread, while still hot, with Broiled Topping. Good warm or cold.

BROILED CAKE TOPPING

60 ml soft butter or margarine	100 ml brown sugar
30 ml milk	150 ml coconut, medium or fine shred

Mix all ingredients in a small bowl. Spread over hot cake. Brown in hot oven 200°C for 10-12 minutes or under broiler until bubbling.

Variation
Add 75-125 ml chopped nuts to coconut mixture.

BASIC WHITE CAKE

Yield: 22 cm square cake
or 2-20 cm round cakes

125 ml shortening
200 ml sugar
  2 eggs
  5 ml vanilla

350 ml cake and pastry flour
  2 ml salt
 10 ml baking powder
175 ml milk

1. Preheat oven to 180°C.
2. Prepare pans by rubbing with shortening and dusting with flour. Use two round 20 cm layer cake pans or one 22 cm square cake pan.
3. Cream shortening well. Gradually add sugar, beating well after each addition, until light and fluffy.
4. Add eggs one at a time, beating well after each addition. Add vanilla.

5. Sift flour with baking powder and salt. Add dry ingredients to creamed mixture alternately with the milk, beginning and ending with dry ingredents and beating smooth after each addition.
6. Place in prepared pan(s) and bake at 180°C. Allow 25-30 minutes for layer cake and 40-45 minutes for single square cake.

Variations

ORANGE — For one of the eggs use 2 yolks. To the mixed batter add 25-30 ml grated orange rind.
SPICE — To the dry ingredients add 5 ml cinnamon, 2 ml cloves and 1 ml nutmeg or mace.
NUT — To the mixed batter stir in 125 ml finely chopped walnuts.
CHOCOLATE — In place of 125 ml shortening use 250 ml butter or margarine. Add 2 squares melted unsweetened chocolate to the creamed fat and sugar mixture. Substitute buttermilk or sour milk for the sweet milk and add 5 ml baking soda to the other dry ingredients.

QUICK MIX CAKE

FULL SIZE	HALF SIZE	FULL SIZE	HALF SIZE
(two 20 cm layers)	(one 20 cm layer)	150 ml milk	75 ml
450 ml sifted cake flour	225 ml	15 ml baking powder	7 ml
300 ml sugar	150 ml	100 ml milk	50 ml
125 ml soft shortening	60 ml	2 eggs	1
4 ml salt	2 ml	5 ml vanilla	2 ml

1. Preheat oven to 190°C.
2. Prepare one or two 20 cm round cake pans depending upon the size of recipe being used. Grease pans and dust lightly with flour.
3. Measure the first 5 ingredients into mixing bowl. Mix thoroughly for about 2 minutes or 300 strokes with a spoon.
4. Stir in baking powder.
5. Add second measure of milk, the

egg and vanilla. Mix again for about 2 minutes.
6. Place in pan(s) and bake at 190°C for 30-35 minutes. The full size cake can be baked in one 22 cm square cake pan. Time will be about 45 minutes. The two layer cake can also be made into 26-28 cupcakes using 30-40 ml batter for each cupcake. Bake at 200°C for 15-20 minutes.

ONE BOWL WHITE CAKE

Yield: 22 cm x 32 cm slab cake

575 ml all purpose flour
450 ml sugar
 25 ml baking powder
  4 ml salt

175 ml shortening, soft
 10 ml vanilla
350 ml milk
  3 eggs

1. Preheat oven to 190°C.
2. Prepare a 22 cm x 32 cm cake pan.
3. Sift dry ingredients into mixing bowl. Add soft shortening, vanilla and

milk. Beat for 2 minutes.
4. Add eggs and beat 1 minute.
5. Pour batter into pan and bake at 190°C for 30-35 minutes.

WHITE LAYER CAKE

FULL SIZE	HALF SIZE
(two 20 cm layers)	(one 20 cm layer)
150 ml shortening	75 ml
350 ml sugar	175 ml
2 eggs	1

FULL SIZE	HALF SIZE
6 ml vanilla	3 ml
500 ml cake and pastry flour	250 ml
12 ml baking powder	6 ml
4 ml salt	2 ml
250 ml milk	125 ml

1. Preheat oven to 180°C.
2. Prepare pans by rubbing with shortening and dusting with flour. Use one or two round 20 cm cake pans.
3. Cream shortening well. Gradually add sugar, beating well after each addition, until light and fluffy.
4. Add eggs one at a time, beating well after each addition. Add vanilla.

5. Sift flour with baking powder and salt. Add dry ingredients to creamed mixture alternately with the milk, beginning and ending with dry ingredients, and beating smooth after each addition.
6. Place in prepared pan(s) and bake at 180°C for 30-35 minutes.

CHOCOLATE LAYER CAKE

Yield: two 20 cm round layer cakes

225 ml shortening
275 ml sugar
5 ml salt
2 eggs
2 squares chocolate, melted

400 ml sifted cake flour
5 ml baking soda
225 ml buttermilk or sour milk
5 ml vanilla

1. Preheat oven to 180°C.
2. Prepare two 20 cm layer cake pans by rubbing with shortening and dusting with flour.
3. Cream shortening. Add sugar gradually, beating well after each addition until light and fluffy (about 3 minutes at medium speed).
4. Add eggs and beat well, about 3 minutes.

5. Stir in melted chocolate. Add vanilla.
6. Combine sifted flour, baking soda and salt. Add dry ingredients alternately with the milk beginning and ending with the dry ingredients. Mix for a total of 3 minutes at low speed.
7. Place in pans and bake at 180°C for about 30 minutes.

BANANA CAKE

Yield: two 20 cm round layer cakes or one 22 cm square cake

125 ml shortening
250 ml sugar
2 eggs
250 ml mashed ripe bananas (3 large)
5 ml vanilla (or 2 ml vanilla and 5 ml orange rind)

450 ml sifted cake and pastry flour
5 ml baking powder
2 ml baking soda
2 ml salt
75 ml sour milk
125 ml finely chopped nuts (optional)

1. Preheat oven to 180°C.
2. Prepare two 20 cm layer cake pans by rubbing with shortening and dusting with flour.
3. Cream shortening. Add sugar gradually, beating well after each addition until mixture is very fluffy.
4. Add eggs one at a time with continued beating until mixture is very fluffy.
5. Beat in mashed bananas and flavouring.

6. Combine sifted flour, baking powder, baking soda and salt. Add dry ingredients alternately with the milk, beginning and ending with dry ingredients. Blend after each addition but do not overmix.
7. Pour the batter into prepared pans. Bake layer cakes at 180°C for 30-35 minutes. Bake a single square or loaf cake for 50-55 minutes.

CHRISTMAS CAKE

125 ml slivered blanched almonds
500 ml candied cherries
500 ml chopped candied mixed peel
500 ml raisins
250 ml currants
250 ml chopped dates
125 ml grape juice (or orange juice)
125 ml all purpose flour
500 ml all purpose flour
  2 ml baking soda

  5 ml cloves
  5 ml allspice
  5 ml cinnamon
  2 ml salt
250 ml butter or margarine
500 ml brown sugar, lightly packed
  6 large eggs
175 ml molasses
200 ml apple juice

1. Combine fruit and nuts. Pour grape juice over, mix well and allow to stand for at least 2 hours or overnight.
2. Preheat oven to 140°C.
3. Prepare pans. Line a 20 cm x 20 cm x 8 cm fruit cake pan or two 20 cm x 12 cm x 8 cm loaf pans by lining with two thicknesses of greased heavy brown paper.
4. Dredge fruit and nuts with 125 ml flour.
5. Sift together remaining dry ingredients.
6. Cream butter. Gradually blend in brown sugar, creaming after each addition until light and fluffy again.
7. Add eggs one at a time with continued creaming after each addition.
8. Mix together apple juice and molasses.
9. Add sifted dry ingredients alternating with liquid ingredients making 4 dry and 3 liquid additions and combining lightly after each addition.
10. Fold in floured fruit. Turn into prepared pans.
11. Bake at 140°C for 3-3½ hours or until cake is done when tested with a toothpick.

CHRISTMAS FRUIT CAKE

450 ml butter or margarine
500 ml brown sugar, packed
 10 large eggs (or 12 medium) separated
1 000 ml sifted all purpose flour
  5 ml cinnamon
  5 ml allspice
  5 ml nutmeg
  2 ml cloves
  2 ml mace
  2 ml salt

500 ml seeded raisins
1 500 ml seedless raisins
750 ml currants
500 ml candied cherries, whole
250 ml sliced candied citron or candied pineapple
250 ml chopped candied mixed peel
250 ml blanched almonds
  1 lemon, juice and rind
125 ml orange juice or grape juice
125 ml cold coffee

1. Prepare fruits. Pour lemon juice and orange juice over them; mix and allow to stand for several hours or overnight. Stir occasionally.
2. Line the pans with 3 thicknesses of heavy brown paper. Carefully grease the last layer.
3. Preheat the oven to 150°C or less.
4. Sift and measure flour. Dredge fruit and nuts with 125 ml of the measured flour.
5. Cream the butter well. Add sugar a little at a time with continued creaming after each addition to maintain the creamy consistency.
6. Add egg yolks one at a time, beating after each addition.
7. Mix spices and salt with remaining flour and sift.
8. Add the dry ingredients alternately with cold coffee beginning and ending with dry ingredients and mixing after each addition.
9. Stir in lemon rind. Add dredged fruit and nuts.
10. Beat egg whites until stiff. Fold into batter last.
11. Spoon batter into prepared pans filling each about ⅔ full. Bake at 150°C or lower, until a toothpick inserted in the centre comes out clean. Times will be approximately:
    Large 20 cm x 20 cm — 3 hours.
    Medium 15 cm x 15 cm — 2¾ hours.
    Small 10 cm x 10 cm — 1¾-2 hours.

DOUBLE BOILER FROSTING

2 egg whites, unbeaten
350 ml granulated sugar
75 ml cold water

15 ml light corn syrup or 2 ml cream of tartar
5 ml vanilla

1. Place all the ingredients except the vanilla in the top part of a double boiler. Beat with a rotary beater until thoroughly mixed.
2. Place over boiling water and beat steadily with the rotary beater until the frosting will form peaks when the beater is lifted. The time will be 7-10 minutes.
3. Remove the top of the double boiler from the heat; add the vanilla; beat until thick enough to spread.

Variations

SEAFOAM DOUBLE BOILER FROSTING — Use brown sugar in place of the granulated sugar. This frosting is especially suitable for spice and banana cakes.

BITTERSWEET SWIRLS — Spread double boiler frosting on cake forming swirls on top of the cake. Melt one square unsweetened chocolate with 3 ml butter. Using a toothpick or narrow blade knife outline swirls of frosting with the melted chocolate.

BOILED WHITE ICING   Yield: 500 ml

500 ml sugar
250 ml water
  1 ml salt
  2 egg whites

1 ml cream of tartar (or few drops lemon juice)
5 ml vanilla

1. Place sugar and water in a saucepan. Stir until the sugar is dissolved. Bring to a boil.
2. Cover and cook for about 3 minutes until the steam has washed down any crystals which may have formed on the sides of the pan.
3. Uncover and cook to 115°C on the candy thermometer. At this temperature the syrup will spin a very thin thread at the end of a coarser thread.
4. Whip the egg whites and salt, until frothy.
5. Add the syrup in a thin stream whipping constantly.
6. When these ingredients are all combined, add cream of tartar and vanilla. Spread immediately.

FUDGE FROSTING   Yield: frosting for 22 cm layer cake (for single layer use half of recipe)

500 ml sugar
  2 ml squares unsweetened chocolate (or 60 ml cocoa and 15 ml more of butter)
60 ml light corn syrup

pinch salt
150 ml milk
 30 ml butter or margarine
  5 ml vanilla

1. Put sugar, chocolate (chopped in pieces), corn syrup, salt and milk into saucepan. Cook slowly over low heat until the sugar is dissolved and the chocolate melted.
2. Bring to the boiling point and cook, stirring occasionally, to the soft ball stage or to a temperature of 112°C on candy thermometer.
3. Remove from heat and add butter. Cool to lukewarm (44°C).
4. When the pan is cool enough add vanilla and begin to beat. Continue beating until icing is of spreading consistency.

DECORATIVE ICING

125 ml shortening
850 ml icing sugar, unsifted
  1 egg white

30 ml cold water
   pinch salt
 2 ml vanilla

Beat these ingredients together for 10 minutes at No. 4 setting of the electric mixer.

BUTTER ICING

50 ml butter or margarine
375 ml icing sugar, unsifted

30 ml milk or cream
3 ml vanilla

1. Cream butter until very soft. Sift icing sugar if desired. Add part of the icing sugar and blend thoroughly.
2. Add milk a few drops at a time with continued beating. Add sugar and liquid alternately until the right spreading consistency is reached.
3. Add flavouring and any colouring.

Variations

ORANGE OR LEMON ICING — Replace the milk with undiluted frozen concentrate or fresh juice. Add 2 ml fresh grated rind if desired.

CHOCOLATE ICING — Add 50 ml cocoa to the sugar or use half to one square melted unsweetened chocolate.

MOCHA ICING — Replace milk with strong cold coffee or mix 3 ml instant coffee with the sugar. Add cocoa to give a light colour (about 25 ml).

ROYAL ICING

Yield: 500 ml

825 ml powdered confectioner's sugar
2 egg whites

1 lemon, juice only
1 or 2 drops glycerin

1. Measure icing sugar, then sift.
2. Beat egg whites until stiff but not dry.
3. Gradually add the sifted sugar, juice of a lemon and glycerin until icing is of a good consistency to be spread.
4. Apply to the cake, using pastry bag.

Notes:

a. *If the icing needs to be stiffer, add a little more sifted icing sugar. To make it softer, thin it very gradually by adding lemon juice, more egg white or water.*

b. *This icing will become very hard. Cover with a damp cloth until ready to use.*

c. *A natural greyish tone that develops during preparation can be prevented by adding a small amount of blue vegetable colouring. Add this only to portions that you want to keep white. Do not add blue to any icing that you plan to colour any pale warm tint.*

Cookies, Slices

HERMITS

Yield: 50 cookies

500 ml flour
3 ml salt
5 ml baking soda
f.g. nutmeg
f.g. allspice
125 ml butter or margarine

250 ml brown sugar
2 eggs
3 ml vanilla
125 ml seedless raisins
125 ml chopped dates
50 ml chopped nuts

1. Sift flour before measuring. Sift flour together with salt, baking soda and spices.
2. Cream fat and add sugar gradually with continued creaming to maintain a fluffy consistency
3. Add eggs one at a time to the creamed mixture. Add vanilla. Beat.
4. Stir in dry ingredients, then nuts and fruit.
5. Drop from spoon onto greased baking sheet, 3 cm apart.
6. Bake at 180°C for 15-18 minutes.

Variations:

1. Omit raisins, dates and spices. Use instead 125 ml shredded coconut and 125 ml currants.
2. Omit chopped nuts and vanilla. Use 50 ml mixed peel, 5 ml grated orange rind and 5 ml orange juice.

ROLLED OAT COOKIES

125 ml shortening
125 ml brown sugar
125 ml granulated sugar
  1 egg, beaten
 30 ml water
  3 ml vanilla

175 ml sifted flour
  2 ml baking soda
  2 ml salt
375 ml uncooked quick cooking oats
300 ml chocolate chips or 250 ml Spanish
      peanuts

1. Cream shortening and sugar thoroughly.
2. Stir in beaten egg, water and vanilla.
3. Sift together flour, salt and baking soda.

4. Add dry ingredients, rolled oats and chocolate chips or peanuts.
5. Drop from a spoon onto a greased baking sheet and bake in a moderate oven 190°C for 10-15 minutes.

CEREAL DROP COOKIES (Whole Grain Cookies)

  2 eggs
175 ml vegetable oil
250 ml light table molasses
175 ml whole wheat flour
125 ml skim milk powder

  5 ml salt
350 ml wheat germ
500 ml rolled oats
125 ml chopped nuts
125 ml raisins

1. Beat eggs well. Add oil and molasses and beat.
2. Stir in flour, milk powder, salt, wheat germ and rolled oats. Mix until smooth.

3. Add raisins and nuts last. Push from a spoon onto a well greased baking sheet.
4. Bake at 180°C for 10-15 minutes.

SUGAR COOKIES

175 ml soft shortening (part butter)
250 ml granulated sugar
  2 eggs
  2 ml flavouring (vanilla or lemon)

625 ml all purpose flour
  5 ml baking powder
  5 ml salt

1. Cream shortening, add sugar gradually continuing to cream until very light and fluffy. Add eggs, one at a time and mix in flavouring.
2. Sift flour, measure, add baking powder and salt, sift over fluffy mixture a little at a time until a stiff dough is formed. Chill at least 1 hour. Form shapes. Bake on an ungreased cookie sheet at 200°C for 6-8 minutes or until delicately browned.

Variations

PLAIN SUGAR COOKIES: Roll out on lightly floured surface to 0.5 cm thickness. Cut desired shapes and sprinkle with sugar.

LEMON SUGAR COOKIES: In place of flavouring use 10 ml grated lemon rind and 5 ml lemon juice.

NUT SUGAR COOKIES: Mix into the dough 250 ml *finely* chopped nuts.

CARAWAY COOKIES: Omit flavouring, sift 125 ml nutmeg with the dry ingredients, then mix 5 ml caraway seeds into the dough.

FILLED SUGAR COOKIES: Before baking, place 2 round cookies shaped together with 5 ml filling (date, fig, raisin). Press edges together with tines of a fork. A solid chocolate mint wafer as the filling is an interesting variation.

CHOCOLATE PINWHEELS: (1) Divide dough into 2 equal parts. Into one part blend 2 squares unsweetened chocolate, melted and cooled. Chill. (2) Roll out white dough to 22 cm x 30 cm. Roll out chocolate dough to same size and lay on top of the white dough. (3) Roll the double layer gently 0.5 cm thick. Roll up tightly beginning at the wide end. Chill. (4) Slice 0.5 cm thick and bake on lightly greased cookie sheet.

PEANUT BUTTER COOKIES

Yield: 35-40 cookies

125 ml margarine
125 ml sugar
 60 ml brown sugar
  1 egg
  5 ml vanilla

125 ml peanut butter
375 ml all purpose flour
  5 ml baking powder
  5 ml baking soda
  5 ml salt

1. Cream fat thoroughly with sugars. Add egg and vanilla and continue creaming. Beat in peanut butter.
2. Sift and measure flour. Sift all dry ingredients together and mix gradually into the creamed mixture.
3. Drop by spoonfuls onto a greased cookie sheet. Flatten with a moistened fork.
4. Bake at 190°C for 10-12 minutes.

CHOCOLATE CHIP COOKIES

Yield: 35-40 cookies

125 ml margarine
125 ml sugar
125 ml brown sugar
  1 egg
  2 ml vanilla

280 ml all purpose flour
  2 ml salt
  2 ml soda
125 ml chocolate chips
125 ml chopped walnuts

1. Thoroughly cream margarine and sugars. Add egg and beat well. Add vanilla.
2. Sift and measure flour. Add baking soda and salt and sift together. Grad-ually stir into creamed mixture.
3. Stir in nuts and chocolate chips.
4. Drop by spoonfuls onto ungreased cookie sheets. Bake at 190°C for ten minutes.

COCONUT MACAROONS

Yield: 30 cookies

125 ml egg whites
250 ml sugar
  1 ml salt

  2 ml vanilla
375 ml moist shredded coconut (medium or fine)

1. Beat egg whites until stiff. Grad-ually beat in sugar, then salt and vanilla. Fold in coconut.
2. Drop from a spoon 5 cm apart on a cookie sheet which has been covered with brown paper.
3. Bake at 150°C for 15-20 minutes.

EASY ROLLED COOKIES

750 ml rolled oats
250 ml all purpose flour
250 ml sugar
250 ml melted butter

  2 ml salt
  5 ml baking soda
 50 ml hot water

1. Combine oats, flour, sugar and salt.
2. Pour melted butter into dry ingre-dients and work dough together.
3. **Dissolve baking soda in hot water.**
4. Add water to dough to form a stiff dough.
5. Chill several hours or overnight.
6. Roll 0.5 cm thick between sheets of waxed paper.
7. Cut with floured cookie cutter into desired shapes.
8. Bake at 190°C until golden and lightly browned around the edges.

Note: Store in container with a loosely fitting lid. Cookies may be sandwiched with date filling. Fill just before serving as cookies will soften.

Date Filling

250 ml dates
125 ml water

 40 ml sugar
 10 ml lemon juice

1. Cut dates into small pieces.
2. Add water and sugar; cook until mixture is quite thick, stirring often to prevent scorching; cool.
3. Keep refrigerated.

GINGERBREAD COOKIES

75 ml soft shortening
250 ml brown sugar
300 ml dark molasses
150 ml cold water

l 500 ml sifted flour
10 ml soda
5 ml each of salt, allspice, ginger, cloves and cinnamon

1. Cream the shortening and sugar together.
2. Add molasses and cold water. Beat well.
3. Combine flour, spices and soda. Add dry ingredients in four parts, beating after each addition.
4. Chill dough for easier handling.
5. Roll dough 0.5 cm thick on a lightly floured board. Cut in desired shapes. Place well apart on a lightly greased baking sheet.
6. Bake until no finger imprint remains in the cookies, 12-15 minutes at 180°C.
7. Decorate as desired with icing or candies. This recipe is suitable for Gingerbread men.

SHORTBREAD

Yield: 45-50 cookies

250 ml butter
125 ml brown sugar

f.g. salt
500 ml all purpose flour

1. Cream butter gradually adding the sugar.
2. Blend in flour and salt until mixture holds together.
3. Knead in the bowl for a few seconds.
4. Chill dough for a few minutes.
5. Roll out 0.5 cm thick and cut in desired shapes.
6. Bake on an ungreased cookie sheet for 20-25 minutes at 150°C or until lightly browned around the edges. Cookies may be decorated before baking.

SWEDISH SPRITZ COOKIES

Yield: 35 cookies

200 ml butter
125 ml sugar
1 egg yolk

2 ml vanilla or almond extract
500 ml sifted cake flour
2 ml salt

1. Thoroughly cream butter, add sugar gradually and continue creaming until very light and fluffy. Add egg yolk and flavouring, mix well.
2. Sift and measure flour, add salt, sift into creamed mixture and mix to a smooth dough. Use hands if necessary.

Note: For best results do not chill dough.

3. Assemble cookie press. Force dough through press to form shapes on the greased cookie sheet. Decorate as desired.
4. Bake at 190°C for 8-10 minutes or until very delicately browned. Remove from pan and cool on cake rack.

CHOCOLATE BROWNIES

Yield: 25 squares

125 ml margarine
250 ml sugar
5 ml vanilla
2 eggs
2 squares unsweetened chocolate, melted

200 ml all purpose flour
3 ml baking powder
2 ml salt
200 ml chopped dates or walnuts

1. Cream margarine and sugar well. Add vanilla.
2. Beat in eggs one at a time. Blend in melted chocolate.
3. Measure and sift dry ingredients together. Stir gradually into creamed mixture.
4. Add nuts and dates.
5. Place in well greased 20 cm square pan and bake at 180°C for 30-35 min.

Variations
Decrease flour to 125 ml. Add 30 ml more margarine. Substitute 125 ml cocoa for the unsweetened chocolate.

BUTTERSCOTCH REFRIGERATOR COOKIES

500 ml all purpose flour
2 ml baking powder
2 ml salt
150 ml table fat

175 ml brown sugar, packed
1 egg, beaten
150 ml nuts, finely chopped (optional)
5 ml vanilla

1. Sift flour, measure, add baking powder and salt and sift together.
2. Cream fat, add sugar gradually, beat until fluffy. Add egg and vanilla.
3. Add dry ingredients slowly mixing to a stiff dough. Stir in nuts if desired.
4. Press dough together and form into cylinders. Wrap in moisture proof paper and refrigerate several hours or overnight.
5. Slice 0.5 cm thick and place on an ungreased cookie sheet. Bake at 200°C for 6-8 minutes.

UNBAKED CHOCOLATE OATMEAL CRUNCHIES

Yield: about 35 cookies

500 ml sugar
125 ml cocoa
125 ml butter
125 ml milk

250 ml coconut
750 ml rolled oats
5 ml vanilla

1. Boil the first four ingredients in a pan for five minutes.
2. Stir in coconut, oats and vanilla.
3. Place on waxed paper by spoonfuls and allow to cool.

DATE AND NUT BARS

Yield: 44 squares

175 ml flour
2 ml salt
5 ml baking powder
2 eggs

250 ml brown sugar
125 ml nuts, chopped
250 ml sliced dates
5 ml vanilla

1. Sift flour, salt and baking powder.
2. Beat eggs well. Beat in the sugar gradually. Stir in the nuts, dates and vanilla. Stir in the dry ingredients.
3. Spread mixture in a shallow pan 22 cm x 22 cm which has been greased and lined on the bottom with waxed paper. The layer of batter should not be more than 2 cm thick.
4. Bake at 180°C for 30 minutes or until the surface springs back when pressed lightly with the finger.
5. Cut into strips 2 cm x 5 cm to serve. Coat with confectioner's sugar if preferred.

RASPBERRY BARS

Yield: 25 squares

125 ml margarine
50 ml sugar
2 eggs, separated
375 ml flour
2 ml salt

raspberry jam
125 ml sugar
5 ml vanilla
50 ml chopped walnuts

1. Cream the margarine and sugar together well. Beat in egg yolks.
2. Sift flour and salt into creamed mixture and combine.
3. Pat into a greased 20 cm square pan. Spread with a thin layer of raspberry jam.
4. Beat egg whites until stiff. Add sugar gradually with continued beating. Add vanilla.
5. Spread topping evenly over jam. Sprinkle nuts on top.
6. Bake at 190°C for 30 minutes. Cut when cooled.

Variation

Omit walnuts. Stir 125-250 ml medium shredded coconut into egg white and sugar mixture before spreading over raspberry-coated base.

NANAIMO BARS

BASE:

125 ml butter
75 ml cocoa
250 ml coconut, finely shredded
125 ml walnuts, chopped
75 ml white sugar
500 ml graham wafer crumbs
1 egg
2 ml vanilla

1. Place soft butter, sugar, cocoa, vanilla and egg in a bowl. Set bowl in a larger bowl of boiling water. Stir gently until butter has melted and mixture is the consistency of custard.
2. Mix crumbs, coconut and nuts together. Stir into cocoa mixture. Pack into ungreased 22 cm pan.

ICING:

60 ml butter
30 ml milk
30 ml vanilla custard pudding powder
500 ml sifted icing sugar

1. Cream butter.
2. Combine milk and custard powder and add to butter.
3. Beat in icing sugar. Spread over the chocolate base and refrigerate to harden.

TOPPING:

2 squares semi-sweet chocolate
30 ml butter

1. Melt chocolate and butter together in top of double boiler. Spread evenly over icing layer. Refrigerate.
2. Cut in small pieces to serve. Keep remainder cold and covered.

Pastry, Pie Fillings

TIME TEMPERATURE CHART FOR BAKING PASTRY

PRODUCT	TEMPERATURE	TIME	CHARACTERISTICS WHEN COOKED
Pie shell	230° C for	10-12 min	Delicate golden brown.
Tart shell, unfilled	230° C for	8-10 min	Delicate golden brown.
Tarts, filled (butter, mincemeat)	190°C	15-20 min	Delicate golden brown.
Single crust filled pies (custard, pumpkin, pecan)	230° C for then 160° C for	15 min 30-40 min	Knife comes out clean. Surface is light brown.
Double crust pie with previously cooked filling (raisin, mincemeat)	230° C for	30-45 min	Crust is golden brown.
Double crust fruit pie with raw fruit.	230° C for then 180° C for	10-15 min 40-45 min	Crust is golden brown. Juices are bubbling. Fruit is tender.
Deep dish fruit pie (top crust only)	230° C for	30-45 min	Delicate golden brown crust.
Turnovers, cooked filling.	230° C for	15 min	Golden brown crust.
Turnovers, raw fruit.	200° C for	35 min	Golden brown crust.
Meringue on cooked filling in prebaked shell.	150° C for or 180° C for or 200° C for	15-20 min 10-15 min 4- 6 min	Pale golden brown. Crisp texture. Light brown. Soft interior. Darker brown peaks. Very soft interior.
Meringue Shells	130° C	50-60 min	Outside is dry. Creamy white colour.

500 ml sifted all purpose flour
5 ml salt

125-150 ml lard or shortening
45- 75 ml cold water

1. Sift and measure flour. Add salt.
2. Cut fat into flour using a pastry blender or two knives until the pieces are the size of peas.
3. Add water by sprinkling a spoon at a time over the flour-fat mixture and

tossing from the bottom of the bowl with a fork. Continue adding, gradually, only until the dough will hold together.
4. Form into a flattened ball and chill for 5 minutes before rolling.

PASTE METHOD FOR PASTRY

Yield: two 22 cm crusts

500 ml sifted all purpose flour
5 ml salt

150 ml shortening
75 ml cold water

1. Sift and measure flour. Add salt.
2. Take out 65 ml of flour and mix with the water in a small bowl. Use a fork to make a paste.
3. Cut shortening into the remaining flour until the pieces are the size of small peas.

4. Add the flour paste to the flour-fat mixture. Scrape the bowl carefully for all the moisture is needed.
5. Mix with a fork until the dough forms a ball that will hold together. Wrap and chill for 20 minutes before rolling if time is available.

HOT WATER PASTRY

Yield: one 20 cm or 22 cm pie or two 20 cm or 22 cm shells or 12-14 medium tarts or 24 small tarts

500 ml sifted all purpose flour
5 ml salt
150 ml shortening

75 ml boiling water
2 ml baking powder (optional)

1. Place shortening in mixing bowl, pour boiling water over it and stir until the shortening has melted.
2. Sift and measure flour. Add salt and baking powder if it is to be used.

3. Combine the dry ingredients with the fat and water, mixing with a fork until a soft dough is formed.
4. Wrap and chill thoroughly before rolling.

OIL PASTRY

Yield: one 20 cm or 22 cm pie or two 20 cm or 22 cm pie shells

500 ml sifted all purpose flour
7 ml salt

125 ml vegetable oil
65 ml cold whole milk

1. Sift and measure flour. Add salt. Make a depression in the centre.
2. Pour the oil and milk into one cup, then all at once pour into the depression in the flour. Stir lightly with a fork until the ingredients are well blended.
3. Press the dough together into a ball, cut in half, and roll each half separately between two sheets of waxed pa-

per. (Lightly dampen the counter top to keep the bottom layer of paper from slipping.)
4. When circle of pastry is the desired size, peel off the top paper. Lift remaining paper and pastry (they will cling together) and place paper side up over pie pan. Carefully peel off paper and continue forming the pie as with any other kind of pastry.

NEVER FAIL PASTRY MIX   Yield: 6 single crusts

1 250 ml sifted all purpose flour
  15 ml salt
   5 ml double-acting baking powder
 550 ml lard

1 egg
15 ml vinegar or lemon juice
   cold water

1. Sift and measure dry ingredients into a very large bowl.
2. Cut in the lard to the consistency of raw oatmeal.
3. Break egg into measuring cup; beat with a fork, add vinegar or lemon juice, then cold water, to make 165 ml. Beat again.

4. Pour liquid ingredients a little at a time over flour-fat mixture and toss lightly with a fork after each addition.
5. Work the dough only until evenly dampened. Form into a ball and divide into six. Wrap balls individually. Refrigerate before using.

Note: This pastry dough keeps well in the refrigerator for several weeks if properly wrapped to prevent drying

CRUMB PIE CRUST

	Amount Before Crushing	Crumbs		Sugar		Butter or Margarine	
	22 cm 20 cm	22 cm	20 cm	22 cm	20 cm	22 cm	20 cm
Graham Wafers	18 wafers	350 ml	300 ml	60 ml	50 ml	75 ml	60 ml
Vanilla Wafers	30 wafers	350 ml	300 ml	—	—	75 ml	60 ml
Chocolate Wafers	30 wafers	350 ml	300 ml	—	—	75 ml	60 ml
Ginger Snaps	30 small cookies	350 ml	300 ml	—	—	100 ml	75 ml
Corn Flakes	1 500 ml	350 ml	300 ml	75 ml	60 ml	125 ml	100 ml

1. Melt the butter. Butter pie plate. Preheat oven to 180°C.
2. Place the cookies or cereal between two sheets of waxed paper or in a plastic bag. Crush with a rolling pin. Measure, and place them in a bowl.
3. Add the sugar to the crumbs, stir and add melted butter and blend well. If desired, save 50-60 ml of this mixture to sprinkle on top of the filling.
4. Press the mixture into the bottom and sides of the pie plate using the back of a spoon or the fingers. Crumbs should be pressed firm into a 0.5 cm thick layer.
5. Bake at 180°C for 5-10 minutes. Cool and fill. Refrigerate for several hours before serving.
6. To make serving easier, wrap a hot wet towel under the bottom and around the sides of the pie plate. Hold towel there for a few minutes before removing a piece of the pie. It should slip out easily.

A NOTE ABOUT CRUMB CRUSTS:

Crumb crusts are especially suited to lemon, cream, gelatin, chiffon or glazed fresh fruit pie fillings and can be topped with meringue or whipped cream. Consider the flavour of the filling being used when you choose the type of crumbs. The addition of 2 - 5 ml cinnamon to graham wafer or corn flake crumbs is a pleasant variation. Alteration of the suggested proportions of the ingredients is possible and will still give good results.

FRUIT	QUANTITY	SUGAR	THICKENER	BUTTER	SALT	FLAVOURING
Apple	1 500 ml sliced	175-200 ml	30 ml flour or 15 ml cornstarch	15 ml	pinch	2 ml cinnamon 1 ml nutmeg
Rhubarb	1 000 ml sliced	250-350 ml	60 ml flour or 30 ml cornstarch or 40 ml tapioca	15 ml	pinch	5 ml grated orange rind
Peach	1 000 ml sliced	125 ml	25 ml cornstarch or 30 ml tapioca	15 ml	pinch	15 ml lemon juice 1 ml almond extract
Cherry	750 ml pitted	250-350 ml	30 ml cornstarch or 40 ml tapioca	15 ml	pinch	1 ml almond extract
Blueberry	750 ml	125 ml	30 ml cornstarch or 40 ml tapioca	15 ml	pinch	2 ml cinnamon
Berry *	1 000 ml	200-250 ml	30 ml cornstarch or 40 ml tapioca	15 ml	pinch	25 ml lemon juice or 2 ml cinnamon

* Berries can be Blackberry, Boysenberry, Currant, Huckleberry, Loganberry, Raspberry, Strawberry.

Note: When preparing fresh fruit pies to be frozen, use tapioca for the thickener and increase the amount by 1/3 to allow for thickening extra juices present when the pie is frozen. Pies frozen unbaked are preferred. See Freezing, page 453.

1. Prepare the fruit; peel, core and slice the apples or peaches; wash rhubarb, cut into 1 cm pieces; wash and pit cherries; pick over berries; wash, hull and slice strawberries.
2. Measure and mix together the sugar, thickener (tapioca should be quick cooking kind), salt and any spices. Mix with the prepared fruit. If tapioca or cornstarch is used as the thickener let this mixture stand for 15 minutes before putting it in the pie shell.
3. Arrange the sugared fruit in an unbaked, unpricked 22 cm pastry shell. Dot with butter. Sprinkle any flavouring over fruit.
4. Cover with upper crust or lattice top. Use cold milk or water to seal two layers. Trim top edge leaving enough pastry to turn under the bottom crust. Flute 3 layers of pastry together.
5. Bake at 230°C for 15 minutes; reduce heat to 180°C and continue baking until fruit is tender and crust browned (40-50 minutes).

MERINGUE SHELLS

2 egg whites, room temperature
f.g. salt

125 ml fine granulated sugar (berry sugar)
2 ml vanilla

1. Beat egg whites and salt until stiff and dry. Beat in about 2/3 of the sugar gradually. Fold in the remainder of the sugar and the vanilla.
2. Cover a baking sheet with brown paper. Place mounds of the meringue mixture on the paper making circles about 5 cm in diameter. Shape scooped centres to place filling in later.
3. Bake in a very slow oven 130°C for about 50-60 minutes. Outside will be dry and a creamy white.
4. Remove from paper while warm; cool, serve with ice cream, fruit, berries or sauce.

APPLE PIE

1 recipe pastry for 2-crust pie
5-6 medium tart apples
200-250 ml sugar (brown sugar)
30 ml flour
pinch salt

3 ml cinnamon
2 ml nutmeg (if desired or cloves or allspice)
15 ml margarine or butter
2 ml lemon juice

1. Prepare pastry and allow to chill until the filling is ready.
2. Wash, peel, core and slice apples making 1 250 ml - 1 500 ml slices.
3. Measure and mix together with the sugar, flour, salt and chosen spices. Place apples in a bowl and toss with sugar mixture.

4. Line a 22 cm pie pan with pastry. Add apples, dot with butter or margarine. Cover with top crust, trim and seal edges well and flute together.
5. Bake in hot oven 230°C for 10 minutes; then reduce the heat to 180°C and bake for 30-45 minutes until apples are tender and juices bubbly.

Quick Apple Pie Variation:

1. Prepare the pastry and allow to chill until the filling is ready.
2. Wash, peel, core, and slice apples making 1 250 - 1 500 ml slices.
3. Measure and combine sugar, flour, salt, spices and butter. Place in heavy skillet or saucepan together with apple slices. Mix.
4. Cover tightly and steam over low heat until the apples are soft but not cooked.
5. Spoon filling into unbaked crust. Cover with top crust, trim, seal edges and flute together.
6. Bake in a very hot oven, 230°C for 15-25 minutes until the pastry is cooked.

BUTTER TARTS

Yield: 12-16 tarts (5 cm)

1 egg
250 ml brown sugar
65 ml butter

30 ml canned milk
2 ml vanilla
250 ml raisins or currants

1. Beat egg, add brown sugar and softened butter and beat until full of bubbles. Add other ingredients and mix well.

2. Pour into uncooked tart shells. Bake at 220°C for 10 minutes. Then reduce heat to 180°C and cook until filling begins to set.

CREAM PIE

Yield: one 22 cm pie

125 ml sugar
90 ml flour
500 ml milk (scalded)
1 ml salt

2 egg yolks or 1 egg
15 ml butter or margarine
3 ml vanilla
1 ml baked 22 cm pie shell

1. Mix the sugar, flour and salt. Gradually add the scalded milk, stirring constantly.
2. Return the mixture to the top of a double boiler. Stir over boiling water until the mixture has thickened. Cover and cook 2 minutes longer.
3. Beat egg yolks. Add part of the hot mixture gradually. Blend until egg

is warmed, then return all of mixture to the double boiler and cook for an additional 2 minutes.
4. Remove from heat. Blend in butter and vanilla. Cook, covered to prevent skin from forming.
5. Place in cooked pie shell and cover with meringue or top with whipping cream just before serving.

Variations:

COCONUT CREAM PIE: Add 250 ml of moist, shredded coconut to cooled filling. Sprinkle 125 ml coconut over meringue before browning or garnish whipped cream topping with plain or toasted coconut.

BANANA CREAM PIE: Arrange a layer of sliced bananas in the bottom of the pastry shell before pouring in cooled filling.

LEMON PIE

315 ml sugar
90 ml cornstarch
1 ml salt
315 ml water (65 ml cold, 250 ml boiling)
2 egg yolks

5 ml grated lemon rind
15 ml butter or margarine
75 ml lemon juice
1 baked pie shell, 20 cm

1. In a saucepan combine the sugar, cornstarch and salt.
2. Add 65 ml of cold water; mix, stir in 250 ml of hot water. Cook over medium heat, stirring constantly until mixture is thick and clear. Allow to bubble one minute.
3. Beat egg yolks. Stir a small amount of hot mixture into the egg, add more gradually and then return all of the warmed mixture to the remaining portion in the pan.
4. Bring to boil again and cook one minute more, stirring constantly. Remove from heat; add butter and lemon rind. Slowly stir in lemon juice. Cool to lukewarm before pouring into pastry shell. Top with meringue if desired.

PIE MERINGUE

2 egg whites, room temperature
pinch salt

1 ml cream of tartar (optional)
60 ml sugar

1. Add salt to egg whites and beat until fluffy. Sprinkle cream of tartar over top and beat until soft peaks form.
2. Add the sugar gradually and continue beating until the meringue is stiff but not dry.
3. Spread meringue on top of filled pastry shell. Begin at the outside edge joining meringue to crust, then fill in the centre and swirl lightly to form attractive peaks.
4. Bake at 150°C for 15-20 minutes until pale golden brown; 180°C for 10-15 minutes until light brown; 200°C for 4-6 minutes until dark peaks form. Cool away from drafts.

CUSTARD PIE

Yield: one 22 cm pie

3 eggs
125 ml sugar
500 ml scalded milk
1 ml salt

1 ml nutmeg
4 ml vanilla
1 uncooked pastry shell, chilled

1. Beat eggs slightly, add sugar and beat.
2. Add hot milk slowly to avoid cooking the egg. Add salt, vanilla and nutmeg.
3. Place chilled raw pastry shell on a low oven rack and pour in the filling.
4. Bake in pre-heated oven at 200°C for 15 minutes, then reduce temperature to 160°C and cook until a knife inserted 2.5 cm from side of the filling comes out clean. The centre may still be soft but will set later.
5. Cool, then refrigerate, if pie is not to be eaten immediately.

PUMPKIN PIE

Yield: filling for one 22 cm pie

2 eggs
400 ml canned pumpkin
175 ml sugar
2 ml salt
5 ml cinnamon

2 ml ginger
1 ml cloves
375 ml evaporated milk
1 unbaked 22 cm pastry shell

1. Beat the eggs slightly, combine with pumpkin.
2. Mix sugar with the salt and spices. (Fewer spices may be preferred.)
3. Add to the pumpkin mixture. Blend in milk. Pour into pastry shell.
4. Bake in a hot oven 220°C for 15 minutes, then reduce the temperature to moderate (180°C) and continue baking for about 45 minutes. A knife inserted near the centre should come out clean when the pie is baked.

LEMON CHIFFON PIE

1 baked 22 cm pie shell (pastry or crumb crust)
15 ml (one envelope) unflavoured gelatin
65 ml cold water

5-10 ml finely grated lemon rind
125 ml lemon juice
pinch salt
250 ml sugar, divided
4 eggs, separated

1. Soften the gelatin in cold water for 5 minutes.
2. Grate the rind of lemon and measure. Extract juice. Measure.
3. Beat egg yolks in top of double boiler, add 125 ml sugar, salt, lemon rind and juice. Cook over boiling water stirring constantly until thick and lemon coloured.
4. Add the gelatin and stir until dissolved. Cool until the mixture mounds

slightly when dropped from a spoon (about one hour in refrigerator or ½ hour over ice water).
5. Beat egg whites until fluffy and gradually add 125 ml sugar. Continue beating until stiff.
6. Fold the cooled gelatin mixture into the beaten egg whites. Pour into cooked pie shell. Chill for several hours before serving.

Desserts

CHOCOLATE PUDDING

Yield: 4 servings

125 ml sugar
60-75 ml cocoa
60 ml cornstarch

f.g. salt
625 ml milk, divided
7 ml vanilla

1. Using a double boiler, scald 500 ml of milk.
2. Place sugar, cornstarch, cocoa and salt in a bowl and mix together well.
3. Add 125 ml cold milk and blend to a smooth paste.
4. Pour cornstarch mixture into scalded milk, stirring constantly. Cook and stir until pudding is smooth and thick.
5. Cover and cook for 15 minutes longer, stirring occasionally.

6. Remove from heat, cool slightly and then stir in vanilla.
7. Pour into individual moulds that have been first rinsed with cold water. Chill until firm. (Waxed paper placed over the pudding during the cooling process will prevent a skin from forming on the surface.)
8. Unmould and serve with fruit (e.g. banana) and/or cream if desired.

Variations:

VANILLA — Omit cocoa and reduce the sugar to 75 ml.

BUTTERSCOTCH — Omit cocoa and vanilla. Substitute sugar with 100 ml brown sugar. Add 30 ml butter to the slightly cooled pudding.

FRUIT WHIP

2 egg whites
50 ml sugar (*a)
250 ml fruit pulp (*b)
15-20 ml lemon juice
*(a) Sugar must be reduced by half or more for any sweetened, cooked fruit.

*(b) Fruit suggestions: prune, apricot, peach, banana, applesauce, grated apple, crushed berries. Canned baby food has a suitable consistency for this dessert.

1. Beat egg whites until stiff but not dry. Add sugar gradually beating to maintain a stiff mixture.
2. Add lemon juice to fruit pulp if

required. Fold pulp into beaten whites.
3. Place into serving dishes and chill before serving. A custard sauce to pour over this may be made from the yolks.

APPLE BROWN BETTY

60 ml table fat	50 ml raisins
500 ml small soft bread cubes	4 medium apples
125 ml brown sugar	30 ml water
1 ml salt	25 ml lemon rind (optional)
3 ml cinnamon	

1. Mix melted fat with bread cubes.
2. In small bowl, mix together sugar, salt, cinnamon, raisins, and lemon rind.
3. Wash, peel, quarter and slice apples into 1 cm slices.
4. Arrange alternate layers of buttered bread cubes and apple slices in 1 litre casserole dish. Begin and end with bread cubes and sprinkle each layer of apples with some of the sugar mixture.
5. Add water.
6. Bake at 190°C for 45 minutes or until top bread cubes are browned.

Variations:
300 ml crushed oatmeal cookies may replace the bread cubes. Adjust the sugar accordingly.

FRUIT CRUMBLE

Fruit Layer	Apple	Rhubarb	Pears
fruit	1 000 ml (6 apples)	1 250 ml	1 000 ml (6 pears)
sugar	75 ml	125-175 ml	50 ml
water*	30 ml*	30 ml*	0-30 ml*
lemon juice	15 ml	—	—
spices	cloves	—	2 ml ginger

* Amount of water needed with pears and apples depends upon the variety of the fruit used. Less water can also be used with frozen apple slices and frozen rhubarb.

1. Place prepared fruit in a greased casserole dish or deep baking pan about 15 cm x 20 cm.
2. Mix well with the dry sugar. Add seasonings if used.
3. Sprinkle water and lemon juice (if used) over top.

Crumb Topping	
100 ml flour	65 ml brown sugar
200 ml rolled oats	100 ml margarine, melted
f.g. salt	5 ml cinnamon
	75 ml chopped walnuts (optional)

1. Combine dry ingredients; add melted fat and mix until crumbly.
2. Sprinkle crumbs over fruit.
3. Bake at 180°C for 40 min or until fruit is tender.
4. Serve with ice cream or lemon sauce.

FRUIT CRISP

Fruit Base	Apple	Rhubarb	Pear
Fruit	1 000 ml	1 250 ml (2 cm slices)	1 000 ml
Sugar	25 ml	75 ml	25 ml
Water	0-25 ml	30 ml	0-25 ml
Lemon juice	15 ml	—	—
Spice	4-5 cloves	—	—

* Prepare fruit as for Fruit Crumble.

Crisp Topping	
125 ml flour	1 ml salt
150 ml brown sugar	5 ml cinnamon
	75 ml margarine

1. Combine flour, sugar, salt and cinnamon in a bowl.
2. Rub in fat until the mixture is the texture of coarse crumbs.
3. Sprinkle topping over fruit. Bake at 170°C until topping is brown and crisp and fruit is tender, about 40 minutes.

TAPIOCA CREAM

1 egg, separated
500 ml milk
50 ml quick cooking tapioca

50 ml sugar
f.g. salt
3 ml vanilla

1. Mix egg yolk with a small amount of milk, add tapioca, sugar, salt and remaining milk.
2. Bring to a boil over medium heat, stirring constantly. Remove from heat.

Mixture will be thin.
3. Fold hot mixture into stiffly beaten egg white. Cool slightly. Add vanilla. Chill thoroughly.

OLD FASHIONED RICE PUDDING

1 000 ml milk
50 ml brown sugar
125 ml short grain rice, uncooked
15 ml margarine

1 ml salt
1 ml cinnamon
5 ml vanilla
175 ml raisins

1. Heat oven to 180°C.
2. Grease 1.5 litre casserole.
3. Combine rice, milk, sugar, margarine, salt, cinnamon and vanilla in casserole.

4. Bake uncovered, stirring frequently for 1½-2 hours.
5. Add raisins, stir gently.
6. Bake 30 minutes or until rice is tender. May be served hot or cold.

FRUIT JELLY

15 ml gelatin
125 ml cold water
75 ml sugar

150 ml juices, (drained from a 400 ml can and water added to make 150 ml)
50 ml lemon juice
250 ml diced mixed fruit

1. Soften gelatin in cold water.
2. Bring sugar and juices to a boil.
3. Add to softened gelatin. Stir until gelatin is dissolved.
4. Cool only until the jelly is of the consistency of thick unbeaten egg white. Then stir in the fruit and pour into mould. Chill until firm.
5. Serve with table or whipped cream, sour cream or custard sauce.

Note: Fruits may be fresh, frozen or canned. Nuts and marshmallows may be added. Fresh or frozen pineapple must be heated to boiling to destroy an enzyme which will keep the gelatin from setting.

QUICK SET JELLY

1 small package jelly powder, any flavour

250 ml boiling water
8-12 ice cubes

1. Dissolve jelly powder completely in boiling water.
2. Add ice cubes and stir constantly for 2-3 minutes or until jelly starts to thicken.

3. Remove unmelted ice. Let stand 3-5 minutes. Stir.
4. Pour into a mould or individual dishes.

QUICK SET SNOW PUDDING

1. Follow steps 1-3 of Quick Set Jelly.
2. Place bowl over ice and water, add 1 egg white and whip with egg beater until fluffy and thick.

3. Pile lightly into sherbet dishes and chill until firm. Serve with custard sauce or with a sauce of crushed sweetened fruit.

Note: This fluffy dessert is very suitable for a crumb crust pie filling.

Jelly	Gelatin	Sugar	Lemon Juice	Water	Other Liquid
Lemon	15 ml	125 ml	2 lemons plus water to make 425 ml		—
Orange	15 ml	125 ml	50 ml	150 ml	2 small cans frozen concentrated orange juice
Apple	15 ml	75 ml	50 ml	—	375 ml apple juice
Coffee	15 ml	50 ml	—	—	400 ml strong black coffee
Ivory	15 ml	50 ml	—	—	450 ml rich milk and 3 ml vanilla

1. Put gelatin in the top of a double boiler; pour in the cold water and leave for 5-10 minutes for gelatin to soften and absorb water.
2. Place pan over boiling water and stir until the gelatin has dissolved. Add sugar; stir until it has dissolved also.
3. Remove from the heat; add remaining water and/or juice. If a clear jelly is desired, strain through a sieve lined with a double thickness of cleansing tissue.
4. Pour into a moistened mould and chill until completely set. Serve with whipped cream, fruit or sauce.

LEMON SNOW PUDDING
Yield: 4-5 servings

10 ml gelatin
125 ml cold water
125 ml sugar

175 ml water
75 ml lemon juice
2 egg whites

1. Put the gelatin in the top of a double boiler, pour the cold water over it and let it stand for 5-10 minutes.
2. Place pan over boiling water and stir until the gelatin has dissolved.
3. Remove from the heat and add remaining water and the lemon juice.
4. Chill to consistency of unbeaten egg white.

5. Beat the egg whites until stiff; beat the jelly until light and fluffy, then combine and beat until the mixture will hold its shape.
6. Pour into a moistened mould or pile lightly into dessert dishes. Chill several hours before serving. Serve with a custard sauce made from the egg yolks.

FRUIT JUICE SNOW
Yield: 8 servings

15 ml gelatin
125 ml sugar
1 ml salt

300 ml water, divided
180 ml frozen fruit juice concentrate
2 egg whites

1. Mix gelatin, sugar and salt thoroughly in a small saucepan.
2. Add 125 ml of the water. Place over low heat, stirring constantly until gelatin is dissolved.
3. Remove from heat and stir in remaining 175 ml water and frozen fruit juice. Stir until melted.
4. Chill until slightly thicker than unbeaten egg white consistency.

5. Add unbeaten egg whites and beat with an electric beater until the mixture begins to hold its shape. If a rotary beater is used the mixture will be light and fluffy in approximately seven minutes. (To speed up hand beating place bowl over ice and water.)
6. Spoon into dessert dishes and chill until firm. Serve with custard sauce or other suitable dessert sauce.

BAVARIAN CREAM

15 ml unflavoured gelatin
125 ml sugar, divided
f.g. salt
2 eggs, separated

200 ml milk
3 ml vanilla
250 ml heavy cream, whipped

1. Mix gelatin, 50 ml of the sugar and salt thoroughly in top of double boiler.
2. Beat egg yolks and milk together. Add to gelatin mixture.
3. Cook over boiling water, stirring constantly until gelatin is dissolved, about 5 minutes.
4. Remove from heat and stir in vanilla. Cool mixture to unbeaten egg white consistency.

5. Beat egg whites until stiff. Beat in remaining 50 ml sugar.
6. Fold the gelatin mixture into stiffly beaten egg whites.
7. Fold whipped cream into gelatin mixture. Turn into a 1 litre mould and chill until firm.
8. Unmould on serving platter and garnish with fruit.

Variations:

COFFEE BAVARIAN — Add 10 ml instant coffee to the sugar and gelatin mixture before adding milk and eggs.

FRUIT AND NUT BAVARIAN — Use 250 ml well drained diced fruit and 50 ml chopped nuts of your choice. Fold these ingredients into mixture together with the whipped cream.

CHOCOLATE BAVARIAN — Add 2 squares grated or chopped sweet chocolate to gelatin and milk mixture in top of double boiler, or reduce milk to 250 ml and use 1 pkg. (250 ml) semi-sweet chocolate pieces.

SPANISH CREAM

15 ml gelatin
50 ml cold water
425 ml milk, scalded
75 ml sugar

f.g. salt
3 ml vanilla
2 eggs

1. Put the gelatin in a small bowl; add the cold water and let stand for 5 minutes.
2. Beat egg yolks slightly; add sugar and beat. Stir hot milk slowly into egg and sugar mixture, return to double boiler and cook over boiling water until thickened. (This is a soft custard; remove it from the heat when the mixture coats the metal spoon.)
3. Dissolve the soaked gelatin in the hot custard. Add vanilla.

4. Chill custard mixture to unbeaten egg white consistency.
5. Add salt to egg whites; beat until stiff. Beat gelatin mixture until light. Fold jellied custard into beaten egg whites.
6. Turn into a 1-litre mould or individual moulds and chill until firm. Unmould onto serving plate and serve plain or with whipped cream, fruit or a sauce.

Variations:

COFFEE SPANISH CREAM — Replace 250 ml of the milk with strong coffee.

PINEAPPLE SPANISH CREAM — Replace the milk by crushed pineapple, undrained; replace vanilla by lemon juice.

LEMON SPANISH CREAM — Use 375 ml milk. Increase sugar to 125 ml. Substitute juice and rind of one lemon for the vanilla.

TWO-LAYERED SPANISH CREAM — To obtain two layers (a jelly on the bottom with custard on top) do not chill the mixture to unbeaten egg white consistency. After removing from the heat, stir in flavouring and fold hot gelatin into beaten egg whites. Turn into a mould.

STRAWBERRY MOUSSE (refrigerated)

250 ml strawberries
125 ml sugar
  5 ml unflavoured gelatin

250 ml whipping cream
  2 egg whites
f.g. salt

1. Hull, wash and crush the strawberries. Frozen berries may be used.
2. Drain the juice from the crushed strawberries, saving the juice.
3. Combine the sugar with the drained strawberries.
4. Add the gelatin to the juice and allow to soak.
5. Place the juice and gelatin over hot water until the gelatin is melted. Cool.

6. When completely cool, beat well, and add sugar-strawberry mixture.
7. Whip cream until just stiff. Add salt to egg whites, then beat until stiff.
8. Fold fruit into whipped cream, then fold into stiffly beaten egg whites.
9. Pour into a tray or mould. Cover with waxed paper. Refrigerate overnight.

CHOCOLATE MOUSSE (frozen)

    3 ml gelatin
  50 ml cold milk
1½ squares chocolate OR
  75 ml cocoa

125 ml milk
150 ml sugar
  5 ml vanilla
500 ml heavy cream, whipped

1. Put gelatin in a small bowl, pour in 50 ml cold milk and let stand for 5 minutes.
2. Put the chocolate and 125 ml milk in the top part of a double boiler and heat over hot water. When the chocolate is melted beat vigorously until smooth.
3. Add the soaked gelatin and the sugar, stirring until both are dissolved.

Cool. (If cocoa is used, mix it with the sugar.)
4. When the mixture begins to thicken, fold it into the whipped cream. Add vanilla.
5. Turn into a refrigerator tray or mould and cover tightly with aluminum foil. Place in freezer or coldest part of freezing compartment of refrigerator.

Variation:

To reduce cost, part or all of the whipping cream can be replaced with an artificial whipped topping. If all the whipping cream is substituted, the amount of sugar should be reduced.

STRAWBERRY CHARLOTTE

Yield: 8-10 servings

  30 ml unflavoured gelatin
175 ml sugar, divided
    1 ml salt
    4 eggs, separated
125 ml water

550-600 ml frozen sliced strawberries
            (2 packages)
  30 ml lemon juice
  10 ml grated lemon rind
250 ml heavy cream

1. Mix gelatin, 50 ml of the sugar and the salt thoroughly in top of a double boiler.
2. Beat egg yolks and water together. Add to gelatin mixture. Add 1 package of the frozen strawberries.
3. Cook over boiling water, stirring constantly until the gelatin is dissolved and strawberries thawed, about 8 minutes.
4. Remove from heat and add remain-

ing package of berries, lemon juice and rind. Stir until berries are thawed.
5. Chill, stirring occasionally, until the mixture mounds when dropped from a spoon.
6. Beat egg whites until stiff. Beat in remaining 125 ml sugar. Fold in gelatin mixture.
7. Whip cream until soft peaks form, fold into gelatin mixture. Turn into mould and chill until firm.

STRAWBERRY CHARLOTTE RUSSE Yield: 10-12 servings

1 recipe Strawberry Charlotte
8-10 lady fingers

whipped cream for garnishing
(about 125 ml)

1. Split lady fingers in half and stand around the edge of a 25 cm spring form pan. Have flat side of cookies turned to centre of pan.

2. Pour Strawberry Charlotte mixture into pan and chill until firm (3-4 hours)

3. Remove from pan and garnish with additional whipped cream and whole berries.

Variations:

1. Instead of lady fingers use sponge cake, jelly roll, soft cookies to line the pan.
2. If a spring form pan is not available, use a loaf pan lined with waxed paper, extending beyond the rim. Approximate pan size of 20 cm x 11 cm x 6 cm. Line the bottom and sides of pan with lady fingers. Pour in ½ of the pudding mixture, add a layer of lady finger halves, then the remaining pudding. Top with remaining cookies. Chill 3-4 hours until firm. Using waxed paper, lift the dessert from the dish and carefully transfer it to a serving plate; remove waxed paper and garnish.

CRAZY CAKE

 7 ml gelatin
50 ml cold water
90 ml boiling water
75 ml sugar

50 ml fine graham wafer crumbs
 2 small egg whites (or 1 large)
 1 ml salt
 5 ml vanilla

1. Place cold water in a large mixing bowl. Sprinkle gelatin on top to soften.
2. Add boiling water and stir until gelatin has dissolved.
3. Stir in sugar, chill slightly, (15 minutes in refrigerator).
4. Meanwhile, sprinkle half of the crumbs over the bottom and sides of a greased loaf cake pan.
5. Add egg white, salt and vanilla to the well chilled gelatin, (it should be syrupy like egg white).
6. Beat with electric or rotary beater about 10 minutes until very light and

fluffy, (mounds will form when beater is lifted).
7. Turn into crumb-lined pan; sprinkle with remaining crumbs.
8. Chill 30 minutes or until ready to serve.
9. Cut into squares and serve with lemon sauce made with egg yolk from recipe. If no sauce is to be used, 1 ml of flavouring and a few drops of suitable food colouring could be added to the mixture before beating. (Examples: peppermint flavour and green colour; orange extract and orange colour.)

Variation:

STRAWBERRY SQUARES:

1. Dissolve 45 ml (½ package) strawberry jello in 125 ml boiling water.
2. Add 4 ice cubes. Stir until mixture begins to set. Remove remaining ice cubes.
3. Add egg white and beat hard. Continue as for Crazy Cake.

ICE CREAM JELLY

 1 package strawberry jelly powder
175 ml boiling water
 30 ml honey

175 ml ice cubes
250 ml vanilla ice cream

1. Use a deep bowl to dissolve the jelly powder in boiling water.
2. Add honey. Mix well.
3. Add ice cubes. Stir until cubes have melted.

4. Using an electric mixer, whip the jelly until it is fluffy.
5. Fold in the ice cream. Spoon into dessert dishes.
6. Chill before serving.

3 ml gelatin
15 ml cold water
30 ml hot water
60 ml sugar
100 ml frozen orange juice (½ small can)

30 ml lemon juice
250 ml milk
1 egg white
f.g. salt

1. Soften gelatin in cold water, dissolve in hot water, add sugar and sufficient orange juice to dissolve the sugar; reheat if necessary.
2. Add remaining orange juice and the lemon juice. Chill until syrupy.
3. Add the milk, pour into refrigerator tray, freeze until firm. The mixture will curdle but will be beaten smooth later.
4. Beat egg white until stiff but not dry. Beat in 30 ml sugar and the salt.
5. Break frozen mixture into chunks and beat until smooth. Fold into egg white mixture. Return to tray; freeze firm.

Variations:

LEMONADE SHERBET — Use 100 ml frozen lemonade (½ small can) to replace frozen orange juice. Reduce lemon juice to 15 ml.

GRAPEFRUIT SHERBET — Use 125 ml grapefruit juice in place of the orange and lemon juices.

VANILLA ICE CREAM

300 ml sugar
75 ml flour
2 ml salt
1 250 ml milk*, scalded
6 eggs

1 000 ml heavy cream
20 ml vanilla
* For extra rich ice cream replace milk with cream.

1. Place sugar, flour and salt in saucepan and mix well.
2. Slowly stir in hot milk. Cook over low heat for about 10 minutes, stirring constantly until mixture is thickened.
3. Beat eggs. Mix a small amount of the hot mixture into beaten eggs, then return to hot mixture and cook 1 minute longer.
4. Chill in refrigerator. Add cream and vanilla. Pour into ice cream freezer.

TO FREEZE ICE CREAM IN AN ICE CREAM FREEZER

1. Scald can, dasher and cover. Assemble parts. Position can in freezer bucket.

2. Pack ice and salt in space around can beginning with ice. Use 50 ml rock salt for each 250 ml finely crushed ice.

3. Pour chilled mixture into can. To allow for expansion, do not fill more than ⅔ full.

4. Let stand until thoroughly chilled. Then turn crank very slowly until mixture is quite stiff. Increase speed gradually until mixture is stiff and of a fine texture and handle is very difficult to turn. OR

5. Start motor and allow the mixture to churn for 20-30 minutes or until the motor slows or stops. Disconnect immediately when motor stops as motor damage can result if left on after stalling.

6. Remove the dasher, scrape ice cream from the sides of the can, and level.

7. Drain water from the freezer bucket and repack with crushed ice and rock salt. If time is short, use 1 part salt to 4 parts ice; if a longer time is available, use 1 part salt to 8 parts ice.

8. Cover well and allow to harden completely for at least 1 hour before serving.

VANILLA ICE CREAM
(using cornstarch or flour)   Yield: 6 servings

125 ml sugar
 15 ml cornstarch (or 30 ml all purpose
    flour)
325 ml coffee cream

  2 eggs, separated
f.g. salt
 10 ml vanilla
250 ml heavy cream

1. Combine the sugar and cornstarch or flour in the top of a double boiler.
2. Gradually add the milk, mix well, place over boiling water and stir until it thickens.
3. Cover and cook for 10 minutes.
4. Beat the egg yolks with a fork in a small mixing bowl.
5. Stir a little of the hot mixture into the beaten egg yolks.
6. Return to the top of the double boiler after all the mixture has been added and continue cooking and stirring for 5 minutes.
7. Remove from the heat and cool.

8. When the custard mixture is cool, beat the egg whites stiff, add the salt and fold into the custard. Add the vanilla.
9. Pour into the refrigerator tray and freeze. Set the control to the lowest temperature.
10. When the mixture is frozen so that it is almost firm, whip the cream.
11. Remove ice cream to a chilled bowl and break it up with a spoon.
12. Beat until free from lumps, then fold in the cream. Beat again.
13. Return to the refrigerator. Set the control to normal operating temperature.

VANILLA ICE CREAM
(using gelatin)

  2 eggs, separated
300 ml milk
125 ml sugar
 10 ml gelatin

 15 ml cold water
  5 ml vanilla
200 ml whipping cream OR
200 ml evaporated milk, chilled icy cold

1. Beat yolks until thick in top of a double boiler, add milk and sugar, stirring.
2. Mix gelatin, with cold water. Set aside for 5 minutes.
3. Cook yolk mixture over hot water until metal spoon is slightly coated.
4. Dissolve gelatin in yolk mixture. Set aside to cool.
5. Beat egg whites to form soft peaks.

Fold cooled egg mixture into whites. Fold in vanilla.
6. Pour into refrigerator tray and freeze to mush consistency.
7. Beat cream or evaporated milk in chilled bowl. Beat quickly with rotary beater until smooth.
8. Fold whipped cream into egg mixture. Beat until smooth. Return to tray and continue freezing.

CAKE DOUGHNUTS

    2 eggs
  250 ml sugar
  250 ml milk
   75 ml oil
1 000 ml all purpose flour
   25 ml double acting baking powder

  1 ml cinnamon
    OR
  5 ml grated lemon rind
  2 ml salt
  1 ml nutmeg

1. Beat eggs and stir in milk and oil.
2. Sift flour before measuring, then add baking powder, cinnamon, nutmeg and salt. Resift and add sugar. (Add lemon rind if used.)
3. Add dry ingredients to wet ingredients.

4. Chill the dough slightly.
5. Roll or pat dough to about 1.5 cm thickness.
6. Deep fry at 190°C for about 3 minutes.

UPSIDE DOWN CAKE

FRUIT LAYER:
- 30 ml table fat
- 125 ml brown sugar

- 15 ml water
- fruit (pineapple, peaches, apricots, plums)
- maraschino cherries

1. Make a syrup of table fat, brown sugar and water. Pour into a 20 cm x 20 cm pan or baking dish.

2. Cut fruit and arrange attractively with cherries on the bottom of the pan.

CAKE LAYER:
- 50 ml shortening
- 150 ml granulated sugar
- 300 ml sifted flour
- 7 ml baking powder

- 1 ml salt
- 1 egg, beaten
- 125 ml milk
- 5 ml vanilla

1. Sift together, flour, baking powder and salt.
2. Work shortening with a spoon until creamy. Slowly add sugar continuing to work until creamy.
3. Add egg, beat well.
4. Add the dry ingredients alternately with milk beginning and ending with the dry mixture and stirring until smooth after each addition. Stir in the vanilla.
5. Pour batter over fruit layer and spread. Bake at 180°C 30-40 minutes or until cake is done.
6. Remove from oven; loosen the edges with a knife and turn out immediately onto a serving plate. Serve in squares, hot or cold, with or without cream.

LEMON CAKE PUDDING (Lemon Sponge Pudding)

Yield: 4-6 servings

- 30 ml table fat
- 175 ml sugar
- 1 ml salt
- 5 ml grated rind of lemon

- 75 ml lemon juice
- 75 ml sifted flour
- 3 eggs, separated
- 375 ml milk

1. Cream fat, sugar and salt together. Gradually add lemon juice, rind and flour.
2. Beat egg whites until stiff; set aside. Beat egg yolks well; add milk and beat.
3. Stir yolk and milk mixture gradually into first mixture. Fold in beaten egg whites.
4. Pour into an ungreased casserole dish or individual custard cups. Place in a pan of water 2-3 cm deep.
5. Bake large casserole at 180°C for 45-50 minutes until top is well browned and sponge on top half of pudding is quite firm and dry. Bake individual desserts at 180°C for 30-35 minutes. Serve warm or cold.

CHOCOLATE SOUFFLÉ

Yield: 4 servings

- 20 ml butter
- 20 ml flour
- 125 ml milk
- f.g. salt
- 30 ml sugar

- 5 ml vanilla
- 2 squares semi-sweetened chocolate
- 2 egg yolks
- 2 egg whites
- 20 ml sugar

1. Melt butter and blend in flour; add milk slowly, stirring constantly. Add salt and sugar and cook until thick; add flavouring.
2. Heat chocolate over hot water just until melted.
3. Beat egg yolks until thick and light. Stir into thickened sauce along with melted chocolate.
4. Beat egg whites until stiff but not dry; gradually add 20 ml sugar, beating well. Fold into chocolate mixture.
5. Turn into buttered dish or custard cups.
6. Place in pan of water and bake at 190°C for 30-35 minutes.
7. Serve at once with whipped cream or custard sauce.

CARROT PUDDING

Yield: 1 large (1 000 ml)
or 2-3 smaller puddings

250 ml grated carrot
250 ml grated apple
250 ml grated potato
250 ml raisins
250 ml currants
125 ml grated or finely ground suet
  2 eggs
250 ml sugar or brown sugar

 15 ml molasses
300 ml all purpose flour
 10 ml baking powder
  5 ml cinnamon
  5 ml allspice
  2 ml baking soda
  5 ml salt

1. Sift all dry ingredients together.
2. Beat eggs until fluffy.
3. Mix together carrot, apple, potato, raisin, currant, suet and sugar. Add eggs and molasses.
4. Add flour mixture and blend well.

5. Place mixture in well greased pudding mould or moulds, filling ½ to ¾ full.
6. Cover with well greased brown paper and tie down.
7. Steam for 3 hours; cool covered; refrigerate.
8. Reheat when needed about 1 hour.

STEAMING:

To improvise a steamer, set the bowl on sealer ring in a deep kettle which has a tight fitting lid. Add boiling water until it comes half way up the mould. When the water boils, adjust the heat so that it will boil gently. Add more boiling water as necessary.

PRESSURE COOKING:

Place stand in pressure cooker. Add sufficient water to come ⅓ up the side of the mould. Use 105 kilopascals pressure. Steam 1 large pudding 1½ hours. Smaller pudding, 1 hour.

PLUM PUDDING

Yield: 10-12 servings

400 ml raisins
250 ml currants
250 ml glacé fruit, mixed
250 ml coarsely chopped walnuts
250 ml finely chopped suet
 10 ml grated orange peel
 50 ml finely chopped crystallized ginger
250 ml sifted all purpose flour, divided
 10 ml baking powder

 10 ml cinnamon
  2 ml nutmeg
  2 ml allspice
  2 ml salt
300 ml brown sugar
  4 eggs
 30 ml cream
 50 ml fruit juice (grape or other)
275 ml graham cracker crumbs

1. Combine the first seven ingredients with 100 ml of the flour. Toss lightly until all the fruit is coated with flour.
2. Sift remaining flour with baking powder, spices and salt.
3. Blend into fruit mixture along with sugar.
4. Beat together eggs, cream and fruit juice until well blended. Add to fruit mixture.
5. Stir in graham cracker crumbs.
6. Grease a large pudding bowl, or two smaller ones, extremely well.

7. Turn pudding mixture into greased moulds.
8. Cover well with heavily greased brown paper. Tie down.
9. Place on a rack in a large saucepan or pressure cooker. Pour about 5 cm water into the bottom of the saucepan and cover tightly.
10. Steam 3½ hours; pressure cook for 1 hour at 105 kilopascals pressure.
11. Remove pudding from steamer and unmould onto platter. Serve hot with hard sauce.

FRUIT LAYER:
640 ml can sweetened fruit
30 ml flour

15 ml table fat
spices as desired

1. Drain fruit reserving liquid. Place fruit in a casserole dish or deep baking pan approximately 20 cm x 20 cm.
2. Add cold water to the fruit syrup to make 250 ml liquid. Blend together the flour with a small amount of the cold liquid to make a smooth paste, then add the rest of the liquid and cook and stir in a saucepan until the mixture thickens.
3. Pour thickened syrup over the fruit and dot with butter. Add spices if desired; e.g., ginger with pears, cloves with apricots.

Note: Unpitted apricots contribute an interesting flavour.

BISCUIT TOPPING:
250 ml flour
15 ml sugar
10 ml baking powder

1 ml salt
50 ml margarine or shortening
1 egg, beaten
50 ml milk

1. Measure and sift dry ingredients into bowl.
2. Cut in fat until it resembles oatmeal.
3. Mix beaten egg and milk together; pour all at once over dry mixture. Toss lightly with a fork until uniformly moistened. Dough should be lumpy.
4. Drop by spoonfuls onto the fruit and sauce mixture. Sprinkle with sugar. Bake at 190°C for 35-40 minutes. Serve hot.

CREAM PUFFS

250 ml all purpose flour
f.g. salt
15 ml sugar
250 ml water or milk

125 ml butter or margarine
4 large eggs (or 5 medium) room temperature

1. Preheat oven to 200°C.
2. Sift and measure flour. Add salt and sugar and sift together.
3. Place water and butter in a heavy pan. Bring to a full boil.
4. Add the dry ingredients all at once and stir quickly with a wooden spoon. Mixture will be lumpy at first. Continue stirring and when it becomes smooth, stir more vigorously. Remove from heat when the paste becomes dry, does not cling to the spoon or the sides of the pan and when pressed lightly the spoon leaves a smooth imprint. Do not overcook for then the dough will fail to puff.
5. Add eggs one at a time, beating vigorously after each addition until the dough no longer looks slippery. For best results eggs must be at room temperature.
6. The paste is ready to bake after the last egg has been incorporated. A small quantity of the dough will stand erect if scooped up at the end of the spoon when the proper consistency is reached. Using a spoon or pastry bag, form mounds or different shapes as desired. Place pastry on an ungreased baking sheet allowing enough space between so that mounds will not touch when they rise.
7. Sprinkle over the shapes on the pan, lightly (as you would laundry), a few drops of water.
8. Bake shapes at 200°C for 10 minutes. Then reduce heat to 180°C and bake for about 25 minutes longer or until quite firm to the touch.
9. Cool shells away from drafts. When cooled, cut them horizontally with a sharp knife and insert filling. If there are any damp dough filaments remaining inside, remove them before filling.

Candies

TEMPERATURES AND TESTS FOR SYRUP AND CANDIES

PRODUCT	SYRUP TEMPERATURE AT SEA LEVEL*	TEST	DESCRIPTION OF TEST
Syrup	110°C to 112°C	Thread	Syrup spins a 5 cm thread when dropped from a fork or spoon.
Fondant Fudge Panocha	112°C to 115°C	Soft ball	Syrup, when dropped into very cold water, forms a soft ball that flattens on removal from water.
Caramels	118°C to 120°C	Firm ball	Syrup, when dropped into very cold water, forms a firm ball that does not flatten on removal from water.
Divinity Marshmallows Popcorn balls	121°C to 130°C	Hard ball	Syrup, when dropped into very cold water, forms a ball that is hard enough to hold its shape, yet plastic.
Butterscotch Toffees	132°C to 143°C	Soft crack	Syrup, when dropped into very cold water, separates into threads that are pliable and not brittle.
Brittle Glace	149°C to 154°C	Hard crack	Syrup, when dropped into very cold water, separates into threads that are hard and brittle.
Barley sugar	160°C	Clear liquid	The sugar liquifies.
Caramel	170°C	Brown liquid	The liquid becomes brown.

* *Elevation Variation*: These syrup temperatures are given for sea level. For each increase of 270 metres in elevation, cook the syrup to a temperature 1°C *lower* than that called for at sea level.

Crystalline candies are hygroscopic in nature and will attract moisture from the air. For this reason, on particularly humid days or very wet days it may be necessary to heat the candy to 1°C hotter than you would if it were a very dry day. This would ensure the right final sugar concentration and would avoid the possibility of a candy that is soft.

An accurate candy thermometer is necessary for best results in making crystalline candies. Test your thermometer by placing it in boiling water and noting the temperature. If your thermometer does not register at 100°C boiling point for water, it will be necessary to make a correction in the final temperature indicated in the candy recipe. Add or subtract the °C necessary to adjust it to your thermometer reading; e.g., if the thermometer registers boiling water at 98°C and the candy recipe requires 112°C, adjust candy temperature to 110°C. These calculations are essential if the candy is to be of correct firmness.

FONDANT

500 ml sugar
40 ml light corn syrup

175 ml water

1. Put sugar, corn syrup and water in saucepan and heat, stirring until the sugar is dissolved.
2. Cover the saucepan when the syrup begins to boil and cook for 3 minutes.
3. Remove cover and boil without stirring until the syrup reaches the soft ball stage,(112°C to 115°C).Wipe off any sugar crystals that may form on the sides of the saucepan above the boiling syrup. This can be done with a clean wet cloth or by wrapping a piece of wet cheesecloth around the tines of a fork.

4. Pour syrup on to a cold wet platter. DO NOT SCRAPE THE SAUCEPAN. Cool until lukewarm. Test by touching bottom of plate with the hand, not by placing finger into the candy mixture.
5. Beat with a spatula until the mixture has crystallized and becomes white and creamy, then knead in the hands until smooth and satiny.
6. If not used immediately, store in a tightly covered container until ready to use.

FIVE-MINUTE FUDGE

150 ml (small can) evaporated milk
400 ml granulated sugar
  2 ml salt
375 ml (16)medium diced marshmallows

125 ml chopped nuts
375 ml semi-sweet chocolate chips
  5 ml vanilla

1. Mix evaporated milk, sugar and salt in a large saucepan. Heat to boiling, then cook 5 minutes, stirring constantly. Begin timing after mixture begins bubbling around the edges of the pan.
2. Remove from the heat, add marsh-

mallows, nuts, chocolate bits and vanilla. Stir fudge until marshmallows and chocolate are melted.
3. Pour fudge into buttered 20 cm x 20 cm pan. Cool. Cut into squares to serve.

PANOCHA (Vanilla Fudge)

750 ml light brown sugar
250 ml evaporated milk or thin cream
 30 ml butter or margarine

  7 ml vanilla
150 ml coarsely chopped nuts (optional)

1. Place the sugar and milk in a saucepan. Stir over low heat until the sugar dissolves.
2. Increase the heat until the mixture boils. Continue boiling with frequent stirring until the thermometer registers 114°C (soft ball stage).
3. Remove from heat, add butter and

set aside to cool without stirring until mixture feels just warm, 44°C.
4. When lukewarm, stir in the vanilla and beat until the candy loses its gloss and becomes thick and creamy. Stir in nuts if desired and turn into slightly buttered pans. Cut in squares when cold.

POPCORN BALLS

500 ml light corn syrup
 15 ml vinegar
  5 ml salt

 10 ml vanilla
3 000 ml popped corn

1. Combine syrup, vinegar and salt in saucepan.
2. Cook, stirring only 3 or 4 times until the thermometer registers 130°C (hard ball stage). Remove from heat, mix vanilla in quickly.

3. Place popcorn in a large bowl and pour syrup over it, tossing with a fork until the popcorn is well coated.
4. When the corn is cool enough to handle, form into balls with lightly buttered hands. Cool on wax paper.

DIVINITY

375 ml granulated sugar
75 ml corn syrup
100 ml boiling water

1 egg white
1 ml vanilla
50 ml chopped nuts

1. Place sugar, syrup and water in a saucepan. Heat slowly stirring until sugar dissolves.
2. Increase the heat and boil steadily without stirring until the thermometer registers 121°C to 130°C, hard ball stage. Remove from heat and cool slightly.
3. Quickly beat egg white until stiff. Gradually add the hot syrup pouring it in a thin stream over the egg and beat-ing constantly.
4. Continue beating with a wooden spoon until the candy will just hold its shape when dropped from the spoon. Stir in vanilla and nuts.
5. Turn into a slightly buttered pan to cool or place the bowl over hot water to keep the mixture soft and drop by spoonfuls onto buttered pan or waxed paper.

MARSHMALLOWS

250 ml coconut, finely shredded
50 ml gelatin
75 ml cold water

750 ml sugar
125 ml boiling water
25 ml vanilla

1. Place coconut in a heavy skillet and stir over medium heat until browned. Cool and spread on cutting board.
2. Place cold water in a large bowl and add gelatin.
3. Place boiling water and sugar in a sauce pan. Heat and stir until sugar dissolves.
4. Pour a little of the syrup over the gelatin and stir well. Add remainder and beat until very thick.
5. When the mixture is nearly thick enough to hold its shape, add vanilla.
6. Continue beating until quite firm. Turn out onto coconut and spread evenly.
7. Cut into cubes and roll remaining sides in coconut.

Variation:

CHOCOLATE MARSHMALLOWS: Add 75 ml cocoa and 60 ml more water to the sugar and water syrup. Continue as above.

WHITE TAFFY

375 ml sugar
1 ml cream of tartar
125 ml light corn syrup

60 ml water
30 ml butter
5 ml vanilla

1. Combine all ingredients except vanilla in a saucepan and blend well.
2. Cook, stirring only occasionally to the hard ball stage, 121°C to 130°C.
3. Remove from heat and stir in vanilla.
4. Pour into a well buttered platter. As candy cools, turn edges toward the centre with a spatula. This helps it to cool evenly.
5. When cooled enough to handle, butter hands, gather candy into a ball and pull it until taffy is snow white and has a satin-like finish.
6. Twist into a rope 1-2 cm in diameter and cut with scissors into pieces 2-3 cm long.

Variations:

PINK MINT TAFFY: Substitute 2 ml peppermint extract for vanilla and add a few drops of red food colouring just before pulling.

GREEN TAFFY: Substitute 2 ml wintergreen extract for vanilla and add a few drops of green food colouring just before pulling.

CANDY CANES: Twist together two colours, cut in lengths and shape with curve at end.

PEANUT BRITTLE

250 ml sugar
125 ml shelled peanuts
  3 ml baking soda

1. Combine baking soda with peanuts.
2. Grease cookie sheet.
3. Put sugar in heavy iron frying pan. Stir constantly over medium heat until all of the sugar has melted. Reduce heat to prevent sugar burning.
4. Add peanuts quickly and stir. Pour into greased pan. Cool.

CANDY APPLES

  8 medium-sized apples
500 ml granulated sugar
150 ml light corn syrup
250 ml water
  3 ml cinnamon
6-8 drops red food colouring

1. Lightly grease a baking sheet.
2. Wash and remove stems from the apples. Insert a wooden meat skewer or stick firmly in the stem end.
3. Combine sugar, syrup and water in saucepan. Cook, stirring until sugar dissolves.
4. Cover and bring to a boil. Wipe inside of pan with moistened clean cloth.
Boil uncovered and without stirring until a few drops in cold water separate into hard brittle threads. This is hard crack stage, 149°C.
5. Blend in cinnamon and food colouring. Remove from heat.
6. Tip saucepan and dip the apples in syrup, turning to coat evenly. Place, stick up, on prepared baking sheet.

Note: The candy mixture will not adhere to apples with a waxy surface.

TURKISH DELIGHT

 45 ml gelatin
125 ml cold water
500 ml sugar
125 ml boiling water
  1 orange, rind and juice
 45 ml lemon juice

1. Soften gelatin in cold water.
2. Make a syrup of sugar and boiling water. When boiling, add gelatin. Boil gently 20 minutes. (Although boiling toughens gelatin, in this confection the toughness is not objectionable.)
3. Remove from heat, add fruit juices and strain. Add rind. Candied fruit and chopped nuts may be added. Food colouring may be added if desired.
4. Pour into moistened pan.
5. When firm, cut into squares using a knife dipped in hot water.
6. Roll in icing sugar or fruit sugar.

Beverages

SUMMER FRESH LEMONADE

Yield: 1 750 ml (about 8 servings)

 15 ml fresh grated lemon peel
375 ml sugar
125 ml water, boiling
375 ml fresh squeezed lemon juice
1 250 ml water

1. In covered jar, combine lemon peel, sugar and boiling water; cover and shake until sugar dissolves.
2. Pour into large pitcher, add lemon juice and water. Store covered in refrigerator. Serve over ice.

FROSTING GLASSES

1. Use attractive glass bowls or cups for fruit cup or small juice glasses for appetizer juice cocktail. Chill glasses.
2. Wipe the rim with a slice of lemon from which the juice is flowing freely or dip the rim in a saucer of lemon juice.
3. Swirl the glass to remove excess moisture, then dip the rim 0.5 cm deep in powdered sugar. Lift the glass and tap it gently to remove any excess sugar.

ICED TEA

4 ml tea

500 ml boiling water

Make tea. Strain leaves or remove tea bags. Sweeten if desired. Pour into tall glasses ⅓ full of chipped ice. Serve with slice of lemon or orange or mint leaf.

FRUIT PUNCH

Yield: 8 litres (serves 40)

4 litres water
750 ml sugar
500 ml strong tea
1 litre apple juice

2 litres pineapple or cranberry juice
500 ml orange juice (or 1 can frozen orange juice)
2 cans frozen lemon concentrate

1. Bring sugar and water to a full rolling boil. Chill.

2. Add the other ingredients. Stir and chill.

EASY FRUIT PUNCH

4 small cans frozen pink lemonade
1 large can unsweetened pineapple juice

2 large bottles 7-Up
ice cubes

1. Dilute lemonade according to label directions.
2. Add pineapple juice.

3. Just before serving stir in 7-Up and ice cubes.

Jams, Pickles

CITRUS MARMALADE

1 grapefruit
2 lemons
3 oranges

sugar
water

1. Wash the fruit. Cut in thin slices, then in thin strips. Discard seeds and hard white centre core of grapefruit. Measure fruit.
2. Add 625 ml boiling water for each 250 ml of fruit. Allow to stand overnight.

3. Next day, boil briskly uncovered for 1½ hours. Measure fruit.
4. Add sugar, using 180 ml sugar for each 250 ml of concentrated fruit.
5. Boil until a little of the syrup will gel on a cold plate, probably about 5 minutes.

RASPBERRY JAM (beater method)

Yield: 2 small jars

350 ml crushed raspberries
250 ml sugar
45 ml lemon juice

1. Pick over berries and mash thoroughly. Measure.
2. Place in saucepan with sugar. Bring to a boil and boil for 5 minutes.
3. Add lemon juice; cook for 5 minutes more.

4. Beat with electric beater for three minutes.
5. Pour into sterilized jars and seal with wax.

FREEZER STRAWBERRY JAM (using pectin crystals)

Yield: 6-8 small jars

549

500 ml crushed strawberries
1 000 ml sugar

1 package pectin crystals
250 ml water

DO NOT DOUBLE THIS RECIPE.
1. Wash, pick over and hull berries. Use only fully ripe fruit.
2. Crush thoroughly. Measure.
3. Add sugar to fruit, mix well and let stand while preparing pectin.
4. Combine water and pectin in saucepan. Bring to a boil and boil hard one minute, stirring constantly.
5. Stir in fruit and sugar mixture.

Continue stirring about three minutes. (There will be a few remaining sugar crystals.)
6. Ladle immediately into clean jars. Cover jam with tight lids or thin coating of paraffin.
7. Let stand for 24 hours. Store in freezer or in refrigerator if to be used within 3 weeks. Once thawed, keep refrigerated.

Note: This jam is easy to make and has a fresh fruit flavour. Because it is uncooked, it will mould and ferment if kept at room temperature. However, it will keep for a month in the refrigerator and for a year in the freezer. Once a jar is opened, it should be used within a few days.

FREEZER BERRY JAM (using liquid pectin)

Yield: 6-8 small jars

500 ml crushed fully ripe fruit (use strawberries, raspberries or blackberries)
1 000 ml sugar

30 ml lemon juice
½ bottle liquid fruit pectin (85 ml)

DO NOT DOUBLE THIS RECIPE.
1. Wash, (if necessary), pick over, and remove stems from berries. Use only ripe fruit.
2. Crush berries thoroughly. Measure.
3. Combine fruit and sugar, stir well and allow to stand for 15-20 minutes while sugar dissolves.
4. Mix liquid pectin and lemon juice well in a small bowl. Stir into mixed fruit and sugar. Continue stirring for

3 minutes. (A few sugar crystals will remain.)
5. Pour immediately into clean jars. Cover at once with tight lids. Allow to set at room temperature for 24 hours. Then store in freezer.
6. To use, allow to thaw at room temperature about 2 hours. Once thawed, keep refrigerated. For use within 3 weeks, jam may be stored in the refrigerator.

PEACH CHUTNEY

Yield: about 1.5 litres

2 kg peaches (16 medium) (2 litres sliced)
250 ml seedless raisins
2 cloves garlic, minced
125 ml chopped onion
175 ml chopped preserved ginger
15-30 ml chili powder

15 ml mustard seed
15 ml curry powder
7 ml salt
50 ml mixed pickling spice
1 000 ml cider vinegar
1 000 ml brown sugar

1. Tie mixed pickling spice in a cheesecloth bag.
2. Peel and slice peaches. Combine with remaining ingredients in a large bowl. Cover and let stand overnight.
3. Place mixture in a heavy kettle.

Bring to boil and simmer uncovered until chutney is the desired consistency. Stir frequently to prevent scorching.
4. Remove spice bag. Ladle chutney into sterilized jars. Seal.

Note: This chutney is similar to Indian mango chutney and is especially good with curry dishes.

TOMATO CHUTNEY

250 ml prepared ripe tomatoes (2-3 whole)
1 medium onion
1 medium apple
125 ml vinegar
125 ml brown sugar
50 ml raisins

2 ml salt
1 ml mustard
3 ml cinnamon
1 ml allspice
1 ml cloves
f.g. cayenne

1. Blanch tomatoes, remove skins and chop before measuring.
2. Peel and chop onion.
3. Wash, quarter, core and chop apple.
4. Place these ingredients in a heavy pot and begin cooking. Add vinegar as required to prevent scorching.
5. Add raisins and spices and cook for 20 minutes or until mixture is thick.
6. Scald jars just before filling. Seal.

DILL PICKLES

fresh cucumbers, 8-12 cm long
fresh dill, whole stalk
small red peppers, dried
bay leaf, dried
garlic cloves, sliced (optional)
horseradish root, sliced (optional)

Brine ingredients:
250 ml coarse pickling salt
1.25 litres vinegar
3.75 litres water

1. Use fresh picked cucumbers of uniform small size (do not cut). Scrub. Cover with cold water and let soak overnight. Add ice cubes to keep cold.
2. Next day, drain and wipe cucumbers. Pack carefully into sterilized jars placing a stalk of dill weed at the bottom and at the top of each jar as well as in the centre if jars are very large.
3. To each litre size jar, add 1 bay leaf, 1 small red pepper, 1 slice garlic clove and 1 slice horseradish root.
4. Prepare brine by combining salt, water and vinegar in stated proportions. Make as much as required for cucumbers used. Heat to boiling.
5. Cover cucumbers with brine. Seal. Store in a cool, dark place for at least 6 weeks before using.

SWEET MIXED PICKLES

1 medium cauliflower, broken in flowerets
1 litre small cucumbers, whole or cut in two
1 litre larger cucumbers, chopped
1 litre onions, chopped
1 litre small whole pickling onions
3 sweet red peppers, chopped
3 green peppers, chopped

Soaking Brine:
250 ml coarse pickling salt
3 litres water

Sweet Pickle Brine:
1 250 ml sugar
125 ml water
1 125 ml vinegar
10 ml celery seed
10 ml mustard seed

Mustard Pickle Ingredients:
200 ml flour
50 ml dry mustard
15 ml tumeric
vinegar

1. Prepare vegetables.
2. Prepare brine by heating salt and water. Cover vegetables with hot brine and leave overnight
3. Next morning, drain and rinse. Prepare vinegar brine in a large canning kettle. Add vegetables and bring to a boil.
4. Put into sterilized jars and seal.

Mustard Pickle Variation:

1. Mix flour and spices. Add just enough cold vinegar to make a smooth paste. Pour over vegetables stirring well as the mixture comes to a boil.
2. When thickened, ladle into sterilized jars and seal.

BREAD AND BUTTER PICKLES

Yield: about 3 litres

- 3 kg cucumbers (about 50 small pickling size: 3-4 cm diameter and 8-10 cm length)
- 1 kg onions (about 16 small white: 4 cm diameter)
- 2 green peppers
- 1 sweet red pepper
- 125 ml coarse pickling salt
- 2 trays ice cubes, cracked
- 1 litre vinegar
- 1 litre sugar
- 15 ml mustard seed
- 15 ml celery seed
- 5 ml tumeric, if desired

1. Wash all vegetables. Slice unpeeled cucumbers as thinly and evenly as possible. Peel onions, slice thinly. Remove seeds from peppers and dice or shred.
2. Place all vegetables together with salt in a large bowl or pot. Bury pieces of cracked ice in the mixture. Cover with a lid, weighted to keep vegetables covered with brine. Let stand about 3 hours.
3. Drain thoroughly.
4. Combine remaining ingredients in a large canning kettle and heat to boiling. Add vegetables. Heat to scalding but do not boil.
5. Pack into sterilized jars. Seal.

CHILI SAUCE

Yield: 1 000 ml

- 6 ripe, large tomatoes
- 1 medium to large onion
- ½ green pepper
- 2 large stalks celery
- 175 ml vinegar
- 75 ml brown sugar
- 2 ml cloves
- 2 ml nutmeg
- 2 ml cinnamon

1. Blanch and peel tomatoes and chop.
2. Chop peeled onion, celery and green pepper into pieces — 1 cm or smaller.
3. Put all vegetables in large enough, heavy saucepan.
4. Add vinegar, sugar and spices and stir well.
5. Bring to boil then turn down to simmer.
6. Simmer for about 2 hours, stirring occasionally to keep from sticking. Should be thick but not dry.
7. Pour into sterilized jars. If sealers with lids are not used, the jars should be sealed with wax.

FRUIT RELISH

Yield: 1 jar (500 ml)

- 5 medium ripe tomatoes
- 1 peach
- 1 pear
- 1 onion
- 1 small red pepper
- 175 ml vinegar
- 150 ml brown sugar
- 5 ml salt
- 15 ml whole mixed pickling spice, tied in a bag.

1. Peel and cube fruit.
2. Peel and chop onion. Chop pepper.
3. Place all the ingredients in a heavy saucepan and simmer slowly until thickened, about 1 hour.
4. Pour into sterilized jar and seal.

PEPPER RELISH

Yield: about 3 000 ml

- 1 kg sweet red peppers (12-15)
- 1 kg green peppers (12-15)
- 1 kg medium onions (12-15)
- 1 000 ml vinegar
- 250 ml sugar
- 5 ml mustard seed
- 15 ml dry mustard
- 15 ml celery seed
- 30 ml salt

1. Wash peppers, remove seed cores. Peel onions.
2. Put all vegetables through a food chopper. Place in large kettle; cover with boiling water and let stand 5 minutes. Drain thoroughly.
3. Add vinegar, sugar, spices and salt. Cook, stirring occasionally, for about 10 minutes or until vegetables are tender.
4. Pour into hot sterilized jars and seal.

Measuring Ingredients

Accurate measurement of ingredients can often make the difference between the success and failure of a recipe. Use standard measures and make all measurements level.

LIQUID INGREDIENTS

Liquid measures are available in 250 ml, 500 ml and 1 000 ml (1 litre) sizes, graduated in 25 ml or 50 ml depending on the total volume of the measure. The top level of the measure should be far enough below the rim so that liquids will not spill out. One made of heatproof, transparent material with a pouring spout will be most useful.

To measure liquids, place the measure on a level surface and pour the liquid to the required mark. When checking accuracy, lower your head so that your eyes are in line with the measurement indicated in the recipe.

DRY INGREDIENTS

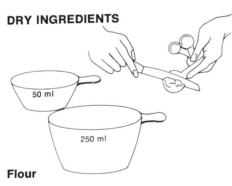

Standard dry measuring sets should be used. These have the full measure right at the rim for easy levelling off. To measure dry ingredients heap the measure to overflowing, then level off the excess with a straight-edged knife or spatula.

Flour

Improved milling techniques now permit accurate measurement of most flour without sifting. However, it is important that the flour not be scooped from a packed container. Stir the flour in the container before heaping it into the measure. Never level flour by shaking the measure or banging it on the table. Cake flour tends to pack more readily. Therefore, recipes usually indicate sifting. When the recipe calls for sifted flour, sift before measuring.

Granulated Sugar

Spoon the sugar into a dry measure until filled to overflowing. Then level off with a straight-edged knife or spatula.

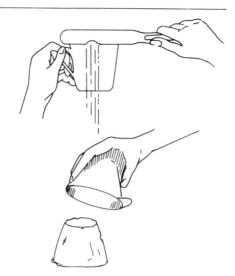

Brown Sugar

Fill the dry measure to overflowing with brown sugar. Press down with the back of a spoon until "lightly packed" to ensure there are no hollows underneath. Level the top with a straight-edged utensil. When turned out of the measure, brown sugar should hold its shape until touched.

SOLID FAT

The method used will depend on the amount being measured and its consistency (soft or hard).

Water displacement – To measure 125 ml margarine place 125 ml water in a liquid measure. Add the margarine in pieces until the water rises to the 250 ml level. Make certain that no fat rises above the water, the measure is on a level surface and the water level is viewed at eye level. Use the same method for measuring other amounts but adjust the volume of water used.

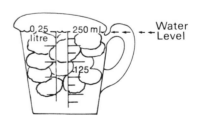

Dry measure—Small amounts of soft fat can be measured in the measures used for dry ingredients or in the spoon-shaped measures. Place the fat in the measure and press down to eliminate air bubbles. Level off with the back of a knife. This method is not as accurate, especially for large portions, since it is difficult to be assured the measure is solidly filled.

FOOD QUANTITIES FOR FIFTY

FOOD	SIZE OF PORTION	AMOUNT TO BUY FOR FIFTY
BEVERAGES:		
Coffee	175 ml beverage	500 g
Coffee (instant)	175 ml beverage	100 ml
Cream	15 ml	1 litre
Sugar, granulated	5 - 10 ml	350 - 500 g
Sugar, lump	2 lumps	500 g
Tea	175 ml beverage	250 g
Fruit Juice	125 ml	6 litres
Whipping cream	as topping	1 litre
MEAT:		
Beef — pot roast (boned)	85 g	12 - 13 kg
Beef — rib roast (rolled)	85 g	13 - 14 kg before boning
Ham — bone in, uncooked	100 g	9 - 10 kg
Ham — cooked, sliced	50 g	3 - 4 kg
Ground meat, (for meat loaf)	100 g	4 kg
Chicken, roast	85 g	18 - 20 kg
Chicken for creaming	125 ml	10 - 12 kg
Turkey, roast	100 g	14 kg
Fish, fillets	100 g	6 kg
Hamburgers	100 - 125 g patty	6 - 8 kg
VEGETABLES:		
Potatoes, boiled	1 medium	9 kg
Potatoes, mashed	125 ml	9 kg
Vegetables, canned	125 ml	20 x 550 ml cans
Vegetables, frozen	125 ml	12 small packages
Lettuce, leaves for salad	2 leaves per serving	4 large heads (2 kg)
Tomatoes, for salad	2 slices (¼ tomato)	25 - 30 tomatoes (4 kg)
Turnips	125 ml	7 - 10 kg
Carrots	125 ml	7 kg
Cabbage, for slaw	125 ml (shredded)	5 kg
MISCELLANEOUS:		
Rolls or biscuits	1½ each	about 75
Butter or margarine	1 pat	300 g
Pickles	2 each	2 - 3 litres
Olives	2 (small)	2 litres
Cookies or squares	2 each	about 100
Cakes	2 pieces	7 x 20 cm cakes each cut into 16 pieces
Ice Cream, bricks	1 slice	10 bricks (5 slices per brick)
Ice Cream, bulk	125 ml or 1 #20 scoop	5 litres
Sauce, for ice cream	30 ml	2 litres
Pies	1/6	6 x 22 cm pies

SANDWICHES
1 large sandwich loaf yields 40 thin slices — makes 40 large sandwiches or 80 small tea sandwiches.
1 small sandwich loaf yields 20 thin slices — makes 20 large sandwiches or 40 small tea sandwiches.

ESTIMATING REQUIREMENTS:
It is impossible to state the exact amount required. When making an estimate consider the time of day that they will be served and whether or not the group members are likely to have hearty appetites. Fancy cut-out sandwiches require more bread. Here is a suggested guide:

Allow 4 - 5 each of tea sandwiches
Allow 3 - 4 each of hearty sandwiches
Allow 300 g soft butter for each large loaf
Allow 225 g soft butter for each small loaf

TEA ESSENCE

Simplify making tea for large numbers by making this essence a few hours ahead of time, then dilute with boiling water to serve.
Pour 1 litre boiling water over 250 ml tea leaves. Allow to stand for 6 minutes. Draw off tea essence. To make the tea, place 125 ml or more tea essence (according to strength desired) into an eight-cup tea pot, and fill with boiling water. (500 g tea yields approximately 1 500 ml tea leaves.)

COFFEE IN QUANTITY

Bring 12 litres water to simmering point. Add 500 g medium grind coffee, tied in a muslin bag large enough to hold twice the amount. Cover tightly and allow to stand 10 minutes or longer at simmering point, until required strength is obtained. Remove coffee bag, cover and let stand over low heat until ready to serve. A bitter flavour will develop if water is allowed to boil after coffee has been added.

DESCRIPTION OF OVEN TEMPERATURES

Very Slow	120°C to 130°C	Hot	200°C to 220°C
Slow	150°C to 160°C	Very Hot	230°C to 250°C
Moderate	170°C to 190°C	Extremely Hot	260°C and up

SUBSTITUTIONS AND EQUIVALENTS

5 ml baking powder	— 2 ml baking soda plus 3 ml cream of tartar
1 square (about 30 g) chocolate	— 45 ml cocoa plus 15 ml fat
15 ml flour, for thickening	— 7 ml cornstarch or 7 ml potato starch or 7 ml arrowroot or 10 ml quick cooking tapioca
250 ml cake flour	— 250 ml all-purpose flour less 10%
250 ml honey	— 250 ml molasses
250 ml sugar	— 250 ml molasses plus 1-3 ml baking soda and omit baking powder
250 ml sugar	— 250 ml honey plus 1-3 ml baking soda used with 50 ml less liquid
250 ml uncooked macaroni	— 500 ml cooked macaroni
250 ml uncooked rice	— 750 ml cooked rice
1 average garlic clove	— 1 ml garlic powder
1 average garlic clove	— 3 ml garlic salt (decrease other salt by 1 ml)
½ medium white onion	— 5 ml onion salt (decrease other salt by 2 ml)
1 medium onion	— 5 ml onion powder
15 ml candied ginger	— 1 ml powdered ginger
15 ml fresh horseradish	— 30 ml prepared horseradish
1 lemon	— 30-50 ml lemon juice
1 lemon	— 10 ml lemon rind
30 ml lemon juice	— 15 ml vinegar
1 medium orange	— 100-125 ml orange juice
1 medium orange	— 30-50 ml orange rind
250 ml sour milk	— 15 ml vinegar or lemon juice plus enough sweet milk to make 250 ml

CHARTS